THE ULTIMATE ASTROLOGER

♈ ♉ ♊ ♋ ♌ ♍ ♎ ♏ ♐ ♑ ♒ ♓

About the Author

Nicholas Campion is an award-winning, internationally recognized authority on astrology, and past President of The Astrological Association of Great Britain and the Astrological Lodge of London. He has written many bestselling books and taught astrology both in the UK and around the world since 1980. He is currently a lecturer with Kepler College in Seattle, where he has helped devise, and is teaching, the first ever B.A. course in astrology in the Western world. His astrological features have appeared in a variety of newspapers and magazines, notably *The Daily Mail*, *Company*, *New Woman*, *Bella*, *Woman's Realm*, *Nineteen*, *Zest*, *Eve*, and *Vogue*. He is on the Web at **www.NickCampion.com.**

By the Same Author

Mundane Astrology: The Astrology of Nations and Organizations
(with Michael Baigent and Charles Harvey)

The Book of World Horoscopes

The New Astrology: The Art and Science of the Stars (with Steve Eddy)

Zodiac: Enhance Your Life Through Astrology

THE ULTIMATE ASTROLOGER

♈ ♉ ♊ ♋ ♌ ♍ ♎ ♏ ♐ ♑ ♒ ♓

A Simple Guide to Calculating and Interpreting Birth Charts for Effective Application in Daily Life

NICHOLAS CAMPION

ASTRO ROOM

A Division of Hay House, Inc.
Carlsbad, California • Sydney, Australia
Canada • Hong Kong • United Kingdom

Published and distributed in the United States by: Hay House, Inc., P.O. Box 5100, Carlsbad, CA 92018-5100 • (800) 654-5126 • (800) 650-5115 (fax) • www.hayhouse.com • **Distributed in Canada by:** Raincoast, 9050 Shaughnessy St., Vancouver, B.C., Canada V6P 6E5

Design: Echelon, Wimborne

First published in 2002 by Rider, an imprint of Ebury Press, Random House, London:
ISBN: 0-7126-1020-0

Includes revised material from *The Practical Astrologer,* first published in 1987 in the UK by Hamlyn Publishing and in the USA by Harry N. Abrams Limited, New York

Library of Congress Control No.: 2002111965

ISBN 1-4019-0081-X

06 05 04 03 4 3 2 1
1st Hay House printing, May 2003

Printed in the United States of America/Canada **[to come]**

CONTENTS

ACKNOWLEDGMENTS

Special thanks to Chester Kemp who has given so generously of his time in producing the tables (with Astrocalc symbols font by permission of Colin Miles), and to Janus software for the chart calculation. Also, my thanks to all the people who have made this book possible, each in their own way, including: Wendy Buonaventura, Michael Baigent, Nick Bantock, Judy Browne, Luisa Calderon, Sue Clayton, Pete Dews, Hugh Elwes, Nicola Glucksmann, Simon Goss, Liz Greene, Eric Griffths, Charles Harvey, Malcolm Love, Michael Lutin, Frances McEvoy, Doreen Montgomery, Joan Quigley, Kim Rogers-Gallagher, Howard Sasportas, Paddy Seymour, Beth Shaw, Ralph Smith, Jonathan Tootell, Helen Vivian, Andy Whitman, my former students at the Camden Institute, members of Aspects, my colleagues at Kepler College and on the Sophia Project steering committee, and the Clifton Poker Group.

INTRODUCTION

Astrology is "the word of the stars" – from the Greek *astra* (star) and *logos* (word). It is the study by which we read significance for our lives into the movements of the stars and planets. Astrology takes the changing patterns of the planets and stars and uses them to understand human life and events on Earth; everything that happens in the heavens above can be taken as a sign of corresponding changes on the Earth below.

Astrology is used to gain understanding of present or past situations and to predict the future, to help people adapt to the unexpected and make the best use of their opportunities. Many people find that it is an extraordinarily accurate description of their personalities, needs, hopes, and aspirations, and of their strengths and weaknesses. Most, though, are also fascinated by astrology's claim to predict the future. Astrologers, meanwhile, advocate it as a fast path to self-understanding, and some psychologists use astrology's language of symbols to help them understand their clients. Astrology can best be described as a celestial mirror, with the movements of the heavens presenting a mythological drama in which we see our lives reflected. *The Ultimate Astrologer* introduces you to the basics of this language of symbols and will, I hope, inspire you to learn it for yourself.

♈ ♉ ♊ ♋ ♌ ♍ ♎ ♏ ♐ ♑ ♒ ♓

CHAPTER 1

THE PLANETS

Everything in astrology begins with the planets, the ten major bodies in the solar system that appear to orbit the Earth: the Sun, the Moon, Mercury, Venus, Mars, Jupiter, Saturn, Uranus, Neptune, and Pluto. These are extremely important, and without them astrology as we know it would not exist. The astronomical definition of a planet is different. In astronomy a planet is a body which orbits a star, while a moon is a body that orbits a planet. However, astrology maintains the ancient meaning of the word "wanderer" – and a planet is thus any body that we see wandering through the heavens. The importance of the planets in human behavior is revealed in the words we still use to describe character traits, including *lunatic, mercurial, venereal, martial, jovial,* and *saturnine.*

THE TEN MAJOR PLANETS

☉

THE SUN

Ruler of Leo

In modern astrology, the Sun is the most important of all the planets. In ancient astral religions it was invariably the focus of worship. The Greeks knew the Sun god as Apollo or Helios, the Egyptians knew it as Ra, Horus, or Aten. The wearing of gold crowns by kings and queens, and the representation of saints with halos, originate from imitation of the Sun god.

"Sun-sign" popular astrology is the form of astrology most familiar to the general public, and it is often possible to produce a detailed character description of a person based solely upon a knowledge of his or her Sun sign (the sign containing the Sun at birth). The Sun is a symbol of creativity, power, and energy, and of life itself, and confers enormous importance on that section of the chart in which it is located. The sign containing the Sun will reveal dominant personality traits, and innate strengths and weaknesses. It will also show the fundamental processes by which individuals may change and grow as well as the type of experience encountered as they pass through life. The Sun is preeminently the planet of the great "I." Some call it the ego, others "the self." It represents both the source of life and our innermost being. It is the creative process and our core potential.

The Sun rules everything associated with gold, honor and power, including monarchs, rulers, and their representatives; generous, proud, and regal behavior; and sunflowers, saffron, and marigolds.

☽

THE MOON

Ruler of Cancer

The Moon is normally considered the most important planet after the Sun, although it has claims to equality with it. The simple reason why the Sun sign has achieved preeminence over the Moon sign in modern astrology is that it's much easier to work out – all you need to know is your date of birth.

The speed with which the Moon moves is important in the assessment of the flow of events. For this reason, it is often the most significant planet in horary, electional, and mundane astrology (Chapter 12) and medical astrology (Chapter 13).

From the Moon's place in the horoscope, the astrologer is able to make deductions about an individual's mother and that person's relationship with her, together with the individual's own maternal and nurturing qualities. For obvious cultural reasons, lunar qualities have often been most clearly expressed by women, but they are no less important for men. The Moon rules the home and family and an individual's family history and relationship with his or her domestic environment. People born with the Moon strong in their horoscopes are often very domesticated, maternal, compassionate, and drawn towards the "caring" professions. Its lesson is that caring for others should be a selfless act, not dependent on what they do for us.

Physically the Moon is responsible for the ebb and flow of the tides, and in astrology it represents fluctuating emotions and moods – and the realization that the entire natural world is in a constant state of flux. In a horoscope, the Moon reveals a person's emotional state and the manner in which it is expressed. It also represents what psychologists call the "persona," the mask or public face that people wear to conceal their true feelings and real sensitivity.

Traditionally, the Moon rules the metal silver and all silver colors. It also has an association with cool and moist weather as well as damp places.

The Moon's Nodes

The Moon has two nodes, the north, drawn as ☊, and the south, shown as ☋. These nodes are not planets, but the two points at which the Moon's monthly path crosses the Sun's annual path (ecliptic) around the Earth. These are abstract points, but astrology accords them the power and effective status of planets. The nodes are considered to be inseparable, each with an individual meaning but together forming a single principle. They are always exactly opposite each other, and the straight line connecting them across the horoscope is seen as the path of the soul through life.

The north node, also called the Dragon's Head, shows the direction in which the individual is heading. This may be difficult, for challenges must be met and new qualities developed.

The south node, also called the Dragon's Tail, shows where the individual is coming from – characteristics and behavior taken for granted that should, perhaps, be left behind. In times of stress, individuals may retreat for safety to the qualities of the south node, but unless they face up to the demands of the north node, there will be a failure to develop the birth potential to the full.

Astrologers who believe in reincarnation claim that the north node represents the present life, while the south node reveals either past actions in the present life or the residue of past lives. This can be interesting, although it is peripheral to practical astrology.

☿

MERCURY

Ruler of Gemini and Virgo

In classical mythology, Mercury, was the messenger of the gods and goddesses on Mount Olympus. In astrology, this planet rules all forms of communication – physical and mental, trivial and profound. For example, a short bus journey to see a friend is a Mercurial experience, as is also the deep process of psychoanalysis.

Mercury is the only planet that combines male and female qualities. As such, it can be used to achieve the fundamental reconciliation between the opposing halves of our personalities. Although Mercury is apparently a superficial planet, its psychological purpose is to facilitate self-transformation by means of self-knowledge and understanding.

Mercury is necessary if we are to know the outside world. It rules short-distance travel, all forms of learning and the acquisition of knowledge, as well as the objects that we use to communicate with one another – telephones, books, trains, cars, newspapers, television, pencils and pens, and so on. In the modern world, thinking machines – computers – are a Mercurial development. In the mystical astrology of the classical world, Mercury was Hermes, who revealed the mysteries of birth, life, and death – and the ultimate wisdom of the universe. He was also the traditional ruler of astrology and magic and, in the modern world, science.

In the birth chart, Mercury reveals the manner in which an individual thinks and speaks, indicating intellectual interests and manner of expression. By examining Mercury in a birth chart, the astrologer can advise on the best way to limit its weaknesses and enhance its strengths. People with Mercury highly developed in their charts should seek careers in the communications field – teaching, journalism, taxi driving, the travel business, or secretarial work, to name a few.

The question Mercury poses is whether truths are relative and change from time to time and place to place – or whether there is an absolute Truth. Its curiosity encourages skepticism and challenges us to question the truths we were born with, as well as those we may have acquired as adults. It teaches us that thinking is a process that may result in more questions – and no final answers.

♀

VENUS

Ruler of Taurus and Libra

Venus was the goddess of love in Roman times, but under other names (Ishtar, Astarte, and Aphrodite) she was worshipped in all ancient cultures. The story of her descent to the underworld (as Inanna) to search for her dead lover, Dumuzzi, is the earliest great romantic epic, written down around 4,000 years ago.

In Western astrology, Venus rules the female half of the human psyche, showing feminine and female qualities in both men and women. To psychologists this is the "anima," the inner feminine and can reveal the woman that women would like to be – and who men dream of. In a woman's horoscope Venus may show the image of female behavior to which the individual aspires. In a man's chart, Venus may reveal his expectations of women and the type of woman he finds attractive.

For the most part, Venusian qualities are soft, loving, diplomatic, artistic, creative and sensitive, but they also have a harder side. In political astrology, Venus rules victory in war. In the earliest Babylonian astrology, Venus could become a destroyer when angered, and we should always remember that love and hate are two sides of the same coin. When passions are roused, anything can happen.

Venus has a particular significance for close partnerships and relationships, including marriage. In order to succeed in relationships, most people develop the Venusian qualities of softness, sensitivity, and diplomacy, but negatively, the planet can become envious, jealous, and aggressive. By examining the position of Venus in the birth chart, the astrologer can deduce how it will affect partnerships, and whether these will be formed easily or not. The lesson it teaches us is that none of us lives alone: we all need other people to survive, let alone to enjoy all that life has to offer.

Venus rules all objects and behavior that are pleasant, pleasurable, beautiful, graceful, and attractive. Some people born with a strong presence of Venus in their birth charts become artists (not forgetting that every activity has an artistic dimension), while others are drawn toward self-indulgence and the pursuit of pleasure – and others to both. It reminds us that, while we all need to receive affection, sometimes the first step can be to give it.

♂

MARS

Ruler of Aries and Scorpio

As the god of war in classical mythology, Mars rules energy, enterprise, dynamism, action, and self-assertion. It also rules all objects connected with heat and violence: knives, guns, explosives, fires, and so on. The colors associated with Mars are red and bright yellow, and its metal is iron.

In medical astrology, Mars is linked to high temperatures, feverish complaints, accidents, and all problems requiring surgery. Its placing in a birth chart indicates the individual's general energy level and overall behavior pattern and can show the manner in which the practical issues, affairs, and problems of the world are approached and handled. Mars reveals a lot about the way we express ourselves to others and therefore has as great a role as Venus in relationships. If Venus is the force of attraction, then Mars reveals the active impulse that causes people to seek each other out. Venus and Mars together reveal all the possibilities in a complete emotional and sexual relationship.

Psychologically, Mars rules the internal image we all have of the ideal man – or what psychologists call the "animus." In a man's chart, it may show the role model he is obliged to live up to or, equally, the one he rejects. In a woman's chart, Mars will show how she manages with her own male half, as well as indicating her expectations of men and the type of man who attracts her.

Mars's lessons teach us how to manage energy, to be assertive rather than aggressive, and to manage anger constructively. It works perfectly when its competitive instincts provide the perfect foil for Venus's cooperative nature.

♃

JUPITER

Ruler of Sagittarius and Pisces

Jupiter in astrology shows two faces, both taken from classical mythology. On the one hand, Jupiter was the great king of the gods, dispensing justice with supreme wisdom, while on the other he was a licentious womanizer and glutton.

In astrology Jupiter is quite simply the planet of growth and expansion, whether spiritual, emotional, mental, or physical. Jupiter does everything on a grandiose and inflated scale. At best it is wise, generous and bountiful, but when it is completely uncontrolled it can become wasteful, extravagant, greedy, and indulgent, always wanting more than is on offer.

Jupiter has specific associations with religion, belief, philosophy, and the law. It shares with Mercury hegemony over reason and the intellectual processes, but whereas Mercury rules knowledge and the communication of knowledge, Jupiter brings the wisdom and understanding that enables the utilization of knowledge.

Like Mercury, Jupiter rules travel, although its journeys are long voyages of exploration and adventure, whether physical, spiritual, or intellectual. These are the means by which Jupiter accomplishes its principal aim – growth.

Traditionally Jupiter has always been known as the planet that brings good fortune, rewards, and opportunities. However, it cannot complete this action on its own, and to make Jupiterian good fortune permanent, Saturn is necessary. Besides, there is no clear distinction between good and bad fortune, for a wonderful opportunity might lead to tragedy, and disaster can result in wonderful consequences. Jupiter's benevolent qualities can take us through many twists and turns, and the planet's ultimate lesson is that we should value everything we're given and use our resources wisely.

♄

SATURN

Ruler of Capricorn and Aquarius

In complete contrast to Jupiter, Saturn rules the principles of limitation and restriction. As Jupiter brings growth, so Saturn provides the structures within which that growth must take place. In its positive form, Saturn represents self-discipline and self-control; while in its negative form, it brings repression and inhibition. As a result, even though Saturn's astrological correlations are quite simple, its psychological manifestations can be complicated. The causes and results of inhibition and repression are many and varied.

It is the planet of time – often pictured as "Old Father Time" – and we become aware of its rulership of old age when we feel our biological clocks ticking. Yet, the defying or transcending of death has always been seen as the greatest possible personal liberation, and in ancient astral religion the goal was to use sacred ritual to break through Saturn and arrive at the stars – representing salvation. Cronos, the Greek Saturn, was also the ruler of the primeval Golden Age – another symbol of personal liberation, and, in this case, freedom from poverty, disease, and death.

Modern astrology has revived the ancient description of Saturn as the "Dark Sun," giving this planet the role of the "shadow," the part of the psyche in which all characteristics and behavior are deposited when considered unacceptable. This material does not disappear, but finds its way into our lives in unwelcome ways – unless we recognize and acknowledge it.

Saturn often provokes difficult or challenging circumstances. Frequently these can be traced to individual behavior and are self-induced, but sometimes they seem to be brought about by fate. These external circumstances force internal change. They can be the testing ground of our lives. If the individual is ready for inner development, then in many cases the pressure of the environment will be alleviated. In general, Saturn indicates delays, obstacles and material difficulties, and it rules tradition, conservatism, established institutions, the authority of the state and religion, the police, and social taboos. In its more positive form it is linked to self-discipline, hard work, organizational ability, and loyalty – and the struggle for perfection.

♅

URANUS

Co-ruler of Aquarius, with Saturn

If Saturn is the planet of order, stability and structure, then Uranus is the planet that tears down all established systems. In Greek myth Uranus was the sky god, but this noble role plays little part in its astrological nature. Astrologers derive the symbolism of Uranus from its eccentric rotation (unlike the other planets, Uranus turns on an east–west axis) and from the fact that its discovery in 1781 came within a few years of the political revolutions in America (1776) and France (1789) and the industrial revolution in England in the late 18th century.

Uranus is revolutionary, radical, individualistic, and independent. It tends to be progressive, but its main need is to be seen to be different; in a progressive atmosphere, it may well be reactionary. Uranus is associated with humanitarianism and philanthropy, but also with chaos and terror. This planet is often antisocial and uncooperative, and its function is to stir up all those who have accepted conventional beliefs and behavior. People with a strong Uranian presence in their chart are often motivated by a desire to separate themselves from what they see as the unthinking masses, and they are often unable to resist the temptation of trying to change society.

In the world of physical objects, Uranus rules all new technology – for example, computers, electronics and nuclear power, the scientific developments that have revolutionized our lives.

Uranus is a planet of personal transformation, a feat accomplished through sudden changes and the raising of new possibilities – sometimes welcome, at other times traumatic. In some cases, the individual may be deprived of a lifestyle that has been safe and secure; while in others, radical changes may open up new vistas.

Uranian individuals often resist close relationships, preferring independence to commitment. This has been explained in terms of the planet's awareness of the possibility of chaos when personal passions are released. This raises fears that in turn lead to a fear of intimacy. Some people might think that this is wise! Above all, the planet symbolizes impermanence, its lesson being that all things must pass.

♆

NEPTUNE

Co-ruler of Pisces, with Jupiter

Neptune in classical mythology ruled the oceans, and in astrology it is a planet of transformation, working like the sea eroding the land, steadily undermining life's physical certainties. Gradual change comes about as old attitudes, beliefs, and lifestyles go out of fashion or are forgotten.

In one form, Neptune represents mystical truth and the universal urge for union with the Divine, and in everyday life it influences the dreams and visions which can represent humanity's strongest motivation. It encourages the charity, sensitivity, and self-sacrifice often necessary to put these into effect. Yet it also signifies illusions and delusions – precisely what some people would say its mystical dreams are! It represents the enchantment that binds us to other people, beliefs, and causes without thinking – it's the triumph of intuition over logical thought. It also indicates greed, fraud, and deception of self and others, for its vision readily turns to disillusionment and cynicism.

Like the sea, Neptune is difficult to pin down. Neptunian people are skilled at changing their disguise in order to adopt different faces. People who externalize this may become performers, gurus, artists, or fashion designers, while others may take refuge in fashion, religion, mysticism, or behind a smokescreen of drink and drugs, legal or otherwise. Some may deny that such activities are escapist: the question which Neptune poses is "who is to say what is real life?"

♇

PLUTO

Co-ruler of Scorpio, with Mars

Pluto is the most distant known planet, although some astronomers insist that it is really too small to be considered a planet. Astrologers combine the distance, mystery, and darkness of the planet with the god Pluto's classical rulership of the underworld to provide the planet's astrological attributes of deep, dark, and unfathomable power.

Pluto is preeminently a planet of transformation. The changes it brings are often of the most profound kind, completely revolutionizing attitudes, beliefs, and behavior. It rules the deepest instincts of the unconscious mind which, when they become dominant, can lead to compulsive and obsessive behavior. Pluto is also connected with underworld crime, fascism – and modern in-depth psychology.

Plutonic individuals often show a passionate interest in the mysteries of life. They tend to be dedicated, persistent, and obstinate in following particular courses of action. Plutonic activities and interests include anything with an element of mystery. Some people take up magic, the occult, spiritual healing, or mystical religion, while others pursue more orthodox scientific investigation and research. In whatever field they are involved Plutonic people make reform and renewal their highest priorities.

RETROGRADE PLANETS

Retrograde planets are those that appear to be traveling backward through the zodiac. This effect is due to an optical illusion created by the varying speeds at which the Earth and other planets orbit the Sun. It is similar to the effect experienced when we look out of a train window and objects which are very close appear to be moving in the opposite direction while those on the horizon seem to be moving in the same direction, if slowly. It's not necessary at this stage to know why this happens, only that it does! Retrograde planets are marked by placing a minus sign next to the planetary glyph. The normal forward motion is known as "direct." The Sun and Moon are never retrograde. The five outer planets, Jupiter, Saturn, Uranus, Neptune, and Pluto, are retrograde so often that this is not taken into account when interpreting a natal chart. However, being retrograde does affect the interpretation of Mercury, Venus, and Mars in a natal chart, for retrograde motion suggests an inward-looking character.

When Mercury is retrograde, the individual may be an introvert, lacking confidence in communicating and expressing ideas. A lot of people think that when Mercury is retrograde, communication is held up and information is lost. However, this is just as likely to happen when the planet is direct. When Venus is retrograde, the individual may be quiet socially, preferring a one-to-one relationship. When Mars is retrograde, the individual may find it difficult to galvanize his or her energies to get things done.

MINOR "PLANETS"

THE CENTAURS

In 1977, a new "planet" was discovered and named Chiron. Astronomers disagreed whether Chiron belonged properly to our solar system, or whether it was a body from outer space captured by the Sun's gravity. Some called it a giant asteroid, others a planetoid. The confusion was caused partly by its highly erratic orbit, but over the next few years more similar bodies were discovered and collectively named Centaurs. It is now thought that they may be comet nuclei sucked into the solar system from a huge group of such bodies which orbit beyond Pluto in the "Kuiper Belt."

Chiron ⚷

Chiron is the most important of the Centaurs astrologically, which is why it is included in the planetary tables at the end of this book. Its meanings are still too speculative, though, to give a sign-by-sign breakdown. Starting with a study of its astronomical characteristics and an examination of the legend of Chiron – who was a centaur (half horse, half human) in Greek mythology – astrologers have applied the following clues to the role of Chiron in the horoscope.

Chiron taught the art of prophecy, among other subjects, to the Greek heroes. Because of this astrologers say the planet Chiron teaches lessons. These lessons may be unusual ("maverick" is one of this planet's key words), startling or sudden. They may also be upsetting, but in the long run, they assist a person who genuinely wishes to discover a deeper purpose in life. Chiron is a healer of emotional, spiritual, and physical ills, the results of which may open doors to new realities and possibilities.

Chiron's orbit is so irregular that at its closest point to the Earth it is inside the orbit of Saturn, and at its furthest it reaches that of Uranus. Astrologically, it forms a bridge from the order, stability and limitation of Saturn to the anarchic individuality of Uranus. Its discovery in 1977 is associated with the rapid spread of psychological counseling and therapy, perhaps, too, with environmentalism and green politics (which seek to "heal" the Earth). Chiron takes the way-out ideas of Uranus and, through Saturn, gives them a practical use.

Pholus and Nessus

Apart from Chiron, the only two Centaurs to have received serious astrological attention are Pholus and Nessus. Pholus is said to represent unconscious impulses and unusual and thoughtless actions that might be either highly creative or self-destructive. Nessus is linked to the awareness of the consequences of our actions.

THE ASTEROIDS

The asteroids are small lumps of rock which orbit the Sun between Mars and Jupiter in the so-called Asteroid belt. The largest, Ceres (60 miles across), was discovered on January 1, 1801, and by 1989 another 5,000 had been charted – and the number is still rising. The first crop of asteroids to be used by astrologers were those with the names of important goddesses – Ceres, Gaea, Demeter, Persephone, Hekate, Astarte, and Aphrodite. The fact that they were all female was thought to correct the heavily male bias in the planets. After 1980, though, the emphasis was broadened to include the so-called "personal asteroids" with familiar names (such as Margaret and Peter), the names of historical figures (such as Attila) or places (such as Moscow). They can be used in interpreting charts but their major fascination lies in the fact that they are often vivid illustrations of astrological coincidences. For example, a man born with Venus conjunct a particular asteroid might marry a woman who shares the same name as that asteroid.

THE PLANETS, THEIR ASSOCIATIONS AND MEANINGS

PLANET	GLYPH	SIGN	SEX	METAL	COLOR	DAY	MEANING
Sun	☉	Leo	M	Gold	Gold	Sunday	Pride, ego
Moon	☽	Cancer	F	Silver	Silver	Monday	Care, nurturing
Mercury	☿	Gemini, Virgo	-	Mercury	Changeable	Wednesday	Thinking, speaking
Venus	♀	Taurus, Libra	F	Copper	Blue/Green	Friday	Love, affection
Mars	♂	Aries, Scorpio	M	Iron	Red	Tuesday	Energy, action
Jupiter	♃	Sagittarius, Pisces	M	Tin	Purple	Thursday	Growth, optimism
Saturn	♄	Capricorn, Aquarius	M	Lead	Sober colors	Saturday	Stability, restriction
Uranus	♅	Aquarius	M	Uranium	Electric blue	-	Change, revolution
Neptune	♆	Pisces	M	Neptunium	Gentle colors	-	Mysticism, illusion
Pluto	♇ or ⯓	Scorpio	M	Plutonium	Black/Deep red	-	Intensity, confrontation

CHAPTER 2

THE ZODIAC

The word *zodiac* can be loosely translated as "circle of animals" (it has the same root as "zoo"). In western astrology the zodiac is based on the ecliptic, the Sun's imaginary path through the sky, dividing it into 12 equal sections. This is known as the *tropical zodiac.* The zodiac used by Western astrologers always begins when the Sun enters Aries at the spring equinox, usually on March 21. It then enters the other 11 signs at aproximately monthly intervals. Indian astrologers use a slightly different zodiac. It contains the same 12 signs as the tropical zodiac but gradually moves with the stars and so is known as the *sidereal zodiac* (from the Latin *sidus*, meaning star). Because of this movement, the Indian sidereal zodiac is no longer aligned with the tropical zodiac. By contrast, the zodiac used by modern astronomers is based on the constellations, huge unequal-sized groupings of stars, and achieved its current form as recently as 1928. It contains 13 signs, the extra one being Ophiucus, which has nothing to do with mainstream astrology.

The tropical zodiac's 12 signs together describe the entire cycle of human experience, analogous to that of the changing seasons. Individually each sign embodies a principle, has a distinct meaning and rules a range of psychological moods, types of behavior, and physical objects. These form the foundation of astrological interpretation.

The signs, in order, are Aries, Taurus, Gemini, Cancer, Leo, Virgo, Libra, Scorpio, Sagittarius, Capricorn, Aquarius, and Pisces. Most people are familiar with them as the Sun signs or birth signs, the signs which contain the Sun at different times of year. The dividing line between two signs is known as the cusp.

Each horoscope, however, contains the entire zodiac and every single person lives out the potential of all 12 signs. We are not, however, solely a product of our Sun sign; most of us are combinations of three, four, or even more major signs, with the others fulfilling less important roles. The interpretation of any one horoscope, therefore, requires a knowledge of the characteristics of every sign.

THE POLARITIES

The signs are divided into two types, male and female. These are sometimes known as positive and negative, although the Chinese philosophical terms *yang* (positive, bright, and masculine) and *yin* (negative, dark, and feminine) probably convey the meaning more accurately.

The sexes of the signs alternate: the male signs are Aries, Gemini, Leo, Libra, Sagittarius, and Aquarius; the female signs are Taurus, Cancer, Virgo, Scorpio, Capricorn, and Pisces.

THE QUALITIES

The qualities, or quadruplicities, are three categories of sign which describe the individual's relationship to the environment.

CARDINAL SIGNS

The cardinal signs are Aries, Cancer, Libra, and Capricorn. Cardinal signs are the most assertive, the most interested in promoting change and influencing the environment. Those born under these signs achieve control by remaining one step ahead of everyone else. Aries seeks leadership and control in general; Cancer controls emotions, home, and family; Libra tries to control partnerships and the social environment; Capricorn controls, uses, and exploits the material environment.

FIXED SIGNS

The fixed signs are Taurus, Leo, Scorpio, and Aquarius. They are the most stable and self-contained. In one sense they tend to leave their environments alone, being more concerned with personal motivations, resisting all attempts by any outside agency to influence their lives. Their strength is their consistency and loyalty, their weakness obstinacy, a refusal to change, and a tendency to hang on to the past. Taurus is the most regular in its behavior and attitudes; Leo finds it difficult to adapt its behavior; Scorpio can get stuck in emotional ruts; Aquarius may become trapped in a negative self-image.

MUTABLE SIGNS

The mutable signs are Gemini, Virgo, Sagittarius, and Pisces. They are the most unstable signs and those most open to influence by the environment. They find it naturally easy to let go, although sometimes too much instability leads to an excessive desire for security. Gemini tends to be changeable in its ideas; Virgo is dominated by its environment; Sagittarius has a continually changing view of life's possibilities; Pisces adapts itself superficially to its environment. While these signs can be infinitely flexible and tolerant, they may also compromise so much that they sacrifice their own interests.

THE ELEMENTS

The elements, or triplicities, are four separate groups of three signs each, described as Fire, Earth, Air, and Water.

FIRE SIGNS

The Fire signs are Aries, Leo, and Sagittarius. Fiery types are energetic, explosive, passionate, and volatile. They live by enthusiasm and faith in the future; they are adventurers, leaders, and innovators. Their weakness is a tendency to burn themselves out, so they should make sure their physical and emotional well-being is not neglected. They are impatient and react badly to obstacles and delays. They are also impractical, and rely on the Earth signs to carry out their requirements.

EARTH SIGNS

The Earth signs are Taurus, Virgo, and Capricorn. Earthy types are literally down to earth. They are practical, cautious, conservative, and reliable. They may lack imagination, but are vital for putting into effect the orders of Fire signs, the ideas of Air signs, and the dreams of Water signs. The Earth signs are essential to the practical implementation of the promise of the horoscope.

AIR SIGNS

The Air signs are Gemini, Libra, and Aquarius. They indicate intellectual activity, thought, and communication. They are logical, rational, and inquisitive; and without the principle they represent, no one would be able to think, let alone communicate ideas to other people. There would be no speech, no memory, no knowledge, and no ability to criticize the excesses of other elements. Like Fire and Water, Air relies upon Earth for practical support.

WATER SIGNS

The Water signs are Cancer, Scorpio, and Pisces. These are the sensitive, emotional signs, those capable of exercising compassion, feeling love (and hate), and expressing affection. They provide the sense of personal meaning to the cold ideas of Air, the unimaginative practicality of Earth, and the careless energy of Fire. With their imagination and dreams, they provide human life with its religious and mystical spirituality.

THE TWELVE SIGNS OF THE ZODIAC

♈ ARIES

ELEMENT: Fire QUALITY: Cardinal
RULING PLANET: Mars SYMBOL: The Ram
The Sun enters Aries on March 20/21.

Aries' reputation for egotism, action, and self-assertion is not based solely upon its fiery, cardinal characteristics, but also upon its position as first sign of the zodiac. At the first degree of Aries the entire cycle of experience represented by the zodiac recommences. It represents the seed moment, the germ of all actions, the point at which movement commences. As such, Ariens are entrepreneurs, leaders, and adventurers; courageous, impulsive, and highly motivated. Ariens spot future possibilities and develop them first, usually pushing their own interests.

Although Aries is the first and fastest of all the signs, it is by no means the noisiest; a great many Ariens are, in fact, quiet and unostentatious. In this respect, Aries takes its character from Mars, a planet concerned solely with action, rather than glamour and the trappings of power.

The animal associated with Aries is the Ram, which is noted in astrology for being aggressive and headstrong. Aries is not a sign of subtlety, and when it meets an obstacle it will, like the ram, charge it. Ariens often bang their heads against walls.

Ariens have so much power and energy that they tend to burn themselves up. To avoid periods of collapse and exhaustion they should take care to replenish their resources.

Myth

The Arien myth is that of the hero – the belief that a single person can save the world. The classic Arien tale relates the exploits of Jason and the Argonauts, the company of heroes who set off in search of the Golden Fleece. In psychological terms the object of the quest, in this case the fleece, symbolizes that part of oneself that one needs to discover in order to become whole.

TAURUS

ELEMENT: Earth QUALITY: Fixed
RULING PLANET: Venus SYMBOL: The Bull
The Sun enters Taurus on April 19/20.

In complete contrast with Aries, Taurus is stable, conservative, and sensual, embodying all the characteristics of fixity and the Earth element. This sign values a comfortable, safe, and unchanging environment, and likes to hold on to the past. Taurus is down to earth and practical, and is also one of the most productive of signs. The bull is an ancient fertility symbol, and Taureans like to be engaged in producing things that can be of practical use. A fine appreciation of beauty and form is combined with creative power, and Taureans often have artistic skills. Often they may become good singers (Taurus rules the throat), but they may also be potters, sculptors, or gardeners, or work with the earth in other ways.

Traditionally, Taureans are said to be of short, stocky stature, with strong shoulders and large necks. Being sensualists, many Taureans are fond of smart clothes, jewelry, and perfume, but their desire for a comfortable and leisured lifestyle can mean quite the opposite – that they prefer their old and comfortable clothes.

Fidelity and consistency are this sign's virtues; obstinacy and a refusal to recognize the necessity for change are its weaknesses. By temperament, Taurus often reflects the nature of the bull. It appears to be passive and contented, but is easily angered when roused.

Myth

The most famous bull myth concerns Theseus, the Greek hero who rescued seven Athenian youths and seven maidens from the half-bull, half-human minotaur, killing the monster in the process. Bull-fighting myths were quite common in the ancient world and may date back to the period before 2000 B.C. when Taurus was the constellation in which the Sun rose at the spring equinox. In a religious sense, these myths may represent the triumph of spring over winter and light over dark. From our modern perspective we could also view such stories as symbolizing the victory of reason over ignorance, or of civilized behavior over the "beast within."

♊ GEMINI

ELEMENT: Air QUALITY: Mutable
RULING PLANET: Mercury SYMBOL: The Twins
The Sun enters Gemini on May 20/21.

Gemini is an Air sign and is ruled by Mercury, so it's preeminently the sign of rational, logical thought, intellectual inquiry, and the gathering of knowledge. The combination of Air with Gemini's mutable quality renders this sign almost impossible to pin down; Geminian thought must have its freedom.

Geminians are often maddeningly inconsistent; they can argue one point of view one day and the completely opposite view on the next. It is the actual process of thinking and communicating that is important to Gemini, not the end result. A firm conclusion is not necessary so long as the mind is kept well exercised. Geminian types often become writers, orators, journalists, teachers, secretaries, lawyers, or computer programmers, or take up other activities in which their mental skills can be exercised. They might also work in the communications industry in other ways – as telephone operators, postal workers, or bus drivers. Their smooth way with words can make them fine salespeople as well.

It has been said that the most natural animal for this sign would be the nervous chattering monkey with its permanently restless habits. The sign is also known as the typical "social butterfly." In fact, the symbol of Gemini is the Twins, embodying the essential split in this sign's nature, the divorce of the intellect from the emotions. Geminians sometimes find it difficult to express emotions as they often rationalize them first, having an ideal of how relationships should work that may not correspond to real situations. They may also be subject to sudden changes of mood, which partners can find confusing, but it may be up to partners to adjust.

Geminians are versatile and can turn their hands to more than one thing at the same time. However, if their talents are spread too thinly, they may not achieve their aims.

Myth

Geminian myths feature twins, such as Cain and Abel, the sons of Adam and Eve in the Old Testament; and Romulus and Remus, the founders of Rome. Often the twins engage in a struggle – Cain kills Abel and Romulus slays Remus. Modern Geminian tales sometimes involve split or dual personalities: in the famous story of Dr. Jekyll and Mr. Hyde, the two personas battle for dominance until the evil Hyde wins, and the only way for Jekyll to triumph is to destroy them both. The lesson is that the "twin" represents those parts of ourselves we would rather not recognize (our "shadow"), but that in acknowledging these characteristics, we can turn them from destructive to positive and constructive qualities.

CANCER

ELEMENT: Water QUALITY: Cardinal
RULING PLANET: The Moon SYMBOL: The Crab
The Sun enters Cancer on June 21/22.

The second of the cardinal signs but the first of the Water signs, Cancer combines the tough self-assertion of the former with the powerful emotions, softness, and sensitivity of the latter. This contrast is embodied in Cancer's animal, the crab, with its soft and fleshy body covered by a hard and protective shell.

Cancer is a sign of compassion and embodies all that is best in the caring, maternal instincts, but it often hides its emotions behind a mask that denies these inner feelings. (In the case of someone born with the Sun in Cancer, the sign containing the Moon may show the nature of the mask.) Cancerians are vulnerable and easily hurt; the confident face they wear in public serves as a defense against the rough and tumble of the world. When upset, Cancerians may withdraw further into their shell, but they can also snap at people, imitating the crab's sharp pincers.

Cancerian emotions fluctuate, but they are tenacious, even ruthless, when it comes to defending their family and friends. Cancer people are renowned as homemakers and usually require domestic stability for happiness. As long as they have a firm base to which they can retreat to recuperate, they are able to venture into the world and make their cardinal presence felt.

Myth

The myths that tell us most about Cancer are those that deal with mother figures and water. Perhaps the most typical is one of the most ancient legends from the Middle East. It's the story of Tiamat, the Salt Water, who was mother to the first generation of gods and goddesses in ancient Babylon. Originally Tiamat was the caring, nurturing mother, but as future generations of deities were born, they began to resent her and she became a monster who was eventually killed by her grandson, Marduk, the new chief god. How could Tiamat, who gave birth to all, eventually be seen as a destroyer? There is a saying that we kill that which we love most. The lesson is that, instead, we should always honor that which gives us life. In our daily lives, we should respect those who do us good turns – and never give in to Cancerian negativity.

♌

LEO

ELEMENT: Fire QUALITY: Fixed
RULING PLANET: The Sun SYMBOL: The Lion
The Sun enters Leo on July 22/23.

A Fire sign, ruled by the Sun and symbolized by the lion, the king of the jungle, this is the most egotistical, proud, and ostentatious of all the signs. At its best, Leo is creative, artistic, colorful, generous, honest, warmhearted, and a natural leader, but can easily cross the line and become excessively vain, flamboyant, extravagant, and selfish. Leos require an audience – and even quiet ones contrive to make an impression, judging their own behavior as reflected in the mirror of audience response. If other people approve, they are happy. Perhaps, though, this indicates a deep insecurity hidden within Leonine confidence; maybe the sign depends too much on others' opinions.

The myth of Leo is the myth of the king – or queen – but in all true kingship, personal power needs to be balanced by obligations and duties. Egocentric Leo must learn social responsibility and tolerance of partners' minor failings. This may mean accepting the need for personal change, but for this obstinate sign, change can be particularly difficult.

Leo's passion is deeply attractive, but the very depth of its feeling means that it can be difficult to love or to work with. Leonine types do not take kindly to limitation of any sort but thrive when given the maximum space and freedom. Their ideal career is acting, and they are often found in work connected with the performing arts. Many other professions, such as teaching, also require acting ability. Classic Leo types are often recognized by their colorful dress, red and gold being their favorite colors – just like the rising Sun.

Myth

Classic Leo myths all involve lions. Two of the greatest heroes of ancient times, Hercules and Samson, both struggled with lions in stories that may date to the time, around 2000 B.C., when Leo ceased to be the sign in which the Sun rose at the summer solstice. Another famous Old Testament story features Daniel, who had the unique distinction of combining in quick succession the jobs of Babylonian court astrologer and Hebrew prophet. The famous tale relates how Daniel was thrown into the lions' den, and how God intervened and the lions left him alone. Because Leo is the royal sign – the lion was a symbol of the Babylonian emperor – the story is a demonstration of God's power over earthly rulers, but it also shows that this power, once recognized, is essentially benign. (In the Middle Ages, when there were moves to replace classical images with Christian ones, there were attempts to rename Leo "one of Daniel's lions.") In a later version of the story, the Christian Androcles, having been thrown into the Roman circus, befriends the lion who is supposed to eat him. In this case, the lion responds to Androcles' kindness and courage with loyalty, an example of positive Leonine qualities resulting in the best possible outcome.

VIRGO

ELEMENT: Earth QUALITY: Mutable
RULING PLANET: Mercury SYMBOL: The Virgin
The Sun enters Virgo on August 22/23.

The key to the understanding of Virgo lies in the symbol of the Virgin. This is not a passive, pure, feeble virgin, but rather a powerful form of the Earth mother, the ancient fertility goddess. In Western mythology, the two greatest examples are Isis, the celestial queen in Egyptian myth; and the Virgin Mary, the queen of heaven in Roman Catholic mythology. The virgin in this sense is pure, but also robust, fertile, and potent. Virgo can be one of the most productive and efficient of signs, and is prepared to sacrifice its own interests in order to complete its allotted tasks. It is above all a sign of service and self-sacrifice.

Mercury's rulership brings to this practical sign the gift of analysis, which is crucial if it is to achieve its practical objectives: thinking a problem through, assessing the facts, and reaching a conclusion.

Virgoans are often too fussy, overconcerned with cleanliness and order, and unable to deal with spontaneity and chaos. Their good-natured willingness to help out lays them open to exploitation by people who are too lazy to do things for themselves. Virgoans are natural bureaucrats, but socially they tend to be shy and lack confidence when expressing their feelings. They can resist anything that threatens to upset the boundaries of their expectations and established order. They have very high standards but can be overcritical. If critical of others, they can offend; if critical of themselves, they can seriously erode their self-confidence. Above all, they need to balance their perfectionism with self-belief and a sense of the possible, perhaps learning from their imaginative opposite sign, Pisces.

Myth

Virgo myths feature one of two key characters – either a virgin/maiden or a celestial mother. The most notable Virgoan figure, combining both characters, is the Roman Catholic Church's Virgin Mary, mother of God, and Queen of Heaven, who cares for sinners so much that she personally intercedes on their behalf with God. Virgo is the only one of the signs, though, to have a distinctly modern myth associated with it. This is the "Gaia hypothesis," invented by the scientist James Lovelock in the 1970s and named after the ancient Greek mother goddess. According to this hypothesis, the Earth is a self-regulating system in which all parts of nature are interdependent with all other parts. As taken up by the millions of people for whom caring for the environment has a spiritual dimension, this means that the earth is alive and that recycling goods or eating organically grown food assumes almost religious overtones. We have here a clear example of a modern myth which encourages us to live a more careful lifestyle, looking after the earth and its natural resources. There could be nothing more typically Virgoan.

LIBRA

ELEMENT: Air QUALITY: Cardinal
RULING PLANET: Venus SYMBOL: The Scales
The Sun enters Libra on September 22/23.

Libra is best understood through its symbol, the scales or balance. The scales were originally those that the Egyptian gods used to weigh the souls of the dead before deciding whether they deserved eternal life, but later became the well-known scales of justice. Libra is also an Air sign and so, in the best circumstances, eminently rational. Libra always weighs up different possibilities, and few signs are so aware of different choices and alternatives. Ideally, Libra's function is to resolve opposing possibilities and to seek a third way, using its mind to help with the resolution of all conflicts. Sometimes, though, Libran types are crippled by indecision, unable to make a firm choice and face the commitment that this involves. Some Librans resolve the dilemma by making an impulsive choice (like its opposite sign, Aries) and, even though it may not be the best option, sticking to it through thick and thin for fear of having to make yet another decision.

This sign is ruled by Venus, and one of its major priorities is to establish harmonious and balanced partnerships. Librans' artistic qualities enable them to create beautiful and pleasing environments, so they can be cordial company both at home and at work. The importance of successful friendships is such that Librans will conceal those parts of their character that they imagine might offend other people, such as displays of anger. They thrive in social groups, being born diplomats, bringing enemies together to make them friends. The sign is always reasonable in the face of criticism and will face prolonged provocation before its good nature cracks. This sign's paradox is that it aims to create a balance that can never really exist in a world undergoing constant change: as soon as a problem is solved, the world moves on and fresh challenges arise. Librans need to learn flexibility and to realize that their efforts to control their environment are unlikely to be successful in a world that contains the competing characters of the other 11 signs.

Myth

Libran myths are divided into two. First there are the relationship myths in which two lovers – the fairy-tale prince and princess, for example – search for each other, and their coming together brings them wholeness and happiness "ever after." The lesson Libra teaches is that ultimately everything we need from other people already lies within us, and that once we recognize that we will form far more harmonious relationships than if we always expect the "other" to supply all our needs. Second are justice myths, in which the evidence is weighed in the Libran balance – the "scales of justice" – and a verdict reached. The scales of justice owe their origin to the Egyptian belief that the souls of the dead, represented by their hearts, were weighed against feathers, symbolizing truth. If the heart was lighter, the dead person was granted everlasting life. Justice, they say, is blind, and one of Libra's strong qualities is its ability to judge impartially issues of right and wrong, regardless of personal loyalties.

SCORPIO

ELEMENT: Water QUALITY: Fixed
RULING PLANET: Mars (with Pluto as co-ruler)
SYMBOL: The Scales
The Sun enters Scorpio on October 23/24.

Scorpio is the deepest of all the signs and takes its cue from the scorpion, a creature that prefers to live in the dark and is liable to react with a sharp sting when disturbed. The sign's intense emotions are toughened by Mars, given an obsessive quality by Pluto, and channeled into a rigid mold by its fixed quality. Scorpio types develop passionate interests and devotion to causes that they pursue with death-defying dedication. Those born under this sign have an instinctive sense of what is right and what is wrong, and though this may be in contradiction to accepted morality, it nevertheless provides a powerful personal motivation. Scorpio types fall deeply in love, but if hurt or rejected can spend hours plotting bitter revenge. They are usually interested in all things deep, dark, or hidden, which covers a wide range of activities: they may become psychologists, therapists, archeologists, historians, healers, miners, speleologists, astronomers, astrologers, detectives, or members of mysterious religious cults or political groups. The Scorpionic solution to any problem is either to hide away, pretending that it doesn't exist, or go to the other extreme and strive for complete and total change (its colors, red and black, are those of the anarchist flag), even at the risk of total and hard-hitting confrontation.

This sign's great weakness is its inflexibility and reluctance to change; its strength is its powerful commitment to its goals.

Myth

Scorpionic myths involve either journeys through the dark or battles with monsters in deep places. Psychologically these represent the confrontation with one's inner demons, fears, hopes, and traumas, and they always end with an optimistic return to the light, representing rebirth. The Egyptians believed that when night fell, the Sun (Ra) journeyed through the underworld in a struggle with the evil Set until eventually Ra triumphed and was reborn at dawn. The Greek hero Hercules engages in a battle with the Lernean hydra, a multiheaded cave-dwelling monster. When he tries to cut off one of its heads, two more grow in its place, so eventually the hero shines a torch in its face and it dies. The Scorpionic lesson is clear: don't repress fears and complexes but talk about them, bring them into the light of day and defuse them.

SAGITTARIUS

ELEMENT: Fire QUALITY: Mutable
RULING PLANET: Jupiter SYMBOL: The Archer
The Sun enters Sagittarius on November 22/23.

The Sagittarian archer is a centaur, a creature with the rear quarters of a horse and the torso, head, and arms of a human being. This suggests a complicated nature, combining beast with human, instinct with reason, body with spirit. Sagittarius's deeper purpose is to reconcile these opposites. This paradox in the sign's nature is difficult to detect, only emerging in the form of sudden changes in interest.

The combination of mutability with Fire makes the sign unstable and its plans are often dropped before completion. In this, Sagittarius takes its nature from the flying arrow – and the fact that it can be more important to travel than to arrive. This sign is marked by long journeys, whether of the mind, spirit or body. As it is the sign of Jupiter, the ruler of wisdom, Sagittarian journeys are often idealistic experiments in religion, philosophy, or the arts, where the desire is to elevate the human spirit. Sometimes the journeys are physical; Sagittarians are often possessed by wanderlust. The purpose is the search for truth. The lesson to be learned by Sagittarians is that, like the arrow in motion, truth is difficult to pin down. When Sagittarius forgets that it is on an endless quest for the truth and imagines that it has arrived at the final answer, it can retreat behind simple dogma.

This sign's great strength lies in its optimism and enthusiasm; its weakness is its impracticality. Yet, if Sagittarians' faith is strong enough, lack of material success may not be a problem.

Myth

Sagittarian myths come in several forms. There are stories about wanderers and explorers who embark on endless journeys, sometimes in search of a mysterious truth. The story of King Arthur's knights and their quest for the Holy Grail is typically Sagittarian, for the point of the story becomes the knights' experiences on the journey, rather than the elusive Grail. In this sense, the Sagittarian lesson is that it is more important to travel than to arrive. Other Sagittarian myths draw on the nature of Jupiter, the king of the classical pantheon and ruler of Sagittarius. Jupiter was alternately supremely wise and noble, and greedy and indulgent. The classic greed myth tells of Midas, king of Phrygia, who wished that everything he touched would turn to gold. When even the food on his plate turned to gold, he realized that before we wish for something, we should make sure it's what we really want. The lesson for Sagittarius is that belief needs to be balanced with fact, theory with practice – and hope with common sense.

CAPRICORN

ELEMENT: Earth **QUALITY:** Cardinal
RULING PLANET: Saturn **SYMBOL:** The Goat (or Goat with Fish Tail)
The Sun enters Capricorn on December 21/22.

The Capricorn is a mythical beast with the head, front legs, and torso of a goat and the tail of a fish. Accordingly, this is a sign with two natures. It is said there are two kinds of goat: the first remains in domestic captivity, tethered to a post; the second is the wild mountain goat, leaping from peak to peak. The first will work hard to be rewarded with a position of minor responsibility, while the second becomes a captain of industry, the multimillionaire of Western capitalism.

The most commonly known side of Capricorn is that described by the combination of the goat, Saturn, and the Earth element: materialistic, practical, serious, and cautious. This Capricorn is the ideal industrialist or businessperson, letting no humanitarian concerns interfere with the important business of making money. Capricorn's central belief is that fancy ideas are far less important than the need to get the job done and keep the world ticking over. However, the tail of the Capricorn rests in the water, revealing quite another dimension to this sign, almost a shadow side. It can indicate an artist, a visionary, or a revolutionary who believes that the regular order of the world must be overthrown.

Capricorns harbor emotions as powerful as those of any other sign but, as it's a Saturnine Earth sign, they may find their feelings difficult to express. They may appear to be shy and happiest in conservative and formal social situations, but if these feelings are not acknowledged they will nag until given adequate expression. It is all too easy to adopt so-called traditional values and then try and impose them on others. Capricorn's great strength, though, is its ability to create tangible, practical gains, not to mention wealth and prosperity – and this should always be valued.

Myth

As the sign which contains the Sun at the winter solstice in the northern hemisphere, Capricorn contains some of the richest and most profound mythology we know of. Christmas, the Christian midwinter festival of hope, light and rebirth, was fixed for just after the solstice because December 25 was the Roman festival of Sol Invictus, when the Sun's rebirth was celebrated. Hannukah, the Jewish Festival of Lights, and Divali, the Hindu midwinter festival, may share common origins with Christmas, Sol Invictus (and the Roman festival of Saturnalia) that go back thousands of years before the individual religions were distinguished. The point is that Capricorn's materialism is about far more than making money. It embodies the endless and interlocking processes of decay and growth to which all natural life is subject. To take an everyday example, Capricorn's attitude toward money puts as much emphasis on using it as making it. One other Capricorn figure is worth noting. The earliest mythical teacher of wisdom in ancient Babylon was Oannes, a creature with the body of a man rather than a goat, but with a fish's tail, just like Capricorn. We can leave this as an open question then: if Capricorn is a teacher, what does it teach each one of us?

AQUARIUS

ELEMENT: Air **QUALITY:** Fixed
RULING PLANET: Saturn (with Uranus as co-ruler)
SYMBOL: The Water Carrier
The Sun enters Aquarius on January 20/21.

This is an enigmatic sign, ruled by two planets with totally incompatible natures, the one desiring order, the other tearing it down. There are many contradictions in this sign's character that make it one of the most interesting.

The water carrier is depicted pouring water out of a vast container, an image that symbolizes the ability of this sign to spread new ideas. Aquarius is concerned, sometimes to the point of obsession, with being new, radical and different. Often it is eccentric, frequently awkward, and always demanding complete personal freedom. Above all, it is idealistic, with strong ideas on how the world should be, although sometimes it shows a disregard for how it actually is.

The Uranian face of Aquarius is an anarchist, yet the Saturnine side believes in authority. The result of this paradox is that Aquarians often try to impose their own unusual ways on other people, against their will if necessary. It is up to them to establish order out of their own chaos, to take charge of their own unconventional instincts, and to define and channel them.

Because Aquarius is a fixed sign, Aquarians often develop a lifestyle, or a set of attitudes, which they find impossible to change. Here is another paradox: Aquarians establish themselves as different from everyone else, but they themselves remain unchanged. Socially and professionally, their partners need to be people who can accept Aquarians' need to say one thing and do another! Aquarians specialize in producing new ideas, but because these are impractical, they need the help of other signs to implement them.

Myth

The most famous Aquarian myths are the flood stories that occur in almost every world culture. Most peoples tell tales of how once, many years ago, when the world was corrupt and decadent, the gods and goddesses, or God, sent a great deluge to cleanse it, allowing only a few humans to survive. This remains one of the guiding Aquarian myths, which is why we expect people associated with this sign to advocate a great revolution that will completely transform the world – as in the Age of Aquarius. The Aquarian lesson is to recognize that while such great dreams may be very worthwhile, and may have admirable consequences, they should never be at the expense of individual freedom. The lesson of the 20th century was that Aquarian utopias go wrong when they fail to recognize that not everyone wants to join in. And in personal relationships Aquarians need to recognize that their partners have minds of their own, that they should respect their ideas – and that change requires consent.

PISCES

ELEMENT: Water QUALITY: Mutable
RULING PLANET: Jupiter (with Neptune as co-ruler)
SYMBOL: The Two Fishes
The Sun enters Pisces on February 18/19.

Pisces is the most unworldly of all the signs. Of its two planetary rulers, Jupiter rules religion, Neptune mysticism. This is hardly a combination to encourage success in worldly pursuits: Pisceans often withdraw from the world into a safe refuge.

Emotional, sensitive, impressionable, and vulnerable, Pisceans lack the hard shell of those under the influence of the other two Water signs, Cancer and Scorpio. Their defense against the world is, therefore, to wear disguises, and they are skilled in adapting to different situations and concealing their real feelings. Pisceans are like chameleons – changing their color at will – and can be criticized for always agreeing with the last person they spoke to. They often appear to be a part of whatever is happening when, in fact, they have drifted off into a private fantasy.

Pisces is exceptionally imaginative – and just as perceptive as Scorpio. If Piscean individuals develop practical skills, they are able to express their talents in a number of ways. They can be excellent artists, but they are also self-sacrificing, wanting to find a role that has a greater meaning. Sometimes they swing into their Virgoan "shadow" and concentrate exclusively on practical matters as a way of silencing their inner world. They are attracted to charitable work, but can be a soft-touch and easily exploited. Their better nature can be their undoing when other people take advantage of them. Pisces longs to do its best for the world and can sacrifice its own interests in both personal and professional relationships. Self-sacrifice may be admirable but is not always a good path to follow.

This is a manipulative sign, often instinctively aware of underlying emotional currents, and Pisceans often succeed on the stage, in religion, and in politics, where performance and ritual enable them to provide illusion and spectacle.

Piscean weakness in handling the real world can lead to chronic indecision. They tend to reject most worldly matters as unimportant, which can be a problem in the materialistic West, but in the East is revered as the principle of "non-attachment," by which mystics can liberate themselves from dependence on the satisfying of physical needs. Pisceans can give the appearance of failing when, in fact, they have made no attempt to succeed. The truth is that they can only throw their full weight into an activity when they truly believe in it, otherwise they go their own way.

Myth

Piscean myths often involve sacrifice, imprisonment, and transformation. Rapunzel's imprisonment in a tower and Sleeping Beauty's long sleep can both be considered Piscean, as can the frog who turns into a prince when shown love. One classic modern Piscean tale is that of Beauty and the Beast, in which the Beast attempts to imprison Beauty but then, after he gives her up, is redeemed by her love and revealed to be a handsome prince. The Piscean lesson is clear: appearances can be deceptive. Never judge people at face value, but try to find the person within and understand their hopes, fears, wishes, and needs. Everyone has a story to tell – and Pisces can tell it.

THE SIGNS OF THE ZODIAC

SIGN	GLYPH	SYMBOL	ELEMENT	QUALITY	SEX	PLANET
Aries	♈	The Ram	Fire	Cardinal	M	Mars
Taurus	♉	The Bull	Earth	Fixed	F	Venus
Gemini	♊	The Twins	Air	Mutable	M	Mercury
Cancer	♋	The Crab	Water	Cardinal	F	The Moon
Leo	♌	The Lion	Fire	Fixed	M	The Sun
Virgo	♍	The Virgin	Earth	Mutable	F	Mercury
Libra	♎	The Scales	Air	Cardinal	M	Venus
Scorpio	♏	The Scorpion	Water	Fixed	F	Mars and Pluto
Sagittarius	♐	The Archer	Fire	Mutable	M	Jupiter
Capricorn	♑	The Goat-Fish	Earth	Cardinal	F	Saturn
Aquarius	♒	The Water Carrier	Air	Fixed	M	Saturn and Uranus
Pisces	♓	The Two Fishes	Water	Mutable	F	Jupiter and Neptune

♈ ♉ ♊ ♋ ♌ ♍ ♎ ♏ ♐ ♑ ♒ ♓

CHAPTER 3

THE PLANETS IN THE SIGNS

In every horoscope, the planets are distributed among the signs of the zodiac in a pattern that is unique, and the interpretation of the planets in the signs is fundamental to all astrological interpretation. A basic formula is used to create the psychological interpretations of planets in signs and, once this is understood, the astrologer is able to interpret these without recourse to books. Such understanding comes with experience, and the beginner has to rely on standard interpretations. The formula assumes that each planet represents a basic function and each sign a basic principle. The function represented by the planet then manifests itself according to the principle of the sign in which it is placed.

THE BASIC PATTERN

The interpretations given here are all general readings, combining the natures of sign and planet, but they by no means represent the last word on the subject. Astrologers create their own subtle differences in the act of reading a horoscope. Most learn by studying set interpretations such as those listed here, and then applying them to the horoscopes of friends and family. In each case, because of the total mix of factors, a slightly different emphasis will be given to each interpretation. The following list, therefore, represents a basic pattern to which the student will be able to add from personal experience.

- Planets in Aries act assertively and powerfully.
- Planets in Taurus become stable and practical.
- Planets in Gemini become more unsettled and intellectual.
- Planets in Cancer become more emotional and cautious.
- Planets in Leo become bolder and more expressive.
- Planets in Virgo become more practical and analytical.
- Planets in Libra become more concerned with relationships and appearances.

- Planets in Scorpio become more perceptive, determined, and emotional.
- Planets in Sagittarius become more unstable and concerned with personal freedom.
- Planets in Capricorn become more practical and cautious.
- Planets in Aquarius become more erratic and in need of freedom.
- Planets in Pisces become more sensitive and emotional.

DIGNITY AND DETRIMENT, EXALTATION AND FALL

Each of the planets is strong or weak when placed in certain signs. In Dignity and Exaltation, the planets are strong and express themselves well; while in Detriment and Fall, they are weak and face difficulties in their expression. Planets are in Dignity in those signs which they rule and in Detriment in the opposing signs. Only the seven traditional planets are included in the Exaltations, and in each case they have both a sign of Exaltation and a single degree within that sign in which the Exaltation is strongest. Planets are in Fall when in the opposing positions to their Exaltation.

At the general level of psychological interpretation, these considerations are already taken into account and need not be considered separately. However, their importance grows as the need for precision increases.

Until the 17th century, astrologers used a complex system of Dignities and "Debilities" (Detriment and Fall) that included the decans – which came about as a result of dividing zodiac signs into three, a system devised by the ancient Egyptians. There has been a revival in their use recently by astrologers using traditional methods of horary astrology (see Chapter 12).

☉

THE SUN

The sign that contains the Sun provides the basic key to personality and life potential. It exposes the individual's major strengths and weaknesses, indicates the lessons to be learned and skills to be tapped. It may also be equated with the male side of the personality as against the Moon's rulership of the female. There are few specifics to consider regarding the Sun, so the following personality descriptions are all brief. They are, however, most important.

♈

SUN IN ARIES (Exaltation)

These people are assertive and self-interested. They are leaders, initiating new ventures, but may rely on others to follow things through. They can make enemies by ignoring other people's welfare.

♉

SUN IN TAURUS

Sun–Taurus types are essentially conservative, requiring stability. They hang on to the past, preserving what is best and refusing to let go what is worst. They are sensual and creative but unambitious, and slow to recognize an opportunity. Their natural fidelity is matched by their stubborn failure to change.

♊

SUN IN GEMINI

Geminians are essentially intellectuals and require constant mental stimulation. Thinkers, talkers, readers and writers, these people need to be involved in acquiring and communicating knowledge. They can also be involved in travel and it is as natural for them to be cab drivers and postal workers as teachers or journalists.

♋

SUN IN CANCER

Sensitive Cancerians are marked by their powerful emotions, but they usually try to conceal these behind a public mask. A valuable clue to interpretation is that the sign containing the Moon (the planet ruling Cancer) gives the nature of the public face adopted by this sign. For example, people with Sun in Cancer but Moon in Aries give an appearance of great self-confidence, while with Moon in Gemini they may give the appearance of cool, intellectual observers. Cancerians place great importance on security and do not like taking risks. Domestic and family security is the key to their happiness and, when they feel safe, they are free to express their caring and compassionate maternal qualities to the full. When deprived of security, they can become sharp-tongued, cynical, and bitter.

♌

SUN IN LEO (Dignity)

Leos are creative in the broadest sense, and for them all the world's a stage. They are either proud, regal, and generous, or vain, egotistical, and wasteful. Even if they are unreliable as far as others are concerned, they are consistent in their own behavior; unpunctuality may be a regular habit. They are instinctively faithful but easily distracted by flattery. Their resistance to change can be a major failing. Sometimes they find that after holding the center stage, the world moves on and leaves them stranded.

♍

SUN IN VIRGO

Idealistic, perfectionist, and practical, Virgos can be self-sacrificing, placing their own interests after those of a greater cause. They require a practical purpose in life and insist that this should show concrete results. High standards can make them excessively critical of others; self-criticism all too often lessens their self-confidence. They have organizational skills and an ability to cope with detail.

♎

SUN IN LIBRA (Fall)

Librans are dominated by an awareness of imbalance and motivated by the need to remedy it. They cannot tolerate a rough environment or uncouth behavior, and often become skilled in creating beautiful and restful surroundings. Usually a sense of balance is achieved through relationships, and a need to succeed in these prompts typically pleasant manners and attractive appearance. Librans can be too dependent on other people's support and approval.

♏

SUN IN SCORPIO

Emotional, intense, and perceptive, Sun-Scorpio types are driven by the instincts of the unconscious. At their best they have deep compassion and a powerful healing energy, but when hurt or rejected they can all too easily retreat to a black depression. Scorpios need to learn to accept, handle, and express their own deep, tempestuous, and sometimes obsessive feelings.

♐

SUN IN SAGITTARIUS

These people are adventurers and seekers after truth. Some are intellectuals who set off on philosophical or religious quests. Others seek experience and personal growth through foreign travel. They can help themselves by establishing a sense of inner security. They can inspire others with their enthusiasm, but can be tactless.

♑

SUN IN CAPRICORN

Conservative and practical, Capricorns often lead very materialistic lives, judging people and opportunities by financial considerations, chasing status, prestige, and possessions. However, they have very deep emotions that often go unrecognized or unacknowledged. It is worth their while to work at expressing their feelings more directly and openly.

♒

SUN IN AQUARIUS (Detriment)

Aquarians aspire to be different. They have a reputation for being progressive, radical, and eccentric, and this is sometimes deserved. In a liberal atmosphere they may express their difference by being authoritarian or conservative. They hate being tied down, and treasure their independence. They often seem to be supremely self-confident but can suffer from a low opinion of their own talents. They need to be more at ease with their feelings and should learn to integrate their radical ideas with practical life.

♓

SUN IN PISCES

Sensitive and emotional, Pisceans are imaginative dreamers. Often they prefer the safety of private fantasy to the fuss and bother of real life. They are impractical, and avoid problems and conflicts by simply slipping away when these appear. Pisceans are impossible to pin down and hate committing themselves or taking decisions. If they discover a cause or a deep personal interest (perhaps artistic, philosophical, or charitable), they will follow it with unshakeable dedication while remaining indifferent to everyday affairs. The symbol of two fishes swimming in opposite directions represents a need to reconcile contrasting possibilities.

☽

THE MOON

The sign containing the Moon provides clues for the astrologer concerning the person's general emotional state, the female half of the psyche, the mother, attitudes to the mother, maternal instincts, the home and family background and the general public face. There are a great many specific statements that can be made about this rich and varied planet, and the following sample interpretations provide a basic summary.

♈

MOON IN ARIES

Generally assertive and emotionally powerful, these people need to control their domestic environments. They are generous in love but require a lot of affection in return. Women with this position are not prepared to take second place; men are likely to seek women with strong personalities. The result of these demands may be argument or friction.

♉

MOON IN TAURUS (Exaltation)

The female archetype embodied here is fertile, maternal, and sexual, and these people can make excellent mothers. Overemphasized, these characteristics can be smothering. These people need domestic security and are practical and competent in running a home.

♊

MOON IN GEMINI

These people rationalize their emotional experiences. As a result, they may lose touch with their real feelings. Their nervous and animated dispositions can be reflected in changeable home conditions. Women with this position are likely to strive for intellectual achievement; men appreciate women with lively minds.

♋

MOON IN CANCER (Dignity)

Highly emotional, these people give a lot of affection, but must feel loved in return if they are to be happy and secure. A stable home life is extremely important as a safe haven for relaxation and privacy. This is one of the archetypal mother images and is strongly expressed in homemaking and domestic skills. Men with this position can be very maternal, and may become strongly attached to a maternal woman.

♌

MOON IN LEO

Self-expressive and extroverted, these people are social performers. Even their apparent emotional honesty can be part of the performance. Domestic life is often lively as the home becomes a stage. Women with this position are warmhearted, generous, and unable to accept a subordinate place. Men may idealize strong and ambitious women, placing them on a pedestal.

♍

MOON IN VIRGO

One of the classic images of the Moon in Virgo is that of the Virgin Mary, the embodiment of purity. Another is of Martha, who faithfully waited on Christ. These people relish order and cleanliness, and abhor crude and uncouth behavior. Domestic order is one of their priorities. They pick their friends carefully and are usually shy.

♎

MOON IN LIBRA

These people need emotional calm. They cannot bear hostility and argument. They preserve the peace in relationships and at home through their diplomatic powers and efforts to create a pleasant environment. Their avoidance of confrontation can lead them to ignore their own feelings, especially their anger.

♏

MOON IN SCORPIO (Fall)

Secretive and intensely emotional, these people often exude an air of mystery. They need stable and secure conditions, which paradoxically are often affected by sudden disruption and confrontations. They are reserved socially, but can be passionate in close relationships.

♐

MOON IN SAGITTARIUS

These people dislike constraints upon their behavior and resist emotional and domestic ties. They need to be given as much freedom as possible. They often leave home to settle abroad. Men with this position are usually attracted to independent, spirited women.

♑

MOON IN CAPRICORN (Detriment)

The Moon in Capricorn reveals conservatism in emotional and domestic matters. These people do not find it easy to show their feelings, and often form relationships for financial reasons, status, or security. They apply their practical skills to maintaining their homes.

♒

MOON IN AQUARIUS

Emotional independence is the key to this position. These people react very badly if they think they are being tied down emotionally or domestically. They resent obligations and responsibilities, and home conditions may be unusual and unsettled.

The Moon in Aquarius is particularly connected to the women's liberation movement, although it is also connected to the traditional ways in which women assert themselves.

♓

MOON IN PISCES

For these sensitive and shy people, the home can provide a refuge from the hard knocks of the real world. They are compassionate and hospitable, but should try to develop a thicker skin without losing their natural kindness. Home life can be disorganized and relationships clouded by unrealistic desires. Men with this position have strong feminine natures.

☿

MERCURY

Mercury's position in the signs reveals the different ways in which people's minds work, their intellectual interests and aptitudes, and how they communicate.

♈

MERCURY IN ARIES

Very self-willed and confident, these people know what they want. In arguments they are combative and convinced they are right. They are fast thinkers and have sharp tongues, and can be intellectually arrogant.

♉

MERCURY IN TAURUS

For Mercury–Taurus types, mental processes are turned to practical problems, and abstract thought is usually considered a waste of time. Thought processes may be slow and attitudes conservative.

♊

MERCURY IN GEMINI (Dignity)

The collection and communication of knowledge is a major priority. These people have clear and logical minds and need mental stimulation. They love debate but their opinions are usually changeable. Physical exercise is necessary to work off nervous tension.

♋

MERCURY IN CANCER

These people have retentive memories. Their thoughts are dominated by their feelings; their attitudes are naturally compassionate and poetic, and attempts to be scientific or objective will be superficial.

♌

MERCURY IN LEO

With a high opinion of their own intellectual powers and plenty of mental energy, these people are quick to form opinions and often do not bother with facts. They like performing and may be attracted to the theater.

♍

MERCURY IN VIRGO (Dignity and Exaltation)

Pedantic, critical, and analytical, these people have no time for frivolous ideas. The less interesting face of this position is to be found in the bureaucrat, the lover of intellectual order; the more interesting in those who use their minds for the practical good of the world.

♎

MERCURY IN LIBRA

These people are born strategists, and use their powers of careful and balanced thought to reconcile opposing factions and forces. Their awareness of contrasting possibilities enables them to increase their choices in life, but can lead to indecision.

♏

MERCURY IN SCORPIO

These people do not have ideas, they have instincts and beliefs, and often follow these with great dedication. They are deeply interested in all things dark, hidden, or mysterious, including religion and political conspiracies, and in all forms of research.

♐

MERCURY IN SAGITTARIUS (Detriment)

These people are philosophers: ideas and opinions are more important to them than facts. They may be careless over detail, but often have an instinctive idea of the truth. They may develop a particular interest in foreign cultures and religion. They are often tactless.

♑

MERCURY IN CAPRICORN

Practically minded and with down-to-earth interests, this is a classic position for engineers or mathematicians as well as people in business. The acquisition of wealth and status is often important.

♒

MERCURY IN AQUARIUS

Independent minded, these people do not like being told what to think. They need the freedom to find their own intellectual interests and they frequently hold radical views. They like issues to be clear-cut.

♓

MERCURY IN PISCES (Detriment and Fall)

Poetic and imaginative, these people have artistic minds and may have difficulty coping with practical and scientific studies. This is the most deceptive and gullible position for Mercury. Confusion can be avoided if attention is paid to detail.

♀

VENUS

The position of Venus in the signs provides clues concerning the individual's female nature, relationships, marriage, and attitudes to pleasure and the arts.

♈

VENUS IN ARIES (Detriment)

These people have a pressing need for attention and affection. They can be passionate lovers, but may also be selfish. They are quick to assert their interests and are often argumentative. Men with this position will be attracted to bold, assertive women.

♉

VENUS IN TAURUS (Dignity)

Physical and emotional love are united by Venus in Taurus. These people are instinctively faithful, but can be too attracted to sensual experience to remain monogamous. Skill in the arts and crafts is likely.

♊

VENUS IN GEMINI

These people distance themselves from emotional contacts by continually analyzing their feelings. They may talk about these without actually facing the real issues. They find it easy to drift in and out of relationships.

♋

VENUS IN CANCER

These people need emotional security. They are caring and sympathetic in emotional relationships, but can be possessive and need to be able to let go when a partnership has run its course. They are often reserved socially.

♌

VENUS IN LEO

Colorful and vivacious, these people are drawn to the social whirl and relationships become a performance. Their egotism can be attractive, but relationships may run into difficulty if they ignore other people's feelings.

♍

VENUS IN VIRGO (Fall)

These people are often shy socially. They make few close friends because most people do not match up to their high standards. Their criticism of other people can be unjustified and result from their own lack of self-confidence. They should learn to trust their own feelings.

♎

VENUS IN LIBRA (Dignity)

Appearances are important and these people rely on making a good impression through pleasant behavior and attractive clothes. They need to be liked and fear arguments and disagreements. Dependence on the latest fashions can result from a lack of emotional confidence. Their expectations of relationships can be too high.

♏

VENUS IN SCORPIO (Detriment)

The female archetype associated with this position is the dark temptress, a potent image throughout the ages. These people are passionate lovers, but sometimes make the mistake of falling in love with the wrong people. Love rejected can lead to bitterness and jealousy. They are often self-sacrificing, but also possessive, and frequently relish emotional confrontation.

♐

VENUS IN SAGITTARIUS

These people need emotional freedom. If successful relationships are to be formed, they must be given the freedom to escape whenever they want to. They cannot tolerate emotional restriction.

♑

VENUS IN CAPRICORN

These people value tradition and seek status and security from emotional partnerships. Common sense is brought to bear on relationships, and personal feelings are pushed to one side.

♒

VENUS IN AQUARIUS

These people require interest, change and stimulation in their relationships. They resist social conventions and do not like to be tied down or forced into a role. The role they choose is often that of the rebel, which can be used to bring partnerships to an end. They tend to have unrealistic intellectual expectations of relationships and can lose touch with their true feelings.

♓

VENUS IN PISCES (Exaltation)

The female image associated with Pisces is that of the ethereal pre-Raphaelite maiden. This is as unrealistic as the rest of this sign's romantic dreams. These people find all relationships a compromise between their fantasies and the reality of human life. They want to be self-sacrificing but are so concerned with their own feelings that they lose touch with their partners.

♂

MARS

Mars in the signs shows the individual's general energy level, the way practical problems are handled, attitudes toward men, and expression of the male psyche.

♈

MARS IN ARIES (Dignity)

Energetic and assertive, these people are leaders in their field. They are impulsive, impatient, and not good at coping with opposition. They exacerbate practical problems by carelessness.

♉

MARS IN TAURUS (Detriment)

Practical, capable, and consistent, these people often get things done in the most sensible way. They are obstinate, however, and not good at adapting to new circumstances.

♊

MARS IN GEMINI

These people often have sharp minds which they can apply to practical problems. They may take on too many tasks at the same time, and by spreading themselves too thinly may delay success.

♋

MARS IN CANCER (Fall)

Actions are dominated by emotional commitment and imagination rather than by practical considerations. They are sometimes prone to emotional outbursts.

♌

MARS IN LEO

Theatrical and dramatic, these people brook no opposition to their grand schemes. Often their actions are impressive and creative, but sometimes they are impractical and lack substance.

♍

MARS IN VIRGO

This is an excellent combination for those involved in crafts or any precise practical activity. They have a flair for detail, thrive on routine, but lack imagination.

♎

MARS IN LIBRA (Detriment)

Energy is best used to restore harmony and balance, perhaps by developing artistic skills, or by reconciling people in conflict. Their awareness of opposing choices can lead to indecision or to an interesting range of experiences and skills in strategy.

♏

MARS IN SCORPIO (Dignity)

These people are invariably drawn to enigmatic and mysterious activities and bring emotional commitment to whatever they do. Their motivations are so strong that it is usually impossible to deflect them from a chosen course of action.

♐

MARS IN SAGITTARIUS

It can take a lifetime for these people to achieve their far-flung ambitions. They set their sights on distant heights and leave others to sort out the details. They often become travelers.

♑

MARS IN CAPRICORN (Exaltation)

These people have a sound practical approach which makes them well fitted to be engineers and mechanics. They are best suited to living and working at a practical level.

♒

MARS IN AQUARIUS

These people seek radical solutions to old problems. Too often these are fine in theory but chaotic in practice. They are idealistic but impractical.

♓

MARS IN PISCES

This is the most impractical position for Mars. Although intuition and imagination helps these people to find the most attractive and, sometimes, the most sensible way of doing things, they usually lack the necessary skills.

♃

JUPITER

Jupiter in each sign gives clues about the way people try to expand and grow. It takes an average of one year to pass through any one sign of the zodiac. Everybody born in a given 12-month period will have Jupiter in the same sign, and it gives false emphasis in a birth chart if too much importance is given to the sign containing Jupiter. Psychologically, this planet should be seen as a general background influence, contributing to other tendencies in the chart.

♈ ♌ ♐

JUPITER IN THE FIRE SIGNS

This reveals a personality with large-scale and personal ambitions, perhaps reaching the top of a career, excelling in a particular skill, or merely striving to be the center of attention. In Aries, these tendencies may be most self-interested, and their nature will be revealed by the other tendencies in the chart. In Leo, ambitions are likely to be grandiose and accomplished with optimism and theatrical flair. In Sagittarius (Dignity), ambitions are more likely to be concerned with intellectual improvement or religious experience, and foreign travel.

♉ ♍ ♑

JUPITER IN THE EARTH SIGNS

These people strive for self-development through practical work in order to achieve material results. Jupiter in Taurus may indicate a love of luxury and sensual experience. In Virgo (Detriment) the purpose is likely to be idealistic but within an orderly structure; in Capricorn (Fall), material wealth may be a priority.

♊ ♎ ♒

JUPITER IN THE AIR SIGNS

In the Air signs, Jupiter stresses personal growth through analysis and the use of the intellect.

Some people may look inward and analyze themselves, examining their own motives; others may concentrate on sharing ideas. In Gemini (Detriment), the collection and communication of facts may be an end in itself. In Libra, Jupiter may emphasize the use of knowledge for promoting peace and harmony, but requires a partnership to function properly. In Aquarius, the emphasis may be on the creation and promotion of new ideas.

♋ ♏ ♓

JUPITER IN THE WATER SIGNS

Jupiter in the Water signs craves emotion. These people need love. While they aspire to the heights of romantic ecstasy, they can also be self-sacrificing and can wallow in self-pity and emotion. In Cancer, (Exaltation) Jupiter emphasises the virtues of helping other people through compassion; in Scorpio, through healing; and in Pisces (Dignity), through prayer and good intentions. Jupiter in Cancer may, on the other hand, lead to indulgence in domestic luxury; in Scorpio it may lead to license in sex and other Scorpionic mysteries; and in Pisces there may be indulgence in escapist fantasies, dreams, religion, or drugs.

♄

SATURN

Saturn rules the principle of limitation. It shows the way in which people control themselves and are inhibited by their environment.

Saturn takes about 29 years to travel around the zodiac, spending almost two and a half years in each sign. Its generational influence is even more pronounced than Jupiter's, and its meaning by sign has a far more general psychological influence in a horoscope than by house and aspect.

♈ ♌ ♐

SATURN IN THE FIRE SIGNS

In the Fire signs, Saturn inhibits the overall energy level, restricts ambitions, and reduces self-confidence. These people may constantly anticipate failure, avoid risks, and reject opportunity, but the fear of failure can lead to concentrated hard work. Conservatism may influence attitudes toward authority when Saturn is in Aries (Fall); creativity, artistic values, and love affairs when it is in Leo (Dettriment); or philosophy, beliefs, and attitudes to foreign cultures when it is in Sagittarius.

♉ ♍ ♑

SATURN IN THE EARTH SIGNS

These people may experience difficulties and challenges in physical and practical affairs. There may be delays or obstacles to work, or financial difficulties. In Taurus, Saturn leads to increased conservatism and stubbornness. In Virgo, it is likely to weaken the self-confidence of this sign, but may increase its capacity for hard work. Saturn in its own sign of Capricorn (Dignity) brings out the individual's materialism and lack of emotion.

♊ ♎ ♒

SATURN IN THE AIR SIGNS

Saturn in the Air signs introduces either mental discipline or intellectual inhibition. There is likely to be conservatism in ideas and attitudes. In Gemini, inability to communicate effectively may be balanced by a determined reliance on the facts. In Libra (Exaltation), there may be an emphasis upon stability in partnerships, and a balance of ideas. In Aquarius (Dignity), ideas and opinions tend to be authoritarian.

♋ ♏ ♓

SATURN IN THE WATER SIGNS

Emotional inhibition is likely to result from Saturn placed in the Water signs. There will certainly be an emphasis on emotional self-control. In Cancer (Detriment), this inclines towards a stable home, although the difficulties this sign has in expressing its feelings will be strengthened. In Scorpio, emotions may become more obsessive but more easily hurt, while Pisces may be more vulnerable than usual.

⚷ ♅ ♆ ♇

CHIRON, URANUS, NEPTUNE AND PLUTO

Chiron takes between 49 and 51 years to complete one cycle of the zodiac. Uranus takes almost 84 years, Neptune almost 164 years, and Pluto just over 245 years. Uranus spends about seven years in each sign, Neptune almost 14 years, and Pluto an average of 21 years. Their meaning by sign in a birth chart is, therefore, so general as to provide only vague background information. To the psychological characteristics of the signs, Uranus brings an unusual quality, Neptune a delicate sensitivity and inspiration, and Pluto determination and power. Psychologically these planets symbolize the character of generations.

THE NODES

The importance attached to the nodes in the signs varies considerably. They are used to give general psychological interpretations.

The nodes should be taken together as a pair, the south node revealing the qualities being left behind, the north node those qualities being developed. There is an element of fate in the nodes due to their connection with the vast issues of reincarnation and karma (the law of cosmic cause and effect).

Astrology argues that individuals can alter their fate by their actions, and the nodes show how this may be done. Hence, the qualities of the south node may be seen as those that should be left behind and those of the north node are those that should be developed.

♈ ♎

NORTH NODE IN ARIES, SOUTH NODE IN LIBRA

These people should be more assertive and not rely on others too much.

♉ ♏

NORTH NODE IN TAURUS, SOUTH NODE IN SCORPIO

These people should be more practical and less emotional.

♊ ♐

NORTH NODE IN GEMINI, SOUTH NODE IN SAGITTARIUS

These people should be more clearheaded, less idealistic.

♋ ♑

NORTH NODE IN CANCER, SOUTH NODE IN CAPRICORN

These people should be more caring and compassionate, and less materialistic.

♌ ♒

NORTH NODE IN LEO, SOUTH NODE IN AQUARIUS

These people should develop their personal authority and be less anarchic.

♍ ♓

NORTH NODE IN VIRGO, SOUTH NODE IN PISCES

These people should be more down-to-earth, less dreamy and disorganized.

♎ ♈

NORTH NODE IN LIBRA, SOUTH NODE IN ARIES

These people should be more considerate to others and less self-interested.

♏ ♉

NORTH NODE IN SCORPIO, SOUTH NODE IN TAURUS

These people should give rein to their feelings and be less concerned with practical issues.

♐ ♊

NORTH NODE IN SAGITTARIUS, SOUTH NODE IN GEMINI

These people should pay less attention to detail and develop a broader vision.

♑ ♋

NORTH NODE IN CAPRICORN, SOUTH NODE IN CANCER

These people should be more practical and less sentimental.

♒ ♌

NORTH NODE IN AQUARIUS, SOUTH NODE IN LEO

These people should be more ready to share and less egotistical.

♓ ♍

NORTH NODE IN PISCES, SOUTH NODE IN VIRGO

These people should develop their sensitivity and emotions, and be less critical of themselves and others.

♈ ♉ ♊ ♋ ♌ ♍ ♎ ♏ ♐ ♑ ♒ ♓

CHAPTER 4

THE TWELVE HOUSES

Interpretation of the signs and planets enables the astrologer to describe character in general psychological terms and to point to likely events in a person's life. However, until the houses are added, astrological interpretation remains necessarily vague. The 12 houses rule specific circumstances and areas of life and enable the astrologer to pinpoint the activities in which the potential of the signs and planets will be expressed.

Each house represents a basic principle, but has a range of manifestations, sometimes sharply different from one another. A prime example of this is the eighth house, which may indicate either a deep involvement in the occult or a career in business, among other possibilities. The astrologer should be aware of these contrasts and try to arrive at the best interpretation, relying on astrological expertise and common sense.

The technical basis of the houses lies in the rotation of the ecliptic around the Earth (the apparent path of the Sun around the Earth on its annual cycle). The ecliptic is divided into four sections equivalent to the Sun's position at dawn, midday, sunset, and midnight, and then each is subdivided into a further three, making 12 in all. These are the 12 houses. Their meanings are related to those of the 12 signs, but to make a neat comparison in which the first house equals Aries, the second Taurus, and so on, removes the differences between them.

Whereas the signs appear to rotate around the Earth once in every 24 hours, the position of the houses is effectively fixed. During a 24-hour period, every possible combination of sign position relative to the houses occurs, and this greatly increases the range of astrological interpretation.

The dividing line between two houses, like that between two signs, is known as the cusp.

THE FOUR ANGLES

The framework upon which the house divisions are based are the four "angles." The Ascendant is the degree of the ecliptic rising over the eastern horizon. That may not be the same as actual sunrise, because the moment at which the Sun comes up in any given place depends on the local geography – it comes up later if there are mountains in the way. The Descendant is the exact opposite of the Ascendant, the degree of the ecliptic setting over the western horizon. The Midheaven is the degree of the zodiac that is at the highest point above the horizon, or culmination. The Latin translation of Midheaven is Medium Coeli (MC). Imum Coeli (IC) is the point directly opposite MC.

In the birth chart, the Ascendant, the cusp of the first house, is as important as the Sun in determining the individual's personality and potential. The sign containing the Ascendant is known as the rising sign.

The Descendant, the cusp of the seventh house, reveals the individual's attitude to partnerships, and what he or she seeks in a relationship.

The MC rules the need for public recognition, status in community and society, and a person's career. It is the cusp of the tenth house in all but the Equal House system.

The IC represents the home, the family background, and the need for psychological roots and stability. It is the cusp of the fourth house in all but the Equal House system.

These four angles correspond to the meanings for the first house (the Ascendant), the fourth house (the IC), the seventh house (the Descendant), and the tenth house (the MC). These four houses, with their corresponding angles, have completely distinct meanings but may, nevertheless, be understood as part of a single process of human experience. The Ascendant symbolizes birth and infancy, the IC represents childhood and the discovery of an individual identity, the Descendant reveals the formation of adult relationships, and the MC represents the culmination of public achievements.

The intermediate eight houses may be understood in the same manner, each having a distinct meaning but also forming part of a process of development through the horoscope, progressing from birth in the first house to dissolution in the twelfth. The beginner must learn the separate meanings of the houses, but an understanding of the process comes with experience.

THE DIFFERENT HOUSE SYSTEMS

There is no astronomically perfect way of calculating the houses. Over the years, astrologers have tried to devise ways of overcoming the weaknesses built into certain systems. The oldest system, dating back some 2,000 years, is the Equal House system, in which the Ascendant is always the cusp (beginning) of the first house and the Descendant is always the cusp of the seventh house. The rest of the ecliptic is divided into 12 equal segments. The weakness of this system is that the MC and IC do not always fall in the same place as their equivalent house cusps (the tenth and the fourth).

All the other common systems place all four angles on their equivalent house cusps, and are known as the Quadrant systems. However, the mathematical and astronomical rationale of each one is different, and astrologers disagree as to which is the most appropriate. The Placidus, Topocentric, and Koch houses are probably the most commonly used, although some astrologers prefer the Porphyry, Regiomontanus, or Campanus systems.

Different arguments are put forward in support of particular house systems, and it is sometimes claimed that each system has a slightly different meaning. This is a genuine problem, for planets that fall in one house under one system may fall in another under a second. Each astrologer must pick the system and techniques that enable him or her to arrive at the most satisfactory interpretation. In this book, the Placidus system is used.

THE TWELVE HOUSES

THE FIRST HOUSE

The first house rules over the entire personality. In practical terms, this means that the sign containing the Ascendant (the rising sign) is as important as the Sun sign, and any planet placed in the first house has enormous influence over the personality.

THE SECOND HOUSE

This house represents money and possessions, attitudes about them, and how they are acquired and used. Psychologically, this house can show how much people value themselves.

THE THIRD HOUSE

The third house reveals the nature of the mind, the style and manner of communication, and the lower levels of education. It rules all the instruments of communication, and short journeys. It also rules brothers and sisters, although this is frequently ignored in psychological interpretation.

THE FOURTH HOUSE

The fourth house symbolizes the home, both the early environment and family background, and the home that the individual creates in later life. It reveals the needs that domestic life is called upon to satisfy, and the conditioning that caused them. Psychologically, it rules the desire for strong roots and positive identity. This house also rules parents, especially the father.

THE FIFTH HOUSE

The fifth house symbolizes the desire to create and all the ways in which creativity manifests itself. The psychological impulse is to leave a personal mark on the world. The specific areas ruled by this house are the arts, leisure, pleasure, romance, children, sport, speculation, and gambling of all kinds.

THE SIXTH HOUSE

The sixth house rules the principle of practical service, the desire to sacrifice the self to the community, or to a greater good. Specifically, this house rules work and health – in particular the healing professions. It also rules the army and bureaucracies on the grounds that these are the armed services and the civil service.

THE SEVENTH HOUSE

This is the house that rules the desire for partnership, the attitudes toward it, and the needs and functions that relationships fulfill. Traditionally this is the house of marriage, although as the institution of marriage becomes less important in Western countries, its meaning has been broadened to include all intimate emotional relationships, particularly one-to-one relationships. This house also rules close working partnerships.

THE EIGHTH HOUSE

The eighth house symbolizes the entire process of life from birth to death. The first house is often considered a house of symbolic birth, being the beginning of the cycle, but the eighth house rules the actual processes of sex, conception, and birth. There is a metaphysical side to this house – it rules reincarnation – and a psychological correlation with profound changes in life; "born-again" Christians may be ruled by it, as may Indian gurus. On the "turning-the-chart" principle, the eighth house also rules other people's money (because it's the second house after the seventh), legacies, investments, and business affairs. Obviously this function overlaps with that of the second house. Its rulership of mystery extends to the occult and magic.

THE NINTH HOUSE

The ninth house represents the desire for union with something greater. This is the house of beliefs, religion, and philosophy. It is also the house of foreign travel, of the desire to leave one's own culture and inhabit another. It rules long journeys of the mind, spirit, and body. Specifically, this house rules higher education, the law, the church, publishing, foreign countries, and overseas travel.

THE TENTH HOUSE

The tenth house reveals the desire to achieve an identity in the community. This is usually expressed through the individual's career, although those without a career must direct their energies through other avenues. Together with the fourth house, this house rules parents, especially the mother. It also rules leaders, governments, and bosses.

THE ELEVENTH HOUSE

The eleventh house rules the desire to integrate with the community. Just as the fifth house rules creativity of a highly personal nature, this house reveals the individual being creative in a social setting. Specifically, it rules the wider social circle of acquaintances and groups, broader ambitions, general hopes and wishes, and political activity.

THE TWELFTH HOUSE

Like the sixth and ninth houses, this house brings a desire for union with a greater reality, but in this case the impulse is far more mystical. The principle represented by this house is one of spiritual service and self-sacrifice. While this house has noble aspirations, it has a bad reputation for being disorganized and escapist. It is the house in which the cycle comes to an end prior to rebirth in the first house, and it embodies all the lessons learnt by the other 11 houses, including their accumulated mistakes. Specifically, it rules all forms of seclusion and privacy – prisons, hospitals, monasteries, dreams, the unconscious. It also rules hidden problems and secret opponents.

♈ ♉ ♊ ♋ ♌ ♍ ♎ ♏ ♐ ♑ ♒ ♓

CHAPTER 5

THE PLANETS IN THE HOUSES

The interpretation of planets in houses at a basic level is relatively simple. The house in which the planet or planets are contained determines the area of life where the tendency indicated will be expressed most strongly. For example, if an individual is born with Mercury in Aries, indicating a tendency to strong opinions, these will be most strongly expressed in the house containing Mercury. If Mercury is in the fourth house, the area of life ruled will be the home and family; if it's in the eleventh, it could be social situations. In other words, the houses indicate people who might be confident in one area of life, but shy in another. Bearing in mind that all the planets rotate completely through the houses once every 24 hours – and will often change their house position after one hour – two individuals born only hours apart on the same day can have utterly different horoscopes.

By examining each planet in its house, it is possible to make more specific judgements about a person's life than is the case with planets and signs alone. The sample interpretations below are all designed to cover the most general eventualities, with an emphasis on psychological inclinations. It is the task of astrologers to decide which of these is most appropriate to a particular person or horoscope. With experience, they will be able to match the planets to the houses and create their own interpretations. Also, it goes without saying that the sign containing the planet is critical. In Chapter 9, we'll see how the interpretation of signs and houses is put together. Plus, if a planet indicates difficulties in a particular area, the rest of the chart will suggest ways in which those difficulties may be dealt with. It should never be accepted at face value that any particular planet in a house is inherently either a negative or positive indicator. In any one situation, the process indicated by a house-planet combination may relate to difficult circumstances one day, easy the next.

THE CHART RULER

The chart ruler, sometimes known as the Ascendant ruler or ruling planet, is the planet that rules the rising sign, and is always one of the most important planets in the chart. For example, if the rising sign is Capricorn, it is ruled by Saturn, which is, therefore, the chart ruler.

If Saturn is then in the sixth house, the importance of health and work issues is emphasized; if it's in the seventh, the emphasis falls on relationship questions.

EMPTY HOUSES

The planets represent the functions that allow the houses to express themselves. When there is no planet in a house, it could be said that there is no obvious way for the house to find expression. There are then two possibilities: either the person ignores the area of life represented by that house or makes a great effort to succeed in that area.

For example, a person with no planets in the fifth house may have little obvious creative talent and leaves it at that, while another may make strenuous efforts to be more creative. However, even if a house contains no planets, it may contain other astrologically significant points. These may include the Moon's nodes or other factors yet to be considered. The full pattern of the chart should reveal whether an empty house is neglected or overdeveloped. In practice, no house is ever truly "empty."

STELLIUM

When five or more planets are gathered in a single house, this is known as a satelletium, or stellium, for short. Naturally, with so many planets in one house, this house becomes extremely important. The role that house plays in the life of the individual will also be quite complicated.

HOUSE CUSP RULERS

The sign on the house cusp is significant and modifies the manifestation of that house. The sign on the cusp of the first house is of great importance and this, the rising sign, is as important as the Sun sign. The signs on the cusps of the fourth, seventh, and tenth houses are also important for these houses, and rule home, marriage, and career. Signs on the cusps of the remaining houses should also be taken into consideration.

The interpretation is quite straightforward once the principles have been grasped. For example, people with Taurus on the second cusp may be cautious (Taurus) with money (second house), Pisces on the fourth cusp may indicate a disorganized (Pisces) home (fourth house), Aries on the seventh cusp might represent people who are assertive and self-interested (Aries) in relationships (seventh house), while with Capricorn on the tenth cusp they may be businesslike (Capricorn) in their career (tenth house).

The possibilities can be increased by looking at the planet that rules the sign on the house cusp. This is most important for the planet that rules the rising sign (known as the chart ruler or ruling planet). The house containing this planet is automatically increased in importance.

Suppose, for example, that the ruler of the fourth cusp is in the tenth house. Perhaps this means that the individual takes advantage of family members for professional purposes, or puts their interests second to career concerns. If the ruler of the first cusp is in the seventh, this may indicate that close relationships are vital to the individual's life in more ways than might initially be suspected.

If the ruler of the seventh cusp is in the eighth, this may indicate that the most important sort of relationships will be financial ones.

PLANETS CLOSE TO CUSPS

A major issue for many astrologers is the question of whether a planet near the end of a house should be considered to belong in the following house. This is a fair enough question given that the movement of houses means that planet will soon change houses anyway. However, until you have learned from your own experience, it's best to regard a planet as being in the house it's actually in.

Remember the golden rule in interpretation – keep it simple.

☉

THE SUN

The house occupied by the Sun is very important in the chart.

THE SUN IN THE FIRST HOUSE

This denotes egotistical and strong-willed people, good at pursuing their own interests and giving orders, but not much interested in cooperation. As it is likely that the Sun and Ascendant will be in the same sign, the influence of this sign is greatly increased.

THE SUN IN THE SECOND HOUSE

Material possessions and financial affairs are extremely important. Self-employment often suits these people because they like to be responsible for their own financial affairs. Some are motivated by a desire for more wealth, others by a fear of poverty, both of which can be manifestations of a deeper insecurity or lack of self-confidence.

THE SUN IN THE THIRD HOUSE

These people are communicators and fall into two types. On the one hand are the intellectuals, writers, teachers, thinkers, and researchers; on the other are postal workers, cab and bus drivers, and so on. For some, such as those in the travel industry, the two types may overlap.

THE SUN IN THE FOURTH HOUSE

Security is important and is found through putting down roots and establishing a stable home. These people need a safe base and like to be part of a large family. There may be a profound awareness of the past and the individual's background.

THE SUN IN THE FIFTH HOUSE

These people retain childlike qualities, and spontaneity remains important throughout adult life. Their creative talents find outlets in the pursuit of love and pleasure as much as in artistic activity, but if the former is developed at the expense of the latter, they will become frustrated.

THE SUN IN THE SIXTH HOUSE

Self-sacrificing, hardworking, and in need of the security provided by routine, these people like to be of service to their families, communities, and employers. Their interest in health inclines them toward medical or charitable work. They are often idealistic, but can be exploited.

THE SUN IN THE SEVENTH HOUSE

These people place enormous emphasis on partnerships. It is vital for them to have somebody to rely upon even though they like to have their own way. This applies to work as much as to marriage and emotional relationships. The partner becomes an intermediary between themselves and the world.

THE SUN IN THE EIGHTH HOUSE

These people are secretive. They are aware of all the deep and intense possibilities in life and are especially interested in the life cycle from birth to death. There is a wide range of manifestations: some become mediums, occultists, therapists, or healers; others enter the world of finance and business. All are interested in self-development, whether through inner exploration or the accumulation of wealth and power.

THE SUN IN THE NINTH HOUSE

This frequently indicates strong overseas connections, periods of travel or life abroad. These people often have strong beliefs that exercise a powerful influence over their actions, and a deep intellectual curiosity, which promotes success in higher education.

THE SUN IN THE TENTH HOUSE

These people require the prestige, status, and recognition that a career brings. Those without a career need to find a substitute that will allow them the same feelings of public identity. This house rules the mother and may show her character and influence.

THE SUN IN THE ELEVENTH HOUSE

These people like to mix in large groups, seeking social variety and stimulation but avoiding the intimacy of close relationships. They join clubs and societies, and are often involved in political action, no matter how small scale.

THE SUN IN THE TWELFTH HOUSE

Secretive and sensitive, these people require privacy and seclusion, if only to recover from the stresses of the world. Their interests are esoteric and they sometimes study psychology or take up mystical practices.

☽

THE MOON

The house occupied by the Moon becomes the focus for the expression of lunar qualities and aspirations: emotional needs and maternal qualities.

THE MOON IN THE FIRST HOUSE

These people have well-developed maternal instincts and can be protective and caring but also possessive. An ability to provide security for others is complicated by a personal need for security. If the latter is satisfied, then the former will operate well. They are particularly vulnerable to changeable emotions and moods.

THE MOON IN THE SECOND HOUSE

Security is found through money and material possessions. But occasionally these people reject materialism, and then a puritanical lifestyle and ideology are reassuring, providing their own certainties. Attitudes to money and changes in income are the result of emotional changes. Women may figure prominently in money matters.

THE MOON IN THE THIRD HOUSE

These are sensitive and poetic communicators and can make excellent teachers, especially of small children. They like to explore and talk about their own feelings. Their restless curiosity keeps them on the move.

THE MOON IN THE FOURTH HOUSE

For these people, domestic security is vital. Even those who travel widely need to have a sure sense of their own roots and identity. Most of them identify strongly with their family and place of origin. In the home, they often play a maternal role.

THE MOON IN THE FIFTH HOUSE

Creative arts fulfill a vital emotional function for these people. There is a strong need for a lively social life and romantic involvement. Pleasure may be gained from caring for children.

THE MOON IN THE SIXTH HOUSE

These people are good employees. They may be drawn to charitable work or the caring professions. They are ready to perform menial tasks at home and at work. Work and health are strongly affected by emotional changes.

THE MOON IN THE SEVENTH HOUSE

These people require close emotional relationships, and often fulfill a maternal role. They attract people who seek security, but they may come to resent this, for their own emotional needs change with the ebb and flow of lunar rhythms.

THE MOON IN THE EIGHTH HOUSE

These people have powerful emotional and sexual needs, but tend to be secretive about them. They have a good business sense, but can be too emotional to make correct decisions.

THE MOON IN THE NINTH HOUSE

For these people, fascination with foreign cultures may bring emotional relationships with foreigners – marriage, and even life abroad. Higher education and religion may attract them ("mother" church or academic institutions may be a refuge from life's problems).

THE MOON IN THE TENTH HOUSE

The career of these people should have significant "female" qualities. It should be emotionally satisfying, involve helping other people and, perhaps, be in one of the caring professions. Career ambitions may be pursued at the expense of domestic interests.

THE MOON IN THE ELEVENTH HOUSE

These people socialize in large groups in which they often take a leading role. Political involvement is likely, especially in "community politics."

THE MOON IN THE TWELFTH HOUSE

Shy and sensitive, these people nevertheless put their compassion and imagination to work for the common good. Their good deeds will be unofficial and behind the scenes. The home is likely to be a place of seclusion and privacy.

☿

MERCURY

The house containing Mercury shows the area of life and the manner in which mental powers are expressed.

MERCURY IN THE FIRST HOUSE

These people have strong minds, and are keen on learning and expressing their ideas. Some may be very talkative, while others prefer to write and think. They are physically restless and may have nervous habits.

MERCURY IN THE SECOND HOUSE

The mind focuses on wealth and material objects, and these people have plenty of ideas for spending as well as earning money. Self-employment is preferable, but work in any part of the communications or travel industry is appropriate.

MERCURY IN THE THIRD HOUSE

These people have active minds and are attracted to all Mercurial activities – studying, teaching, communicating, and traveling. They are often restless and dislike staying too long in the same place.

MERCURY IN THE FOURTH HOUSE

These people often study at home. They develop interests in their own past, family history, environment, and any subject that helps them establish a sense of identity.

MERCURY IN THE FIFTH HOUSE

Intellectual aptitudes are combined with creative desires. These people may write, perhaps music or fiction, and have a talent for communication. The theater is a likely medium for expression, and children appreciate their skill in telling stories.

MERCURY IN THE SIXTH HOUSE

If these people are mentally stimulated and allowed to express their own ideas at work, then they may be methodical and precise employees, depending on the sign containing the planet. Employment in Mercurial fields is likely. They take a keen interest in health matters, but their own wellness can be affected by nervous tension.

MERCURY IN THE SEVENTH HOUSE

Mental rapport in partnerships, including marriage, is essential. These people like to share interests, hobbies, and attitudes with close friends. They are also interested in other people's problems, partly out of curiosity.

MERCURY IN THE EIGHTH HOUSE

These people have intense and secretive minds, and a fascination for all things arcane and mysterious. This may lead to serious study of psychology, sex, the occult, and the roots of human behavior. Their perception may also be the basis of a sound business sense.

MERCURY IN THE NINTH HOUSE

Fascinated by knowledge and with a desire for understanding, these people may reach academic heights. They often become perpetual students. A particular interest in religion, philosophy, the law, and foreign cultures is likely.

MERCURY IN THE TENTH HOUSE

Careers must provide mental stimulation and utilize ideas and communicative skills. Job satisfaction is more important than monetary rewards. A career in teaching, journalism, secretarial work, or travel is appropriate.

MERCURY IN THE ELEVENTH HOUSE

These people are very sociable. They use their friends and acquaintances as sounding boards for their ideas. They are often to be found in groups or societies, perhaps connected with local politics.

MERCURY IN THE TWELFTH HOUSE

These people are shy and secretive. This is reflected in their interests, which include psychology, mysticism, and the occult. They need to develop greater confidence in expressing their ideas, for these are often carefully considered.

♀

VENUS

The house containing Venus shows the area of life in which Venusian affairs will be expressed, especially artistic skills and the need for partnership.

VENUS IN THE FIRST HOUSE

Friendship is all-important to these people. Their need to be liked is the main motivation behind their attractive image and charming manners. Many take an active interest in the arts and fashion.

VENUS IN THE SECOND HOUSE

These people can earn money through the arts and in partnerships, especially with women. It may be spent in the pursuit of social activities or in buying luxuries. Self-confidence is established through partnerships and material success.

VENUS IN THE THIRD HOUSE

These people have a persuasive charm and are good raconteurs. They make effective sales people. They are sociable and treat friends as part of their family. At school, they do best in arts subjects.

VENUS IN THE FOURTH HOUSE

The home must be a peaceful and pleasant place, because these people find if difficult to cope with domestic disorder or family quarrels. They are perfectionists at home – good at creating a friendly atmosphere and defusing arguments.

VENUS IN THE FIFTH HOUSE

These people put a lot of energy into socializing and go to great lengths to be popular. They have creative talents and even their entertaining takes on a dramatic dimension. They form easy and affectionate relationships with children.

VENUS IN THE SIXTH HOUSE

Working conditions must be harmonious, preferably in a cooperative and sociable atmosphere. Competition or hostility at work is difficult to cope with. Venus indicates work with women, the arts, property, and in leisure activities.

VENUS IN THE SEVENTH HOUSE

Sociable, charming, and diplomatic, these people are often popular and attractive. However, they may rely too much on other people for approval and make unrealistic emotional demands in partnerships.

VENUS IN THE EIGHTH HOUSE

These people can be possessive and jealous. Sexual experience is a vital part of their emotional relationships, and their sexual relationships require a deep and intense emotional commitment. Secrecy causes misunderstandings.

VENUS IN THE NINTH HOUSE

Emotional attraction to foreign cultures can lead to marriage or life abroad for these people. Friends come from a variety of backgrounds. There is an affinity with religion, and artistic interests will have religious and philosophical overtones.

VENUS IN THE TENTH HOUSE

For these people, social skills prove an asset in a career connected with the arts, property, or other Venusian areas. Work involving other people is appropriate. Social life may revolve around work.

VENUS IN THE ELEVENTH HOUSE

These people find social satisfaction in large groups and have a wide circle of acquaintances.

VENUS IN THE TWELFTH HOUSE

These people tend to be rather shy and have few close friends. They can benefit from being more confident and open in their feelings and emotional needs.

♂

MARS

The house containing Mars reveals a major outlet for the planet's energetic, active, and assertive qualities.

MARS IN THE FIRST HOUSE

Assertive and energetic, these people usually put their own interests first. However, they apply equal vigor and flair when doing things for other people.

MARS IN THE SECOND HOUSE

A great deal of energy is put into earning and spending money. Self-employment is attractive to these people. They are competitive in business and inclined to take risks.

MARS IN THE THIRD HOUSE

These people are quick in mind and speech. They are forceful in putting their own ideas across, tactless, and argumentative. They are restless and fond of travel. Their interests may lie in research work.

MARS IN THE FOURTH HOUSE

Domestic concerns occupy a good deal of energy, both in terms of practical jobs to be done and difficult relationships to be resolved. These people like to be in control in the home and do not take kindly to opposition.

MARS IN THE FIFTH HOUSE

This position brings energy and vigor to all creative, social, and romantic activities. If too much time is spent entertaining, it will detract from artistic development. These people may put pressure on their children to succeed.

MARS IN THE SIXTH HOUSE

Hardworking, conscientious, and competitive, these people are good employees as long as they have the chance to get ahead. They are impatient and do not find it easy to handle delays or obstacles. They will clash with colleagues who stand in their way. Health may be affected by impatient and reckless behavior.

MARS IN THE SEVENTH HOUSE

These people are sociable and outgoing and tend to organize other people's affairs. Their energy makes them popular, but they can offend with their forthright and outspoken ways. Emotional relationships may be formed and broken on impulse.

MARS IN THE EIGHTH HOUSE

These people have intense and deep motivations. Some develop an interest in the occult or mysticism, some form a series of sexual relationships, and others become involved in business and high finance.

MARS IN THE NINTH HOUSE

Travel is vital for these people, as it absorbs their surplus energy. They have strong beliefs and will promote them passionately.

MARS IN THE TENTH HOUSE

Ambitious and competitive, these people choose careers that provide the best opportunities for personal advancement. They perform better as employers than employees, but can be too ruthless.

MARS IN THE ELEVENTH HOUSE

These individuals attract a vast number of casual acquaintances, all of whom are superficially close. They are attracted to political and organized groups, but their abrasive manners may antagonize people.

MARS IN THE TWELFTH HOUSE

Work behind the scenes, perhaps dedicated to a cause, is likely for these people, but so is conspiracy and plotting. Unless a cause is found, there is a lack of purpose and direction. Anger tends to be bottled up.

♃

JUPITER

The house containing Jupiter shows the area of life in which growth, expansion, and wisdom is sought, and which offers an opportunity for the fulfillment of personal ambitions.

JUPITER IN THE FIRST HOUSE

Outgoing and optimistic, these people have the enthusiasm to create fresh possibilities and opportunities wherever they go. They seek control over their lives and environment. Their weakness is overconfidence.

JUPITER IN THE SECOND HOUSE

These people divide into those who take an idealistic view of money and possessions, rejecting them in favor of "higher" priorities, and those who work hard to acquire material wealth. Even if greedy, they are often generous and extravagant. Money is rarely a problem.

JUPITER IN THE THIRD HOUSE

These people have grand ideas and a strong desire to inflict them on others. They may be skilled communicators and drawn to work in the media. They also enjoy traveling and may work in the travel industry.

JUPITER IN THE FOURTH HOUSE

There is usually a desire for a large or grandly decorated home. Periodic moves are likely, and may include living abroad. Pride in family and the immediate environment are important.

JUPITER IN THE FIFTH HOUSE

Self-confidence and idealism often carry these people to creative success. They are attracted to the performing arts, and their romantic and leisure activities are often theatrical in style.

JUPITER IN THE SIXTH HOUSE

These people are usually hard workers, especially if their work serves some larger cause. Job satisfaction is more important than money; in a job with no purpose, they can be lazy. Health may be weakened by self-indulgence.

JUPITER IN THE SEVENTH HOUSE

Apparently friendly to all, these people often take the initiative in new relationships. They are generous, but also attracted to people who can be of benefit to them. They present a highly confident public image.

JUPITER IN THE EIGHTH HOUSE

The eighth house manifests itself in several distinct ways. Some of these people will concentrate on acquiring sexual experience, some are drawn to the occult, seeking esoteric knowledge, while others go into business, concentrating on acquiring wealth. If Jupiter is badly aspected, money can be lost.

JUPITER IN THE NINTH HOUSE

These people divide into two types: intellectuals and students of religion, or travelers seeking answers to their personal problems. Often they become dogmatic in their beliefs.

JUPITER IN THE TENTH HOUSE

These people are faced with a choice in their careers – to work in pursuit of their ideals and gain wisdom, or to work for status and power. Those denied respect and recognition will give their best in work.

JUPITER IN THE ELEVENTH HOUSE

Gregarious and sociable, these people have a wide circle of acquaintances, few of whom will be real friends. They have broad ambitions and enlist their colleagues to assist them.

JUPITER IN THE TWELFTH HOUSE

Dissatisfied with the material world and attracted by mystical and religious solutions, these people are idealistic and may prefer the private world of the imagination to harsh reality.

♄

SATURN

The house containing Saturn shows the area of life in which Saturnine obstacles and difficulties are met and lessons are learned.

SATURN IN THE FIRST HOUSE

Instinctively conservative and sensitive to the restrictions of authority and their environment, these people often lose self-confidence. Some meet failure at every turn, while others achieve success by sheer hard work and dedication. To succeed, they need to develop a sense of inner authority and self-discipline.

SATURN IN THE SECOND HOUSE

There may be a fear of poverty; as a result these people are careful with money. But excessive caution or stinginess can lead to lost financial opportunities.

SATURN IN THE THIRD HOUSE

These people have structured and methodical minds well fitted to solving practical problems. Lack of confidence, however, may restrict full use of the imagination and can hinder academic success.

SATURN IN THE FOURTH HOUSE

Domestic responsibilities or difficulties are likely. In childhood, these may be the result of others' actions, but adults invariably attract these commitments. There is a need for domestic security – often provided by physical ties.

SATURN IN THE FIFTH HOUSE

These people lack confidence in their creative abilities and social skills. Artistic potential will only be developed if practical skills are acquired. There is a formality in social relationships and in dealings with children.

SATURN IN THE SIXTH HOUSE

Security may be found in hard work. These people have high expectations and meet challenges, delays, and difficulties at work. Efforts are rewarded by slow advancement. They may worry unduly about their health.

SATURN IN THE SEVENTH HOUSE

There is a need for stability in partnerships, but there will usually be delays, sometimes caused by external obstacles such as parental opposition or financial difficulties, which can be used as excuses. These people have high expectations. They are often attracted to those who are older and more experienced, sometimes committed elsewhere. Few friends are allowed to get really close.

SATURN IN THE EIGHTH HOUSE

There is often a deep interest in occult mysteries. Attitudes to sex are serious and can be inhibited. These people are usually responsible with money, but need to take care of investments.

SATURN IN THE NINTH HOUSE

These people are influenced by the religious and traditional values of their background. Even rebellion will change only the form and not the reality of their basic beliefs. Life or travel in foreign countries may be most successful if connected with work. Care should be taken to avoid difficulties in travel.

SATURN IN THE TENTH HOUSE

There may be delays in finding a career, but once the search is over, these people will be stable and responsible workers, overcoming difficulties with effort and gaining gradual promotion. Work should be practical, and bring status and authority.

SATURN IN THE ELEVENTH HOUSE

These people either keep themselves to themselves or overcome their shyness by joining societies in which social life is centered around a purpose, sometimes political. Friends are often older and more experienced.

SATURN IN THE TWELFTH HOUSE

These people need a sense of inner purpose and make good behind-the-scenes organizers. They often suffer from an inexplicable fear of authority or concern about the future, and should find a way to develop self-confidence.

♅

URANUS

The house containing Uranus shows the area of life in which individuals may experience sudden changes, or a pressing need for personal freedom.

URANUS IN THE FIRST HOUSE

These people hate to be tied down and resent limits on their personal freedom. They are individualists and are afraid of being submerged in the mass. They are innovators and inventors, better at competing than cooperating.

URANUS IN THE SECOND HOUSE

Financial affairs may be subject to unusual conditions, sudden gains, or unexpected losses. Income may be earned in original or inventive work. These people may have strong ideas about how money should be used.

URANUS IN THE THIRD HOUSE

These people have original minds and may find it difficult to cope with the limitations of an orthodox educational system. They use their talents in idealistic ways such as teaching, in technology (perhaps within the communications industry), or in other inventive ways, such as advertising.

URANUS IN THE FOURTH HOUSE

Domestic conditions may be out of the ordinary, unsettled, or subject to unexpected changes. Chaos may be preferred to domestic routine, and family ties are not welcomed. There is a dislike of domestic responsibility.

URANUS IN THE FIFTH HOUSE

For these people creative flair may be expressed in art that extends the boundaries of the acceptable by using new techniques – abstract art, experimental theater, electronic music, and so on. Romantic attachments may be unorthodox. Their children may be unusual and stimulating.

URANUS IN THE SIXTH HOUSE

These people are attracted to work which is inventive, technical, unusual, or idealistic. Stimulation at work is more important than financial gain, and frustration and friction result from dull working conditions. Health may be affected by nervous tension.

URANUS IN THE SEVENTH HOUSE

Friends and friendships are unusual and ideas about marriage unorthodox. These people are afraid of being tied down and losing their emotional independence; partners must give them plenty of space. Partnerships can be made and unmade without warning.

URANUS IN THE EIGHTH HOUSE

There is a fascination for the occult and unusual answers to life's mysteries. These people need sexual variety. They have unconventional schemes for making money.

URANUS IN THE NINTH HOUSE

Beliefs may be unusual; these people are attracted to oriental religions and new cults. Foreign travel may be motivated by a search for unusual experiences.

URANUS IN THE TENTH HOUSE

These people may be reluctant to settle into a career unless it offers scope for their unusual talents or a challenge to their idealism. They need to be able to make personal decisions, and in an unsuitable career will be restless and likely to leave.

URANUS IN THE ELEVENTH HOUSE

Long-term ambitions are unusual, and these people are often found in groups that have common inventive or ideological interests. There may be a large circle of acquaintances, although these change frequently.

URANUS IN THE TWELFTH HOUSE

These people have strange and wonderful imaginations, and are often interested in subjects such as yoga, psychology, mysticism, and other ways of extending the consciousness.

♆

NEPTUNE

The house containing Neptune shows where ideals are expressed, but also where confusion may arise.

NEPTUNE IN THE FIRST HOUSE

Sensitive and imaginative, these people are often involved in the arts and fashion. They are gullible, but capable of deceiving others. They are idealistic, and attracted to philanthropic work and mystical beliefs.

NEPTUNE IN THE SECOND HOUSE

In financial matters, these people can be confused, wasteful, deceptive, idealistic, generous, or greedy. They either love money for the fantasies it can buy or despise it for being worldly. Their best way of earning money is through putting the imagination to use, for example, in the arts.

NEPTUNE IN THE THIRD HOUSE

These people have poetic imaginations and are skilled in communicating fantasies and fiction. They make good journalists and teachers. They may find it difficult to express facts clearly, concentrating on images and theories.

NEPTUNE IN THE FOURTH HOUSE

The home background may have elements of mystery or confusion. These people have an image of their dream home, a haven of peace and quiet, and they prefer comfortable chaos to domestic routine.

NEPTUNE IN THE FIFTH HOUSE

These people have an artistic talent founded on a vivid imagination. They yearn for romance. Their relations with children may be loving but confused.

NEPTUNE IN THE SIXTH HOUSE

Self-sacrificing instincts often attract these people to employment in which they are overworked and underpaid, perhaps charitable or medical work. Others find jobs in the arts or entertainment world. If in meaningless jobs, they will be lazy and disorganized. Their health may be undermined by a sensitivity to harsh conditions.

NEPTUNE IN THE SEVENTH HOUSE

These people are idealistic in relationships, but their romantic expectations can be too high and result in disappointment. They are often attracted by superficial appearances, misunderstanding the realities of a situation.

NEPTUNE IN THE EIGHTH HOUSE

Sexual relationships may be colored by fantasies and unrealistic expectations. These people are fascinated by the mysteries of life, and they have an interest in magic and the occult. They have imaginative business ideas but may lack the practical expertise to carry them out.

NEPTUNE IN THE NINTH HOUSE

These people are attracted to mystical beliefs, and foreign cultures fascinate them, sometimes unrealistically. They are easily impressed by religious ritual and dogma. Legal matters should be approached with caution.

NEPTUNE IN THE TENTH HOUSE

In ordinary careers, these people may have unrealistic aspirations and be disorganized. In careers where they can express their idealism or imagination – charitable and social work, films, fashion, advertising and the arts – great dedication is likely.

NEPTUNE IN THE ELEVENTH HOUSE

The long-term ambitions of these people may be idealistic but difficult to define. They are easily influenced by the latest fashions, and are shy in public.

NEPTUNE IN THE TWELFTH HOUSE

These people have sensitive dreams that may never be expressed in everyday life. There is often an interest in mysticism and psychology.

♇

PLUTO

The house containing Pluto reveals an area of life that may be the subject of compulsive interest and activity, and in which profound changes are likely.

PLUTO IN THE FIRST HOUSE

These people are usually determined and intense, and they work hard to achieve their personal goals. They may often conceal their turbulent personalities, but may be subject to periodic revolutions in lifestyle.

PLUTO IN THE SECOND HOUSE

Money and possessions are important to these people, not necessarily in themselves but as catalysts for personal transformation. Their finances may be subject to sudden changes, and they may swing from rags to riches and back again, probably as a result of taking risks.

PLUTO IN THE THIRD HOUSE

The minds of these people harbor deep, dark, and hidden interests. They are very perceptive and may be dissatisfied with an ordinary education.

PLUTO IN THE FOURTH HOUSE

Domestic upheavals are likely, partly provoked by the desire for change and partly by other people and circumstances. If domestic change is blocked, these people will bottle things up until an explosion occurs.

PLUTO IN THE FIFTH HOUSE

These people have a compulsive creative urge and may work hard to be accepted as artists. They may also direct their energies into frenetic social activity. Relations with children may be emotional but difficult: the rest of the chart will indicate how such difficulties may be overcome.

PLUTO IN THE SIXTH HOUSE

These people throw an enormous amount of energy into their work and will not tolerate inefficiency or obstruction from colleagues, nor will they obey unreasonable orders. If personally motivated, they are capable of bringing their healing energies to any situation. Emotional stress and strain may undermine their health.

PLUTO IN THE SEVENTH HOUSE

These people often expect partners to satisfy impossible emotional demands and will put them through grueling tests to see if they are committed to the relationship. If their love is reciprocated, they will respond with devotion and passion.

PLUTO IN THE EIGHTH HOUSE

Fascinated by the mysteries of the life force from birth to death, reincarnation and the occult, these people may develop a devotion to spiritual practices. Those who are more materially minded may become involved in sexual, business, or financial adventures.

PLUTO IN THE NINTH HOUSE

These people hold deep beliefs that they will fight to defend. They may be morally self-righteous. Travel to distant countries is important to help in their search for other faiths.

PLUTO IN THE TENTH HOUSE

For these people, work should be a vehicle for the expression and acquisition of personal power, sometimes matched, paradoxically, by a desire to serve the community. Suitable careers include medicine, psychology, religion, politics, and detective work.

PLUTO IN THE ELEVENTH HOUSE

These people find personal power in group situations and are often attracted to politics. They become personally involved in political situations and expect politics to solve their individual problems.

PLUTO IN THE TWELFTH HOUSE

These people often develop an interest in psychology or the occult as a means of discovering their deeper natures. There may be a desire for union with the cosmos.

♈ ♉ ♊ ♋ ♌ ♍ ♎ ♏ ♐ ♑ ♒ ♓

CHAPTER 6

CALCULATING THE HOROSCOPE

Unfamiliar technical jargon can make astrological calculation seem excessively complicated, but, in fact, the calculations themselves are straightforward and, with the aid of calculators, have been made as easy as simple mathematics. Many astrologers have given up calculation altogether in favor of computers, although the astrologer who has no knowledge of calculation will be at a severe disadvantage when a computer is not available. It is very useful to be able to look at the astrological tables and perform in one's head the rough calculations that reveal where a planet is at the moment – or what sign is rising.

There are a number of tables at the back of this book that will enable you to calculate a horoscope by hand.

THE EPHEMERIS

An ephemeris (ephemerides in the plural) is a listing of the positions of the planets in the zodiac for particular days of the year. The level of detail supplied varies and most astrologers use two versions, one a general edition containing basic information for a period of perhaps 50 years, and the other a detailed edition covering only one year. The ephemeris at the back of this book contains the planetary positions required for simple calculation. These tables run from 1960 to 2010 and include positions for the Sun ☉, Moon ☽, Mercury ☿, Venus ♀, and Mars ♂ for midnight (00.00 hrs) Greenwich Mean Time (GMT) for every day; for Jupiter ♃ for the 1st, 6th, 11th, 16th, 21st, 26th, and 31st; for Saturn ♄, Chiron ⚷, and the Moon's North Node ☊ for the 1st, 11th, 21st, and 31st; and for Uranus ♅, Neptune ♆, and Pluto ♇ for the 1st and 16th.

Find the year and month you are interested in, look for the relevant planetary symbol on the left and then read across to the right to find the exact degree and sign of the zodiac for each planet on a particular day. For July 2010, for example, you will see that on the 1st, the Sun is at 9 degrees Cancer and, reading to the right, on the 23rd it's at 0 degrees Leo. For all normal uses, there is no need to calculate these positions more precisely. Only for the Moon, because it moves so fast, will you need to work out exactly where it was at any particular time. For example, if it is at 29 degrees Aquarius at midnight on July 1, 2010, and at 11 degrees Pisces at midnight on the 2nd, then you will need to work out where it was at, say, 3 P.M. This is not difficult, and the simple math is set out in the box on page 86. You can check your results at: www.astro.com/p/nc1 (go to the Chart Drawing option and follow the instructions).

SIDEREAL TIME TABLES

Sidereal time measures the Earth's rotation against the stars rather than against the Sun, and it is necessary to convert ordinary clock time into sidereal time in order to calculate the Ascendant and houses. There are two tables. The first one gives the sidereal time for 00.00 hrs for each day of the month. The bottom table shows the adjustment needed for each year, following the example given.

TABLES OF HOUSES

These tables give you the Ascendant and Midheaven. There are different editions computed for the various house systems. Once you have worked out the sidereal time for birth, find the relevant time on the left-hand vertical scale. Then read across to the right to find the nearest latitude. If birth was in the southern hemisphere, look for the nearest equivalent northern latitude (eg, for 26 degrees south look up 26 degrees north). The relevant rules are given in the calculation example on page 84. For example, if the sidereal time at birth was 20.00 (8 P.M.), then the column to the right gives the Midheaven (MC) – 28 degrees Capricorn – and the columns to the right of that the Ascendant at different intervals of latitude. For example, the Ascendant at 33 degrees north was 13 degrees Taurus, and at 52 degrees north it was 0 degrees Gemini.

To insert equal houses, mark the house cusps off at 30-degree intervals from the Ascendant. If, for example, the Ascendant is 0 degrees Gemini, the second house cusp is 0 degrees Cancer, the third 0 degrees Leo and so on. To check the cusps in the Placidus or in any other house system, go to www.astro.com/p/nc1 and input the relevant data.

SUN SIGN CHANGES

This table shows the minute that the Sun changes from one zodiac sign to another, from 1960 to 2010. For individuals born close to the cusp, this information is essential in order to ascertain which sign they were born in. For example, in August 1965, the Sun moved into Virgo at 8:44 A.M. on the 23rd. All these times are given in Greenwich Mean Time (GMT), so you may need to make an initial adjustment to work out the time of birth in GMT (see page 82).

LONGITUDE EQUIVALENT, ACCELERATION ON THE INTERVAL, DAYLIGHT SAVING TIME

These tables will be necessary when you come to calculate a chart, and their use is explained in the examples given.

The calculation of horoscopes can be taken to whatever level of detail is required. It is usually enough to know a planet's position to the nearest degree. Minutes rarely make much difference, seconds are usually irrelevant, and there is never any need to use fractions of seconds, as some astrologers have done. In the tables in this book, the planetary positions are set out to the nearest degree. This means that, in effect, most of the planetary positions can be read off from the tables. However, the rules for calculating planetary positions to the nearest minute for the exact time of day have also been set out so that you will be able to do it when you need to. In the sample chart on page 92, only the Moon needs to be calculated.

All astrologers can make mistakes in their calculations. Even computers produce erroneous charts when they are given the wrong information. The fact that errors can occur only reinforces the need for careful checking of data. Hours can be wasted if an interpretation of an inaccurate horoscope is prepared, and it is always best to double-check calculations before drawing up a horoscope.

There are two stages in casting a horoscope: calculation of the position of the planets in the signs of the zodiac (see page 83), and calculation of the positions of the houses and rising sign (see page 85). The first step, converting the time of birth into Greenwich Mean Time, is the same in each stage (see page 82).

MEASURING TIME AND SPACE

The basic coordinates of all astrological celestial measurement are the *ecliptic*, the Sun's apparent path around the Earth and the basis of the zodiac, and the *equator*, which is projected into space as the *celestial equator.*

Greenwich Mean Time is set for zero degrees of longitude, the line of longitude that runs north–south through Greenwich in London. It is the basis of all time zones in the world. Places to the east of Greenwich are always in advance of Greenwich in time, and places to the west are always behind in time. When it is 12 noon at Greenwich, for example, in Berlin, which is to the east, it is usually 1 P.M. and in Sydney it's 10 P.M. Meanwhile, in New York, which is west of Greenwich, the time is 7 A.M. and in Los Angeles it's 4 A.M.

If we used just the Sun as a measure of time, places only a few miles part could have different times. However, modern mass-communications, beginning with railway timetables in the 19th century, have required standardization of times. There are now, therefore, 24 time zones spanning the globe, each one an hour in front of the zone to its west. The USA, for instance, is divided into four time zones. When the time is noon at Greenwich it is 7 A.M. in the eastern USA, 4 A.M. in the west, and 5 A.M. and 6 A.M. in the two central zones.

SPACE

The circle of the zodiac is divided into 360 degrees (as are all circles), or 12 signs of 30 degrees each. Each degree consists of 60 minutes and each minute of 60 seconds, though seconds are rarely used. The symbol ° stands for degree; " for minute, and " for second. If, for example, the Moon was at 1 degree, 16 minutes, and 28 seconds in Gemini, this could be written in any of the following forms, depending on how much detail is required.

1° 16' 28" or 1° 16' or 1°

This type of measurement around the zodiac is based on the ecliptic and is known as *celestial longitude.*

Absolute longitude measures planetary positions in terms of the entire 360-degree circle. For example, 1 degree Taurus is 31 degrees of absolute longitude, 1 degree Gemini is 61 degrees of absolute longitude, and so on, right around to 1 degree Pisces, which is 331 degrees of absolute longitude.

There are three other methods of defining a planet's location. *Celestial latitude* measures distances north and south of the ecliptic, *declination* measures distances north and south of the equator, and *right ascension* measures distances around the equator. None of these is essential to horoscope calculation at this stage. (Latitude and declination are both used to work out parallel aspects, and right ascension is the basis of a form of prediction known as primary directions.)

Latitude and longitude

The two coordinates used on the Earth to establish the location of a place are lines of latitude, which run east–west and are either north or south of the equator. Both measurements use degrees, minutes, and seconds, although in practice, seconds are rarely used. The latitude of Greenwich, for example, is 51 degrees north, while Buenos Aires, the capital of Argentina, is 34 degrees south. Lines of longitude run from north to south and measure positions east and west. For example, Cape Town in South Africa is 18 degrees east – and all places directly north or south of Cape Town are also 18 degrees east.

The Sun passes through 10 degrees of longitude in four minutes. The time that it takes the Sun to travel from Greenwich to a particular place is known as the Longitude Equivalent in Time (LET). For example, the LET of a place 12 degrees east or west of Greenwich is 49 minutes and 56 seconds.

TIME

Astrological calculation uses two separate but interlocking systems of measuring time. The first is the familiar system of seconds, minutes, hours, days of 24 hours, and years of 365 days (or 366 in a leap year). This is the normal system in which all events on Earth are measured. The year in this system is known as the *tropical year.*

The second system is that of *sidereal time*, based on the Earth's rotation in relation to the stars rather than to the Sun (*sidus* is the Latin word for *star*). The sidereal year is longer than the tropical year, being 365 days, 6 hours, 9 minutes, and 9.5 seconds in duration. The sidereal day is shorter than the ordinary day, and is 23 hours, 56 minutes, 4.09 seconds long. If tropical and sidereal time are synchronized at the beginning of the day, by midnight tropical time sidereal time will be 11:56:06 P.M. After 17 days the difference between the two systems amounts to just over one hour. Sidereal time is a vital part of the astrological calculation and must be worked out before the horoscope can be cast (see tables in the back of this book). Tropical time is always converted into sidereal time during the calculation of the Ascendant and houses.

To avoid confusion over A.M. and P.M. times it is often safer to use the 24-hour clock, in which 1 P.M. is 13:00 hrs, 2 P.M. is 14:00 hrs, and so on.

EQUIPMENT

The astrologer must have access to certain items of equipment and reference tables before calculating a horoscope. A ruler and set of different colored pens are the most obvious. Most astrologers also use printed chart wheels (if you visit www.astro.com/p/ncl you can calculate a chart wheel and print it off). Other necessary reference material is listed below.

The appropriate *ephemeris* (see page 75).

The *Tables of Houses* (see page 76).

An *atlas* is necessary to look up the longitude and latitude for the place of birth or other locations for which the chart is to be cast.

It is also very useful to have a *calculator* that uses both degrees, minutes, and seconds; and hours, minutes, and seconds.

For *software packages*, see Resources.

CHART RECTIFICATION

The problem of the uncertain birth time has bedeviled astrology for the past 2,000 years. Many astrologers solve this difficulty by attempting to work out an exact birth time by a process known as *rectification*. There is no uniformly accepted procedure, but the standard practice is to take major events from the individual's life and correlate these with the expected transits over the Ascendant and Midheaven. This is relatively simple if the approximate birth time is known and all the astrologer has to establish is the degree of the Ascendant. However, if there is not even an approximate birth time, the astrologer has to cope with many different possibilities.

A guess at a likely rising sign might be made in the light of the individual's known behavior and by looking at characteristics that are not accounted for by the Sun and Moon signs. Some astrologers take notice of the physical appearance, for this is often partly signified by the Ascendant. For example, if a person has red hair this may indicate an Ascendant in one of the Fire signs – Aries, Leo, or Sagittarius – while dark, intense eyes are often a sign of a Scorpio Ascendant. Once a possible Ascendant has been established, the other houses can be filled in and the distribution of planets in houses correlated with the person's interests and circumstances.

The first events the astrologer considers are those that happen in early childhood – especially serious illness, accidents, or other traumatic events, which should be shown by major transits over the Ascendant or perhaps by major aspects from the progressed Ascendant. For example, if the astrologer has decided on a Virgo Ascendant and finds that at the age of three, when Mars and Uranus were conjunct at 10 degrees Virgo, the child's life went through a series of major changes, this would be taken as evidence in favor of an Ascendant of 10 degrees Virgo.

Events in later life, such as marriage, can also be used to indicate the Ascendant and birth time. Princess Diana's engagement to Prince Charles gives us a suitable example. Her accepted birth time gives an Ascendant of 18 degrees Sagittarius and a Midheaven of 23 degrees Libra, but, at the time of her engagement, progressed Venus (indicating love) was at 16 degrees Gemini approaching an opposition to her natal Ascendant, and transiting Pluto (indicating transformation in lifestyle) was at 21 degrees Libra, approaching a conjunction with her Midheaven. An astrologer rectifying her chart might decide that, at her engagement, progressed Venus and transiting Pluto must have been in exact aspect with her birth chart, giving her an Ascendant of 16 degrees Sagittarius and a Midheaven of 21 degrees Libra, and a birth time eight minutes prior to the recorded time.

Rectification, however, is a subtle procedure which depends very much on the impressions of the astrologer. There is nothing scientific in it and to imagine that a rectified time is the objectively "correct" birth time is simply not the case. There is always evidence to suggest a different birth time. For example, in Princess Diana's case, transiting Neptune at her engagement was at 22 degrees Sagittarius, suggesting an Ascendant of 22 degrees Sagittarius and a birth time 16 minutes later than the recorded time.

DATA

Since it is extremely important to obtain accurate data to guarantee confidence in the interpretation, it is best if clients write down their own birth data as they are then responsible for any errors. If the astrologer is taking information over the telephone, it should be read back to the client for confirmation. It is especially important to check whether the time was morning (A.M.) or afternoon and evening (P.M.).

The date of birth when written in figures can cause confusion, so it is best that the month should always be written down in full. For example, 7.4.1987 is July 4, 1987 in the USA but 7 April 1987 in Europe.

The place of birth should be as exact as possible. If the person was born in a large city such as London or Los Angeles, it is not strictly necessary to worry about the exact location, even though there may be minute differences in the horoscope from one side of the city to the other. If a person was born in a small village, its distance from the nearest large town must be ascertained as the village itself might not be shown in any available atlas.

The time of birth needs to be known as precisely as possible, although most recorded birth times are technically inaccurate, and may differ by 15 or 30 minutes from the actual time of birth. Most people give their birth time as being on the quarter-hour, half-hour, or hour, yet nature is never so regular. However, when a client does specify an exact time, the astrologer may assume it is accurate. When the time is stated only approximately, the astrologer faces a dilemma. If the subject reports that birth occurred "between four and half-past," or "between seven and eight," the astrologer should question this to see if the time can be pinpointed more accurately. If not the horoscope may be cast for the halfway-point between the two times, 4:15 and 7:30, respectively. It should be interpreted with an open mind, and if the subject disagrees sharply with any statements that are made, this may help to clarify the time of birth.

Some people give their birth time as "in the early hours," "before dawn," or "around lunchtime." The astrologer should question the client and then estimate the approximate time. For example, "around lunchtime" could indicate 12 P.M. The resulting horoscope will be speculative but, by interpreting it, the astrologer may be able to work out a more accurate chart.

If the birth time is entirely unknown, then there are two options. The first is to cast a *solar chart*. This is set for midnight, dawn, or noon, depending on the astrologer's preference. Most solar charts are cast for noon. Although the resulting chart is speculative, it can still yield accurate interpretations. The other option is to employ *rectification* (see page 80).

CALCULATIONS

– 1 –

CONVERTING GIVEN TIME TO GREENWICH MEAN TIME

The given time is the time for which the horoscope must be cast – the time given by the client to the astrologer. In the case of the birth chart this is the time of birth. It is essential that this is converted to Greenwich Mean Time (GMT), which is the standard time upon which all world time zones are based. It is also sometimes referred to as Universal Time (UT). The first step in all astrological calculation is to change the time to GMT, and for one simple reason – this is what is used in all astrological tables.

In many countries, the clocks are advanced by one hour during the summer months. This is known as *daylight saving time*, although it is sometimes referred to as *summer time*. If two hours are added, it is known as *double summer time*.

Local Mean Time (LMT) is local time fixed in relation to the Sun. In most countries it has now been replaced by zone standard time. Standard time zones were instituted in the USA in 1883. However, the zones have changed over time, and shifts still occasionally occur. Additionally, births early this century in Africa and Asia may have been recorded in LMT, and this should be checked by the astrologer.

Method

1 Make adjustment for zone standard time: if the zone is west of Greenwich, add zone standard to birth time; if east of Greenwich, subtract zone standard from birth time.

2 If daylight saving time (summer time) was in use, subtract one hour from birth time (see table in the back of this book).

3 If the birth time is given in LMT, calculate the Longitude Equivalent in Time (LET), using the table in the back of this book. If place of birth is west of Greenwich, add LET to birth time. If place of birth is east of Greenwich, subtract LET from birth time.

Conversion of birth time to GMT can result in a *change of date*. Should this happen, it is the GMT date that is used to calculate the horoscope. In the case of an individual born in Washington D.C. at 10 P.M. on September 6, the date to use would be September 7, because the time in Greenwich at the moment of birth was 3 A.M. the following day.

– 2 –

FINDING THE ZODIACAL POSITION OF THE PLANETS

The planets' positions are generally calculated to approximately the nearest degree and minute, and a variation of one or two minutes is acceptable. If logarithms, calculators, or computers are used, positions may be calculated to the nearest second, although this is unusual.

The planetary positions in the ephemeris are all given for midnight GMT and are rounded to the nearest whole degree. This means that no calculation is required to find the approximate position for any of the planets, except the Moon.

The Proportional Method, as set out below, can be used to calculate the position of the Moon to the nearest whole degree, and the position of a planet to the nearest minute.

Method

1 Convert the given time of birth to GMT.

2 Calculate the interval between midnight GMT and the time of birth. For example, if birth was at 7 A.M. GMT the interval is seven hours; at 3 P.M. GMT it is 15 hours.

3 Calculate the daily motion of the planet; that is, the distance traveled by the planet during the day of birth. This can be worked out by subtracting the position at the beginning of the day from the position at the end of the day.

4 Divide the daily motion by 24 to find out how far the planet moved in one hour.

5 Multiply this result by the interval. If a computer or calculator is not available, and unless absolute accuracy is required, it is permissible to simplify this calculation by rounding the interval to the nearest hour.

6 Add this result to the position of the planet at the beginning of the day. If the planet is retrograde, subtract the result from the planet's position at the beginning of the day.

7 The final result is the *approximate* position of the planet for the time of birth.

The same method can be used to find the *exact* position of a planet to the nearest degree and minute, assuming an ephemeris giving positions in degrees and minutes is used.

CALCULATING THE ASCENDANT AND MIDHEAVEN FOR A BIRTH IN THE SOUTHERN HEMISPHERE

Date of birth: (GMT): August 5, 1974
Time of birth: (GMT): 10:10 A.M.
Place of birth: Melbourne, Australia
Latitude: 37° 47' south
Longitude: 144° 58' east

Sidereal time, midnight GMT August 5, 1974 (to nearest minute): 20 hrs 53 mins

Interval between midnight and birth time: 10 hrs 10 mins

Add together the previous two figures: 31 hrs 3 mins

Acceleration on interval (to nearest minute): 2 mins

Add together the previous two figures: 31 hrs 5 mins
(sidereal time at Greenwich at birth)

Longitude Equivalent in Time: 9 hrs 40 mins

Add together the previous two figures (because east): 40 hrs 45 mins

Add 12 hrs: 52 hrs 45 mins.

Subtract 24 hrs if necessary: 28 hrs 45 mins

Subtract 24 hrs again: 4 hrs 45 mins.

Because northern tables are used to mirror the southern latitudes, refer first to the Tables of Houses and you will see the Midheaven (MC) is correctly given as 13 degrees Sagittarius.

Now look to the opposite side and under an MC of 13 degrees Sagittarius, find the Ascendant under 38 degrees North. This gives an Ascendant of 15 degrees Pisces.

– 3 –

CALCULATING THE HOUSES AND ASCENDANT

This calculation takes into account the longitude and latitude of the place of birth and sidereal time. The key reference here is Tables of Houses for Northern Latitudes (see back of book). An adjustment is made in the final calculation to work out houses for the southern latitudes (see page 86).

Method 1 (for northern latitudes)

1 Convert birth time to GMT.

2 Look up longitude and latitude of place of birth, using any good atlas.

3 Look up the sidereal time for midnight GMT for the date of birth, remembering to use the new date if an adjustment has been made to this for GMT (see tables in the back of this book).

4 Work out the interval between midnight GMT and the GMT time of birth.

5 Add the interval to the sidereal time for midnight.

6 Work out the acceleration on the interval and add this to the previous figure (see table in the back of this book). The result is the sidereal time at Greenwich at birth.

7 Calculate the longitude equivalent in time or LET (see table in the back of this book). If longitude of birthplace is east of Greenwich, add the LET to the sidereal time at Greenwich at birth. If longitude of birthplace is west of Greenwich, subtract the LET from the sidereal time at Greenwich at birth. The result is the local sidereal time at birth.

8 If the result is more than 24 hours, subtract 24 hours.

9 Turn to the Tables of Houses for northern latitudes. Find the column for the latitude of the place of birth, look down the sidereal time column until you find the time closest to the local sidereal time at birth, and read off the Ascendant and the Midheaven.

Method 2 (for southern latitudes)

1 Follow steps 1–7 above.

2 Add 12 hours.

3 If the result is more than 24 hours, subtract 24 hours. If this result is still more than 24 hours, subtract a further 24 hours.

4 Turn to the Tables of Houses for the equivalent northern latitude. For example, for 43 degrees south, look up tables for 43 degrees north.

5 Look up the Ascendant and Midheaven.

6 *Reverse the signs.* For example, Aries becomes Libra and Scorpio becomes Taurus.

CALCULATING A PLANET'S DAILY MOTION

Once an astrologer has calculated a planet's daily motion to the nearest minute, the planet's exact position at any time of the day can be worked out, as the following samples show.

1	Planet's position at end of day	18°	13'	
	Planet's position at beginning of day	16°	23'	
	Daily motion is therefore	1°	50'	
2	Planet's position at end of day	18°		
	Planet's position at beginning of day	17°		
	Daily motion is therefore	1°		

3 If the planet is retrograde, then the calculation must be reversed.

Planet's position at beginning of day	12°	41'	
Planet's position at end of day	11°	43'	
Daily motion is therefore	-0°	58'	(i.e., retrograde)

– 4 –

CALCULATING THE EXACT ASCENDANT AND MIDHEAVEN, IN DEGREES AND MINUTES

Having calculated the approximate Ascendant and Midheaven, it is possible to draw up and interpret the chart – but it is customary to calculate the angles exactly. This is not necessary for the ordinary reading of a birth chart, but the rules are given here should you wish to perfect your calculation skills.

Method

1 Work out the local sidereal time at birth, then look in the Tables of Houses for the sidereal times immediately before and after this, and then the Ascendant and Midheaven for both these times.

2 Subtract the earlier sidereal time from the later sidereal time. Convert the result into seconds. For example, 3' 10" converts to 190". Call this A.

3 Subtract the earlier sidereal time from the local sidereal time at birth. Convert the result into seconds and call this B.

4 Subtract the Midheaven at the earlier time from the Midheaven at the later time. Convert the result into minutes. For example, 1° 0' converts to 60'. Call this C.

5 Subtract the Ascendant at the earlier time from the Ascendant at the later time. Convert the result into minutes and call this D.

6 Multiply B by D and divide the result by A. If you are using ordinary mathematics, it is sufficient to arrive at a result in minutes alone, but using a pocket calculator will give you a result with seconds, too. Add this result to the earlier Ascendant to give the exact Ascendant at birth.

7 Multiply B by C and divide the result by A. Again, ordinary mathematics, will give a result in minutes alone, but a calculator will give minutes and seconds.

8 Add the result to the earlier Midheaven to give the exact Midheaven at birth.

DRAWING UP THE HOROSCOPE

There are various styles used to draw up horoscopes, depending on the preferences of individual astrologers and on the different house systems employed. Whatever style is used, neatness is an essential requirement, otherwise no other astrologer can read the chart. For hand-drawn charts, most astrologers use printed chart forms with a circle drawn out to show divisions for the signs and each degree, with spaces for writing information about the horoscope. Some astrologers add more detail, such as aspect lines (drawn between the planets to indicate the aspects – usually blue or green for harmonious, red for tense, straight for major, broken for minor), others prefer a simpler presentation. Even with computerized charts, the main software packages offer a wide variety of styles (see Resources).

Check your horoscope calculations on the web at www.astro.com/p/nc1 (select Chart Drawing and follow the instructions).

READING THE EPHEMERIS

The ephemeris is a simple guide to planetary positions. The position of each planet is always given for midnight GMT (00.00). The positions of the Sun, Moon, Mercury, Venus, and Mars are always given for each day; those of the remaining planets are given for every day or less frequently, depending on how much detail is required. If you check the tables at the end of this book you will see that at midnight on January 1, 2000, the Sun was at 10 degrees Capricorn, the Moon was at 7 degrees Scorpio, and so on. By February 1, the Sun was at 11 degrees Capricorn, the Moon was at 22 degrees Sagittarius.

SAMPLE HOROSCOPE CALCULATION

This interpretation example uses the data for writer and dancer Wendy Buonaventura, born at 10:25 P.M. on July 4, 1950, in Fulham, west London.

Method

1 Convert birth time to GMT. Because Wendy was born in the UK, no time zone adjustment is necessary. However, because she was born during daylight saving time (summer time), we have to subtract one hour from her birth time, giving 9:25 P.M. GMT.

2 Calculate the positions of the planets. We can calculate positions to the nearest degree by simply looking them up in the ephemeris for 1950 (pages 90–91), or we can work them out to the exact minute (see box on page 86).

3 Calculate the position of the Moon. Because the Moon moves by up to 12 degrees per day, it is not enough to simply look up its position in the ephemeris. It is very useful to remember that the Moon moves by 30', or half a degree, per hour. To the nearest degree, the Moon at midnight at the

beginning of July 4, 1950 was 6 degrees Pisces. By the following midnight it was 18 degrees. Therefore we know it did indeed move around 12 degrees during the day at a rate of half a degree per hour. By 9 P.M. GMT on July 4, it would therefore have moved by 10 degrees and 30 minutes and would have arrived at 16 degrees and 30 minutes. By 10 P.M. GMT, it would have arrived at roughly 17 degrees Pisces. Therefore, a rough computation indicates that at 9:25 P.M. GMT, when Wendy was born, the Moon would have been at 16 degrees and 45 minutes in Pisces. In fact, checking with the Janus software indicates that at 9:25P.M. GMT the Moon was at exactly 17 degrees Pisces. However, this 15-minute difference is so slight as to have no effect at all on the interpretation of the chart and we can rely on our simple math to arrive at a chart which is sufficiently accurate for almost any eventuality.

4 Calculate the Ascendant and Midheaven (MC), as follows:

a) Look up sidereal time for midnight GMT, July 4, 1950 (to nearest minute): 18 hrs 45 mins
b) Work out interval between midnight and birth (9:25 P.M. GMT): 21 hrs 25 mins
c) Add a and b together: 40 hrs 10 mins
d) Look up acceleration on interval (to nearest minute): 4 mins
e) Add c and d together: 40 hrs 14 mins (= sidereal time at Greenwich at birth).
f) Look up longitude equivalent in time (to nearest minute): 1 min
g) Subtract f from e (because Fulham is west of Greenwich): 40 hrs 13 mins
h) Subtract 24 hrs (because previous figure is more than 24 hrs): 16 hrs 13 mins
i) Look up Ascendant and MC in Tables of Houses for 51 degrees north: Ascendant = 5 degrees Aquarius, MC = 5 degrees Sagittarius.

If you check these calculations at www.astro.com/p/nc1, you'll find that the exact Ascendant is 5 degrees and 32 minutes Aquarius and the exact MC is 5 degrees and 17 minutes Sagittarius. Janus software (see Resources) confirms these figures.

The chart on page 92 was drawn up for Wendy using Janus software. The numbers on the inner wheel are the numbers of the houses. The outer wheel shows the exact zodiac sign position of each house cusp, starting with the Ascendant at 5 degrees and 32 minutes Aquarius on the left-hand side. The planets are given in their exact zodiac positions.

EPHEMERIS

1950

JAN

	1	2	3	4	5	6	7	8	9	10	11	12	13	14	15	16	17	18	19	20	21	22	23	24	25	26	27	28	29	30	31
☉	10♑	11	12	13	14	15	16	17	18	19	20	21	22	23	24	25	26	27	28	29	0♒	1	2	3	4	5	6	8	9	10	11
☽	1♊	14	26	9♋	22	6♌	19	3♍	17	0♎	14	29	13♏	27	11♐	25	9♑	23	7♒	20	3♓	15	28	10♈	22	3♉	15	27	9♊	22	4♋
☿	29♑	0♒	1	2	3	3	4	4	4	4	4	3	2	1	0	29♑	28	27	25	24	23	22	21	20	19	19	18	18	18	18	18
♀	17♒	17	18	18	18	18	18	19	19	19	19	19	19	18	18	18	18	18	17	17	17	16	16	15	15	14	13	13	12	12	11
♂	2♎	3	3	3	4	4	4	5	5	5	6	6	6	6	7	7	7	8	8	8	8	9	9	9	9	9	10	10	10	10	10
	1	6	11	16	21	26	31		1	11	21	31		1	11	21	31		1	16		1	16		1	16		1	11	21	31
♃	7♒	8	9	10	11	12	14	♄	19♍	19	19	19	⚷	16♐	17	18	19	♅	3♋	2	♆	17♎	17	♇	18♌	17	☊	12♈	12	11	11

FEB

	1	2	3	4	5	6	7	8	9	10	11	12	13	14	15	16	17	18	19	20	21	22	23	24	25	26	27	28			
☉	12♒	13	14	15	16	17	18	19	20	21	22	23	24	25	26	27	28	29	30	1♓	2	3	4	5	6	7	8	9			
☽	17♋	1♌	15	28	13♍	27	11♎	25	10♏	24	8♐	22	5♑	19	2♒	15	28	11♓	23	6♈	18	29	11♉	23	5♊	17	29	12♋			
☿	19♑	19	19	20	21	21	22	23	24	25	26	27	28	29	0♒	1	3	4	5	6	8	9	11	12	13	15	16	18			
♀	10♒	10	9	9	8	7	7	6	6	5	5	5	4	4	4	4	3	3	3	3	3	3	3	3	3	4	4	4			
♂	10♎	10	11	11	11	11	11	11	11	11	11	11	11	11	11	11	11	11	11	11	11	10	10	10	10	10	10	9			
	1	6	11	16	21	26			1	11	21			1	11	21			1	16		1	16		1	16		1	11	21	
♃	14♒	15	16	17	19	20		♄	18♍	18	17		⚷	19♐	20	20		♅	2♋	1	♆	17♎	17	♇	17♌	17	☊	10♈	10	9	

MAR

	1	2	3	4	5	6	7	8	9	10	11	12	13	14	15	16	17	18	19	20	21	22	23	24	25	26	27	28	29	30	31
☉	10♓	11	12	13	14	15	16	17	18	19	20	21	22	23	24	25	26	27	28	29	30	1♈	2	3	4	5	6	7	8	9	10
☽	25♋	9♌	23	7♍	21	6♎	21	6♏	20	4♐	18	2♑	16	29	12♒	25	7♓	20	2♈	14	26	8♉	19	1♊	13	25	8♋	20	3♌	17	1♍
☿	19♒	21	22	24	25	27	29	0♓	2	3	5	7	9	10	12	14	16	17	19	21	23	25	27	29	1♈	3	5	7	9	11	13
♀	4♒	5	5	5	6	6	7	7	8	8	9	9	10	11	11	12	13	13	14	15	16	16	17	18	19	20	20	21	22	23	24
♂	9♎	9	9	9	8	8	8	7	7	7	7	6	6	6	5	5	4	4	4	3	3	3	2	2	1	1	1	0	30♍	29	29
	1	6	11	16	21	26	31		1	11	21	31		1	11	21	31		1	16		1	16		1	16		1	11	21	31
♃	20♒	22	23	24	25	26	27	♄	17♍	16	15	14	⚷	21♐	21	22	22	♅	1♋	1	♆	17♎	17	♇	16♌	16	☊	9♈	8	8	7

APR

	1	2	3	4	5	6	7	8	9	10	11	12	13	14	15	16	17	18	19	20	21	22	23	24	25	26	27	28	29	30	
☉	11♈	12	13	14	15	16	17	18	19	20	21	22	23	23	24	25	26	27	28	29	0♉	1	2	3	4	5	6	7	8	9	
☽	15♍	30	15♎	30	15♏	30	14♐	29	12♑	26	9♒	22	4♓	17	29	11♈	23	4♉	16	28	10♊	22	4♋	16	29	12♌	25	9♍	23	8♎	
☿	15♈	17	19	21	23	25	27	29	1♉	3	5	7	8	10	12	13	15	16	18	19	20	21	22	23	24	25	25	26	27	27	
♀	25♒	26	27	28	28	29	0♓	1	2	3	4	5	6	7	8	9	10	11	12	13	14	15	16	17	18	19	21	22	23	24	
♂	29♍	28	28	28	27	27	27	26	26	26	25	25	25	25	24	24	24	24	23	23	23	23	23	23	22	22	22	22	22	22	
	1	6	11	16	21	26			1	11	21			1	11	21			1	16		1	16		1	16		1	11	21	
♃	27♒	28	29	0♓	1	2		♄	14♍	14	13		⚷	22♐	22	21		♅	1♋	2	♆	16♎	16	♇	16♌	16	☊	7♈	7	6	

MAY

	1	2	3	4	5	6	7	8	9	10	11	12	13	14	15	16	17	18	19	20	21	22	23	24	25	26	27	28	29	30	31
☉	10♉	11	12	13	14	15	16	17	18	19	20	21	22	23	24	25	26	26	27	28	29	0♊	1	2	3	4	5	6	7	8	9
☽	23♎	8♏	23	8♐	23	8♑	22	5♒	19	1♓	14	26	8♈	20	1♉	13	25	7♊	19	1♋	13	26	8♌	21	5♍	18	2♎	16	1♏	16	1♐
☿	27♉	27	28	28	27	27	27	27	26	26	25	25	24	24	23	23	22	21	21	20	20	19	19	19	19	19	19	19	19	19	19
♀	25♓	26	27	28	29	0♈	1	2	3	5	6	7	8	9	10	11	12	13	15	16	17	18	19	20	21	22	24	25	26	27	28
♂	22♍	22	22	22	22	22	22	22	22	22	22	22	23	23	23	23	23	23	23	24	24	24	24	24	25	25	25	25	26	26	26
	1	6	11	16	21	26	31		1	11	21	31		1	11	21	31		1	16		1	16		1	16		1	11	21	31
♃	3♓	3	4	5	5	6	6	♄	13♍	13	13	13	⚷	21♐	21	20	19	♅	2♋	3	♆	15♎	15	♇	16♌	16	☊	6♈	5	5	4

JUN

	1	2	3	4	5	6	7	8	9	10	11	12	13	14	15	16	17	18	19	20	21	22	23	24	25	26	27	28	29	30	
☉	10♊	11	12	13	14	15	16	17	18	19	20	20	21	22	23	24	25	26	27	28	29	0♋	1	2	3	4	5	6	7	8	
☽	17♐	2♑	16	0♒	14	27	10♓	23	5♈	17	28	10♉	22	4♊	16	28	10♋	23	5♌	18	1♍	15	28	12♎	26	11♏	25	10♐	25	10♑	
☿	19♉	20	20	21	21	22	23	23	24	25	26	27	28	29	0♊	2	3	4	6	7	9	10	12	14	15	17	19	21	23	25	
♀	29♈	0♉	2	3	4	5	6	7	9	10	11	12	13	14	15	17	18	19	20	21	22	24	25	26	27	28	29	1♊	2	3	
♂	26♍	27	27	27	28	28	28	29	29	29	30	0♎	0	1	1	2	2	2	3	3	4	4	4	5	5	6	6	7	7	8	
	1	6	11	16	21	26			1	11	21			1	11	21			1	16		1	16		1	16		1	11	21	
♃	6♓	7	7	7	7	7		♄	13♍	13	14		⚷	19♐	19	18		♅	4♋	5	♆	15♎	15	♇	16♌	16	☊	4♈	4	3	

EPHEMERIS

1950

JUL

JUL	1	2	3	4	5	6	7	8	9	10	11	12	13	14	15	16	17	18	19	20	21	22	23	24	25	26	27	28	29	30	31
☉	9♋	10	11	11	12	13	14	15	16	17	18	19	20	21	22	23	24	25	26	27	28	29	30	1♌	1	2	3	4	5	6	7
☽	24♑	9♒	22	6♓	18	1♈	13	25	7♉	19	0♊	12	25	7♋	19	2♌	15	28	12♍	25	9♎	23	7♏	21	5♐	20	4♑	19	3♒	17	0♓
☿	27♊	29	1♋	3	5	7	9	11	14	16	18	20	22	24	26	29	1♌	3	5	7	9	11	12	14	16	18	20	21	23	25	27
♀	4♊	5	7	8	9	10	11	12	14	15	16	17	18	20	21	22	23	24	26	27	28	29	0♋	2	3	4	5	6	8	9	10
♂	8♎	8	9	9	10	10	11	11	12	12	13	13	14	14	15	15	16	17	17	18	18	19	19	20	20	21	21	22	23	23	24
	1	6	11	16	21	26	31		1	11	21	31		1	11	21	31		1	16		1	16		1	16		1	11	21	31
♃	7♓	7	7	7	7	6	6	♄	14♍	15	16	17	⚷	17♐	17	16	16	♅	5♋	6	♆	15♎	15	♇	17♌	17	☊	3♈	2	1	1

AUG

AUG	1	2	3	4	5	6	7	8	9	10	11	12	13	14	15	16	17	18	19	20	21	22	23	24	25	26	27	28	29	30	31
☉	8♌	9	10	11	12	13	14	15	16	17	18	19	20	21	22	23	24	24	25	26	27	28	29	0♍	1	2	3	4	5	6	7
☽	14♓	26	9♈	21	3♉	15	27	9♊	21	3♋	15	28	11♌	24	8♍	22	6♎	20	4♏	18	2♐	16	0♑	14	28	12♒	26	9♓	22	4♈	17
☿	28♌	30	1♍	3	4	6	7	9	10	12	13	14	16	17	18	19	20	22	23	24	25	26	27	27	28	29	30	0♎	1	1	2
♀	11♋	12	14	15	16	17	18	20	21	22	23	24	26	27	28	29	0♌	2	3	4	5	7	8	9	10	11	13	14	15	16	18
♂	24♎	25	25	26	27	27	28	28	29	30	0♏	1	1	2	3	3	4	4	5	6	6	7	8	8	9	9	10	11	11	12	13
	1	6	11	16	21	26	31		1	11	21	31		1	11	21	31		1	16		1	16		1	16		1	11	21	31
♃	6♓	5	4	4	3	3	2	♄	17♍	18	19	21	⚷	16♐	16	16	16	♅	7♋	8	♆	15♎	15	♇	18♌	18	☊	1♈	0	30♓	29

SEP

SEP	1	2	3	4	5	6	7	8	9	10	11	12	13	14	15	16	17	18	19	20	21	22	23	24	25	26	27	28	29	30
☉	8♍	9	10	11	12	13	14	15	16	17	18	19	20	21	22	23	24	25	25	26	27	28	29	0♎	1	2	3	4	5	6
☽	29♈	11♉	23	5♊	16	29	11♋	23	6♌	19	3♍	17	1♎	15	30	14♏	29	13♐	27	11♑	25	8♒	22	5♓	18	0♈	13	25	7♉	19
☿	2♎	2	2	2	2	2	2	2	1	1	30♍	29	28	27	26	25	24	23	22	21	20	20	19	18	18	18	18	18	18	19
♀	19♌	20	21	23	24	25	26	27	29	30	1♍	2	4	5	6	7	9	10	11	12	14	15	16	17	18	20	21	22	23	25
♂	13♏	14	15	15	16	17	17	18	19	19	20	21	21	22	23	23	24	25	25	26	27	27	28	29	29	0♐	1	2	2	3
	1	6	11	16	21	26			1	11	21			1	11	21			1	16		1	16		1	16		1	11	21
♃	2♓	1	0	30♒	29	29		♄	21♍	22	23		⚷	16♐	16	16		♅	9♋	9	♆	16♎	16	♇	18♌	19	☊	29♓	29	28

OCT

OCT	1	2	3	4	5	6	7	8	9	10	11	12	13	14	15	16	17	18	19	20	21	22	23	24	25	26	27	28	29	30	31
☉	7♎	8	9	10	11	12	13	14	15	16	17	18	19	20	21	22	23	24	25	26	27	28	29	0♏	1	2	3	4	5	6	7
☽	1♊	13	25	7♋	19	1♌	14	27	11♍	25	9♎	24	9♏	24	9♐	23	8♑	22	5♒	19	2♓	14	27	9♈	21	3♉	15	27	9♊	21	3♋
☿	20♍	20	21	22	24	25	26	28	29	1♎	2	4	5	7	9	11	12	14	16	17	19	21	22	24	26	28	29	1♏	3	4	6
♀	26♍	27	28	30	1♎	2	3	5	6	7	8	10	11	12	13	15	16	17	18	20	21	22	23	25	26	27	28	30	1♏	2	3
♂	4♐	4	5	6	6	7	8	9	9	10	11	11	12	13	14	14	15	16	16	17	18	19	19	20	21	22	22	23	24	25	25
	1	6	11	16	21	26	31		1	11	21	31		1	11	21	31		1	16		1	16		1	16		1	11	21	31
♃	28♒	28	28	28	28	28	28	♄	25♍	26	27	28	⚷	17♐	18	19	19	♅	9♋	9	♆	17♎	17	♇	19♌	20	☊	28♓	27	27	26

NOV

NOV	1	2	3	4	5	6	7	8	9	10	11	12	13	14	15	16	17	18	19	20	21	22	23	24	25	26	27	28	29	30
☉	8♏	9	10	11	12	13	14	15	16	17	18	19	20	21	22	23	24	25	26	27	28	29	0♐	1	2	3	4	5	6	7
☽	15♋	27	10♌	22	5♍	19	3♎	17	2♏	17	3♐	18	3♑	17	2♒	15	29	11♓	24	6♈	18	0♉	12	24	6♊	18	30	12♋	24	6♌
☿	8♏	9	11	12	14	16	17	19	20	22	24	25	27	28	30	1♐	3	4	6	7	9	11	12	14	15	17	18	20	21	23
♀	5♏	6	7	8	10	11	12	14	15	16	17	19	20	21	22	24	25	26	27	29	30	1♐	2	4	5	6	7	9	10	11
♂	26♐	27	28	28	29	30	1♑	1	2	3	4	4	5	6	7	7	8	9	10	10	11	12	13	13	14	15	16	17	17	18
	1	6	11	16	21	26			1	11	21			1	11	21			1	16		1	16		1	16		1	11	21
♃	28♒	28	28	28	29	29		♄	28♍	29	0♎		⚷	19♐	20	22		♅	9♋	9	♆	18♎	18	♇	20♌	20	☊	26♓	25	25

DEC

DEC	1	2	3	4	5	6	7	8	9	10	11	12	13	14	15	16	17	18	19	20	21	22	23	24	25	26	27	28	29	30	31
☉	8♐	9	10	11	12	13	14	15	16	17	18	19	20	21	22	23	24	25	27	28	29	30	1♑	2	3	4	5	6	7	8	9
☽	18♌	1♍	14	27	11♎	26	10♏	25	11♐	26	11♑	26	10♒	24	8♓	21	3♈	15	27	9♉	21	3♊	15	27	9♋	21	3♌	16	28	11♍	24
☿	24♐	26	27	28	30	1♑	3	4	5	7	8	9	11	12	13	14	15	16	16	17	18	18	18	18	18	18	17	16	15	14	13
♀	12♐	14	15	16	17	19	20	21	22	24	25	26	27	29	0♑	1	3	4	5	6	8	9	10	11	13	14	15	16	18	19	20
♂	19♑	20	20	21	22	23	23	24	25	26	27	27	28	29	30	0♒	1	2	3	4	4	5	6	7	8	8	9	10	11	11	12
	1	6	11	16	21	26	31		1	11	21	31		1	11	21	31		1	16		1	16		1	16		1	11	21	31
♃	30♒	1♓	1	2	3	4	5	♄	1♎	1	2	2	⚷	23♐	24	25	26	♅	9♋	8	♆	19♎	19	♇	20♌	20	☊	24♓	24	23	23

Wendy Buonaventura
Natal Chart
4 Jul 1950 AD GC
10:25:00 PM
BST -01:00:00
Fulham
England
0w13'00
51n28'00
Geocentric
Tropical
Placidus
True Node

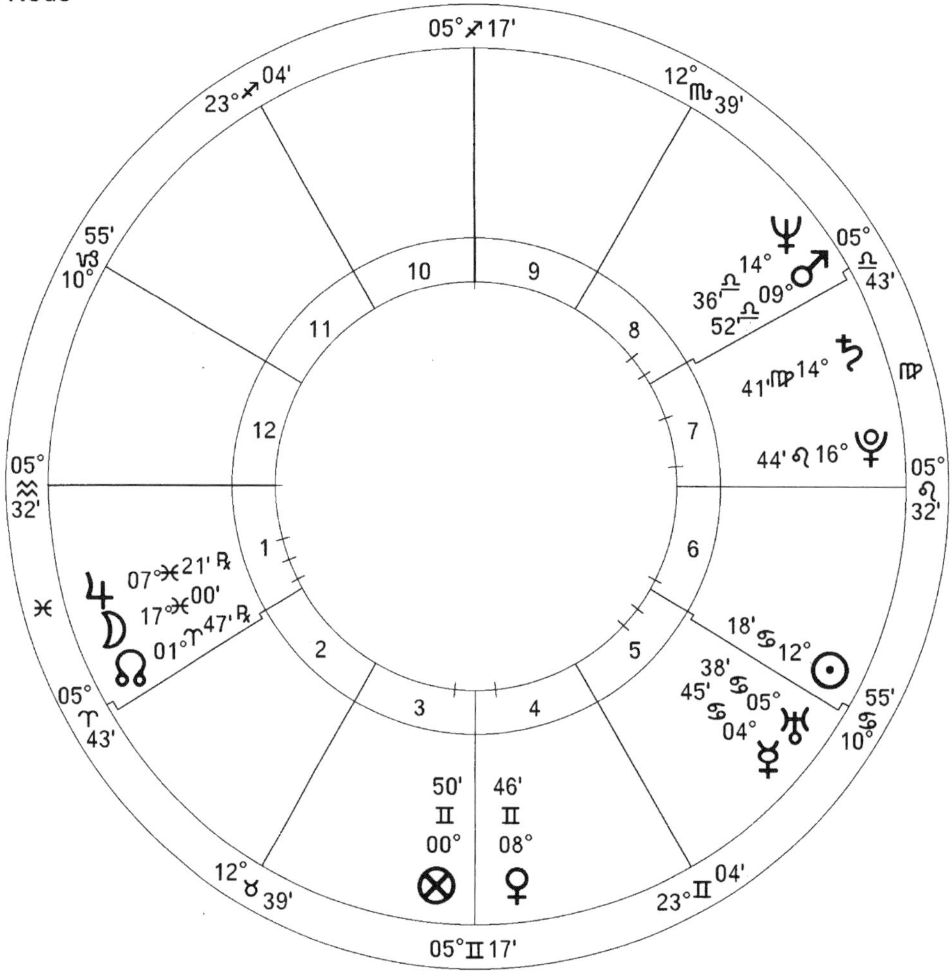

♈ ♉ ♊ ♋ ♌ ♍ ♎ ♏ ♐ ♑ ♒ ♓

CHAPTER 7

THE ASPECTS

An aspect is the precise distance between any two points in a horoscope. Almost all aspects measure distances around the ecliptic (i.e., in the zodiac) – the zodiacal aspects – although others measure distances such as the distance above or below the ecliptic. Usually aspects are formed between two planets, although aspects between any one planet and the angles (Ascendant, Descendant, MC and IC) are also considered. We also find aspect patterns which link three or more planets.

The aspects are used to establish how the planetary symbols combine. For example, an aspect between Mercury and Jupiter brings together the planets of thought and expansion – and produces big ideas. An aspect between Venus and Saturn links the planets of love and limitation and indicates formal relationships.

MAJOR AND MINOR ASPECTS

Aspects are formed by division of the circle of 360 degrees by certain numbers, and may be understood through the rules of numerology. Division of the circle by 3, 6, and 12 is harmonious and flowing; while division by 2, 4, and 8 is rigid, structured, and difficult. Originally there were just five zodiacal aspects – the conjunction, sextile, square, trine, and opposition – and these are still regarded as the strongest. They are known as the *major* aspects, as opposed to the *minor* aspects, which were all devised more recently and are generally considered weaker, although in specific situations it might be a minor aspect that offers the best perspective. The minor aspects were created when astrologers began to drop some of the ways that planetary meanings were worked out, such as the essential dignities (see Chapter 3). The most commonly used aspects are the semi-sextile, semi-square, sesquiquadrate, and quincunx. There are also aspects based on division of the 360 degrees of the zodiac by 5 (the quintile, 72 degrees), by 7 (the septile, 52 degrees), by 9 (novile, 40 degrees), and by 10 (the decile, 36 degrees). Since the theory of harmonics was worked out in the 1950s and 60s, all planets are linked whether they're in a recognized aspect or not. The major aspects, though, retain their overwhelming importance.

HARMONIOUS AND TENSE ASPECTS

The other major division of aspects is into *harmonious/easy* or *tense/challenging*. Some astrologers call these aspects "good" and "bad," but such descriptions are misleading for they imply that the outcome is preordained. In any case, what is "bad" in one set of circumstances or to one person, might be "good" to another or in a different situation. Harmonious aspects link planets in ways that come naturally, providing a helpful environment for the development of innate abilities, whereas tense ones may raise awkward questions and require hard work. In coping with the problems represented by tense aspects, many people may experience failure, but some will be driven to overcome their difficulties and in the process develop their astrological potential. For example, an individual with Venus and Saturn in an easy relationship might naturally fit into conventional relationships, but someone who has the two planets in a difficult relationship might try to form conventional relationships but have difficulty making them work. Sometimes, though, harmonious aspects can indicate complacency and a failure to make the most of one's talents, while tense aspects encourage extra effort and ambition – almost as if the individual has something to prove. Tense aspects can be the grit in the oyster that creates the pearl.

Each type of aspect, therefore, has two faces. The tense aspects bring difficulties which can result in great achievement, while the harmonious aspects bring easy conditions which can lead to wasted opportunities.

It is preferable to have a balance of tense and harmonious aspects. Individuals with only harmonious aspects may have plenty of potential but no drive to develop it, while those with only tense aspects may lack the faith and optimism to overcome difficulties. In effect, even people who are born with a predominance of harmonious or tense aspects will find that as time moves on the transits and progressions (see Chapter 10) mean that the balance is constantly changing.

THE MEANING OF THE ASPECTS

The *conjunction* is the most powerful aspect and combines two planets in a single force.

The *opposition* is extremely powerful and places the planets in conflict with each other, producing difficulties but increasing the range of possibilities open to the individual.

The *trine* is the most powerful harmonious aspect, bringing the planets together in an easy combination.

The *square* is strong, but less powerful than opposition, and symbolizes friction between planets.

The *sextile* is a strong, harmonious aspect, but less powerful than the trine.

Semi-square, *sesquiquadrate*, and *quincunx* are all minor tense aspects. Psychologically their effect may be seen as a very weak version of the square. Some astrologers give them additional importance in predicting events.

Semi-sextile is the main minor harmonious aspect, and psychologically is a weak version of the sextile.

CHARACTERISTICS OF THE ASPECTS

ASPECT	GLYPH	DEGREES APART WHEN EXACT	ORB IN DEGREES	RANGE OF OPERATION IN DEGREES	STRENGTH	NATURE
Conjunction	☌	0	8	0–8	Major	Neutral
Semi-sextile	⚺	30	2	28–32	Minor	Harmonious
Semi-square	∠	45	2	43–47	Minor	Tense
Sextile	⚹	60	6	56–64	Major	Harmonious
Quintile	Q	72	2	70–74	Minor	Harmonious
Square	□	90	8	82–98	Major	Tense
Trine	△	120	8	112–128	Major	Harmonious
Sesquiquadrate	⚼	135	2	133–137	Minor	Tense
Bi-quintile	Bq	144	2	142–146	Minor	Harmonious
Quincunx or Inconjunct	⚻	150	2	148–152	Minor	Tense
Opposition	☍	180	8	172–188	Major	Tense
Parallel of declination	∥	0	8	0–8	Major	Neutral

APPLYING AND SEPARATING ASPECTS

When two planets are moving together to form an exact aspect they are *applying*. When they are moving apart from the exact aspect they are *separating*. Applying aspects are usually seen as stronger psychologically than separating aspects. When looking at events, separating aspects refer to past events and applying aspects refer to future events.

ORBS

An orb is the distance by which a planet is allowed to deviate from the exact aspect. Each aspect has an orb, and the deviation allowed is usually up to 8 degrees. The more exact the aspect, the stronger the influence; the looser the aspect, the weaker the influence. The more powerful aspects are allowed wider orbs than the less powerful ones. There is slight disagreement as to the extent of the orbs but usually the conjunction, opposition, trine, and square have 8 degrees; the sextile 6 degrees; and the minor aspects 2 degrees.

There is an older system in which the planets themselves, rather than the aspects, had orbs, but the aspect orb system, devised in the late 19th century, is the one in universal use today.

ASPECT PATTERNS

When three or more planets are connected to each other by aspect, they form a pattern with a meaning of its own.

"T" Square

Two planets in opposition are both in square to a third planet. This brings tension and sharp, pressing problems, the result of which may be great energy and consequently a better than average chance of success throughout life.

When interpreting a "T" Square, all the factors involved – planets, signs, and houses – must be taken separately and then built up into a picture of the choices, difficulties, and solutions that each planet suggests.

When the "T" Square is in:

- *cardinal signs*, people have exceptional dynamism and energy
- *fixed signs*, people may be excessively stubborn, fighting personal battles to the bitter end
- *mutable signs*, people may try to solve, or even avoid, the problems associated with the "T" Square by being flexible and adaptable

Grand Cross

The Grand Cross consists of four planets connected by four squares and two oppositions. In effect, this consists of four "T" Squares and, although the process of interpretation is essentially the same as that for a single "T" Square, the complexity and possibilities are considerably more varied. This pattern is not necessarily more dynamic than the "T" Square.

When the Grand Cross is in:

- cardinal signs, people's problems and difficulties are more likely to result in energetic and assertive behavior
- fixed signs, people may hang on to their problems and be exceptionally stubborn and resistant to change
- mutable signs, people may be very adaptable, but may also exacerbate their problems by evading them

Grand Trine

Three planets are connected by three trines to form a triangle, the Grand Trine, around which planetary influences circulate with ease. This brings a wealth of natural talent, indicated by the signs and houses containing the planets, but may require tense aspects to provide the motivation for its expression.

When the Grand Trine is in:

- *Fire signs*, talents include enthusiasm and the search for new possibilities
- *Earth signs*, talents lie in practical work and experience
- *Air signs*, talents lie in intellectual work and the communication of ideas
- *Water signs*, talents are rooted in sympathy, compassion, and intuition

Yod

Also known as the Finger of Fate or the Finger of God, Yod is the name given to two planets in opposition connected to two other planets, one by semi-sextiles and the other by quincunxes. There is a consensus that this pattern is important, but few astrologers make much use of it. The two additional planets provide a choice of paths for the individual to express or discharge the tension of the opposition.

Mystic Rectangle

This consists of four planets connected in a rectangle of two squares and two trines, together with two oppositions connecting the opposite planets. Despite the name there is nothing mystical about this pattern. The combination of tense and harmonious aspects produces the best possible potential for the constructive use of natural talents.

Kite

The person with a kite pattern may be a "highflyer." All three planets in a grand trine are connected to a fourth planet, one by an opposition and the other two by sextiles. This is a useful combination of tense and harmonious aspects in which the two planets connected by trines and sextiles provide outlets for the tension of the opposition.

ASPECTS ON THE CHART

The chart below shows how the aspects are drawn on a chart. Each line in the wheel at the center represents an aspect between two planets, including the Ascendant and Midheaven (astrologers differ on whether to include these two points). The grid below shows all the aspects between planets.

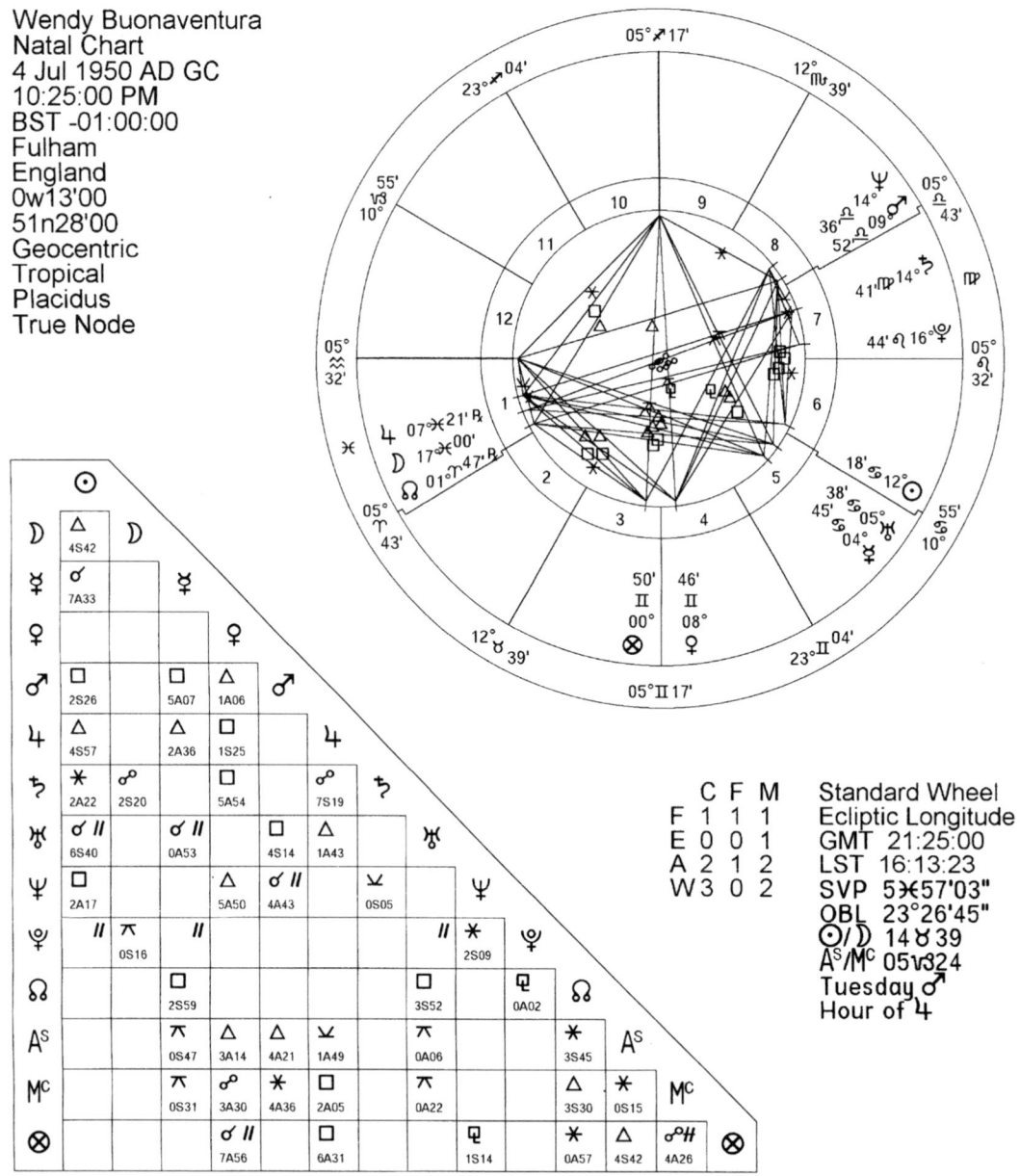

Wendy Buonaventura
Natal Chart
4 Jul 1950 AD GC
10:25:00 PM
BST -01:00:00
Fulham
England
0w13'00
51n28'00
Geocentric
Tropical
Placidus
True Node

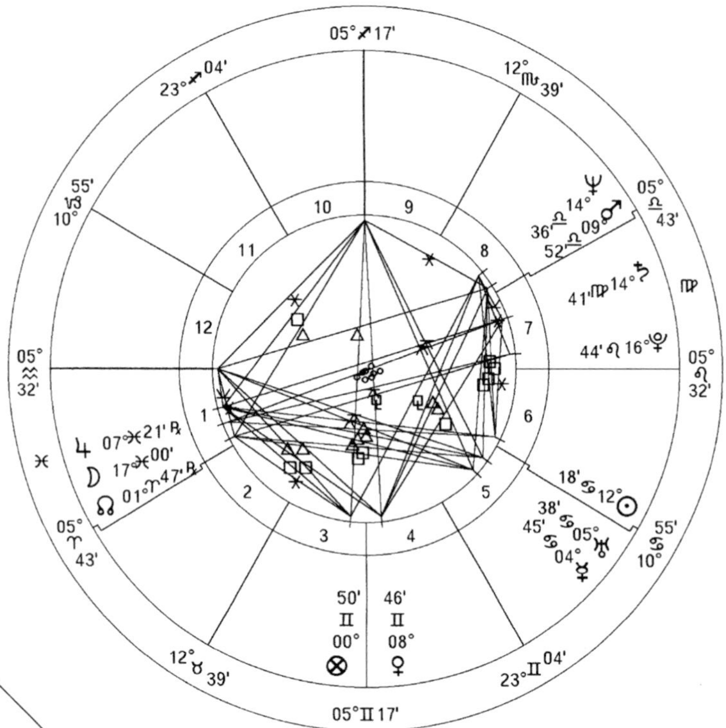

	☉	☽	☿	♀	♂	♃	♄	♅	♆	♇	☊	As	Mc
☽	△ 4S42												
☿	☌ 7A33												
♀													
♂	□ 2S26		□ 5A07	△ 1A06									
♃	△ 4S57		△ 2A36	□ 1S25									
♄	✶ 2A22	☍ 2S20		□ 5A54		☍ 7S19							
♅	☌ ∥ 6S40		☌ ∥ 0A53		□ 4S14	△ 1A43							
♆	□ 2A17			△ 5A50	☌ ∥ 4A43		⚺ 0S05						
♇	∥	⚻ 0S16	∥					∥	✶ 2S09				
☊			□ 2S59					□ 3S52		Q 0A02			
As			⚻ 0S47	△ 3A14	△ 4A21	⚺ 1A49		⚻ 0A06			✶ 3S45		
Mc			⚻ 0S31	☍ 3A30	✶ 4A36	□ 2A05		⚻ 0A22			△ 3S30	✶ 0S15	
⊗				☌ ∥ 7A56		□ 6A31			Q 1S14		✶ 0A57	△ 4S42	☍ # 4A26

	C	F	M
F	1	1	1
E	0	0	1
A	2	1	2
W	3	0	2

Standard Wheel
Ecliptic Longitude
GMT 21:25:00
LST 16:13:23
SVP 5♓57'03"
OBL 23°26'45"
☉/☽ 14♉39
As/Mc 05♑24
Tuesday ♂
Hour of ♃

♈ ♉ ♊ ♋ ♌ ♍ ♎ ♏ ♐ ♑ ♒ ♓

CHAPTER 8

INTERPRETING THE ASPECTS

The planetary aspects are the connecting threads that knit together all the apparently separate interpretations of the planets in their signs and houses, welding them into a whole. Understanding of the aspects is vital to the work of the astrologer, but beginners usually start by using standard interpretations, such as those given in pages 103–115.

The interpretations are summarized under three headings, which refer specifically to the major aspects: *harmonious aspects* (trine and sextile), *conjunction*, and *tense aspects* (opposition and square). In fact, there is usually an overlap of meaning and it is useful to read all three in order to gain a full understanding of the ways in which any two planets combine. For the semi-sextile, use the interpretations for harmonious aspects, and for the semi-square, sesquiquadrate, and quincunx use those given for the tense aspects. But it should be understood that in the case of these minor aspects, the interpretations will often have only a slight significance.

To understand how a planet operates in an aspect it is worthwhile examining its aspects with a variety of planets. For example, by studying the aspects of Uranus with Venus and the Moon, a more complete picture will be gained of the effect Uranus has on the emotions than if only Uranus–Venus aspects are checked.

Each aspect has a personality which may be described in human terms; for example, the astrologer may remark that Mercury opposed to Jupiter is extremist or that Moon trine Venus is pleasant.

In most cases the language used is very general because this allows as many manifestations as possible to be encompassed. It is then the astrologer's task to make the generalizations more specific in the light of common sense, knowledge of the person and astrological experience. For example, Mercury in opposition to Mars is very impatient. The astrologer may conclude that this raises the risk of hasty, wrongheaded decisions and physical accidents, problems which can be avoided by the cultivation of care, patience, and attention to detail. Any of the sample interpretations may be extended in this way, and the astrologer should look for ways to bring out the positive potential of the tense aspects and guard against the negative potential of the harmonious aspects.

Each sign and planet has both positive and negative, easy and difficult, manifestations. Difficult aspects to a planet may stimulate the negative qualities, whereas harmonious aspects may stimulate the positive qualities of the planet and the house or sign in which it is placed. For example, Mercury in Pisces can be either intuitive or confused. A harmonious aspect to Mercury may enhance intuition, while a tense aspect may stimulate confusion. Jupiter in the fourth house may lead to either pride or selfishness at home. Harmonious aspects to Jupiter may enhance pride and generosity, while tense aspects stimulate selfishness.

PSYCHOLOGICAL PROCESSES: STRATEGIES FOR SURVIVAL AND SELF-IMPROVEMENT

Each aspect represents a psychological process that can be worked out by considering the nature of each planet and the ways in which they interact (harmonious or tense). If the aspects are analyzed in this way it becomes easier for the astrologer to offer advice. For example, if the individual's aspects are reflected in a Sun–Uranus opposition, then life may be constantly disrupted by losses and unexpected events that appear to be outside personal control. Yet the astrologer may be able to identify ways in which these problems may be partly of the individual's own making, and that it is the individual's own disruptive behavior, perhaps linked to a deep desire for independence and resistance to commitment, which contributes to the problem. If the underlying situation is understood, it can often be turned to personal advantage. Perhaps, for example, a talent for independent thought and unconventional solutions can be put to positive use. Approaching the horoscope in this way allows us to develop strategies both for survival and self-improvement.

PROBLEMS AND SOLUTIONS

Tense aspects bring problems, the solution to which is often provided by the harmonious aspects between the same planets. For example, a Mercury–Saturn may indicate that Saturn inhibits Mercury (thought and verbal self-expression). At its most negative, the opposition might reflect a serious lack of confidence that can encourage failure at school. Yet a way around this can be provided by developing the clear and logical skills of the Mercury–Saturn trine (formal and logical thought). Everyone will experience several harmonious aspects from Mercury to their natal Saturn as the planets transit around the chart (see Chapter 11), and major harmonious aspects from Saturn to Mercury every few years. Astrologers will read these as the perfect moments for self-improvement and, if there is a problem with communication, confidence-building measures. But the opposition should not always be seen as negative. Although for one individual it might signify a serious lack of confidence, for another it might be perfect for serious, disciplined, and narrowly focused thought.

A Mars–Saturn opposition may signify Saturn's restriction of Martian energy. This might be reflected in a hypersensitivity to obstacles. In a sense it doesn't matter if these are real or imagined; what matters is that their combined effect may be to crush the individual's enthusiasm or confidence and create failure through a lack of nerve. Jobs may be abandoned before they are completed, or even never started because the fear of failure is so great. People who experience such a Saturn–Mars dynamic can help themselves by developing the self-discipline of the Mars–Saturn trine. We also need to consider the signs containing the planets. For example, Saturn's restrictive function might be easier to deal with if the planet is in Libra (where it's exalted) or Capricorn (which it rules). Similarly, if both planets are in Aries, and because Mars is at home in Aries, Martian energy might be enough to sweep aside Saturnine obstacles.

NEEDS AND CIRCUMSTANCES

Although harmonious and tense aspects tend to produce easy and awkward behavior, respectively, each contains a little of the other and the final manifestation is often based on a person's circumstances. The key to a psychological reading of the aspect can therefore be found in a consideration of the needs that each aspect brings. For example, an emotionally volatile aspect such as a Moon–Pluto conjunction brings an awareness of the depth (Pluto) of family relationships (the Moon). This might in turn suggest a consciousness of past family difficulties, perhaps over the generations (Pluto can be a symbol of confrontation in the quest for the truth, and moves slowly, linking long periods of time). One possible reaction from the individual concerned is a need for commitment – for close family members and partners to prove that they are always going to stick around. If this commitment is forthcoming, the individual may be contented (even if he or she tends to Plutonic qualities such as jealousy, or sets tests for partners to test their commitment). If it is not, the result may be angry confrontation and disruption.

In part the nature of the signs and houses containing the planets provides a clue. For example, a Moon–Pluto conjunction in vibrant Leo is more likely to be explosive than one in diplomatic Libra.

On a larger scale it is obvious that an individual in Los Angeles is likely to behave differently to one in Afghanistan, even if their charts were to be identical. Quite simply, a woman in Los Angeles with a Moon–Pluto aspect can walk out on her marriage, whereas one in Afghanistan cannot. Thus, to make precise predictions of how any individual will behave in any given astrological situation, knowledge of his or her cultural background is required. If anything, this is an indication that while astrology can be applied to any question, by itself it cannot provide universal answers.

ASPECTS BETWEEN THE OUTER PLANETS

Aspects between the outer planets – Jupiter, Saturn, Uranus, Neptune, and Pluto – are far less specific from an individual point of view than are aspects that involve the inner planets. Their interpretations in natal astrology tend to be vague because they can be in orb for months – as in the case of Jupiter–Saturn aspects – or even much longer. For example, the Neptune–Pluto sextile signifies the entire period from around 1943 to roughly 2004. Such long-term aspects therefore signify major historical events, the character of generations and the nature of cultural changes, so they are not listed below. It is up to each astrologer to decide whether these aspects will have a noticeable role in the natal chart. Aspects with tighter orbs are more likely to be influential than those with looser orbs, and applying aspects should be more significant than those that are separating.

However, it is the aspects to inner planets that give these impersonal outer planet aspects personal relevance. For example, millions of people may be born with a Neptune–Pluto conjunction, but for many this will have no individual psychological significance. Yet the people who have these two planets in conjunction with the Sun, the Moon, the Ascendant, or MC, may be those who in some way express the character of the times. The latest Neptune–Pluto sextile, for example, would be ignored in most normal chart readings. However, an individual who was born, say, with the Sun conjunct Neptune and the Moon conjunct Pluto would naturally be given a very "Neptune–Pluto" reading by the astrologer, and might experience precisely the idealistic, romantic, and confrontational events symbolized by the two planets. A noticeable example is provided by the Uranus–Pluto conjunction in Virgo in the mid-1960s. At the time this aspect coincided with a wave of revolutions across the world, from upheavals in China to riots in Paris and the anti-Vietnam war protests and hippie ideology in the USA. All children born in the mid-1960s have this aspect, but those who were born with conjunctions, squares or oppositions from the Sun, Moon, and Ascendant to Uranus or Pluto often exhibit a sense of mission, a feeling that life is to be lived to the full, and a reluctance to compromise their personal positions. For the duration and meaning of these planetary cycles see the table in Chapter 12.

PLANETS IN ASPECT TO ANGLES

Aspects between planets and the four angles are significant for the general character, home, family, partnerships, and career. The most important aspect is the conjunction, and this is always vital to interpretation of the birth chart. Sample interpretations are not listed here, but the examples given in Chapter 5 for planets in houses may be used. For planets conjunct the Ascendant, look up the interpretations for planets in the first house; for conjunctions with the IC, those for planets in the fourth house; for conjunctions with the Descendant, those for planets in the seventh house; and for conjunctions with the MC, those for planets in the tenth house.

Planets in square to the angles bring tension and those in trines or sextiles signify harmony.

THE PLANETARY ASPECTS

Remember, all these sample interpretations indicate the basic ways in which planetary symbols interact. As you become more familiar with them you will be able to look at a chart and understand instinctively what each combination of planets signifies, as follows.

☉ ☽

SUN–MOON

Harmonious aspects: contribute toward a balanced, peaceful, settled nature and increase the general chances of satisfaction and success in life. Relations with home and family and with the opposite sex should be good.

Conjunction: indicates that people may be individualistic and encounter problems in dealing with changing circumstances. Relations with the home and family may be so strong that it is difficult to escape their influence.

Tense aspects: reflect fundamental conflict, perhaps between parents, between parents and children, or between career or public affairs and domestic or private interests. Emotions may be strong and difficult to control.

☉ ☿

SUN–MERCURY

These two planets are never more than 28 degrees apart so the only major aspect that occurs is the *conjunction*: it signifies people who are subjective and creative, good at expressing opinions and working in the arts, but poor at handling logic, detail, and technical studies. There is often intellectual arrogance and prejudice. This is an excellent aspect for performers.

☉ ♀

SUN–VENUS

These planets are never more than 48 degrees apart so the only major aspect that occurs is the conjunction: it strengthens the female nature in both men and women, and is excellent for all creative and artistic activities. There is a love of refined pursuits and sensual pleasures, a need for partnership, a flair for fashion and style, and charming manners. Vanity and self-centered behavior are failings.

☉ ♂

SUN–MARS

Harmonious aspects: indicate that the personality is self-motivated, adventurous, energetic, competitive, decisive, and impatient. These people may become investigators, researchers, and seekers after hidden truths.

Conjunction: the aspect of the explorer and the warrior. These people have a vast amount of energy, although sometimes they push themselves to the point of exhaustion.

Tense aspects: increase the tendency to overwork, to take risks, and put up with personal discomfort. These people are good-natured and warmhearted, but they are also impulsive, excitable, reckless, and egotistical.

☉ ♃

SUN-JUPITER

Harmonious aspects: give a generally sensible, optimistic, and good-humored personality. These people divide into those who receive their inspiration from travel and adventure, and those who seek inner inspiration from religion or intellectual studies. Their idealism and optimism attract opportunities.

Conjunction: confers both intellectual wisdom and material benefit. These people are often proud and worldly, and even those who follow an ascetic or religious path tend to be self-important.

Tense aspects: signifies strong idealism. These people espouse causes, often impractical or unpopular, and pursue them to the point of self-sacrifice. They have a strong faith in their own destiny, a deep need for personal freedom, dislike order and routine, and often become travelers.

☉ ♄

SUN-SATURN

Harmonious aspects: indicate people who are conscientious workers, fulfilling obligations and observing responsibilities. There may be some self-inhibition.

Conjunction: signifies plenty of self-discipline and fondness for a routine life with a sense of order. These people often face difficult material circumstances, conflict with authority, or obstacles and delays. Difficulties erode their self-confidence, but this can be restored by hard work.

Tense aspects: divides people into two types: those who give in to the failure and frustration and those who react to this with such disciplined hard work that they achieve great things. They put up with difficult circumstances, if necessary.

☉ ♅

SUN-URANUS

Harmonious aspects: indicate people who are independent and unconventional. They are idealistic, and associate themselves with causes and movements. They often become leaders because other people admire their unusual way of doing things.

Conjunction: a sign of people who are inventive, independent, radical, and unconventional. By their refusal to accept established beliefs and behavior they force other people to reconsider their ways.

Tense aspects: reflect an individualist, egotistical, eccentric, and unconventional personality. Independence is prized above all else. Often these people are reckless and disorganized in their behavior. Nervous exhaustion and carelessness are possible.

☉ ♆

SUN-NEPTUNE

Harmonious aspects: signify people who are sentimental, kindly, and inclined to charitable work. They have a good creative imagination, are attracted to the arts and mysticism, and prefer a pleasant life.

Conjunction: intuition, imagination, sensitivity, self-sacrifice, compassion, and impracticality are the main qualities. There are two types: those who find their purpose in asceticism, mysticism, and selfless charitable work, and those who are drawn to the world of fashion, glamour, art, and style.

Tense aspects: indicate too much compassion and selflessness, making these people vulnerable to exploitation and deception. Sometimes they sacrifice their own interests. They may turn to religion, fashion, drink, or drugs as a means of shutting out the real world.

☉ ♇

SUN-PLUTO

Harmonious aspects: add emotional power and determination to the personality. These people can be obstinate, secretive, and interested in the deeper and darker mysteries of life.

Conjunction: an intense, emotional, and volcanic aspect, indicating that life is often disrupted by profound upheavals. These people use different means to help them cope with this: some may choose psychoanalysis or therapy, others religion, magic, or politics.

Tense aspects: signify people who thrive on emotional confrontation. They are obstinate, determined, and dedicated, and challenge other people to change their ways.

☽ ☿

MOON-MERCURY

Harmonious aspects: indicate a good memory, a poetic mind, and common sense. These people make fine journalists or teachers. They are interested in their background and environment.

Conjunction: strengthens the poetic and common-sense qualities of the harmonious aspects. Clear thought and analysis may be the best ways to resolve emotional problems. There is a love of gossip, and contacts with family members are often close.

Tense aspects: indicate there may be nervous tension, domestic misunderstandings, and a tendency to jump to hasty conclusions. These people have a sharp perception of the truth.

☽ ♀

MOON-VENUS

Harmonious aspects: reflected in an even temperament, graceful manners, and often an attractive appearance. These people cultivate social success. Their artistic talents are frequently turned to the creation of a pleasant domestic environment.

Conjunction: indicates that success in life is achieved more through natural charm than through work or skill. There is a taste for the finer things in life and a love of luxury. These people need a pleasant and balanced environment, especially in the home and family, and use all their diplomatic skills to create it.

Tense aspects: suggest there is often confusion about true feelings and emotional needs. There may be difficult domestic choices, and external obstacles such as rivals in love.

☽ ♂

MOON–MARS

Harmonious aspects: indicate the personality is generally constructive and practical. There is usually a good understanding of domestic problems, and a positive will to resolve them. There is honesty in the expression of feelings and a warm, hospitable manner.

Conjunction: sign of people who are emotional, courageous, daring, and adventurous, who take personal risks. In the family and home, they know just what they want and are unprepared to take second place. They are often entrepreneurs, explorers, and travelers.

Tense aspects: bring emotional tension, impulsive, and reckless behavior, a readiness to face personal danger and confrontation within the family. Domestically there are three types: the compulsive homemaker, always putting things up and taking them down; the emotional fighter who seeks confrontation; and the wanderer who is too restless to create a home.

☽ ♃

MOON–JUPITER

Harmonious aspects: signify those who are sympathetic, generous, helpful, and optimistic, people who attract good fortune by their very openness. They are idealistic, but appreciate a pleasant and comfortable home. Like all harmonious aspects to Jupiter, they assist in legal affairs and higher education.

Conjunction: has two sides: on the one hand it indicates those who are very generous, spontaneous, warm, and hospitable, but, on the other, those who can be very demanding, requiring affection, love, large families, luxurious homes, foreign travel and, for the more introverted, religious experience and intellectual study. There can be selfishness in achieving these ambitions. Life abroad is likely.

Tense aspects: indicate a continual desire for "more"; more emotion, affection, luxury or, for the introverted type, more religion. Emotional needs may be temporarily satisfied by material consumption, religious obsessions, or extreme beliefs. These people need to find personal motivation in order to alleviate their dependence upon external stimuli.

☽ ♄

MOON–SATURN

Harmonious aspects: a sign of people who regulate their emotional and family lives by doing what they consider to be right: being faithful, practical, and punctual.

Conjunction: indicates people who are faithful, reliable, and loyal, even in times of difficulty. They lack confidence in their feelings, possibly avoiding emotional entanglement by being cold, or burying themselves in work and domestic cares. Men will be attracted to older women. Emotional relationships may be delayed, but once formed are very stable.

Tense aspects: suggest difficulty in expressing emotion, and feelings are often concealed behind a mask. There is a need for a stable and secure home, but often domestic responsibilities are allowed to dominate family life.

☽ ♅

MOON–URANUS

Harmonious aspects: indicate emotional and domestic independence is important. These people resent social pressures, and conditions in the home are often unusual.

Conjunction: signifies a need for emotional and domestic freedom so strong that all ties will be resisted, and cooperation with partners and family members will be difficult. These people need variety. Expression of the emotions may be superficially open, but feelings are often ignored, only to explode later.

Tense aspects: reflect uncooperative attitudes that may bring about unexpected domestic upheavals. Domestic chaos is preferred to routine. These people are attracted to "alternative" lifestyles such as communal living, but their individualism works against such ventures.

☽ ♆

MOON–NEPTUNE

Harmonious aspects: bring a kindly and compassionate personality, making the home a pleasant and hospitable place, if a little disorganized. The home and family may be romanticized.

Conjunction: indicates a deep yearning for something greater than the self. This may be found through mystical religion, in romantic love, or by attachment to the family. There are often self-sacrificing tendencies and other people may take advantage. There is an attraction for art and fashion. The home may be exotic and mysterious, if rather disorganized.

Tense aspects: have qualities similar to those of the conjunction, but heighten the tendencies to confusion, especially in the home. Unrealistic fantasies tend to obscure daily reality. There is a vivid artistic imagination and a feeling for fashion and style.

☽ ♇

MOON–PLUTO

Harmonious aspects: suggest emotional intensity and a desire for change and improvement in the home. These people bring their emotional problems to the surface, even if this causes domestic confrontation.

Conjunction: indicates people who are very obstinate, especially over domestic issues; their refusal to compromise often guarantees conflict. They try to bottle up their feelings, but the more they do this, the more likely they are to explode. Such explosions may be the catalyst for complete revolution in home and lifestyle. These people can choose to use their emotional energy for either destructive or constructive purposes.

Tense aspects: suggest the emotions are deep, and that relationships and domestic affairs can be complicated. Domestic upheavals may be caused by events apparently outside personal control. The interests of these people are deep and often include psychology, the occult, revolutionary lifestyles, and healing.

☿ ♀

MERCURY–VENUS

Mercury and Venus make two major aspects – conjunction and sextile.

Sextile: brings balance, common sense, and pleasant, charming manners. All social, emotional and educational affairs benefit, and communication is straightforward.

Conjunction: brings eloquence, social charm, teaching skills, persuasive powers, and balanced opinions. These people are able to understand their emotions, but if too rational they may deny their true feelings.

☿ ♂

MERCURY–MARS

Harmonious aspects: strengthen the mind, which is energetic and perceptive. There is a liking for practical research and investigation, which will be tackled with common sense and precision.

Conjunction: indicates the mind is sharp, perceptive, and witty, with a feel for sarcasm and satire. These people love argument. They are strongly drawn to research in practical subjects, but often exhaust themselves mentally through overwork. Their weakness is impatience.

Tense aspects: indicate people with strong and energetic minds, but who can be too argumentative and impatient. Sometimes they attach themselves to causes, becoming determined reformers, attacking abuses in society; investigative journalists come under these aspects.

☿ ♃

MERCURY–JUPITER

Harmonious aspects: signifies people who are optimistic, philosophical, good-natured, and open to new ideas. Intellectual interests are often pursued at the expense of worldly considerations. There is a restlessness and love of travel.

Conjunction: brings a love of ideas and a thirst for knowledge, which may be expressed in a variety of ways. Some people will be collectors of facts, others study philosophy or religion, while still others travel the world. There is a belief in freedom of speech and dislike of orthodox education, which may limit academic success.

Tense aspects: indicate people who are extremists, swinging between scepticism and belief. They find it difficult to reconcile facts with theory, or to think clearly. There is great restlessness and curiosity, and they frequently travel or reside in foreign countries. As with all tense Jupiter aspects, there may be difficulties with the law.

☿ ♄

MERCURY–SATURN

Harmonious aspects: suggest people who deal well with routine, tend towards conservative opinions, think clearly and are attracted to practical subjects. An ability to work hard and consistently enhances academic success.

Conjunction: denotes the mind is serious, attitudes conservative and practical. These people lack confidence in their ideas and imagination and find security in detail and precision. They work hard academically, but difficulty with expressing ideas can limit their success.

Tense aspects: bring the same conservatism and preference for practical studies as the conjunction, but emphasize a lack of confidence in personal ideas and imagination. These people, however, are often hardheaded, materialistic, and businesslike, and in their struggle to overcome the prospect of educational failure, they achieve undreamed-of success.

☿ ♅

MERCURY–URANUS

Harmonious aspects: Uranus brings its electric qualities to the mind and these aspects are quick-witted, inventive, and skilled in finding new solutions to old problems. Such solutions may lie in high technology – or in new possibilities in human thought and awareness. These people thrive on debate and argument.

Conjunction: indicates people who are independently minded. Their main interest is to challenge accepted values and they easily become eccentric reactionaries or flag-waving anarchists. Those with more practical interests are usually drawn towards new technology. Nervous tension is common.

Tense aspects: signifies people who can be extremist in their opinions, vain and arrogant in their beliefs and ideas, which are often highly unusual and completely impractical. They become members of odd religious cults or fringe political groups. They are often in the intellectual vanguard, for today's fringe idea can be tomorrow's accepted belief.

☿ ♆

MERCURY–NEPTUNE

Harmonious aspects: indicate people who are imaginative, idealistic, refined, and artistic, but are not good with detail. They may be at home with such diverse interests as photography, fashion, and mysticism. They may be gullible.

Conjunction: brings intuition, imagination, mysticism, intellectual sensitivity, and breadth of vision. These are expressed best through the arts or idealistic work, but there may be an inability to handle practical studies. These people may be unwilling to face difficult choices and often retreat into a dream world.

Tense aspects: a sign of artists or mystics, and people who are very highly motivated. Their opinions are flexible, although deep beliefs may be held with sincere conviction. Too often they resort to deceiving themselves, or others, as an easy way out of a complicated situation.

☿ ♇

MERCURY–PLUTO

Harmonious aspects: indicate people who are obstinate, perceptive, and interested in research into deep and mysterious subjects such as psychology, magic, criminology, and subatomic physics. They like argument and debate.

Conjunction: reflects the merging of unconscious and conscious minds, with beliefs and ideas becoming as one. As a result, these people are obstinate, opinionated, and argumentative. Some study subjects such as astronomy or physics, while others become involved in the occult, psychotherapy, or healing.

Tense aspects: indicate a mind dominated by beliefs and instincts. These people often have many prejudices. They study in short intense bursts followed by exhaustion. There is a relentless search for truth, and practical considerations are usually ignored.

♀ ♂

VENUS–MARS

Harmonious aspects: indicate that these people are passionate with lovers, warm and friendly with strangers, and have a fondness for the pleasures of the flesh and leisure activities. They are energetic, with a relaxed and easy attitude towards work.

Conjunction: indicates people with warm and powerful emotions, and a continual need for social, physical, and sexual experience. They are energetic, assertive, self-interested, and often popular. Quick to anger, they do not bear grudges and find it easy to make amends.

Tense aspects: are as vigorous as the conjunction, but indicate that these people are more ready to take offense – friendly one moment, hostile the next. They are impatient and impulsive, placing unrealistic emotional demands on partners. They are likely to have sudden enthusiasms that they drop without warning.

♀ ♃

VENUS–JUPITER

Harmonious aspects: reflect a personality that is affectionate, with graceful manners. These people sense the prevailing social mood and fit in with the latest fashion. They are usually hospitable and generous. This aspect benefits all legal and financial matters.

Conjunction: indicates people who are exceptionally generous and loving, but require a great deal of affection and social stimulation in return. There is often an expectation that partners provide material support. Social confidence and optimism are the keys to their success. They can be very needy, craving affection, but also very giving.

Tense aspects: a sign of people who are spontaneous and vivacious, but who at times can be emotionally demanding. Friendships are often disrupted by Jupiterian activities: religion, travel, or devotion to idealistic causes. They possess artistic ambitions, but not necessarily any talent. These people do best in independent enterprises where conflicts with others will not arise.

♀ ♄

VENUS–SATURN

Harmonious aspects: indicate people who are quiet, responsible, and faithful in all social and emotional affairs. Conventional behavior and stable relationships provide security and counteract fears of rejection and lack of confidence. Often these people are attracted to friends who are older than themselves. They are usually careful with money and resources.

Conjunction: repeats the qualities of the harmonious aspects, but is much stronger. There may be delays in forming relationships, but once formed these will be stable. Traditional values are favored in relationships: fidelity is taken to such lengths that a marriage may be maintained when there is no love left. These people need to develop confidence in their own feelings.

Tense aspects: similar to the harmonious aspects but indicate a tendency to encounter delays and obstacles – from parents, lack of money, or work. Loyal and faithful, these people usually subordinate their own feelings to practical considerations; they may marry for security. They need to develop confidence in their own emotional needs. Sometimes they suffer from a fear of poverty, and need to take care of resources.

♀ ♅

VENUS–URANUS

Harmonious aspects: reflect a need for change and interest in all friendships. These people preserve their emotional independence even in marriage, and reduce ties to a minimum. Their original and unusual behavior is a source of social popularity.

Conjunction: stresses the importance of emotional independence. These people resent obligations and expectations. They are superficially direct and open with their emotions, but keep their feelings to themselves. If they feel their independence is threatened, they may become cold and distant or leave without warning, but given their freedom they are devoted and loyal. Artistic talents are original and may be combined with an interest in technology.

Tense aspects: reflect a need for emotional independence so great that any commitment is seen as a threat. The emotions fluctuate, and these people may experience many partnerships in their search for the ideal. Their expectations are high; they prefer emotional conflict to remaining in an unsatisfactory relationship. In the arts they are eccentric and original. There are likely to be sudden monetary gains and losses.

♀ ♆

VENUS–NEPTUNE

Harmonious aspects: bring romance, compassion, and intuition to all relationships. These people have inventive imaginations, which is advantageous in artistic activities. They are conscious of style, image, and fashion.

Conjunction: indicates people who are highly sensitive, romantic, and idealistic in relationships; consequently they are often confused and muddled. They are shy and sometimes prefer fantasy to a real relationship. Once the ideal partner is found, they are self-sacrificing and devoted. Artistic imagination is vivid and there may be a fascination with film, photography, and fashion.

Tense aspects: signify people who are extremely romantic, with the result that confusion and misunderstanding are common. Fantasy may be preferred to the reality of relationships. Sometimes they divert their energies into mysticism or the arts. They need to develop a clear head and a thick skin.

♀ ♇

VENUS–PLUTO

Harmonious aspects: indicate people who tend to be serious and committed in relationships. They have high expectations of partners and are prepared to risk confrontation when these are not satisfied.

Conjunction: suggests deep, intense, and inflexible emotions, and a need for passionate, emotional, and sexual commitment. These people are fiercely jealous and do not take kindly to rejection. They are secretive and bottle up their feelings.

Tense aspects: indicate people who may love and hate with equal intensity. They are secretive and conceal their true passions. There is a deep brooding imagination, often expressed through the arts. Their pursuit of emotional power may be channeled into business activities and the quest for money.

♂ ♃

MARS–JUPITER

Harmonious aspects: bring action and energy. These people are always looking for ways to improve themselves through sport and physical fitness, travel, or education.

Conjunction: suggests crusaders opening up opportunities for themselves and others. These people sometimes become athletes, adventurers, or explorers. Their weaknesses are self-importance and pursuit of personal power and wealth.

Tense aspects: signify people who are restless and reckless, tending towards extremes. Some are greedy for possessions, power, and money; others renounce their personal interests for an idealistic cause. There is a love of adventure and travel.

♂ ♄

MARS–SATURN

Harmonious aspects: indicate people who are hard workers. They make good entrepreneurs for, although cautious, they can withstand personal hardship and danger. They lack imagination, an advantage for those with dangerous tasks to perform.

Conjunction: also indicates hard workers. These people are practical organizers, careful with resources and good at dealing with the obstacles and delays they often encounter. They value security and stability, and do not take risks.

Tense aspects: indicate people who develop sudden enthusiasms for practical projects but then often give them up, as a result of either an external obstacle – lack of money, opposition from authority – or a failure of will, confidence, or energy. They need to be more consistent.

♂ ♅

MARS–URANUS

Harmonious aspects: suggest strong individualists with unusual activities. They may participate in fringe political and reformist movements, or apply their inventive skills to technology and engineering.

Conjunction: indicates people who are independent, individualist, and inventive. They may find it difficult to follow a routine or cooperate at work. They must take responsibility for their own actions.

Tense aspects: signify eccentric and individualistic people who sometimes join fringe religious or political groups but are too restless to be committed. Only by developing practical skills can they turn their plans into action.

♂ ♆

MARS–NEPTUNE

Harmonious aspects: suggest impractical people who do well in work that requires imagination, artistic skill, or idealism.

Conjunction: indicates the need for a greater purpose in life. If this is satisfied, these people will put their dreams into practice. Otherwise they will be impractical and confused. Imaginative and idealistic work is often found in the arts, fashion, or films.

Tense aspects: bring increased feeling for music, the arts, fantasy, and mysticism. There is a tendency to be impractical, and some people sacrifice their lives to their imagination. Others become revolutionaries or mystics, attacking materialist society.

♂ ♇

MARS–PLUTO

Harmonious aspects: bring dedication, persistence and emotional commitment to all work and activities. These people are obstinate and difficult to divert from a chosen course of action.

Conjunction: indicates people who are self-willed and determined, and listen to no advice. If they are attracted to religious or political causes, they become strong leaders.

Tense aspects: suggest major confrontations and revolutions in lifestyle. These people are determined, persistent, obstinate, and perceptive, with an unrealistic belief in absolute truth and their own destiny.

♃ ♄

JUPITER–SATURN

Harmonious aspects: are extremely beneficial and constructive, provide a firm base from which to develop potential of the whole chart.

Conjunction: reflects a choice between restricting Saturn and expansive Jupiter. If a balance is reached, considerable achievement is possible.

Tense aspects: indicate conflicting possibilities – whether to change or remain the same, to take a risk or refuse an opportunity. If these problems can be overcome, much may be achieved.

♃ ♅

JUPITER–URANUS

Harmonious aspects: bring idealism, thoughtfulness and independence.

Conjunction: indicates people who are optimistic, expansive, and adventurous, with grand ambitions and desires that may be difficult to control or implement. They have great faith in their own originality and a belief in the future.

Tense aspects: signify a reckless and all-consuming need for experience, variety, and independence. Sometimes this results not in originality and inventiveness, but dogmatic beliefs.

♃ ♆

JUPITER–NEPTUNE

Harmonious aspects: bring compassion, reforming ideals, artistic inclinations, a wandering spirit, and sometimes a religious vision. These tendencies are subtle and are easily overwhelmed by more forceful ones.

Conjunction: is excessively sensitive. Often there is exceptional idealism and a love of religion. There may be a fascination for travel, the arts, and fashion.

Tense aspects: are confused and oversensitive. They lead people to sacrifice themselves to great causes, escape into private fantasies or lives of rootless wandering.

♃ ♇

JUPITER–PLUTO

Harmonious aspects: indicate tenacity, determination, and the desire for self-improvement.

Conjunction: inclines to interests in art, religion, politics, psychology, and endless foreign travel. These people fight for the truth, but also seek personal power.

Tense aspects: reflect a need for personal exploration through travel, revolution, or religion, often accompanied by a self-interested, obstinate, and militant attitude.

♄ ♅

SATURN–URANUS

Harmonious aspects: combine sound practical skills with innovative and original abilities that form an extremely useful foundation for developing the birth potential.

Conjunction: indicates determination and hard work combined with originality, offering new solutions to old problems. These people have democratic ideals, but are authoritarian in practice.

Tense aspects: lead to erratic behavior, ranging from an authoritarian need for order to a belief in total anarchy.

♄ ♆

SATURN–NEPTUNE

Harmonious aspects: enable dreams, imagination and inspiration to become the basis for practical action. Beliefs tend to be conservative.

Conjunction: if the opposing principles of these two planets can be reconciled, the imagination will be disciplined and dreams realized. If not resolved, confusion may upset practical ambitions. Attitudes to religion are conservative.

Tense aspects: tend to block the satisfactory expression of the imagination and create muddle in practical affairs. Beliefs and opinions are inclined to be reactionary.

♄ ♇

SATURN–PLUTO

Harmonious aspects: bring a sense of purpose, a desire for self-improvement, and an emotional commitment to ambition.

Conjunction: brings a profound desire for personal change and development. These people are often very stubborn and ambitious. They tend to be self-controlled.

Tense aspects: indicate a desire to revolutionize personal life or reform society, but aspirations are confused and there is a tendency to confrontation.

♅ ♆

URANUS–NEPTUNE

Harmonious aspects: increase the imagination and desire for meaning in life, but the influence is subtle.

Conjunction: brings a profound desire for change, extending beyond the individual into political and mystical revolution. Only those people who are in the vanguard of their generation will truly manifest this aspect. For most, it will be experienced in terms of the unsettling events through which they live.

Tense aspects: indicate a potential for chaos and upheaval, a willingness to tear down the old and welcome the new. For many people, these aspects will be experienced in terms of external events that affect their lives.

♅ ♇

URANUS–PLUTO

Harmonious aspects: reinforce the emotional commitment to change and a desire for personal transformation. Most people experience these aspects through external events.

Conjunction: suggests people will experience profound revolutionary change in their lives. This conjunction is very infrequent and coincides with periods of historic upheaval.

Tense aspects: are similar in effect to the conjunction. Psychologically they indicate tension and need for change.

♆ ♇

NEPTUNE–PLUTO

Harmonious aspects: the two planets were in sextile continuously from 1945 to 1995, so associated with the massive changes that have taken place since the Second World War.

Conjunction: brings historic upheaval. The people born under this aspect in the 1890s were the generation that lived through the First World War. If especially prominent in a natal chart, it signifies emotional intensity, mysticism, and a need for personal revolution.

♈ ♉ ♊ ♋ ♌ ♍ ♎ ♏ ♐ ♑ ♒ ♓

CHAPTER 9

NATAL ASTROLOGY

This chapter examines the interpretation of birth charts. Other sorts of horoscopes are looked at in Chapter 12.

INTERPRETING THE HOROSCOPE

Most astrology revolves around the interpretation of the horoscope, a process that often seems mysterious to the uninitiated but is second nature to the experienced. Experience is gained by endless practice, for which there is no substitute. Moreover, when casting charts for other people there is an overriding consideration – a duty of care on the part of the astrologer towards the client.

CULTURAL FACTORS

There is one preliminary step in interpretation – to ascertain exactly what the horoscope is set for (it can be cast for relationships, questions, countries, and sporting contests, for instance). If an astrologer shows you a horoscope and challenges you to interpret it, you'll have no idea whether it's set for a frog, a person, or a theatrical production. And if you find out that it's for a person, you won't know if it's for an infant or an octogenarian. If you know it's for an adult, you won't know whether it's for a man, a woman, a New York executive, or a New Guinean villager. No astrological interpretation exists in isolation and as much information as possible is required before a meaningful interpretation can be attempted. In this sense an astrologer is in exactly the same position as a doctor who needs all the available evidence before a reliable diagnosis is possible.

PREPARATIONS

Only by making copious notes on a chart and producing detailed written interpretations is it possible to become familiar with the meanings of the astrological significators – the signs, planets, houses, and aspects. As you become more familiar with the meanings of these symbols, it will gradually become unnecessary to write notes and increasingly easy to interpret horoscopes spontaneously. Even experienced astrologers often need a few hours to prepare a chart before seeing a client, and although most record their readings on to tape, preparing a written interpretation is by far the best way to develop a sound appreciation of how to read a chart methodically and creatively. Remember, you're converting images and symbols into words: start doing this in a routine manner, learn the basics and soon you'll be improvising. And one other thing – astrology is a lifelong study; astrologers who have been practicing for 30 or 40 years still go back and find new ways of looking at charts.

But there is one overriding rule: keep it simple. The purpose of astrology, especially when dealing with other people, is to use the chart to shed light on particular problems, or give meaning to otherwise inexplicable situations. Start by looking at what's most important in the chart, then look at what's less important, and only add more minor aspects, or midpoints, asteroids, harmonics, or any other complication when you are happy that you have mastered the basics. Each level of detail that's added will introduce complications into the interpretations. For example, an individual with the Sun in Taurus might be inflexible. Add a Piscean Moon and that person becomes flexible. Place the Sun in the sixth house and the Moon in the fourth and the individual might be flexible at home and inflexible at work. Yet what happens if the Sun is conjunct changeable Neptune and the Moon conjunct disciplined Saturn? Very soon the picture becomes extremely complicated and the interpretation correspondingly rich. But all astrologers set their own limits on how much detail they are going to consider.

Also, when working with individuals, keep in mind the need to listen to them rather than impose astrological preconceptions on them. Don't imagine that astrological terms such as "rule" and "influence" mean that they are the passive recipients of planetary forces. It's much more useful to see the horoscope as a mirror, reflecting their life, symbolizing, signifying, or representing the matters which are important to them in such a way that a dialogue between astrologer and client will shed light on them.

THE THREE STAGES OF INTERPRETATION

The first stage of a written interpretation is *analysis*. Each of the major significators is taken in order of priority and a brief interpretation is written alongside, copied, or summarized from one of the sample interpretations in Chapters 3, 5, and 8. The second stage is *integration*. The different general themes and areas of life to be considered must all be gathered together under common headings. The third stage is *synthesis*, in which all the different sections of the second stage are incorporated into a single report.

ANALYSIS

The significators should be taken in the following order.

1 Factors indicating major tendencies:
   a) balance of elements – is there an emphasis on one or two?
   b) balance of qualities – is there an emphasis on one or two?
   c) strong aspect patterns – is there a "T" Square, Grand Cross, Grand Trine, or other significant pattern?

2 The Ascendant and the rising sign; position by sign and house of the Ascendant ruler (the planet ruling the rising sign); aspects made by the Ascendant and Ascendant ruler (also known as the chart ruler or ruling planet).

3 The Sun sign, house, and aspects.

4 The Sun ruler (the planet ruling the sign containing the Sun), its sign, house, and aspects.

5 The Moon sign, and house and aspects made by the Moon.

6 The remaining planets – in order from Mercury to Pluto – and their houses, signs, and aspects.

7 The nodes and any other factors to be considered.

It is helpful to read through the notes on the chart analysis and insert next to each interpretation the subheading under which it should be considered. Most of the interpretations will fall naturally under one subheading, but some may have to be considered under two or even three.

When looking at a house, consider the planets in the house first, then the sign on the cusp, and then the house ruler (the planet ruling the sign on the cusp). Consideration of the house ruler should be left to last because although it provides more information it can be confusing for the beginner. Interpretation of the house ruler becomes more important when there are no planets in a house.

The following subheadings are useful as a rough guide for a thorough interpretation, although these may be combined or added to as necessary. For example, emotions and relationships may be considered either together or separately.

General character

The Ascendant; planets in the first house; the Sun and Moon; major patterns and outstanding features such as element emphasis; Ascendant ruler; any other general features.

Family

Planets in the fourth house; fourth house ruler (planet ruling the sign on the cusp of the fourth house); fifth house (children); third house (brothers and sisters); tenth house and the tenth house ruler, if relevant; Moon (mother); fourth house with Sun and Saturn (father), if relevant.

Emotions

The Moon, Venus, planets in water signs.

Relationships

The Descendant; planets in the seventh house and the seventh house ruler (close partnerships and marriage); planets in the fifth house and the fifth house ruler (romance); planets in the eleventh house and the eleventh house ruler (groups, acquaintances); planets in Libra (partnerships); Mars (social energy); Moon, Venus, and planets in water signs, if relevant.

Mind, intellect, and education

Mercury; planets in the third house and the third house ruler (ability to communicate, school education, general interests, and mental skills); Jupiter; planets in the ninth house and the ninth house ruler (higher education, philosophical outlook); eighth and twelfth houses (indications of intuitive skills); Neptune (imagination); planets in Gemini and Virgo, if relevant.

Artistic and creative ability

Planets in the fifth house and the fifth house ruler; Mercury, Venus, Mars, and Neptune, if relevant; planets in Earth signs (practical skill).

Career, work

MC; planets in the tenth house and the tenth house ruler (career); planets in the sixth house and the sixth house ruler (working conditions, nature of job); Mars (practical energy); Saturn (self-organization and discipline).

Money

Planets in the second house and the second house ruler; planets in the eighth house and the eighth house ruler.

Travel

Planets in the third house (short journeys); planets in the ninth house (long journeys).

Health

Planets in the sixth house and the sixth house ruler; general indications from other significators.

Should any other information be required, turn to the relevant house in the horoscope and examine the planets it contains, the sign on its cusp and the planet ruling this sign, and the general planetary ruler. Thus, for the law, turn first to the ninth house (which rules the law), the planet it contains and the planet which rules its cusp, and then to Jupiter, the general ruler of the law. For leisure activities, examine Venus, the fifth house, and general factors such as the Sun sign.

The beginner will find it very useful to rewrite the notes of the analysis under these separate headings, but with a little experience this stage can be dropped or shortened to the point where all that is needed is a note of the relevant subheading next to each interpretation in the analysis.

INTEGRATION

Integrating the analysis of the horoscope is not solely a matter of rearranging all the individual interpretations under their separate headings. It is necessary to make connections between different factors in the chart, combining interpretations which go well together and attempting to reconcile the contradictions between those that do not. It is through examining the contradictions contained in any chart that the true complexity of an individual character may be understood.

For example, we might look at an individual's Sun and conclude that this person is shy, sensitive and impractical – but an insensitive Arien Moon and a practical Taurean Ascendant would in turn mean the Sun is placed in the sociable eleventh house. Meanwhile, the impulsive Arien Moon and cautious Taurean Ascendant lead to very different conclusions, and that's before we consider the fact that the outgoing Moon would probably be in the reclusive twelfth house. Ultimately each individual is unique; no two people can ever share the same horoscope, and astrology always reveals that each one of us is a mass of contradictions. Perhaps we could say that this is precisely why human beings are so impossible to understand. A hundred years of psychology, with dozens of theories, hundreds of experts, thousands of books, and hundreds of thousands of students, have certainly done little to illuminate the problems inherent in human nature, although Jungian psychology could be singled out as being particularly helpful for astrologers.

SYNTHESIS

The astrologer may now proceed to the third stage, in which the whole interpretation is written out in a form which is easy for the subject to read and understand.

Most professional astrologers give only verbal consultations, but these can easily be taped for the client. (In the USA, where distances are often great, telephone consultations are common.) A verbal consultation is usually given because full written reports are laborious to complete and do not take into account any dialogue between astrologer and client. Nevertheless, the written report has its advantages, especially as the client can refer far more easily to a sentence on a page than to a passage on a tape. For the student, the preparation of written reports is the best way to learn the meanings of astrological symbols, become familiar with the process of interpretation, and develop confidence as an astrologer.

In the final interpretation, it is open to the astrologer to use examples, figures of speech, and metaphors in order to make the interpretation more colorful and to emphasize certain points. Astrological jargon should be left out of the final draft as this is usually meaningless to the client, although the technical information, such as the positions of the planets, should be listed separately. Psychological jargon should also be avoided as this often serves only to obscure the real issues.

SAMPLE INTERPREATION

This interpretation refers to the chart on page 92, drawn up for dancer and writer Wendy Buonaventura.

ANALYSIS

Dominance of water: generally emotional, sensitive, imaginative.

Dominance of cardinal/mutable: changeable, restless, unstable.

"T" Square in mutable: tension, energy directed into search for change, new circumstances.

Ascendant – Aquarius: requires independence and freedom, needs to be different, intellectual, idealistic, impractical, resents restrictions.

Ascendant ruler – Saturn in Virgo: need for physical order.

Saturn in the eighth house: needs to work very hard in business; possibility of losses, delays in business.

Saturn sextile Sun: self-discipline, good sense of order, ability to cope with responsibilities and routine.

Saturn opposition Moon: emotionally reserved; difficulty in expressing feelings; needs emotional stability; material difficulties in the home, eg, lack of money, disagreements between parents, opposition from family members.

Saturn square Venus: difficulties and delays in forming relationships; shy in expressing feelings; needs emotional security; faithful in relationships; conservative in artistic attitudes; possibility of financial restrictions.

Saturn opposition Jupiter: the basic need for order and restriction is in conflict with the desire for expansion and growth – there may be continual difficulties posed by the demand for change on the one hand and for stability on the other.

Saturn semi-sextile Neptune: ability to express the imagination through practical skills.

Ascendant co-ruler Uranus in Cancer: seeks emotional independence, domestic change. In most cases the position of Uranus by sign has only a general psychological meaning, but this is heightened by the conjunction of Uranus with the Sun.

Uranus in the fifth house: requires independence in leisure activities and romance; artistically original; relations with children unusual; the children themselves will be independent.

Uranus on the sixth cusp: technically Uranus is in the fifth house, but it is an exact conjunction with the sixth cusp so it may be considered to have a role in sixth house matters. Work will be highly original; there will be a need to work independently and a dislike of routine. Health may be affected by nervous tension.

Uranus conjunct Sun: the orb is wide and the aspect is separating, but it is important because of the Sun's general significance. There is an exceptionally strong need for independence and a desire to follow an original and unusual lifestyle; resists commitments and routine.
Uranus conjunct Mercury: an orb of less than 1 degree makes this a very strong aspect. Strong, unusual, original, independent ideas; needs mental stimulation; likes debate and argument.

Uranus square Mars: individualistic behavior; prefers acting alone to obeying orders; impatient with established routine; needs to innovate.

Uranus trine Jupiter: beliefs tend to be independent, unusual.

Uranus quincunx Ascendant: independent spirit.
Uranus quincunx MC: requires independence and change in career.

Sun in Cancer: Sun-sign characteristics are exceptionally important. Emotional, sensitive, compassionate, maternal; needs secure home and stable family life; moods fluctuate.

Sun in the sixth house: conscientious worker; likes to look after people; worries about health (Cancer types are worriers); physical health subject to emotional moods.

Sun trine Moon: well-balanced; home and family life harmonious; generally well-integrated personality.

Sun conjunct Mercury: the orb for this aspect is very wide but it is applying and therefore given added importance. Strong-minded, strong-willed; the mind is subjective and the ideas are personal; impatient with clear or logical thought.

Sun square Mars: adventurous; fights battles with little thought of personal welfare; likes a challenge; can be reckless and impatient.

Sun trine Jupiter: optimistic, expansive, and self-confident.

Sun square Neptune: vivid imagination but tendency to confusion and dismissal of practical considerations.

Moon in Pisces: extreme sensitivity, deep imagination, changeable, dreamy, impractical; home and family life need to be calm, peaceful, and relaxed, but may be disorganized with an element of mystery.

Moon in the second house: financial affairs fluctuate; money earned through women; attitudes to money and possessions based on emotions, not practical needs.

Moon quincunx Pluto: need for renewal.

Mercury in Cancer: the mind, ideas, and ideals are dominated by the emotions; better at intuitive rather than rational thought; good memory.

Mercury in the fifth house: intellect and skills need to be used creatively in communication.

Mercury on the sixth cusp: Like Uranus, Mercury is in an exact conjunction with the sixth cusp and so may be considered to have a sixth house function. Needs mental stimulation in work; must utilize communicative skills.

Mercury square Mars: impatient, fond of argument and debate; seeks truth; sharp-tongued; must have intellectual stimulation; restless; fond of travel; may suffer from nervous tension.

Mercury trine Jupiter: good common sense; beliefs and ideas harmonize.

Mercury quincunx Ascendant: mental tension increases need for intellectual achievement.

Mercury quincunx MC: mental tension leads to need for intellectual stimulation in career.

Venus in Gemini: socially lively and vivacious; rationalizes emotions; likes to talk about feelings; intellectual approach to the arts.

Venus in the fifth house: emotional energy is directed into artistic activity; likes entertaining; needs mental rapport with friends; relations with children lively and affectionate.

Venus trine Mars: warm, hospitable, sociable; well-balanced emotionally and socially; charm assists in achievement of aims and ambitions; financial affairs balanced.

Venus square Jupiter: strong need for affection; love of luxury and comfort; high artistic ambitions; perfectionist.

Venus trine Neptune: very romantic; idealistic and imaginative in the arts.

Venus trine Ascendant: sense of beauty; social charm and grace.

Venus opposition MC: likelihood of disagreements with colleagues at work; emotional need for a beautiful and pleasant home.

Mars in Libra: indecision in practical affairs; energy best expressed through the arts, creation of a pleasant environment; diplomatic and social skills.

Mars in the ninth house: strong beliefs; will fight for what is right; need to travel and work abroad.

Mars conjunct Neptune: confusion in practical affairs; does best in work requiring inspiration, imagination, artistic skill, e.g. theater, films; lofty ambitions.

Mars trine Ascendant: good practical energy. *Mars sextile MC*: sound practical attitude to career.

Jupiter in Pisces: sense of justice, wisdom, sensitivity.

Jupiter in the second house: extravagant; idealistic; possessions not valued highly; prefers beautiful objects to practical ones; possibility of unexpected financial windfalls.

Jupiter square MC: desire for status, success, and recognition in the career; high ambitions.

Neptune in Libra: belief in justice, fairness, idealistic in partnerships. Unless it is especially emphasized, the sign position of Neptune has little psychological significance. In this case Neptune is the co-ruler of Pisces, the Moon sign, but is not itself of special importance.

Neptune in the ninth house: beliefs are mystical and idealistic; deep inspiration is gained from foreign travel and cultures.

Neptune sextile Pluto: desire for a sense of personal purpose and meaning. This aspect was in orb for about 60 years, from 1942 until the turn of the century, and except in rare cases has little individual psychological significance.

Pluto in Leo: Pluto was in Leo from 1939 to 1957. This has no individual psychological significance unless it is heavily emphasized in a chart.

Pluto in the seventh house: relationships are dominated by deep expectations influenced by the past; strong personal needs, perfectionism and personal commitment.

INTEGRATION

Wendy's chart contains several basic contradictions in her life in terms of difficult choices and conflicts of interest. The most obvious of these is between the need for security represented by the Sun in Cancer and the Moon–Saturn opposition, and the desire for independence and change revealed in the Aquarian Ascendant and the Sun-Uranus conjunction. Supporting factors may be found for each possibility, not least of which is Saturn's dual role as bringer of security and ruler of Aquarian independence. The astrologer can see the tension that these opposites bring to the character, and by looking at the entire chart can build up a comprehensive picture of their effect. As Cancer and the Moon both rule the home, the pressure is felt most keenly in the conflicting desires for a stable home life and Uranian–Aquarian change and upheaval. A resolution is offered astrologically through the harmonious trine of the Moon to Uranus and the sextile of the Sun to Saturn. In practical terms, the best compromise is a secure home base combined with plenty of personal freedom.

Venus is another focus for contradictions. On the one hand, it is in Gemini and squared Jupiter, a combination that indicates the subject is lively, talkative, and prepared to discuss emotions. On the other, it is square Saturn, indicating reserve and shyness, a characteristic backed up by the Sun in Cancer (naturally reserved) and the Moon in opposition to Saturn. Indications of reserve are the stronger, so while Wendy can be socially vivacious, she is usually rather quiet and shy.

It is also necessary to draw links between planets, signs, houses, and aspects that are not spelled out in the analysis. For example, the Sun in the sixth house indicates a conscientious worker, but the Sun in Cancer indicates someone who seeks personal emotional fulfilment. The result is that Wendy is a conscientious worker as long as she is emotionally committed to her work.

Similarly with the Saturn–Jupiter opposition: this reflects a general conflict that reinforces the need for security versus the need for change symbolized by the Sun in Cancer and the Aquarian Ascendant. However, when it is seen that Jupiter is in the second house and Saturn in the eighth, the aspect has particular significance for Wendy's financial affairs. These may be subject to sharp fluctuations as the two planets alternate in dominance, and the desire to spend (symbolized by Jupiter) is held in check by restricted business possibilities (symbolized by Saturn). In Wendy's life, this relates to the difficulties involved in making a living as an artist.

In this interpretation, house cusp rulers have been used only sparingly to provide additional information. The main example concerns the eleventh house, ruler of acquaintances and the larger social circle. In Wendy's chart, Sagittarius is on the cusp of the eleventh house, and this sign is ruled by Jupiter. By examining Jupiter's location and aspects, further information can be gathered about Wendy's social life. The indications are contradictory, as Jupiter's opposition to Saturn shows reserve but its square to Venus is vivacious. The astrologer adds this information to what is already known to build up a more comprehensive interpretation.

From Wendy's chart, an astrologer can deduce the following information.

General character

Sun, Cancer, sixth aspects; Moon Pisces second plus aspects; Ascendant Aquarius, plus aspects, general condition of chart rulers, Saturn and Uranus (as there are two rulers, Saturn, the traditional, should be taken as more important), water-cardinal-mutable emphasis.

This person is obviously highly emotional (Sun, Cancer, square, Neptune, Moon, Pisces) and requires complete personal independence (the Sun, in conjunction with Uranus; Ascendant Aquarius). There will be many difficult choices to make between the desire for change and travel (the Sun in conjunction with Uranus; Sun square Mars, ninth) and the need for security and stability (Sun, Cancer, Moon in opposition Saturn; Jupiter opposition Saturn). She is naturally hardworking (the Sun in sixth sextile

Saturn) but requires emotional commitment to any practical activity (Sun, Cancer in sixth, Moon in Pisces). She tends to be impractical (Sun square Neptune, Mars in conjunction with Neptune) and her practical energies fluctuate with her emotions.

The tension between her opposing needs for change and stability is channeled into artistic work (Jupiter in opposition Saturn). In spite of her sensitivity, she is remarkably tough (cardinal emphasis) and can adapt to change ("T" Square mutable).

Family

Moon, Pisces and aspects, fourth house and Venus, ruler of the fourth cusp, fifth house and Mercury, ruler of the fifth cusp. The Moon stands out as by far the strongest significator of domestic conditions, so much so that in this case, the others may be virtually ignored unless specific questions arise.

There is a strong need for a pleasant, peaceful, and imaginative home environment (Moon in Pisces), although there are strong indications of domestic problems – lack of money and difficulties either between or with parents (Moon in opposition Saturn), particularly conflict with the father (Wendy, symbolized by the Moon ruler of women, is opposed to Saturn, ruler of the father). However, there are excellent signs that such difficulties will be overcome and domestic harmony restored (Moon trine Sun). The home will probably be quite stable (fourth cusp in Taurus) although there is a restless desire for change (Venus, ruler of fourth, in Gemini). A desire for a large family (Venus in fifth square Jupiter) is balanced by a reluctance to take on responsibility (Venus in fifth square Saturn). The astrologer must work out which planet is stronger, Jupiter or Saturn. Each has a claim: Jupiter is strong in its own sign, Pisces, but Saturn exerts a powerfully restrictive opposition on the Moon.

Emotions and relationships

Planets in water signs, Venus and Mars, planets in Libra, the seventh and eleventh houses. This person is clearly exceptionally emotional and sensitive (Sun in Cancer square Neptune, Moon in Pisces) and comes to terms quite well with her strong feelings (Sun trine Moon). She needs security and stability but she must also have independence, freedom, variety, and stimulation (Ascendant Aquarius, Sun in conjunction with Uranus, Venus in Gemini). She is extremely romantic (Sun in Cancer square Neptune, Moon in Pisces), but her moods can change without warning (Sun square Mars, Sun square Neptune), though she tends to be discreet in public (Sun in opposition with Saturn, Sun in Cancer).

Mind, intellect, education

The mind is completely dominated by the emotions and imagination (Mercury in Cancer in conjunction with Sun) and is unusual, independent, and inventive (Mercury in conjunction with Uranus). Ideas are strongly held and there is a reluctance to compromise (Mercury in conjunction with the Sun, Mercury square Mars). Behind the emotional front, she displays common sense and is fair-minded (Mercury trine Jupiter).

Beliefs are strong and balanced (Mars ruler of third in Libra, ninth). There are strong indications of a creative imagination, which will be expressed through artistic activity (Venus ruler of ninth cusp in fifth), probably writing (Venus in Gemini fifth trine Mars ruler of third), signifying creative energy. Attitudes to the arts will be quite conservative (Venus in fifth square Jupiter, Jupiter square MC), original (Uranus in conjunction with Mercury, ruler of fifth), and extremely enthusiastic (Venus in fifth square Jupiter). There is a strong ambition to succeed (Venus in fifth square Jupiter, Jupiter square MC).

Artistic skills and an intuitive mind indicate that Wendy will always do better in the arts than in the sciences.

Career, work

Wendy is a conscientious worker (Sun in sixth sextile Saturn) and drawn toward work that is personally satisfying and can help others (Sun in Cancer sixth, ruler of sixth in Pisces). Her attitude to work is basically idealistic and imaginative but unworldly (Sun in sixth square Neptune, Moon ruler of sixth in Pisces). She will work hard to get things right, often sacrificing her own interests (Sun in sixth square Neptune) sometimes to the point of physical exhaustion (Sun in sixth square Mars). Her work involves her intellectual and communicative talents, although the nervous tension this creates may affect her health (Mercury in conjunction with Uranus on the sixth cusp of work and health). Her career may involve foreign countries and travel (Mars ruler of MC in ninth), the arts, or public relations (Mars ruler of MC in Libra trine Venus).

Money

Money will be earned through women (Moon general significator of women in the second house), the arts, or imagination (Moon in second in Pisces). There may be a fear of poverty, and lean times in business alternating with times of plenty (Moon in second in conjunction with Jupiter, opposition Saturn). Extravagance is tempered by caution (Jupiter in second in opposition Saturn in eighth), but she can be hardheaded in business (Saturn in eighth).

Health

Health problems are likely to arise from nervous tension (Mercury in conjunction with Uranus on the sixth cusp) and worry (Cancers are great worriers), and are subject to emotional changes and sensitivity (Moon ruler of the sixth house in Pisces).

SYNTHESIS

The subject of our horoscope, Wendy, is a writer and dancer. The chart clearly indicates an interest in writing, through Venus in Gemini in the fifth house, and by the trine to Mars in Libra (ruled by Venus) in the ninth house of higher education (Wendy studied literature in college). Her published work has been well received. Success is also shown by the trine to Mars in Libra in the ninth house, this house being the ruler of publishers. Less obvious from the chart is Wendy's skill as a dancer. However, to the astrologer versed in symbolism, dancing is represented by Pisces, the sign that rules the feet. The Moon in Pisces emphasizes the sign and also rules Cancer, the sign on the cusp of the sixth house of work. The astrologer may, therefore, make a connection between her work and a flair for dance.

There is a clear contradiction in the chart between conservatism and originality in the field of art. Feedback from the subject shows how these have been reconciled. Wendy specializes in the traditional solo dances of the Middle East, dances that are thousands of years old. She has pioneered their acceptance in Britain, thus introducing an unusual dance form to Western society. In this she has expressed her own conjunction of Uranus with the Sun (natural ruler of the fifth house of creativity) and Mercury (ruler of the fifth cusp in the birth chart). The fact that she is the exponent of an ancient art form is reflected in the conservative square of Saturn to Venus in the fifth house. Mars, ruler of the MC (career) in the ninth house (foreign countries) indicates both the foreign inspiration of Wendy's dances and the frequency with which she works abroad.

Wendy's income – like that of most artists – tends to fluctuate and, as the chart suggests, times of plenty alternate with periods when funds are low. Remarkably, with the Moon in the second house, she does indeed earn her money through women, for her dances are traditional female dances, and only women attend her classes.

Wendy works independently with great dedication and energy, frequently sacrificing material interests to the cause of perfecting her art, tendencies that are clearly shown in the conjunction of the Sun with Uranus and its squares to Neptune and Mars. In fact, she works to exhaustion (Sun square Mars), and the strain of self-employment is a factor which can affect her health (Mercury conjunct Uranus indicates nervous tension). She has in the past collaborated with other dancers, but these partnerships have tended to be short-lived (Mars square Sun, ruler of the seventh cusp of partnerships outweighs the harmonious effect of the Mars–Venus trine).

It is interesting to see how one theme in Wendy's life, her dancing, draws together so many significators in the horoscope, including the second, fifth, sixth, seventh, eighth, ninth, and tenth houses.

Before becoming a dancer, Wendy worked in public relations (Mars in Libra) for a community arts cooperative, which she left because she was too independent minded for the organization. By chec-king back with the chart, the astrologer is able to see that Jupiter, ruler of the eleventh house of the community, is in a difficult square to Venus, ruling public relations in Gemini, sign of ideas, in the fifth house of the arts. It is doubtful if any astrologer could have achieved such an exact interpretation from this configuration, but by getting feedback from the client the astrologer will be able to make more fruitful use of the chart.

The astrological conclusions concerning Wendy's emotions, home, and family also prove correct. She is highly romantic, but dislikes formal ties, partly a reflection of her need to feel independent. A major influence on her life has been the restricted financial circumstances of her childhood (Moon opposition Saturn), and while her attitude to money is basically idealistic (Jupiter in the second house), she nonetheless needs material comforts for her peace of mind.

A consistent and difficult choice that Wendy has had to face reflects the larger issue in her life: whether to seek stability or change. The need for a stable home (fourth cusp in Taurus, Sun in Cancer, Moon opposed Saturn) has been contradicted by a desire to live and travel abroad (Sun conjunct Uranus, square Mars in the ninth house). Possibly due to the strength of the Moon–Saturn opposition, she has established a settled home in England, but one with few responsibilities, thus making possible the frequent journeys attendant on her work.

THE FINAL CONSULTATION

Once the horoscope had been studied and an interpretation prepared, a dialogue took place between Wendy and the astrologer. The astrologer provided the basic interpretation, Wendy reacted to this, and the astrologer was then able to clarify and elaborate the interpretation, playing down certain factors while highlighting others. The final interpretation was, therefore, the result of a collaboration between the astrologer and the client, a process which is more fruitful for both than if the horoscope is prepared in a vacuum. At this stage of the consultation, no predictions were necessary, but the simple character delineation itself was extremely useful. Clarification of the major issues in the horoscope, especially the sharp conflict between the opposing needs for change and stability, enabled Wendy to understand her life with greater confidence and certainty.

SUMMARY

Astrologers should not play at being God. They do not have access to some absolute truth, even if astrology is capable of providing answers that other disciplines cannot. Astrologers should always listen to the client. In some cases they may accept the client's criticism of the interpretation and modify it accordingly. In others, where they may feel that the client is refusing to face up to some awkward implication, they must try to find another way of explaining it.

Above all, the qualities demanded of an astrologer are sensitivity, tact, humility, and consideration for the problems and circumstances of the client. People go to astrologers with a great deal of trust, and it is up to the astrologer to respect this confidence.

♈ ♉ ♊ ♋ ♌ ♍ ♎ ♏ ♐ ♑ ♒ ♓

CHAPTER 10

PREDICTION: TRANSITS AND PROGRESSIONS

Most people associate astrology with prediction of the future. This is indeed one of its most fascinating uses. However, prediction of events in people's lives is very difficult, perhaps even impossible in most circumstances. Most astrologers use the birth chart to anticipate possible future options, all of which will be dependent on the actions taken now, in the present. To look into the future using astrology is to anticipate periods that bring different sorts of potential – either relaxed or stressful, personal or professional, and so on.

The first step in prediction is the analysis of the patterns of the birth chart. The analysis is then brought up to the present and projected into the future so that the astrologer can give practical and relevant advice. It is best to start by looking at changing psychological moods, predicting, for example, periods of optimism or pessimism, of intense emotion, or of levelheaded, practical effort. The astrologer also looks in general at the person's changing circumstances, anticipating periods of restriction or of opportunity, of change or stability. Such general prediction is commonly known as the "analysis of future trends."

Transits are based on the actual movements of the planets in real, current time, whereas progressions, also sometimes known as directions, are based on symbolic movements of the planets.

THE TRANSITS

The transits are the day-by-day and hour-by-hour movements of the planets through the zodiac. We talk about them moving over the birth chart as if that were something that actually exists. In reality, though, the birth chart is just a snapshot of a moment in time, and the transiting planets 20 or 30 years later relate to that moment in time, not to any current physical reality. The principle here is that time is the central organizing principle in human life. Quite simply, there is a time to act and a time to stay still.

Students of astrology often look for textbooks that will give them sample interpretations of the transiting planets. In fact, there is no inherent difference between a transiting position and a natal one: the symbolism of planet in house, sign, and aspect is built up in exactly the same way. Thus the essence of an aspect between natal Sun and transiting Pluto is the same as that between natal Sun and natal Pluto. The difference in interpretation is based on the fact that natal aspects are considered to describe an individual's entire life, whereas transiting aspects are temporary.

TRANSITS AND THE BIRTH CHART

Astrologers often say that the transits "release" or "trigger" the potential, or promise, of the birth chart. This doesn't imply that they "cause" change. Perhaps it's better to say that they are signposts that show the way forward into the future, but that can only be read in relation to the birth chart. Therefore, the interpretation of a transit by sign, house, or aspect must take into account the natal sign, house, and aspect of that planet. For example, a person who has Mars in Pisces in the fifth house, signifying imagination and creative energy, will retain these initial natal characteristics regardless of which house or sign Mars subsequently transits. If Mars transits the sixth house in Aries, indicating effort at work, the intuition of Pisces and the creativity of the fifth house will still be of paramount importance.

The same principle applies to aspects. For example, if Mercury is opposed to Mars in the natal chart, a person may take hurried decisions without thinking the issues through properly. However, at a particular time, he or she may experience a trine from transiting Mercury to natal Mars, an aspect that indicates firm and positive decisions. In spite of this harmonious transiting aspect, there will still be a marked tendency with respect to the impatience and recklessness of the natal aspect.

To get around this problem, astrologers couch their predictions in general terms, forecasting tendencies rather than specific events, except when the indications are especially strong. The astrologer must also take into account the general disposition of the birth chart, because this shows how people will react to future events. For example, two people may have transiting Uranus in opposition to the natal Sun, an aspect that can bring shattering changes. One of these people may be a Capricorn who hates change, while the other may be a Piscean who thrives on uncertainty. The Capricorn will have a miserable time, experiencing the collapse of a structured existence, whereas the Piscean will have a great time relishing the new possibilities that Uranus brings.

It often happens that a planet turns retrograde and returns to aspect a natal planet over which it has recently passed. The same planet will then change direction and aspect the natal planet for a third time. The effective duration of a transiting aspect is then substantially increased and is exact on three occasions. Each time the aspect will be experienced in a different way in line with the person's changing circumstances. It is often said that on the first occasion, the issues or problems associated with the aspect are raised. On the second occasion, the person learns how to deal with them. On the third, all being well, a solution is successfully implemented, and life moves forward to a new phase.

Transits not only bring changing moods and circumstances, they bring lessons to learn, and it can be useful if a planet does indeed turn retrograde. In learning such lessons, individuals mature and gain in experience and wisdom, and astrology becomes less a means to mere prediction and more a guide to self-development.

TIMING

Since all the planets move at different speeds, the transits last for different periods of time. A transit of Pluto, for example, can last for 18 months, but a transit of the Moon can be over in an hour. The more exact the aspect from a transiting planet to a natal planet, the more intense is the psychological experience and the more likely it is that significant events will occur. Frequently, a number of transiting planets make aspects to the same part of the birth chart, with the result that major changes become more likely. For example, a square from transiting Pluto to the natal Moon may be joined by a trine from transiting Saturn and a conjunction from transiting Mars. Such a build-up of aspects would almost certainly indicate a move of home (the Moon ruling the home), while a single aspect might bring only minor changes.

The transits of the three outermost planets, Uranus, Neptune, and Pluto, indicate periods of between 6 and 18 months in which profound change takes place, bringing events that can alter the direction of life. Transits of Saturn may last between one and nine months, bringing difficulties and restriction, while transits of Jupiter may last between one week and nine months and bring opportunity. Transits of Mercury, Venus, and Mars may last anything from one day to several weeks, depending on the speed of motion, and are psychologically far more superficial. The events they cause may be trivial, but they can also act as catalysts for creating the life-shattering events symbolized by the slow-moving outer planets. Transits of the Sun last for two days and, if combined with other planetary transits, often indicate the days on which major events occur.

Transits of the Moon last for one or two hours and often indicate the time at which an event takes place. New Moons and full Moons are always important, and when a new or full Moon makes powerful aspects to a birth chart, this indicates that major events are likely to occur within a few days.

New Moons represent the birth of a new cycle, and full Moons show the culmination of an old cycle. The period between the new Moon and the full Moon – the waxing Moon – is considered a period of increasing energy, and the period from the full Moon to the new Moon – the waning Moon – is considered a period of declining energy.

Eclipses strengthen the significance of a new or full Moon. There are several eclipses each year, and these often bring to a head crises that have been building up for some time.

It is also possible to use the transiting Ascendant and MC, which can be calculated for any particular time. Aspects from the transiting Ascendant and MC to the birth chart often indicate the exact time at which an event takes place, but few astrologers go into such detail when making predictions.

LIFE CYCLES

The aspects made by transits of the slower moving planets to their places in the birth chart indicate major phases of life and the turning points at which people mature. Adolescence is the first such point and coincides, approximately, with Jupiter's return to its position at birth (age 12) and transiting Saturn's opposition to its natal place (age 14–15). Jupiter's need for growth and Saturn's for order describe some of the difficulties of this age. Change also often occurs at age 29 when Saturn returns to its birth position. This frequently coincides with an individual's profound dissatisfaction at what has been achieved in life so far, and can thus be a time of crisis. People who made young and inappropriate marriages sometimes split up, while those who have resisted commitment suddenly settle down. The end result is usually a greater sense of stability and maturity. The "midlife" crisis, now a recognized feature of the early 40s, coincides with an impressive series of aspects, including revolutionary Uranus's opposition to its natal position. During this period, many people rebel against the home life and career that they have spent so long creating.

TRANSITS THROUGH HOUSES AND SIGNS

The principles of interpretation for transiting are the same as those for natal planets, bearing in mind that the passage of a planet through a sign or house represents only one phase in a person's life. To interpret the transits through houses and signs, refer to the standard interpretations for natal planets in houses and signs in Chapters 4 and 6. Generally, little attention is paid to transits through signs because these only lightly modify the overwhelming strength of the natal positions. However, transits through houses are extremely important for they show changing circumstances.

INTERPRETING THE ASPECTS

Brief interpretations are listed here for all the main combinations of aspects from transiting planets to natal planets. Detail can be added by referring to the more thorough interpretations for natal aspects in Chapter 9.

It is extremely important to draw distinctions between aspects from transiting outer planets to natal inner planets on the one hand, and transiting inner planets to natal outer planets on the other. The effect of the former will be profound and long lasting, while that of the latter will be over quite quickly and often cause only trivial events. This must be borne in mind when using the sample interpretations. For example, the Sun conjunct Pluto brings psychological and emotional intensity and the prospect of major changes. If the transiting Sun is making a conjunction to natal Pluto, as it does once a year, then the psychological mood will pass in two days and the event may be significant but not revolutionary. However, if transiting Pluto is making a conjunction to the natal Sun, the person may enter a period of up to 18 months when his or her mood is obsessive, deep and intense, and an entire way of life may be turned upside down.

In general it is best to use only major aspects in transits – the conjunction, sextile, square, trine, and opposition. Minor aspects may be added later if more detail is required.

Orbs should be kept as tight as possible; the standard orb is one degree.

PREDICTING EVENTS

The standard interpretations are all worked out for general situations and, therefore, tend to be vague and psychological. Events can be predicted only by looking at a combination of transits, and when several transits point to the same conclusion, it is a fair bet that event will take place. Events occur as much under tense aspects as under harmonious ones, although it is, of course, necessary to understand the precise nature of the planets involved.

Harmonious aspects bring benefits, but do not guarantee success; tense aspects bring difficulties, but do not guarantee failure. To predict a particular event, look for when there are a number of relevant transits occurring at the same time.

General changes: transits to the natal Ascendant, Sun, and Moon.

Moves of home: transits to the natal Moon and IC and through the fourth house.

Marriage: the same as for moves of home, combined with transits to natal Venus, Descendant, and planets in the seventh house.

Career: transits to natal MC and through the natal tenth house.

Money: transits through the natal second and eighth houses and to natal planets in these houses.

Health: transits through the natal sixth house and to planets in the sixth house. Astrology alone should never be used to make any more than the most general statements about health. For example, it may shed light on the causes of stress. For all detailed analysis serious medical experience is required.

Education: transits to natal Mercury and the third house (school), to natal Jupiter and the ninth house (higher education).

Signing contracts: transits to natal Mercury and the natal third house.

Travel: transits to natal Mercury and the natal third house (short journeys), to natal Jupiter and the natal ninth house (long journeys).

THE PROGRESSIONS

Behind the principle of progression lies the ancient belief that any complete unit of time shares the same essential quality as every other complete unit, even those of a different duration. Thus, each day, week, month, and year represents in its own way the same basic cycle of experience: the day moves on its endless cycle symbolizing a phase in the life of the Sun; the seven days of the week symbolize one complete journey through the seven traditional planets; the month is based on the vital passage of the Moon from new to full and back again; and the year moves through the cycle of the seasons.

SECONDARY PROGRESSIONS

There are about 20 different types of progression, although only a few are in common use. Those used most often are the secondary progressions, popularly known as "Day for a Year" progressions. If the type of progression used is not specified, it is always assumed that the Day for a Year method is used. In the Day for a Year system, each day of life is regarded as equivalent to one year of life. The planetary positions for each day are used to make predictions for the equivalent year: those for the first day are used to make predictions for the first year, those for the second day for the second year, and so on. If a child experiences a major astrological configuration ten days after birth, there will be significant developments at around ten years of age. The infant who has a dramatic astrological pattern on the 50th day after birth will experience great upheavals in the 50th year of life. Day for a Year progressions are simple to calculate and require no expertise in interpretation beyond that needed for transits.

CALCULATING "DAY FOR A YEAR" PROGRESSIONS

The first stage is to work out the day for which the progressed planets must be calculated. If the subject's date of birth is March 4, 1953, and you want to work out progressions for age 17, add 17 to the day (4) of the birth month: 17 + 4 = 21. Planetary positions on March 21, 1953 are then equivalent to progressed planets for 1970 at age 17. This is the progressed date.

Frequently the exact progressed date will fall in the month following the month of birth (or even the month after that). This problem can be solved by adding the relevant age to the date of birth, then subtracting the number of days in the month (or months) preceding that in which the progressed date falls, as in the following example.

To work out progressions for someone at age 30 (born on March 4, 1953), we add 30 to 4, giving 34. Because there is no such date as March 34, we have to subtract the number of days in March (31), giving a real date of April 3. Therefore the planetary positions on April 3, 1953 are the progressed planets for 1983, at age 30. The planets are then looked up in the ephemeris in the usual way (the planets for one day referring to the whole of the equivalent year). For example, on April 3, the Sun was at 13 degrees Aries approaching an exact conjunction with natal Mars. This aspect was actually exact on April 8, when the subject was 35 years old. This was indeed an excellent and busy year for the subject's professional life.

For all planets except the Moon this is sufficient. The Moon moves so fast that it progresses approximately one degree every month, We therefore need to be able to work out the exact positions of the progressed planets for any day.

The progressed planets and angles (Ascendant and Midheaven) should be calculated for the birthday each year. Follow the normal procedure for casting a horoscope using the GMT time of birth, the place of birth, and the sidereal time and planetary positions for the progressed day.

By working out the progressed horoscope for two successive birthdays (i.e., two successive days in the ephemeris), it is possible to work out how far a planet or angle progresses in one year. Division of the annual motion by 12 gives the monthly motion, from which it is possible to work out the exact progressed positions for any day of the year.

Sample calculation

The progressed positions on a person's birthday at any given age can be worked out following a simple, logical sequence. The data here refers to Wendy Buonaventura – born at 10:25 P.M. BST (9:25 GMT) on July 4, 1950 – whose chart appears in Chapter 6.

First, following the instructions in the first paragraph of this section, work out the progressed positions for Wendy, age 1 (1 + 4 = 5, therefore 9:25 P.M. GMT July 5, 1950 = July 4, 1951, age 1). It is then easy to calculate the positions for subsequent years:

9.25 P.M. GMT July 6, 1950 = July 4, 1952, age 2
9.25 P.M. GMT July 7, 1950 = July 4, 1953, age 3
9.25 P.M. GMT July 8, 1950 = July 4, 1953, age 4

then

9.25 P.M. GMT August 7, 1950 = July 4, 1984, age 34
9.25 P.M. GMT August 8, 1950 = July 4, 1985, age 35

and

9.25 P.M. GMT August 23, 1950 = July 4, 2000, age 50
9.25 P.M. GMT August 24, 1950 = July 4, 2001, age 51

and so on.

INTERPRETING THE PROGRESSIONS

The principles of interpretation are exactly the same as those governing transits. Usually only the first five planets – Sun, Moon, Mercury, Venus and Mars – are used, together with the Ascendant and MC. The outer five planets progress so slowly that they sometimes scarcely move. The progressed planets make aspects to the natal planets that should be interpreted exactly like transiting aspects to natal planets, with the qualification that they last much longer and are, therefore, more profound; for example, an aspect from the progressed Sun to the birth chart lasts two years. The orb for aspects should be one degree, the same as for transiting aspects; minor aspects should also be used.

Aspects between the progressed MC and Ascendant always indicate significant points in life and take their character from the nature of the planet, which is aspected in exactly the same way as aspects between natal MC and Ascendant and transiting planets.

The movement of a progressed planet into a new house or sign of the birth chart always marks a significant development, bringing a change in character or a new focus of attention.

Interpretations for all the progressions can be based on the standard interpretations for natal positions and transits given in previous chapters. For example, an interpretation of progressed Mercury conjunct natal Sun will be essentially the same as natal Mercury conjunct natal Sun or transiting Mercury conjunct natal Sun, given that the duration of effect is different in each case. The aspect from natal Mercury to the Sun indicates the basic lifelong character, progressed Mercury indicates a phase of mental development over one or two years, and transiting Mercury indicates a lively and interesting day.

CHAPTER 11

RELATIONSHIPS AND THE COMPARISON OF CHARTS

The general nature and circumstances of one person's relationships can be worked out quite simply from the birth chart, mainly by studying the seventh house, Venus, and all associated factors. There are also special techniques for examining individual relationships that a person may form, whether with husband or wife, parents or children, brothers or sisters, employers or employees, or anybody else with whom he or she might come into contact.

The process in which one horoscope is compared with another is known technically as *synastry*. At its simplest level, synastry works by comparing Sun signs, a process that offers remarkably deep insights into the mysterious sources of attraction between two people. There are certain classic combinations of Sun signs that often produce close relationships. The most common of these are relationships between signs of the same element, and between opposite signs, although people born under adjacent Sun signs also often experience a deep attraction. Each combination of signs produces difficulties as well as benefits, and the easiest way to understand these is by looking at the combination of elements.

ELEMENT RELATIONSHIPS

Fire–Fire

These people share their enthusiasm, energy, and adventurous spirits, but a distaste for compromise and an inability to cooperate can lead to disagreement.

Fire–Earth

This is an interesting combination for, ironically, the attraction between these signs rests in their profound differences. The energetic Fire person is able to give full vent to that element's adventurous instincts in the full knowledge that the Earth partner will provide security, continuity, and stability.

Meanwhile the Earth partner can remain as stodgy as desired, relying on the Fire partner to work for change and create opportunities. But there can be sharp differences: the Earth partner may resent Fire's impulsive need for change, and Fire can become impossibly irritated with Earth's lack of ambition.

Fire–Air

This relationship is often extremely lively because Air's intellect and Fire's enthusiasm spark off interesting ideas and a willingness to change. Differences are often settled quickly. However, difficulty in expressing feelings and a tendency to ignore practical necessities can produce long-term problems.

Fire–Water

These elements share powerful emotions, but their feelings are of a very different kind, and misunderstanding is more common than understanding. Water is dismayed by Fire's complete lack of sensitivity, and Fire is completely baffled by Water's quiet, introverted secrecy and apparent lack of worldly ambition. Casual friendships work better than close relationships, for the latter often suffer from deep emotional conflict.

Earth–Earth

Two people both with Suns in Earth signs share a common outlook on life, and a joint fondness for stability and routine can lead to long-lasting relationships. However, there can be a lack of stimulation, emotional depth, and ambition, and even when these relationships last for a long time, there can be an absence of real feeling.

Earth–Air

These elements can be brought together by self-interest. Earth benefits from Air's ideas, and Air gains from Earth's practical skills. The result is a relationship founded on common sense, but together these elements lack emotional depth and worldly ambition.

Earth–Water

Earth and Water often form deep and lasting friendships. They are comfortable with each other, and Water admires Earth's practical skills as much as Earth is fascinated by Water's emotional depth and sensitivity. But if the relationship is too close, long-term irritation can set in: Earth loses patience with Water's muddled impracticality and Water becomes bored by Earth's love of order and routine.

Air–Air

People with Suns in Air signs share a lively and curious approach to life and can find each other immensely stimulating. There is usually a great deal of communication, but deeper feelings are all too easily ignored with the result that long-term problems can arise. The relationship tends to be impractical, although this is not necessarily a problem.

Air–Water

This can be a highly stimulating combination: Air's clarity of thought and Water's intuition and sensitivity produce an interesting and imaginative relationship. In closer relationships, misunderstandings may arise that make for difficulties in dealing with practical issues.

Water–Water

Mutual understanding is often deep, and a shared longing for romantic love can take these people into a world of dreams and fantasy. When things go wrong, however, they tend to wallow in their troubles. They may find it impossible to plan for the future.

In general, the presence of Suns in the same sign is not an indication of a long-term relationship because, with both partners having the same basic strengths and weakness, it is possible they may fail to provide either mutual stimulation or balance. People with Suns in adjacent signs (such as Aries–Taurus or Capricorn–Sagittarius) and opposite signs (such as Taurus–Scorpio or Aries–Libra) are often very close, because each provides something that the other needs, bringing a welcome balance. However, serious differences can lead to deep arguments. Suns in signs that are in a sextile to each other (such as Pisces–Taurus or Aquarius–Aries) can produce good friendships, but the differences between them may work against long-term relationships. Suns in signs that are in a square to each other (such as Pisces–Gemini or Aries–Capricorn) are often extremely stimulating, but the very differences that make for a lively friendship may place obstacles in the way of closer relationships. Most favored of all are relationships produced by Suns in signs that are in trine to each other (such as Pisces–Scorpio or Libra–Gemini), for these have enough similarities to provide deep understanding but sufficient differences to create interest and stimulation.

COMPARING CHARTS

A comparison of two horoscopes is based mainly on the aspects made between the planets in one chart and those in the other.

ASPECTS

The interpretation of aspects between planets in two charts follows exactly the same principle as the interpretation of aspects in a single chart. For example, if a Sun–Moon sextile in a natal chart is a harmonious indication, then an individual with the Sun in Pisces is likely to get on well with an individual with the Moon in Gemini. Just as to be born with the Sun and Moon in the same sign indicates a personality with a powerful direction, so people born with the Sun and Moon in conjunction may form a powerful relationship. It should be remembered, though, that whereas the psychological processes indicated in a birth chart are often "internal," in relationships two people play out a joint drama. It is not always clear who will play which role: if one person was born with the Sun opposite another's Saturn, it is not always clear who will play the Saturnine role. When two people have the same planet conjunct, they may share a common perspective in the area of life represented by that planet (although with the slower moving planets entire generations have them in conjunction).

The aspects between any two charts can be divided into six categories.

1 Aspects between the Sun, Moon, and angles (Ascendant and Midheaven) of one chart and those of the other are exceptionally important. Conjunctions between one person's Moon and the other's Sun reveal a deep attraction, and the conjunction of one person's Sun or Moon with the other's Ascendant or Descendant often indicates a long-lasting relationship.

2 Aspects between one person's Sun, Moon, and angles and the other's Mercury, Venus, or Mars do not in themselves lead to a close relationship, but to compatibility in certain areas and activities.

3 Aspects between Mercury, Venus, and Mars in both charts can be important indicators of compatibility. These are most significant when the aspect involves the same planet in each chart. For example, aspects between two Mercurys indicate intellectual compatibility or incompatibility, aspects between two Venuses indicate mutual affection or antipathy, and aspects between two Mars reveal either harmony in joint activities or strong antagonism.

4 Aspects between inner planets of one chart and outer planets of the other usually seem to be less significant and often contribute little to an understanding of the relationship. These aspects occur most importantly between contemporaries. For example, the child with Sun squared Pluto will also have the Sun squared to the Plutos of all other children of the same age. All the child's relationships will be colored by this aspect and it will, therefore, be less significant for judging particular partnerships. Such aspects are also often found between parents and children, in which case they should be given slightly more significance.

5 Aspects between the outer planets of two charts have still less significance. They usually occur in the horoscopes of people from different generations. For example, people born at 29-year intervals have their Saturns in a conjunction. All children born in 1966 have Pluto squared to the Plutos of people born in 1900, and those born in 1982 have Saturn in conjunction with the Plutos of those born in 1979. These aspects show how people relate to each other en masse, and their use in the comparison of two charts must always take this into account.

Unless it is necessary to take an in-depth look at one particular factor in a chart, only the major aspects should be used. This cuts down the amount of information the astrologer has to consider and allows the most important features to stand out. As a general rule, the greater the number of strong aspects between significant planets and angles in two charts, the greater the prospect of a close relationship. It often happens that a planet in one chart aspects a strong configuration – such as a "T" Square – in another. The prospects of a close relationship are then dramatically emphasized.

6 Progressed aspects, especially between the Sun, Moon, and angles in two people's charts, can be very effective in explaining why sudden, unexpected encounters occur – why two strangers fall in love at first sight, for example. It might be, as one possibility, that one's progressed Sun or Moon is exactly conjunct the other's Sun, Moon, or angles, within an orb of no more than 1 degree. When the aspects become exact, the relationship starts. If there are difficulties in sustaining the relationship, it may not last when the aspects move on.

ORBS

There is no consensus concerning the width of orbs to be used for aspects between natal planets in one chart and those in another. However, a general rule is that wider orbs should be given to aspects between the most significant planets, and more attention should be given to the stronger aspects – a conjunction is always far more significant than a sextile.

Conventionally, astrologers do not usually require any orb for relationships between Suns and Moons. It is common to hear conversations in which they compare themselves by sign – one might be "a Taurean" and the other "a Virgo." However, the more factors that are to be considered, the greater the need for tighter discipline. Generally, aspects between the Sun, Moon, and angles need an 8-degree orb, those between the inner planets a 6- or even 4-degree orb, and those between the outer planets a 1- or 2-degree orb.

HOUSES

An in-depth comparison of charts goes a step beyond the analysis of aspects and also examines house positions. The planets from one chart are superimposed on to the houses of the other, enabling the astrologer to see in which area of life each partner will experience the relationship most intensely. For example, if partner A's planets fall in partner B's second house, then B may be concerned with joint security and finances, while if B's planets fall in A's fifth house, this relationship may add zest and sparkle to A's life. One classic contact in the charts of married couples is the location of one partner's Sun in the other's seventh house. This often explains compatibility between couples whose Suns and Moons make no aspects to each other.

SIGNS

The signs may also be brought into use in detailed examination of a particular aspect, but, as with the use of houses, the possibilities are both complex and subtle, and it is not feasible to go into every variation.

An understanding of houses and signs in synastry can only be acquired gradually, by building on the experience of ordinary chart interpretation.

COMPOSITE CHARTS

The composite chart is a single horoscope that can prove remarkably effective in demonstrating the salient points in a relationship. Whereas chart comparison complicates matters because two horoscopes create so many interpretative possibilities, the composite chart provides stunningly simple insights into any partnership.

SAMPLE COMPOSITE CHART CALCULATION

For person A with the Sun at 13 degrees Pisces and person B with the Sun at 27 degrees Leo.

A's Sun is 343 degrees in absolute longitude (i.e., 343 degrees after the beginning of Aries) and B's is 147 degrees. To arrive at the composite Sun, these two figures are added together (490 degrees) and then divided by two, giving a result of 245 degrees.
This equates to 5 degrees Sagittarius.

For simplicity, use the nearest midpoint to the two Suns, in this case 5 degrees Gemini.

There are two types of composite chart. One, known as the relationship chart, is based on the exact point in time halfway between the births of the two people, and the exact halfway point between their birth places, both in latitude and longitude. As this is very complicated to calculate without a computer, most astrologers use the second type, which is worked out by adding up the position of each pair of planets – Ascendants, Midheavens, Suns, Moons, and so on – and then dividing the result by two. The position of each planet is converted into absolute longitude – its position in terms of the whole zodiac of 360 degrees – and then added to its equivalent planet. Division of the result by two gives the composite position. If the Equal House system is used, only the composite Ascendant and MC need be calculated – all the other house cusps will follow the usual order at 30-degree intervals after the Ascendant.

The method for interpreting a composite horoscope is exactly the same as that for any natal chart, except of course that the readings apply to a relationship, not a person. Aspects, sign, and house position can all be used to build up a picture of the relationship, its strengths and weaknesses and what each partner has to gain from it. Transits over the composite chart indicate major stages in the relationship, and most composite charts are affected by very strong transits at the time when the two people met.

In another variation on this theme, a composite chart can be based on the partners' progressed charts for a certain moment in time. For example, a progressed composite chart for the time of a marriage would be based on each person's progressions for the marriage. However, in practice, few astrologers go into this kind of detail.

COMPATIBILITY

The table below uses the position of the Sun to indicate the basic patterns of compatibility between signs. It could also be used to illustrate combinations of the Sun, Moon, and Ascendant. For example, people with the Sun and Moon in signs of the same element may have a similar relationship to individuals with the Sun in the same element. It is misleading to speak of signs being compatible or incompatible with each other. The truth is that each sign has a different sort of relationship with each of the others. Some combinations may work better as friends than lovers, others as colleagues rather than friends. Besides, different people need different relationships: some marriages thrive on agreement, others on argument.

THE ASTROLOGICAL RELATIONSHIP BETWEEN SIGNS

SUN IN	HARMONIOUS	DIFFICULT
Same sign	Often an immediate close rapport and mutual understanding	Lack of stimulation, shared weaknesses and negative habits are emphasized
Adjacent signs	Profound differences in personality and lifestyle can produce mutual fascination. The strengths of one compensate for the weakness of the other	Complete antipathy, little in common
Alternate signs	Sufficient similarities to create an easy, friendly relationship. Sufficient differences to create stimulation and interest	Few difficulties, disagreements tend to be mild, but there may be a lack of commitment to the long term
Signs in same quality (cardinal, fixed, or mutable)	Sufficient differences to provide strong mutual fascination. Good for deep friendship	Fundamentally different attitudes to life bring disagreement in close partnership
Signs in same element (Fire, Earth, Air, or Water)	The best combination for compatibility in friendships and close partnerships of all kinds	Joint weaknesses may be emphasized
Signs in quincunx	Similar to adjacent signs.	Similar to adjacent signs.
Opposite signs	Often produces a deep attraction. Each partner exactly balances the other, compensates for their weaknesses and provides an extra dimension that is otherwise lacking	In close long-term relationships, deep attraction often gives way to irritation and disagreement as differences in attitude and behavior become more marked

♈ ♉ ♊ ♋ ♌ ♍ ♎ ♏ ♐ ♑ ♒ ♓

CHAPTER 12

HORARY, ELECTIONAL, MUNDANE, AND FINANCIAL ASTROLOGY

So far, we have dealt solely with the branch of astrology that interests most people – character analysis and the forecast of future trends for individuals. However, there are other important applications of astrology. These are discussed in this chapter.

HORARY ASTROLOGY: ASKING QUESTIONS

Horoscopes cast to answer questions are known as horary charts (set for the time and place that the question is asked). Like any other branch of astrology, horary can be practiced at either a simple or complex technical level. However, what it requires is precision in both the use of astrological factors and thought on the part of the astrologer. Whereas most modern psychological astrology is designed to enable people to find meaning in their lives, horary predictions are either right or wrong. There is no middle way. We can also use horary questions to find meaning in everyday events as well as big questions, but they are used mainly when we want to know exactly what will happen. Often the horary chart can provide a prediction of a future event when the natal chart can give only a rough indication of future trends. Does that mean that the future is predetermined? Perhaps. But we can also use horary astrology in order to find ways to manage our lives better rather than submit to events we cannot control.

Great attention should be paid to the way in which the question is phrased. For example, a simple "will such-and-such happen?" question can elicit only a yes or no answer. However, "what will be the consequences if such-and-such a course of action is pursued?" obtains an answer that will enable the questioner to decide what steps are desirable or necessary.

The first step is to find out which are the significant planets – known as the significators – and there are two ways of doing this. The first and most important way is to work out which houses rule the question and then look at the planets ruling the cusp. For example, if the question concerns career, we look to the tenth house and then to the planet ruling the sign containing the cusp. The second, and less important, way is to take into account any planet that might be a "general significator"; this may, if the main significators don't provide an immediate answer, point to a solution. For example, in a question about relationships, Venus is always likely to be an important factor. Last, the Moon is always important.

The person asking the question is always ruled by the planet ruling the Ascendant: if the Ascendant is Scorpio, the person asking the question is Mars. Mars, we would say, is the significator of the questioner. The subject of the question is signified by the planet ruling the relevant house: if the question concerns career matters, then the tenth house is responsible, and if Gemini is on the cusp of the tenth, then Mercury rules the question.

Horary astrology also relies on the traditional definitions of planets as either "benefic," or helpful, and "malefic," or easy. Saturn is the most difficult, followed by Mars, and Jupiter is the easiest, followed by Venus. Although the three planets discovered in the modern times, Uranus, Neptune, and Pluto, are often not used at all, they would generally be considered difficult.

Similarly, trines and sextiles are considered helpful aspects and square and opposition difficult. Applying aspects (when the two planets are still forming the past) indicate future events, and separating ones (when the two planets have already made their aspect and are moving apart) indicate past events. When one or more significant planets is retrograde (moving backwards), this introduces further complications by delaying a future aspect or returning two planets to an aspect they have already made. As will by now be clear, most horary charts contain a combination of helpful and difficult indications, and the astrologer has to be very clear about both the rules of interpretation and the nature of the question in order to arrive at an answer.

"Yes" answers may be indicated if:

1 the significators are in an applying conjunction, trine, or sextile.

2 one or all significators are in an applying aspect to Venus or Jupiter, especially a trine or sextile or conjunction.

3 the Moon is aspected to both of the other significators even when they are not aspected.

4 the significators are strongly placed by house (such as in the house which rules the question) or sign (such as in its own sign).

"No" answers may be indicated if:

1 the significators are in a separating trine or sextile, are applying to a square or opposition, or are not in aspect.

2 the significators are aspected to Mars or Saturn, especially in a square or opposition.

3 the significators are poorly placed by sign (for example, in its opposite sign) or house (for example, in a house which undermines the question).

Questions that ask "What should I do?" are less likely to achieve a precise answer – but may be the most effective for people who are concerned to live their lives to the fullest.

ELECTIONAL ASTROLOGY: CHOOSING AUSPICIOUS MOMENTS

When astrologers calculate the most auspicious hour for an event to begin, it is said that they elect the time – hence, electional astrology. If the one purpose of astrology is to develop freedom of choice, electional astrology sees that purpose fulfilled. If astrology is the study of the changing quality of time and human submission to it, then electional astrology sees the astrologer becoming an active participant in this process.

The aim of electional astrology is to harmonize with the universe, not to control it. Its purpose is to assess the best moment to begin any undertaking, using the shifting nature of time as much as a bird uses currents of air to facilitate flight.

It must be understood, however, that the best elected chart in the world will not guarantee success in a project that is fundamentally flawed. If you asked an astrologer to elect the best time to fly to the most distant star, he or she could choose the most auspicious hour and you still wouldn't succeed. Thus, electional astrology deals only with matters that are strictly possible. On the other hand, even a difficult chart can be improved by dedication, hard work, and the will to succeed. No elected chart will ever be perfect, and even a chart with one ideal pattern may contain another that promises difficulties. The best the astrologer can do is achieve a sensible balance so that difficult and easy factors work together, the former bringing the testing circumstances that are necessary for personal growth, and the latter bringing the optimism and opportunity to win through in the end.

Another limitation on electional astrology is the simple fact that some planetary configurations cannot be avoided. For example, all charts elected from July 2001 to June 2002 have a Saturn–Pluto opposition, and all those from around 2010 to 2016 a Uranus–Pluto square. Sometimes the pressure of time means that unwanted aspects cannot be avoided: when the Roman emperor Nero's astrologers were ordered to choose the time for his proclamation they probably had only a matter of hours to choose from.

There is also one philosophical consideration. Electional astrology carries with it the assumption that we can consciously select auspicious times. But, if we suppose, as some astrologers do, that many events have a purpose that is predetermined, the astrologer's election of the auspicious moment may also be preordained. Often astrologers must begin work with a consideration of the circumstances rather than of the planetary positions. The reason is obvious: day and night, public and religious holidays, and just plain common sense all determine whether an event is possible or not. For example, it is unlikely that a public meeting will be held at the dead of night, or a book launched before it is printed. Sometimes simple physical pressures cannot be overcome. Any astrologer deciding that a ship should be launched when the Moon is on the Ascendant or Descendant would be sending it straight into the mud, for the tide would be low. There is no astrological way to avoid such a fate – apart from launching the ship in a floating harbor, protected from the tides. In most matters, such considerations limit the number of possibilities open to the astrologer.

Nevertheless, in many cases astrology is the paramount consideration: in the southeast-Asian state of Myanmar, formerly called Burma, astrologers insisted that independence from the British on January 4, 1948 be granted at 4:20 A.M. Opponents of electional astrology point out that Myanmar's post-colonial history has been disastrous, but its defenders reply that without such an auspicious chart life would have been much worse. What the truth is, we really can't say!

What we do know, though, is that even the most auspicious charts eventually experience difficult transits or progressions, and that these coincide with problematic events.

In the United States, Ronald Reagan received astrological advice throughout his political career. His inauguration as governor of California was timed by his astrologers for the unusual hour of 16 minutes past midnight on January 1, 1967 in Sacramento. The major newspapers were perplexed by this choice of time (gubernatorial inaugurations always take place at noon) and Reagan's officials were forced to state that "this will be no star-gazing administration." Reagan's most well-known astrologer, Joan Quigley, elected the time for his inauguration as President in 1981 and then went on to advise him until 1988. Quigley's craft was essentially electional astrology in that she was arranging the President's schedule in line with the planets. Her advice to Reagan to say nothing during the "Iran-Contra-gate" investigation into an arms selling scandal probably saved his presidency.

While such political work is rare in the West, it is common in Asia: Myanmar and Sri Lanka, for example, both have horoscopes chosen by the government astrologers. In India, astrologers are usually involved in the election of auspicious times for marriage and business events.

GUIDELINES

The principles used to elect an auspicious moment to begin an enterprise are similar to the horary rules that are used to predict whether an enterprise will have a successful outcome.

1 Select the houses that indicate the planned event, such as the ninth house for a long journey, or the seventh for marriage. The first house always indicates the event as a whole.

2 Make sure that the relevant planets are well aspected to each other.

3 Make sure that the house cusps are ruled by signs whose ruling planets are well aspected and well placed.

4 Make sure difficult indications in the chart contribute positively to the whole picture.

Remember that there is no such thing as a perfect moment, only one that offers the best possible combination of factors. Whatever the planets indicate, it is what the people themselves do that determines the outcome: the planets themselves provide only a guide.

MUNDANE ASTROLOGY: LOOKING AT HISTORY AND POLITICS

Mundane astrology is the astrology of world affairs. The term "mundane" is derived from the Latin word *mundus* meaning "world." The Roman writer Pliny wrote that "The Greeks have designated the world by a word that means 'ornament,' and we have given it the name of *mundus*, because of its perfect finish and grace." Mundane astrology takes as its subject the entire sweep of world history, the rise and fall of nations and even religions. Its scope extends from human affairs – politics, economics, fashion, the arts, war, and revolution – to the physical environment in all its forms – from plant growth to the weather, and disturbances such as volcanic eruptions and earthquakes.

In practice, the subject is so broad that it is best to recognize different areas of interest and expertise so that political astrology can be distinguished from financial astrology, and these in turn can be separated from the study of the physical environment. Mundane horoscopes are cast both for events and for groups of people: for battles and wars, the launching of ships and spacecraft, the independence of nations, general elections, the coronation of kings and queens, and for organizations such as trade unions and political parties. The simplest form of mundane horoscope is the composite chart, which is drawn for the relationship between two people and which overlaps with natal astrology. At the other end of the scale, the horoscope for communist China represents hundreds of millions of people, and the chart for the foundation of the United Nations organization signifies a common venture involving almost the entire population of the earth.

Mundane astrology differs from the other branches of the art in that horoscopes are drawn not only for human affairs, but also for astronomical events, which are then used to indicate the general trends for the coming weeks, months, or years. The principal charts are those for the ingresses – the times of the entry of planets into new signs (especially the entry of the Sun into the four cardinal signs: Aries, Cancer, Libra, and Capricorn) – and the semimontly new Moons and full Moons.

The political astrologer also uses the techniques of the other branches of astrology, studying the natal charts of politicians and public figures, or asking horary questions to gain insights into specific situations. It is necessary to understand and study all the other forms of astrology and to have a grasp of current affairs.

We also need to say a word about the philosophy of mundane astrology. While it can make use of what are often called the "divinatory" techniques of horary astrology or the psychological approaches of modern natal astrology, it relies heavily on the correlation of important global events with the long-term cycles of the outer planets. This focuses our attention on the concept of long-term cycles in human affairs, almost as if human society itself is a living organism which grows and decays in complex rhythms. Society therefore constitutes itself into what used to be known as a "body politic," in which individuals play their role as part of a larger whole. This idea has been out of fashion in the West for the last 50 years but is demonstrated by astrology: some of mundane astrology's most effective predictions are made by looking at the current phase in a cycle and then examining the equivalent past phases to identify common patterns.

CORRECT PREDICTIONS

Predicting the future is a delicate business, and many astrological forecasts are as inaccurate as those made using any other technique. However, astrology can make political predictions that exceed in their ability to sum up the nature and timing of events anything attempted by other methods. One problem, of course, is that the same events can never recur, so we are always faced with entirely new situations. We cannot say that X occurred at the last planetary conjunction, so it will occur again. What we can say, though, is that something of a similar nature may occur again. Clarity of thought and a familiarity with politics are probably more important in reaching a reasonable prediction than a grasp of complex astrological techniques. Also, of course, we have to ask what exactly is the point of making such forecasts. True, sometimes we can try to avert disaster. For example, in 1987 British astrologer Dennis Elwell decided that there was a threat of losses at sea. He wrote to the P&O shipping company to warn of the danger, but they replied that they were happy with their safety procedures – all of which is documented in Elwell's book, *The Cosmic Loom.* A few weeks later, the ferry the *Herald of Free Enterprise* sank outside Zeebrugge with huge loss of life. In other instances, it's not so easy to see how astrology can help. For example, in the *Astrological Journal* of summer 1980, Michael Baigent predicted that the Soviet Union might disintegrate between January 1989 and November 1991, mainly because of the transits of Pluto over the Russian Sun. This is exactly what happened. Baigent's prediction was reinforced by at least five other forecasts of revolution in the Soviet Union made as early as 1950, and it more than makes up for most astrologers' failure to predict the Second World War in the 1930s. It is clear that astrology can forecast turning points in world history, but what exactly do we make of this remarkable ability? It appears that human societies do indeed grow and decay in the same way as other natural organisms.

THE CYCLES OF THE OUTER PLANETS AND THEIR MEANINGS

The cycles of the outer planets, from one conjunction to the next, are used to describe the character of particular periods. When each combination of planets reaches a major aspect – especially conjunction, square, and opposition, but also trine and sextile – we expect their quality to be reflected in world events.

CYCLE	AVERAGE DURATION BETWEEN CONJUNCTION IN YEARS	MEANINGS
Jupiter–Saturn	20	Varies, depending on the sign, but should be seen as the basic cycle of historical change
Jupiter–Uranus	14	Enterprise, freedom, innovation, expansion, discovery, exploration
Jupiter–Neptune	13	Religion, mysticism, ideologies, speculation, inflation
Jupiter–Pluto	12	Power struggles, violent conflicts, excessive optimism, intense beliefs
Saturn–Uranus	45 Current cycle began 1988, ends 2032	The polarization of authority and anarchy, right wing and authoritarian politics and ideas, material innovation
Saturn–Neptune	36 Current cycle began 1989, ends 2026	Democracy, idealism, philanthropy, and socialism
Saturn–Pluto	33 Current cycle began 1982, ends 2020	The structuring of intense passions and ancient forces, political restructuring, violent confrontation, organized crime
Uranus–Neptune	172 Current cycle began 1993, ends c. 2165	Revolutions, especially in ideologies and religion, enlightenment
Uranus–Pluto	127 Current cycle began 1965–6, ends c. 2092	Social upheaval, revolution
Neptune–Pluto	492 Current cycle began 1891, ends c. 2383	Major historical change

FINANCIAL ASTROLOGY

Financial astrology, sometimes known by the grand title astro-economics, is technically included under the umbrella of mundane astrology, although many natal astrologers are approached for business advice. The risks are great, for, on the astrologer's advice, large sums of money can be made or lost. Some brokers and businessmen use astrology themselves, and there is no doubt that profits are made on astrological principles.

However, there is no simple method – if there were, astrologers would all be millionaires. The situation is analagous to that of the gambler who discovers a system that "works" for him or her but not for anybody else. Each successful financial astrologer must evolve a method that suits his or her own particular experience and expertise.

The September 11, 1995 issue of *Forbes* magazine, the journal for millionaires – and would-be billionaires – drew attention to the astonishing success of financial analyst Arch Crawford. His newsletter, *Crawford Perspectives*, was one of the top-performing financial newsletters of the previous five years. Interestingly, Crawford is an astrologer, relying heavily on the correlation of planetary motions with business cycles in order to forecast the future. The article claimed that "there has long been a thriving astrological subculture within the investment world."

The Jupiter–Uranus cycle, being the supreme significator of individual enterprise, is regarded as the ruler of "free-market" capitalism. In 1983, when these planets were in a conjunction, the Western world, led by the United States, shook itself out of the recession that had gripped it since 1979. Under the pressure of high interest rates, market prices reached their highest-ever levels. On January 8, 1986, the two planets reached the next phase of their cycle, the sextile. Although they later recovered, stock prices on this day experienced their biggest fall since the Wall Street crash of 1929.

Guidelines for financial success

1 The second and eighth houses, the planets in them, and the planets ruling them are the main indication of financial conditions.

2 Jupiter and Venus are generally the most benevolent planets, indicating profit and growth – but also inflation and recklessness.

3 Saturn is the most inauspicious planet, indicating cuts and recession, but also caution, common sense, and saving.

4 In general economic cycles, prices tend to rise when planets are approaching a trine or sextile and then fall, and fall while planets are approaching squares or oppositions and then rise.

♈ ♉ ♊ ♋ ♌ ♍ ♎ ♏ ♐ ♑ ♒ ♓

CHAPTER 13

MEDICAL ASTROLOGY

The application of astrology to the healing arts has a long history. Today, the principles of medical astrology are frequently combined with the techniques of complementary medicine such as homeopathy, acupuncture, or ayurvedic medicine, which is closely linked to Indian astrology.

The underlying theory of astrological medicine is that of "as above, so below," with the Earth being seen as an exact mirror of heaven, with each human body reflecting the astrological cosmos of planet, signs and houses – an "internal" zodiac to match the one in the sky. The horoscope sheds light on the state of health of both body and mind, and in the past a training in medicine was considered an essential part of the astrologer's work. According to this theory, true health occurs when the individual is in a state of harmony with nature, which may be described as being in a state of "ease." Disease, or dis-ease, occurs when the state of harmony is destroyed, and it is the task of the astrological physician to help maintain a state of ease or perfect health. This is an impossible goal, for astrology itself assumes that the cosmos is in a state of perpetual change. Human beings are, therefore, engaged in a search for perfect health, a goal as elusive as a mirage in the desert. In the astrological scheme of things, the pursuit of health is a continual process, not something to take up when a mild state of disease gives way to an acute or chronic condition. The goal is to maintain balance.

Even when physical symptoms are apparently dominant, the astrologer considers that emotional and mental symptoms, normally lumped together as "psychological," are of vital importance. However, while astrologers may be good at dealing with stress in their counseling role, they would never attempt to diagnose or treat a physical problem without the necessary medical training.

THE SIGNS

Each sign of the zodiac rules a part of the body – and any physiological processes – starting with Aries at the head and moving down to Pisces at the feet.

- Aries rules the head (a classic Aries complaint is the headache caused by stress and overwork).
- Taurus rules the throat.
- Gemini rules the lungs, nerves, shoulders, arms, hands, and fingers (Geminian types may suffer from nervous complaints).
- Cancer rules the breast, chest area, and stomach (some people link a Cancerian tendency to worry with digestive complaints).
- Leo rules the heart and spine.
- Virgo rules the intestines (as with Cancer, the worrying to which this sign is prone may result in digestive troubles).
- Libra rules the loins and kidneys (the sign's perfectionism is reflected in the kidney's cleansing functions).
- Scorpio rules the reproductive and excretory organs.
- Sagittarius rules the thighs.
- Capricorn rules the knees.
- Aquarius rules the ankles.
- Pisces rules the feet.

THE PLANETS

Although in some modern books on astrology, health issues are focused on the signs, these relate mainly to the planets, whose sign positions can then give further indications.

☉

The SUN is quite simply the symbol of life itself, and is associated with growth and well being. It is specifically associated with ailments of the heart and hot, feverish complaints. The part of the body ruled by the sign in which the Sun is found should be emphasized.

☽

The MOON is connected with the regulation of fluids and water in the body, and the physical problems that occur when these are in excess or insufficient. Typical symptoms include feeling cold and shivery. The Moon is always linked to changing emotional moods, which suggests a relationship between an excess (or perhaps lack) of water in the body and difficulty in expressing emotions.

☿

MERCURY is ruler of the nervous system. It is associated with nervous disorders and problems arising from too much mental stimulation – exhaustion, headaches, loss of memory.

♀

VENUS is literally associated with venereal diseases and all problems caused by self-indulgence. This is an emotional planet with a cool and watery nature, and may be related to problems of water retention. It is certainly connected to kidney disorders.

♂

MARS, always a planet associated with heat and aggression, rules hot, feverish, and angry complaints; inflammation; hemorrhages; high blood pressure; deep, burning pains; violent, contagious and eruptive diseases; and all treatment by surgery. Superficial problems ruled by Mars include insect stings and bites, burns and scalds, and accidents caused by hasty or impulsive action. It is clear that at both chronic and acute levels, Martian problems may be self-inflicted due to aggressive and unthinking or uncoordinated behavior, or overwork.

♃

JUPITER rules the liver. Its general effect on the body is to speed things up, encourage growth, and increase the circulation. It rules tumors and other growths, whether malignant or benign, and is also associated with problems arising from being overweight or the excessive consumption of food, drugs, or alcohol.

♄

SATURN rules the skin and the entire bone structure, and is the essential principle that holds the body together. This planet slows everything down, producing blockages and underfunction, poor growth, and poorly functioning organs.

♅

URANUS connects with all dramatic or sudden events, perhaps a violent rupture or hemorrhage, or an unexpected cure. It is also associated with accidents, nervous problems, and fast or erratic functions.

♆

NEPTUNE rules the gradual erosion of physical powers and can be associated with lethargy or wasting diseases. A strong Neptunian type will also easily suffer the negative effects of alcohol or drugs (prescribed or otherwise).

♇

PLUTO is associated with complaints of the reproductive or excretory system and with deep changes, either sudden or long-term, in the physical condition. It is also linked to conditions caused by intense emotions.

FORMS OF TREATMENT

The astrologer's task is to restore balance once the essential problem has been diagnosed. There are two traditional approaches to treatment. The simplest is the prescription of a remedy whose qualities are opposite those of the symptoms. For example, if the basic problem is Venusian, a Martian remedy should be applied. More complicated is the principle of treatment through "sympathy." In this case, a Venusian remedy would be applied to a Venusian problem. The more confused the symptoms and obscure the causes, the greater the difficulty in settling on an appropriate remedy. It goes without saying that only trained and qualified medical practitioners should attempt the diagnosis and treatment of serious ailments.

EXERCISE

Generally the Sun sign is seen as embodying the physical disposition, and the methods of exercise that are recommended usually reflect this. The patterns are fairly predictable. Aries needs energetic exercise and enjoys competitive sports; Taurus moves slowly; and Geminians are obliged to work off nervous tension in physical exercise (running and walking being two common activities). Cancer may enjoy water sports, as might Scorpio and Pisces. Theatrical Leo enjoys dancing, as does Pisces, whose sign rules the feet. Aquarius may be attracted to new sports and Libra to graceful ones (synchronized swimming or tai chi). Sagittarius is a runner and jogger, while Capricorn may set off hiking (like the mountain goat), and Virgo is attracted to sports which require precision. Although such recommendations are usually given only to the Sun signs, the disposition of the entire chart is important and the Moon sign or Ascendant may be more significant than the Sun.

CHANGE OF LIFESTYLE

Sometimes the remedy lies in a change of lifestyle rather than in medical treatment. For example, the lazy Venus–Jupiter person might benefit from developing the qualities of Mars and taking regular exercise. On the other hand, the tense and nervous Mars–Mercury individual might benefit from some Venus–Jupiter self-indulgence. Marsilio Ficino, the Italian Renaissance philosopher, thought that the best remedy for reclusive, intellectual, saturnine types (like himself) was to develop the properties of Venus–Jupiter by getting drunk and chasing the opposite sex.

HERBS

Herbal remedies lie at the very core of traditional astrological medicine, and every herb and plant is ruled by one of the seven traditional planets. In basic treatment, an herb is prescribed to counteract the physical symptoms, so that an herb under the rulership of cold-moist Venus may be given to alleviate the problems caused by hot-dry Mars . One of the classic remedies for migraine, a typical Mars complaint, is the Venusian herb fever-few. Interestingly, this is also used by orthodox doctors, who have been unable to find any other cure for this problem.

HOMEOPATHY

Homeopathic diagnosis and treatment is usually practiced separately from astrology, although the two systems have strong affinities and are often used together. Homeopathy uses the principle of healing by sympathy, with a remedy similar to the symptoms being administered. For example, coffee, which induces a state of high nervousness, is ruled by Mars (perhaps with Mercury), yet in its homeopathic form, coffee is also a remedy for such a condition. In the case of broken bones, ruled by Saturn, the remedy is symphitum, made from the herb comfrey, known as "knit-bone" and also ruled by Saturn. In other words, a Saturn herb comes to the aid of a Saturn problem. In spite of its apparent simplicity, considerable expertise in homeopathy is required before such treatments can be effectively applied.

There is no systematic correlation of homeopathic remedies with astrological conditions, and with two such subtle disciplines, a fixed system would probably create problems. However, many of those trained in the two practices are well aware of the close correspondences. It is interesting to note that there are 12 homeopathic remedies (Cell Salts), that correspond to the 12 signs, and which are routinely taken as a tonic. In general, the salt used is the one which corresponds to the Ascendant, Sun, or Moon sign, depending on which is most appropriate.

BACH FLOWER REMEDIES

The flower remedies invented by Edward Bach are based on the principle of homeopathy. Each remedy equates to a certain emotional and mental type – one may be full of anger, one cold and distant, another full of fear – and is prescribed for someone whose psychological state equates with the remedy's "symptom picture." As with homeopathy, there is no standard correlation with astrology; the astrologer analyzes the overall disposition of the chart and selects the most appropriate remedy. For example, a remedy associated with fear might be prescribed for a very Saturnine person.

One remedy that is of general use is Olive flower, prescribed for complete mental exhaustion. The remedy is equated with Virgo and, because the olive tree itself is ruled by Jupiter, has been successfully prescribed for the conditions of physical and mental collapse that can overtake the overworked Piscean. The connections are subtle and flexible, but effective.

ACUPUNCTURE

Traditional acupuncture, which is becoming increasing popular in the West, is intimately connected with Chinese astrology, with the acupuncturist taking into account the individual's natal disposition, the season, the weather, and other relevant information. As an oriental system, acupuncture does not correspond exactly to Western astrology, but work is in progress to enable the two systems to be used together.

♈ ♉ ♊ ♋ ♌ ♍ ♎ ♏ ♐ ♑ ♒ ♓

CHAPTER 14

ASTROLOGICAL GARDENING

The entire universe pulsates to an intricate series of beats and rhythms. We are coming to understand some of these, such as the circadian (daily) rhythms that drive our bodies in line with the Sun. We are also discovering others, such as the radio signals received from distant stars known as pulsars, which are so regular it was originally thought they were sent by intelligent life forms. Out of all the uses of astrology, the regulation of gardening and agriculture according to cosmic cycles has the greatest practical potential, although it is one that is sadly ignored by all but a few organic gardeners and farmers.

THE TRADITION

Astrology lays down clear guidelines for obtaining the greatest benefit from planting, growing, and harvesting plants. They state that the crucial stages of each plant's life must occur during certain favorable times, based on the belief that every type of plant is ruled by a planet whose nature it shares. For example, ginger, a typically hot spice ruled by Mars, should if possible be planted with Mars in Dignity by sign (in Aries or Scorpio), or in its Exaltation (in Capricorn), in the sixth house (in which it is said to "rejoice"), and in good aspects, such as applying trines to the Moon, Jupiter, and Venus. If such perfect conditions never arise, then the astrologer must find the next best! Similarly, Sun-ruled plants need to be sown under a strong Sun, Moon-ruled plants under a strong Moon, and so on.

Astrological gardening of this precision takes on a ritual quality, and its function is indicated by recent evidence suggesting connections between the health of plants and their environment. It is no longer considered unusual that plants are more robust after being talked to or being exposed to sensitive music. In strict astrological gardening, the effect is much the same. By taking a ritualistic approach, the gardener adopts a certain attitude, and as a result, the cultivation of the plant is enhanced.

Whatever their specific rulerships, all plants come under the general sway of the Moon. The principal lunar cycle is the full Moon–new Moon cycle, but traditions differ on the question of whether plants should be sown around new Moon (the beginning of the waning phase). Generally, the new Moon is favored. Some say that only root crops should be planted during the waning Moon.

The rules are based on the proposition that just before new Moon energy reaches a trough, after which growth accelerates, reaching a peak at full Moon. At the new Moon, moisture absorption is at its lowest and at full Moon at its highest. For this reason, crops should be harvested for storage at the new Moon (when they are driest) and for immediate consumption at full Moon (when they are most succulent). In France, from 1669 until the Revolution of 1789, it was the law that timber could be felled only at new Moon.

THE ZODIAC GARDEN

Naturally, each sign of the zodiac can be associated with a different style of garden, although it does not follow that people born with the Sun in a certain sign will relate to a particular kind of garden. There might be times when we prefer to live through our Moon signs, Ascendants, or some other part of our chart.

ARIES

♈ Aries is associated with all plants that are fiery, spiky, and sharp, hence its rulership of, for example, red roses. Stinging nettles and thistles are probably among the less welcome Arien plants. The Arien garden should contain plenty of bright colors, especially reds and scarlets, and vivid, lively scents.

TAURUS

♉ The Taurean garden should be a place to relax, filled with delicate scents and colors, including subtle blues, pinks, and greens. An ideal addition to the Taurean garden are fruit trees, especially those which produce rich and sweet fruits such as peaches, figs, plums, or apples.

GEMINI

♊ Gemini is a sign of change and variety, and the main consideration of the Geminian garden is that there should be plenty to interest and stimulate. Plants of various types and colors, and from every part of the globe, should compete for attention.

CANCER

Cancer is a watery sign, which means quite simply that it is associated with all plants with juicy and succulent leaves and fruit, especially those that like to live near water. This sign is also associated with trailing plants and white flowers. Ideally, a water garden should be lunar.

LEO

The Leo garden should be bold and theatrical, with groups of plants designed to create a dramatic impression. Typical leonine plants are those which evoke this sign's ruling planet, the Sun. The sunflower is the obvious Leo plant, the marigold another. Gold and scarlet are the favored colors. Not surprisingly, plenty of sunlight is essential.

VIRGO

The Virgo garden should include plants that are useful at the same time as producing beautiful flowers or scents. For example, a herb garden could be a centerpiece, as could a number of fruit trees, providing homegrown food. Virgo likes variety, and its colors are grey and navy blue.

LIBRA

Libra is a sign that delights in beauty and delicate hues and sweet scents. Its special colors are blues and pinks, and its favorite plants are those which produce rich fruits – a peach or a plum tree forms an ideal centerpiece to a Libran garden.

SCORPIO

Scorpio delights in dark colors, such as deep blues and dark reds, as well as in plants which are tough and spiky; a deep-red rose is ideally Scorpionic. Many Scorpionic plants are happy growing near water or in shade.

SAGITTARIUS

Sagittarius is associated with bright colors, especially purple and blue, although reds are permissible. Rich and impressive flowers from the far corners of the world appeal to the adventurous Sagittarian mentality.

CAPRICORN

As a sign with a conservative reputation, Capricorn is associated with carefully laid out and formal gardens, designed to impress as much as to please. Old varieties of plants appeal to the sign's sense of tradition; its favorite colors tend to be dark.

AQUARIUS

♒ The Aquarian garden should be a place to challenge all accepted ideas of garden design, reflecting only the personality of its creator. Its favorite colors are bright and garish, including a vivid electric blue, and it favors an unlikely but stimulating contrast of plants.

PISCES

♓ The Piscean garden should be secluded, pleasing, and relaxing, and if possible should include a pool or pond as a centerpiece. The Piscean individual adores delicate flowers and subtle scents, and the sign's favorite colors are turquoise and sea green.

BIODYNAMIC GARDENING

In the 1950s, a comprehensive system of lunar gardening was worked out by Maria Thun, a follower of the mystic Rudolf Steiner. Thun's main innovation was to relate plant structure to the four elements. Previously, tradition had regarded the three Water signs as ideal for the sowing and germination of seeds, the Earth signs, especially Taurus and Capricorn, as suitable for root crops (though not as beneficial as Water signs), the Air signs as indifferent, and the hot-dry Fire signs as harmful and likely to lead to famine.

Thun divided plants into four sections – the root (related to Earth), the leaf (related to Water), the flower (related to Air), and the fruit or seed (related to Fire). Next she classified different crops under these categories so that, for example, potato equates to root/Earth and cabbage to leaf/Water.

The basic practice is quite simple – crops should be sown or planted when the Moon is in the relevant element. However, there is one major drawback. Thun used the sidereal zodiac of Indian astrology, not the standard tropical zodiac of the west, because the sidereal zodiac produced the required result. Unfortunately, an ordinary ephemeris shows only the tropical signs, although converting these into sidereal is a simple but laborious process. Luckily, in the 1970s two British experts, Simon Best and Nick Kollerstrom, solved this problem by publishing a yearly calendar containing gardening instruction (see Resources).

Tests have shown that when this system is applied, crop yields may increase by as much as 54 percent, but that the use of chemical fertilizers destroys the beneficial effect. The Biodynamic system is thus both a powerful argument in favor of the use of organic farming methods and a pointer to the most positive help that astrology can offer.

THE LUNAR CALENDAR IN BIODYNAMIC GARDENING

LUNAR PHASE	PHYSIOLOGY	ACTION
New Moon	Water intake at a minimum	Harvest for storage. Plant seeds after New Moon
First quarter	Growth accelerates	Plant seeds
Full Moon	Water intake and growth peak	Harvest for immediate consumption
Last quarter	Growth declines	No planting

THE LUNAR METABOLISM

The metabolism of a range of plants, measured by changes in oxygen consumption, varies with the position of the Moon. A sharp increase in oxygen intake takes place shortly before the Moon rises, a trough is reached when it is on the MC, and a second peak when it is on the Descendant. Biodynamic gardeners tend to plant seeds when the Moon is in the tenth, eleventh, or twelfth houses – in other words, when it is rising.

Also, results obtained by recent research show that plants respond to changes in the Earth's magnetic field caused by the cycles of the Sun and the Moon; plant growth speeds up around the full Moon, sap rises faster, and up to 35 percent more water is absorbed than at the new Moon. The metabolic rate of even the humble potato is up to 15 percent greater at full Moon than at the new Moon.

Some cycles peak at both the new and full Moons – the electricity potential of trees and the amount of oxygen absorbed by seeds both seem to maximize at these times. Other cycles vary depending on the needs of the plant at different phases – at new Moon more potassium is absorbed and at full Moon phosphorus intake is maximized, a fact that should be taken into account if chemical fertilizers are used.

♈ ♉ ♊ ♋ ♌ ♍ ♎ ♏ ♐ ♑ ♒ ♓

CHAPTER 15

INDIAN ASTROLOGY

The astrology practiced in India today is known as Jyotish, which loosely translates as the "science of light" or "wisdom of the heavens." It is regarded as one of the six vedangas, or "limbs," of the Hindu religion, but it is not necessary to be a Hindu in order to practice or use it (there are also Sikh and Muslim practitioners in India). Indian astrology is becoming increasingly popular in the West, where it is usually known as Vedic astrology, after the Vedas, the Hindu sacred texts. We cannot say when astrology developed in India, although we can assume that between 3,000 and 4,000 years ago it was being used to arrange the sacred calendar and to time religious rites.

A huge amount of creative development took place in astrology between 2,000 and 2,500 years ago, mainly in the Middle East and Egypt. Many cultures contributed to the philosophy of astrology, but the international language of the time was Greek, so eventually most texts that dealt with the new techniques, such as the calculation and interpretation of birth charts, were written in Greek. These texts then spread west to Europe and east to Persia and India. Around 2,000 years ago, the astrology practiced in Rome, Egypt, and India would have been the same. However, because of the vast distances between these places and the fact that lines of communication were frequently ruptured by wars and invasions, variations began to appear.

The first major change occurred around A.D. 120, when the idea of the tropical zodiac was introduced into the West (see Chapter 2). Increasingly, Western astrologers began to use the spring equinox, March 21, to mark zero degrees Aries and the beginning of the zodiac. In India, meanwhile, astrologers continued to use the older sidereal zodiac, based on the stars. Due to the "precession of the equinoxes," the stars shift against the spring equinox by about 1 degree every 72 years. As a result, the sidereal and tropical zodiacs are now totally out of sync. If you were born with the Sun in one sign in the tropical zodiac, you almost certainly have it in a different sign in the sidereal zodiac. To work out approximately where a planet is in the sidereal zodiac, add 6 degrees to its western (tropical) position, subtract 30 degrees and move it back to the previous sign. Thus, a planet at 14 degrees Pisces moves to 20 degrees Aquarius in the sidereal zodiac.

In addition, Indian astrologers still use many of the techniques developed in classical times – which fell out of use in the West 300 years ago – as well as others which they developed themselves. Indian astrologers make great use of electional astrology, particularly in arranging auspicious times for marriages, and chart comparison, especially assessing the compatibility of potential marriage partners. Some rules are quite simple – weddings are never held on Saturday, because Saturn is deemed to be inauspicious, but are best celebrated on Thursday, ruled by optimistic Jupiter. Others are much more complex. Although most Indian astrologers do not use the sophisticated psychological astrology which has been developed in the West, they often have a far higher level of technical skill than their Western counterparts.

Because of its intimate relationship with Hinduism, Indian astrology (at least, as practiced by Hindus) has a spiritual dimension that is lacking in Western astrology (though individual Western astrologers may incorporate their own beliefs in their astrology). In particular, Indian astrologers rely on the doctrines of *reincarnation* (according to which the soul lives through endless lives, gradually discovering the purpose of its existence) and *karma* (which holds that all current conditions are the result of our previous actions, and our present actions sow the seeds for all future conditions). Traditionally, all Indian astrologers were priests, although in the 21st century a class of secular professional astrologers exists, just as in the West. In everyday life, astrology's spiritual dimension can be reflected in the carrying out of pujas (purification rituals) or meditation in temples containing planetary shrines. Indian astrologers, too, take on a counseling role, listening to their clients' problems and advising them on the most appropriate course of action.

The final difference between Indian and Western astrology is that Indian astrologers still draw their horoscopes in a square format, as did Western astrologers until the 19th century. However, the differences between Western and Indian astrology are, in one sense, just an extreme form of the smaller differences that exist between different schools of thought and technical approaches within Western astrology. Most astrologers do not see these differences as a problem. In fact, they are often seen as an advantage, opening up many ways of reading one horoscope. Some astrologers say that there are many different paths to truth – or paths up a mountain.

Indian astrologers also use what in the West are known as harmonic charts. For example, the Western ninth harmonic chart has long been cast in India as the *navamsa* chart. It indicates relationships – and the future marriage partner – and so is extremely important. Sixteen other harmonic – or *shodasavarga* – charts are also used.

THE SIGNS, PLANETS, AND HOUSES

There are obviously differences in terminology between Indian and Western astrology. In India, the planets are known as *grahas*; the Moon's north and south nodes, which have particular importance, are known as Rahu and Ketu; the zodiac signs are known as *rashis*; and the houses are known as *bhavas*. However, the relationships between them are mostly the same as in Western astrology; for example, Aries is ruled by Mars and the tenth house rules the career. But Indian astrology pays more attention to the lunar cycle, including the phase of the Moon at birth. The waxing phase, from new Moon to full, is considered more auspicious than the waning phase, from full Moon to new. Every day of the lunar month is known as a *tithi*, and this determines whether a particular day might be auspicious for a particular action. The whole lunar cycle through the zodiac is divided into 27 *nakshatras*, each of which is ruled by a planet and has a range of meanings. On average, the Moon passes through one nakshatra in a day. Uranus, Neptune, and Pluto are not part of the traditional structure of Indian astrology, although some Indian astrologers now use these planets, adopting the same meanings as they have in the west.

THE SIGNS OF THE ZODIAC AND THE RASHIS

WESTERN SIGN	INDIAN NAME (English spelling may vary)	DATE THAT THE SUN ENTERS (may be a day either side)
Aries	Mesha	April 14
Taurus	Vrishaba	May 15
Gemini	Mithuna	June 15
Cancer	Kataka	July 17
Leo	Simha	August 17
Virgo	Kanya	September 17
Libra	Thula	October 18
Scorpio	Vrischika	November 17
Sagittarius	Dhanus	December 16
Capricorn	Makara	January 14
Aquarius	Kumbha	February 13
Pisces	Meena	March 15

THE PLANETS IN INDIAN ASTROLOGY

PLANET	INDIAN NAME	GOD OR GODDESS
Sun	Ravi or Surya	Shiva
Moon	Chandra	Parvati
Mercury	Budha or Buddha	Vishnu
Venus	Sukra or Shukra	Lakshmi
Mars	Kuja, Kartika, or Mangala	Kamara
Jupiter	Brihaspati or Guru	Brahma
Saturn	Sani	Yama

THE NAKSHATRAS

There are 27 nakshatras in all and, in effect, they constitute a lunar zodiac separate from the 12-sign solar zodiac. They are used for interpreting the natal chart, arranging auspicious moments and predicting the future. The meanings of the nakshatras are as rich as those of the regular zodiac signs. One point to consider is the planet ruling the nakshatra. For example, if you were born with the Sun in the second nakshatra, Bharani, you might be a Venusian person – very charming – but if it was in Punavasu, the seventh nakshatra, you might be Jupiterian – jovial and optimistic. Remember, though, that the positions given below are in the solar zodiac (the Indian one, not the Western). The following list includes the degree and minute at which each nakshatra begins.

1 Ashwini, 0 degrees Aries, ruled by Ketu (the Moon's south node).

2 Bharani, 13 degrees 20 minutes Aries, ruled by Venus.

3 Kritikka, 26 degrees 40 minutes Taurus, ruled by the Sun.

4 Rohini, 10 degrees Taurus, ruled by the Moon.

5 Mrigasira, 23 degrees 20 minutes Taurus, ruled by Mars.

6 Ardra, 6 degrees 40 minutes Gemini, ruled by Rahu (the Moon's north node).

7 Punavasu, 20 degrees Gemini, ruled by Jupiter.

8 Pushya, 3 degrees 20 minutes Cancer, ruled by Saturn.

9 Ashlesha, 16 degrees 40 minutes Cancer, ruled by Mercury.

10 Magha, 0 degrees Leo, ruled by Ketu.

11 Purva Phalguni, 13 degrees 20 minutes Leo, ruled by Venus.

12 Uttara Phalguni, 26 degrees 40 minutes Leo, ruled by the Sun.

13 Hasta, 10 degrees Virgo, ruled by the Moon.

14 Chitra, 23 degrees 20 minutes Virgo, ruled by Mars.

15 Swati, 6 degrees 40 minutes Libra, ruled by Rahu.

16 Vishakha, 20 degrees Libra, ruled by Jupiter.

17 Anuradha, 3 degrees 20 minutes Scorpio, ruled by Saturn.

18 Jyeshta, 16 degrees 40 minutes Scorpio, ruled by Mercury.

19 Mula, 0 degrees Sagittarius, ruled by Ketu.

20 Purvashadha, 13 degrees, 20 minutes Sagittarius, ruled by Venus.

21 Uttarashadha, 26 degrees, 40 minutes Sagittarius, ruled by the Sun.

22 Shravana, 10 degrees Capricorn, ruled by the Moon.

23 Dhanishta, 23 degrees 20 minutes Capricorn, ruled by Mars.

24 Shatabhishak, 6 degrees 40 minutes Aquarius, ruled by Rahu.

25 Purva Bhadra, 20 degrees Aquarius, ruled by Jupiter.

26 Uttara Bhadra, 3 degrees 20 minutes Pisces.

27 Revati, 16 degrees 40 minutes Pisces.

♈ ♉ ♊ ♋ ♌ ♍ ♎ ♏ ♐ ♑ ♒ ♓

CHAPTER 16

CHINESE ASTROLOGY

Chinese astrology is increasingly familiar in the West, although its roots are entirely different from those of both Indian and Western astrology. A few very minor pieces of Western astrology are found in China, probably because the relevant texts were carried along the ancient silk routes across central Asia. But in general the two systems are utterly different, although this doesn't mean that they can't be used together – far from it. Just as different branches of Western astrology may provide different insights, so Chinese astrology can offer a fresh perspective. Technically, Chinese astrology is every bit as complex as its Western counterpart, and in many cases more so than the astrology used by most Western practitioners of psychological astrology. Chinese astrology uses the stars and planets, though the main coordinates are the equator and the north and south poles rather than the ecliptic. The year is divided into 24 periods known as ch'i, each of which corresponds roughly to a half of one Western zodiac sign, and there are 28 "lunar mansions" based on a principle similar to the 27 Indian nakshatras (though there may be no common origin). The time of day is also crucial, as in Western astrology.

Chinese astrology is part of a cosmology that also includes healing methods such as acupuncture and herbalism; martial arts and exercise systems such as judo, karate, and tai chi; and feng shui, the art of arranging the environment in harmony with invisible natural energies. These energies, known as chi, are constantly moving between an active, positive form, known as yang, and a passive, negative one, known as yin (traditionally these are regarded as male and female). Astrology is a means of mapping these constantly shifting energies so that the nature of the times can be understood and auspicious moments can be selected for initiating new enterprises.

THE ANIMAL SIGNS

The best-known feature of Chinese astrology in the West – due to accessibility rather than traditional importance – is the allocation of animal signs to each year in a 12-year cycle. The origin of this practice is far more recent than that of Chinese astrology as a whole – probably no earlier than the sixth century. According to myth, the Buddha summoned all the animals on Earth to say farewell to him before he died, but only 12 turned up. As a reward, he named a year after each of the animals, in the order that they appeared. Astronomically, the years relate to the 11.87-year Jupiter cycle, but there is no direct correspondence. Nor do they correspond exactly to Western years, because the Chinese year is lunar. The animal signs are rarely used in sophisticated Chinese astrological texts, but they are a quick and easy reference for popular astrology, like the Western Sun signs. Many people are now aware of both their Western Sun sign and their Chinese year sign. For example, a Pisces born in 1953 is a Piscean Snake, while a 1965 Leo is a Leonine Snake, but a Pisces and a Leo born in 1998 will be a Tiger-Pisces and a Tiger-Leo, respectively.

There are no exact correspondences between the Chinese animals and the Western signs, but there are similarities, as pointed out below. Some Western signs have obvious Chinese counterparts; others have none, so there is no neat system.

The Rat is charming, intelligent, witty, sociable, fun-loving, and has a good memory (which sounds like Gemini).

The Ox, as we would expect, is slow moving, methodical, stable, determined, tenacious, dutiful, and reliable (much like the Western Taurus).

The Tiger, like its real-life counterpart, is competitive, courageous, reckless, charismatic, and proud (similar to Leo).

The Rabbit, or Hare, is sociable, compassionate, intuitive, modest, sensitive, refined, creative, and a seeker after Truth (not unlike the Western Pisces).

The Dragon, the only mythical creature, is charismatic, outgoing, independent, decisive, volatile, confident, energetic, and sociable (like Aries with a dash of Leo).

The Snake is wise (yet often naive), reserved, subtle, prudent, graceful, stylish, shrewd, and sensual (similar to Scorpio).

The Horse is sociable, generous, kind, optimistic, talkative, honest, energetic, strong-willed, opinionated, sporty, and sometimes careless (much like Sagittarius).

The Sheep is persevering, sensitive, idealistic, conservative, fussy, emotional, impressionable, moody, and kind (which sounds like Pisces with a small dash of Virgo or Capricorn).

The Monkey is active, agile, inventive, restless, plausible, stubborn, inquisitive, manipulative, quick-witted, and optimistic (not unlike a combination of Aries, Gemini, and Sagittarius).

The Rooster is artistic, practical, shrewd, alert, extravagant, flamboyant, protective, sensitive, and showy (qualities that combine elements of Cancer with parts of Leo).

The Dog (like man's – or woman's – best friend) is loyal, honest, friendly, reliable, generous, trustworthy and dutiful, and needs affection (a mixture, perhaps, of Taurus and Leo).

The Pig, or Boar, is pleasure-loving, self-indulgent, contented, home-loving, practical, sincere, hard-working, virtuous, and sometimes solitary (combining elements of Cancer and Capricorn).

Because each year is ruled by a different animal, each animal has its easy and challenging years. For example, a loyal Dog might be more at ease in a stable Ox year than a lively Dragon one, although it should stay alert for the opportunities the latter might offer.

On the question of compatibility, some books give rules for the relationships between each animal, but, as with Western astrology, it is best to go back to first principles.

THE ANIMAL YEARS

The Chinese year always begins on the day corresponding to the new Moon in Aquarius in the Western zodiac. The table overleaf can be used to calculate the starting date for years prior to 1912 and beyond 2007 using this simple principle. (These dates may sometimes vary by a day either way if the new Moon occurred near midnight.)

THE ANIMAL YEARS
1912–2007

ANIMAL	STARTING DATES (MONTH, DAY, YEAR)							
Rat	2.18.1912	2.5.1924	1.24.1936	2.10.1948	1.28.1960	2.15.1972	2.2.1984	2.9.1996
Ox	2.6.1913	1.24.1925	2.11.1937	1.29.1949	2.15.1961	2.3.1973	2.20.1985	2.7.1997
Tiger	1.26.1914	2.13.1926	1.31.1938	1.17.1950	2.5.1962	1.23.1974	2.9.1986	1.28.1998
Rabbit	2.14.1915	2.2.1927	2.19.1939	2.6.1951	1.25.1963	2.11.1975	1.29.1987	2.16.1999
Dragon	2.4.1916	1.23.1928	2.8.1940	1.27.1952	2.13.1964	1.31.1976	2.17.1988	2.5.2000
Snake	1.23.1917	2.10.1929	1.27.1941	2.14.1953	2.2.1965	2.18.1977	2.6.1989	1.24.2001
Horse	2.11.1918	1.30.1930	2.15.1942	2.3.1954	1.21.1966	2.7.1978	1.27.1990	2.12.2002
Goat	2.1.1919	2.17.1931	2.5.1943	1.24.1955	2.9.1967	1.28.1979	2.16.1991	2.1.2003
Monkey	2.20.1920	2.6.1932	1.25.1944	2.12.1956	1.30.1968	2.16.1980	2.4.1992	1.22.2004
Rooster	2.8.1921	1.26.1933	2.13.1945	1.31.1957	2.17.1969	2.5.1981	1.23.1993	2.9.2005
Dog	1.28.1922	2.14.1934	2.2.1946	2.18.1958	2.6.1970	1.25.1982	2.10.1994	1.29.2006
Pig	2.16.1923	2.4.1935	1.22.1947	2.8.1959	1.27.1971	2.13.1983	1.31.1995	2.18.2007

THE ELEMENTS AND THE 60-YEAR CYCLE

Whereas Western astrologers use four elements (Fire, Earth, Air, and Water), the Chinese use five (Fire, Earth, Metal, Water, Wood). Each element has a relationship with the others as the chi moves between them.

- *Fire*, ruled by Mars, is energetic, active, forceful, ambitious, impulsive, and commanding.
- *Earth*, ruled by Saturn, is solid, reliable, capable, efficient, reasonable, cautious, and conservative.
- *Metal*, ruled by Venus, is ambitious, rigid, resolute, determined, and guided by strong feelings.
- *Water*, ruled by Mercury, is intellectual, observant, communicative, subtle, flexible, and manipulative.
- *Wood*, ruled by Jupiter, is ethical, moral, confident, generous, persuasive, and versatile.

At every moment, the balance of the elements is in a state of flux, but each two-year period is ruled by one element, as in the following sample:

1986 and 1987:	Fire
1988 and 1989:	Earth
1990 and 1991:	Metal
1992 and 1993:	Water
1994 and 1995:	Wood

Elements for years before or after the above dates can be worked out by repeating this two-year pattern. In addition, each animal year (see table on previous page) is ruled by an element. So, for example, a 1953 Snake is a Water snake, combining Water's fluidity with the Snake's wisdom, while a 1965 Snake combines Wood's confidence, generosity, versatility, and ethical standards with Snake's wisdom. Also, each year is alternately yin or yang. In the 1980s, for example, 1986 was yang, 1987 yin, 1988 yang, 1989 yin, and so on.

The total cycle of 12 animals and 5 elements takes 60 years. The whole sequence dates back to the beginning of the calendar in 2367 B.C., so the 78th cycle started in 1984.

♈ ♉ ♊ ♋ ♌ ♍ ♎ ♏ ♐ ♑ ♒ ♓

CHAPTER 17

BECOMING A PROFESSIONAL ASTROLOGER

How do you set up as a professional astrologer? This is a question asked by most aspiring professionals – but one to which they rarely find an answer. Although there are good schools of astrology, there are no coordinated professional training programs. Few people set out to become professional astrologers, but many who have studied the subject read charts for friends and family – and occasionally charge a small fee. The number of full-time professionals is in fact very small in the Western world, where, unlike in India, astrology ceased to be part of mainstream culture and is only now making a comeback.

TRAINING

The first step in becoming a professional astrologer is to receive some training. There are systems of education in place (see the links on the web at www.NickCampion.com), although many of the finest astrologers are self-taught. Of the schools that do teach astrology, few give professional instruction. The UK-based Faculty of Astrological Studies' diploma is recognized as a professional-level qualification, while the London-based Centre for Psychological Astrology is the only school to incorporate psychoanalysis in its program. For anyone wishing to deal with people on a deep, psychological level, it is often necessary to receive some sort of training in counseling. This is the only way to ensure that psychological astrology can be of real benefit to people – and that astrologers can operate within a safe framework. This kind of training can help them deal with issues such as dependency (some clients project their own needs on to the astrologer and develop a dependent relationship) and help them guard against any tendency to abuse their own power. Most psychological astrologers aim to empower their clients, so that they will be able to make their own decisions and choices.

The priorities are obviously different for financial, horary, and medical astrologers, but they all recognize that they need professional experience in a particular field before they can give detailed advice in that area. Without such experience or qualifications, they should confine themselves to their own area of competence and refer clients seeking specialist advice to the relevant professionals.

PRACTICALITIES

Once you have received some training, you will need an office or suitable space away from your ordinary domestic circumstances where you can see clients in peace. You will also need to decide what fees to charge. The top professionals charge around $150 for a reading; some limit this to an hour, while others charge a set fee no matter how long the reading lasts. If this seems expensive, remember that it needs to cover the necessary preparation time – which can be hours, although this time will decrease with experience. Obviously, beginners are going to charge a lower rate, depending both on their experience and what local conditions can support: astrologers in cosmopolitan cities such as Paris, London, or Los Angeles are inevitably able to charge more than those who live in smaller or more remote communities. The whole process of seeing clients can be time consuming, and many professionals are happy to see only a few clients a week.

It used to be common for astrologers to provide long written analyses, often by mail. However, new technology has enabled working practices to change. Astrologers who see clients face-to-face invariably tape their consultations, while others who deal with long-distance clients (which is very common) give phone consultations. These can also be taped. Technology is only part of the process, though.

AN ASTROLOGICAL CODE OF ETHICS

Many professionally trained astrologers now sign a code of ethics. The code reproduced below was one of the first; it was devised by the Faculty of Astrological Studies, founded in London in 1948. Although some clauses, such as 2 and 3, deal principally with the Faculty and its attitudes to astrology, most set out broad rules of ethical conduct to which nobody could object. Clauses 4d, e, and f set up standards to which all the helping professions aspire.

SAMPLE CODE OF ETHICS

I accept without reservation the conditions and propositions set out here, and undertake to fulfill these to the best of my ability.

1 I will endeavor to act at all times in such a way as to enhance the good name of astrology, explaining its true nature as I understand it to all interested persons and defending it against unjust aspersions or ill-informed attacks.

2 I will similarly seek to promote the welfare and good name of the Faculty of Astrological Studies by all appropriate and honorable means.

3 I undertake not to use my Diploma qualification in connection with "Sun sign" forecasting for the media.

4 In all my astrological work, whether professional or otherwise, I will abide by the following rules:

a) When undertaking natal work, I will explain clearly that unless the time and place of birth can be given with reasonable accuracy, any interpretation supplied must be regarded as incomplete or inadequate.

b) For all professional work, I will charge an adequate fee except in the case of a client who is in genuine need of help but is unable to pay, in which case I will adjust or waive my fee.

c) I will make an individual and original study of each case, and will not use any form of duplication; nor will I use the writings of others without due acknowledgement. If a computer analysis forms all or part of my work, I will advise my client in advance, and will give a clear explanation of how it differs from an individual, noncomputerized analysis.

d) In work stated to be astrological, I will not insert anything that is not founded on astrological symbolism. Should I wish to give advice or information derived from other sources, I will do this separately, making clear to the client that it is not based on astrology.

e) I agree to respect strictly all confidences made to me.

f) I will not use for my own advantage any knowledge of others gained in the course of my work; nor will I keep for private gain any discoveries I might make which could benefit astrologers generally.

g) I will use discretion in making any public statement regarding political matters or persons prominent in public life, and will avoid all such as are contrary to good taste or undesirable in the public interest.

Finally, I admit the right of the Council of the Faculty in the event of willful or grave violation of this Code of Ethics to withdraw my Diploma and erase my name from the Register of Diploma Holders of the said Faculty.

ORGANIZATIONS FOR PROFESSIONAL ASTROLOGERS

Many astrologers enjoy their independence and prefer to work alone, but others feel the need for professional support. The Organization of Professional Astrologers (www.professionalastrologers.org) is based in the USA, and the Association of Professional Astrologers (www.professional-astrology.org) in the UK, but both will accept suitably qualified members from any country.

RESOURCES

This book contains all you need to know to cast and interpret birth charts. *The Ultimate Astrologer* also serves as an introduction to much else that astrology has to offer. But if you wish to investigate further, read on.

WEBSITES

All websites are eventually linked to all others, such is the nature of the worldwide web. One of the best places to start is www.NickCampion.com. This site includes the free chart calculation service set up for *The Ultimate Astrologer*, information on books, schools and societies (particularly in the USA, e.g., the National Council for Geocosmic Research, the International Society for Astrological Research, and the Association for Astrological Networking), and a range of links to the most popular sites on science and astrology.

The Astrological Association of Great Britain is one of the most respected astrological societies in the Western world. It publishes the highly regarded *Astrological Journal*, as well as a research journal, *Correlation*, the *Astrology and Medicine Newsletter*, and an online newsletter, *Transit*. It has members from all over the world and maintains close links with other astrological organizations, especially in the USA. Visit the AA on line at www.AstrologicalAssociation.com. You will find there a link to the Astrological Lodge of London (www.astrology.co.uk), which publishes an excellent quarterly magazine.

Check out www.astrodienst.com for the website of Liz Greene, the world's most influential psychological astrologer. If you wish, you can purchase one of her highly recommended computerized astrology reports. The longest-established commercial provider of horoscope interpretations is Equinox, based in the UK and online at www.equinox.uk.com.

If you are seeking a professional astrologer, go to www.NickCampion.com/livelink for a constantly updated directory.

SOFTWARE

There is now some superb astrological software on the market that is enabling astrologers to work with techniques that in the past were too time-consuming and complicated. If you want to do more than just cast a chart, and wish to experiment with a wide range of astrological techniques, look out for the software produced by Janus in New Zealand, Solar Fire in Australia, and Matrix in the USA. It is difficult to say which is best – each has its supporters. But they will all provide a complete package that will enable you to pursue any technique described in this book. You will find up-to-date links to these software packages (and others) through www.NickCampion.com.

EDUCATIONAL PROGRAMS

Information on the changing world of astrological education is kept up to date on the website www.NickCampion.com (go to "Education" on the menu). The broadest and best-known astrological educational programs are run by the Faculty of Astrological Studies in the UK, the National Council for Geocosmic Research in the USA, and, as of July 2000, Kepler College in Seattle. This college offers the first-ever BA in astrological studies in the Western world (with an MA launched in 2002). It's a web-based distance-learning program, although students are expected to attend a weeklong symposium in Seattle once a term. It is also becoming possible to study astrology at university level in the UK. Such courses are not vocational in that they do not train professional astrologers; rather, they investigate astrology from a historical or cultural perspective. Again, you'll find up-to-date details at www.NickCampion.com.

BOOKS

Many books on astrology have small print runs, so are consequently hard to get and often go out of print. All the following titles are recommended. If you have difficulty finding one, try a secondhand book search service (on the web, one is offered through Amazon) – or try your local library.

A general guide to astrology in the context of astronomy, cosmology and myths of the stars is *The New Astrology* by Nicholas Campion and Steve Eddy (Bloomsbury, 1999), and an examination of astrology as a journey through the year is Nicholas Campion's *Zodiac* (Quadrille, 2000). An excellent illustrated book on astrology is Warren Kenton's *Astrology: The Celestial Mirror* (Thames & Hudson, 1974).

If you're interested in books on the planets, a list is given on www.NickCampion.com (refer to "Books" on the main menu). The best technical explanation of the houses is given by Ralph William Holden in *The*

Elements of House Division, published originally by the AFA but now available through the Faculty of Astrological Studies. One of the best guides to the aspects is Sue Tompkins' *Aspects in Astrology* (Rider, 2002). An excellent examination of the use of midpoints is *Working With Astrology* by Michael Harding and Charles Harvey (Arkana, 1990). A detailed set of interpretations for transiting planets is to be found in Robert Hand's *Planets in Transit* (Whitford Press 1976). For composite charts see the same author's *Planets in Composite* (Whitford Press, 1975). For the application of chart dynamics to family relationships, look for *The Astrology of Family Dynamics* by Erin Sullivan (Weiser Books, 2001) and Lynn Bell's *Planetary Threads: Patterns of Relating Among Family and Friends* (CPA Press, 1999 [Lynn Bell's website www.fainc.org.au]). Also, check out two books by Liz Greene: *Astrology for Lovers* (Unwin 1986) and *Relationships and How to Survive Them* (CPA Press), as well as *Love and Sexuality* by Babs Kirby and Janey Stubbs (Element Books, 1992).

If you want to find out about horary astrology, the art of answering precise questions, excellent books include Derek Appleby's *Horary Astrology* (Aquarian Press, 1985) and Barbara H. Waters' *Horary Astrology and the Judgement of Events* (Valhalla, 1973). Olivia Barclay's *Horary Astrology Rediscovered* (Whitford Press, 1990) includes some of the more traditional and, until recently, lost rules for the interpretation of horary charts.

The complete modern work on mundane astrology (the application of astrology to history and politics) is *Mundane Astrology: An introduction to the astrology of nations* by Michael Baigent, Nicholas Campion and Charles Harvey (revised edition, HarperCollins, 1992). This is currently out of print but is available through the Urania Trust (e-mail: urania@globalnet.co.uk). For non-English language editions see www.NickCampion.com. The complete collection of horoscopes for countries is Nicholas Campion's *The Book of World Horoscopes* (Cinnabar Books, 1997). For details of how to order, see www.NickCampion.com.

Jane Ridder-Patrick's *A Handbook of Medical Astrology* (Arkana, 1991) is the best all-round introduction to medical astrology. Graeme Tobyn's *Culpeper's Medicine* (Element Books, 1997) is an excellent examination of traditional western medical astrology, while Michel Gauquelin's *How Cosmic and Atmospheric Energies Influence Your Health* (Aurora Press, 1970) examines the evidence for cosmic influences. Elisabeth Brooke's *A Woman's Book of Herbs* (Women's Press, 1992) gives useful ideas for the astrological use of herbs as tonics and supplements.

Nick Kollerstrom's *Planting by the Moon: A Gardeners' Calendar* is published annually by Prospect Books (Allaleigh House, Blackawton, Totnes, Devon TQ9 7DL, UK). The 1999 and 2000 editions contain extensive discussions of all the evidence on lunar gardening. Kollerstrom also runs the BBC's lunar gardening site at www.bbbc.co.uk/gardening/lunar. Michel Gauquelin's *The Cosmic Clocks* (Astro Computing Services, San Diego 1982) also contains much interesting material about the Moon and biological cycles.

There are a number of excellent introductions to Indian astrology. One is Ronnie Gale Dreyer's *Vedic Astrology* (Samuel Weiser, 1997); another is Komilla Sutton's *The Essentials of Vedic Astrology* (The

Wessex Astrologer, 1999). For the nakshatras see Dennis M. Harness's *Nakshatras*, (Lotus Press, 1999). Most software packages calculate charts in the sidereal zodiac, but to study Indian astrology seriously you will need an ephemeris: *Lahiri's Indian Ephemeris of Planetary Positions* is published annually by the Astro-Research Bureau, Calcutta.

The best, indeed the only, all-around introduction to detailed Chinese astrology is Derek Walters' *Chinese Astrology* (Aquarian Press, 1987). Theodora Lau's *The Handbook of Chinese Horoscopes* (Arrow Books, 1979) was one of the first books on the 12 animal signs to be published in English, and it remains the best. For Tibetan astrology see Philippe Cornu's *Tibetan Astrology* (Shambhala, 1997) and Michael Erlewine's chapter on Tibetan Astrology in Thomas Moore, *Eastern Systems for Western Astrologers* (Samuel Weiser, 1997).

Mayan and Aztec astrology constitutes another entirely different system. The most detailed account of what we know of Mayan cosmology to date is *Maya Cosmos: Three Thousand Years on the Shaman's Path* by David Friedel, Linda Schele, and Joy Parker (William Morrow & Co., 1993). Bruce Scofield's *Day-Signs: Native American Astrology from Ancient Mexico* (One Reed Publications, 1991) is a modern reconstruction of Mayan astrology, while *The Mayan Oracle* by Ariel Spilsbury and Michael Bryner (Bear & Co., 1992) is an imaginative, modern divinatory tool applying the symbols of Mayan astrology.

There are a number of books that deal with the profound issues raised by astrology, but these are probably best left until the subject has been studied for some time. Recommended titles are Liz Greene's *The Astrology of Fate* (originally published by Allan & Unwin in 1984), Dennis Elwell's *The Cosmic Loom* (Urania Trust, 2001), Michael Harding's *Hymns to the Ancient Gods* (Arkana, 1992) and Geoffrey Cornelius's *The Moment of Astrology* (Arkana, 1994).

Nicholas Campion's *Cosmos: a Cultural History of Astrology* published by London Books in 2002, is a comprehensive study of astrology. Campion's *Astrology, History and Apocalypse* (CPA Press, 2000) contains a more general overview of the history of Western astrology.

For summaries of scientific investigations of astrology, see *Astrology: Science or Superstition?* by Hans Eysenck and David Nias (Pelican, 1982) or Percy Seymour's *Astrology: The Evidence of Science* (Penguin-Arkana, 1990).

Astrology has changed considerably over the last 200 years, so if you should become interested in what we know as "traditional" astrology – the astrology practiced before 1700 – look for a copy of William Lilly's *Christian Astrology*, a great compendium of medieval astrology (originally published in 1647, reprinted in 1985 by Regulus Publishing, London). Lastly, Lee Lehman's *Classical Astrology for Modern Living* (Whitford Press 1996) shows how some of these ancient approaches to astrology have a modern application.

GLOSSARY

Ascendant: The degree of the zodiac rising over the eastern horizon.

Aspect: A precise distance between two planets in the zodiac. There are five main aspects – conjunction, sextile, square, trine, and opposition.

Astrology: The use of celestial phenomena, especially the movements of the planets, to attribute meaning to life on Earth, to analyze events and predict the future.

Astronomy: The physical study of celestial phenomena.

Chart: A diagram of the heavens drawn for the time of a particular event; see horoscope.

Cusp: The dividing point between any two signs or houses.

Degree: The basic unit used to measure a circle. The zodiac is divided into 360 degrees.

Descendant: The exact opposite of the Ascendant, i.e., the degree of the zodiac descending over the western horizon.

Ecliptic: The apparent path of the Sun around the Earth.

Electional Astrology: The astrology used to plan the future.

Element: Four different types of sign – Fire, Air, Earth, and Water.

Ephemeris: Table of planetary positions.

Horary Astrology: The astrology used to answer precise questions.

Horoscope: A diagram of the heavens drawn for the time of a particular event. Also known as a chart. When drawn for the moment of birth, it is usually known as a birth chart.

House: One of 12 sections of the horoscope ruling different circumstances and activities.

IC: The Imum Coeli – the nadir, or lowest point, of the horoscope.

Midheaven: The Medium Coeli, usually known as MC – the zenith, or highest point, of the horoscope.

Midpoint: The halfway point between two planets.

Minute: One sixtieth of a degree.

Moon's Nodes: The points at which the Moon's apparent path around the Earth crosses the Sun's apparent path.

Mundane Astrology: The astrology used in politics, history, and general world affairs.

Natal Astrology: The astrology used to analyze personality and make predictions for individuals.

Planet: One of the ten bodies that appear to orbit the Earth: the Sun, the Moon, Mercury, Venus, Mars, Jupiter, Saturn, Uranus, Neptune, and Pluto. In 1977, an eleventh, Chiron, was discovered.

Polarity: The division of the signs of the zodiac into two groups, described as either male or female, or negative or positive.

Progression: The symbolic movement of the planets around the horoscope, used for prediction.

Quality: Three different types of sign – Cardinal, Fixed, and Mutable.

Retrograde: The apparent backward movement of planets in the zodiac.

Rising Sign: The sign of the zodiac rising over the eastern horizon.

Sign: One of 12 divisions of the zodiac – Aries, Taurus, Gemini, Cancer, Leo, Virgo, Libra, Scorpio, Sagittarius, Capricorn, Aquarius, Pisces.

Solstice: The point at which the Sun reaches its furthest extent north and south, usually on June 21 and December 21.

Star: Any physical body in the sky used in astrology. The "fixed" stars are distinguished from the "wandering" stars, or planets.

Synastry: The use of astrology to analyze human relationships through the comparison of horoscopes.

Transit: The movement of planets through the zodiac, used in prediction.

Zodiac: A band of sky extending on either side of the ecliptic.

TABLES

1960

JAN

	1	2	3	4	5	6	7	8	9	10	11	12	13	14	15	16	17	18	19	20	21	22	23	24	25	26	27	28	29	30	31
☉	10♑	11	12	13	14	15	16	17	18	19	20	21	22	23	24	25	26	27	28	29	30	1♒	2	3	4	5	6	7	8	9	10
☽	10♒	25	8♓	22	5♈	17	29	11♉	23	5♊	17	29	11♋	23	5♌	17	30	13♍	26	9♎	22	6♏	20	4♐	19	4♑	19	3♒	18	2♓	16
☿	25♐	26	28	29	1♑	3	4	6	7	9	10	12	13	15	17	18	20	21	23	25	26	28	30	1♒	3	5	6	8	10	11	13
♀	28♏	30	1♐	2	3	4	6	7	8	9	10	12	13	14	15	16	18	19	20	21	22	24	25	26	27	29	30	1♑	2	3	5
♂	20♐	21	22	22	23	24	25	25	26	27	28	28	29	30	1♑	1	2	3	4	4	5	6	7	7	8	9	10	10	11	12	12
	1	6	11	16	21	26	31		1	11	21	31		1	11	21	31		1	16		1	16		1	16		1	11	21	31
♃	19♐	20	21	22	23	24	25	♄	9♑	11	12	13	⚷	24♒	25	26	26	♅	21♌	20	♆	9♏	9	♇	6♍	6	☊	29♍	28	28	27

FEB

	1	2	3	4	5	6	7	8	9	10	11	12	13	14	15	16	17	18	19	20	21	22	23	24	25	26	27	28	29		
☉	11♒	12	13	14	15	16	17	18	19	20	21	22	23	24	25	26	27	28	29	0♓	1	2	3	4	5	6	7	8	9		
☽	30♓	13♈	25	8♉	20	1♊	13	25	7♋	19	1♌	14	27	9♍	22	6♎	19	3♏	16	0♐	15	29	13♑	28	12♒	26	10♓	24	7♈		
☿	15♒	17	18	20	22	24	26	27	29	1♓	3	5	6	8	10	11	13	15	16	18	19	20	21	22	23	24	25	25	26		
♀	6♑	7	8	10	11	12	13	14	16	17	18	19	21	22	23	24	25	27	28	29	0♒	2	3	4	5	7	8	9	10		
♂	13♑	14	15	15	16	17	18	19	19	20	21	22	22	23	24	25	25	26	27	28	28	29	30	1♒	1	2	3	4	4		
	1	6	11	16	21	26			1	11	21			1	11	21			1	16		1	16		1	16		1	11	21	
♃	25♐	26	27	28	29	29		♄	13♑	14	15		⚷	26♒	27	28		♅	19♌	19	♆	9♏	9	♇	5♍	5	☊	27♍	27	26	

MAR

	1	2	3	4	5	6	7	8	9	10	11	12	13	14	15	16	17	18	19	20	21	22	23	24	25	26	27	28	29	30	31
☉	10♓	11	12	13	14	15	16	17	18	19	20	21	22	23	24	25	26	27	28	29	0♈	1	2	3	4	5	6	7	8	9	10
☽	20♈	3♉	15	27	9♊	21	3♋	15	27	10♌	22	5♍	18	2♎	15	29	13♏	27	11♐	26	10♑	24	8♒	22	6♓	19	2♈	16	28	11♉	23
☿	26♓	26	26	25	25	24	24	23	22	21	20	19	18	17	16	16	15	14	14	13	13	12	12	12	12	12	12	13	13	14	14
♀	11♒	13	14	15	16	18	19	20	21	23	24	25	26	27	29	30	1♓	2	4	5	6	7	9	10	11	12	13	15	16	17	18
♂	5♒	6	7	7	8	9	10	11	11	12	13	14	14	15	16	17	17	18	19	20	21	21	22	23	24	24	25	26	27	27	28
	1	6	11	16	21	26	31		1	11	21	31		1	11	21	31		1	16		1	16		1	16		1	11	21	31
♃	30♐	1♑	1	2	2	3	3	♄	16♑	17	17	18	⚷	28♒	29	30	0♓	♅	18♌	18	♆	9♏	9	♇	5♍	4	☊	26♍	25	24	24

APR

	1	2	3	4	5	6	7	8	9	10	11	12	13	14	15	16	17	18	19	20	21	22	23	24	25	26	27	28	29	30	
☉	11♈	12	13	14	15	16	17	18	19	20	21	22	23	24	25	26	27	28	29	30	1♉	2	3	4	5	6	7	8	9	10	
☽	5♊	17	29	11♋	23	5♌	17	30	13♍	26	10♎	24	8♏	23	8♐	22	7♑	21	5♒	19	2♓	16	29	12♈	24	7♉	19	1♊	13	25	
☿	15♓	15	16	17	18	19	19	20	22	23	24	25	26	27	29	30	1♈	3	4	5	7	8	10	11	13	15	16	18	20	21	
♀	20♓	21	22	23	25	26	27	28	29	1♈	2	3	4	6	7	8	9	11	12	13	14	15	17	18	19	20	22	23	24	25	
♂	29♒	30	1♓	1	2	3	4	4	5	6	7	8	8	9	10	11	11	12	13	14	14	15	16	17	18	18	19	20	21	21	
	1	6	11	16	21	26			1	11	21			1	11	21			1	16		1	16		1	16		1	11	21	
♃	3♑	3	3	4	4	4		♄	18♑	18	18		⚷	0♓	1	1		♅	17♌	17	♆	8♏	8	♇	4♍	4	☊	24♍	23	23	

MAY

	1	2	3	4	5	6	7	8	9	10	11	12	13	14	15	16	17	18	19	20	21	22	23	24	25	26	27	28	29	30	31
☉	11♉	12	13	14	15	15	16	17	18	19	20	21	22	23	24	25	26	27	28	29	30	1♊	2	3	4	5	6	7	8	9	10
☽	7♋	19	1♌	13	25	8♍	21	4♎	18	2♏	17	2♐	17	2♑	17	1♒	15	29	13♓	26	9♈	21	4♉	16	28	10♊	22	4♋	16	28	10♌
☿	23♈	25	27	29	1♉	2	4	6	8	10	12	15	17	19	21	23	25	27	30	2♊	4	6	8	11	13	15	17	19	21	23	25
♀	27♈	28	29	0♉	1	3	4	5	6	8	9	10	11	12	14	15	16	17	19	20	21	22	24	25	26	27	28	30	1♊	2	3
♂	22♓	23	24	24	25	26	27	27	28	29	30	1♈	1	2	3	4	4	5	6	7	7	8	9	10	10	11	12	13	13	14	15
	1	6	11	16	21	26	31		1	11	21	31		1	11	21	31		1	16		1	16		1	16		1	11	21	31
♃	3♑	3	3	3	2	2	1	♄	18♑	18	18	18	⚷	2♓	2	2	2	♅	17♌	17	♆	8♏	7	♇	4♍	4	☊	22♍	22	21	21

JUN

	1	2	3	4	5	6	7	8	9	10	11	12	13	14	15	16	17	18	19	20	21	22	23	24	25	26	27	28	29	30	
☉	10♊	11	12	13	14	15	16	17	18	19	20	21	22	23	24	25	26	27	28	29	30	1♋	2	2	3	4	5	6	7	8	
☽	22♌	4♍	16	29	12♎	26	11♏	25	10♐	26	11♑	26	11♒	25	9♓	22	6♈	18	1♉	13	25	7♊	19	1♋	13	25	7♌	18	1♍	13	
☿	27♊	28	0♋	2	4	5	7	9	10	12	13	14	16	17	18	19	20	22	23	24	24	25	26	27	27	28	29	29	29	30	
♀	5♊	6	7	8	10	11	12	13	14	16	17	18	19	21	22	23	24	25	27	28	29	0♋	2	3	4	5	7	8	9	10	
♂	16♈	16	17	18	19	19	20	21	22	22	23	24	25	25	26	27	28	28	29	30	0♉	1	2	3	3	4	5	6	6	7	
	1	6	11	16	21	26			1	11	21			1	11	21			1	16		1	16		1	16		1	11	21	
♃	1♑	0	30♐	29	29	28		♄	18♑	17	16		⚷	2♓	2	2		♅	18♌	18	♆	7♏	7	♇	4♍	4	☊	21♍	20	20	

1960

EPHEMERIS

JUL

	1	2	3	4	5	6	7	8	9	10	11	12	13	14	15	16	17	18	19	20	21	22	23	24	25	26	27	28	29	30	31
☉	9♋	10	11	12	13	14	15	16	17	18	19	20	21	22	22	23	24	25	26	27	28	29	0♌	1	2	3	4	5	6	7	8
☽	25♍	8♎	21	5♏	19	4♐	19	4♑	19	5♒	19	4♓	18	2♈	15	27	10♉	22	4♊	16	28	10♋	22	4♌	16	28	10♍	22	5♎	18	1♏
☿	30♋	0♌	0	0	0	0	30♋	29	29	29	28	28	27	26	26	25	24	24	23	23	22	21	21	21	20	20	20	20	20	20	20
♀	11♋	13	14	15	16	18	19	20	21	23	24	25	26	27	29	30	1♌	2	4	5	6	7	9	10	11	12	13	15	16	17	18
♂	8♉	8	9	10	11	11	12	13	13	14	15	15	16	17	18	18	19	20	20	21	22	22	23	24	24	25	26	27	27	28	29
	1	6	11	16	21	26	31		1	11	21	31		1	11	21	31		1	16		1	16		1	16		1	11	21	31
♃	27♐	27	26	26	25	25	24	♄	16♑	15	14	13	⚷	2♓	2	1	1	♅	19♌	20	♆	6♏	6	♇	4♍	4	☊	19♍	19	18	17

AUG

	1	2	3	4	5	6	7	8	9	10	11	12	13	14	15	16	17	18	19	20	21	22	23	24	25	26	27	28	29	30	31
☉	9♌	10	11	12	13	14	14	15	16	17	18	19	20	21	22	23	24	25	26	27	28	29	30	1♍	2	3	4	5	6	7	8
☽	15♏	29	13♐	28	13♑	28	13♒	28	12♓	26	10♈	23	6♉	19	1♊	13	25	7♋	18	0♌	12	25	7♍	19	2♎	15	28	12♏	25	9♐	23
☿	21♋	21	22	23	23	24	25	26	28	29	0♌	2	3	5	7	8	10	12	14	16	18	20	22	24	26	28	30	2♍	4	6	8
♀	20♌	21	22	23	25	26	27	28	29	1♍	2	3	4	6	7	8	9	11	12	13	14	15	17	18	19	20	22	23	24	25	27
♂	29♉	30	1♊	1	2	3	3	4	4	5	6	6	7	8	8	9	10	10	11	11	12	13	13	14	15	15	16	16	17	18	18
	1	6	11	16	21	26	31		1	11	21	31		1	11	21	31		1	16		1	16		1	16		1	11	21	31
♃	24♐	24	24	24	24	24	24	♄	13♑	13	12	12	⚷	1♓	0	30♒	29	♅	21♌	22	♆	6♏	7	♇	5♍	5	☊	17♍	17	16	16

SEP

	1	2	3	4	5	6	7	8	9	10	11	12	13	14	15	16	17	18	19	20	21	22	23	24	25	26	27	28	29	30	
☉	9♍	10	10	11	12	13	14	15	16	17	18	19	20	21	22	23	24	25	26	27	28	29	30	1♎	2	3	4	5	6	7	
☽	8♑	22	7♒	22	6♓	20	4♈	18	1♉	14	27	9♊	21	3♋	15	27	9♌	21	3♍	16	28	11♎	25	8♏	22	6♐	20	4♑	18	3♒	
☿	10♍	11	13	15	17	19	21	23	24	26	28	30	1♎	3	5	6	8	9	11	13	14	16	17	19	20	22	23	25	26	28	
♀	28♍	29	0♎	1	3	4	5	6	8	9	10	11	13	14	15	16	17	19	20	21	22	24	25	26	27	29	30	1♏	2	3	
♂	19♊	19	20	21	21	22	22	23	23	24	25	25	26	26	27	27	28	28	29	29	30	0♋	1	1	2	2	3	3	4	4	
	1	6	11	16	21	26			1	11	21			1	11	21			1	16		1	16		1	16		1	11	21	
♃	24♐	24	24	25	25	26		♄	12♑	12	12		⚷	29♒	29	28		♅	23♌	23	♆	7♏	7	♇	6♍	6	☊	16♍	15	15	

OCT

	1	2	3	4	5	6	7	8	9	10	11	12	13	14	15	16	17	18	19	20	21	22	23	24	25	26	27	28	29	30	31
☉	8♎	9	10	11	12	13	14	15	16	17	18	19	20	21	22	23	24	25	26	27	28	29	30	1♏	2	3	4	5	6	7	8
☽	17♒	1♓	15	29	13♈	26	9♉	22	5♊	17	29	11♋	23	4♌	16	29	11♍	24	7♎	20	4♏	18	2♐	17	1♑	15	29	14♒	27	11♓	25
☿	29♎	0♏	2	3	4	6	7	8	10	11	12	13	14	15	16	17	18	19	20	21	22	23	23	23	24	24	24	24	24	24	23
♀	5♏	6	7	8	10	11	12	13	14	16	17	18	19	21	22	23	24	25	27	28	29	0♐	2	3	4	5	6	8	9	10	11
♂	5♋	5	6	6	7	7	8	8	8	9	9	10	10	10	11	11	12	12	12	13	13	13	14	14	14	15	15	15	15	16	16
	1	6	11	16	21	26	31		1	11	21	31		1	11	21	31		1	16		1	16		1	16		1	11	21	31
♃	26♐	27	28	28	29	30	1♑	♄	12♑	12	13	13	⚷	28♒	28	28	27	♅	24♌	25	♆	8♏	8	♇	7♍	7	☊	14♍	14	13	13

NOV

	1	2	3	4	5	6	7	8	9	10	11	12	13	14	15	16	17	18	19	20	21	22	23	24	25	26	27	28	29	30	
☉	9♏	10	11	12	13	14	15	16	17	18	19	20	21	22	23	24	25	26	27	28	29	30	1♐	2	3	4	5	6	7	8	
☽	8♈	22	5♉	17	0♊	13	25	7♋	19	0♌	12	24	6♍	19	2♎	15	28	12♏	27	11♐	26	11♑	26	10♒	24	8♓	22	5♈	18	1♉	
☿	23♏	22	21	20	19	18	16	15	14	12	11	10	9	9	8	8	8	8	8	9	9	10	11	12	13	14	15	16	18	19	
♀	13♐	14	15	16	17	19	20	21	22	23	25	26	27	28	30	1♑	2	3	4	6	7	8	9	10	12	13	14	15	16	18	
♂	16♋	16	17	17	17	17	17	18	18	18	18	18	18	18	18	19	19	19	19	19	19	19	19	19	19	18	18	18	18	18	
	1	6	11	16	21	26			1	11	21			1	11	21			1	16		1	16		1	16		1	11	21	
♃	1♑	2	3	4	5	6		♄	14♑	14	15		⚷	27♒	27	28		♅	25♌	26	♆	9♏	9	♇	8♍	8	☊	13♍	12	12	

DEC

	1	2	3	4	5	6	7	8	9	10	11	12	13	14	15	16	17	18	19	20	21	22	23	24	25	26	27	28	29	30	31
☉	9♐	10	11	12	13	14	15	16	17	18	19	20	21	22	23	24	25	26	27	28	29	0♑	1	2	3	4	5	6	7	8	9
☽	14♉	26	9♊	21	3♋	15	27	9♌	20	2♍	14	27	9♎	23	6♏	20	5♐	20	5♑	20	5♒	20	4♓	18	2♈	15	28	11♉	23	6♊	18
☿	20♏	22	23	25	26	27	29	0♐	2	3	5	6	8	9	11	12	14	16	17	19	20	22	23	25	26	28	30	1♑	3	4	6
♀	19♑	20	21	22	24	25	26	27	28	30	1♒	2	3	4	5	7	8	9	10	11	13	14	15	16	17	18	20	21	22	23	24
♂	18♋	18	18	17	17	17	17	17	16	16	16	15	15	15	15	14	14	14	13	13	12	12	12	11	11	11	10	10	9	9	9
	1	6	11	16	21	26	31		1	11	21	31		1	11	21	31		1	16		1	16		1	16		1	11	21	31
♃	7♑	8	9	10	12	13	14	♄	16♑	17	18	19	⚷	28♒	28	28	29	♅	26♌	26	♆	10♏	10	♇	8♍	8	☊	11♍	10	10	9

1961

JAN

	1	2	3	4	5	6	7	8	9	10	11	12	13	14	15	16	17	18	19	20	21	22	23	24	25	26	27	28	29	30	31
☉	10♑	11	12	13	14	15	16	17	18	20	21	22	23	24	25	26	27	28	29	30	1♒	2	3	4	5	6	7	8	9	10	11
☽	30♊	12♋	24	5♌	17	29	11♍	23	5♎	18	1♏	14	28	13♐	28	13♑	28	13♒	28	13♓	27	11♈	25	8♉	20	3♊	15	27	9♋	21	2♌
☿	7♑	9	11	12	14	15	17	19	20	22	24	25	27	29	0♒	2	4	5	7	9	11	12	14	16	17	19	21	22	24	26	27
♀	25♒	26	28	29	30	1♓	2	3	4	5	7	8	9	10	11	12	13	14	15	16	17	19	20	21	22	23	24	25	26	27	28
♂	8♋	8	7	7	7	6	6	5	5	5	4	4	4	4	3	3	3	2	2	2	2	1	1	1	1	1	1	1	0	0	0
	1	6	11	16	21	26	31		1	11	21	31		1	11	21	31		1	16		1	16		1	16		1	11	21	31
♃	14♑	15	16	18	19	20	21	♄	20♑	21	22	23	⚷	29♒	29	30	1♓	♅	25♌	25	♆	11♏	11	♇	8♍	8	☊	9♍	9	8	8

FEB

	1	2	3	4	5	6	7	8	9	10	11	12	13	14	15	16	17	18	19	20	21	22	23	24	25	26	27	28			
☉	12♒	13	14	15	16	17	18	19	20	21	22	23	24	25	26	27	28	29	0♓	1	2	3	4	5	6	7	8	9			
☽	14♌	26	8♍	20	2♎	15	27	10♏	24	7♐	22	6♑	21	6♒	21	6♓	21	6♈	20	3♉	16	29	11♊	24	6♋	17	29	11♌			
☿	29♒	0♓	2	3	4	5	6	7	8	8	9	9	9	9	9	8	8	7	6	5	4	3	2	1	30♒	29	28	27			
♀	29♓	30	1♈	2	3	4	5	6	6	7	8	9	10	11	12	13	14	14	15	16	17	17	18	19	20	20	21	22			
♂	0♋	0	0	0	0	30♊	30	0♋	0	0	0	0	0	0	0	1	1	1	1	1	1	1	2	2	2	2	2	3			
	1	6	11	16	21	26			1	11	21			1	11	21			1	16		1	16		1	16		1	11	21	
♃	21♑	22	23	25	26	27		♄	23♑	24	25		⚷	1♓	1	2		♅	24♌	24	♆	11♏	11	♇	7♍	7	☊	8♍	7	7	

MAR

	1	2	3	4	5	6	7	8	9	10	11	12	13	14	15	16	17	18	19	20	21	22	23	24	25	26	27	28	29	30	31
☉	10♓	11	12	13	14	15	16	17	18	19	20	21	22	23	24	25	26	27	28	29	0♈	1	2	3	4	5	6	7	8	9	10
☽	23♌	5♍	17	29	12♎	24	7♏	20	4♐	18	2♑	16	0♒	15	30	14♓	29	13♈	27	11♉	24	7♊	20	2♋	14	26	7♌	19	1♍	13	26
☿	26♒	26	25	25	25	24	24	24	25	25	25	26	26	27	27	28	29	30	1♓	1	2	3	5	6	7	8	9	10	12	13	14
♀	22♈	23	24	24	25	25	26	26	26	27	27	28	28	28	28	29	29	29	29	29	29	29	29	29	29	29	28	28	28	27	27
♂	3♋	3	3	4	4	4	4	5	5	5	6	6	6	7	7	7	8	8	8	9	9	9	10	10	11	11	11	12	12	13	13
	1	6	11	16	21	26	31		1	11	21	31		1	11	21	31		1	16		1	16		1	16		1	11	21	31
♃	27♑	28	29	0♒	1	2	3	♄	26♑	27	28	29	⚷	3♓	3	4	4	♅	23♌	22	♆	11♏	11	♇	7♍	6	☊	6♍	6	5	5

APR

	1	2	3	4	5	6	7	8	9	10	11	12	13	14	15	16	17	18	19	20	21	22	23	24	25	26	27	28	29	30	
☉	11♈	12	13	14	15	16	17	18	19	20	21	22	23	24	25	26	27	28	29	30	1♉	2	3	4	5	6	6	7	8	9	
☽	8♎	21	4♏	17	1♐	14	28	12♑	26	11♒	25	9♓	24	8♈	22	6♉	19	2♊	15	28	10♋	22	4♌	15	27	9♍	21	4♎	17	30	
☿	16♓	17	19	20	22	23	25	26	28	29	1♈	3	4	6	8	10	11	13	15	17	19	21	23	25	27	29	1♉	3	5	7	
♀	27♈	26	26	25	25	24	23	23	22	21	21	20	20	19	18	18	17	17	16	16	15	15	14	14	14	14	13	13	13	13	
♂	13♋	14	14	15	15	16	16	16	17	17	18	18	19	19	20	20	21	21	22	22	22	23	23	24	24	25	25	26	26	27	
	1	6	11	16	21	26			1	11	21			1	11	21			1	16		1	16		1	16		1	11	21	
♃	3♒	3	4	5	5	6		♄	29♑	29	30		⚷	5♓	5	6		♅	22♌	22	♆	11♏	10	♇	6♍	6	☊	5♍	4	4	

MAY

	1	2	3	4	5	6	7	8	9	10	11	12	13	14	15	16	17	18	19	20	21	22	23	24	25	26	27	28	29	30	31
☉	10♉	11	12	13	14	15	16	17	18	19	20	21	22	23	24	25	26	27	28	29	30	1♊	2	3	4	5	5	6	7	8	9
☽	13♏	27	11♐	25	9♑	23	7♒	22	6♓	20	3♈	17	1♉	14	28	10♊	23	6♋	18	30	11♌	23	5♍	17	29	12♎	25	8♏	22	6♐	20
☿	9♉	11	14	16	18	20	22	24	26	29	1♊	3	5	7	9	10	12	14	16	18	19	21	22	24	25	27	28	29	0♋	1	3
♀	13♈	13	13	13	13	13	13	13	14	14	14	15	15	15	16	16	17	17	18	18	19	19	20	21	21	22	23	23	24	25	25
♂	27♋	28	28	29	29	30	0♌	1	2	2	3	3	4	4	5	5	6	6	7	7	8	8	9	10	10	11	11	12	12	13	13
	1	6	11	16	21	26	31		1	11	21	31		1	11	21	31		1	16		1	16		1	16		1	11	21	31
♃	6♒	7	7	7	7	7	7	♄	30♑	30	30	29	⚷	6♓	6	7	7	♅	22♌	22	♆	10♏	10	♇	6♍	6	☊	3♍	2	2	1

JUN

	1	2	3	4	5	6	7	8	9	10	11	12	13	14	15	16	17	18	19	20	21	22	23	24	25	26	27	28	29	30	
☉	10♊	11	12	13	14	15	16	17	18	19	20	21	22	23	24	25	26	27	27	28	29	0♋	1	2	3	4	5	6	7	8	
☽	5♑	19	4♒	18	2♓	17	0♈	14	27	11♉	24	7♊	19	2♋	14	26	8♌	20	1♍	13	25	7♎	20	3♏	16	30	14♐	29	14♑	29	
☿	4♋	4	5	6	7	8	8	9	9	10	10	10	10	10	10	10	10	10	10	9	9	9	8	8	7	6	6	5	5	4	
♀	26♈	27	28	29	29	0♉	1	2	3	4	4	5	6	7	8	9	10	11	12	13	14	15	16	17	18	19	20	21	22	23	
♂	14♌	15	15	16	16	17	17	18	18	19	20	20	21	21	22	22	23	24	24	25	25	26	26	27	28	28	29	29	0♍	1	
	1	6	11	16	21	26			1	11	21			1	11	21			1	16		1	16		1	16		1	11	21	
♃	7♒	7	7	6	6	6		♄	29♑	29	29		⚷	7♓	7	7		♅	22♌	23	♆	9♏	9	♇	6♍	6	☊	1♍	1	0	

1961

JUL

	1	2	3	4	5	6	7	8	9	10	11	12	13	14	15	16	17	18	19	20	21	22	23	24	25	26	27	28	29	30	31
☉	9♋	10	11	12	13	14	15	16	17	17	18	19	20	21	22	23	24	25	26	27	28	29	30	1♌	2	3	4	5	6	7	8
☽	13♒	28	13♓	27	11♈	24	8♉	21	3♊	16	28	11♋	23	4♌	16	28	10♍	22	4♎	16	28	11♏	24	8♐	22	7♑	22	7♒	22	7♓	22
☿	4♋	3	3	2	2	2	1	1	1	1	2	2	2	3	3	4	4	5	6	7	8	9	10	11	13	14	16	17	19	21	22
♀	24♉	25	26	27	28	29	30	1♊	2	3	4	5	6	7	8	9	10	12	13	14	15	16	17	18	19	20	21	23	24	25	26
♂	1♍	2	2	3	4	4	5	5	6	7	7	8	8	9	10	10	11	11	12	13	13	14	14	15	16	16	17	17	18	19	19
	1	6	11	16	21	26	31		1	11	21	31		1	11	21	31		1	16		1	16		1	16		1	11	21	31
♃	5♒	5	4	3	3	2	2	♄	28♑	27	26	26	⚷	6♓	6	6	6	♅	23♌	24	♆	9♏	9	♇	6♍	6	☊	30♌	29	29	28

AUG

	1	2	3	4	5	6	7	8	9	10	11	12	13	14	15	16	17	18	19	20	21	22	23	24	25	26	27	28	29	30	31
☉	9♌	9	10	11	12	13	14	15	16	17	18	19	20	21	22	23	24	25	26	27	28	29	30	1♍	2	3	3	4	5	6	7
☽	7♈	21	4♉	18	0♊	13	25	8♋	20	1♌	13	25	7♍	19	1♎	13	25	7♏	20	3♐	17	1♑	16	0♒	15	1♓	16	1♈	15	30	13♉
☿	24♋	26	28	30	2♌	4	6	8	10	12	14	16	18	20	22	24	26	28	0♍	2	4	6	8	10	12	13	15	17	19	20	22
♀	27♊	28	29	0♋	2	3	4	5	6	7	8	10	11	12	13	14	15	16	18	19	20	21	22	23	25	26	27	28	29	0♌	2
♂	20♍	21	21	22	22	23	24	24	25	26	26	27	27	28	29	29	30	1♎	1	2	3	3	4	4	5	6	6	7	8	8	9
	1	6	11	16	21	26	31		1	11	21	31		1	11	21	31		1	16		1	16		1	16		1	11	21	31
♃	1♒	1	0	30♑	29	29	28	♄	26♑	25	24	24	⚷	5♓	5	5	4	♅	25♌	26	♆	9♏	9	♇	7♍	7	☊	28♌	28	27	27

SEP

	1	2	3	4	5	6	7	8	9	10	11	12	13	14	15	16	17	18	19	20	21	22	23	24	25	26	27	28	29	30
☉	8♍	9	10	11	12	13	14	15	16	17	18	19	20	21	22	23	24	25	26	27	28	29	30	1♎	2	3	4	5	6	7
☽	27♉	10♊	22	5♋	17	29	10♌	22	4♍	16	28	10♎	22	4♏	17	0♐	13	27	11♑	25	9♒	24	9♓	24	9♈	24	8♉	22	5♊	18
☿	24♍	25	27	29	0♎	2	3	5	6	8	9	11	12	13	15	16	18	19	20	21	23	24	25	26	27	28	29	0♏	1	2
♀	3♌	4	5	6	8	9	10	11	12	14	15	16	17	18	20	21	22	23	24	26	27	28	29	0♍	2	3	4	5	7	8
♂	10♎	10	11	12	12	13	13	14	15	15	16	17	17	18	19	19	20	21	21	22	23	23	24	25	25	26	27	27	28	29
	1	6	11	16	21	26			1	11	21			1	11	21			1	16		1	16		1	16		1	11	21
♃	28♑	28	28	27	27	27		♄	24♑	23	23		⚷	4♓	4	3		♅	27♌	28	♆	9♏	9	♇	8♍	8	☊	26♌	26	25

OCT

	1	2	3	4	5	6	7	8	9	10	11	12	13	14	15	16	17	18	19	20	21	22	23	24	25	26	27	28	29	30	31
☉	8♎	9	10	11	12	12	13	14	15	16	17	18	19	20	21	22	23	24	25	26	27	28	29	0♏	1	2	3	4	5	6	7
☽	1♋	13	25	7♌	19	1♍	12	24	7♎	19	1♏	14	27	10♐	24	7♑	21	5♒	19	4♓	18	3♈	17	2♉	16	30	13♊	26	9♋	21	3♌
☿	3♏	4	5	6	6	7	7	8	8	8	8	8	8	7	7	6	6	5	4	3	1	0	29♎	28	26	25	24	24	23	23	22
♀	9♍	10	11	13	14	15	16	18	19	20	21	22	24	25	26	27	29	30	1♎	2	4	5	6	7	9	10	11	12	13	15	16
♂	29♎	0♏	1	1	2	3	4	4	5	6	6	7	8	8	9	10	10	11	12	12	13	14	15	15	16	17	17	18	19	19	20
	1	6	11	16	21	26	31		1	11	21	31		1	11	21	31		1	16		1	16		1	16		1	11	21	31
♃	27♑	28	28	28	29	29	30	♄	23♑	23	24	24	⚷	3♓	2	2	2	♅	29♌	29	♆	10♏	10	♇	9♍	9	☊	25♌	24	24	23

NOV

	1	2	3	4	5	6	7	8	9	10	11	12	13	14	15	16	17	18	19	20	21	22	23	24	25	26	27	28	29	30
☉	8♏	9	10	11	12	13	14	15	16	17	18	19	20	21	22	23	24	25	26	27	28	29	0♐	1	2	3	5	6	7	8
☽	15♌	27	9♍	21	3♎	15	28	10♏	23	7♐	20	4♑	18	2♒	16	30	14♓	28	12♈	26	10♉	24	8♊	21	4♋	17	29	11♌	23	5♍
☿	22♎	22	23	23	24	25	26	27	28	29	0♏	1	3	4	5	7	8	10	11	13	14	16	18	19	21	22	24	25	27	29
♀	17♎	18	20	21	22	23	25	26	27	28	30	1♏	2	3	5	6	7	8	10	11	12	13	15	16	17	19	20	21	22	24
♂	21♏	22	22	23	24	24	25	26	26	27	28	29	29	0♐	1	1	2	3	4	4	5	6	7	7	8	9	9	10	11	12
	1	6	11	16	21	26			1	11	21			1	11	21			1	16		1	16		1	16		1	11	21
♃	30♑	0♒	1	2	2	3		♄	24♑	25	26		⚷	2♓	2	2		♅	30♌	0♍	♆	11♏	12	♇	10♍	10	☊	23♌	23	22

DEC

	1	2	3	4	5	6	7	8	9	10	11	12	13	14	15	16	17	18	19	20	21	22	23	24	25	26	27	28	29	30	31
☉	9♐	10	11	12	13	14	15	16	17	18	19	20	21	22	23	24	25	26	27	28	29	30	1♑	2	3	4	5	6	7	8	9
☽	17♍	28	11♎	23	6♏	19	2♐	16	30	14♑	28	12♒	27	11♓	25	9♈	23	6♉	20	3♊	17	30	12♋	25	7♌	19	1♍	13	24	6♎	18
☿	0♐	2	3	5	6	8	9	11	13	14	16	17	19	20	22	24	25	27	28	30	2♑	3	5	6	8	10	11	13	14	16	18
♀	25♏	26	27	29	30	1♐	2	4	5	6	7	9	10	11	12	14	15	16	17	19	20	21	22	24	25	26	27	29	30	1♑	3
♂	12♐	13	14	15	15	16	17	18	18	19	20	20	21	22	23	23	24	25	26	26	27	28	29	29	0♑	1	2	2	3	4	5
	1	6	11	16	21	26	31		1	11	21	31		1	11	21	31		1	16		1	16		1	16		1	11	21	31
♃	4♒	5	6	7	8	9	10	♄	26♑	27	28	30	⚷	2♓	2	3	3	♅	1♍	1	♆	12♏	13	♇	10♍	10	☊	22♌	21	21	20

1962

JAN

	1	2	3	4	5	6	7	8	9	10	11	12	13	14	15	16	17	18	19	20	21	22	23	24	25	26	27	28	29	30	31
☉	10♑	11	12	13	14	15	16	17	18	19	20	21	22	23	24	25	26	27	28	29	0♒	1	3	4	5	6	7	8	9	10	11
☽	1♏	13	26	10♐	24	8♑	23	7♒	22	7♓	21	6♈	20	3♉	17	0♊	13	26	9♋	21	3♌	15	27	9♍	21	3♎	14	26	9♏	21	4♐
☿	19♑	21	22	24	26	27	29	1♒	2	4	5	7	8	10	11	13	14	16	17	18	19	20	21	22	22	23	23	23	23	22	22
♀	4♑	5	6	8	9	10	11	13	14	15	16	18	19	20	21	23	24	25	26	28	29	0♒	1	3	4	5	6	8	9	10	11
♂	5♑	6	7	8	9	9	10	11	12	12	13	14	15	15	16	17	18	18	19	20	21	22	22	23	24	25	25	26	27	28	28
	1	6	11	16	21	26	31		1	11	21	31		1	11	21	31		1	16		1	16		1	16		1	11	21	31
♃	10♒	12	13	14	15	16	17	♄	30♑	1♒	2	3	⚷	3♓	4	4	5	♅	0♍	30♌	♆	13♏	13	♇	10♍	10	☊	20♌	19	19	18

FEB

	1	2	3	4	5	6	7	8	9	10	11	12	13	14	15	16	17	18	19	20	21	22	23	24	25	26	27	28		
☉	12♒	13	14	15	16	17	18	19	20	21	22	23	24	25	26	27	28	29	30	1♓	2	3	4	5	6	7	8	9		
☽	18♐	2♑	16	1♒	16	1♓	16	1♈	15	30	14♉	27	10♊	23	6♋	18	30	12♌	24	6♍	18	29	11♎	23	5♏	18	0♐	13		
☿	21♒	20	19	18	17	16	15	13	12	11	10	9	9	8	8	7	7	7	7	7	8	8	9	9	10	10	11	12		
♀	13♒	14	15	17	18	19	20	22	23	24	25	27	28	29	0♓	2	3	4	5	7	8	9	10	12	13	14	15	17		
♂	29♑	0♒	1	2	2	3	4	5	5	6	7	8	9	9	10	11	12	12	13	14	15	16	16	17	18	19	20	20		
	1	6	11	16	21	26			1	11	21			1	11	21			1	16		1	16		1	16		1	11	21
♃	18♒	19	20	21	22	24		♄	3♒	5	6		⚷	5♓	5	6		♅	29♌	29	♆	13♏	13	♇	10♍	9	☊	18♌	18	17

MAR

	1	2	3	4	5	6	7	8	9	10	11	12	13	14	15	16	17	18	19	20	21	22	23	24	25	26	27	28	29	30	31
☉	10♓	11	12	13	14	15	16	17	18	19	20	21	22	23	24	25	26	27	28	29	30	1♈	2	3	4	5	6	7	8	9	10
☽	26♐	10♑	24	9♒	24	9♓	24	9♈	24	9♉	23	6♊	20	2♋	15	27	9♌	21	3♍	14	26	8♎	20	2♏	15	27	10♐	22	6♑	19	3♒
☿	13♒	14	15	16	17	18	19	20	21	23	24	25	27	28	29	1♓	2	4	5	7	8	10	11	13	14	16	18	19	21	23	24
♀	18♓	19	20	22	23	24	25	27	28	29	0♈	2	3	4	5	7	8	9	10	11	13	14	15	16	18	19	20	21	23	24	25
♂	21♒	22	23	23	24	25	26	27	27	28	29	30	1♓	1	2	3	4	4	5	6	7	8	8	9	10	11	12	12	13	14	15
	1	6	11	16	21	26	31		1	11	21	31		1	11	21	31		1	16		1	16		1	16		1	11	21	31
♃	24♒	26	27	28	29	0♓	1	♄	7♒	8	8	9	⚷	7♓	7	8	8	♅	28♌	27	♆	13♏	13	♇	9♍	8	☊	17♌	16	16	15

APR

	1	2	3	4	5	6	7	8	9	10	11	12	13	14	15	16	17	18	19	20	21	22	23	24	25	26	27	28	29	30
☉	11♈	12	13	14	15	16	17	18	19	20	21	22	23	24	25	26	27	27	28	29	0♉	1	2	3	4	5	6	7	8	9
☽	17♒	2♓	17	2♈	17	2♉	17	1♊	15	28	11♋	24	6♌	18	30	11♍	23	5♎	17	29	11♏	24	7♐	19	3♑	16	29	13♒	27	12♓
☿	26♓	28	30	2♈	3	5	7	9	11	13	15	17	19	21	23	25	28	30	2♉	4	6	8	10	12	14	16	18	20	22	24
♀	26♈	28	29	0♉	1	3	4	5	6	7	9	10	11	12	14	15	16	17	19	20	21	22	23	25	26	27	28	30	1♊	2
♂	15♓	16	17	18	19	19	20	21	22	22	23	24	25	26	26	27	28	29	29	0♈	1	2	3	3	4	5	6	6	7	8
	1	6	11	16	21	26			1	11	21			1	11	21			1	16		1	16		1	16		1	11	21
♃	1♓	2	3	4	5	6		♄	9♒	10	11		⚷	9♓	9	10		♅	27♌	27	♆	13♏	13	♇	8♍	8	☊	15♌	15	14

MAY

	1	2	3	4	5	6	7	8	9	10	11	12	13	14	15	16	17	18	19	20	21	22	23	24	25	26	27	28	29	30	31
☉	10♉	11	12	13	14	15	16	17	18	19	20	21	22	23	24	25	26	27	28	29	29	0♊	1	2	3	4	5	6	7	8	9
☽	26♓	11♈	26	11♉	25	9♊	23	6♋	19	2♌	14	26	8♍	20	1♎	13	26	8♏	20	3♐	16	29	13♑	26	10♒	24	8♓	22	6♈	21	5♉
☿	26♉	28	30	1♊	3	4	6	7	9	10	11	12	13	14	15	16	17	18	18	19	19	20	20	20	20	20	20	20	20	20	20
♀	3♊	4	6	7	8	9	10	12	13	14	15	17	18	19	20	21	23	24	25	26	27	29	30	1♋	2	3	5	6	7	8	9
♂	9♈	9	10	11	12	13	13	14	15	16	16	17	18	19	19	20	21	22	22	23	24	25	25	26	27	28	29	29	0♉	1	2
	1	6	11	16	21	26	31		1	11	21	31		1	11	21	31		1	16		1	16		1	16		1	11	21	31
♃	7♓	8	9	9	10	11	11	♄	11♒	11	11	11	⚷	10♓	10	11	11	♅	26♌	26	♆	12♏	12	♇	8♍	8	☊	14♌	13	13	12

JUN

	1	2	3	4	5	6	7	8	9	10	11	12	13	14	15	16	17	18	19	20	21	22	23	24	25	26	27	28	29	30
☉	10♊	11	12	13	14	15	16	17	18	19	20	21	22	22	23	24	25	26	27	28	29	0♋	1	2	3	4	5	6	7	8
☽	20♉	4♊	18	1♋	14	27	10♌	22	4♍	16	28	9♎	22	4♏	16	29	12♐	25	9♑	23	7♒	21	5♓	19	3♈	17	1♉	15	29	13♊
☿	19♊	19	18	18	17	17	16	16	15	15	14	14	13	13	13	12	12	12	12	12	12	12	12	13	13	14	14	15	15	16
♀	11♋	12	13	14	15	17	18	19	20	21	23	24	25	26	27	29	30	1♌	2	3	4	6	7	8	9	10	11	13	14	15
♂	2♉	3	4	4	5	6	7	7	8	9	10	10	11	12	13	13	14	15	16	16	17	18	18	19	20	21	21	22	23	23
	1	6	11	16	21	26			1	11	21			1	11	21			1	16		1	16		1	16		1	11	21
♃	11♓	12	12	12	12	13		♄	11♒	11	11		⚷	11♓	11	11		♅	27♌	27	♆	11♏	11	♇	8♍	8	☊	12♌	11	11

EPHEMERIS

1962

JUL

	1	2	3	4	5	6	7	8	9	10	11	12	13	14	15	16	17	18	19	20	21	22	23	24	25	26	27	28	29	30	31
☉	9♋	10	11	12	13	13	14	15	16	17	18	19	20	21	22	23	24	25	26	27	28	29	30	1♌	2	3	3	4	5	6	7
☽	26♊	10♋	23	5♌	18	30	12♍	24	6♎	17	29	12♏	24	7♐	20	4♑	18	2♒	16	1♓	15	30	14♈	28	12♉	26	10♊	23	6♋	19	1♌
☿	17♊	18	19	20	21	22	24	25	26	28	29	1♋	3	4	6	8	10	12	14	16	18	20	22	24	26	28	0♌	3	5	7	9
♀	16♌	17	19	20	21	22	23	24	25	27	28	29	0♍	1	2	4	5	6	7	8	9	10	11	13	14	15	16	17	18	19	20
♂	24♉	25	26	26	27	28	28	29	30	1♊	1	2	3	3	4	5	5	6	7	8	8	9	10	10	11	12	12	13	14	14	15
	1	6	11	16	21	26	31		1	11	21	31		1	11	21	31		1	16		1	16		1	16		1	11	21	31
♃	13♓	13	13	12	12	12	11	♄	10♒	10	9	8	⚷	11♓	11	10	10	♅	28♌	29	♆	11♏	11	♇	8♍	8	☊	10♌	10	9	9

AUG

	1	2	3	4	5	6	7	8	9	10	11	12	13	14	15	16	17	18	19	20	21	22	23	24	25	26	27	28	29	30	31
☉	8♌	9	10	11	12	13	14	15	16	17	18	19	20	21	22	23	24	25	26	26	27	28	29	0♍	1	2	3	4	5	6	7
☽	14♌	26	8♍	20	2♎	14	26	8♏	20	2♐	15	28	12♑	26	10♒	25	10♓	25	10♈	24	9♉	23	7♊	20	3♋	16	28	11♌	23	5♍	17
☿	11♌	13	15	17	19	21	23	25	27	29	0♍	2	4	6	7	9	11	12	14	16	17	19	20	22	23	25	26	28	29	0♎	2
♀	22♍	23	24	25	26	27	28	29	0♎	1	2	4	5	6	7	8	9	10	11	12	13	14	15	16	17	18	19	20	21	22	23
♂	16♊	16	17	18	18	19	20	21	21	22	22	23	24	24	25	26	26	27	28	28	29	30	0♋	1	2	2	3	4	4	5	5
	1	6	11	16	21	26	31		1	11	21	31		1	11	21	31		1	16		1	16		1	16		1	11	21	31
♃	11♓	11	10	10	9	8	8	♄	8♒	7	7	6	⚷	10♓	9	9	9	♅	29♌	0♍	♆	11♏	11	♇	9♍	9	☊	9♌	8	8	7

SEP

	1	2	3	4	5	6	7	8	9	10	11	12	13	14	15	16	17	18	19	20	21	22	23	24	25	26	27	28	29	30
☉	8♍	9	10	11	12	13	14	15	16	17	18	19	20	21	22	23	24	25	26	27	28	29	29	0♎	1	2	3	4	5	6
☽	29♍	10♎	22	4♏	16	28	11♐	23	6♑	20	4♒	18	3♓	18	3♈	19	4♉	18	3♊	16	30	13♋	25	8♌	20	2♍	14	25	7♎	19
☿	3♎	4	6	7	8	9	10	11	13	14	15	15	16	17	18	19	19	20	20	21	21	22	22	22	22	22	21	21	20	20
♀	24♎	25	26	27	28	29	30	1♏	2	3	4	5	5	6	7	8	9	10	11	11	12	13	14	15	15	16	17	18	18	19
♂	6♋	7	7	8	9	9	10	10	11	12	12	13	13	14	15	15	16	16	17	18	18	19	19	20	21	21	22	22	23	23
	1	6	11	16	21	26			1	11	21			1	11	21			1	16		1	16		1	16		1	11	21
♃	8♓	7	6	6	5	5		♄	6♒	5	5		⚷	9♓	8	8		♅	1♍	2	♆	11♏	11	♇	10♍	10	☊	7♌	7	6

OCT

	1	2	3	4	5	6	7	8	9	10	11	12	13	14	15	16	17	18	19	20	21	22	23	24	25	26	27	28	29	30	31
☉	7♎	8	9	10	11	12	13	14	15	16	17	18	19	20	21	22	23	24	25	26	27	28	29	0♏	1	2	3	4	5	6	7
☽	1♏	13	25	7♐	20	2♑	15	29	12♒	27	11♓	26	12♈	27	12♉	27	11♊	25	9♋	22	4♌	17	29	11♍	22	4♎	16	28	10♏	22	4♐
☿	19♎	18	17	16	15	14	13	11	10	9	8	8	7	7	7	7	7	7	8	8	9	10	11	12	13	15	16	17	19	20	22
♀	20♏	20	21	21	22	23	23	24	24	25	25	25	26	26	26	27	27	27	27	27	28	28	28	28	28	27	27	27	27	27	26
♂	24♋	25	25	26	26	27	27	28	28	29	29	0♌	1	1	2	2	3	3	4	4	5	5	6	6	7	7	8	8	9	9	9
	1	6	11	16	21	26	31		1	11	21	31		1	11	21	31		1	16		1	16		1	16		1	11	21	31
♃	4♓	4	3	3	3	3	3	♄	5♒	5	5	5	⚷	7♓	7	6	6	♅	3♍	4	♆	12♏	12	♇	11♍	11	☊	6♌	5	4	4

NOV

	1	2	3	4	5	6	7	8	9	10	11	12	13	14	15	16	17	18	19	20	21	22	23	24	25	26	27	28	29	30
☉	8♏	9	10	11	12	13	14	15	16	17	18	19	20	21	22	23	24	25	26	27	28	29	0♐	1	2	3	4	5	6	7
☽	17♐	29	12♑	25	8♒	22	6♓	20	5♈	20	5♉	20	5♊	20	4♋	17	0♌	13	25	7♍	19	1♎	13	25	7♏	19	1♐	14	26	9♑
☿	23♎	25	27	28	30	1♏	3	5	6	8	10	11	13	14	16	18	19	21	22	24	26	27	29	0♐	2	4	5	7	8	10
♀	26♏	26	25	25	24	24	23	23	22	22	21	20	20	19	19	18	17	17	16	16	15	15	14	14	14	13	13	13	13	12
♂	10♌	10	11	11	12	12	13	13	13	14	14	15	15	15	16	16	17	17	17	18	18	18	19	19	19	20	20	20	21	21
	1	6	11	16	21	26			1	11	21			1	11	21			1	16		1	16		1	16		1	11	21
♃	3♓	3	3	3	4	4		♄	5♒	6	6		⚷	6♓	6	6		♅	5♍	5	♆	13♏	14	♇	12♍	12	☊	4♌	3	3

DEC

	1	2	3	4	5	6	7	8	9	10	11	12	13	14	15	16	17	18	19	20	21	22	23	24	25	26	27	28	29	30	31
☉	8♐	9	10	11	12	13	14	15	16	17	18	19	20	22	23	24	25	26	27	28	29	30	1♑	2	3	4	5	6	7	8	9
☽	22♑	5♒	19	2♓	16	0♈	15	29	14♉	29	13♊	27	11♋	25	8♌	21	3♍	15	27	9♎	21	3♏	15	27	10♐	22	5♑	18	2♒	15	29
☿	11♐	13	15	16	18	19	21	22	24	26	27	29	0♑	2	3	5	6	8	10	11	13	14	16	17	19	20	22	23	25	26	27
♀	12♏	12	12	12	12	12	12	13	13	13	13	14	14	14	15	15	16	16	17	17	18	18	19	20	20	21	22	22	23	24	24
♂	21♌	21	22	22	22	22	23	23	23	23	23	24	24	24	24	24	24	24	24	25	25	25	25	25	25	25	25	25	25	25	25
	1	6	11	16	21	26	31		1	11	21	31		1	11	21	31		1	16		1	16		1	16		1	11	21	31
♃	5♓	5	6	6	7	8	9	♄	7♒	8	9	10	⚷	6♓	6	7	7	♅	5♍	5	♆	14♏	15	♇	12♍	12	☊	2♌	2	1	1

1963

EPHEMERIS

JAN

	1	2	3	4	5	6	7	8	9	10	11	12	13	14	15	16	17	18	19	20	21	22	23	24	25	26	27	28	29	30	31
☉	10♑	11	12	13	14	15	16	17	18	19	20	21	22	23	24	25	26	27	28	29	0♒	1	2	3	4	5	6	7	8	9	10
☽	13♓	27	11♈	26	10♉	24	8♊	22	6♋	19	3♌	16	28	11♍	23	5♎	17	29	11♏	23	5♐	17	0♑	13	27	11♒	25	9♓	24	8♈	22
☿	29♑	30	1♒	2	3	4	5	6	6	6	7	7	6	6	6	5	4	3	2	0	29♑	28	26	25	24	23	22	22	21	21	21
♀	25♏	26	27	28	29	29	0♐	1	2	3	4	5	6	7	8	8	9	10	11	12	13	14	15	16	17	18	20	21	22	23	24
♂	25♌	24	24	24	24	24	24	24	24	23	23	23	23	22	22	22	22	21	21	21	20	20	20	19	19	19	18	18	18	17	17
	1	6	11	16	21	26	31		1	11	21	31		1	11	21	31		1	16		1	16		1	16		1	11	21	31
♃	9♓	10	11	12	13	14	15	♄	10♒	11	12	13	⚷	7♓	8	8	9	♅	5♍	5	♆	15♏	15	♇	12♍	12	☊	1♌	0	30♋	29

FEB

	1	2	3	4	5	6	7	8	9	10	11	12	13	14	15	16	17	18	19	20	21	22	23	24	25	26	27	28			
☉	11♒	12	13	14	15	16	17	18	20	21	22	23	24	25	26	27	28	29	30	1♓	2	3	4	5	6	7	8	9			
☽	7♉	21	5♊	18	2♋	15	28	11♌	24	6♍	19	1♎	13	25	7♏	19	1♐	13	25	8♑	21	5♒	19	3♓	18	3♈	18	3♉			
☿	21♑	21	21	21	22	22	23	23	24	25	26	27	27	28	30	1♒	2	3	4	5	7	8	9	10	12	13	15	16			
♀	25♐	26	27	28	29	0♑	1	2	3	5	6	7	8	9	10	11	12	13	15	16	17	18	19	20	21	23	24	25			
♂	16♌	16	16	15	15	14	14	14	13	13	12	12	12	11	11	11	10	10	10	9	9	9	8	8	8	8	7	7			
	1	6	11	16	21	26			1	11	21			1	11	21			1	16		1	16		1	16		1	11	21	
♃	15♓	16	18	19	20	21		♄	14♒	15	16		⚷	9♓	9	10		♅	4♍	4	♆	16♏	16	♇	12♍	11	☊	29♋	29	28	

MAR

	1	2	3	4	5	6	7	8	9	10	11	12	13	14	15	16	17	18	19	20	21	22	23	24	25	26	27	28	29	30	31
☉	10♓	11	12	13	14	15	16	17	18	19	20	21	22	23	24	25	26	27	28	29	30	1♈	2	3	4	5	6	7	8	9	10
☽	17♉	1♊	15	29	12♋	25	8♌	20	3♍	15	27	9♎	21	3♏	15	27	9♐	21	3♑	16	29	13♒	27	12♓	26	12♈	27	12♉	27	11♊	25
☿	17♒	19	20	22	23	25	26	28	30	1♓	3	5	6	8	10	11	13	15	17	18	20	22	24	26	28	30	2♈	4	6	8	10
♀	26♑	27	28	29	1♒	2	3	4	5	6	8	9	10	11	12	13	15	16	17	18	19	20	22	23	24	25	26	28	29	30	1♓
♂	7♌	7	7	6	6	6	6	6	6	6	6	5	5	5	5	5	5	5	5	5	5	6	6	6	6	6	6	6	6	6	7
	1	6	11	16	21	26	31		1	11	21	31		1	11	21	31		1	16		1	16		1	16		1	11	21	31
♃	22♓	23	24	25	27	28	29	♄	17♒	18	19	20	⚷	10♓	11	12	12	♅	3♍	2	♆	16♏	15	♇	11♍	11	☊	28♋	27	27	26

APR

	1	2	3	4	5	6	7	8	9	10	11	12	13	14	15	16	17	18	19	20	21	22	23	24	25	26	27	28	29	30	
☉	11♈	12	13	14	14	15	16	17	18	19	20	21	22	23	24	25	26	27	28	29	0♉	1	2	3	4	5	6	7	8	9	
☽	9♋	22	5♌	17	30	12♍	24	6♎	18	30	12♏	24	6♐	18	30	12♑	25	8♒	21	5♓	20	5♈	20	5♉	20	6♊	20	4♋	18	1♌	
☿	12♈	14	16	18	20	22	24	26	28	0♉	2	4	6	8	10	11	13	15	16	18	19	21	22	23	24	25	26	27	28	28	
♀	2♓	4	5	6	7	8	9	11	12	13	14	15	17	18	19	20	21	23	24	25	26	27	29	30	1♈	2	3	5	6	7	
♂	7♌	7	7	7	7	8	8	8	8	9	9	9	9	10	10	10	10	11	11	11	12	12	12	13	13	13	14	14	14	15	
	1	6	11	16	21	26			1	11	21			1	11	21			1	16		1	16		1	16		1	11	21	
♃	29♓	0♈	2	3	4	5		♄	20♒	21	22		⚷	12♓	13	13		♅	2♍	1	♆	15♏	15	♇	10♍	10	☊	26♋	25	25	

MAY

	1	2	3	4	5	6	7	8	9	10	11	12	13	14	15	16	17	18	19	20	21	22	23	24	25	26	27	28	29	30	31
☉	10♉	11	12	13	14	15	16	17	18	19	20	21	22	22	23	24	25	26	27	28	29	0♊	1	2	3	4	5	6	7	8	9
☽	14♌	27	9♍	21	3♎	15	27	9♏	21	3♐	15	27	9♑	22	4♒	17	1♓	15	29	14♈	29	14♉	29	14♊	29	13♋	27	10♌	23	6♍	18
☿	29♉	30	30	0♊	0	1	1	1	0	0	30♉	30	29	29	28	28	27	27	26	25	25	24	24	23	23	23	22	22	22	22	22
♀	8♈	9	11	12	13	14	15	17	18	19	20	21	23	24	25	26	28	29	30	1♉	2	4	5	6	7	8	10	11	12	13	14
♂	15♌	16	16	16	17	17	18	18	18	19	19	20	20	20	21	21	22	22	23	23	24	24	25	25	25	26	26	27	27	28	28
	1	6	11	16	21	26	31		1	11	21	31		1	11	21	31		1	16		1	16		1	16		1	11	21	31
♃	6♈	7	8	9	10	11	12	♄	22♒	23	23	23	⚷	14♓	14	15	15	♅	1♍	1	♆	14♏	14	♇	10♍	10	☊	24♋	24	23	23

JUN

	1	2	3	4	5	6	7	8	9	10	11	12	13	14	15	16	17	18	19	20	21	22	23	24	25	26	27	28	29	30	
☉	10♊	11	12	13	14	15	16	17	17	18	19	20	21	22	23	24	25	26	27	28	29	30	1♋	2	3	4	5	6	7	8	
☽	30♍	12♎	24	6♏	18	29	12♐	24	6♑	19	1♒	14	28	11♓	25	9♈	23	8♉	23	8♊	22	7♋	21	5♌	18	1♍	14	26	8♎	20	
☿	22♉	22	22	22	23	23	24	24	25	26	26	27	28	29	0♊	1	2	3	5	6	7	9	10	12	13	15	17	18	20	22	
♀	16♉	17	18	19	21	22	23	24	25	27	28	29	0♊	1	3	4	5	6	7	9	10	11	12	14	15	16	17	18	20	21	
♂	29♌	29	30	0♍	1	1	2	2	3	3	4	4	5	6	6	7	7	8	8	9	9	10	10	11	11	12	13	13	14	14	
	1	6	11	16	21	26			1	11	21			1	11	21			1	16		1	16		1	16		1	11	21	
♃	12♈	13	14	15	16	16		♄	23♒	23	23		⚷	15♓	15	15		♅	1♍	2	♆	14♏	13	♇	10♍	10	☊	23♋	22	22	

1963

EPHEMERIS

JUL

	1	2	3	4	5	6	7	8	9	10	11	12	13	14	15	16	17	18	19	20	21	22	23	24	25	26	27	28	29	30	31
☉	8♋	9	10	11	12	13	14	15	16	17	18	19	20	21	22	23	24	25	26	27	28	28	29	0♌	1	2	3	4	5	6	7
☽	2♏	14	26	8♐	20	3♑	15	28	11♒	24	8♓	22	6♈	20	4♉	18	3♊	17	1♋	15	29	13♌	26	9♍	22	4♎	16	28	10♏	22	4♐
☿	24♊	26	28	30	2♋	4	6	8	10	12	15	17	19	21	23	25	27	29	2♌	4	6	8	10	12	13	15	17	19	21	23	24
♀	22♊	23	25	26	27	28	29	1♋	2	3	4	6	7	8	9	10	12	13	14	15	17	18	19	20	21	23	24	25	26	28	29
♂	15♍	15	16	16	17	18	18	19	19	20	20	21	22	22	23	23	24	25	25	26	26	27	27	28	29	29	30	0♎	1	2	2
	1	6	11	16	21	26	31		1	11	21	31		1	11	21	31		1	16		1	16		1	16		1	11	21	31
♃	17♈	18	18	19	19	19	19	♄	23♒	22	21	21	⚷	15♓	15	14	14	♅	2♍	3	♆	13♏	13	♇	10♍	10	☊	21♋	21	20	20

AUG

	1	2	3	4	5	6	7	8	9	10	11	12	13	14	15	16	17	18	19	20	21	22	23	24	25	26	27	28	29	30	31
☉	8♌	9	10	11	12	13	14	15	16	17	18	19	20	20	21	22	23	24	25	26	27	28	29	0♍	1	2	3	4	5	6	7
☽	16♐	28	11♑	24	7♒	20	4♓	18	2♈	17	1♉	15	29	13♊	27	11♋	25	8♌	21	4♍	17	30	12♎	24	6♏	18	30	12♐	24	6♑	19
☿	26♌	28	29	1♍	3	4	6	7	9	10	12	13	14	16	17	18	20	21	22	23	24	25	26	27	28	29	0♎	1	2	2	3
♀	0♌	1	3	4	5	6	7	9	10	11	12	14	15	16	17	19	20	21	22	24	25	26	27	28	30	1♍	2	3	5	6	7
♂	3♎	4	4	5	5	6	7	7	8	8	9	10	10	11	12	12	13	14	14	15	15	16	17	17	18	19	19	20	21	21	22
	1	6	11	16	21	26	31		1	11	21	31		1	11	21	31		1	16		1	16		1	16		1	11	21	31
♃	19♈	19	19	19	19	19	19	♄	21♒	20	19	18	⚷	14♓	14	13	13	♅	4♍	5	♆	13♏	13	♇	11♍	11	☊	19♋	19	18	18

SEP

	1	2	3	4	5	6	7	8	9	10	11	12	13	14	15	16	17	18	19	20	21	22	23	24	25	26	27	28	29	30
☉	8♍	9	10	11	12	13	14	15	16	17	18	19	19	20	21	22	23	24	25	26	27	28	29	0♎	1	2	3	4	5	6
☽	2♒	15	29	13♓	28	12♈	27	12♉	26	10♊	24	8♋	21	5♌	18	1♍	13	26	8♎	20	2♏	14	26	8♐	20	2♑	14	27	10♒	23
☿	4♎	4	4	5	5	5	5	5	5	5	4	4	3	2	2	1	30♍	29	28	27	26	25	24	23	22	21	21	21	21	21
♀	8♍	10	11	12	13	15	16	17	18	20	21	22	23	25	26	27	28	29	1♎	2	3	4	6	7	8	9	11	12	13	14
♂	23♎	23	24	24	25	26	26	27	28	28	29	30	0♏	1	2	2	3	4	4	5	6	6	7	8	9	9	10	11	11	12
	1	6	11	16	21	26			1	11	21			1	11	21			1	16		1	16		1	16		1	11	21
♃	19♈	18	18	17	17	16		♄	18♒	18	17		⚷	13♓	12	12		♅	6♍	7	♆	13♏	14	♇	12♍	12	☊	18♋	17	17

OCT

	1	2	3	4	5	6	7	8	9	10	11	12	13	14	15	16	17	18	19	20	21	22	23	24	25	26	27	28	29	30	31
☉	7♎	8	9	10	11	12	13	14	15	16	17	18	19	20	21	22	23	24	25	26	27	28	29	30	1♏	2	3	4	5	6	7
☽	7♓	22	6♈	21	6♉	21	6♊	21	5♋	18	2♌	15	28	10♍	23	5♎	17	29	11♏	23	5♐	16	28	10♑	23	5♒	18	1♓	15	30	14♈
☿	21♍	21	22	22	23	24	25	26	28	29	0♎	2	3	5	7	8	10	12	13	15	17	18	20	22	24	25	27	29	0♏	2	4
♀	16♎	17	18	19	21	22	23	24	26	27	28	29	1♏	2	3	4	6	7	8	9	11	12	13	14	16	17	18	19	21	22	23
♂	13♏	13	14	15	15	16	17	17	18	19	20	20	21	22	22	23	24	24	25	26	27	27	28	29	29	0♐	1	2	2	3	4
	1	6	11	16	21	26	31		1	11	21	31		1	11	21	31		1	16		1	16		1	16		1	11	21	31
♃	15♈	15	14	13	13	12	12	♄	17♒	17	16	17	⚷	11♓	11	11	10	♅	8♍	8	♆	14♏	15	♇	13♍	13	☊	16♋	16	15	15

NOV

	1	2	3	4	5	6	7	8	9	10	11	12	13	14	15	16	17	18	19	20	21	22	23	24	25	26	27	28	29	30
☉	8♏	9	10	11	12	13	14	15	16	17	18	19	20	21	22	23	24	25	26	27	28	29	30	1♐	2	3	4	5	6	7
☽	30♈	15♉	0♊	15	30	14♋	28	11♌	25	7♍	20	2♎	14	26	8♏	20	2♐	13	25	7♑	19	2♒	14	27	10♓	24	8♈	23	8♉	23
☿	5♏	7	9	10	12	13	15	17	18	20	21	23	25	26	28	29	1♐	2	4	5	7	9	10	12	13	15	16	18	19	21
♀	24♏	26	27	28	29	1♐	2	3	4	6	7	8	9	11	12	13	14	16	17	18	19	20	22	23	24	25	27	28	29	0♑
♂	5♐	5	6	7	7	8	9	10	10	11	12	13	13	14	15	15	16	17	18	18	19	20	21	21	22	23	24	24	25	26
	1	6	11	16	21	26			1	11	21			1	11	21			1	16		1	16		1	16		1	11	21
♃	11♈	11	11	10	10	10		♄	17♒	17	17		⚷	10♓	10	10		♅	9♍	10	♆	15♏	16	♇	14♍	14	☊	15♋	14	14

DEC

	1	2	3	4	5	6	7	8	9	10	11	12	13	14	15	16	17	18	19	20	21	22	23	24	25	26	27	28	29	30	31
☉	8♐	9	10	11	12	13	14	15	16	17	18	19	20	21	22	23	24	25	26	27	28	29	0♑	1	2	3	4	6	7	8	9
☽	8♊	23	8♋	23	7♌	20	4♍	16	29	11♎	23	5♏	17	29	10♐	22	4♑	16	29	11♒	24	7♓	20	4♈	18	2♉	16	1♊	16	1♋	16
☿	22♐	24	25	27	28	30	1♑	3	4	5	7	8	10	11	12	13	14	16	17	18	18	19	20	20	21	21	21	20	20	19	19
♀	2♑	3	4	5	7	8	9	10	12	13	14	15	17	18	19	20	22	23	24	25	27	28	29	0♒	2	3	4	5	6	8	9
♂	27♐	27	28	29	30	0♑	1	2	3	4	4	5	6	7	7	8	9	10	10	11	12	13	13	14	15	16	17	17	18	19	20
	1	6	11	16	21	26	31		1	11	21	31		1	11	21	31		1	16		1	16		1	16		1	11	21	31
♃	10♈	10	10	10	10	10	11	♄	18♒	19	19	20	⚷	10♓	10	11	11	♅	10♍	10	♆	16♏	17	♇	14♍	14	☊	13♋	12	12	11

1964

JAN

	1	2	3	4	5	6	7	8	9	10	11	12	13	14	15	16	17	18	19	20	21	22	23	24	25	26	27	28	29	30	31
☉	10♑	11	12	13	14	15	16	17	18	19	20	21	22	23	24	25	26	27	28	29	30	1♒	2	3	4	5	6	7	8	9	10
☽	1♌	15	28	12♍	25	7♎	19	1♏	13	25	7♐	19	1♑	13	25	8♒	21	4♓	17	0♈	14	28	12♉	26	11♊	25	10♋	24	8♌	22	6♍
☿	18♑	17	15	14	13	11	10	9	8	7	6	5	5	5	5	5	5	5	5	6	6	7	8	9	9	10	11	12	13	15	16
♀	10♒	11	13	14	15	16	18	19	20	21	22	24	25	26	27	29	30	1♓	2	4	5	6	7	8	10	11	12	13	14	16	17
♂	20♑	21	22	23	24	24	25	26	27	27	28	29	30	1♒	1	2	3	4	5	5	6	7	8	8	9	10	11	12	12	13	14
	1	6	11	16	21	26	31		1	11	21	31		1	11	21	31		1	16		1	16		1	16		1	11	21	31
♃	11♈	11	12	12	13	14	15	♄	20♒	21	23	24	⚷	11♓	11	12	12	♅	10♍	10	♆	17♏	18	♇	14♍	14	☊	11♋	11	10	10

FEB

	1	2	3	4	5	6	7	8	9	10	11	12	13	14	15	16	17	18	19	20	21	22	23	24	25	26	27	28	29		
☉	11♒	12	13	14	15	16	17	18	19	20	21	22	23	24	25	26	27	28	29	0♓	1	2	3	4	5	6	7	8	9		
☽	19♍	2♎	15	27	9♏	21	3♐	15	27	9♑	21	4♒	17	30	13♓	27	11♈	25	9♉	23	7♊	21	5♋	19	3♌	17	1♍	14	27		
☿	17♑	18	19	21	22	23	25	26	27	29	0♒	2	3	4	6	7	9	11	12	14	15	17	18	20	22	23	25	27	28		
♀	18♓	19	21	22	23	24	25	27	28	29	0♈	1	3	4	5	6	7	8	10	11	12	13	14	16	17	18	19	20	21		
♂	15♒	16	16	17	18	19	19	20	21	22	23	23	24	25	26	27	27	28	29	30	1♓	1	2	3	4	4	5	6	7		
	1	6	11	16	21	26			1	11	21			1	11	21			1	16		1	16		1	16		1	11	21	
♃	15♈	16	17	17	18	19		♄	24♒	25	26		⚷	12♓	13	14		♅	9♍	9	♆	18♏	18	♇	14♍	13	☊	10♋	9	9	

MAR

	1	2	3	4	5	6	7	8	9	10	11	12	13	14	15	16	17	18	19	20	21	22	23	24	25	26	27	28	29	30	31
☉	10♓	11	12	13	14	15	16	17	18	19	20	21	22	23	24	25	26	27	28	29	0♈	1	2	3	4	5	6	7	8	9	10
☽	10♎	23	5♏	17	29	11♐	23	5♑	17	29	12♒	25	8♓	22	6♈	21	5♉	20	4♊	18	2♋	16	30	13♌	27	10♍	23	6♎	19	1♏	13
☿	0♓	2	4	5	7	9	11	13	14	16	18	20	22	24	26	28	0♈	2	4	6	8	10	12	14	16	18	20	22	23	25	27
♀	23♈	24	25	26	27	28	29	1♉	2	3	4	5	6	7	8	10	11	12	13	14	15	16	17	18	19	20	22	23	24	25	26
♂	8♓	8	9	10	11	12	12	13	14	15	16	16	17	18	19	19	20	21	22	23	23	24	25	26	27	27	28	29	30	0♈	1
	1	6	11	16	21	26	31		1	11	21	31		1	11	21	31		1	16		1	16		1	16		1	11	21	31
♃	20♈	21	22	24	25	26	27	♄	27♒	29	30	1♓	⚷	14♓	15	15	16	♅	8♍	7	♆	18♏	18	♇	13♍	13	☊	8♋	8	7	7

APR

	1	2	3	4	5	6	7	8	9	10	11	12	13	14	15	16	17	18	19	20	21	22	23	24	25	26	27	28	29	30	
☉	11♈	12	13	14	15	16	17	18	19	20	21	22	23	24	25	26	27	28	29	30	1♉	2	3	4	5	6	7	8	9	10	
☽	25♏	7♐	19	1♑	13	25	7♒	20	3♓	16	1♈	15	30	14♉	29	14♊	29	13♋	27	10♌	24	7♍	20	3♎	15	27	10♏	22	4♐	15	
☿	28♈	30	1♉	3	4	5	6	7	8	9	10	10	11	11	11	11	12	11	11	11	11	10	10	9	9	8	7	7	6	5	
♀	27♉	28	29	30	1♊	2	3	4	5	6	7	8	9	10	11	12	13	13	14	15	16	17	18	19	20	20	21	22	23	24	
♂	2♈	3	4	4	5	6	7	7	8	9	10	10	11	12	13	14	14	15	16	17	17	18	19	20	20	21	22	23	23	24	
	1	6	11	16	21	26			1	11	21			1	11	21			1	16		1	16		1	16		1	11	21	
♃	27♈	28	30	1♉	2	3		♄	1♓	2	3		⚷	16♓	17	17		♅	7♍	6	♆	17♏	17	♇	12♍	12	☊	7♋	6	5	

MAY

	1	2	3	4	5	6	7	8	9	10	11	12	13	14	15	16	17	18	19	20	21	22	23	24	25	26	27	28	29	30	31
☉	11♉	12	13	14	15	15	16	17	18	19	20	21	22	23	24	25	26	27	28	29	30	1♊	2	3	4	5	6	7	8	9	10
☽	27♐	9♑	21	3♒	15	28	11♓	25	9♈	23	8♉	23	8♊	23	8♋	23	7♌	20	4♍	17	30	12♎	24	7♏	19	0♐	12	24	6♑	18	30
☿	5♉	4	4	3	3	2	2	2	2	2	2	2	2	2	2	3	3	4	4	5	5	6	7	8	9	10	11	12	13	14	16
♀	24♊	25	26	27	27	28	29	29	30	1♋	1	2	2	3	3	4	4	5	5	5	6	6	6	6	6	7	7	7	7	7	7
♂	25♈	26	27	27	28	29	30	0♉	1	2	3	3	4	5	6	6	7	8	9	9	10	11	11	12	13	14	14	15	16	17	17
	1	6	11	16	21	26	31		1	11	21	31		1	11	21	31		1	16		1	16		1	16		1	11	21	31
♃	4♉	6	7	8	9	10	11	♄	3♓	4	5	5	⚷	18♓	18	18	19	♅	6♍	6	♆	17♏	16	♇	12♍	12	☊	5♋	4	4	3

JUN

	1	2	3	4	5	6	7	8	9	10	11	12	13	14	15	16	17	18	19	20	21	22	23	24	25	26	27	28	29	30	
☉	11♊	11	12	13	14	15	16	17	18	19	20	21	22	23	24	25	26	27	28	29	30	1♋	2	3	3	4	5	6	7	8	
☽	12♒	24	7♓	20	3♈	17	2♉	16	1♊	17	2♋	17	1♌	16	30	13♍	26	9♎	21	4♏	16	28	9♐	21	3♑	15	27	9♒	21	4♓	
☿	17♉	18	20	21	23	24	26	27	29	1♊	2	4	6	8	10	12	14	16	18	20	22	24	26	28	1♋	3	5	7	9	12	
♀	7♋	7	6	6	6	6	5	5	5	4	4	3	3	2	2	1	0	30♊	29	29	28	27	27	26	26	25	24	24	23	23	
♂	18♉	19	20	20	21	22	22	23	24	25	25	26	27	28	28	29	30	0♊	1	2	3	3	4	5	5	6	7	7	8	9	
	1	6	11	16	21	26			1	11	21			1	11	21			1	16		1	16		1	16		1	11	21	
♃	12♉	13	14	15	16	17		♄	5♓	5	5		⚷	19♓	19	19		♅	6♍	6	♆	16♏	15	♇	12♍	12	☊	3♋	3	2	

1964

JUL

	1	2	3	4	5	6	7	8	9	10	11	12	13	14	15	16	17	18	19	20	21	22	23	24	25	26	27	28	29	30	31
☉	9♋	10	11	12	13	14	15	16	17	18	19	20	21	22	23	23	24	25	26	27	28	29	0♌	1	2	3	4	5	6	7	8
☽	16♓	30	13♈	27	11♉	25	10♊	25	10♋	25	10♌	24	8♍	22	5♎	18	0♏	12	24	6♐	18	30	12♑	24	6♒	18	1♓	13	26	10♈	23
☿	14♋	16	18	20	22	24	26	28	30	2♌	4	6	7	9	11	13	14	16	18	19	21	22	24	25	27	28	29	1♍	2	3	4
♀	23♊	22	22	21	21	21	21	21	20	20	20	20	20	20	21	21	21	21	21	22	22	22	23	23	24	24	24	25	25	26	27
♂	10♊	10	11	12	12	13	14	14	15	16	17	17	18	19	19	20	21	21	22	23	23	24	25	25	26	27	27	28	29	29	0♋
	1	6	11	16	21	26	31		1	11	21	31		1	11	21	31		1	16		1	16		1	16		1	11	21	31
♃	18♉	19	20	21	21	22	23	♄	5♓	5	4	3	⚷	19♓	19	18	18	♅	7♍	8	♆	15♏	15	♇	12♍	12	☊	2♋	1	1	0

AUG

	1	2	3	4	5	6	7	8	9	10	11	12	13	14	15	16	17	18	19	20	21	22	23	24	25	26	27	28	29	30	31
☉	9♌	10	11	12	13	14	15	15	16	17	18	19	20	21	22	23	24	25	26	27	28	29	30	1♍	2	3	4	5	6	7	8
☽	7♉	21	5♊	20	4♋	19	4♌	18	2♍	16	0♎	13	26	9♏	21	3♐	14	26	8♑	20	2♒	15	27	10♓	23	7♈	20	4♉	18	2♊	16
☿	6♍	7	8	9	10	11	12	13	13	14	15	15	16	16	17	17	17	18	18	18	18	18	17	17	17	16	15	15	14	13	12
♀	27♊	28	28	29	30	0♋	1	2	3	3	4	5	6	6	7	8	9	10	11	12	12	13	14	15	16	17	18	19	20	21	22
♂	1♋	1	2	3	3	4	5	5	6	7	7	8	9	9	10	11	11	12	13	13	14	15	15	16	17	17	18	19	19	20	20
	1	6	11	16	21	26	31		1	11	21	31		1	11	21	31		1	16		1	16		1	16		1	11	21	31
♃	23♉	24	24	25	25	25	26	♄	3♓	3	2	1	⚷	18♓	18	17	17	♅	8♍	9	♆	15♏	15	♇	13♍	13	☊	0♋	30♊	29	28

SEP

	1	2	3	4	5	6	7	8	9	10	11	12	13	14	15	16	17	18	19	20	21	22	23	24	25	26	27	28	29	30	
☉	9♍	10	11	11	12	13	14	15	16	17	18	19	20	21	22	23	24	25	26	27	28	29	30	1♎	2	3	4	5	6	7	
☽	30♊	14♋	28	13♌	27	11♍	25	8♎	21	4♏	16	29	11♐	22	4♑	16	28	10♒	23	6♓	19	2♈	16	0♉	14	28	13♊	27	11♋	25	
☿	11♍	10	9	8	7	7	6	5	5	5	4	4	4	5	5	6	6	7	8	9	11	12	13	15	16	18	20	21	23	25	
♀	23♋	24	25	26	27	28	29	30	1♌	2	3	4	5	6	7	8	9	10	11	12	14	15	16	17	18	19	20	21	22	23	
♂	21♋	22	22	23	24	24	25	26	26	27	27	28	29	29	30	0♌	1	2	2	3	4	4	5	5	6	7	7	8	8	9	
	1	6	11	16	21	26			1	11	21			1	11	21			1	16		1	16		1	16		1	11	21	
♃	26♉	26	26	26	26	26		♄	1♓	0	30♒		⚷	17♓	16	16		♅	10♍	11	♆	15♏	16	♇	14♍	14	☊	28♊	28	27	

OCT

	1	2	3	4	5	6	7	8	9	10	11	12	13	14	15	16	17	18	19	20	21	22	23	24	25	26	27	28	29	30	31
☉	8♎	9	10	11	12	13	14	15	16	17	18	19	20	21	22	23	24	25	26	27	28	29	30	1♏	2	3	4	5	6	7	8
☽	9♌	23	6♍	20	3♎	17	29	12♏	24	7♐	18	0♑	12	24	6♒	18	1♓	14	27	11♈	25	9♉	24	8♊	23	7♋	22	6♌	20	3♍	17
☿	26♍	28	30	2♎	4	5	7	9	11	12	14	16	18	19	21	23	25	26	28	30	1♏	3	4	6	8	9	11	12	14	16	17
♀	25♌	26	27	28	29	0♍	1	3	4	5	6	7	8	9	11	12	13	14	15	16	18	19	20	21	22	24	25	26	27	28	30
♂	10♌	10	11	11	12	13	13	14	14	15	15	16	17	17	18	18	19	19	20	21	21	22	22	23	23	24	25	25	26	26	27
	1	6	11	16	21	26	31		1	11	21	31		1	11	21	31		1	16		1	16		1	16		1	11	21	31
♃	26♉	25	25	25	24	23	23	♄	29♒	29	28	28	⚷	15♓	15	15	14	♅	12♍	13	♆	16♏	17	♇	15♍	15	☊	27♊	26	26	25

NOV

	1	2	3	4	5	6	7	8	9	10	11	12	13	14	15	16	17	18	19	20	21	22	23	24	25	26	27	28	29	30	
☉	9♏	10	11	12	13	14	15	16	17	18	19	20	21	22	23	24	25	26	27	28	29	30	1♐	2	3	4	5	6	7	8	
☽	30♍	13♎	26	8♏	20	3♐	15	27	8♑	20	2♒	14	26	9♓	22	5♈	19	3♉	18	2♊	17	2♋	17	2♌	16	30	14♍	27	10♎	22	
☿	19♏	20	22	23	25	26	28	29	1♐	2	4	5	7	8	10	11	12	14	15	17	18	19	21	22	23	25	26	27	28	29	
♀	1♎	2	3	4	6	7	8	9	10	12	13	14	15	16	18	19	20	21	23	24	25	26	27	29	30	1♏	2	4	5	6	
♂	27♌	28	28	29	29	30	0♍	1	1	2	3	3	4	4	5	5	6	6	7	7	8	8	9	9	9	10	10	11	11	12	
	1	6	11	16	21	26			1	11	21			1	11	21			1	16		1	16		1	16		1	11	21	
♃	23♉	22	21	21	20	19		♄	28♒	28	29		⚷	14♓	14	14		♅	14♍	14	♆	17♏	18	♇	16♍	16	☊	25♊	25	24	

DEC

	1	2	3	4	5	6	7	8	9	10	11	12	13	14	15	16	17	18	19	20	21	22	23	24	25	26	27	28	29	30	31
☉	9♐	10	11	12	13	14	15	16	17	18	19	20	21	22	23	24	25	26	27	28	29	0♑	1	2	3	4	5	6	7	8	9
☽	5♏	17	29	11♐	23	5♑	17	29	10♒	22	5♓	17	30	13♈	27	11♉	25	10♊	26	11♋	26	11♌	25	10♍	23	7♎	19	2♏	14	26	8♐
☿	0♑	1	2	3	3	4	4	5	5	5	5	4	4	3	2	1	29♐	28	27	25	24	23	22	21	20	19	19	19	19	19	19
♀	7♏	9	10	11	12	13	15	16	17	18	20	21	22	23	25	26	27	28	30	1♐	2	3	5	6	7	8	10	11	12	13	15
♂	12♍	13	13	14	14	14	15	15	16	16	17	17	17	18	18	18	19	19	20	20	20	21	21	21	22	22	22	23	23	23	24
	1	6	11	16	21	26	31		1	11	21	31		1	11	21	31		1	16		1	16		1	16		1	11	21	31
♃	19♉	18	18	17	17	17	16	♄	29♒	30	0♓	1	⚷	14♓	14	14	15	♅	15♍	15	♆	18♏	19	♇	16♍	16	☊	24♊	23	23	22

1965

JAN

	1	2	3	4	5	6	7	8	9	10	11	12	13	14	15	16	17	18	19	20	21	22	23	24	25	26	27	28	29	30	31
☉	10♑	11	12	13	14	15	16	18	19	20	21	22	23	24	25	26	27	28	29	30	1♒	2	3	4	5	6	7	8	9	10	11
☽	20♐	2♑	14	26	7♒	19	1♓	14	26	9♈	22	6♉	19	4♊	18	3♋	19	4♌	19	4♍	18	2♎	15	28	11♏	23	5♐	17	29	11♑	22
☿	19♐	20	20	21	22	22	23	24	25	26	28	29	30	1♑	2	4	5	6	8	9	10	12	13	14	16	17	19	20	22	23	25
♀	16♐	17	18	20	21	22	23	25	26	27	28	30	1♑	2	3	5	6	7	8	10	11	12	13	15	16	17	18	20	21	22	23
♂	24♍	24	24	25	25	25	25	26	26	26	26	26	27	27	27	27	27	27	27	28	28	28	28	28	28	28	28	28	28	28	28
	1	6	11	16	21	26	31		1	11	21	31		1	11	21	31		1	16		1	16		1	16		1	11	21	31
♃	16♉	16	16	16	16	17	17	♄	1♓	2	3	4	⚷	15♓	15	16	16	♅	15♍	15	♆	19♏	20	♇	16♍	16	☊	22♊	21	21	20

FEB

	1	2	3	4	5	6	7	8	9	10	11	12	13	14	15	16	17	18	19	20	21	22	23	24	25	26	27	28			
☉	12♒	13	14	15	16	17	18	19	20	21	22	23	24	25	26	27	28	29	0♓	1	2	3	4	5	6	7	8	9			
☽	4♒	16	29	11♓	23	6♈	19	2♉	15	29	13♊	27	12♋	27	12♌	27	12♍	26	10♎	24	7♏	19	2♐	14	25	7♑	19	1♒			
☿	26♑	28	29	1♒	3	4	6	7	9	11	12	14	16	17	19	21	22	24	26	28	30	1♓	3	5	7	9	11	13			
♀	25♑	26	27	28	30	1♒	2	3	5	6	7	8	10	11	12	13	15	16	17	18	20	21	22	23	25	26	27	28			
♂	28♍	28	28	28	28	28	28	27	27	27	27	27	27	26	26	26	26	25	25	25	25	24	24	24	23	23	23	22			
	1	6	11	16	21	26			1	11	21			1	11	21			1	16		1	16		1	16		1	11	21	
♃	17♉	17	18	18	19	20		♄	5♓	6	7		⚷	16♓	17	17		♅	14♍	13	♆	20♏	20	♇	16♍	15	☊	20♊	20	19	

MAR

	1	2	3	4	5	6	7	8	9	10	11	12	13	14	15	16	17	18	19	20	21	22	23	24	25	26	27	28	29	30	31
☉	10♓	11	12	13	14	15	16	17	18	19	20	21	22	23	24	25	26	27	28	29	0♈	1	2	3	4	5	6	7	8	9	10
☽	13♒	25	7♓	20	3♈	16	29	12♉	26	10♊	24	8♋	22	6♌	21	5♍	20	4♎	18	1♏	14	27	9♐	21	3♑	15	27	9♒	21	3♓	16
☿	14♓	16	18	20	22	24	26	28	30	2♈	4	5	7	9	10	12	14	15	16	17	19	20	20	21	22	22	23	23	23	23	23
♀	30♒	1♓	2	3	5	6	7	8	10	11	12	13	15	16	17	18	20	21	22	23	25	26	27	28	29	1♈	2	3	4	6	7
♂	22♍	22	21	21	20	20	20	19	19	19	18	18	17	17	17	16	16	15	15	15	14	14	14	13	13	13	12	12	12	12	11
	1	6	11	16	21	26	31		1	11	21	31		1	11	21	31		1	16		1	16		1	16		1	11	21	31
♃	20♉	21	22	22	23	24	25	♄	8♓	9	10	11	⚷	18♓	18	19	20	♅	13♍	12	♆	20♏	20	♇	15♍	15	☊	19♊	18	18	17

APR

	1	2	3	4	5	6	7	8	9	10	11	12	13	14	15	16	17	18	19	20	21	22	23	24	25	26	27	28	29	30	
☉	11♈	12	13	14	15	16	17	18	19	20	21	22	23	24	25	26	27	28	29	30	1♉	2	3	4	5	6	7	7	8	9	
☽	29♓	12♈	25	9♉	23	6♊	20	4♋	19	3♌	17	1♍	15	29	13♎	26	9♏	22	5♐	17	29	11♑	23	5♒	17	29	11♓	24	7♈	20	
☿	23♈	23	22	22	21	20	20	19	18	17	17	16	15	14	14	13	13	12	12	12	12	12	12	12	12	12	13	13	14	14	
♀	8♈	9	11	12	13	14	16	17	18	19	21	22	23	24	26	27	28	29	0♉	2	3	4	5	7	8	9	10	12	13	14	
♂	11♍	11	11	10	10	10	10	10	9	9	9	9	9	9	9	9	9	9	9	9	9	9	9	9	9	9	9	9	9	9	
	1	6	11	16	21	26			1	11	21			1	11	21			1	16		1	16		1	16		1	11	21	
♃	25♉	26	27	29	30	1♊		♄	12♓	13	14		⚷	20♓	20	21		♅	12♍	11	♆	20♏	19	♇	14♍	14	☊	17♊	17	16	

MAY

	1	2	3	4	5	6	7	8	9	10	11	12	13	14	15	16	17	18	19	20	21	22	23	24	25	26	27	28	29	30	31
☉	10♉	11	12	13	14	15	16	17	18	19	20	21	22	23	24	25	26	27	28	29	30	1♊	2	3	4	5	5	6	7	8	9
☽	4♉	18	2♊	16	1♋	15	30	14♌	28	12♍	25	9♎	22	5♏	18	1♐	13	25	7♑	19	1♒	13	25	7♓	19	2♈	15	28	12♉	26	11♊
☿	15♈	15	16	17	18	19	20	21	22	23	24	25	27	28	29	1♉	2	3	5	6	8	10	11	13	15	16	18	20	22	24	26
♀	15♉	17	18	19	20	21	23	24	25	26	28	29	0♊	1	3	4	5	6	7	9	10	11	12	14	15	16	17	19	20	21	22
♂	9♍	10	10	10	10	10	10	11	11	11	11	11	12	12	12	12	13	13	13	14	14	14	14	15	15	15	16	16	17	17	17
	1	6	11	16	21	26	31		1	11	21	31		1	11	21	31		1	16		1	16		1	16		1	11	21	31
♃	2♊	3	4	5	6	8	9	♄	15♓	15	16	17	⚷	21♓	22	22	22	♅	11♍	11	♆	19♏	18	♇	14♍	14	☊	16♊	15	15	14

JUN

	1	2	3	4	5	6	7	8	9	10	11	12	13	14	15	16	17	18	19	20	21	22	23	24	25	26	27	28	29	30	
☉	10♊	11	12	13	14	15	16	17	18	19	20	21	22	23	24	25	26	27	27	28	29	0♋	1	2	3	4	5	6	7	8	
☽	26♊	10♋	25	10♌	24	8♍	22	6♎	19	2♏	15	27	10♐	22	4♑	16	28	9♒	21	3♓	15	28	10♈	23	7♉	20	5♊	19	4♋	19	
☿	28♉	30	2♊	4	6	8	10	12	14	17	19	21	23	25	28	30	2♋	4	6	8	10	12	14	16	18	20	22	24	25	27	
♀	23♊	25	26	27	28	30	1♋	2	3	4	6	7	8	9	11	12	13	14	15	17	18	19	20	22	23	24	25	26	28	29	
♂	18♍	18	18	19	19	20	20	20	21	21	22	22	22	23	23	24	24	25	25	26	26	27	27	28	28	28	29	29	30	0♎	
	1	6	11	16	21	26			1	11	21			1	11	21			1	16		1	16		1	16		1	11	21	
♃	9♊	10	11	13	14	15		♄	17♓	17	17		⚷	22♓	22	23		♅	11♍	11	♆	18♏	18	♇	14♍	14	☊	14♊	13	13	

1965

EPHEMERIS

JUL

	1	2	3	4	5	6	7	8	9	10	11	12	13	14	15	16	17	18	19	20	21	22	23	24	25	26	27	28	29	30	31
☉	9♋	10	11	12	13	14	15	16	17	18	18	19	20	21	22	23	24	25	26	27	28	29	30	1♌	2	3	4	5	6	7	8
☽	4♌	19	4♍	19	2♎	16	29	12♏	24	7♐	19	1♑	13	25	6♒	18	0♓	12	24	7♈	19	2♉	15	29	13♊	28	13♋	28	13♌	28	13♍
☿	29♋	1♌	2	4	5	7	8	10	11	13	14	15	16	18	19	20	21	22	23	24	25	26	26	27	28	28	29	29	29	30	30
♀	0♌	1	3	4	5	6	7	9	10	11	12	13	15	16	17	18	20	21	22	23	24	26	27	28	29	0♍	2	3	4	5	7
♂	1♎	1	2	3	3	4	4	5	5	6	6	7	7	8	8	9	9	10	11	11	12	12	13	13	14	15	15	16	16	17	17
	1	6	11	16	21	26	31		1	11	21	31		1	11	21	31		1	16		1	16		1	16		1	11	21	31
♃	16♊	17	18	19	20	21	22	♄	17♓	17	17	16	⚷	23♓	22	22	22	♅	12♍	12	♆	17♏	17	♇	14♍	14	☊	12♊	12	11	11

AUG

	1	2	3	4	5	6	7	8	9	10	11	12	13	14	15	16	17	18	19	20	21	22	23	24	25	26	27	28	29	30	31
☉	9♌	9	10	11	12	13	14	15	16	17	18	19	20	21	22	23	24	25	26	27	28	29	30	1♍	2	3	4	4	5	6	7
☽	28♍	12♎	25	9♏	21	4♐	16	28	10♑	22	3♒	15	27	9♓	21	4♈	16	29	12♉	25	8♊	22	7♋	21	6♌	21	7♍	21	6♎	20	4♏
☿	0♍	0	0	30♌	30	29	29	28	28	27	27	26	25	24	23	23	22	21	20	20	19	18	18	18	18	18	18	18	18	19	20
♀	8♍	9	10	11	13	14	15	16	17	19	20	21	22	23	25	26	27	28	29	1♎	2	3	4	5	7	8	9	10	11	12	14
♂	18♎	19	19	20	20	21	22	22	23	23	24	25	25	26	27	27	28	28	29	30	0♏	1	2	2	3	3	4	5	5	6	7
	1	6	11	16	21	26	31		1	11	21	31		1	11	21	31		1	16		1	16		1	16		1	11	21	31
♃	22♊	23	24	25	26	27	28	♄	16♓	16	15	14	⚷	22♓	22	21	21	♅	13♍	14	♆	17♏	17	♇	15♍	15	☊	11♊	10	10	9

SEP

	1	2	3	4	5	6	7	8	9	10	11	12	13	14	15	16	17	18	19	20	21	22	23	24	25	26	27	28	29	30
☉	8♍	9	10	11	12	13	14	15	16	17	18	19	20	21	22	23	24	25	26	27	28	29	30	1♎	2	3	4	5	6	7
☽	17♏	30	12♐	25	7♑	18	0♒	12	24	6♓	18	1♈	13	26	9♉	22	5♊	18	2♋	16	1♌	16	0♍	15	30	14♎	28	12♏	25	8♐
☿	20♌	21	22	23	25	26	27	29	0♍	2	4	6	7	9	11	13	15	17	18	20	22	24	26	28	30	1♎	3	5	7	9
♀	15♎	16	17	18	20	21	22	23	24	25	27	28	29	0♏	1	3	4	5	6	7	8	10	11	12	13	14	15	17	18	19
♂	7♏	8	9	9	10	11	11	12	13	13	14	15	15	16	17	17	18	19	19	20	21	21	22	23	24	24	25	26	26	27
	1	6	11	16	21	26			1	11	21			1	11	21			1	16		1	16		1	16		1	11	21
♃	28♊	28	29	29	30	0♋		♄	14♓	13	13		⚷	21♓	20	20		♅	15♍	16	♆	18♏	18	♇	16♍	16	☊	9♊	9	8

OCT

	1	2	3	4	5	6	7	8	9	10	11	12	13	14	15	16	17	18	19	20	21	22	23	24	25	26	27	28	29	30	31
☉	8♎	9	10	11	12	13	14	14	15	16	17	18	19	20	21	22	23	24	25	26	27	28	29	0♏	1	2	3	4	5	6	7
☽	21♐	3♑	15	27	8♒	20	2♓	15	27	9♈	22	5♉	18	2♊	15	29	13♋	27	11♌	26	10♍	24	9♎	23	7♏	20	3♐	16	28	11♑	23
☿	10♎	12	14	15	17	19	20	22	24	25	27	29	0♏	2	3	5	6	8	9	11	12	14	15	17	18	20	21	23	24	26	27
♀	20♏	21	22	23	25	26	27	28	29	0♐	1	3	4	5	6	7	8	9	11	12	13	14	15	16	17	18	19	20	22	23	24
♂	28♏	28	29	30	1♐	1	2	3	3	4	5	5	6	7	8	8	9	10	11	11	12	13	13	14	15	16	16	17	18	19	19
	1	6	11	16	21	26	31		1	11	21	31		1	11	21	31		1	16		1	16		1	16		1	11	21	31
♃	1♋	1	1	1	1	1	1	♄	12♓	11	11	11	⚷	19♓	19	19	18	♅	17♍	18	♆	18♏	19	♇	17♍	17	☊	8♊	7	6	6

NOV

	1	2	3	4	5	6	7	8	9	10	11	12	13	14	15	16	17	18	19	20	21	22	23	24	25	26	27	28	29	30
☉	8♏	9	10	11	12	13	14	15	16	17	18	19	20	21	22	23	24	25	26	27	28	29	0♐	1	3	4	5	6	7	8
☽	5♒	16	28	10♓	23	5♈	18	1♉	14	28	12♊	26	10♋	24	8♌	22	7♍	21	5♎	18	2♏	15	28	11♐	24	6♑	18	0♒	12	24
☿	28♏	30	1♐	2	4	5	6	7	9	10	11	12	13	14	15	16	17	17	18	18	19	19	19	19	19	18	18	17	16	15
♀	25♐	26	27	28	29	0♑	1	2	3	4	5	6	7	9	10	11	12	13	14	15	15	16	17	18	19	20	21	22	23	24
♂	20♐	21	22	22	23	24	25	25	26	27	28	28	29	30	1♑	1	2	3	4	4	5	6	7	7	8	9	10	10	11	12
	1	6	11	16	21	26			1	11	21			1	11	21			1	16		1	16		1	16		1	11	21
♃	1♋	1	0	0	30♊	29		♄	11♓	10	11		⚷	18♓	18	18		♅	18♍	19	♆	19♏	20	♇	18♍	18	☊	6♊	5	5

DEC

	1	2	3	4	5	6	7	8	9	10	11	12	13	14	15	16	17	18	19	20	21	22	23	24	25	26	27	28	29	30	31
☉	9♐	10	11	12	13	14	15	16	17	18	19	20	21	22	23	24	25	26	27	28	29	30	1♑	2	3	4	5	6	7	8	9
☽	6♓	18	0♈	13	26	9♉	22	6♊	20	5♋	20	4♌	19	3♍	17	1♎	15	29	12♏	25	7♐	20	2♑	15	27	9♒	20	2♓	14	26	8♈
☿	14♐	12	11	10	8	7	6	5	4	4	3	3	3	3	3	4	4	5	5	6	7	8	9	10	11	13	14	15	16	18	19
♀	25♑	26	27	27	28	29	30	1♒	1	2	3	4	4	5	6	6	7	8	8	9	9	10	10	11	11	12	12	12	13	13	13
♂	13♑	13	14	15	16	17	17	18	19	20	20	21	22	23	24	24	25	26	27	27	28	29	30	1♒	1	2	3	4	5	5	6
	1	6	11	16	21	26	31		1	11	21	31		1	11	21	31		1	16		1	16		1	16		1	11	21	31
♃	29♊	28	27	27	26	25	25	♄	11♓	11	12	12	⚷	18♓	18	18	18	♅	19♍	20	♆	20♏	21	♇	18♍	18	☊	4♊	4	3	3

1966

EPHEMERIS

JAN

	1	2	3	4	5	6	7	8	9	10	11	12	13	14	15	16	17	18	19	20	21	22	23	24	25	26	27	28	29	30	31
☉	10♑	11	12	13	14	15	16	17	18	19	20	21	22	23	24	25	26	27	28	29	0♒	2	3	4	5	6	7	8	9	10	11
☽	21♈	3♉	16	30	14♊	28	13♋	28	13♌	28	13♍	28	12♎	25	9♏	22	4♐	17	29	11♑	23	5♒	17	29	11♓	23	5♈	17	29	12♉	25
☿	20♐	22	23	25	26	27	29	0♑	2	3	5	6	8	9	11	12	14	15	17	19	20	22	23	25	26	28	30	1♒	3	5	6
♀	13♒	14	14	14	14	14	14	14	14	13	13	13	13	12	12	12	11	11	10	10	9	9	8	7	7	6	6	5	4	4	3
♂	7♒	8	8	9	10	11	12	12	13	14	15	16	16	17	18	19	19	20	21	22	23	23	24	25	26	27	27	28	29	30	1♓
	1	6	11	16	21	26	31		1	11	21	31		1	11	21	31		1	16		1	16		1	16		1	11	21	31
♃	24♊	24	23	23	22	22	22	♄	12♓	13	14	15	⚷	18♓	19	19	20	♅	20♍	19	♆	21♏	22	♇	18♍	18	☊	3♊	2	2	1

FEB

	1	2	3	4	5	6	7	8	9	10	11	12	13	14	15	16	17	18	19	20	21	22	23	24	25	26	27	28			
☉	12♒	13	14	15	16	17	18	19	20	21	22	23	24	25	26	27	28	29	30	1♓	2	3	4	5	6	7	8	9			
☽	8♊	22	6♋	21	6♌	22	7♍	22	7♎	21	5♏	18	1♐	14	26	8♑	20	2♒	14	26	8♓	20	2♈	14	26	8♉	21	4♊			
☿	8♒	10	11	13	15	17	18	20	22	24	26	27	29	1♓	3	5	7	8	10	12	14	16	17	19	21	23	24	26			
v	3♒	2	2	1	1	0	30♑	29	29	29	29	29	28	28	28	28	28	28	28	29	29	29	29	30	30	0♒	1	1			
♂	1♓	2	3	4	5	5	6	7	8	8	9	10	11	12	12	13	14	15	16	16	17	18	19	19	20	21	22	23			
	1	6	11	16	21	26			1	11	21			1	11	21			1	16		1	16		1	16		1	11	21	
♃	22♊	21	21	21	21	21		♄	15♓	17	18		⚷	20♓	20	21		♅	19♍	18	♆	22♏	22	♇	18♍	18	☊	1♊	0	30♉	

MAR

	1	2	3	4	5	6	7	8	9	10	11	12	13	14	15	16	17	18	19	20	21	22	23	24	25	26	27	28	29	30	31
☉	10♓	11	12	13	14	15	16	17	18	19	20	21	22	23	24	25	26	27	28	29	30	1♈	2	3	4	5	6	7	8	9	10
☽	17♊	1♋	15	29	14♌	30	15♍	0♎	15	30	14♏	27	10♐	23	5♑	17	29	11♒	23	5♓	17	29	11♈	23	5♉	18	1♊	14	27	11♋	25
☿	27♓	29	30	1♈	2	3	4	5	5	5	6	6	6	5	5	5	4	3	3	2	1	0	29♓	28	27	27	26	25	25	24	24
♀	1♒	2	2	3	3	4	5	5	6	6	7	8	9	9	10	11	12	12	13	14	15	16	16	17	18	19	20	21	22	23	24
♂	23♓	24	25	26	26	27	28	29	30	0♈	1	2	3	3	4	5	6	7	7	8	9	10	10	11	12	13	13	14	15	16	17
	1	6	11	16	21	26	31		1	11	21	31		1	11	21	31		1	16		1	16		1	16		1	11	21	31
♃	22♊	22	22	23	23	24	24	♄	19♓	20	21	22	⚷	21♓	22	23	23	♅	18♍	17	♆	22♏	22	♇	17♍	17	☊	30♉	29	28	28

APR

	1	2	3	4	5	6	7	8	9	10	11	12	13	14	15	16	17	18	19	20	21	22	23	24	25	26	27	28	29	30	
☉	11♈	12	13	14	15	16	17	18	19	20	21	22	23	24	25	26	27	28	28	29	0♉	1	2	3	4	5	6	7	8	9	
☽	9♌	24	8♍	23	8♎	23	7♏	22	5♐	18	1♑	13	26	8♒	20	1♓	13	25	7♈	20	2♉	15	28	11♊	24	7♋	21	5♌	19	4♍	
☿	23♓	23	23	23	23	23	23	23	24	24	25	25	26	27	27	28	29	0♈	1	2	3	4	5	7	8	9	11	12	13	15	
♀	25♒	25	26	27	28	29	0♓	1	2	3	4	5	6	7	8	9	10	12	13	14	15	16	17	18	19	20	21	22	23	24	
♂	17♈	18	19	20	20	21	22	23	23	24	25	26	26	27	28	29	29	0♉	1	2	2	3	4	5	5	6	7	8	8	9	
	1	6	11	16	21	26			1	11	21			1	11	21			1	16		1	16		1	16		1	11	21	
♃	24♊	25	26	27	27	28		♄	22♓	24	25		⚷	23♓	24	24		♅	17♍	16	♆	22♏	21	♇	17♍	16	☊	28♉	27	27	

MAY

	1	2	3	4	5	6	7	8	9	10	11	12	13	14	15	16	17	18	19	20	21	22	23	24	25	26	27	28	29	30	31
☉	10♉	11	12	13	14	15	16	17	18	19	20	21	22	23	24	25	26	27	28	29	29	0♊	1	2	3	4	5	6	7	8	9
☽	18♍	3♎	17	2♏	16	30	13♐	26	9♑	21	4♒	16	28	9♓	21	3♈	16	28	11♉	24	7♊	20	4♋	18	2♌	16	0♍	15	29	13♎	27
☿	16♈	18	19	21	22	24	26	27	29	1♉	2	4	6	8	10	12	14	16	18	20	22	24	26	28	1♊	3	5	7	9	12	14
♀	25♓	26	28	29	30	1♈	2	3	4	5	6	8	9	10	11	12	13	14	15	17	18	19	20	21	22	23	25	26	27	28	29
♂	10♉	10	11	12	13	13	14	15	16	16	17	18	19	19	20	21	21	22	23	24	24	25	26	26	27	28	29	29	0♊	1	1
	1	6	11	16	21	26	31		1	11	21	31		1	11	21	31		1	16		1	16		1	16		1	11	21	31
♃	29♊	0♋	1	2	3	4	5	♄	26♓	27	28	28	⚷	25♓	25	26	26	♅	16♍	16	♆	21♏	21	♇	16♍	16	☊	26♉	26	25	25

JUN

	1	2	3	4	5	6	7	8	9	10	11	12	13	14	15	16	17	18	19	20	21	22	23	24	25	26	27	28	29	30	
☉	10♊	11	12	13	14	15	16	17	18	19	20	21	22	22	23	24	25	26	27	28	29	0♋	1	2	3	4	5	6	7	8	
☽	11♏	25	8♐	21	4♑	17	29	12♒	24	5♓	17	29	11♈	24	6♉	19	2♊	15	29	14♋	28	12♌	27	11♍	26	10♎	24	7♏	21	4♐	
☿	16♊	18	20	22	24	26	28	0♋	2	4	6	8	10	11	13	15	16	18	20	21	22	24	25	27	28	29	0♌	1	2	3	
♀	0♉	1	3	4	5	6	7	8	10	11	12	13	14	15	17	18	19	20	21	22	24	25	26	27	28	29	1♊	2	3	4	
♂	2♊	3	4	4	5	6	6	7	8	9	9	10	11	11	12	13	13	14	15	16	16	17	18	18	19	20	20	21	22	22	
	1	6	11	16	21	26			1	11	21			1	11	21			1	16		1	16		1	16		1	11	21	
♃	5♋	6	8	9	10	11		♄	28♓	29	29		⚷	26♓	26	26		♅	16♍	16	♆	20♏	20	♇	16♍	16	☊	25♉	24	24	

EPHEMERIS

1966

JUL

	1	2	3	4	5	6	7	8	9	10	11	12	13	14	15	16	17	18	19	20	21	22	23	24	25	26	27	28	29	30	31
☉	9♋	10	11	12	13	13	14	15	16	17	18	19	20	21	22	23	24	25	26	27	28	29	30	1♌	2	3	4	4	5	6	7
☽	17♐	0♑	13	25	8♒	20	2♓	14	25	7♈	19	2♉	14	27	10♊	24	8♋	22	7♌	22	7♍	22	6♎	20	4♏	18	1♐	14	27	9♑	22
☿	4♌	5	6	7	8	8	9	10	10	11	11	11	11	11	11	11	11	11	11	10	10	9	9	8	8	7	6	5	5	4	3
♀	5♊	7	8	9	10	11	12	14	15	16	17	18	20	21	22	23	24	26	27	28	29	0♋	2	3	4	5	6	8	9	10	11
♂	23♊	24	24	25	26	27	27	28	29	29	30	1♋	1	2	3	3	4	5	5	6	7	7	8	9	9	10	11	11	12	13	13
	1	6	11	16	21	26	31		1	11	21	31		1	11	21	31		1	16		1	16		1	16		1	11	21	31
♃	12♋	13	14	15	17	18	19	♄	30♓	30	30	29	⚷	26♓	26	26	26	♅	16♍	17	♆	20♏	19	♇	16♍	16	☊	23♉	23	22	21

AUG

	1	2	3	4	5	6	7	8	9	10	11	12	13	14	15	16	17	18	19	20	21	22	23	24	25	26	27	28	29	30	31
☉	8♌	9	10	11	12	13	14	15	16	17	18	19	20	21	22	23	24	25	26	27	27	28	29	0♍	1	2	3	4	5	6	7
☽	4♒	16	28	10♓	22	4♈	16	28	10♉	22	5♊	18	2♋	16	1♌	16	1♍	16	1♎	16	0♏	14	28	11♐	24	6♑	19	1♒	13	25	7♓
☿	3♌	2	2	1	1	1	0	0	0	1	1	1	2	2	3	4	5	6	7	9	10	11	13	14	16	18	20	22	23	25	27
♀	12♋	14	15	16	17	18	20	21	22	23	24	26	27	28	29	1♌	2	3	4	5	7	8	9	10	12	13	14	15	16	18	19
♂	14♋	15	15	16	17	17	18	19	19	20	21	21	22	22	23	24	24	25	26	26	27	28	28	29	30	0♌	1	1	2	3	3
	1	6	11	16	21	26	31		1	11	21	31		1	11	21	31		1	16		1	16		1	16		1	11	21	31
♃	19♋	20	21	22	23	24	25	♄	29♓	29	28	28	⚷	26♓	25	25	25	♅	17♍	18	♆	19♏	19	♇	17♍	17	☊	21♉	21	20	20

SEP

	1	2	3	4	5	6	7	8	9	10	11	12	13	14	15	16	17	18	19	20	21	22	23	24	25	26	27	28	29	30
☉	8♍	9	10	11	12	13	14	15	16	17	18	19	20	21	22	23	24	25	26	27	28	29	30	1♎	1	2	3	4	5	6
☽	19♓	1♈	13	25	7♉	19	1♊	14	27	11♋	25	9♌	24	9♍	25	10♎	25	9♏	23	7♐	20	3♑	16	28	10♒	22	4♓	16	28	10♈
☿	29♌	1♍	3	5	7	9	11	13	15	17	18	20	22	24	26	28	29	1♎	3	5	6	8	10	11	13	15	16	18	19	21
♀	20♌	21	23	24	25	26	28	29	0♍	1	2	4	5	6	7	9	10	11	12	14	15	16	17	19	20	21	22	24	25	26
♂	4♌	5	5	6	7	7	8	8	9	10	10	11	12	12	13	14	14	15	15	16	17	17	18	19	19	20	20	21	22	22
	1	6	11	16	21	26			1	11	21			1	11	21			1	16		1	16		1	16		1	11	21
♃	25♋	26	27	28	29	30		♄	28♓	27	26		⚷	25♓	24	24		♅	19♍	20	♆	20♏	20	♇	18♍	18	☊	20♉	19	19

OCT

	1	2	3	4	5	6	7	8	9	10	11	12	13	14	15	16	17	18	19	20	21	22	23	24	25	26	27	28	29	30	31
☉	7♎	8	9	10	11	12	13	14	15	16	17	18	19	20	21	22	23	24	25	26	27	28	29	0♏	1	2	3	4	5	6	7
☽	22♈	4♉	16	28	11♊	23	6♋	20	4♌	18	3♍	18	3♎	18	3♏	18	2♐	16	29	12♑	24	7♒	19	1♓	13	25	6♈	18	0♉	13	25
☿	23♎	24	26	27	29	0♏	2	3	4	6	7	9	10	11	13	14	15	17	18	19	20	22	23	24	25	26	27	28	29	30	1♐
♀	27♍	29	30	1♎	2	4	5	6	7	9	10	11	12	14	15	16	17	19	20	21	22	24	25	26	27	29	30	1♏	2	4	5
♂	23♌	23	24	25	25	26	26	27	28	28	29	30	0♍	1	1	2	3	3	4	4	5	6	6	7	7	8	8	9	10	10	11
	1	6	11	16	21	26	31		1	11	21	31		1	11	21	31		1	16		1	16		1	16		1	11	21	31
♃	1♌	1	2	2	3	3	4	♄	25♓	25	24	24	⚷	23♓	23	22	22	♅	21♍	22	♆	20♏	21	♇	19♍	19	☊	18♉	18	17	17

NOV

	1	2	3	4	5	6	7	8	9	10	11	12	13	14	15	16	17	18	19	20	21	22	23	24	25	26	27	28	29	30
☉	8♏	9	10	11	12	13	14	15	16	17	18	19	20	21	22	23	24	25	26	27	28	29	0♐	1	2	3	4	5	6	7
☽	8♊	20	3♋	17	0♌	14	28	12♍	27	12♎	26	11♏	25	10♐	23	7♑	20	3♒	15	27	9♓	21	3♈	15	27	9♉	21	4♊	17	0♋
☿	1♐	2	2	3	3	3	3	3	3	2	2	1	0	29♏	28	27	25	24	23	21	20	19	18	18	17	17	17	17	18	18
♀	6♏	7	9	10	11	12	14	15	16	17	19	20	21	22	24	25	26	27	29	30	1♐	2	4	5	6	7	9	10	11	13
♂	11♍	12	13	13	14	14	15	15	16	17	17	18	18	19	19	20	21	21	22	22	23	23	24	25	25	26	26	27	27	28
	1	6	11	16	21	26			1	11	21			1	11	21			1	16		1	16		1	16		1	11	21
♃	4♌	4	4	4	4	4		♄	23♓	23	23		⚷	22♓	22	22		♅	23♍	24	♆	21♏	22	♇	20♍	20	☊	17♉	16	15

DEC

	1	2	3	4	5	6	7	8	9	10	11	12	13	14	15	16	17	18	19	20	21	22	23	24	25	26	27	28	29	30	31
☉	8♐	9	10	11	12	13	14	15	16	17	18	20	21	22	23	24	25	26	27	28	29	30	1♑	2	3	4	5	6	7	8	9
☽	14♋	27	11♌	25	9♍	23	7♎	22	6♏	20	4♐	18	1♑	15	28	10♒	23	5♓	17	29	11♈	22	4♉	17	29	12♊	26	9♋	23	7♌	21
☿	19♏	19	20	21	22	23	24	25	27	28	29	0♐	2	3	5	6	7	9	10	12	13	15	16	18	19	21	22	24	25	27	28
♀	14♐	15	16	18	19	20	21	23	24	25	26	28	29	0♑	1	3	4	5	6	8	9	10	11	13	14	15	16	18	19	20	21
♂	28♍	29	29	30	1♎	1	2	2	3	3	4	4	5	5	6	6	7	7	8	8	9	9	10	10	11	11	12	12	13	13	14
	1	6	11	16	21	26	31		1	11	21	31		1	11	21	31		1	16		1	16		1	16		1	11	21	31
♃	4♌	4	4	4	3	3	2	♄	23♓	23	23	24	⚷	22♓	22	22	22	♅	24♍	24	♆	23♏	23	♇	21♍	21	☊	15♉	14	14	13

1967

JAN

	1	2	3	4	5	6	7	8	9	10	11	12	13	14	15	16	17	18	19	20	21	22	23	24	25	26	27	28	29	30	31
☉	10♑	11	12	13	14	15	16	17	18	19	20	21	22	23	24	25	26	27	28	29	0♒	1	2	3	4	5	6	7	8	9	10
☽	6♍	20	4♎	18	2♏	16	30	13♐	27	10♑	23	6♒	18	1♓	13	25	6♈	18	0♉	12	24	7♊	20	3♋	17	2♌	16	1♍	16	0♎	15
☿	30♐	1♑	3	5	6	8	9	11	12	14	16	17	19	21	22	24	25	27	29	0♒	2	4	6	7	9	11	12	14	16	18	19
♀	23♑	24	25	26	28	29	0♒	1	3	4	5	6	8	9	10	12	13	14	15	17	18	19	20	22	23	24	25	27	28	29	0♓
♂	14♎	15	15	16	16	16	17	17	18	18	19	19	19	20	20	21	21	22	22	22	23	23	23	24	24	25	25	25	26	26	26
	1	6	11	16	21	26	31		1	11	21	31		1	11	21	31		1	16		1	16		1	16		1	11	21	31
♃	2♌	1	1	0	29♋	29	28	♄	24♓	25	26	26	⚷	22♓	22	23	23	♅	24♍	24	♆	24♏	24	♇	21♍	21	☊	13♉	13	12	12

FEB

	1	2	3	4	5	6	7	8	9	10	11	12	13	14	15	16	17	18	19	20	21	22	23	24	25	26	27	28
☉	11♒	12	13	14	15	16	18	19	20	21	22	23	24	25	26	27	28	29	30	1♓	2	3	4	5	6	7	8	9
☽	29♎	13♏	27	10♐	23	6♑	19	2♒	14	27	9♓	21	3♈	15	26	8♉	20	2♊	15	28	11♋	25	10♌	24	9♍	24	10♎	24
☿	21♒	23	25	26	28	30	2♓	3	5	7	8	10	11	12	14	15	16	17	17	18	18	19	19	19	19	18	18	17
♀	2♓	3	4	5	6	8	9	10	11	13	14	15	16	18	19	20	21	23	24	25	26	28	29	0♈	1	3	4	5
♂	27♎	27	27	28	28	28	29	29	29	29	30	30	0♏	0	1	1	1	1	1	2	2	2	2	2	2	3	3	3
	1	6	11	16	21	26			1	11	21			1	11	21			1	16		1	16		1	16		1
♃	28♋	27	27	26	26	25		♄	27♓	28	29		⚷	23♓	24	24		♅	24♍	23	♆	24♏	24	♇	20♍	20	☊	12♉

	29	30
	11	21
♃	11	11

MAR

	1	2	3	4	5	6	7	8	9	10	11	12	13	14	15	16	17	18	19	20	21	22	23	24	25	26	27	28	29	30	31
☉	10♓	11	12	13	14	15	16	17	18	19	20	21	22	23	24	25	26	27	28	29	30	1♈	2	3	4	5	6	7	8	9	10
☽	9♏	23	7♐	20	3♑	16	29	11♒	24	6♓	18	30	11♈	23	5♉	17	29	11♊	24	6♋	20	3♌	18	2♍	17	3♎	18	3♏	18	2♐	16
☿	16♓	15	14	13	12	11	10	9	8	8	7	6	6	5	5	5	5	5	5	5	5	5	6	6	7	8	8	9	10	11	12
♀	6♈	7	9	10	11	12	14	15	16	17	19	20	21	22	23	25	26	27	28	29	1♉	2	3	4	6	7	8	9	10	12	13
♂	3♏	3	3	3	3	3	3	3	3	3	3	3	3	3	3	3	3	3	3	2	2	2	2	2	2	1	1	1	1	0	0
	1	6	11	16	21	26	31		1	11	21	31		1	11	21	31		1	16		1	16		1	16		1	11	21	31
♃	25♋	25	25	24	24	24	25	♄	30♓	1♈	2	3	⚷	25♓	25	26	27	♅	23♍	22	♆	24♏	24	♇	20♍	19	☊	10♉	10	9	9

APR

	1	2	3	4	5	6	7	8	9	10	11	12	13	14	15	16	17	18	19	20	21	22	23	24	25	26	27	28	29	30
☉	11♈	12	13	14	15	16	16	17	18	19	20	21	22	23	24	25	26	27	28	29	0♉	1	2	3	4	5	6	7	8	9
☽	30♐	13♑	26	8♒	21	3♓	15	27	8♈	20	2♉	14	26	8♊	20	3♋	16	29	13♌	27	11♍	26	11♎	26	11♏	26	11♐	25	9♑	22
☿	13♓	14	15	16	17	18	20	21	22	23	25	26	28	29	1♈	2	4	5	7	8	10	12	13	15	17	19	21	22	24	26
♀	14♉	15	16	18	19	20	21	22	24	25	26	27	28	30	1♊	2	3	4	5	7	8	9	10	11	12	14	15	16	17	18
♂	30♎	29	29	29	29	28	28	28	27	27	26	26	26	25	25	25	24	24	23	23	23	22	22	22	21	21	21	20	20	20
	1	6	11	16	21	26			1	11	21			1	11	21			1	16		1	16		1	16		1	11	21
♃	25♋	25	25	25	26	26		♄	3♈	5	6		⚷	27♓	27	28		♅	22♍	21	♆	24♏	24	♇	19♍	18	☊	9♉	8	7

MAY

	1	2	3	4	5	6	7	8	9	10	11	12	13	14	15	16	17	18	19	20	21	22	23	24	25	26	27	28	29	30	31
☉	10♉	11	12	13	14	15	16	17	18	19	20	21	22	23	23	24	25	26	27	28	29	0♊	1	2	3	4	5	6	7	8	9
☽	5♒	17	30	12♓	24	5♈	17	29	11♉	23	5♊	17	30	13♋	26	9♌	23	6♍	21	5♎	20	5♏	19	4♐	19	3♑	17	0♒	13	26	8♓
☿	28♈	0♉	2	4	6	8	10	12	14	17	19	21	23	25	28	30	2♊	4	6	8	10	12	14	16	18	20	22	24	25	27	29
♀	19♊	21	22	23	24	25	26	27	29	30	1♋	2	3	4	5	6	8	9	10	11	12	13	14	15	16	18	19	20	21	22	23
♂	19♎	19	19	18	18	18	17	17	17	17	17	16	16	16	16	16	16	15	15	15	15	15	15	15	15	15	15	15	15	15	15
	1	6	11	16	21	26	31		1	11	21	31		1	11	21	31		1	16		1	16		1	16		1	11	21	31
♃	27♋	28	28	29	30	0♌	1	♄	7♈	8	9	10	⚷	28♓	29	29	29	♅	21♍	20	♆	23♏	23	♇	18♍	18	☊	7♉	6	6	5

JUN

	1	2	3	4	5	6	7	8	9	10	11	12	13	14	15	16	17	18	19	20	21	22	23	24	25	26	27	28	29	30
☉	10♊	11	12	13	14	15	16	17	17	18	19	20	21	22	23	24	25	26	27	28	29	30	1♋	2	3	4	5	6	7	8
☽	20♓	2♈	14	26	7♉	19	2♊	14	27	10♋	23	6♌	19	3♍	17	1♎	15	30	14♏	29	13♐	27	11♑	25	8♒	21	4♓	16	28	10♈
☿	0♋	2	3	5	6	8	9	10	11	12	14	15	16	16	17	18	19	19	20	20	21	21	22	22	22	22	22	22	22	21
♀	24♋	25	26	27	28	29	0♌	1	2	3	4	5	6	7	8	9	10	11	12	13	14	15	16	17	18	19	20	21	22	23
♂	15♎	15	15	15	16	16	16	16	16	16	16	17	17	17	17	18	18	18	18	19	19	19	19	20	20	20	21	21	21	22
	1	6	11	16	21	26			1	11	21			1	11	21			1	16		1	16		1	16		1	11	21
♃	1♌	2	3	4	5	6		♄	10♈	11	11		⚷	29♓	30	30		♅	20♍	20	♆	23♏	22	♇	18♍	18	☊	5♉	5	4

1967

EPHEMERIS

JUL

	1	2	3	4	5	6	7	8	9	10	11	12	13	14	15	16	17	18	19	20	21	22	23	24	25	26	27	28	29	30	31
☉	8♋	9	10	11	12	13	14	15	16	17	18	19	20	21	22	23	24	25	26	27	28	29	29	0♌	1	2	3	4	5	6	7
☽	22♈	4♉	16	28	10♊	23	6♋	19	2♌	16	30	14♍	28	12♎	26	10♏	25	9♐	22	6♑	20	3♒	16	29	12♓	24	6♈	18	30	11♉	23
☿	21♋	21	20	20	19	19	18	18	17	16	16	15	15	14	14	13	13	13	12	12	12	12	13	13	13	14	14	15	16	17	18
♀	23♌	24	25	26	27	28	28	29	0♍	1	2	2	3	4	4	5	6	6	7	8	8	9	9	10	10	11	11	12	12	12	13
♂	22♎	22	23	23	24	24	24	25	25	26	26	26	27	27	28	28	29	29	30	0♏	0	1	1	2	2	3	3	4	4	5	6
	1	6	11	16	21	26	31		1	11	21	31		1	11	21	31		1	16		1	16		1	16		1	11	21	31
♃	7♌	8	9	10	11	13	14	♄	12♈	12	12	12	⚷	30♓	30	30	29	♅	21♍	21	♆	22♏	22	♇	18♍	19	☊	4♉	3	3	2

AUG

	1	2	3	4	5	6	7	8	9	10	11	12	13	14	15	16	17	18	19	20	21	22	23	24	25	26	27	28	29	30	31
☉	8♌	9	10	11	12	13	14	15	16	17	18	19	20	21	21	22	23	24	25	26	27	28	29	0♍	1	2	3	4	5	6	7
☽	6♊	18	1♋	14	27	11♌	25	10♍	24	9♎	23	7♏	21	5♐	19	3♑	16	29	12♒	25	8♓	20	2♈	14	26	8♉	19	1♊	14	26	9♋
☿	19♋	20	21	22	24	25	27	28	0♌	2	4	6	7	9	11	13	15	17	19	21	23	25	27	29	1♍	3	5	7	9	11	13
♀	13♍	13	13	14	14	14	14	14	14	14	14	14	14	13	13	13	13	12	12	11	11	10	10	9	9	8	8	7	6	6	5
♂	6♏	7	7	8	8	9	9	10	10	11	12	12	13	13	14	14	15	16	16	17	17	18	19	19	20	20	21	22	22	23	24
	1	6	11	16	21	26	31		1	11	21	31		1	11	21	31		1	16		1	16		1	16		1	11	21	31
♃	14♌	15	16	17	18	19	20	♄	12♈	12	12	11	⚷	29♓	29	29	28	♅	22♍	23	♆	22♏	22	♇	19♍	19	☊	2♉	2	1	1

SEP

	1	2	3	4	5	6	7	8	9	10	11	12	13	14	15	16	17	18	19	20	21	22	23	24	25	26	27	28	29	30
☉	8♍	9	10	11	12	13	14	15	16	17	18	19	20	20	21	22	23	24	25	26	27	28	29	0♎	1	2	3	4	5	6
☽	22♋	6♌	20	4♍	19	4♎	18	3♏	18	2♐	16	30	13♑	26	9♒	22	4♓	16	29	11♈	22	4♉	16	28	10♊	22	4♋	17	0♌	14
☿	15♍	17	18	20	22	24	25	27	29	0♎	2	4	5	7	9	10	12	13	15	16	18	19	20	22	23	25	26	27	29	30
♀	5♍	4	3	3	2	2	1	1	0	30♌	29	29	29	28	28	28	28	28	28	28	28	28	28	28	28	28	28	29	29	29
♂	24♏	25	25	26	27	27	28	29	29	30	1♐	1	2	3	3	4	5	5	6	7	7	8	9	9	10	11	11	12	13	13
	1	6	11	16	21	26			1	11	21			1	11	21			1	16		1	16		1	16		1	11	21
♃	21♌	22	23	24	25	26		♄	11♈	11	10		⚷	28♓	28	28		♅	24♍	25	♆	22♏	22	♇	20♍	21	☊	0♉	30♈	29

OCT

	1	2	3	4	5	6	7	8	9	10	11	12	13	14	15	16	17	18	19	20	21	22	23	24	25	26	27	28	29	30	31
☉	7♎	8	9	10	11	12	13	14	15	16	17	18	19	20	21	22	23	24	25	26	27	28	29	30	1♏	2	3	4	5	6	7
☽	28♌	12♍	27	12♎	27	12♏	27	12♐	26	10♑	23	6♒	19	1♓	13	26	7♈	19	1♉	13	25	7♊	19	1♋	13	26	9♌	22	6♍	21	5♎
☿	1♏	2	4	5	6	7	8	9	10	11	12	13	14	15	15	16	16	17	17	17	17	17	17	17	16	16	15	14	13	12	11
♀	30♌	0♍	1	1	1	2	2	3	4	4	5	5	6	7	7	8	9	10	10	11	12	13	14	14	15	16	17	18	19	20	21
♂	14♐	15	16	16	17	18	18	19	20	21	21	22	23	23	24	25	26	26	27	28	28	29	30	1♑	1	2	3	4	4	5	6
	1	6	11	16	21	26	31		1	11	21	31		1	11	21	31		1	16		1	16		1	16		1	11	21	31
♃	27♌	28	29	29	0♍	1	2	♄	9♈	8	8	7	⚷	27♓	27	26	26	♅	26♍	27	♆	22♏	23	♇	21♍	22	☊	29♈	28	28	27

NOV

	1	2	3	4	5	6	7	8	9	10	11	12	13	14	15	16	17	18	19	20	21	22	23	24	25	26	27	28	29	30
☉	8♏	9	10	11	12	13	14	15	16	17	18	19	20	21	22	23	24	25	26	27	28	29	30	1♐	2	3	4	5	6	7
☽	20♎	5♏	21	6♐	21	5♑	19	2♒	15	28	10♓	23	4♈	16	28	10♉	22	4♊	16	28	10♋	23	5♌	18	2♍	15	30	14♎	29	14♏
☿	9♏	8	7	6	4	4	3	2	2	1	1	2	2	2	3	4	5	6	7	8	9	10	12	13	14	16	17	19	20	22
♀	22♍	22	23	24	25	26	27	28	29	0♎	1	2	3	4	5	6	8	9	10	11	12	13	14	15	16	17	18	19	21	22
♂	7♑	7	8	9	10	10	11	12	13	13	14	15	16	16	17	18	19	19	20	21	22	22	23	24	25	26	26	27	28	29
	1	6	11	16	21	26			1	11	21			1	11	21			1	16		1	16		1	16		1	11	21
♃	2♍	3	3	4	4	5		♄	7♈	6	6		⚷	26♓	26	25		♅	27♍	28	♆	23♏	24	♇	22♍	22	☊	27♈	27	26

DEC

	1	2	3	4	5	6	7	8	9	10	11	12	13	14	15	16	17	18	19	20	21	22	23	24	25	26	27	28	29	30	31
☉	8♐	9	10	11	12	13	14	15	16	17	18	19	20	21	22	23	24	25	26	27	28	29	0♑	1	2	4	5	6	7	8	9
☽	29♏	14♐	29	13♑	27	11♒	24	7♓	19	1♈	13	25	7♉	18	0♊	12	25	7♋	20	2♌	15	29	12♍	26	10♎	24	8♏	23	7♐	22	7♑
☿	23♏	25	26	28	29	1♐	2	4	5	7	8	10	11	13	15	16	18	19	21	22	24	25	27	29	0♑	2	3	5	7	8	10
♀	23♎	24	25	26	27	28	30	1♏	2	3	4	5	6	8	9	10	11	12	13	15	16	17	18	19	21	22	23	24	25	26	28
♂	29♑	0♒	1	2	2	3	4	5	6	6	7	8	9	9	10	11	12	13	13	14	15	16	16	17	18	19	20	20	21	22	23
	1	6	11	16	21	26	31		1	11	21	31		1	11	21	31		1	16		1	16		1	16		1	11	21	31
♃	5♍	5	6	6	6	6	6	♄	6♈	6	6	6	⚷	25♓	25	25	26	♅	29♍	29	♆	25♏	25	♇	23♍	23	☊	26♈	25	25	24

1968

JAN

	1	2	3	4	5	6	7	8	9	10	11	12	13	14	15	16	17	18	19	20	21	22	23	24	25	26	27	28	29	30	31
☉	10♑	11	12	13	14	15	16	17	18	19	20	21	22	23	24	25	26	27	28	29	0♒	1	2	3	4	5	6	7	8	9	10
☽	21♑	5♒	19	2♓	15	27	9♈	21	3♉	15	27	9♊	21	3♋	16	29	12♌	25	9♍	23	6♎	20	4♏	19	3♐	17	1♑	15	29	13♒	27
☿	11♑	13	15	16	18	20	21	23	24	26	28	29	1♒	3	5	6	8	10	11	13	14	16	18	19	21	22	24	25	26	27	29
♀	29♏	0♐	1	2	4	5	6	7	8	10	11	12	13	15	16	17	18	19	21	22	23	24	25	27	28	29	0♑	2	3	4	5
♂	23♒	24	25	26	27	27	28	29	30	0♓	1	2	3	4	4	5	6	7	7	8	9	10	11	11	12	13	14	14	15	16	17
	1	6	11	16	21	26	31		1	11	21	31		1	11	21	31		1	16		1	16		1	16		1	11	21	31
♃	6♍	5	5	5	4	4	3	♄	6♈	7	7	8	⚷	26♓	26	26	27	♅	29♍	29	♆	26♏	26	♇	23♍	23	☊	24♈	23	23	22

FEB

	1	2	3	4	5	6	7	8	9	10	11	12	13	14	15	16	17	18	19	20	21	22	23	24	25	26	27	28	29
☉	11♒	12	13	14	15	16	17	18	19	20	21	22	23	24	25	26	27	28	29	0♓	1	2	3	4	5	6	7	8	9
☽	10♓	22	5♈	17	29	11♉	23	4♊	16	29	11♋	24	7♌	21	5♍	19	3♎	17	1♏	15	30	14♐	28	11♑	25	9♒	22	5♓	18
☿	30♒	0♓	1	2	2	2	2	2	2	1	1	30♒	29	28	27	26	24	23	22	21	20	19	19	18	18	17	17	17	17
♀	6♑	8	9	10	11	13	14	15	16	17	19	20	21	22	24	25	26	27	29	30	1♒	2	3	5	6	7	8	10	11
♂	18♓	18	19	20	21	21	22	23	24	25	25	26	27	28	28	29	30	1♈	1	2	3	4	4	5	6	7	8	8	9

	1	6	11	16	21	26			1	11	21			1	11	21			1	16		1	16		1	16		1	11	21	
♃	3♍	3	2	1	1	0		♄	8♈	9	10		⚷	27♓	27	28		♅	29♍	28	♆	26♏	26	♇	23♍	22	☊	22♈	22	21	

MAR

	1	2	3	4	5	6	7	8	9	10	11	12	13	14	15	16	17	18	19	20	21	22	23	24	25	26	27	28	29	30	31
☉	10♓	11	12	13	14	15	16	17	18	19	20	21	22	23	24	25	26	27	28	29	0♈	1	2	3	4	5	6	7	8	9	10
☽	0♈	13	25	7♉	19	0♊	12	24	6♋	19	2♌	15	29	13♍	27	12♎	27	11♏	26	10♐	24	8♑	22	5♒	19	1♓	14	27	9♈	21	3♉
☿	17♒	17	18	18	19	19	20	21	21	22	23	24	25	26	27	28	29	0♓	2	3	4	5	7	8	10	11	12	14	15	17	18
♀	12♒	13	15	16	17	18	19	21	22	23	24	26	27	28	29	1♓	2	3	4	5	7	8	9	10	12	13	14	15	17	18	19
♂	10♈	11	11	12	13	14	14	15	16	17	17	18	19	20	20	21	22	23	23	24	25	26	26	27	28	29	29	0♉	1	1	2
	1	6	11	16	21	26	31		1	11	21	31		1	11	21	31		1	16		1	16		1	16		1	11	21	31
♃	30♌	29	28	28	27	27	27	♄	11♈	12	13	15	⚷	28♓	29	29	30	♅	28♍	27	♆	27♏	26	♇	22♍	21	☊	21♈	20	20	19

APR

	1	2	3	4	5	6	7	8	9	10	11	12	13	14	15	16	17	18	19	20	21	22	23	24	25	26	27	28	29	30
☉	11♈	12	13	14	15	16	17	18	19	20	21	22	23	24	25	26	27	28	29	30	1♉	2	3	4	5	6	7	8	9	10
☽	15♉	27	9♊	20	2♋	15	27	10♌	23	7♍	21	5♎	20	5♏	20	5♐	20	5♑	19	2♒	16	29	11♓	24	6♈	18	30	12♉	24	5♊
☿	20♓	22	23	25	27	28	30	2♈	3	5	7	9	11	13	15	16	18	20	22	24	26	29	1♉	3	5	7	9	11	13	16
♀	20♓	21	23	24	25	26	28	29	0♈	1	3	4	5	6	7	9	10	11	12	14	15	16	17	19	20	21	22	23	25	26
♂	3♉	4	4	5	6	7	7	8	9	10	10	11	12	12	13	14	15	15	16	17	17	18	19	20	20	21	22	22	23	24

	1	6	11	16	21	26			1	11	21			1	11	21			1	16		1	16		1	16		1	11	21	
♃	27♌	26	26	26	26	26		♄	15♈	16	17		⚷	30♓	1♈	1		♅	27♍	26	♆	26♏	26	♇	21♍	21	☊	19♈	19	18	

MAY

	1	2	3	4	5	6	7	8	9	10	11	12	13	14	15	16	17	18	19	20	21	22	23	24	25	26	27	28	29	30	31
☉	11♉	12	13	14	15	16	16	17	18	19	20	21	22	23	24	25	26	27	28	29	30	1♊	2	3	4	5	6	7	8	9	10
☽	17♊	29	11♋	23	6♌	19	2♍	15	29	14♎	28	14♏	29	14♐	29	14♑	28	12♒	25	8♓	21	3♈	15	27	9♉	21	2♊	14	26	8♋	20
☿	18♉	20	22	24	26	28	0♊	2	4	6	8	9	11	13	14	16	17	18	20	21	22	23	24	25	26	27	28	29	29	0♋	1
♀	27♈	28	30	1♉	2	3	5	6	7	8	9	11	12	13	14	16	17	18	19	21	22	23	24	25	27	28	29	0♊	2	3	4
♂	25♉	25	26	27	27	28	29	30	0♊	1	2	2	3	4	4	5	6	7	7	8	9	9	10	11	11	12	13	14	14	15	16
	1	6	11	16	21	26	31		1	11	21	31		1	11	21	31		1	16		1	16		1	16		1	11	21	31
♃	26♌	26	26	27	27	28	28	♄	19♈	20	21	22	⚷	2♈	2	2	3	♅	26♍	25	♆	26♏	25	♇	20♍	20	☊	18♈	17	17	16

JUN

	1	2	3	4	5	6	7	8	9	10	11	12	13	14	15	16	17	18	19	20	21	22	23	24	25	26	27	28	29	30
☉	11♊	12	12	13	14	15	16	17	18	19	20	21	22	23	24	25	26	27	28	29	30	1♋	2	3	3	4	5	6	7	8
☽	3♌	15	28	11♍	24	8♎	22	7♏	22	7♐	22	7♑	22	7♒	21	4♓	17	30	12♈	24	6♉	18	29	11♊	23	5♋	17	30	12♌	25
☿	1♋	1	2	2	2	2	2	2	2	2	1	1	0	30♊	29	29	28	28	27	27	26	26	25	25	24	24	24	23	23	23
♀	5♊	6	8	9	10	11	13	14	15	16	18	19	20	21	22	24	25	26	27	29	30	1♋	2	4	5	6	7	8	10	11
♂	16♊	17	18	18	19	20	20	21	22	22	23	24	24	25	26	26	27	28	29	29	30	1♋	1	2	3	3	4	5	5	6

	1	6	11	16	21	26			1	11	21			1	11	21			1	16		1	16		1	16		1	11	21	
♃	28♌	29	29	0♍	1	2		♄	22♈	23	24		⚷	3♈	3	3		♅	25♍	25	♆	25♏	24	♇	20♍	20	☊	16♈	15	15	

EPHEMERIS

1968

JUL

	1	2	3	4	5	6	7	8	9	10	11	12	13	14	15	16	17	18	19	20	21	22	23	24	25	26	27	28	29	30	31
☉	9♋	10	11	12	13	14	15	16	17	18	19	20	21	22	23	24	24	25	26	27	28	29	0♌	1	2	3	4	5	6	7	8
☽	8♍	21	4♎	18	2♏	17	1♐	16	1♑	16	1♒	15	29	12♓	25	8♈	20	2♉	14	26	8♊	20	2♋	14	26	9♌	22	5♍	18	1♎	15
☿	23♊	23	24	24	24	25	25	26	26	27	28	29	30	1♋	2	3	5	6	8	9	11	12	14	16	18	20	21	23	25	27	29
♀	12♋	13	15	16	17	18	19	21	22	23	24	26	27	28	29	1♌	2	3	4	5	7	8	9	10	12	13	14	15	17	18	19
♂	7♋	7	8	9	9	10	11	11	12	13	13	14	15	15	16	16	17	18	18	19	20	20	21	22	22	23	24	24	25	26	26
	1	6	11	16	21	26	31		1	11	21	31		1	11	21	31		1	16		1	16		1	16		1	11	21	31
♃	2♍	3	4	5	6	7	8	♄	24♈	25	25	26	⚷	3♈	3	3	3	♅	25♍	26	♆	24♏	24	♇	20♍	21	☊	14♈	14	13	13

AUG

	1	2	3	4	5	6	7	8	9	10	11	12	13	14	15	16	17	18	19	20	21	22	23	24	25	26	27	28	29	30	31
☉	9♌	10	11	12	13	14	15	16	17	18	19	20	21	22	23	24	24	25	26	27	28	29	30	1♍	2	3	4	5	6	7	8
☽	29♎	13♏	27	11♐	26	10♑	25	9♒	23	7♓	20	3♈	16	28	10♉	22	4♊	16	28	10♋	22	5♌	18	1♍	14	28	12♎	26	10♏	24	8♐
☿	2♌	4	6	8	10	12	14	16	18	20	22	24	26	28	30	2♍	4	6	7	9	11	13	14	16	18	19	21	23	24	26	27
♀	20♌	21	23	24	25	26	28	29	0♍	1	3	4	5	6	7	9	10	11	12	14	15	16	17	19	20	21	22	24	25	26	27
♂	27♋	28	28	29	30	0♌	1	1	2	3	3	4	5	5	6	7	7	8	9	9	10	10	11	12	12	13	14	14	15	16	16
	1	6	11	16	21	26	31		1	11	21	31		1	11	21	31		1	16		1	16		1	16		1	11	21	31
♃	8♍	9	10	11	12	13	14	♄	26♈	26	25	25	⚷	3♈	3	3	2	♅	27♍	27	♆	24♏	24	♇	21♍	22	☊	13♈	12	12	11

SEP

	1	2	3	4	5	6	7	8	9	10	11	12	13	14	15	16	17	18	19	20	21	22	23	24	25	26	27	28	29	30
☉	9♍	10	11	12	12	13	14	15	16	17	18	19	20	21	22	23	24	25	26	27	28	29	0♎	1	2	3	4	5	6	7
☽	22♐	6♑	20	4♒	18	2♓	15	28	11♈	24	6♉	18	0♊	12	24	6♋	18	0♌	13	26	9♍	23	7♎	21	6♏	20	4♐	19	3♑	17
☿	29♍	0♎	2	3	5	6	8	9	10	12	13	14	16	17	18	19	20	21	22	23	24	25	26	27	28	28	29	30	0♏	1
♀	28♍	30	1♎	2	3	5	6	7	8	9	11	12	13	14	16	17	18	19	21	22	23	24	25	27	28	29	0♏	2	3	4
♂	17♌	18	18	19	19	20	21	21	22	23	23	24	24	25	26	26	27	28	28	29	30	0♍	1	1	2	3	3	4	5	5
	1	6	11	16	21	26			1	11	21			1	11	21			1	16		1	16		1	16		1	11	21
♃	15♍	16	17	18	19	20		♄	25♈	25	24		⚷	2♈	2	1		♅	28♍	29	♆	24♏	24	♇	22♍	23	☊	11♈	11	10

OCT

	1	2	3	4	5	6	7	8	9	10	11	12	13	14	15	16	17	18	19	20	21	22	23	24	25	26	27	28	29	30	31
☉	8♎	9	10	11	12	13	14	15	16	17	18	19	20	21	22	23	24	25	26	27	28	29	30	1♏	2	3	4	5	6	7	8
☽	1♒	15	28	11♓	24	7♈	20	2♉	14	26	8♊	20	2♋	14	26	8♌	21	4♍	17	1♎	15	30	15♏	30	15♐	29	14♑	28	12♒	25	8♓
☿	1♏	1	1	1	1	1	0	30♎	29	29	28	27	26	24	23	22	21	20	19	18	17	16	16	16	16	16	16	17	17	18	19
♀	5♏	6	8	9	10	11	13	14	15	16	18	19	20	21	22	24	25	26	27	29	30	1♐	2	3	5	6	7	8	9	11	12
♂	6♍	6	7	8	8	9	10	10	11	11	12	13	13	14	14	15	16	16	17	18	18	19	19	20	21	21	22	23	23	24	24
	1	6	11	16	21	26	31		1	11	21	31		1	11	21	31		1	16		1	16		1	16		1	11	21	31
♃	21♍	22	23	24	25	26	27	♄	23♈	22	22	21	⚷	1♈	0	30♓	30	♅	0♎	1	♆	25♏	25	♇	23♍	24	☊	9♈	9	8	8

NOV

	1	2	3	4	5	6	7	8	9	10	11	12	13	14	15	16	17	18	19	20	21	22	23	24	25	26	27	28	29	30
☉	9♏	10	11	12	13	14	15	16	17	18	19	20	21	22	23	24	25	26	27	28	29	30	1♐	2	3	4	5	6	7	8
☽	21♓	4♈	16	28	11♉	23	5♊	16	28	10♋	22	4♌	16	29	12♍	25	9♎	23	8♏	23	8♐	23	9♑	23	8♒	22	5♓	18	1♈	13
☿	20♎	21	22	24	25	26	28	29	1♏	2	4	5	7	9	10	12	13	15	16	18	20	21	23	24	26	28	29	1♐	2	4
♀	13♐	14	16	17	18	19	20	22	23	24	25	26	28	29	0♑	1	3	4	5	6	7	9	10	11	12	13	15	16	17	18
♂	25♍	26	26	27	27	28	29	29	30	0♎	1	2	2	3	3	4	5	5	6	7	7	8	8	9	10	10	11	11	12	13
	1	6	11	16	21	26			1	11	21			1	11	21			1	16		1	16		1	16		1	11	21
♃	27♍	28	29	0♎	1	2		♄	21♈	20	20		⚷	30♓	29	29		♅	2♎	3	♆	26♏	26	♇	24♍	25	☊	8♈	7	7

DEC

	1	2	3	4	5	6	7	8	9	10	11	12	13	14	15	16	17	18	19	20	21	22	23	24	25	26	27	28	29	30	31
☉	9♐	10	11	12	13	14	15	16	17	18	19	20	21	22	23	24	25	26	27	28	29	0♑	1	2	3	4	5	6	7	8	9
☽	25♈	8♉	20	1♊	13	25	7♋	19	1♌	13	25	8♍	21	4♎	17	1♏	16	1♐	16	2♑	17	2♒	16	1♓	14	27	10♈	22	5♉	17	28
☿	5♐	7	9	10	12	13	15	16	18	20	21	23	24	26	27	29	1♑	2	4	5	7	9	10	12	13	15	17	18	20	21	23
♀	19♑	21	22	23	24	25	27	28	29	0♒	1	2	4	5	6	7	8	9	11	12	13	14	15	16	18	19	20	21	22	23	25
♂	13♎	14	14	15	15	16	17	17	18	18	19	20	20	21	21	22	23	23	24	24	25	25	26	27	27	28	28	29	29	0♏	1
	1	6	11	16	21	26	31		1	11	21	31		1	11	21	31		1	16		1	16		1	16		1	11	21	31
♃	2♎	3	4	4	5	5	5	♄	19♈	19	19	19	⚷	29♓	29	29	29	♅	3♎	4	♆	27♏	27	♇	25♍	25	☊	6♈	6	5	5

EPHEMERIS

1969

JAN

	1	2	3	4	5	6	7	8	9	10	11	12	13	14	15	16	17	18	19	20	21	22	23	24	25	26	27	28	29	30	31
☉	10♑	11	12	13	14	15	17	18	19	20	21	22	23	24	25	26	27	28	29	30	1♒	2	3	4	5	6	7	8	9	10	11
☽	10♊	22	4♋	16	28	10♌	22	5♍	17	0♎	13	27	11♏	25	10♐	25	10♑	25	10♒	24	9♓	22	6♈	18	1♉	13	25	7♊	19	1♋	13
☿	25♑	26	28	29	1♒	2	4	5	7	8	9	10	12	13	13	14	15	15	16	16	16	16	15	15	14	13	12	11	10	8	7
♀	26♒	27	28	29	0♓	1	2	4	5	6	7	8	9	10	11	12	13	14	16	17	18	19	20	21	22	23	24	25	26	27	28
♂	1♏	2	2	3	3	4	5	5	6	6	7	7	8	8	9	10	10	11	11	12	12	13	13	14	14	15	16	16	17	17	18
	1	6	11	16	21	26	31		1	11	21	31		1	11	21	31		1	16		1	16		1	16		1	11	21	31
♃	5♎	6	6	6	6	6	6	♄	19♈	19	20	20	⚷	29♓	29	30	0♈	♅	4♎	4	♆	28♏	28	♇	25♍	25	☊	5♈	4	4	3

FEB

	1	2	3	4	5	6	7	8	9	10	11	12	13	14	15	16	17	18	19	20	21	22	23	24	25	26	27	28			
☉	12♒	13	14	15	16	17	18	19	20	21	22	23	24	25	26	27	28	29	0♓	1	2	3	4	5	6	7	8	9			
☽	25♋	7♌	19	2♍	14	27	10♎	24	7♏	21	5♐	19	4♑	19	3♒	18	2♓	16	0♈	13	26	9♉	21	3♊	15	27	9♋	21			
☿	6♒	5	4	3	2	2	1	1	0	0	0	0	1	1	1	2	3	3	4	5	6	7	7	8	10	11	12	13			
♀	29♓	30	1♈	2	3	4	5	5	6	7	8	9	10	11	12	12	13	14	15	15	16	17	18	18	19	20	20	21			
♂	18♏	19	19	20	20	21	21	22	22	23	23	24	24	25	25	26	26	27	27	28	28	29	29	29	30	0♐	1	1			
	1	6	11	16	21	26			1	11	21			1	11	21			1	16		1	16		1	16		1	11	21	
♃	6♎	6	5	5	5	4		♄	20♈	21	22		⚷	0♈	1	1		♅	4♎	3	♆	28♏	29	♇	25♍	24	☊	3♈	2	2	

MAR

	1	2	3	4	5	6	7	8	9	10	11	12	13	14	15	16	17	18	19	20	21	22	23	24	25	26	27	28	29	30	31
☉	10♓	11	12	13	14	15	16	17	18	19	20	21	22	23	24	25	26	27	28	29	0♈	1	2	3	4	5	6	7	8	9	10
☽	3♌	15	28	11♍	24	7♎	20	4♏	18	2♐	16	0♑	14	29	13♒	27	11♓	25	8♈	21	4♉	17	29	11♊	23	5♋	17	29	11♌	23	6♍
☿	14♒	15	17	18	19	21	22	23	25	26	28	29	1♓	2	4	5	7	8	10	12	13	15	17	18	20	22	24	26	27	29	1♈
♀	21♈	22	23	23	24	24	24	25	25	25	26	26	26	26	27	27	27	27	27	27	27	27	26	26	26	26	25	25	25	24	24
♂	2♐	2	3	3	3	4	4	5	5	5	6	6	7	7	7	8	8	9	9	9	10	10	10	11	11	11	12	12	12	12	13
	1	6	11	16	21	26	31		1	11	21	31		1	11	21	31		1	16		1	16		1	16		1	11	21	31
♃	4♎	3	3	2	1	1	30♍	♄	23♈	24	25	26	⚷	1♈	2	3	3	♅	3♎	2	♆	29♏	29	♇	24♍	24	☊	1♈	1	0	30♓

APR

	1	2	3	4	5	6	7	8	9	10	11	12	13	14	15	16	17	18	19	20	21	22	23	24	25	26	27	28	29	30	
☉	11♈	12	13	14	15	16	17	18	19	20	21	22	23	24	25	26	27	28	29	30	1♉	2	3	4	5	6	7	8	9	9	
☽	19♍	2♎	16	30	14♏	28	13♐	27	11♑	25	9♒	23	7♓	20	4♈	17	30	12♉	25	7♊	19	1♋	13	25	7♌	19	1♍	14	27	10♎	
☿	3♈	5	7	9	11	13	15	17	19	21	23	25	27	29	2♉	4	6	8	10	12	14	16	18	19	21	23	25	26	28	29	
♀	23♈	23	22	21	21	20	20	19	18	18	17	17	16	15	15	14	14	13	13	12	12	12	11	11	11	11	11	11	11	10	
♂	13♐	13	13	14	14	14	14	15	15	15	15	15	16	16	16	16	16	16	16	16	17	17	17	17	17	17	17	17	17	17	
	1	6	11	16	21	26			1	11	21			1	11	21			1	16		1	16		1	16		1	11	21	
♃	30♍	29	29	28	28	27		♄	26♈	28	29		⚷	3♈	4	4		♅	2♎	1	♆	28♏	28	♇	23♍	23	☊	30♓	29	29	

MAY

	1	2	3	4	5	6	7	8	9	10	11	12	13	14	15	16	17	18	19	20	21	22	23	24	25	26	27	28	29	30	31
☉	10♉	11	12	13	14	15	16	17	18	19	20	21	22	23	24	25	26	27	28	29	30	1♊	2	3	4	5	6	6	7	8	9
☽	24♎	8♏	23	8♐	23	7♑	22	6♒	20	4♓	17	0♈	13	26	9♉	21	3♊	15	27	9♋	21	3♌	15	27	9♍	22	5♎	18	2♏	17	2♐
☿	0♊	2	3	4	5	6	7	8	9	10	10	11	11	11	12	12	12	12	12	12	12	11	11	11	10	10	9	9	8	8	7
♀	11♈	11	11	11	11	11	11	12	12	12	13	13	14	14	15	15	16	16	17	17	18	19	19	20	21	21	22	23	23	24	25
♂	17♐	17	17	16	16	16	16	16	16	16	16	15	15	15	15	15	14	14	14	14	13	13	13	12	12	12	12	11	11	11	10
	1	6	11	16	21	26	31		1	11	21	31		1	11	21	31		1	16		1	16		1	16		1	11	21	31
♃	27♍	27	26	26	26	26	26	♄	0♉	1	3	4	⚷	5♈	5	6	6	♅	0♎	0	♆	28♏	27	♇	23♍	22	☊	28♓	28	27	27

JUN

	1	2	3	4	5	6	7	8	9	10	11	12	13	14	15	16	17	18	19	20	21	22	23	24	25	26	27	28	29	30	
☉	10♊	11	12	13	14	15	16	17	18	19	20	21	22	23	24	25	26	27	28	28	29	0♋	1	2	3	4	5	6	7	8	
☽	17♐	2♑	17	2♒	16	0♓	14	27	10♈	23	6♉	18	0♊	12	24	6♋	18	30	12♌	24	6♍	18	0♎	13	27	11♏	25	10♐	25	10♑	
☿	6♊	6	5	5	5	4	4	4	4	3	3	3	4	4	4	5	5	5	6	7	7	8	9	10	11	12	13	14	16	17	
♀	26♈	27	27	28	29	30	1♉	2	3	3	4	5	6	7	8	9	10	11	12	13	14	15	16	17	18	19	20	21	22	23	
♂	10♐	10	9	9	9	8	8	8	7	7	7	6	6	6	5	5	5	4	4	4	4	4	3	3	3	3	3	2	2	2	
	1	6	11	16	21	26			1	11	21			1	11	21			1	16		1	16		1	16		1	11	21	
♃	26♍	26	27	27	27	28		♄	4♉	5	6		⚷	6♈	7	7		♅	30♍	30	♆	27♏	27	♇	22♍	22	☊	27♓	26	26	

EPHEMERIS

1969

JUL

	1	2	3	4	5	6	7	8	9	10	11	12	13	14	15	16	17	18	19	20	21	22	23	24	25	26	27	28	29	30	31
☉	9♋	10	11	12	13	14	15	16	17	18	19	19	20	21	22	23	24	25	26	27	28	29	30	1♌	2	3	4	5	6	7	8
☽	26♑	11♒	26	10♓	24	7♈	20	3♉	15	27	9♊	21	3♋	15	27	9♌	21	3♍	15	27	10♎	23	6♏	20	4♐	19	4♑	19	4♒	19	4♓
☿	18♊	20	21	23	25	26	28	30	2♋	3	5	7	9	11	13	16	18	20	22	24	26	28	0♌	3	5	7	9	11	13	15	17
♀	24♉	25	26	27	28	29	0♊	1	2	3	4	5	6	8	9	10	11	12	13	14	15	16	17	19	20	21	22	23	24	25	26
♂	2♐	2	2	2	2	2	2	2	2	2	2	2	2	2	2	2	2	2	2	3	3	3	3	3	4	4	4	4	5	5	5
	1	6	11	16	21	26	31		1	11	21	31		1	11	21	31		1	16		1	16		1	16		1	11	21	31
♃	28♍	29	29	0♎	1	2	2	♄	7♉	8	8	9	⚷	7♈	7	7	7	♅	0♎	1	♆	26♏	26	♇	23♍	23	☊	25♓	25	24	23

AUG

	1	2	3	4	5	6	7	8	9	10	11	12	13	14	15	16	17	18	19	20	21	22	23	24	25	26	27	28	29	30	31
☉	9♌	10	10	11	12	13	14	15	16	17	18	19	20	21	22	23	24	25	26	27	28	29	30	1♍	2	3	4	5	5	6	7
☽	18♓	2♈	16	29	12♉	24	6♊	18	0♋	12	24	6♌	18	30	12♍	24	7♎	20	3♏	16	30	14♐	28	13♑	28	13♒	28	12♓	26	10♈	24
☿	19♌	21	22	24	26	28	30	1♍	3	5	7	8	10	11	13	14	16	17	19	20	22	23	25	26	27	28	30	1♎	2	3	4
♀	27♊	29	30	1♋	2	3	4	5	7	8	9	10	11	12	13	15	16	17	18	19	20	22	23	24	25	26	28	29	30	1♌	2
♂	5♐	6	6	6	7	7	7	8	8	8	9	9	10	10	10	11	11	12	12	13	13	13	14	14	15	15	16	16	17	17	18
	1	6	11	16	21	26	31		1	11	21	31		1	11	21	31		1	16		1	16		1	16		1	11	21	31
♃	2♎	3	4	5	6	7	8	♄	9♉	9	9	9	⚷	7♈	6	6	6	♅	1♎	2	♆	26♏	26	♇	23♍	24	☊	23♓	23	22	22

SEP

	1	2	3	4	5	6	7	8	9	10	11	12	13	14	15	16	17	18	19	20	21	22	23	24	25	26	27	28	29	30
☉	8♍	9	10	11	12	13	14	15	16	17	18	19	20	21	22	23	24	25	26	27	28	29	30	1♎	2	3	4	5	6	7
☽	7♉	20	2♊	15	27	8♋	20	2♌	14	26	9♍	21	4♎	17	30	13♏	27	11♐	25	9♑	23	8♒	22	6♓	21	5♈	18	2♉	15	28
☿	5♎	6	7	8	9	10	11	12	12	13	13	14	14	15	15	15	15	15	15	14	14	13	12	12	11	10	9	8	7	5
♀	3♌	5	6	7	8	9	11	12	13	14	15	17	18	19	20	21	23	24	25	26	27	29	30	1♍	2	3	5	6	7	8
♂	18♐	19	19	20	21	21	22	22	23	23	24	24	25	26	26	27	27	28	29	29	30	0♑	1	2	2	3	4	4	5	5
	1	6	11	16	21	26			1	11	21			1	11	21			1	16		1	16		1	16		1	11	21
♃	8♎	9	10	11	12	13		♄	9♉	9	8		⚷	6♈	5	5		♅	3♎	4	♆	26♏	26	♇	24♍	25	☊	22♓	21	21

OCT

	1	2	3	4	5	6	7	8	9	10	11	12	13	14	15	16	17	18	19	20	21	22	23	24	25	26	27	28	29	30	31
☉	8♎	9	10	11	12	13	14	15	16	17	18	18	19	20	21	22	23	24	25	26	27	28	29	0♏	1	2	3	4	5	6	7
☽	10♊	23	5♋	16	28	10♌	22	4♍	17	30	13♎	26	9♏	23	7♐	21	6♑	20	4♒	18	2♓	16	30	13♈	27	10♉	23	6♊	18	0♋	12
☿	4♎	3	2	2	1	0	0	30♍	30	0♎	0	1	2	2	3	4	6	7	8	10	11	13	14	16	17	19	21	22	24	26	27
♀	10♍	11	12	13	14	16	17	18	19	21	22	23	24	26	27	28	29	1♎	2	3	4	5	7	8	9	10	12	13	14	15	17
♂	6♑	7	7	8	9	9	10	11	11	12	13	13	14	15	15	16	17	17	18	19	20	20	21	22	22	23	24	24	25	26	27
	1	6	11	16	21	26	31		1	11	21	31		1	11	21	31		1	16		1	16		1	16		1	11	21	31
♃	14♎	16	17	18	19	20	21	♄	8♉	7	6	5	⚷	4♈	4	4	3	♅	5♎	6	♆	27♏	27	♇	25♍	26	☊	20♓	20	19	19

NOV

	1	2	3	4	5	6	7	8	9	10	11	12	13	14	15	16	17	18	19	20	21	22	23	24	25	26	27	28	29	30
☉	8♏	9	10	11	12	13	14	15	16	17	18	19	20	21	22	23	24	25	26	27	29	30	1♐	2	3	4	5	6	7	8
☽	24♋	6♌	18	30	12♍	25	8♎	21	4♏	18	3♐	17	2♑	16	1♒	15	29	13♓	26	10♈	23	6♉	19	2♊	14	26	8♋	20	2♌	14
☿	29♎	0♏	2	4	5	7	9	10	12	14	15	17	18	20	22	23	25	26	28	30	1♐	3	4	6	7	9	11	12	14	15
♀	18♎	19	20	22	23	24	25	27	28	29	0♏	2	3	4	5	7	8	9	10	12	13	14	15	17	18	19	20	22	23	24
♂	27♑	28	29	29	0♒	1	2	2	3	4	4	5	6	7	7	8	9	10	10	11	12	13	13	14	15	15	16	17	18	18
	1	6	11	16	21	26			1	11	21			1	11	21			1	16		1	16		1	16		1	11	21
♃	21♎	22	23	24	25	26		♄	5♉	4	4		⚷	3♈	3	3		♅	6♎	7	♆	28♏	28	♇	26♍	27	☊	19♓	18	17

DEC

	1	2	3	4	5	6	7	8	9	10	11	12	13	14	15	16	17	18	19	20	21	22	23	24	25	26	27	28	29	30	31
☉	9♐	10	11	12	13	14	15	16	17	18	19	20	21	22	23	24	25	26	27	28	29	30	1♑	2	3	4	5	6	7	8	9
☽	26♌	8♍	20	2♎	15	29	12♏	27	11♐	26	11♑	26	11♒	25	9♓	23	7♈	20	3♉	16	28	11♊	23	5♋	17	29	11♌	22	4♍	16	28
☿	17♐	18	20	21	23	25	26	28	29	1♑	2	4	5	7	8	10	11	13	14	16	17	18	20	21	22	24	25	26	27	28	28
♀	25♏	27	28	29	0♐	2	3	4	6	7	8	9	11	12	13	14	16	17	18	19	21	22	23	24	26	27	28	29	1♑	2	3
♂	19♒	20	21	21	22	23	24	24	25	26	27	27	28	29	30	0♓	1	2	3	3	4	5	6	6	7	8	9	9	10	11	11
	1	6	11	16	21	26	31		1	11	21	31		1	11	21	31		1	16		1	16		1	16		1	11	21	31
♃	27♎	28	29	30	1♏	1	2	♄	3♉	3	2	2	⚷	2♈	2	2	3	♅	8♎	8	♆	29♏	29	♇	27♍	27	☊	17♓	16	16	15

1970

JAN

	1	2	3	4	5	6	7	8	9	10	11	12	13	14	15	16	17	18	19	20	21	22	23	24	25	26	27	28	29	30	31
☉	10♑	11	12	13	14	15	16	17	18	19	20	21	22	23	24	25	26	27	28	30	1♒	2	3	4	5	6	7	8	9	10	11
☽	11♎	23	7♏	20	4♐	19	4♑	19	5♒	20	5♓	19	3♈	17	30	13♉	25	8♊	20	2♋	14	26	8♌	19	1♍	13	25	7♎	20	2♏	15
☿	29♑	30	30	30	30	30	29	29	28	27	26	25	23	22	21	19	18	17	16	15	15	14	14	14	14	14	14	15	15	16	16
♀	4♑	6	7	8	9	11	12	13	15	16	17	18	20	21	22	23	25	26	27	28	30	1♒	2	3	5	6	7	8	10	11	12
♂	12♓	13	14	14	15	16	17	17	18	19	20	20	21	22	23	23	24	25	26	26	27	28	29	29	0♈	1	2	2	3	4	5
	1	6	11	16	21	26	31		1	11	21	31		1	11	21	31		1	16		1	16		1	16		1	11	21	31
♃	2♏	3	4	4	5	5	5	♄	2♉	2	2	3	⚷	3♈	3	3	3	♅	9♎	9	♆	30♏	0♐	♇	27♍	27	☊	15♓	15	14	14

FEB

	1	2	3	4	5	6	7	8	9	10	11	12	13	14	15	16	17	18	19	20	21	22	23	24	25	26	27	28			
☉	12♒	13	14	15	16	17	18	19	20	21	22	23	24	25	26	27	28	29	30	1♓	2	3	4	5	6	7	8	9			
☽	29♏	13♐	27	12♑	27	12♒	28	13♓	27	12♈	25	9♉	22	4♊	17	29	11♋	23	4♌	16	28	10♍	22	4♎	17	29	12♏	25			
☿	17♑	18	18	19	20	21	22	23	25	26	27	28	29	1♒	2	3	5	6	7	9	10	12	13	14	16	18	19	21			
♀	13♒	15	16	17	18	20	21	22	23	25	26	27	28	30	1♓	2	3	5	6	7	8	10	11	12	13	15	16	17			
♂	5♈	6	7	7	8	9	10	10	11	12	13	13	14	15	16	16	17	18	18	19	20	21	21	22	23	23	24	25			
	1	6	11	16	21	26			1	11	21			1	11	21			1	16		1	16		1	16		1	11	21	
♃	5♏	6	6	6	6	6		♄	3♉	3	4		⚷	3♈	4	4		♅	9♎	8	♆	1♐	1	♇	27♍	27	☊	14♓	13	13	

MAR

	1	2	3	4	5	6	7	8	9	10	11	12	13	14	15	16	17	18	19	20	21	22	23	24	25	26	27	28	29	30	31
☉	10♓	11	12	13	14	15	16	17	18	19	20	21	22	23	24	25	26	27	28	29	30	1♈	2	3	4	5	6	7	8	9	10
☽	9♐	22	7♑	21	6♒	21	6♓	21	5♈	20	4♉	17	0♊	13	25	7♋	19	1♌	13	25	7♍	19	1♎	14	26	9♏	22	6♐	19	3♑	17
☿	22♒	24	25	27	29	0♓	2	4	5	7	9	11	12	14	16	18	20	22	24	25	27	29	1♈	3	5	7	9	11	13	16	18
♀	18♓	20	21	22	23	25	26	27	28	30	1♈	2	3	5	6	7	8	10	11	12	13	15	16	17	18	20	21	22	23	25	26
♂	26♈	26	27	28	29	29	30	1♉	1	2	3	4	4	5	6	6	7	8	9	9	10	11	11	12	13	13	14	15	16	16	17
	1	6	11	16	21	26	31		1	11	21	31		1	11	21	31		1	16		1	16		1	16		1	11	21	31
♃	6♏	6	5	5	5	4	4	♄	5♉	6	7	8	⚷	5♈	5	6	7	♅	8♎	7	♆	1♐	1	♇	26♍	26	☊	12♓	12	11	11

APR

	1	2	3	4	5	6	7	8	9	10	11	12	13	14	15	16	17	18	19	20	21	22	23	24	25	26	27	28	29	30	
☉	11♈	12	13	14	15	16	17	18	19	20	21	22	23	24	25	26	27	28	29	30	0♉	1	2	3	4	5	6	7	8	9	
☽	1♒	15	30	15♓	29	13♈	28	12♉	25	8♊	21	3♋	15	27	9♌	21	3♍	15	27	10♎	22	5♏	19	2♐	16	30	14♑	28	12♒	26	
☿	20♈	22	24	26	27	29	1♉	3	5	7	8	10	11	13	14	15	16	17	18	19	20	21	21	22	22	22	22	22	22	22	
♀	27♈	28	29	1♉	2	3	4	6	7	8	9	11	12	13	14	15	17	18	19	20	22	23	24	25	27	28	29	0♊	1	3	
♂	18♉	18	19	20	20	21	22	23	23	24	25	25	26	27	27	28	29	29	0♊	1	2	2	3	4	4	5	6	6	7	8	
	1	6	11	16	21	26			1	11	21			1	11	21			1	16		1	16		1	16		1	11	21	
♃	4♏	3	2	2	1	1		♄	8♉	9	11		⚷	7♈	7	8		♅	7♎	6	♆	1♐	0	♇	26♍	25	☊	11♓	10	9	

MAY

	1	2	3	4	5	6	7	8	9	10	11	12	13	14	15	16	17	18	19	20	21	22	23	24	25	26	27	28	29	30	31
☉	10♉	11	12	13	14	15	16	17	18	19	20	21	22	23	24	25	26	27	28	29	30	0♊	1	2	3	4	5	6	7	8	9
☽	10♓	24	8♈	22	6♉	20	3♊	16	29	11♋	23	5♌	17	29	11♍	23	5♎	18	1♏	14	28	12♐	26	10♑	24	9♒	23	7♓	21	5♈	19
☿	22♉	22	22	21	21	20	20	19	19	18	17	17	16	16	15	15	14	14	14	13	13	13	13	13	13	14	14	14	15	15	16
♀	4♊	5	6	7	9	10	11	12	14	15	16	17	18	20	21	22	23	24	26	27	28	29	0♋	2	3	4	5	6	8	9	10
♂	8♊	9	10	10	11	12	12	13	14	14	15	16	16	17	18	18	19	20	20	21	22	22	23	24	24	25	26	26	27	28	28
	1	6	11	16	21	26	31		1	11	21	31		1	11	21	31		1	16		1	16		1	16		1	11	21	31
♃	30♎	29	29	28	28	27	27	♄	12♉	13	14	16	⚷	8♈	9	9	10	♅	5♎	5	♆	0♐	30♏	♇	25♍	25	☊	9♓	8	8	7

JUN

	1	2	3	4	5	6	7	8	9	10	11	12	13	14	15	16	17	18	19	20	21	22	23	24	25	26	27	28	29	30	
☉	10♊	11	12	13	14	15	16	17	18	19	20	21	22	23	23	24	25	26	27	28	29	0♋	1	2	3	4	5	6	7	8	
☽	2♉	16	29	12♊	25	7♋	19	1♌	13	25	7♍	19	1♎	13	26	9♏	22	6♐	20	5♑	20	4♒	19	3♓	18	2♈	16	29	12♉	25	
☿	17♉	17	18	19	20	21	22	23	24	25	27	28	29	1♊	2	4	5	7	8	10	12	14	15	17	19	21	23	25	27	29	
♀	11♋	12	14	15	16	17	18	20	21	22	23	24	26	27	28	29	0♌	1	3	4	5	6	7	9	10	11	12	13	14	16	
♂	29♊	30	0♋	1	2	2	3	4	4	5	6	6	7	8	8	9	10	10	11	12	12	13	14	14	15	16	16	17	18	18	
	1	6	11	16	21	26			1	11	21			1	11	21			1	16		1	16		1	16		1	11	21	
♃	27♎	27	26	26	26	26		♄	16♉	17	18		⚷	10♈	10	10		♅	5♎	5	♆	29♏	29	♇	25♍	25	☊	7♓	7	6	

1970

EPHEMERIS

JUL

	1	2	3	4	5	6	7	8	9	10	11	12	13	14	15	16	17	18	19	20	21	22	23	24	25	26	27	28	29	30	31
☉	9♋	10	11	12	13	14	14	15	16	17	18	19	20	21	22	23	24	25	26	27	28	29	30	1♌	2	3	4	5	5	6	7
☽	8♊	21	3♋	16	28	10♌	22	3♍	15	27	9♎	21	4♏	17	0♐	14	29	13♑	28	13♒	28	13♓	28	12♈	26	9♉	23	5♊	18	0♋	13
☿	2♋	4	6	8	10	12	15	17	19	21	23	25	27	29	1♌	3	5	7	9	11	13	15	16	18	20	22	23	25	27	28	30
♀	17♌	18	19	20	21	23	24	25	26	27	28	29	1♍	2	3	4	5	6	7	9	10	11	12	13	14	15	16	17	19	20	21
♂	19♋	19	20	21	21	22	23	23	24	25	25	26	27	27	28	29	29	30	0♌	1	2	2	3	4	4	5	6	6	7	8	8
	1	6	11	16	21	26	31		1	11	21	31		1	11	21	31		1	16		1	16		1	16		1	11	21	31
♃	26♎	26	27	27	27	28	28	♄	19♉	20	21	22	⚷	10♈	10	10	10	♅	5♎	5	♆	29♏	28	♇	25♍	25	☊	6♓	5	5	4

AUG

	1	2	3	4	5	6	7	8	9	10	11	12	13	14	15	16	17	18	19	20	21	22	23	24	25	26	27	28	29	30	31
☉	8♌	9	10	11	12	13	14	15	16	17	18	19	20	21	22	23	24	25	26	27	28	28	29	0♍	1	2	3	4	5	6	7
☽	25♋	7♌	18	0♍	12	24	6♎	18	0♏	13	26	9♐	23	7♑	22	7♒	22	7♓	22	7♈	21	5♉	19	2♊	15	27	10♋	22	4♌	15	27
☿	1♍	3	4	6	7	8	10	11	12	13	15	16	17	18	19	20	21	22	23	24	24	25	26	26	27	27	28	28	28	28	28
♀	22♍	23	24	25	26	27	28	30	1♎	2	3	4	5	6	7	8	9	10	11	12	13	14	15	16	17	18	19	20	21	22	23
♂	9♌	9	10	11	11	12	13	13	14	15	15	16	16	17	18	18	19	20	20	21	22	22	23	24	24	25	25	26	27	27	28
	1	6	11	16	21	26	31		1	11	21	31		1	11	21	31		1	16		1	16		1	16		1	11	21	31
♃	28♎	29	29	0♏	1	2	2	♄	22♉	22	22	23	⚷	10♈	10	10	9	♅	6♎	6	♆	28♏	28	♇	26♍	26	☊	4♓	4	3	2

SEP

	1	2	3	4	5	6	7	8	9	10	11	12	13	14	15	16	17	18	19	20	21	22	23	24	25	26	27	28	29	30
☉	8♍	9	10	11	12	13	14	15	16	17	18	19	20	21	22	23	24	25	26	27	28	29	30	1♎	2	2	3	4	5	6
☽	9♍	21	3♎	15	27	9♏	22	5♐	18	2♑	16	0♒	15	0♓	15	0♈	15	30	14♉	28	11♊	24	6♋	19	1♌	12	24	6♍	18	30
☿	28♍	28	27	27	26	26	25	24	23	22	21	20	19	18	17	17	16	15	15	14	14	14	14	14	15	15	16	17	18	19
♀	24♎	25	26	27	28	29	30	1♏	2	3	4	4	5	6	7	8	9	9	10	11	12	13	13	14	15	15	16	17	17	18
♂	29♌	29	30	1♍	1	2	2	3	4	4	5	6	6	7	7	8	9	9	10	11	11	12	13	13	14	14	15	16	16	17
	1	6	11	16	21	26			1	11	21			1	11	21			1	16		1	16		1	16		1	11	21
♃	2♏	3	4	5	6	7		♄	23♉	23	22		⚷	9♈	9	9		♅	7♎	8	♆	28♏	28	♇	27♍	27	☊	2♓	2	1

OCT

	1	2	3	4	5	6	7	8	9	10	11	12	13	14	15	16	17	18	19	20	21	22	23	24	25	26	27	28	29	30	31
☉	7♎	8	9	10	11	12	13	14	15	16	17	18	19	20	21	22	23	24	25	26	27	28	29	0♏	1	2	3	4	5	6	7
☽	12♎	24	6♏	19	2♐	15	28	12♑	26	10♒	24	9♓	24	9♈	23	8♉	22	6♊	19	2♋	15	27	9♌	21	2♍	14	26	8♎	21	3♏	16
☿	20♍	21	23	24	26	27	29	0♎	2	4	6	7	9	11	12	14	16	18	19	21	23	25	26	28	30	1♏	3	5	6	8	9
♀	19♏	19	20	20	21	21	22	22	23	23	23	24	24	24	25	25	25	25	25	25	25	25	25	25	25	25	24	24	24	23	23
♂	18♍	18	19	20	20	21	21	22	23	23	24	25	25	26	27	27	28	28	29	30	0♎	1	2	2	3	4	4	5	5	6	7
	1	6	11	16	21	26	31		1	11	21	31		1	11	21	31		1	16		1	16		1	16		1	11	21	31
♃	8♏	9	10	11	12	13	14	♄	22♉	21	21	20	⚷	8♈	8	7	7	♅	9♎	10	♆	29♏	29	♇	28♍	28	☊	1♓	0	30♒	29

NOV

	1	2	3	4	5	6	7	8	9	10	11	12	13	14	15	16	17	18	19	20	21	22	23	24	25	26	27	28	29	30
☉	8♏	9	10	11	12	13	14	15	16	17	18	19	20	21	22	23	24	25	26	27	28	29	0♐	1	2	3	4	5	6	7
☽	29♏	12♐	25	9♑	22	6♒	20	4♓	19	3♈	18	2♉	16	0♊	14	27	10♋	23	5♌	17	29	10♍	22	4♎	16	29	11♏	24	8♐	21
☿	11♏	13	14	16	17	19	21	22	24	25	27	28	30	1♐	3	5	6	8	9	11	12	14	15	17	18	19	21	22	24	25
♀	23♏	22	22	21	21	20	20	19	18	18	17	17	16	15	15	14	14	13	13	12	12	11	11	11	11	10	10	10	10	10
♂	7♎	8	9	9	10	11	11	12	12	13	14	14	15	16	16	17	17	18	19	19	20	21	21	22	23	23	24	24	25	26
	1	6	11	16	21	26			1	11	21			1	11	21			1	16		1	16		1	16		1	11	21
♃	15♏	16	17	18	19	20		♄	20♉	19	18		⚷	7♈	6	6		♅	11♎	12	♆	30♏	0♐	♇	29♍	29	☊	29♒	29	28

DEC

	1	2	3	4	5	6	7	8	9	10	11	12	13	14	15	16	17	18	19	20	21	22	23	24	25	26	27	28	29	30	31
☉	8♐	9	10	11	12	13	14	15	16	18	19	20	21	22	23	24	25	26	27	28	29	30	1♑	2	3	4	5	6	7	8	9
☽	5♑	19	3♒	17	1♓	15	29	13♈	27	11♉	25	9♊	22	5♋	18	0♌	13	25	6♍	18	30	12♎	24	7♏	19	3♐	16	30	14♑	29	13♒
☿	27♐	28	29	1♑	2	3	5	6	7	8	9	10	11	12	13	13	14	14	14	14	14	13	13	12	11	10	9	7	6	5	3
♀	10♏	10	10	10	10	10	10	11	11	11	12	12	12	13	13	14	14	15	16	16	17	17	18	19	19	20	21	22	22	23	24
♂	26♎	27	28	28	29	30	0♏	1	1	2	3	3	4	5	5	6	7	7	8	8	9	10	10	11	12	12	13	14	14	15	15
	1	6	11	16	21	26	31		1	11	21	31		1	11	21	31		1	16		1	16		1	16		1	11	21	31
♃	21♏	22	23	24	25	26	27	♄	18♉	17	16	16	⚷	6♈	6	6	6	♅	13♎	13	♆	1♐	1	♇	29♍	30	☊	28♒	27	27	26

1971

JAN	1	2	3	4	5	6	7	8	9	10	11	12	13	14	15	16	17	18	19	20	21	22	23	24	25	26	27	28	29	30	31
☉	10♑	11	12	13	14	15	16	17	18	19	20	21	22	23	24	25	26	27	28	29	0♒	1	2	3	4	5	6	7	8	9	10
☽	28♒	12♓	26	10♈	24	8♉	22	5♊	18	1♋	14	26	8♌	21	2♍	14	26	8♎	20	2♏	14	27	10♐	24	8♑	22	7♒	22	7♓	22	6♈
☿	2♑	1	30♐	29	29	28	28	28	28	28	28	29	29	30	1♑	1	2	3	4	5	6	7	9	10	11	12	13	15	16	17	19
♀	25♏	26	26	27	28	29	30	1♐	2	3	4	5	6	6	7	8	9	10	11	12	13	14	15	17	18	19	20	21	22	23	24
♂	16♏	17	17	18	19	19	20	20	21	22	22	23	24	24	25	26	26	27	27	28	29	29	30	1♐	1	2	2	3	4	4	5
	1	6	11	16	21	26	31		1	11	21	31		1	11	21	31		1	16		1	16		1	16		1	11	21	31
♃	28♏	29	29	0♐	1	2	3	♄	16♉	16	16	16	⚷	6♈	6	6	7	♅	13♎	14	♆	2♐	2	♇	30♍	30	☊	26♒	25	25	24

FEB	1	2	3	4	5	6	7	8	9	10	11	12	13	14	15	16	17	18	19	20	21	22	23	24	25	26	27	28			
☉	11♒	12	14	15	16	17	18	19	20	21	22	23	24	25	26	27	28	29	30	1♓	2	3	4	5	6	7	8	9			
☽	21♈	5♉	18	2♊	15	28	10♋	23	5♌	17	29	11♍	23	5♎	16	28	10♏	23	5♐	18	2♑	16	0♒	15	30	15♓	0♈	15			
☿	20♑	22	23	24	26	27	29	0♒	2	3	5	6	8	9	11	13	14	16	17	19	21	22	24	26	28	29	1♓	3			
♀	25♐	26	27	28	29	0♑	2	3	4	5	6	7	8	9	10	12	13	14	15	16	17	18	20	21	22	23	24	25			
♂	6♐	6	7	7	8	9	9	10	11	11	12	12	13	14	14	15	16	16	17	17	18	19	19	20	21	21	22	22			
	1	6	11	16	21	26			1	11	21			1	11	21			1	16		1	16		1	16		1	11	21	
♃	3♐	3	4	5	5	5		♄	16♉	16	17		⚷	7♈	7	8		♅	13♎	13	♆	3♐	3	♇	29♍	29	☊	24♒	24	23	

MAR	1	2	3	4	5	6	7	8	9	10	11	12	13	14	15	16	17	18	19	20	21	22	23	24	25	26	27	28	29	30	31
☉	10♓	11	12	13	14	15	16	17	18	19	20	21	22	23	24	25	26	27	28	29	30	1♈	2	3	4	5	6	7	8	9	10
☽	0♉	14	28	12♊	25	7♋	20	2♌	14	26	8♍	20	1♎	13	25	7♏	19	2♐	15	27	11♑	24	9♒	23	8♓	23	8♈	24	9♉	23	7♊
☿	5♓	7	8	10	12	14	16	18	20	22	24	26	28	30	2♈	4	6	7	9	11	13	15	17	18	20	22	23	25	26	27	28
♀	26♑	28	29	30	1♒	2	3	5	6	7	8	9	10	12	13	14	15	16	17	19	20	21	22	23	25	26	27	28	29	0♓	2
♂	23♐	24	24	25	25	26	27	27	28	29	29	30	0♑	1	2	2	3	3	4	5	5	6	6	7	8	8	9	9	10	11	11
	1	6	11	16	21	26	31		1	11	21	31		1	11	21	31		1	16		1	16		1	16		1	11	21	31
♃	6♐	6	6	6	6	6	6	♄	17♉	18	19	20	⚷	8♈	9	9	10	♅	13♎	12	♆	3♐	3	♇	29♍	28	☊	23♒	22	22	21

APR	1	2	3	4	5	6	7	8	9	10	11	12	13	14	15	16	17	18	19	20	21	22	23	24	25	26	27	28	29	30	
☉	11♈	12	13	14	15	16	17	18	18	19	20	21	22	23	24	25	26	27	28	29	0♉	1	2	3	4	5	6	7	8	9	
☽	21♊	4♋	17	29	11♌	23	5♍	17	28	10♎	22	4♏	17	29	11♐	24	7♑	21	4♒	18	2♓	17	2♈	17	2♉	17	1♊	15	29	12♋	
☿	29♈	0♉	1	2	3	3	3	4	4	4	4	3	3	3	2	2	1	1	30♈	29	29	28	27	26	26	25	25	24	24	24	
♀	3♓	4	5	6	8	9	10	11	12	14	15	16	17	18	20	21	22	23	24	26	27	28	29	0♈	2	3	4	5	6	8	
♂	12♑	12	13	13	14	15	15	16	16	17	17	18	19	19	20	20	21	21	22	23	23	24	24	25	25	26	26	27	27	28	
	1	6	11	16	21	26			1	11	21			1	11	21			1	16		1	16		1	16		1	11	21	
♃	6♐	6	6	6	5	5		♄	20♉	21	23		⚷	10♈	10	11		♅	12♎	11	♆	3♐	3	♇	28♍	28	☊	21♒	21	20	

MAY	1	2	3	4	5	6	7	8	9	10	11	12	13	14	15	16	17	18	19	20	21	22	23	24	25	26	27	28	29	30	31
☉	10♉	11	12	13	14	15	16	17	18	19	20	21	22	23	24	24	25	26	27	28	29	0♊	1	2	3	4	5	6	7	8	9
☽	25♋	7♌	20	1♍	13	25	7♎	19	1♏	13	26	8♐	21	4♑	18	1♒	15	28	13♓	27	11♈	26	11♉	25	9♊	23	7♋	20	3♌	15	28
☿	23♈	23	23	23	23	23	24	24	24	25	25	26	27	27	28	29	30	1♉	2	3	4	5	6	8	9	10	12	13	14	16	18
♀	9♈	10	11	12	14	15	16	17	18	20	21	22	23	25	26	27	28	29	1♉	2	3	4	5	7	8	9	10	11	13	14	15
♂	28♑	29	30	0♒	1	1	2	2	3	3	4	4	5	5	6	6	7	7	7	8	8	9	9	10	10	11	11	11	12	12	13
	1	6	11	16	21	26	31		1	11	21	31		1	11	21	31		1	16		1	16		1	16		1	11	21	31
♃	4♐	4	3	3	2	1	1	♄	24♉	25	26	28	⚷	12♈	12	13	13	♅	10♎	10	♆	2♐	2	♇	27♍	27	☊	20♒	19	19	18

JUN	1	2	3	4	5	6	7	8	9	10	11	12	13	14	15	16	17	18	19	20	21	22	23	24	25	26	27	28	29	30	
☉	10♊	11	12	13	14	15	16	17	18	18	19	20	21	22	23	24	25	26	27	28	29	30	1♋	2	3	4	5	6	7	8	
☽	10♍	21	3♎	15	27	9♏	22	5♐	17	1♑	14	28	11♒	25	9♓	23	8♈	22	6♉	20	4♊	18	2♋	15	28	11♌	23	5♍	17	29	
☿	19♉	21	22	24	26	28	29	1♊	3	5	7	9	11	13	15	18	20	22	24	26	28	1♋	3	5	7	9	11	14	16	18	
♀	16♉	18	19	20	21	22	24	25	26	27	28	30	1♊	2	3	5	6	7	8	9	11	12	13	14	15	17	18	19	20	22	
♂	13♒	13	14	14	15	15	15	16	16	16	17	17	17	18	18	18	18	19	19	19	19	20	20	20	20	21	21	21	21	21	
	1	6	11	16	21	26			1	11	21			1	11	21			1	16		1	16		1	16		1	11	21	
♃	1♐	30♏	29	29	28	28		♄	28♉	29	0♊		⚷	13♈	13	14		♅	10♎	9	♆	1♐	1	♇	27♍	27	☊	18♒	17	17	

1971

EPHEMERIS

JUL

	1	2	3	4	5	6	7	8	9	10	11	12	13	14	15	16	17	18	19	20	21	22	23	24	25	26	27	28	29	30	31
☉	9♋	9	10	11	12	13	14	15	16	17	18	19	20	21	22	23	24	25	26	27	28	29	30	0♌	1	2	3	4	5	6	7
☽	11♎	23	5♏	17	0♐	13	26	10♑	23	7♒	22	6♓	20	4♈	19	3♉	17	1♊	14	28	11♋	24	7♌	19	1♍	14	25	7♎	19	1♏	13
☿	20♋	22	24	26	27	29	1♌	3	5	6	8	10	11	13	14	16	17	19	20	22	23	24	26	27	28	29	0♍	1	2	3	4
♀	23♊	24	25	26	28	29	0♋	1	3	4	5	6	7	9	10	11	12	14	15	16	17	18	20	21	22	23	25	26	27	28	30
♂	21♒	21	22	22	22	22	22	22	22	22	22	22	22	22	22	22	22	22	22	21	21	21	21	21	21	21	20	20	20	20	20
	1	6	11	16	21	26	31		1	11	21	31		1	11	21	31		1	16		1	16		1	16		1	11	21	31
♃	27♏	27	27	27	27	27	27	♄	1♊	3	4	4	⚷	14♈	14	14	14	♅	10♎	10	♆	1♐	1	♇	27♍	27	☊	16♒	16	15	15

AUG

	1	2	3	4	5	6	7	8	9	10	11	12	13	14	15	16	17	18	19	20	21	22	23	24	25	26	27	28	29	30	31
☉	8♌	9	10	11	12	13	14	15	16	17	18	19	20	21	22	22	23	24	25	26	27	28	29	0♍	1	2	3	4	5	6	7
☽	25♏	8♐	21	4♑	18	2♒	16	1♓	16	0♈	15	29	14♉	28	11♊	25	8♋	21	3♌	16	28	10♍	22	4♎	16	27	9♏	21	4♐	16	29
☿	5♍	6	7	7	8	9	9	10	10	10	10	11	11	10	10	10	10	9	9	8	8	7	6	5	4	3	2	2	1	30♌	29
♀	1♌	2	3	4	6	7	8	9	11	12	13	14	16	17	18	19	20	22	23	24	25	27	28	29	0♍	2	3	4	5	7	8
♂	19♒	19	19	19	18	18	18	18	17	17	17	17	16	16	16	16	15	15	15	15	14	14	14	14	13	13	13	13	13	13	12
	1	6	11	16	21	26	31		1	11	21	31		1	11	21	31		1	16		1	16		1	16		1	11	21	31
♃	27♏	27	27	27	28	28	29	♄	4♊	5	6	6	⚷	14♈	14	13	13	♅	10♎	11	♆	0♐	0	♇	28♍	28	☊	15♒	14	14	13

SEP

	1	2	3	4	5	6	7	8	9	10	11	12	13	14	15	16	17	18	19	20	21	22	23	24	25	26	27	28	29	30
☉	8♍	9	10	11	12	13	14	15	16	17	18	19	20	21	22	22	23	24	25	26	27	28	29	0♎	1	2	3	4	5	6
☽	12♑	26	10♒	25	9♓	24	10♈	25	9♉	24	8♊	21	5♋	18	0♌	13	25	7♍	19	1♎	12	24	6♏	18	0♐	12	25	8♑	21	4♒
☿	29♌	28	28	27	27	27	28	28	28	29	30	1♍	2	3	4	5	7	8	10	11	13	15	17	18	20	22	24	26	27	29
♀	9♍	10	12	13	14	15	17	18	19	20	21	23	24	25	26	28	29	0♎	1	3	4	5	6	8	9	10	11	13	14	15
♂	12♒	12	12	12	12	12	12	12	12	12	12	12	12	12	12	12	12	12	12	13	13	13	13	13	13	14	14	14	14	15
	1	6	11	16	21	26			1	11	21			1	11	21			1	16		1	16		1	16		1	11	21
♃	29♏	29	30	1♐	1	2		♄	6♊	6	7		⚷	13♈	13	12		♅	12♎	13	♆	0♐	1	♇	29♍	29	☊	13♒	13	12

OCT

	1	2	3	4	5	6	7	8	9	10	11	12	13	14	15	16	17	18	19	20	21	22	23	24	25	26	27	28	29	30	31
☉	7♎	8	9	10	11	12	13	14	15	16	17	18	19	20	21	22	23	24	25	26	27	28	29	30	1♏	2	3	4	5	6	7
☽	18♒	3♓	18	3♈	18	3♉	18	3♊	17	1♋	14	27	10♌	22	4♍	16	28	9♎	21	3♏	15	27	9♐	22	4♑	17	30	13♒	27	11♓	26
☿	1♎	3	5	7	8	10	12	14	15	17	19	20	22	24	25	27	29	0♏	2	4	5	7	8	10	12	13	15	16	18	19	21
♀	16♎	18	19	20	21	23	24	25	26	28	29	0♏	1	3	4	5	6	8	9	10	11	13	14	15	16	18	19	20	21	22	24
♂	15♒	15	15	16	16	16	17	17	17	18	18	18	19	19	20	20	20	21	21	22	22	22	23	23	24	24	25	25	26	26	27
	1	6	11	16	21	26	31		1	11	21	31		1	11	21	31		1	16		1	16		1	16		1	11	21	31
♃	3♐	4	5	6	7	8	9	♄	6♊	6	6	5	⚷	12♈	11	11	10	♅	14♎	14	♆	1♐	1	♇	30♍	0♎	☊	12♒	11	10	10

NOV

	1	2	3	4	5	6	7	8	9	10	11	12	13	14	15	16	17	18	19	20	21	22	23	24	25	26	27	28	29	30
☉	8♏	9	10	11	12	13	14	15	16	17	18	19	20	21	22	23	24	25	26	27	28	29	0♐	1	2	3	4	5	6	7
☽	11♈	26	11♉	27	11♊	26	10♋	23	6♌	18	1♍	13	25	6♎	18	0♏	12	24	6♐	19	1♑	14	27	10♒	23	7♓	21	5♈	20	5♉
☿	22♏	24	25	27	28	30	1♐	2	4	5	7	8	9	11	12	13	15	16	17	19	20	21	22	23	24	25	26	26	27	28
♀	25♏	26	27	29	30	1♐	2	4	5	6	7	9	10	11	12	14	15	16	17	19	20	21	22	24	25	26	27	29	30	1♑
♂	27♒	28	28	29	29	30	0♓	1	1	2	2	3	3	4	5	5	6	6	7	7	8	9	9	10	10	11	12	12	13	13
	1	6	11	16	21	26			1	11	21			1	11	21			1	16		1	16		1	16		1	11	21
♃	9♐	10	11	12	13	14		♄	5♊	4	3		⚷	10♈	10	10		♅	15♎	16	♆	2♐	2	♇	1♎	1	☊	10♒	9	9

DEC

	1	2	3	4	5	6	7	8	9	10	11	12	13	14	15	16	17	18	19	20	21	22	23	24	25	26	27	28	29	30	31
☉	8♐	9	10	11	12	13	14	15	16	17	18	19	20	21	22	23	24	25	26	27	28	29	0♑	2	3	4	5	6	7	8	9
☽	20♉	5♊	19	4♋	18	1♌	14	27	9♍	21	3♎	15	27	8♏	21	3♐	15	28	11♑	24	7♒	20	4♓	18	2♈	16	0♉	15	29	13♊	28
☿	28♐	28	28	28	28	28	27	26	25	24	23	21	20	19	17	16	15	14	13	13	12	12	12	12	12	13	13	14	15	15	16
♀	2♑	4	5	6	7	9	10	11	12	14	15	16	17	19	20	21	22	23	25	26	27	28	30	1♒	2	3	5	6	7	8	10
♂	14♓	15	15	16	16	17	18	18	19	19	20	21	21	22	23	23	24	24	25	26	26	27	28	28	29	30	0♈	1	1	2	3
	1	6	11	16	21	26	31		1	11	21	31		1	11	21	31		1	16		1	16		1	16		1	11	21	31
♃	15♐	16	18	19	20	21	22	♄	3♊	2	1	0	⚷	10♈	9	9	9	♅	17♎	18	♆	3♐	4	♇	2♎	2	☊	8♒	8	7	7

1972

EPHEMERIS

JAN

	1	2	3	4	5	6	7	8	9	10	11	12	13	14	15	16	17	18	19	20	21	22	23	24	25	26	27	28	29	30	31
☉	10♑	11	12	13	14	15	16	17	18	19	20	21	22	23	24	25	26	27	28	29	0♒	1	2	3	4	5	6	7	8	9	10
☽	12♋	25	9♌	22	4♍	17	29	11♎	23	4♏	16	28	11♐	23	6♑	19	3♒	16	0♓	14	28	13♈	27	11♉	25	9♊	23	7♋	20	4♌	17
☿	17♐	18	19	20	21	23	24	25	26	28	29	0♑	2	3	4	6	7	9	10	12	13	15	16	18	19	21	22	24	25	27	28
♀	11♒	12	13	14	16	17	18	19	21	22	23	24	26	27	28	29	0♓	2	3	4	5	7	8	9	10	11	13	14	15	16	17
♂	3♈	4	5	5	6	7	7	8	9	9	10	11	11	12	12	13	14	14	15	16	16	17	18	18	19	20	20	21	22	22	23
	1	6	11	16	21	26	31		1	11	21	31		1	11	21	31		1	16		1	16		1	16		1	11	21	31
♃	22♐	23	25	26	27	28	29	♄	0♊	30♉	30	30	⚷	9♈	10	10	10	♅	18♎	18	♆	4♐	5	♇	2♎	2	☊	7♒	6	6	5

FEB

	1	2	3	4	5	6	7	8	9	10	11	12	13	14	15	16	17	18	19	20	21	22	23	24	25	26	27	28	29		
☉	11♒	12	13	14	15	16	17	18	19	20	21	22	23	24	25	26	27	28	29	0♓	1	2	3	4	5	6	8	9	10		
☽	30♌	12♍	24	6♎	18	0♏	12	24	6♐	19	1♑	14	27	11♒	25	9♓	24	9♈	23	8♉	22	6♊	20	3♋	17	30	13♌	25	8♍		
☿	0♒	2	3	5	7	8	10	11	13	15	17	18	20	22	24	25	27	29	1♓	3	5	6	8	10	12	14	16	18	20		
♀	19♓	20	21	22	24	25	26	27	28	29	1♈	2	3	4	5	7	8	9	10	11	13	14	15	16	17	18	20	21	22		
♂	24♈	24	25	26	26	27	28	28	29	30	0♉	1	2	2	3	4	4	5	6	6	7	8	8	9	10	10	11	11	12		
	1	6	11	16	21	26			1	11	21			1	11	21			1	16		1	16		1	16		1	11	21	
♃	29♐	30	1♑	2	3	3		♄	30♉	30	30		⚷	10♈	11	11		♅	18♎	18	♆	5♐	5	♇	2♎	2	☊	5♒	4	4	

MAR

	1	2	3	4	5	6	7	8	9	10	11	12	13	14	15	16	17	18	19	20	21	22	23	24	25	26	27	28	29	30	31
☉	11♓	12	13	14	15	16	17	18	19	20	21	22	23	24	25	26	27	27	28	29	0♈	1	2	3	4	5	6	7	8	9	10
☽	20♍	3♎	15	27	8♏	20	2♐	14	26	9♑	22	5♒	19	3♓	18	3♈	18	3♉	18	2♊	16	0♋	14	27	10♌	22	5♍	17	29	11♎	23
☿	21♓	23	25	27	29	1♈	2	4	5	7	8	10	11	12	13	14	14	15	15	16	16	16	16	16	15	15	14	14	13	12	11
♀	23♈	24	25	26	28	29	30	1♉	2	3	4	5	7	8	9	10	11	12	13	14	15	16	18	19	20	21	22	23	24	25	26
♂	13♉	13	14	15	15	16	17	17	18	19	19	20	21	21	22	23	23	24	25	25	26	27	27	28	29	29	30	1♊	1	2	2
	1	6	11	16	21	26	31		1	11	21	31		1	11	21	31		1	16		1	16		1	16		1	11	21	31
♃	4♑	5	5	6	6	7	7	♄	0♊	1	2	3	⚷	11♈	12	13	13	♅	18♎	17	♆	5♐	5	♇	1♎	1	☊	3♒	3	2	2

APR

	1	2	3	4	5	6	7	8	9	10	11	12	13	14	15	16	17	18	19	20	21	22	23	24	25	26	27	28	29	30	
☉	11♈	12	13	14	15	16	17	18	19	20	21	22	23	24	25	26	27	28	29	0♉	1	2	3	4	5	6	7	8	9	10	
☽	5♏	17	29	11♐	23	5♑	17	0♒	13	27	11♓	26	11♈	26	12♉	27	12♊	26	10♋	24	7♌	19	2♍	14	26	8♎	20	2♏	14	26	
☿	10♈	10	9	8	7	7	6	5	5	4	4	4	4	4	4	4	4	4	5	5	6	6	7	8	8	9	10	11	12	13	
♀	27♉	28	29	0♊	1	2	3	4	5	6	7	8	9	10	11	12	13	13	14	15	16	17	18	19	19	20	21	22	23	23	
♂	3♊	4	4	5	6	6	7	8	8	9	10	10	11	12	12	13	14	14	15	15	16	17	17	18	19	19	20	21	21	22	
	1	6	11	16	21	26			1	11	21			1	11	21			1	16		1	16		1	16		1	11	21	
♃	7♑	8	8	8	8	8		♄	3♊	4	5		⚷	13♈	14	14		♅	17♎	16	♆	5♐	5	♇	0♎	0	☊	2♒	1	1	

MAY

	1	2	3	4	5	6	7	8	9	10	11	12	13	14	15	16	17	18	19	20	21	22	23	24	25	26	27	28	29	30	31
☉	11♉	12	13	14	15	16	17	17	18	19	20	21	22	23	24	25	26	27	28	29	0♊	1	2	3	4	5	6	7	8	9	10
☽	8♐	20	2♑	14	27	9♒	22	6♓	20	5♈	19	5♉	20	5♊	20	5♋	19	2♌	16	28	11♍	23	5♎	17	29	11♏	23	5♐	17	29	11♑
☿	14♈	15	16	17	19	20	21	23	24	25	27	28	0♉	2	3	5	7	8	10	12	14	15	17	19	21	23	25	27	29	2♊	4
♀	24♊	25	25	26	27	27	28	29	29	30	0♋	1	1	2	2	2	3	3	4	4	4	4	4	5	5	5	5	5	5	5	4
♂	23♊	23	24	25	25	26	26	27	28	28	29	30	0♋	1	2	2	3	3	4	5	5	6	7	7	8	9	9	10	11	11	12
	1	6	11	16	21	26	31		1	11	21	31		1	11	21	31		1	16		1	16		1	16		1	11	21	31
♃	8♑	8	8	8	7	7	6	♄	6♊	7	9	10	⚷	15♈	15	16	16	♅	15♎	15	♆	5♐	4	♇	30♍	29	☊	0♒	30♑	29	29

JUN

	1	2	3	4	5	6	7	8	9	10	11	12	13	14	15	16	17	18	19	20	21	22	23	24	25	26	27	28	29	30	
☉	11♊	12	13	13	14	15	16	17	18	19	20	21	22	23	24	25	26	27	28	29	30	1♋	2	3	4	4	5	6	7	8	
☽	24♑	6♒	19	2♓	16	30	14♈	29	13♉	28	13♊	28	13♋	27	11♌	24	7♍	19	2♎	14	26	8♏	19	1♐	13	26	8♑	20	3♒	16	
☿	6♊	8	10	12	15	17	19	21	23	25	28	30	2♋	4	6	8	10	12	14	16	17	19	21	23	24	26	27	29	0♌	2	
♀	4♋	4	4	4	3	3	2	2	1	1	0	30♊	29	29	28	28	27	26	26	25	24	24	23	23	22	22	21	21	20	20	
♂	12♋	13	14	14	15	16	16	17	18	18	19	19	20	21	21	22	23	23	24	25	25	26	26	27	28	28	29	30	0♌	1	
	1	6	11	16	21	26			1	11	21			1	11	21			1	16		1	16		1	16		1	11	21	
♃	6♑	6	5	5	4	3		♄	10♊	11	13		⚷	16♈	17	17		♅	14♎	14	♆	4♐	3	♇	29♍	29	☊	29♑	28	28	

1972

JUL

	1	2	3	4	5	6	7	8	9	10	11	12	13	14	15	16	17	18	19	20	21	22	23	24	25	26	27	28	29	30	31
☉	9♋	10	11	12	13	14	15	16	17	18	19	20	21	22	23	24	25	25	26	27	28	29	0♌	1	2	3	4	5	6	7	8
☽	29♒	13♓	26	10♈	24	9♉	23	8♊	22	7♋	21	5♌	19	2♍	15	28	10♎	22	4♏	16	28	10♐	22	4♑	17	29	12♒	26	9♓	23	7♈
☿	3♌	5	6	7	9	10	11	12	13	14	15	16	17	18	19	19	20	20	21	21	22	22	22	22	22	22	22	22	22	21	21
♀	20♊	19	19	19	19	18	18	18	18	18	18	18	18	19	19	19	19	20	20	20	21	21	22	22	22	23	24	24	25	25	26
♂	1♌	2	3	3	4	5	5	6	7	7	8	8	9	10	10	11	12	12	13	14	14	15	15	16	17	17	18	19	19	20	20
	1	6	11	16	21	26	31		1	11	21	31		1	11	21	31		1	16		1	16		1	16		1	11	21	31
♃	3♑	2	1	1	0	30♐	29	♄	14♊	15	16	17	⚷	17♈	17	17	17	♅	14♎	14	♆	3♐	3	♇	29♍	30	☊	27♑	26	26	25

AUG

	1	2	3	4	5	6	7	8	9	10	11	12	13	14	15	16	17	18	19	20	21	22	23	24	25	26	27	28	29	30	31
☉	9♌	10	11	12	13	14	15	16	16	17	18	19	20	21	22	23	24	25	26	27	28	29	30	1♍	2	3	4	5	6	7	8
☽	21♈	5♉	20	4♊	18	2♋	16	0♌	14	27	10♍	23	5♎	18	30	12♏	24	6♐	18	30	12♑	25	8♒	21	5♓	19	3♈	18	2♉	16	1♊
☿	20♌	20	19	18	18	17	16	15	14	14	13	12	12	11	11	11	11	10	11	11	11	11	12	13	14	15	16	17	18	19	21
♀	26♊	27	28	29	29	30	1♋	1	2	3	4	5	5	6	7	8	9	10	11	11	12	13	14	15	16	17	18	19	20	21	22
♂	21♌	22	22	23	24	24	25	26	26	27	27	28	29	29	30	1♍	1	2	3	3	4	4	5	6	6	7	8	8	9	10	10
	1	6	11	16	21	26	31		1	11	21	31		1	11	21	31		1	16		1	16		1	16		1	11	21	31
♃	29♐	29	29	29	29	28	29	♄	17♊	18	19	20	⚷	17♈	17	17	17	♅	15♎	15	♆	3♐	2	♇	0♎	0	☊	25♑	25	24	24

SEP

	1	2	3	4	5	6	7	8	9	10	11	12	13	14	15	16	17	18	19	20	21	22	23	24	25	26	27	28	29	30
☉	9♍	10	11	12	13	13	14	15	16	17	18	19	20	21	22	23	24	25	26	27	28	29	0♎	1	2	3	4	5	6	7
☽	15♊	29	13♋	26	10♌	23	6♍	19	1♎	14	26	8♏	20	2♐	13	25	8♑	20	3♒	16	29	13♓	28	12♈	27	12♉	27	11♊	26	9♋
☿	22♌	24	26	27	29	1♍	3	5	7	8	10	12	14	16	18	20	22	24	25	27	29	1♎	3	4	6	8	10	11	13	15
♀	23♋	24	25	26	27	28	29	0♌	1	2	3	4	5	6	7	8	10	11	12	13	14	15	16	17	18	19	21	22	23	24
♂	11♍	11	12	13	13	14	15	15	16	17	17	18	18	19	20	20	21	22	22	23	24	24	25	26	26	27	27	28	29	29
	1	6	11	16	21	26			1	11	21			1	11	21			1	16		1	16		1	16		1	11	21
♃	29♐	29	29	29	30	0♑		♄	20♊	20	20		⚷	17♈	16	16		♅	16♎	17	♆	3♐	3	♇	1♎	2	☊	24♑	23	23

OCT

	1	2	3	4	5	6	7	8	9	10	11	12	13	14	15	16	17	18	19	20	21	22	23	24	25	26	27	28	29	30	31
☉	8♎	9	10	11	12	13	14	15	16	17	18	19	20	21	22	23	24	25	26	27	28	29	30	1♏	2	3	4	5	6	7	8
☽	23♋	6♌	19	2♍	15	28	10♎	22	4♏	16	28	10♐	22	4♑	16	28	11♒	24	7♓	21	6♈	21	6♉	21	6♊	21	6♋	20	3♌	17	29
☿	16♎	18	20	21	23	25	26	28	29	1♏	2	4	5	7	8	10	11	13	14	16	17	18	20	21	23	24	25	26	28	29	0♐
♀	25♌	26	27	28	30	1♍	2	3	4	5	6	8	9	10	11	12	13	15	16	17	18	19	21	22	23	24	25	27	28	29	0♎
♂	0♎	1	1	2	3	3	4	5	5	6	6	7	8	8	9	10	10	11	12	12	13	14	14	15	16	16	17	18	18	19	20
	1	6	11	16	21	26	31		1	11	21	31		1	11	21	31		1	16		1	16		1	16		1	11	21	31
♃	1♑	1	2	2	3	4	5	♄	21♊	21	20	20	⚷	15♈	15	15	14	♅	18♎	19	♆	3♐	4	♇	2♎	3	☊	22♑	22	21	21

NOV

	1	2	3	4	5	6	7	8	9	10	11	12	13	14	15	16	17	18	19	20	21	22	23	24	25	26	27	28	29	30
☉	9♏	10	11	12	13	14	15	16	17	18	19	20	21	22	23	24	25	26	27	28	29	30	1♐	2	3	4	5	6	7	8
☽	12♍	25	7♎	19	1♏	13	25	7♐	19	0♑	12	24	7♒	19	2♓	16	30	14♈	29	14♉	29	15♊	30	14♋	29	13♌	26	9♍	22	4♎
☿	1♐	3	4	5	6	7	8	9	9	10	11	11	12	12	12	12	12	12	12	11	10	9	8	7	6	4	3	2	0	29♏
♀	1♎	3	4	5	6	7	9	10	11	12	13	15	16	17	18	20	21	22	23	24	26	27	28	29	1♏	2	3	4	5	7
♂	20♎	21	21	22	23	23	24	25	25	26	27	27	28	29	29	0♏	1	1	2	3	3	4	5	5	6	7	7	8	9	9
	1	6	11	16	21	26			1	11	21			1	11	21			1	16		1	16		1	16		1	11	21
♃	5♑	6	7	8	9	10		♄	20♊	19	19		⚷	14♈	14	13		♅	20♎	21	♆	4♐	5	♇	3♎	4	☊	20♑	20	19

DEC

	1	2	3	4	5	6	7	8	9	10	11	12	13	14	15	16	17	18	19	20	21	22	23	24	25	26	27	28	29	30	31
☉	9♐	10	11	12	13	14	15	16	17	18	19	20	21	22	23	24	25	26	27	28	29	0♑	1	2	3	4	5	6	7	8	9
☽	16♎	28	10♏	22	4♐	16	27	9♑	21	4♒	16	29	12♓	25	9♈	23	7♉	22	7♊	22	8♋	22	7♌	21	4♍	18	0♎	13	25	7♏	19
☿	28♏	27	27	26	26	26	26	27	27	28	28	29	0♐	1	2	3	4	5	7	8	9	10	12	13	15	16	17	19	20	22	23
♀	8♏	9	10	12	13	14	15	17	18	19	20	22	23	24	25	27	28	29	0♐	2	3	4	5	7	8	9	10	12	13	14	15
♂	10♏	11	11	12	13	13	14	15	15	16	17	17	18	19	19	20	21	21	22	23	23	24	25	25	26	27	28	28	29	30	0♐
	1	6	11	16	21	26	31		1	11	21	31		1	11	21	31		1	16		1	16		1	16		1	11	21	31
♃	11♑	12	13	14	15	16	18	♄	18♊	17	16	15	⚷	13♈	13	13	13	♅	22♎	22	♆	5♐	6	♇	4♎	4	☊	19♑	18	18	17

1973

EPHEMERIS

		1	2	3	4	5	6	7	8	9	10	11	12	13	14	15	16	17	18	19	20	21	22	23	24	25	26	27	28	29	30	31
JAN	☉	10♑	11	12	13	15	16	17	18	19	20	21	22	23	24	25	26	27	28	29	30	1♒	2	3	4	5	6	7	8	9	10	11
	☽	1♐	12	24	6♑	18	1♒	13	26	9♓	22	5♈	19	3♉	17	1♊	16	1♋	16	0♌	15	29	12♍	26	8♎	21	3♏	15	27	9♐	21	3♑
	☿	25♐	26	28	29	1♑	2	4	5	7	8	10	11	13	14	16	18	19	21	22	24	26	27	29	1♒	2	4	6	7	9	11	13
	♀	16♐	18	19	20	21	23	24	25	26	28	29	0♑	1	3	4	5	7	8	9	10	12	13	14	15	17	18	19	20	22	23	24
	♂	1♐	2	2	3	4	4	5	6	6	7	8	8	9	10	10	11	12	13	13	14	15	15	16	17	17	18	19	19	20	21	21
		1	6	11	16	21	26	31		1	11	21	31		1	11	21	31		1	16		1	16		1	16		1	11	21	31
	♃	18♑	19	20	21	22	24	25	♄	15♊	15	14	14	⚷	13♈	13	13	13	♅	23♎	23	♆	6♐	7	♇	4♎	4	☊	17♑	17	16	16

		1	2	3	4	5	6	7	8	9	10	11	12	13	14	15	16	17	18	19	20	21	22	23	24	25	26	27	28			
FEB	☉	12♒	13	14	15	16	17	18	19	20	21	22	23	24	25	26	27	28	29	0♓	1	2	3	4	5	6	7	8	9			
	☽	15♑	27	9♒	22	5♓	19	2♈	16	29	13♉	28	12♊	26	10♋	25	9♌	23	7♍	20	3♎	16	29	11♏	23	5♐	17	28	10♑			
	☿	14♒	16	18	20	21	23	25	27	29	0♓	2	4	6	8	9	11	13	14	16	18	19	21	22	23	24	25	26	27			
	♀	25♑	27	28	29	0♒	2	3	4	5	7	8	9	10	12	13	14	15	17	18	19	20	22	23	24	25	27	28	29			
	♂	22♐	23	24	24	25	26	26	27	28	28	29	30	1♑	1	2	3	3	4	5	5	6	7	8	8	9	10	10	11			
		1	6	11	16	21	26			1	11	21			1	11	21			1	16		1	16		1	16		1	11	21	
	♃	25♑	26	27	28	29	1♒		♄	14♊	14	14		⚷	14♈	14	14		♅	23♎	23	♆	7♐	7	♇	4♎	4	☊	16♑	15	15	

		1	2	3	4	5	6	7	8	9	10	11	12	13	14	15	16	17	18	19	20	21	22	23	24	25	26	27	28	29	30	31
MAR	☉	10♓	11	12	13	14	15	16	17	18	19	20	21	22	23	24	25	26	27	28	29	0♈	1	2	3	4	5	6	7	8	9	10
	☽	23♑	5♒	18	1♓	14	28	12♈	26	10♉	24	9♊	23	7♋	21	5♌	18	2♍	15	28	11♎	24	7♏	19	1♐	13	24	6♑	18	0♒	13	26
	☿	28♓	28	28	29	29	28	28	28	27	26	26	25	24	23	22	21	20	19	18	18	17	16	16	16	15	15	15	15	15	15	16
	♀	0♓	2	3	4	5	7	8	9	10	12	13	14	15	16	18	19	20	21	23	24	25	26	28	29	0♈	1	3	4	5	6	8
	♂	12♑	12	13	14	15	15	16	17	17	18	19	19	20	21	22	22	23	24	24	25	26	27	27	28	29	29	0♒	1	2	2	3
		1	6	11	16	21	26	31		1	11	21	31		1	11	21	31		1	16		1	16		1	16		1	11	21	31
	♃	1♒	2	3	4	5	6	7	♄	14♊	14	15	15	⚷	15♈	15	16	16	♅	23♎	22	♆	7♐	7	♇	4♎	3	☊	14♑	14	13	13

		1	2	3	4	5	6	7	8	9	10	11	12	13	14	15	16	17	18	19	20	21	22	23	24	25	26	27	28	29	30	
APR	☉	11♈	12	13	14	15	16	17	18	19	20	21	22	23	24	25	26	27	28	29	30	1♉	2	3	4	5	6	7	8	9	10	
	☽	9♓	23	7♈	21	5♉	20	5♊	19	4♋	18	1♌	15	28	12♍	25	8♎	20	3♏	15	27	9♐	21	3♑	14	26	8♒	21	4♓	17	1♈	
	☿	16♓	16	17	18	18	19	20	21	21	22	23	24	25	27	28	29	0♈	1	3	4	5	7	8	10	11	13	14	16	18	19	
	♀	9♈	10	11	13	14	15	16	18	19	20	21	23	24	25	26	27	29	30	1♉	2	4	5	6	7	9	10	11	12	14	15	
	♂	4♒	4	5	6	6	7	8	9	9	10	11	11	12	13	14	14	15	16	16	17	18	19	19	20	21	21	22	23	24	24	
		1	6	11	16	21	26			1	11	21			1	11	21			1	16		1	16		1	16		1	11	21	
	♃	7♒	8	8	9	10	10		♄	16♊	16	17		⚷	16♈	17	18		♅	21♎	21	♆	7♐	7	♇	3♎	2	☊	12♑	12	11	

		1	2	3	4	5	6	7	8	9	10	11	12	13	14	15	16	17	18	19	20	21	22	23	24	25	26	27	28	29	30	31
MAY	☉	10♉	11	12	13	14	15	16	17	18	19	20	21	22	23	24	25	26	27	28	29	30	1♊	2	3	4	5	6	7	7	8	9
	☽	15♈	29	14♉	29	14♊	29	14♋	28	12♌	25	9♍	22	4♎	17	29	12♏	24	6♐	17	29	11♑	23	5♒	17	29	12♓	25	9♈	23	8♉	23
	☿	21♈	23	24	26	28	30	2♉	4	5	7	9	11	13	16	18	20	22	24	26	28	1♊	3	5	7	9	12	14	16	18	20	22
	♀	16♉	17	18	20	21	22	23	25	26	27	28	30	1♊	2	3	4	6	7	8	9	11	12	13	14	16	17	18	19	20	22	23
	♂	25♒	26	26	27	28	28	29	30	1♓	1	2	3	3	4	5	6	6	7	8	8	9	10	10	11	12	12	13	14	15	15	16
		1	6	11	16	21	26	31		1	11	21	31		1	11	21	31		1	16		1	16		1	16		1	11	21	31
	♃	11♒	11	12	12	12	12	12	♄	18♊	20	21	22	⚷	18♈	19	19	20	♅	20♎	20	♆	7♐	6	♇	2♎	2	☊	11♑	10	10	9

		1	2	3	4	5	6	7	8	9	10	11	12	13	14	15	16	17	18	19	20	21	22	23	24	25	26	27	28	29	30	
JUN	☉	10♊	11	12	13	14	15	16	17	18	19	20	21	22	23	24	25	26	27	28	29	29	0♋	1	2	3	4	5	6	7	8	
	☽	8♊	23	8♋	23	7♌	21	5♍	18	1♎	14	26	9♏	21	3♐	14	26	8♑	20	2♒	14	26	9♓	21	5♈	18	2♉	16	1♊	16	1♋	
	☿	24♊	26	28	30	1♋	3	5	7	8	10	12	13	14	16	17	19	20	21	22	23	25	26	27	27	28	29	30	0♌	1	2	
	♀	24♊	25	27	28	29	0♋	1	3	4	5	6	8	9	10	11	12	14	15	16	17	19	20	21	22	23	25	26	27	28	30	
	♂	17♓	17	18	19	19	20	21	21	22	23	23	24	25	25	26	27	27	28	29	29	0♈	1	1	2	3	3	4	5	5	6	
		1	6	11	16	21	26			1	11	21			1	11	21			1	16		1	16		1	16		1	11	21	
	♃	12♒	12	12	12	11	11		♄	22♊	24	25		⚷	20♈	20	20		♅	19♎	19	♆	6♐	6	♇	2♎	2	☊	9♑	9	8	

1973

EPHEMERIS

JUL

	1	2	3	4	5	6	7	8	9	10	11	12	13	14	15	16	17	18	19	20	21	22	23	24	25	26	27	28	29	30	31
☉	9♋	10	11	12	13	14	15	16	17	18	19	20	20	21	22	23	24	25	26	27	28	29	0♌	1	2	3	4	5	6	7	8
☽	16♋	1♌	16	0♍	14	28	11♎	23	6♏	18	30	11♐	23	5♑	17	29	11♒	23	6♓	18	1♈	14	28	12♉	26	10♊	25	10♋	25	10♌	24
☿	2♌	2	3	3	3	3	3	3	3	3	3	2	2	1	1	0	30♋	29	28	28	27	26	26	25	24	24	24	23	23	23	23
♀	1♌	2	3	4	6	7	8	9	10	12	13	14	15	17	18	19	20	21	23	24	25	26	27	29	30	1♍	2	4	5	6	7
♂	7♈	7	8	8	9	10	10	11	12	12	13	13	14	15	15	16	16	17	17	18	19	19	20	20	21	21	22	22	23	23	24
	1	6	11	16	21	26	31		1	11	21	31		1	11	21	31		1	16		1	16		1	16		1	11	21	31
♃	11♒	10	10	9	8	8	7	♄	26♊	27	29	30	⚷	21♈	21	21	21	♅	19♎	19	♆	5♐	5	♇	2♎	2	☊	8♑	7	7	6

AUG

	1	2	3	4	5	6	7	8	9	10	11	12	13	14	15	16	17	18	19	20	21	22	23	24	25	26	27	28	29	30	31
☉	9♌	10	11	11	12	13	14	15	16	17	18	19	20	21	22	23	24	25	26	27	28	29	30	1♍	2	3	4	5	6	6	7
☽	9♍	23	6♎	19	2♏	14	26	8♐	20	2♑	14	26	8♒	20	3♓	15	28	11♈	25	8♉	22	6♊	20	5♋	19	4♌	18	3♍	17	1♎	14
☿	23♋	23	23	24	24	25	26	26	27	28	29	1♌	2	3	5	6	8	10	11	13	15	17	19	21	23	25	27	29	1♍	3	5
♀	8♍	10	11	12	13	14	16	17	18	19	20	22	23	24	25	26	28	29	30	1♎	2	4	5	6	7	8	9	11	12	13	14
♂	24♈	25	26	26	26	27	27	28	28	29	29	30	0♉	1	1	1	2	2	3	3	3	4	4	4	5	5	5	6	6	6	7
	1	6	11	16	21	26	31		1	11	21	31		1	11	21	31		1	16		1	16		1	16		1	11	21	31
♃	7♒	6	6	5	5	4	4	♄	30♊	1♋	2	3	⚷	21♈	21	21	20	♅	19♎	20	♆	5♐	5	♇	2♎	3	☊	6♑	5	5	4

SEP

	1	2	3	4	5	6	7	8	9	10	11	12	13	14	15	16	17	18	19	20	21	22	23	24	25	26	27	28	29	30
☉	8♍	9	10	11	12	13	14	15	16	17	18	19	20	21	22	23	24	25	26	27	28	29	30	1♎	2	3	4	5	6	7
☽	27♎	10♏	22	4♐	16	28	10♑	22	4♒	16	29	11♓	24	8♈	21	5♉	19	3♊	17	1♋	15	29	14♌	28	12♍	25	9♎	22	5♏	18
☿	7♍	9	10	12	14	16	18	20	22	24	25	27	29	1♎	2	4	6	7	9	11	12	14	15	17	18	20	21	23	24	26
♀	15♎	17	18	19	20	21	23	24	25	26	27	28	30	1♏	2	3	4	5	7	8	9	10	11	12	14	15	16	17	18	19
♂	7♉	7	7	7	8	8	8	8	8	9	9	9	9	9	9	9	9	9	9	9	9	9	9	9	9	9	9	9	9	9
	1	6	11	16	21	26			1	11	21			1	11	21			1	16		1	16		1	16		1	11	21
♃	3♒	3	3	3	2	2		♄	3♋	4	4		⚷	20♈	20	20		♅	21♎	22	♆	5♐	5	♇	3♎	4	☊	4♑	4	3

OCT

	1	2	3	4	5	6	7	8	9	10	11	12	13	14	15	16	17	18	19	20	21	22	23	24	25	26	27	28	29	30	31
☉	8♎	9	10	11	12	13	14	15	16	17	18	19	20	21	21	22	23	24	25	26	27	28	29	0♏	1	2	3	4	5	6	7
☽	0♐	12	24	6♑	18	30	12♒	24	7♓	20	3♈	17	1♉	15	29	14♊	28	12♋	26	10♌	24	8♍	21	5♎	18	1♏	13	26	8♐	20	2♑
☿	27♎	29	0♏	2	3	4	6	7	8	10	11	12	13	15	16	17	18	19	20	21	22	23	23	24	25	25	26	26	26	27	27
♀	20♏	22	23	24	25	26	27	28	30	1♐	2	3	4	5	6	8	9	10	11	12	13	14	15	16	17	19	20	21	22	23	24
♂	8♉	8	8	8	8	7	7	7	7	6	6	6	6	5	5	5	4	4	4	3	3	3	2	2	2	1	1	1	0	30♈	30
	1	6	11	16	21	26	31		1	11	21	31		1	11	21	31		1	16		1	16		1	16		1	11	21	31
♃	2♒	2	3	3	3	4	4	♄	5♋	5	5	5	⚷	19♈	19	18	18	♅	22♎	23	♆	5♐	6	♇	4♎	5	☊	3♑	2	2	1

NOV

	1	2	3	4	5	6	7	8	9	10	11	12	13	14	15	16	17	18	19	20	21	22	23	24	25	26	27	28	29	30
☉	8♏	9	10	11	12	13	14	15	16	17	18	19	20	21	22	23	24	26	27	28	29	30	1♐	2	3	4	5	6	7	8
☽	14♑	26	7♒	20	2♓	15	28	11♈	25	9♉	24	9♊	23	8♋	23	7♌	21	5♍	18	1♎	15	27	10♏	22	4♐	16	28	10♑	22	4♒
☿	26♏	26	26	25	24	23	22	21	20	18	17	16	15	14	13	12	11	11	11	11	11	11	12	12	13	14	15	16	17	18
♀	25♐	26	27	28	29	0♑	1	2	3	5	6	7	8	9	10	11	12	13	14	14	15	16	17	18	19	20	21	22	23	24
♂	29♈	29	29	28	28	28	28	27	27	27	27	27	26	26	26	26	26	26	26	26	25	25	25	25	25	25	25	25	25	25
	1	6	11	16	21	26			1	11	21			1	11	21			1	16		1	16		1	16		1	11	21
♃	4♒	5	5	6	7	7		♄	5♋	4	4		⚷	18♈	17	17		♅	24♎	25	♆	6♐	7	♇	6♎	6	☊	1♑	1	0

DEC

	1	2	3	4	5	6	7	8	9	10	11	12	13	14	15	16	17	18	19	20	21	22	23	24	25	26	27	28	29	30	31
☉	9♐	10	11	12	13	14	15	16	17	18	19	20	21	22	23	24	25	26	27	28	29	30	1♑	2	3	4	5	6	7	8	9
☽	16♒	28	10♓	23	6♈	19	3♉	17	2♊	17	2♋	17	2♌	17	1♍	15	28	12♎	24	7♏	19	1♐	13	25	7♑	19	1♒	12	24	6♓	19
☿	19♏	20	22	23	24	26	27	29	0♐	2	3	5	6	8	9	11	12	14	15	17	18	20	21	23	24	26	27	29	1♑	2	4
♀	24♑	25	26	27	28	29	29	0♒	1	2	2	3	4	4	5	5	6	7	7	8	8	9	9	9	10	10	10	11	11	11	11
♂	25♈	26	26	26	26	26	26	26	26	27	27	27	27	27	28	28	28	28	28	28	29	29	29	30	0♉	1	1	1	1	2	2
	1	6	11	16	21	26	31		1	11	21	31		1	11	21	31		1	16		1	16		1	16		1	11	21	31
♃	8♒	9	10	11	12	13	14	♄	3♋	2	1	1	⚷	17♈	17	16	16	♅	26♎	27	♆	7♐	8	♇	6♎	7	☊	30♐	29	29	28

1974

JAN

	1	2	3	4	5	6	7	8	9	10	11	12	13	14	15	16	17	18	19	20	21	22	23	24	25	26	27	28	29	30	31
☉	10♑	11	12	13	14	15	16	17	18	19	20	21	22	23	24	25	26	28	29	30	1♒	2	3	4	5	6	7	8	9	10	11
☽	1♈	14	27	11♉	25	10♊	25	10♋	25	10♌	25	10♍	24	8♎	21	4♏	16	28	10♐	22	4♑	16	28	9♒	21	4♓	16	28	11♈	24	7♉
☿	5♑	7	8	10	12	13	15	16	18	20	21	23	25	26	28	30	1♒	3	5	7	8	10	12	13	15	17	19	20	22	24	25
♀	11♒	11	11	11	11	11	11	11	11	10	10	10	9	9	9	8	8	7	6	6	5	5	4	3	3	2	2	1	0	30♑	29
♂	3♉	3	3	4	4	4	5	5	6	6	6	7	7	8	8	9	9	9	10	10	11	11	12	12	13	13	14	14	15	15	16
	1	6	11	16	21	26	31		1	11	21	31		1	11	21	31		1	16		1	16		1	16		1	11	21	31
♃	14♒	16	17	18	19	20	21	♄	1♋	30♊	29	28	⚷	16♈	16	17	17	♅	27♎	28	♆	8♐	9	♇	7♎	7	☊	28♐	27	27	26

FEB

	1	2	3	4	5	6	7	8	9	10	11	12	13	14	15	16	17	18	19	20	21	22	23	24	25	26	27	28			
☉	12♒	13	14	15	16	17	18	19	20	21	22	23	24	25	26	27	28	29	30	1♓	2	3	4	5	6	7	8	9			
☽	20♉	4♊	18	3♋	18	3♌	18	3♍	18	2♎	16	29	12♏	25	7♐	19	1♑	13	24	6♒	18	0♓	13	25	8♈	21	4♉	17			
☿	27♒	29	0♓	2	3	4	6	7	8	9	10	11	11	12	12	12	12	11	11	10	10	9	8	7	6	5	4	3			
♀	29♑	28	28	28	27	27	27	26	26	26	26	26	26	26	26	26	26	26	26	27	27	27	28	28	28	29	29	30			
♂	16♉	17	17	18	18	19	19	20	20	21	21	22	22	23	23	24	24	25	25	26	26	27	28	28	29	29	30	0♊			
	1	6	11	16	21	26			1	11	21			1	11	21			1	16		1	16		1	16		1	11	21	
♃	22♒	23	24	25	26	28		♄	28♊	28	28		⚷	17♈	17	18		♅	28♎	28	♆	9♐	9	♇	7♎	6	☊	26♐	26	25	

MAR

	1	2	3	4	5	6	7	8	9	10	11	12	13	14	15	16	17	18	19	20	21	22	23	24	25	26	27	28	29	30	31
☉	10♓	11	12	13	14	15	16	17	18	19	20	21	22	23	24	25	26	27	28	29	30	1♈	2	3	4	5	6	7	8	9	10
☽	0♊	14	28	13♋	27	12♌	27	11♍	26	10♎	24	7♏	20	3♐	15	27	9♑	21	3♒	15	27	9♓	21	4♈	17	0♉	14	27	11♊	25	9♋
☿	2♓	1	30♒	29	28	28	28	27	27	27	27	27	28	28	28	29	29	0♓	1	2	2	3	4	5	6	7	8	10	11	12	13
♀	0♒	1	1	2	2	3	4	4	5	6	6	7	8	9	9	10	11	12	13	14	14	15	16	17	18	19	20	21	22	23	24
♂	1♊	1	2	3	3	4	4	5	5	6	6	7	8	8	9	9	10	10	11	12	12	13	13	14	15	15	16	16	17	17	18
	1	6	11	16	21	26	31		1	11	21	31		1	11	21	31		1	16		1	16		1	16		1	11	21	31
♃	28♒	29	1♓	2	3	4	5	♄	28♊	28	28	29	⚷	18♈	19	19	20	♅	27♎	27	♆	10♐	10	♇	6♎	6	☊	25♐	24	24	23

APR

	1	2	3	4	5	6	7	8	9	10	11	12	13	14	15	16	17	18	19	20	21	22	23	24	25	26	27	28	29	30	
☉	11♈	12	13	14	15	16	17	18	19	20	21	22	23	24	25	26	27	28	29	30	1♉	1	2	3	4	5	6	7	8	9	
☽	23♋	7♌	22	6♍	20	4♎	18	2♏	15	28	11♐	23	5♑	17	29	11♒	23	5♓	17	30	13♈	26	10♉	24	7♊	22	6♋	20	4♌	18	
☿	15♓	16	17	19	20	21	23	24	26	27	29	1♈	2	4	6	7	9	11	12	14	16	18	20	22	24	26	28	30	2♉	4	
♀	25♒	25	26	27	28	29	0♓	1	2	3	4	5	7	8	9	10	11	12	13	14	15	16	17	18	19	20	21	22	24	25	
♂	19♊	19	20	20	21	22	22	23	23	24	24	25	26	26	27	27	28	29	29	30	0♋	1	2	2	3	3	4	5	5	6	
	1	6	11	16	21	26			1	11	21			1	11	21			1	16		1	16		1	16		1	11	21	
♃	5♓	6	7	8	9	10		♄	29♊	29	0♋		⚷	20♈	20	21		♅	26♎	26	♆	10♐	9	♇	5♎	5	☊	23♐	23	22	

MAY

	1	2	3	4	5	6	7	8	9	10	11	12	13	14	15	16	17	18	19	20	21	22	23	24	25	26	27	28	29	30	31
☉	10♉	11	12	13	14	15	16	17	18	19	20	21	22	23	24	25	26	27	28	29	30	1♊	1	2	3	4	5	6	7	8	9
☽	2♍	16	0♎	14	27	11♏	24	6♐	19	1♑	13	25	7♒	18	0♓	13	25	8♈	21	4♉	18	2♊	17	1♋	16	0♌	15	29	13♍	27	11♎
☿	6♉	8	10	12	14	17	19	21	23	25	27	30	2♊	4	6	8	10	12	14	15	17	19	21	22	24	25	27	28	30	1♋	2
♀	26♓	27	28	29	0♈	1	2	4	5	6	7	8	9	10	11	12	14	15	16	17	18	19	20	22	23	24	25	26	27	28	30
♂	6♋	7	8	8	9	9	10	11	11	12	12	13	14	14	15	15	16	17	17	18	18	19	20	20	21	21	22	23	23	24	24
	1	6	11	16	21	26	31		1	11	21	31		1	11	21	31		1	16		1	16		1	16		1	11	21	31
♃	11♓	12	13	14	14	15	16	♄	1♋	2	3	4	⚷	22♈	22	23	23	♅	25♎	25	♆	9♐	9	♇	5♎	4	☊	22♐	21	21	20

JUN

	1	2	3	4	5	6	7	8	9	10	11	12	13	14	15	16	17	18	19	20	21	22	23	24	25	26	27	28	29	30	
☉	10♊	11	12	13	14	15	16	17	18	19	20	21	22	23	24	24	25	26	27	28	29	0♋	1	2	3	4	5	6	7	8	
☽	24♎	7♏	20	2♐	15	27	9♑	21	3♒	15	27	9♓	21	3♈	16	29	13♉	26	11♊	25	10♋	25	10♌	25	10♍	24	7♎	21	4♏	17	
☿	3♋	4	6	7	7	8	9	10	11	11	12	12	13	13	13	14	14	14	14	13	13	13	13	12	12	11	11	10	10	9	
♀	1♉	2	3	4	5	7	8	9	10	11	12	14	15	16	17	18	19	21	22	23	24	25	26	28	29	0♊	1	2	4	5	
♂	25♋	26	26	27	28	28	29	29	30	1♌	1	2	2	3	4	4	5	5	6	7	7	8	9	9	10	10	11	12	12	13	
	1	6	11	16	21	26			1	11	21			1	11	21			1	16		1	16		1	16		1	11	21	
♃	16♓	16	17	17	17	18		♄	5♋	6	7		⚷	23♈	24	24		♅	24♎	24	♆	8♐	8	♇	4♎	4	☊	20♐	19	19	

1974

JUL

	1	2	3	4	5	6	7	8	9	10	11	12	13	14	15	16	17	18	19	20	21	22	23	24	25	26	27	28	29	30	31
☉	9♋	10	11	12	13	14	15	15	16	17	18	19	20	21	22	23	24	25	26	27	28	29	30	1♌	2	3	4	5	6	6	7
☽	29♏	12♐	24	6♑	18	30	11♒	23	5♓	17	29	12♈	24	7♉	21	5♊	19	4♋	19	4♌	19	4♍	19	3♎	17	1♏	14	26	9♐	21	3♑
☿	9♋	8	7	7	6	6	5	5	5	5	4	4	4	5	5	5	5	6	7	7	8	9	10	11	12	13	14	16	17	19	20
♀	6♊	7	8	9	11	12	13	14	15	17	18	19	20	21	23	24	25	26	27	29	30	1♋	2	3	5	6	7	8	9	11	12
♂	13♌	14	15	15	16	17	17	18	18	19	20	20	21	22	22	23	23	24	25	25	26	27	27	28	28	29	30	0♍	1	2	2
	1	6	11	16	21	26	31		1	11	21	31		1	11	21	31		1	16		1	16		1	16		1	11	21	31
♃	18♓	18	18	18	18	17	17	♄	8♋	10	11	12	⚷	24♈	24	24	24	♅	24♎	24	♆	7♐	7	♇	4♎	4	☊	18♐	18	17	17

AUG

	1	2	3	4	5	6	7	8	9	10	11	12	13	14	15	16	17	18	19	20	21	22	23	24	25	26	27	28	29	30	31
☉	8♌	9	10	11	12	13	14	15	16	17	18	19	20	21	22	23	24	25	26	27	28	29	29	0♍	1	2	3	4	5	6	7
☽	15♑	27	8♒	20	2♓	14	26	9♈	21	4♉	17	30	14♊	28	12♋	27	12♌	28	13♍	28	12♎	26	10♏	23	5♐	18	30	12♑	24	5♒	17
☿	22♋	24	25	27	29	1♌	3	5	7	9	11	13	15	17	19	21	23	25	27	29	1♍	3	5	7	9	11	13	14	16	18	20
♀	13♋	14	15	17	18	19	20	21	23	24	25	26	28	29	0♌	1	2	4	5	6	7	9	10	11	12	13	15	16	17	18	20
♂	3♍	3	4	5	5	6	7	7	8	8	9	10	10	11	12	12	13	13	14	15	15	16	17	17	18	19	19	20	20	21	22
	1	6	11	16	21	26	31		1	11	21	31		1	11	21	31		1	16		1	16		1	16		1	11	21	31
♃	17♓	17	16	15	15	14	14	♄	12♋	14	15	16	⚷	24♈	24	24	24	♅	24♎	25	♆	7♐	7	♇	5♎	5	☊	17♐	16	16	15

SEP

	1	2	3	4	5	6	7	8	9	10	11	12	13	14	15	16	17	18	19	20	21	22	23	24	25	26	27	28	29	30
☉	8♍	9	10	11	12	13	14	15	16	17	18	19	20	21	22	23	24	25	26	27	28	29	30	1♎	2	3	4	4	5	6
☽	29♒	11♓	23	6♈	18	1♉	13	26	10♊	23	7♋	22	6♌	21	6♍	21	6♎	20	4♏	18	1♐	14	26	8♑	20	2♒	14	26	8♓	20
☿	21♍	23	25	26	28	30	1♎	3	4	6	7	9	10	12	13	15	16	17	19	20	22	23	24	25	27	28	29	30	1♏	2
♀	21♌	22	23	25	26	27	28	29	1♍	2	3	4	6	7	8	9	11	12	13	14	16	17	18	19	21	22	23	24	26	27
♂	22♍	23	24	24	25	26	26	27	28	28	29	29	0♎	1	1	2	3	3	4	5	5	6	7	7	8	9	9	10	11	11
	1	6	11	16	21	26			1	11	21			1	11	21			1	16		1	16		1	16		1	11	21
♃	14♓	13	12	12	11	10		♄	16♋	17	17		⚷	24♈	24	23		♅	25♎	26	♆	7♐	7	♇	6♎	6	☊	15♐	15	14

OCT

	1	2	3	4	5	6	7	8	9	10	11	12	13	14	15	16	17	18	19	20	21	22	23	24	25	26	27	28	29	30	31
☉	7♎	8	9	10	11	12	13	14	15	16	17	18	19	20	21	22	23	24	25	26	27	28	29	0♏	1	2	3	4	5	6	7
☽	2♈	15	28	10♉	23	7♊	20	4♋	18	2♌	16	1♍	15	30	14♎	29	12♏	26	9♐	22	4♑	16	28	10♒	22	4♓	16	28	11♈	24	7♉
☿	3♏	4	5	6	7	7	8	9	9	10	10	10	11	11	11	10	10	9	9	8	7	6	5	4	2	1	30♎	29	28	27	26
♀	28♍	29	0♎	2	3	4	5	7	8	9	10	12	13	14	15	17	18	19	20	22	23	24	25	27	28	29	1♏	2	3	4	6
♂	12♎	13	13	14	14	15	16	16	17	18	18	19	20	20	21	22	22	23	24	24	25	26	26	27	28	28	29	30	0♏	1	2
	1	6	11	16	21	26	31		1	11	21	31		1	11	21	31		1	16		1	16		1	16		1	11	21	31
♃	10♓	9	9	9	8	8	8	♄	18♋	19	19	19	⚷	23♈	22	22	22	♅	27♎	28	♆	7♐	8	♇	7♎	7	☊	13♐	13	12	12

NOV

	1	2	3	4	5	6	7	8	9	10	11	12	13	14	15	16	17	18	19	20	21	22	23	24	25	26	27	28	29	30
☉	8♏	9	10	11	12	13	14	15	16	17	18	19	20	21	22	23	24	25	26	27	28	29	0♐	1	2	3	4	5	6	7
☽	20♉	3♊	17	1♋	14	29	13♌	27	11♍	25	9♎	23	7♏	21	4♐	17	30	12♑	24	6♒	18	30	12♓	24	6♈	19	2♉	15	28	12♊
☿	25♎	25	25	25	25	25	26	27	27	28	29	0♏	2	3	4	5	7	8	10	11	13	14	16	17	19	20	22	23	25	26
♀	7♏	8	9	11	12	13	14	16	17	18	19	21	22	23	24	26	27	28	29	1♐	2	3	4	6	7	8	9	11	12	13
♂	2♏	3	4	5	5	6	7	7	8	9	9	10	11	11	12	13	13	14	15	15	16	17	18	18	19	20	20	21	22	22
	1	6	11	16	21	26			1	11	21			1	11	21			1	16		1	16		1	16		1	11	21
♃	8♓	8	8	8	9	9		♄	19♋	19	19		⚷	21♈	21	21		♅	29♎	30	♆	8♐	9	♇	8♎	8	☊	12♐	11	11

DEC

	1	2	3	4	5	6	7	8	9	10	11	12	13	14	15	16	17	18	19	20	21	22	23	24	25	26	27	28	29	30	31
☉	8♐	9	10	11	12	13	14	16	17	18	19	20	21	22	23	24	25	26	27	28	29	30	1♑	2	3	4	5	6	7	8	9
☽	26♊	10♋	25	9♌	24	8♍	22	6♎	20	3♏	17	30	13♐	25	8♑	20	2♒	14	26	8♓	20	2♈	14	26	9♉	22	6♊	20	5♋	19	4♌
☿	28♏	30	1♐	3	4	6	7	9	11	12	14	15	17	18	20	21	23	25	26	28	29	1♑	3	4	6	7	9	11	12	14	15
♀	14♐	16	17	18	19	21	22	23	24	26	27	28	30	1♑	2	3	5	6	7	8	10	11	12	13	15	16	17	18	20	21	22
♂	23♏	24	24	25	26	27	27	28	29	29	0♐	1	1	2	3	4	4	5	6	6	7	8	9	9	10	11	11	12	13	14	14
	1	6	11	16	21	26	31		1	11	21	31		1	11	21	31		1	16		1	16		1	16		1	11	21	31
♃	9♓	10	10	11	12	12	13	♄	18♋	17	17	16	⚷	20♈	20	20	20	♅	1♏	1	♆	9♐	10	♇	9♎	9	☊	10♐	10	9	9

1975

EPHEMERIS

JAN

	1	2	3	4	5	6	7	8	9	10	11	12	13	14	15	16	17	18	19	20	21	22	23	24	25	26	27	28	29	30	31
☉	10♑	11	12	13	14	15	16	17	18	19	20	21	22	23	24	25	26	27	28	29	0♒	1	2	3	4	5	6	7	8	9	10
☽	19♌	4♍	18	3♎	17	0♏	13	26	9♐	22	4♑	16	28	10♒	22	4♓	16	28	10♈	22	4♉	17	0♊	14	28	13♋	27	13♌	28	13♍	28
☿	17♑	19	20	22	24	25	27	28	0♒	2	3	5	7	8	10	11	13	14	16	17	18	20	21	22	23	24	24	25	25	25	25
♀	23♑	25	26	27	28	30	1♒	2	3	5	6	7	8	10	11	12	13	15	16	17	18	20	21	22	23	25	26	27	28	30	1♓
♂	15♐	16	16	17	18	19	19	20	21	21	22	23	24	24	25	26	27	27	28	29	29	0♑	1	2	2	3	4	5	5	6	7
	1	6	11	16	21	26	31		1	11	21	31		1	11	21	31		1	16		1	16		1	16		1	11	21	31
♃	13♓	14	15	16	17	18	19	♄	16♋	15	14	14	⚷	20♈	20	20	20	♅	2♏	2	♆	10♐	11	♇	9♎	9	☊	9♐	8	8	7

FEB

	1	2	3	4	5	6	7	8	9	10	11	12	13	14	15	16	17	18	19	20	21	22	23	24	25	26	27	28			
☉	11♒	13	14	15	16	17	18	19	20	21	22	23	24	25	26	27	28	29	30	1♓	2	3	4	5	6	7	8	9			
☽	13♎	27	10♏	23	6♐	19	1♑	13	25	7♒	19	1♓	13	25	7♈	19	1♉	13	26	9♊	22	6♋	21	5♌	21	6♍	21	6♎			
☿	25♒	25	24	24	23	22	21	19	18	17	16	15	14	13	12	11	11	10	10	10	10	10	10	11	11	11	12	13			
♀	2♓	3	5	6	7	8	10	11	12	13	15	16	17	18	20	21	22	23	25	26	27	28	29	1♈	2	3	4	6			
♂	7♑	8	9	10	10	11	12	13	13	14	15	16	16	17	18	19	19	20	21	22	22	23	24	25	25	26	27	28			
	1	6	11	16	21	26			1	11	21			1	11	21			1	16		1	16		1	16		1	11	21	
♃	19♓	20	22	23	24	25		♄	13♋	13	12		⚷	20♈	21	21		♅	2♏	2	♆	11♐	12	♇	9♎	9	☊	7♐	6	6	

MAR

	1	2	3	4	5	6	7	8	9	10	11	12	13	14	15	16	17	18	19	20	21	22	23	24	25	26	27	28	29	30	31
☉	10♓	11	12	13	14	15	16	17	18	19	20	21	22	23	24	25	26	27	28	29	30	1♈	2	3	4	5	6	7	8	9	10
☽	21♎	6♏	19	3♐	16	28	10♑	22	4♒	16	28	10♓	22	4♈	16	28	10♉	23	5♊	18	2♋	16	30	14♌	29	14♍	29	15♎	29	14♏	28
☿	13♒	14	15	16	17	18	19	20	21	22	23	24	25	27	28	29	1♓	2	3	5	6	8	9	11	12	14	16	17	19	20	22
♀	7♈	8	9	11	12	13	14	15	17	18	19	20	22	23	24	25	26	28	29	0♉	1	3	4	5	6	7	9	10	11	12	13
♂	28♑	29	30	1♒	1	2	3	4	4	5	6	7	7	8	9	10	10	11	12	13	13	14	15	16	16	17	18	19	19	20	21
	1	6	11	16	21	26	31		1	11	21	31		1	11	21	31		1	16		1	16		1	16		1	11	21	31
♃	26♓	27	28	29	1♈	2	3	♄	12♋	12	12	12	⚷	21♈	22	23	23	♅	2♏	2	♆	12♐	12	♇	9♎	8	☊	5♐	5	4	4

APR

	1	2	3	4	5	6	7	8	9	10	11	12	13	14	15	16	17	18	19	20	21	22	23	24	25	26	27	28	29	30	
☉	11♈	12	13	14	15	16	17	18	19	20	20	21	22	23	24	25	26	27	28	29	0♉	1	2	3	4	5	6	7	8	9	
☽	11♐	24	7♑	19	1♒	13	25	7♓	19	1♈	13	25	7♉	20	3♊	15	29	12♋	26	10♌	24	9♍	23	8♎	23	7♏	22	6♐	19	2♑	
☿	24♓	26	27	29	1♈	3	5	6	8	10	12	14	16	18	20	22	24	26	28	1♉	3	5	7	9	11	13	15	17	20	22	
♀	15♉	16	17	18	19	21	22	23	24	25	27	28	29	0♊	1	2	4	5	6	7	8	9	11	12	13	14	15	16	18	19	
♂	22♒	23	23	24	25	26	26	27	28	29	29	0♓	1	2	2	3	4	5	5	6	7	8	9	9	10	11	12	12	13	14	
	1	6	11	16	21	26			1	11	21			1	11	21			1	16		1	16		1	16		1	11	21	
♃	3♈	4	6	7	8	9		♄	12♋	13	13		⚷	23♈	24	24		♅	1♏	1	♆	12♐	12	♇	8♎	7	☊	4♐	3	3	

MAY

	1	2	3	4	5	6	7	8	9	10	11	12	13	14	15	16	17	18	19	20	21	22	23	24	25	26	27	28	29	30	31
☉	10♉	11	12	13	14	15	16	17	18	19	20	21	22	23	24	25	25	26	27	28	29	0♊	1	2	3	4	5	6	7	8	9
☽	15♑	27	9♒	21	3♓	15	27	9♈	21	4♉	16	29	12♊	25	9♋	23	7♌	21	5♍	19	4♎	18	2♏	16	0♐	14	27	10♑	23	5♒	17
☿	23♉	25	27	29	1♊	3	4	6	7	9	10	12	13	14	15	16	17	18	19	20	21	21	22	22	23	23	23	23	24	24	24
♀	20♊	21	22	23	24	26	27	28	29	0♋	1	2	4	5	6	7	8	9	10	11	12	14	15	16	17	18	19	20	21	22	23
♂	15♓	15	16	17	18	18	19	20	21	21	22	23	24	24	25	26	27	27	28	29	30	0♈	1	2	3	3	4	5	6	6	7
	1	6	11	16	21	26	31		1	11	21	31		1	11	21	31		1	16		1	16		1	16		1	11	21	31
♃	10♈	11	12	14	15	16	17	♄	14♋	15	16	17	⚷	25♈	26	26	27	♅	0♏	29♎	♆	11♐	11	♇	7♎	7	☊	2♐	2	1	1

JUN

	1	2	3	4	5	6	7	8	9	10	11	12	13	14	15	16	17	18	19	20	21	22	23	24	25	26	27	28	29	30	
☉	10♊	11	12	13	14	15	16	17	18	19	19	20	21	22	23	24	25	26	27	28	29	30	1♋	2	3	4	5	6	7	8	
☽	29♒	11♓	23	5♈	17	29	12♉	25	8♊	21	5♋	19	3♌	17	2♍	16	0♎	14	28	12♏	26	9♐	22	5♑	18	1♒	13	25	7♓	19	
☿	23♊	23	23	23	22	22	21	21	20	20	19	19	18	17	17	17	16	16	15	15	15	15	15	15	15	15	16	16	17	17	
♀	24♋	25	26	27	28	30	1♌	2	3	4	5	6	7	8	9	10	11	12	12	13	14	15	16	17	18	19	20	21	22	22	
♂	8♈	9	9	10	11	12	12	13	14	15	15	16	17	18	18	19	20	21	21	22	23	23	24	25	26	26	27	28	28	29	
	1	6	11	16	21	26			1	11	21			1	11	21			1	16		1	16		1	16		1	11	21	
♃	17♈	18	19	19	20	21		♄	17♋	18	19		⚷	27♈	27	27		♅	29♎	29	♆	10♐	10	♇	7♎	6	☊	1♐	0	30♏	

1975

EPHEMERIS

JUL

	1	2	3	4	5	6	7	8	9	10	11	12	13	14	15	16	17	18	19	20	21	22	23	24	25	26	27	28	29	30	31
☉	9♋	10	10	11	12	13	14	15	16	17	18	19	20	21	22	23	24	25	26	27	28	29	30	1♌	1	2	3	4	5	6	7
☽	1♈	13	25	7♉	20	3♊	16	30	14♋	28	13♌	28	12♍	27	11♎	25	9♏	22	6♐	19	2♑	14	27	9♒	21	4♓	15	27	9♈	21	3♉
☿	18♊	18	19	20	21	22	23	24	25	27	28	29	1♋	2	4	6	7	9	11	13	15	17	19	21	23	25	27	29	1♌	4	6
♀	23♌	24	25	26	27	27	28	29	30	0♍	1	2	2	3	4	4	5	6	6	7	7	8	8	9	9	9	10	10	10	11	11
♂	30♈	1♉	1	2	3	3	4	5	6	6	7	8	8	9	10	10	11	12	12	13	14	14	15	16	17	17	18	19	19	20	21
	1	6	11	16	21	26	31		1	11	21	31		1	11	21	31		1	16		1	16		1	16		1	11	21	31
♃	22♈	22	23	23	24	24	24	♄	21♋	22	23	24	⚷	28♈	28	28	28	♅	28♎	28	♆	10♐	9	♇	7♎	7	☊	29♏	28	28	27

AUG

	1	2	3	4	5	6	7	8	9	10	11	12	13	14	15	16	17	18	19	20	21	22	23	24	25	26	27	28	29	30	31
☉	8♌	9	10	11	12	13	14	15	16	17	18	19	20	21	22	23	23	24	25	26	27	28	29	0♍	1	2	3	4	5	6	7
☽	15♉	28	11♊	24	8♋	22	7♌	22	7♍	22	7♎	21	6♏	19	3♐	16	29	11♑	24	6♒	18	0♓	12	24	6♈	18	30	12♉	24	6♊	19
☿	8♌	10	12	14	16	18	20	22	24	26	28	30	1♍	3	5	7	8	10	12	14	15	17	18	20	22	23	25	26	28	29	0♎
♀	11♍	11	12	12	12	12	12	12	12	11	11	11	11	11	10	10	9	9	9	8	8	7	6	6	5	5	4	3	3	2	2
♂	21♉	22	22	23	24	24	25	26	26	27	28	28	29	29	0♊	1	1	2	3	3	4	4	5	6	6	7	7	8	8	9	10
	1	6	11	16	21	26	31		1	11	21	31		1	11	21	31		1	16		1	16		1	16		1	11	21	31
♃	24♈	25	25	25	25	24	24	♄	25♋	26	27	28	⚷	28♈	28	28	28	♅	29♎	29	♆	9♐	9	♇	7♎	7	☊	27♏	27	26	26

SEP

	1	2	3	4	5	6	7	8	9	10	11	12	13	14	15	16	17	18	19	20	21	22	23	24	25	26	27	28	29	30
☉	8♍	9	10	11	12	13	14	15	16	17	18	19	20	21	22	23	23	24	25	26	27	28	29	0♎	1	2	3	4	5	6
☽	2♋	16	1♌	15	0♍	16	1♎	16	1♏	15	29	13♐	26	8♑	21	3♒	15	27	9♓	21	3♈	15	27	9♉	21	3♊	15	28	12♋	25
☿	2♎	3	4	6	7	8	10	11	12	13	14	15	16	17	18	19	20	21	21	22	23	23	24	24	24	24	24	24	24	24
♀	1♍	0	30♌	29	29	28	28	27	27	27	26	26	26	26	26	26	25	25	25	26	26	26	26	26	26	27	27	27	28	28
♂	10♊	11	11	12	12	13	13	14	14	15	15	16	17	17	18	18	18	19	19	20	20	21	21	22	22	23	23	23	24	24
	1	6	11	16	21	26			1	11	21			1	11	21			1	16		1	16		1	16		1	11	21
♃	24♈	24	24	23	23	22		♄	28♋	29	0♌		⚷	28♈	27	27		♅	30♎	0♏	♆	9♐	9	♇	8♎	8	☊	26♏	25	25

OCT

	1	2	3	4	5	6	7	8	9	10	11	12	13	14	15	16	17	18	19	20	21	22	23	24	25	26	27	28	29	30	31
☉	7♎	8	9	10	11	12	13	14	15	16	17	18	19	20	21	22	23	24	25	26	27	28	29	30	1♏	2	3	4	5	6	7
☽	9♌	24	9♍	24	9♎	24	9♏	24	8♐	21	5♑	17	30	12♒	24	6♓	18	30	12♈	24	6♉	18	0♊	13	25	8♋	21	5♌	19	3♍	18
☿	23♎	23	22	21	21	20	18	17	16	15	14	13	12	11	10	10	9	9	9	9	10	10	11	12	13	14	15	16	17	19	20
♀	28♌	29	29	30	0♍	1	2	2	3	3	4	5	5	6	7	8	8	9	10	11	12	12	13	14	15	16	17	18	19	20	21
♂	25♊	25	25	26	26	27	27	27	28	28	28	29	29	29	29	30	30	0♋	0	1	1	1	1	1	2	2	2	2	2	2	2
	1	6	11	16	21	26	31		1	11	21	31		1	11	21	31		1	16		1	16		1	16		1	11	21	31
♃	21♈	21	20	19	19	18	17	♄	1♌	2	2	3	⚷	27♈	26	26	25	♅	1♏	2	♆	9♐	10	♇	9♎	10	☊	24♏	24	23	23

NOV

	1	2	3	4	5	6	7	8	9	10	11	12	13	14	15	16	17	18	19	20	21	22	23	24	25	26	27	28	29	30
☉	8♏	9	10	11	12	13	14	15	16	17	18	19	20	21	22	23	24	25	26	27	28	29	0♐	1	2	3	4	5	6	7
☽	3♎	17	2♏	17	2♐	16	30	13♑	26	8♒	21	3♓	15	26	8♈	20	2♉	14	27	9♊	22	5♋	18	2♌	15	29	13♍	28	12♎	27
☿	22♎	23	25	26	28	29	1♏	3	4	6	7	9	11	12	14	16	17	19	20	22	24	25	27	28	30	1♐	3	5	6	8
♀	22♍	22	23	24	25	26	27	28	29	0♎	1	2	4	5	6	7	8	9	10	11	12	13	14	15	16	18	19	20	21	22
♂	2♋	3	3	3	3	3	3	3	3	3	3	2	2	2	2	2	2	2	2	1	1	1	1	0	0	30♊	30	29	29	29
	1	6	11	16	21	26			1	11	21			1	11	21			1	16		1	16		1	16		1	11	21
♃	17♈	17	16	16	15	15		♄	3♌	3	3		⚷	25♈	25	24		♅	3♏	4	♆	10♐	11	♇	10♎	11	☊	22♏	22	21

DEC

	1	2	3	4	5	6	7	8	9	10	11	12	13	14	15	16	17	18	19	20	21	22	23	24	25	26	27	28	29	30	31
☉	8♐	9	10	11	12	13	14	15	16	17	18	19	20	21	22	23	24	25	26	27	28	30	1♑	2	3	4	5	6	7	8	9
☽	11♏	25	10♐	24	7♑	21	4♒	16	29	11♓	23	4♈	16	28	10♉	23	5♊	18	1♋	15	28	12♌	26	10♍	24	9♎	23	7♏	21	5♐	18
☿	9♐	11	12	14	16	17	19	20	22	23	25	27	28	30	1♑	3	4	6	8	9	11	12	14	15	17	19	20	22	23	25	26
♀	23♎	24	25	27	28	29	30	1♏	2	3	5	6	7	8	9	10	12	13	14	15	16	17	19	20	21	22	23	25	26	27	28
♂	28♊	28	28	27	27	27	26	26	26	25	25	24	24	24	23	23	22	22	22	21	21	21	20	20	19	19	19	19	18	18	18
	1	6	11	16	21	26	31		1	11	21	31		1	11	21	31		1	16		1	16		1	16		1	11	21	31
♃	15♈	15	15	15	15	15	15	♄	3♌	2	2	1	⚷	24♈	24	24	24	♅	5♏	6	♆	11♐	12	♇	11♎	11	☊	21♏	20	20	19

1976

EPHEMERIS

JAN

	1	2	3	4	5	6	7	8	9	10	11	12	13	14	15	16	17	18	19	20	21	22	23	24	25	26	27	28	29	30	31
☉	10♑	11	12	13	14	15	16	17	18	19	20	21	22	23	24	25	26	27	28	29	0♒	1	2	3	4	5	6	7	8	9	10
☽	2♑	15	29	11♒	24	6♓	18	0♈	12	24	6♉	18	0♊	13	26	10♋	23	8♌	22	6♍	21	5♎	20	4♏	18	1♐	15	28	11♑	24	7♒
☿	27♑	29	0♒	2	3	4	5	6	7	8	8	9	9	9	9	9	9	8	7	6	5	4	3	1	0	29♑	28	27	26	25	24
♀	29♏	1♐	2	3	4	5	7	8	9	10	11	13	14	15	16	18	19	20	21	22	24	25	26	27	28	30	1♑	2	3	5	6
♂	17♊	17	17	17	16	16	16	16	16	16	15	15	15	15	15	15	15	15	15	15	15	15	15	15	15	15	15	15	15	15	15
	1	6	11	16	21	26	31		1	11	21	31		1	11	21	31		1	16		1	16		1	16		1	11	21	31
♃	16♈	16	16	17	18	18	19	♄	1♌	0	29♋	29	⚷	24♈	24	24	24	♅	6♏	7	♆	13♐	13	♇	12♎	12	☊	19♏	19	18	18

FEB

	1	2	3	4	5	6	7	8	9	10	11	12	13	14	15	16	17	18	19	20	21	22	23	24	25	26	27	28	29		
☉	11♒	12	13	14	15	16	17	18	19	20	21	22	23	24	25	26	27	28	29	0♓	1	2	3	5	6	7	8	9	10		
☽	20♒	2♓	14	26	8♈	20	2♉	14	26	8♊	21	4♋	17	1♌	16	1♍	16	0♎	15	30	14♏	28	12♐	25	8♑	21	4♒	16	29		
☿	24♑	24	23	23	23	24	24	24	25	25	26	27	27	28	29	0♒	1	2	3	4	6	7	8	9	11	12	13	15	16		
♀	7♑	8	9	11	12	13	14	16	17	18	19	21	22	23	24	25	27	28	29	0♒	2	3	4	5	7	8	9	10	11		
♂	15♊	16	16	16	16	16	16	17	17	17	17	18	18	18	18	19	19	19	19	20	20	20	21	21	21	22	22	22	23		
	1	6	11	16	21	26			1	11	21			1	11	21			1	16		1	16		1	16		1	11	21	
♃	19♈	20	21	22	23	24		♄	29♋	28	27		⚷	24♈	24	25		♅	7♏	7	♆	13♐	14	♇	12♎	11	☊	18♏	17	17	

MAR

	1	2	3	4	5	6	7	8	9	10	11	12	13	14	15	16	17	18	19	20	21	22	23	24	25	26	27	28	29	30	31
☉	11♓	12	13	14	15	16	17	18	19	20	21	22	23	24	25	26	27	28	29	30	1♈	1	2	3	4	5	6	7	8	9	10
☽	11♓	23	5♈	17	28	10♉	22	4♊	16	29	12♋	25	9♌	24	9♍	24	9♎	24	9♏	24	8♐	22	5♑	18	1♒	13	26	8♓	20	2♈	13
☿	17♒	19	20	22	23	25	26	28	29	1♓	2	4	6	7	9	11	12	14	16	18	19	21	23	25	27	29	1♈	3	5	7	9
♀	13♒	14	15	16	18	19	20	21	23	24	25	26	27	29	30	1♓	2	4	5	6	7	9	10	11	12	14	15	16	17	18	20
♂	23♊	23	24	24	24	25	25	26	26	26	27	27	28	28	28	29	29	30	0♋	1	1	2	2	2	3	3	4	4	5	5	6
	1	6	11	16	21	26	31		1	11	21	31		1	11	21	31		1	16		1	16		1	16		1	11	21	31
♃	24♈	25	27	28	29	30	1♉	♄	27♋	26	26	26	⚷	25♈	25	26	27	♅	7♏	7	♆	14♐	14	♇	11♎	11	☊	16♏	16	15	15

APR

	1	2	3	4	5	6	7	8	9	10	11	12	13	14	15	16	17	18	19	20	21	22	23	24	25	26	27	28	29	30	
☉	11♈	12	13	14	15	16	17	18	19	20	21	22	23	24	25	26	27	28	29	0♉	1	2	3	4	5	6	7	8	9	10	
☽	25♈	7♉	19	1♊	13	25	8♋	21	4♌	18	2♍	17	2♎	17	2♏	17	2♐	17	1♑	14	27	10♒	23	5♓	17	29	11♈	22	4♉	16	
☿	11♈	13	15	17	19	21	23	25	27	29	1♉	3	5	7	9	11	13	15	16	18	19	21	22	24	25	26	27	28	29	0♊	
♀	21♓	22	23	25	26	27	28	30	1♈	2	3	4	6	7	8	9	11	12	13	14	16	17	18	19	20	22	23	24	25	27	
♂	6♋	7	7	8	8	9	9	10	10	11	11	12	12	13	13	14	14	15	15	16	16	17	17	18	18	19	19	20	20	21	
	1	6	11	16	21	26			1	11	21			1	11	21			1	16		1	16		1	16		1	11	21	
♃	1♉	2	4	5	6	7		♄	26♋	26	27		⚷	27♈	27	28		♅	6♏	6	♆	14♐	14	♇	10♎	10	☊	14♏	14	13	

MAY

	1	2	3	4	5	6	7	8	9	10	11	12	13	14	15	16	17	18	19	20	21	22	23	24	25	26	27	28	29	30	31
☉	11♉	12	13	14	15	16	17	18	18	19	20	21	22	23	24	25	26	27	28	29	0♊	1	2	3	4	5	6	7	8	9	10
☽	28♉	10♊	22	5♋	17	0♌	14	27	12♍	26	11♎	26	11♏	26	10♐	25	9♑	23	6♒	19	1♓	14	25	7♈	19	1♉	13	25	7♊	19	2♋
☿	1♊	1	2	3	3	3	4	4	4	4	4	3	3	3	2	2	2	1	0	30♉	29	29	28	28	27	27	26	26	26	25	25
♀	28♈	29	0♉	2	3	4	5	6	8	9	10	11	13	14	15	16	18	19	20	21	22	24	25	26	27	29	30	1♊	2	3	5
♂	22♋	22	23	23	24	24	25	25	26	26	27	28	28	29	29	30	0♌	1	1	2	3	3	4	4	5	5	6	7	7	8	8
	1	6	11	16	21	26	31		1	11	21	31		1	11	21	31		1	16		1	16		1	16		1	11	21	31
♃	8♉	10	11	12	13	14	15	♄	27♋	28	29	29	⚷	28♈	29	30	0♉	♅	5♏	4	♆	13♐	13	♇	10♎	9	☊	13♏	12	12	11

JUN

	1	2	3	4	5	6	7	8	9	10	11	12	13	14	15	16	17	18	19	20	21	22	23	24	25	26	27	28	29	30	
☉	11♊	12	13	14	14	15	16	17	18	19	20	21	22	23	24	25	26	27	28	29	30	1♋	2	3	4	5	5	6	7	8	
☽	14♋	27	11♌	24	8♍	22	6♎	20	5♏	20	4♐	19	3♑	17	1♒	14	27	9♓	22	4♈	16	27	9♉	21	3♊	16	28	11♋	24	7♌	
☿	25♉	25	25	25	25	26	26	26	27	27	28	29	29	0♊	1	2	3	4	5	6	8	9	10	12	13	15	16	18	20	21	
♀	6♊	7	8	10	11	12	13	15	16	17	18	19	21	22	23	24	26	27	28	29	1♋	2	3	4	5	7	8	9	10	12	
♂	9♌	9	10	11	11	12	12	13	13	14	15	15	16	16	17	18	18	19	19	20	20	21	22	22	23	23	24	25	25	26	
	1	6	11	16	21	26			1	11	21			1	11	21			1	16		1	16		1	16		1	11	21	
♃	16♉	17	18	19	20	21		♄	30♋	1♌	2		⚷	0♉	1	1		♅	4♏	3	♆	13♐	12	♇	9♎	9	☊	11♏	11	10	

1976

EPHEMERIS

JUL

	1	2	3	4	5	6	7	8	9	10	11	12	13	14	15	16	17	18	19	20	21	22	23	24	25	26	27	28	29	30	31
☉	9♋	10	11	12	13	14	15	16	17	18	19	20	21	22	23	24	25	25	26	27	28	29	0♌	1	2	3	4	5	6	7	8
☽	21♌	5♍	19	3♎	17	1♏	15	29	14♐	28	12♑	26	9♒	22	5♓	17	30	12♈	24	5♉	17	29	11♊	24	7♋	20	3♌	17	1♍	15	29
☿	23♊	25	27	29	1♋	3	5	7	9	11	13	15	18	20	22	24	26	28	0♌	2	5	7	9	11	12	14	16	18	20	22	24
♀	13♋	14	15	16	18	19	20	21	23	24	25	26	28	29	0♌	1	2	4	5	6	7	9	10	11	12	14	15	16	17	18	20
♂	26♌	27	28	28	29	29	0♍	1	1	2	2	3	4	4	5	5	6	7	7	8	9	9	10	10	11	12	12	13	13	14	15
	1	6	11	16	21	26	31		1	11	21	31		1	11	21	31		1	16		1	16		1	16		1	11	21	31
♃	22♉	23	24	25	26	27	27	♄	3♌	4	5	7	⚷	1♉	2	2	2	♅	3♏	3	♆	12♐	12	♇	9♎	9	☊	10♏	9	9	8

AUG

	1	2	3	4	5	6	7	8	9	10	11	12	13	14	15	16	17	18	19	20	21	22	23	24	25	26	27	28	29	30	31
☉	9♌	10	11	12	13	14	15	16	17	17	18	19	20	21	22	23	24	25	26	27	28	29	30	1♍	2	3	4	5	6	7	8
☽	13♎	28	12♏	26	10♐	24	7♑	21	4♒	18	1♓	13	26	8♈	20	1♉	13	25	7♊	19	2♋	15	28	12♌	26	10♍	25	9♎	24	8♏	23
☿	25♌	27	29	1♍	2	4	5	7	8	10	11	13	14	16	17	18	20	21	22	24	25	26	27	28	29	0♎	1	2	3	4	4
♀	21♌	22	23	25	26	27	28	30	1♍	2	3	4	6	7	8	9	11	12	13	14	16	17	18	19	20	22	23	24	25	27	28
♂	15♍	16	17	17	18	18	19	20	20	21	22	22	23	23	24	25	25	26	27	27	28	29	29	30	0♎	1	2	2	3	4	4
	1	6	11	16	21	26	31		1	11	21	31		1	11	21	31		1	16		1	16		1	16		1	11	21	31
♃	27♉	28	29	29	30	0♊	1	♄	7♌	8	9	11	⚷	2♉	2	2	2	♅	3♏	4	♆	11♐	11	♇	9♎	10	☊	8♏	7	7	6

SEP

	1	2	3	4	5	6	7	8	9	10	11	12	13	14	15	16	17	18	19	20	21	22	23	24	25	26	27	28	29	30
☉	9♍	10	11	12	13	14	14	15	16	17	18	19	20	21	22	23	24	25	26	27	28	29	0♎	1	2	3	4	5	6	7
☽	7♐	21	4♑	18	1♒	14	27	9♓	22	4♈	16	28	10♉	21	3♊	15	27	10♋	23	6♌	20	4♍	19	3♎	18	3♏	18	3♐	17	1♑
☿	5♎	6	6	7	7	7	8	8	8	8	8	7	7	6	6	5	4	3	2	1	0	29♍	28	27	26	25	25	24	24	23
♀	29♍	0♎	2	3	4	5	6	8	9	10	11	13	14	15	16	18	19	20	21	22	24	25	26	27	29	30	1♏	2	3	5
♂	5♎	6	6	7	8	8	9	10	10	11	11	12	13	13	14	15	15	16	17	17	18	19	19	20	21	21	22	23	23	24
	1	6	11	16	21	26			1	11	21			1	11	21			1	16		1	16		1	16		1	11	21
♃	1♊	1	1	1	1	1		♄	11♌	12	13		⚷	2♉	1	1		♅	4♏	5	♆	11♐	11	♇	10♎	11	☊	6♏	6	5

OCT

	1	2	3	4	5	6	7	8	9	10	11	12	13	14	15	16	17	18	19	20	21	22	23	24	25	26	27	28	29	30	31
☉	8♎	9	10	11	12	13	14	15	16	17	18	19	20	21	22	23	24	25	26	27	28	29	30	1♏	2	3	4	5	6	7	8
☽	15♑	28	11♒	24	6♓	18	1♈	13	24	6♉	18	30	12♊	24	6♋	18	1♌	14	28	12♍	27	12♎	27	12♏	27	12♐	26	11♑	24	8♒	21
☿	23♍	23	23	24	24	25	26	27	28	29	1♎	2	3	5	6	8	10	11	13	14	16	18	20	21	23	25	26	28	30	1♏	3
♀	6♏	7	8	10	11	12	13	14	16	17	18	19	21	22	23	24	25	27	28	29	0♐	2	3	4	5	6	8	9	10	11	13
♂	25♎	25	26	27	27	28	29	29	0♏	1	1	2	3	3	4	5	6	6	7	8	8	9	10	10	11	12	12	13	14	15	15
	1	6	11	16	21	26	31		1	11	21	31		1	11	21	31		1	16		1	16		1	16		1	11	21	31
♃	1♊	1	0	0	30♉	29	29	♄	14♌	15	16	16	⚷	1♉	0	30♈	29	♅	6♏	7	♆	12♐	12	♇	11♎	12	☊	5♏	4	4	3

NOV

	1	2	3	4	5	6	7	8	9	10	11	12	13	14	15	16	17	18	19	20	21	22	23	24	25	26	27	28	29	30
☉	9♏	10	11	12	13	14	15	16	17	18	19	20	21	22	23	24	25	26	27	28	29	30	1♐	2	3	4	5	6	7	8
☽	3♓	15	28	10♈	21	3♉	15	27	9♊	21	3♋	15	28	10♌	23	7♍	21	5♎	20	5♏	20	5♐	20	5♑	19	3♒	17	30	12♓	24
☿	5♏	6	8	10	11	13	14	16	18	19	21	22	24	26	27	29	0♐	2	3	5	7	8	10	11	13	14	16	17	19	20
♀	14♐	15	16	17	19	20	21	22	23	25	26	27	28	29	1♑	2	3	4	5	7	8	9	10	11	13	14	15	16	17	19
♂	16♏	17	17	18	19	19	20	21	21	22	23	24	24	25	26	26	27	28	29	29	0♐	1	1	2	3	4	4	5	6	6
	1	6	11	16	21	26			1	11	21			1	11	21			1	16		1	16		1	16		1	11	21
♃	28♉	28	27	26	26	25		♄	16♌	17	17		⚷	29♈	29	28		♅	8♏	8	♆	12♐	13	♇	13♎	13	☊	3♏	3	2

DEC

	1	2	3	4	5	6	7	8	9	10	11	12	13	14	15	16	17	18	19	20	21	22	23	24	25	26	27	28	29	30	31
☉	9♐	10	11	12	13	14	15	16	17	18	19	20	21	22	23	24	25	26	27	28	29	0♑	1	2	3	4	5	6	7	8	9
☽	6♈	18	0♉	12	24	6♊	18	30	12♋	25	7♌	20	3♍	17	0♎	14	29	13♏	28	13♐	28	13♑	27	11♒	25	8♓	20	3♈	15	27	8♉
☿	22♐	23	25	26	28	29	1♑	2	4	5	7	8	10	11	12	14	15	16	17	18	19	20	21	22	22	23	23	23	23	23	23
♀	20♑	21	22	23	25	26	27	28	29	1♒	2	3	4	5	6	8	9	10	11	12	13	15	16	17	18	19	20	21	23	24	25
♂	7♐	8	9	9	10	11	12	12	13	14	14	15	16	17	17	18	19	20	20	21	22	23	23	24	25	26	26	27	28	28	29
	1	6	11	16	21	26	31		1	11	21	31		1	11	21	31		1	16		1	16		1	16		1	11	21	31
♃	24♉	24	23	23	22	22	22	♄	17♌	17	16	16	⚷	28♈	28	27	27	♅	9♏	10	♆	14♐	14	♇	14♎	14	☊	2♏	1	0	30♎

1977

EPHEMERIS

JAN

	1	2	3	4	5	6	7	8	9	10	11	12	13	14	15	16	17	18	19	20	21	22	23	24	25	26	27	28	29	30	31
☉	10♑	11	13	14	15	16	17	18	19	20	21	22	23	24	25	26	27	28	29	30	1♒	2	3	4	5	6	7	8	9	10	11
☽	20♉	2♊	14	26	9♋	21	4♌	17	0♍	14	27	11♎	25	9♏	23	8♐	22	7♑	21	5♒	19	2♓	16	28	11♈	23	5♉	16	28	10♊	22
☿	22♑	21	20	19	18	16	15	14	12	11	10	9	9	8	7	7	7	7	7	8	8	8	9	10	10	11	12	13	14	15	16
♀	26♒	27	28	29	1♓	2	3	4	5	6	7	8	9	10	11	13	14	15	16	17	18	19	20	21	22	23	24	25	26	27	28
♂	30♐	1♑	1	2	3	4	4	5	6	7	7	8	9	10	11	11	12	13	14	14	15	16	17	17	18	19	20	20	21	22	23
	1	6	11	16	21	26	31		1	11	21	31		1	11	21	31		1	16		1	16		1	16		1	11	21	31
♃	22♉	21	21	21	21	21	22	♄	16♌	15	14	14	⚷	27♈	27	27	28	♅	11♏	11	♆	15♐	15	♇	14♎	14	☊	30♎	29	29	28

FEB

	1	2	3	4	5	6	7	8	9	10	11	12	13	14	15	16	17	18	19	20	21	22	23	24	25	26	27	28			
☉	12♒	13	14	15	16	17	18	19	20	21	22	23	24	25	26	27	28	29	0♓	1	2	3	4	5	6	7	8	9			
☽	4♋	17	30	13♌	26	10♍	24	8♎	22	6♏	20	4♐	18	2♑	16	0♒	14	27	11♓	23	6♈	18	0♉	12	24	6♊	18	30			
☿	17♑	18	20	21	22	23	25	26	27	29	0♒	1	3	4	6	7	9	10	12	13	15	16	18	19	21	23	24	26			
♀	29♓	30	1♈	2	3	3	4	5	6	7	8	9	10	10	11	12	13	13	14	15	16	16	17	18	18	19	19	20			
♂	23♑	24	25	26	27	27	28	29	30	0♒	1	2	3	3	4	5	6	7	7	8	9	10	10	11	12	13	14	14			
	1	6	11	16	21	26			1	11	21			1	11	21			1	16		1	16		1	16		1	11	21	
♃	22♉	22	22	23	23	24		♄	14♌	13	12		⚷	28♈	28	28		♅	12♏	12	♆	16♐	16	♇	14♎	14	☊	28♎	28	27	

MAR

	1	2	3	4	5	6	7	8	9	10	11	12	13	14	15	16	17	18	19	20	21	22	23	24	25	26	27	28	29	30	31
☉	10♓	11	12	13	14	15	16	17	18	19	20	21	22	23	24	25	26	27	28	29	0♈	1	2	3	4	5	6	7	8	9	10
☽	12♋	25	8♌	21	5♍	19	3♎	18	2♏	16	1♐	15	29	13♑	27	10♒	23	6♓	19	2♈	14	26	8♉	20	2♊	14	26	8♋	20	3♌	16
☿	28♒	29	1♓	3	5	6	8	10	12	14	15	17	19	21	23	25	27	29	1♈	3	5	7	9	11	13	15	17	19	21	23	25
♀	20♈	21	21	22	22	23	23	23	24	24	24	24	24	24	25	25	25	24	24	24	24	24	24	23	23	23	22	22	21	21	20
♂	15♒	16	17	17	18	19	20	21	21	22	23	24	24	25	26	27	28	28	29	30	1♓	1	2	3	4	5	5	6	7	8	9
	1	6	11	16	21	26	31		1	11	21	31		1	11	21	31		1	16		1	16		1	16		1	11	21	31
♃	24♉	25	26	27	27	28	29	♄	11♌	11	10	10	⚷	29♈	29	30	0♉	♅	12♏	11	♆	16♐	16	♇	14♎	13	☊	27♎	26	26	25

APR

	1	2	3	4	5	6	7	8	9	10	11	12	13	14	15	16	17	18	19	20	21	22	23	24	25	26	27	28	29	30	
☉	11♈	12	13	14	15	16	17	18	19	20	21	22	23	24	25	26	27	28	29	30	1♉	2	3	4	5	6	7	8	9	10	
☽	29♌	13♍	27	12♎	26	11♏	26	11♐	25	10♑	24	7♒	20	3♓	16	29	11♈	23	5♉	17	29	11♊	22	4♋	16	29	11♌	24	7♍	21	
☿	26♈	28	30	1♉	3	4	6	7	8	9	10	11	12	13	13	14	14	14	14	15	14	14	14	14	13	13	12	12	11	11	
♀	20♈	19	18	18	17	17	16	15	15	14	13	13	12	12	11	11	10	10	10	9	9	9	9	8	8	8	8	8	8	8	
♂	9♓	10	11	12	12	13	14	15	16	16	17	18	19	19	20	21	22	23	23	24	25	26	26	27	28	29	29	0♈	1	2	
	1	6	11	16	21	26			1	11	21			1	11	21			1	16		1	16		1	16		1	11	21	
♃	29♉	0♊	1	3	4	5		♄	10♌	10	10		⚷	0♉	1	1		♅	11♏	10	♆	16♐	16	♇	13♎	12	☊	25♎	25	24	

MAY

	1	2	3	4	5	6	7	8	9	10	11	12	13	14	15	16	17	18	19	20	21	22	23	24	25	26	27	28	29	30	31
☉	11♉	11	12	13	14	15	16	17	18	19	20	21	22	23	24	25	26	27	28	29	30	1♊	2	3	4	5	6	7	8	8	9
☽	5♎	20	5♏	20	5♐	20	5♑	19	3♒	17	0♓	13	26	8♈	20	2♉	14	26	7♊	19	1♋	13	25	8♌	20	3♍	16	30	14♎	28	13♏
☿	10♉	9	9	8	8	7	6	6	6	5	5	5	5	5	5	5	5	5	6	6	7	7	8	9	9	10	11	12	13	14	15
♀	8♈	9	9	9	9	10	10	10	11	11	12	12	12	13	14	14	15	15	16	17	17	18	19	19	20	21	22	22	23	24	25
♂	3♈	3	4	5	6	6	7	8	9	9	10	11	12	13	13	14	15	16	16	17	18	19	19	20	21	22	22	23	24	25	25
	1	6	11	16	21	26	31		1	11	21	31		1	11	21	31		1	16		1	16		1	16		1	11	21	31
♃	6♊	7	8	9	10	11	13	♄	10♌	11	11	12	⚷	2♉	3	3	4	♅	10♏	9	♆	16♐	15	♇	12♎	12	☊	24♎	23	22	22

JUN

	1	2	3	4	5	6	7	8	9	10	11	12	13	14	15	16	17	18	19	20	21	22	23	24	25	26	27	28	29	30	
☉	10♊	11	12	13	14	15	16	17	18	19	20	21	22	23	24	25	26	27	28	29	30	0♋	1	2	3	4	5	6	7	8	
☽	28♏	13♐	29	14♑	28	13♒	26	10♓	22	5♈	17	29	11♉	23	5♊	16	28	10♋	22	5♌	17	30	13♍	26	9♎	23	7♏	22	7♐	22	
☿	16♉	17	19	20	21	23	24	25	27	29	0♊	2	4	5	7	9	11	13	15	17	19	21	23	25	27	29	2♋	4	6	8	
♀	25♈	26	27	28	29	30	1♉	2	2	3	4	5	6	7	8	9	10	11	12	13	14	15	16	17	18	19	20	21	22	23	
♂	26♈	27	28	28	29	30	1♉	1	2	3	4	4	5	6	7	7	8	9	10	10	11	12	12	13	14	15	15	16	17	17	
	1	6	11	16	21	26			1	11	21			1	11	21			1	16		1	16		1	16		1	11	21	
♃	13♊	14	15	16	17	19		♄	12♌	13	14		⚷	4♉	4	5		♅	9♏	8	♆	15♐	14	♇	12♎	11	☊	22♎	21	21	

1977

JUL

	1	2	3	4	5	6	7	8	9	10	11	12	13	14	15	16	17	18	19	20	21	22	23	24	25	26	27	28	29	30	31
☉	9♋	10	11	12	13	14	15	16	17	18	19	20	20	21	22	23	24	25	26	27	28	29	0♌	1	2	3	4	5	6	7	8
☽	7♑	22	7♒	21	5♓	18	1♈	14	26	8♉	20	1♊	13	25	7♋	19	2♌	14	27	10♍	23	6♎	20	3♏	17	2♐	16	1♑	16	1♒	15
☿	10♋	12	15	17	19	21	23	25	27	29	1♌	3	5	7	8	10	12	14	15	17	19	20	22	24	25	27	28	29	1♍	2	3
♀	24♉	25	26	27	28	29	0♊	1	3	4	5	6	7	8	9	10	11	12	13	15	16	17	18	19	20	21	22	23	25	26	27
♂	18♉	19	20	20	21	22	23	23	24	25	25	26	27	27	28	29	30	0♊	1	2	2	3	4	4	5	6	6	7	8	9	9
	1	6	11	16	21	26	31		1	11	21	31		1	11	21	31		1	16		1	16		1	16		1	11	21	31
♃	20♊	21	22	23	24	25	26	♄	15♌	16	17	19	⚷	5♉	5	6	6	♅	8♏	8	♆	14♐	14	♇	11♎	12	☊	20♎	20	19	19

AUG

	1	2	3	4	5	6	7	8	9	10	11	12	13	14	15	16	17	18	19	20	21	22	23	24	25	26	27	28	29	30	31
☉	9♌	10	11	12	12	13	14	15	16	17	18	19	20	21	22	23	24	25	26	27	28	29	30	1♍	2	3	4	5	6	7	7
☽	29♒	13♓	26	9♈	22	4♉	16	28	10♊	21	3♋	16	28	11♌	23	6♍	20	3♎	16	0♏	14	28	12♐	27	11♑	25	10♒	24	8♓	21	4♈
☿	5♍	6	7	8	10	11	12	13	14	15	15	16	17	18	18	19	19	20	20	20	21	21	21	21	21	20	20	19	19	18	17
♀	28♊	29	0♋	1	3	4	5	6	7	8	9	11	12	13	14	15	16	18	19	20	21	22	23	25	26	27	28	29	0♌	2	3
♂	10♊	11	11	12	13	13	14	15	15	16	17	17	18	19	19	20	20	21	22	22	23	24	24	25	26	26	27	27	28	29	29
	1	6	11	16	21	26	31		1	11	21	31		1	11	21	31		1	16		1	16		1	16		1	11	21	31
♃	26♊	27	28	29	0♋	1	2	♄	19♌	20	21	23	⚷	6♉	6	6	6	♅	8♏	8	♆	14♐	13	♇	12♎	12	☊	19♎	18	18	17

SEP

	1	2	3	4	5	6	7	8	9	10	11	12	13	14	15	16	17	18	19	20	21	22	23	24	25	26	27	28	29	30
☉	8♍	9	10	11	12	13	14	15	16	17	18	19	20	21	22	23	24	25	26	27	28	29	30	1♎	2	3	4	5	6	7
☽	17♈	30	12♉	24	6♊	18	29	11♋	24	6♌	19	2♍	15	29	13♎	27	11♏	25	9♐	23	8♑	22	6♒	19	3♓	16	30	13♈	25	8♉
☿	17♍	16	15	14	13	12	11	10	9	9	8	7	7	7	7	7	7	8	8	9	10	11	12	13	15	16	18	19	21	22
♀	4♌	5	6	8	9	10	11	12	14	15	16	17	18	20	21	22	23	24	26	27	28	29	0♍	2	3	4	5	7	8	9
♂	30♊	1♋	1	2	2	3	4	4	5	5	6	7	7	8	8	9	10	10	11	11	12	12	13	14	14	15	15	16	16	17
	1	6	11	16	21	26			1	11	21			1	11	21			1	16		1	16		1	16		1	11	21
♃	2♋	3	3	4	4	5		♄	23♌	24	25		⚷	6♉	5	5		♅	9♏	9	♆	13♐	13	♇	13♎	13	☊	17♎	16	16

OCT

	1	2	3	4	5	6	7	8	9	10	11	12	13	14	15	16	17	18	19	20	21	22	23	24	25	26	27	28	29	30	31
☉	8♎	9	10	11	12	13	14	15	16	17	18	19	20	21	22	23	24	25	25	26	27	28	29	0♏	1	2	3	4	5	6	7
☽	20♉	2♊	14	25	7♋	19	2♌	14	27	10♍	23	7♎	21	6♏	21	5♐	20	4♑	19	3♒	16	30	13♓	26	9♈	21	4♉	16	28	10♊	22
☿	24♍	26	28	29	1♎	3	5	6	8	10	12	13	15	17	19	20	22	24	26	27	29	1♏	2	4	5	7	9	10	12	13	15
♀	10♍	11	13	14	15	16	18	19	20	21	23	24	25	26	27	29	30	1♎	2	4	5	6	7	9	10	11	12	14	15	16	17
♂	17♋	18	19	19	20	20	21	21	22	22	23	23	24	24	25	25	26	26	27	27	27	28	28	29	29	30	0♌	1	1	1	2
	1	6	11	16	21	26	31		1	11	21	31		1	11	21	31		1	16		1	16		1	16		1	11	21	31
♃	5♋	6	6	6	6	6	6	♄	26♌	27	28	29	⚷	5♉	4	4	3	♅	10♏	11	♆	14♐	14	♇	14♎	14	☊	15♎	15	14	14

NOV

	1	2	3	4	5	6	7	8	9	10	11	12	13	14	15	16	17	18	19	20	21	22	23	24	25	26	27	28	29	30
☉	8♏	9	10	11	12	13	14	15	16	17	18	19	20	22	23	24	25	26	27	28	29	30	1♐	2	3	4	5	6	7	8
☽	4♋	15	27	10♌	22	5♍	18	1♎	15	30	14♏	29	14♐	29	14♑	29	13♒	27	10♓	23	6♈	18	0♉	13	25	7♊	18	0♋	12	24
☿	17♏	18	20	21	23	24	26	27	29	0♐	2	3	5	6	8	9	11	12	14	15	17	18	19	21	22	23	25	26	27	28
♀	19♎	20	21	22	24	25	26	27	29	30	1♏	2	4	5	6	7	9	10	11	12	14	15	16	17	19	20	21	22	24	25
♂	2♌	3	3	3	4	4	4	5	5	5	6	6	6	7	7	7	8	8	8	8	9	9	9	9	10	10	10	10	10	11
	1	6	11	16	21	26			1	11	21			1	11	21			1	16		1	16		1	16		1	11	21
♃	6♋	6	6	5	5	4		♄	29♌	30	0♍		⚷	3♉	3	2		♅	12♏	13	♆	15♐	15	♇	15♎	16	☊	14♎	13	13

DEC

	1	2	3	4	5	6	7	8	9	10	11	12	13	14	15	16	17	18	19	20	21	22	23	24	25	26	27	28	29	30	31
☉	9♐	10	11	12	13	14	15	16	17	18	19	20	21	22	23	24	25	26	27	28	29	0♑	1	2	3	4	5	6	7	8	9
☽	6♌	18	0♍	13	26	9♎	23	7♏	22	7♐	23	8♑	23	8♒	22	6♓	20	3♈	15	28	10♉	22	4♊	15	27	9♋	21	3♌	15	27	10♍
☿	30♐	1♑	2	3	4	5	5	6	7	7	7	7	7	7	7	6	5	4	3	2	0	29♐	28	26	25	24	23	22	22	21	21
♀	26♏	27	29	30	1♐	2	4	5	6	7	9	10	11	12	14	15	16	18	19	20	21	23	24	25	26	28	29	0♑	1	3	4
♂	11♌	11	11	11	11	11	11	11	11	12	12	12	12	12	12	11	11	11	11	11	11	11	11	11	11	10	10	10	10	10	9
	1	6	11	16	21	26	31		1	11	21	31		1	11	21	31		1	16		1	16		1	16		1	11	21	31
♃	4♋	3	3	2	1	1	30♊	♄	0♍	1	0	0	⚷	2♉	2	1	1	♅	14♏	15	♆	16♐	16	♇	16♎	16	☊	12♎	12	11	11

1978

EPHEMERIS

JAN

	1	2	3	4	5	6	7	8	9	10	11	12	13	14	15	16	17	18	19	20	21	22	23	24	25	26	27	28	29	30	31
☉	10♑	11	12	13	14	15	16	17	18	19	20	21	22	23	24	26	27	28	29	30	1♒	2	3	4	5	6	7	8	9	10	11
☽	22♍	5♎	18	2♏	16	1♐	15	1♑	16	1♒	16	1♓	15	28	11♈	24	6♉	18	0♊	12	24	6♋	18	30	12♌	24	7♍	19	2♎	15	28
☿	21♐	21	21	22	22	23	24	24	25	26	27	28	29	0♑	1	3	4	5	6	8	9	10	12	13	14	16	17	19	20	21	23
♀	5♑	6	8	9	10	11	13	14	15	16	18	19	20	21	23	24	25	27	28	29	0♒	2	3	4	5	7	8	9	10	12	13
♂	9♌	9	9	8	8	8	7	7	7	6	6	6	5	5	4	4	4	3	3	2	2	2	1	1	0	0	30♋	29	29	29	28
	1	6	11	16	21	26	31		1	11	21	31		1	11	21	31		1	16		1	16		1	16		1	11	21	31
♃	30♊	29	29	28	28	27	27	♄	0♍	30♌	29	28	⚷	1♉	1	1	1	♅	15♏	16	♆	17♐	17	♇	17♎	17	☊	11♎	10	9	9

FEB

	1	2	3	4	5	6	7	8	9	10	11	12	13	14	15	16	17	18	19	20	21	22	23	24	25	26	27	28			
☉	12♒	13	14	15	16	17	18	19	20	21	22	23	24	25	26	27	28	29	30	1♓	2	3	4	5	6	7	8	9			
☽	12♏	26	10♐	25	9♑	24	9♒	24	9♓	23	6♈	19	2♉	15	27	9♊	21	3♋	14	26	9♌	21	3♍	16	29	12♎	25	9♏			
☿	24♑	26	27	29	1♒	2	4	5	7	8	10	12	13	15	17	18	20	22	23	25	27	29	1♓	2	4	6	8	10			
♀	14♒	15	17	18	19	20	22	23	24	25	27	28	29	0♓	2	3	4	5	7	8	9	10	12	13	14	15	17	18			
♂	28♋	27	27	27	26	26	26	26	25	25	25	24	24	24	24	24	23	23	23	23	23	23	23	23	22	22	22	22			
	1	6	11	16	21	26			1	11	21			1	11	21			1	16		1	16		1	16		1	11	21	
♃	27♊	26	26	26	26	26		♄	28♌	28	27		⚷	1♉	2	2		♅	16♏	16	♆	18♐	18	♇	17♎	16	☊	9♎	8	8	

MAR

	1	2	3	4	5	6	7	8	9	10	11	12	13	14	15	16	17	18	19	20	21	22	23	24	25	26	27	28	29	30	31
☉	10♓	11	12	13	14	15	16	17	18	19	20	21	22	23	24	25	26	27	28	29	0♈	1	2	3	4	5	6	7	8	9	10
☽	22♏	6♐	20	5♑	19	4♒	18	3♓	17	0♈	14	27	10♉	22	5♊	17	29	10♋	22	4♌	17	29	12♍	25	8♎	21	5♏	19	3♐	17	2♑
☿	12♓	14	15	17	19	21	23	25	27	29	1♈	3	5	7	8	10	12	13	15	16	18	19	20	22	23	23	24	25	25	26	26
♀	19♓	20	22	23	24	25	27	28	29	0♈	2	3	4	5	7	8	9	10	12	13	14	15	17	18	19	20	21	23	24	25	26
♂	22♋	22	22	22	22	22	22	22	23	23	23	23	23	23	23	23	24	24	24	24	24	24	25	25	25	25	26	26	26	26	27
	1	6	11	16	21	26	31		1	11	21	31		1	11	21	31		1	16		1	16		1	16		1	11	21	31
♃	26♊	26	27	27	27	28	28	♄	26♌	25	25	24	⚷	2♉	3	3	4	♅	16♏	16	♆	18♐	18	♇	16♎	16	☊	7♎	7	6	6

APR

	1	2	3	4	5	6	7	8	9	10	11	12	13	14	15	16	17	18	19	20	21	22	23	24	25	26	27	28	29	30	
☉	11♈	12	13	14	15	16	17	18	19	20	21	22	23	24	25	26	27	28	29	30	1♉	2	2	3	4	5	6	7	8	9	
☽	16♑	30	14♒	28	12♓	26	9♈	22	5♉	18	0♊	12	25	6♋	18	0♌	12	24	7♍	20	3♎	16	0♏	14	29	13♐	28	12♑	27	11♒	
☿	26♈	26	26	26	26	25	25	24	23	23	22	21	20	20	19	18	18	17	16	16	16	15	15	15	15	15	15	15	15	16	
♀	28♈	29	0♉	1	3	4	5	6	8	9	10	11	12	14	15	16	17	19	20	21	22	23	25	26	27	28	30	1♊	2	3	
♂	27♋	27	27	28	28	28	29	29	29	30	0♌	0	1	1	2	2	2	3	3	3	4	4	5	5	5	6	6	7	7	8	
	1	6	11	16	21	26			1	11	21			1	11	21			1	16		1	16		1	16		1	11	21	
♃	29♊	29	30	1♋	1	2		♄	24♌	24	24		⚷	4♉	4	5		♅	16♏	15	♆	18♐	18	♇	15♎	15	☊	6♎	5	5	

MAY

	1	2	3	4	5	6	7	8	9	10	11	12	13	14	15	16	17	18	19	20	21	22	23	24	25	26	27	28	29	30	31
☉	10♉	11	12	13	14	15	16	17	18	19	20	21	22	23	24	25	26	27	28	29	30	1♊	2	2	3	4	5	6	7	8	9
☽	25♒	9♓	22	5♈	18	1♉	14	26	9♊	21	3♋	15	26	8♌	20	2♍	15	28	11♎	24	8♏	23	8♐	23	8♑	23	7♒	21	5♓	19	2♈
☿	16♈	17	17	18	18	19	20	21	22	23	24	25	26	27	28	30	1♉	2	4	5	6	8	9	11	13	14	16	18	19	21	23
♀	4♊	6	7	8	9	11	12	13	14	15	17	18	19	20	21	23	24	25	26	27	29	30	1♋	2	4	5	6	7	8	9	11
♂	8♌	8	9	9	10	10	11	11	12	12	13	13	13	14	14	15	15	16	16	17	17	18	18	19	19	20	20	21	21	22	22
	1	6	11	16	21	26	31		1	11	21	31		1	11	21	31		1	16		1	16		1	16		1	11	21	31
♃	3♋	4	5	6	7	8	9	♄	24♌	24	24	25	⚷	6♉	6	7	7	♅	15♏	14	♆	18♐	18	♇	15♎	14	☊	4♎	4	3	3

JUN

	1	2	3	4	5	6	7	8	9	10	11	12	13	14	15	16	17	18	19	20	21	22	23	24	25	26	27	28	29	30	
☉	10♊	11	12	13	14	15	16	17	18	19	20	21	22	23	24	25	25	26	27	28	29	0♋	1	2	3	4	5	6	7	8	
☽	15♈	28	11♉	23	5♊	17	29	11♋	23	5♌	17	29	11♍	23	6♎	19	3♏	17	1♐	16	1♑	17	2♒	17	1♓	15	29	12♈	25	8♉	
☿	25♉	27	29	1♊	3	5	7	9	11	13	15	18	20	22	24	26	29	1♋	3	5	7	9	11	13	15	17	19	21	23	25	
♀	12♋	13	14	15	17	18	19	20	21	23	24	25	26	27	29	30	1♌	2	3	4	6	7	8	9	10	11	13	14	15	16	
♂	23♌	24	24	25	25	26	26	27	27	28	28	29	29	30	0♍	1	2	2	3	3	4	4	5	5	6	7	7	8	8	9	
	1	6	11	16	21	26			1	11	21			1	11	21			1	16		1	16		1	16		1	11	21	
♃	9♋	10	11	12	13	15		♄	25♌	25	26		⚷	8♉	8	9		♅	13♏	13	♆	17♐	17	♇	14♎	14	☊	3♎	2	1	

EPHEMERIS

1978

JUL

	1	2	3	4	5	6	7	8	9	10	11	12	13	14	15	16	17	18	19	20	21	22	23	24	25	26	27	28	29	30	31
☉	9♋	10	11	12	13	14	15	15	16	17	18	19	20	21	22	23	24	25	26	27	28	29	30	1♌	2	3	4	5	6	6	7
☽	20♉	2♊	14	26	8♋	20	2♌	14	26	8♍	20	2♎	15	28	11♏	25	10♐	25	10♑	25	10♒	25	10♓	24	8♈	21	4♉	17	29	11♊	23
☿	27♋	28	0♌	2	3	5	7	8	10	11	13	14	15	17	18	19	20	22	23	24	25	26	27	28	28	29	30	0♍	1	2	2
♀	17♌	18	20	21	22	23	24	25	26	28	29	30	1♍	2	3	4	6	7	8	9	10	11	12	13	15	16	17	18	19	20	21
♂	9♍	10	11	11	12	12	13	14	14	15	15	16	16	17	18	18	19	19	20	21	21	22	22	23	24	24	25	25	26	27	27
	1	6	11	16	21	26	31		1	11	21	31		1	11	21	31		1	16		1	16		1	16		1	11	21	31
♃	16♋	17	18	19	20	21	22	♄	27♌	28	29	1♍	⚷	9♉	9	10	10	♅	12♏	12	♆	16♐	16	♇	14♎	14	☊	1♎	0	30♍	29

AUG

	1	2	3	4	5	6	7	8	9	10	11	12	13	14	15	16	17	18	19	20	21	22	23	24	25	26	27	28	29	30	31
☉	8♌	9	10	11	12	13	14	15	16	17	18	19	20	21	22	23	24	25	26	27	28	29	30	0♍	1	2	3	4	5	6	7
☽	5♋	17	29	11♌	23	5♍	17	29	12♎	24	8♏	21	5♐	19	4♑	19	4♒	19	4♓	18	3♈	17	30	13♉	26	8♊	20	2♋	14	26	8♌
☿	2♍	3	3	3	3	3	3	3	2	2	1	1	0	29♌	29	28	27	26	25	25	24	23	22	22	21	21	21	20	20	20	21
♀	22♍	23	24	26	27	28	29	30	1♎	2	3	4	5	6	7	8	9	10	11	12	13	14	15	16	17	18	19	20	21	22	23
♂	28♍	29	29	30	0♎	1	2	2	3	3	4	5	5	6	7	7	8	9	9	10	10	11	12	12	13	14	14	15	16	16	17
	1	6	11	16	21	26	31		1	11	21	31		1	11	21	31		1	16		1	16		1	16		1	11	21	31
♃	23♋	24	25	26	27	28	29	♄	1♍	2	3	4	⚷	10♉	10	10	10	♅	12♏	13	♆	16♐	16	♇	14♎	15	☊	29♍	29	28	28

SEP

	1	2	3	4	5	6	7	8	9	10	11	12	13	14	15	16	17	18	19	20	21	22	23	24	25	26	27	28	29	30
☉	8♍	9	10	11	12	13	14	15	16	17	18	19	20	21	22	23	24	25	26	27	28	29	30	1♎	2	3	4	5	5	6
☽	20♌	2♍	14	26	9♎	22	5♏	18	1♐	15	29	14♑	28	13♒	27	12♓	27	11♈	25	8♉	21	4♊	16	28	10♋	22	4♌	16	28	10♍
☿	21♌	22	22	23	24	25	26	27	29	0♍	2	3	5	7	8	10	12	14	16	18	19	21	23	25	27	29	1♎	2	4	6
♀	24♎	25	26	27	28	29	30	1♏	2	2	3	4	5	6	7	7	8	9	10	11	11	12	13	13	14	15	15	16	17	17
♂	18♎	18	19	19	20	21	21	22	23	23	24	25	25	26	27	27	28	29	29	0♏	1	1	2	3	3	4	5	5	6	7
	1	6	11	16	21	26			1	11	21			1	11	21			1	16		1	16		1	16		1	11	21
♃	29♋	0♌	1	2	3	4		♄	5♍	6	7		⚷	10♉	9	9		♅	13♏	14	♆	16♐	16	♇	15♎	16	☊	28♍	27	27

OCT

	1	2	3	4	5	6	7	8	9	10	11	12	13	14	15	16	17	18	19	20	21	22	23	24	25	26	27	28	29	30	31
☉	7♎	8	9	10	11	12	13	14	15	16	17	18	19	20	21	22	23	24	25	26	27	28	29	0♏	1	2	3	4	5	6	7
☽	22♍	5♎	18	1♏	15	28	12♐	26	10♑	24	8♒	23	7♓	21	5♈	19	3♉	16	29	12♊	24	6♋	18	30	12♌	24	6♍	18	1♎	13	27
☿	8♎	10	11	13	15	16	18	20	21	23	25	26	28	30	1♏	3	4	6	7	9	11	12	14	15	17	18	20	21	22	24	25
♀	18♏	18	19	19	20	20	21	21	21	22	22	22	22	22	23	23	23	23	23	23	23	23	22	22	22	22	21	21	20	20	20
♂	8♏	8	9	10	10	11	12	12	13	14	14	15	16	17	17	18	19	19	20	21	21	22	23	24	24	25	26	26	27	28	29
	1	6	11	16	21	26	31		1	11	21	31		1	11	21	31		1	16		1	16		1	16		1	11	21	31
♃	4♌	5	6	6	7	8	8	♄	8♍	9	10	11	⚷	9♉	8	8	7	♅	14♏	15	♆	16♐	16	♇	16♎	17	☊	26♍	26	25	25

NOV

	1	2	3	4	5	6	7	8	9	10	11	12	13	14	15	16	17	18	19	20	21	22	23	24	25	26	27	28	29	30
☉	8♏	9	10	11	12	13	14	15	16	17	18	19	20	21	22	23	24	25	26	27	28	29	0♐	1	2	3	4	5	6	7
☽	10♏	24	8♐	22	7♑	21	5♒	19	3♓	17	1♈	15	28	11♉	24	7♊	20	2♋	14	26	8♌	20	2♍	14	26	8♎	21	5♏	19	3♐
☿	27♏	28	30	1♐	2	4	5	6	8	9	10	11	12	14	15	16	17	18	18	19	20	21	21	21	22	22	22	21	21	20
♀	19♏	19	18	17	17	16	16	15	14	14	13	13	12	12	11	11	10	10	9	9	9	8	8	8	8	7	7	7	7	7
♂	29♏	30	1♐	1	2	3	4	4	5	6	6	7	8	9	9	10	11	12	12	13	14	15	15	16	17	17	18	19	20	20
	1	6	11	16	21	26			1	11	21			1	11	21			1	16		1	16		1	16		1	11	21
♃	8♌	8	9	9	9	9		♄	11♍	12	13		⚷	7♉	7	6		♅	16♏	17	♆	17♐	17	♇	17♎	18	☊	24♍	24	23

DEC

	1	2	3	4	5	6	7	8	9	10	11	12	13	14	15	16	17	18	19	20	21	22	23	24	25	26	27	28	29	30	31
☉	8♐	9	10	11	12	14	15	16	17	18	19	20	21	22	23	24	25	26	27	28	29	30	1♑	2	3	4	5	6	7	8	9
☽	17♐	2♑	17	1♒	16	0♓	14	28	11♈	25	8♉	21	3♊	16	28	10♋	22	4♌	16	28	10♍	22	4♎	16	29	13♏	26	11♐	25	11♑	26
☿	19♐	18	17	16	15	13	12	11	9	8	7	7	6	6	5	5	6	6	6	7	7	8	9	10	11	12	13	14	15	17	18
♀	7♏	8	8	8	8	8	9	9	9	10	10	11	11	12	12	13	13	14	15	15	16	17	17	18	19	20	20	21	22	23	24
♂	21♐	22	23	23	24	25	26	26	27	28	29	29	0♑	1	2	2	3	4	5	6	6	7	8	9	9	10	11	12	12	13	14
	1	6	11	16	21	26	31		1	11	21	31		1	11	21	31		1	16		1	16		1	16		1	11	21	31
♃	9♌	9	9	8	8	8	7	♄	13♍	14	14	14	⚷	6♉	6	5	5	♅	18♏	19	♆	18♐	18	♇	18♎	19	☊	23♍	22	22	21

1979

EPHEMERIS

JAN

	1	2	3	4	5	6	7	8	9	10	11	12	13	14	15	16	17	18	19	20	21	22	23	24	25	26	27	28	29	30	31
☉	10♑	11	12	13	14	15	16	17	18	19	20	21	22	23	24	25	26	27	28	29	0♒	1	2	3	4	5	6	7	8	9	11
☽	11♒	26	10♓	24	8♈	22	5♉	18	0♊	13	25	7♋	19	1♌	13	25	6♍	18	0♎	12	25	8♏	21	5♐	19	3♑	18	4♒	19	4♓	19
☿	19♐	20	22	23	24	26	27	29	0♑	2	3	4	6	7	9	10	12	13	15	16	18	20	21	23	24	26	28	29	1♒	2	4
♀	24♏	25	26	27	28	29	30	1♐	2	3	4	4	5	6	7	8	9	10	11	12	14	15	16	17	18	19	20	21	22	23	24
♂	15♑	15	16	17	18	19	19	20	21	22	22	23	24	25	26	26	27	28	29	29	0♒	1	2	3	3	4	5	6	6	7	8
	1	6	11	16	21	26	31		1	11	21	31		1	11	21	31		1	16		1	16		1	16		1	11	21	31
♃	7♌	6	6	5	5	4	3	♄	14♍	14	13	13	⚷	5♉	5	5	5	♅	20♏	20	♆	19♐	19	♇	19♎	19	☊	21♍	21	20	20

FEB

	1	2	3	4	5	6	7	8	9	10	11	12	13	14	15	16	17	18	19	20	21	22	23	24	25	26	27	28			
☉	12♒	13	14	15	16	17	18	19	20	21	22	23	24	25	26	27	28	29	30	1♓	2	3	4	5	6	7	8	9			
☽	3♈	17	1♉	14	27	10♊	22	4♋	16	28	10♌	21	3♍	15	27	9♎	22	4♏	17	0♐	14	28	12♑	27	12♒	27	12♓	27			
☿	6♒	7	9	11	12	14	16	18	19	21	23	25	27	28	0♓	2	4	6	8	10	11	13	15	17	19	20	22	24			
♀	25♐	26	27	28	30	1♑	2	3	4	5	6	7	8	10	11	12	13	14	15	16	18	19	20	21	22	23	25	26			
♂	9♒	10	10	11	12	13	14	14	15	16	17	17	18	19	20	21	21	22	23	24	25	25	26	27	28	29	29	0♓			
	1	6	11	16	21	26			1	11	21			1	11	21			1	16		1	16		1	16		1	11	21	
♃	3♌	2	2	1	1	0		♄	13♍	12	11		⚷	5♉	5	6		♅	21♏	21	♆	20♐	20	♇	19♎	19	☊	20♍	19	19	

MAR

	1	2	3	4	5	6	7	8	9	10	11	12	13	14	15	16	17	18	19	20	21	22	23	24	25	26	27	28	29	30	31
☉	10♓	11	12	13	14	15	16	17	18	19	20	21	22	23	24	25	26	27	28	29	30	1♈	2	3	4	5	6	7	8	9	10
☽	12♈	26	10♉	23	6♊	18	1♋	13	25	6♌	18	0♍	12	24	6♎	19	1♏	14	27	10♐	24	8♑	22	6♒	21	5♓	20	5♈	20	4♉	18
☿	26♓	27	29	0♈	2	3	4	5	6	7	7	8	8	8	9	8	8	8	7	7	6	6	5	4	3	2	1	0	30♓	29	28
♀	27♑	28	29	0♒	1	3	4	5	6	7	9	10	11	12	13	14	16	17	18	19	20	22	23	24	25	26	27	29	30	1♓	2
♂	1♓	2	2	3	4	5	6	6	7	8	9	10	10	11	12	13	14	14	15	16	17	17	18	19	20	21	21	22	23	24	24
	1	6	11	16	21	26	31		1	11	21	31		1	11	21	31		1	16		1	16		1	16		1	11	21	31
♃	30♋	30	29	29	29	29	29	♄	11♍	10	9	8	⚷	6♉	6	7	8	♅	21♏	21	♆	20♐	20	♇	19♎	18	☊	18♍	18	17	17

APR

	1	2	3	4	5	6	7	8	9	10	11	12	13	14	15	16	17	18	19	20	21	22	23	24	25	26	27	28	29	30	
☉	11♈	12	13	14	15	16	17	18	19	20	21	21	22	23	24	25	26	27	28	29	0♉	1	2	3	4	5	6	7	8	9	
☽	1♊	14	27	9♋	21	3♌	15	27	8♍	20	3♎	15	28	11♏	24	7♐	21	4♑	18	2♒	16	1♓	15	29	14♈	28	12♉	26	9♊	22	
☿	28♓	27	27	26	26	26	26	26	26	26	26	27	27	28	28	29	30	0♈	1	2	3	4	5	6	7	8	10	11	12	13	
♀	3♓	5	6	7	8	9	11	12	13	14	15	17	18	19	20	21	23	24	25	26	27	29	30	1♈	2	3	5	6	7	8	
♂	25♓	26	27	28	28	29	30	1♈	2	2	3	4	5	5	6	7	8	8	9	10	11	12	12	13	14	15	15	16	17	18	
	1	6	11	16	21	26			1	11	21			1	11	21			1	16		1	16		1	16		1	11	21	
♃	29♋	29	29	30	0♌	0		♄	8♍	8	7		⚷	8♉	8	9		♅	20♏	20	♆	20♐	20	♇	18♎	18	☊	16♍	16	15	

MAY

	1	2	3	4	5	6	7	8	9	10	11	12	13	14	15	16	17	18	19	20	21	22	23	24	25	26	27	28	29	30	31
☉	10♉	11	12	13	14	15	16	17	18	19	20	21	22	23	24	25	26	26	27	28	29	0♊	1	2	3	4	5	6	7	8	9
☽	5♋	17	29	11♌	23	5♍	16	29	11♎	23	6♏	20	3♐	17	1♑	15	29	13♒	27	12♓	26	10♈	23	7♉	21	4♊	17	0♋	13	25	7♌
☿	15♈	16	18	19	21	22	24	25	27	28	0♉	2	4	5	7	9	11	13	15	17	19	21	23	25	27	29	1♊	4	6	8	10
♀	9♈	11	12	13	14	15	17	18	19	20	22	23	24	25	26	28	29	30	1♉	2	4	5	6	7	8	10	11	12	13	15	16
♂	18♈	19	20	21	22	22	23	24	25	25	26	27	28	28	29	30	1♉	1	2	3	4	4	5	6	7	7	8	9	10	10	11
	1	6	11	16	21	26	31		1	11	21	31		1	11	21	31		1	16		1	16		1	16		1	11	21	31
♃	1♌	2	2	3	3	4	5	♄	7♍	7	7	7	⚷	9♉	10	11	11	♅	19♏	19	♆	20♐	20	♇	17♎	17	☊	15♍	14	14	13

JUN

	1	2	3	4	5	6	7	8	9	10	11	12	13	14	15	16	17	18	19	20	21	22	23	24	25	26	27	28	29	30	
☉	10♊	11	12	13	14	15	16	17	18	19	19	20	21	22	23	24	25	26	27	28	29	0♋	1	2	3	4	5	6	7	8	
☽	19♌	1♍	12	24	6♎	19	2♏	15	28	12♐	26	11♑	25	10♒	24	8♓	22	6♈	20	4♉	17	0♊	13	26	9♋	21	3♌	15	27	9♍	
☿	12♊	15	17	19	21	23	25	27	29	1♋	3	5	7	9	11	13	14	16	18	19	21	22	24	25	27	28	29	1♌	2	3	
♀	17♉	18	19	21	22	23	24	25	27	28	29	0♊	2	3	4	5	6	8	9	10	11	12	14	15	16	17	19	20	21	22	
♂	12♉	13	13	14	15	15	16	17	18	18	19	20	21	21	22	23	23	24	25	26	26	27	28	29	29	30	1♊	1	2	3	
	1	6	11	16	21	26			1	11	21			1	11	21			1	16		1	16		1	16		1	11	21	
♃	5♌	6	7	8	9	10		♄	8♍	8	9		⚷	11♉	12	12		♅	18♏	18	♆	19♐	19	♇	17♎	16	☊	13♍	13	12	

1979

JUL

	1	2	3	4	5	6	7	8	9	10	11	12	13	14	15	16	17	18	19	20	21	22	23	24	25	26	27	28	29	30	31
☉	9♋	10	10	11	12	13	14	15	16	17	18	19	20	21	22	23	24	25	26	27	28	29	30	1♌	1	2	3	4	5	6	7
☽	21♍	2♎	15	27	10♏	23	6♐	20	5♑	19	4♒	19	4♓	19	3♈	17	1♉	14	27	10♊	23	5♋	18	30	12♌	24	5♍	17	29	11♎	23
☿	4♌	5	6	7	8	9	10	11	11	12	13	13	13	14	14	14	14	14	14	14	14	14	13	13	12	12	11	11	10	9	8
♀	23♊	25	26	27	28	30	1♋	2	3	4	6	7	8	9	11	12	13	14	15	17	18	19	20	22	23	24	25	27	28	29	0♌
♂	3♊	4	5	6	6	7	8	8	9	10	11	11	12	13	13	14	15	15	16	17	17	18	19	20	20	21	22	22	23	24	24
	1	6	11	16	21	26	31		1	11	21	31		1	11	21	31		1	16		1	16		1	16		1	11	21	31
♃	11♌	12	13	14	15	16	17	♄	9♍	10	11	12	⚷	13♉	13	14	14	♅	17♏	17	♆	19♐	18	♇	16♎	17	☊	12♍	11	11	10

AUG

	1	2	3	4	5	6	7	8	9	10	11	12	13	14	15	16	17	18	19	20	21	22	23	24	25	26	27	28	29	30	31
☉	8♌	9	10	11	12	13	14	15	16	17	18	19	20	21	22	23	24	24	25	26	27	28	29	0♍	1	2	3	4	5	6	7
☽	5♏	18	1♐	15	29	13♑	28	13♒	28	13♓	28	13♈	27	11♉	24	7♊	20	2♋	15	27	9♌	21	2♍	14	26	8♎	20	2♏	14	27	10♐
☿	8♌	7	6	6	5	4	4	4	3	3	3	3	3	4	4	5	5	6	7	8	9	10	11	13	14	16	17	19	21	23	25
♀	1♌	3	4	5	6	8	9	10	11	13	14	15	16	17	19	20	21	22	24	25	26	27	29	30	1♍	2	4	5	6	7	9
♂	25♊	26	26	27	28	28	29	30	0♋	1	2	2	3	4	4	5	6	6	7	8	8	9	9	10	11	11	12	13	13	14	15
	1	6	11	16	21	26	31		1	11	21	31		1	11	21	31		1	16		1	16		1	16		1	11	21	31
♃	17♌	18	20	21	22	23	24	♄	12♍	13	15	16	⚷	14♉	14	14	14	♅	17♏	17	♆	18♐	18	♇	17♎	17	☊	10♍	9	9	8

SEP

	1	2	3	4	5	6	7	8	9	10	11	12	13	14	15	16	17	18	19	20	21	22	23	24	25	26	27	28	29	30
☉	8♍	9	10	11	12	13	14	15	16	17	18	19	20	21	22	23	24	24	25	26	27	28	29	0♎	1	2	3	4	5	6
☽	23♐	7♑	21	6♒	21	6♓	21	7♈	21	6♉	20	3♊	17	29	12♋	24	6♌	18	29	11♍	23	5♎	17	29	11♏	24	7♐	20	3♑	17
☿	26♌	28	0♍	2	4	6	8	10	12	14	16	18	19	21	23	25	27	29	0♎	2	4	6	7	9	11	12	14	16	17	19
♀	10♍	11	12	13	15	16	17	18	20	21	22	23	25	26	27	28	30	1♎	2	3	5	6	7	8	10	11	12	13	15	16
♂	15♋	16	17	17	18	18	19	20	20	21	22	22	23	23	24	25	25	26	26	27	28	28	29	29	0♌	1	1	2	2	3
	1	6	11	16	21	26			1	11	21			1	11	21			1	16		1	16		1	16		1	11	21
♃	24♌	25	26	27	28	29		♄	16♍	17	19		⚷	14♉	14	13		♅	17♏	18	♆	18♐	18	♇	18♎	18	☊	8♍	8	7

OCT

	1	2	3	4	5	6	7	8	9	10	11	12	13	14	15	16	17	18	19	20	21	22	23	24	25	26	27	28	29	30	31
☉	7♎	8	9	10	11	12	13	14	15	16	17	18	19	20	21	22	23	24	25	26	27	28	29	30	1♏	2	3	4	5	6	7
☽	1♒	15	30	15♓	30	15♈	30	14♉	28	12♊	25	8♋	20	2♌	14	26	8♍	20	2♎	14	26	8♏	21	4♐	17	30	13♑	27	11♒	25	9♓
☿	20♎	22	24	25	27	28	30	1♏	3	4	6	7	9	10	11	13	14	15	17	18	19	21	22	23	24	25	27	28	29	30	1♐
♀	17♎	18	20	21	22	23	25	26	27	28	29	1♏	2	3	4	6	7	8	9	11	12	13	14	16	17	18	19	21	22	23	24
♂	4♌	4	5	5	6	7	7	8	8	9	9	10	11	11	12	12	13	13	14	14	15	16	16	17	17	18	18	19	19	20	20
	1	6	11	16	21	26	31		1	11	21	31		1	11	21	31		1	16		1	16		1	16		1	11	21	31
♃	0♍	1	2	3	4	5	6	♄	20♍	21	22	23	⚷	13♉	13	12	12	♅	19♏	20	♆	18♐	18	♇	19♎	19	☊	7♍	6	6	5

NOV

	1	2	3	4	5	6	7	8	9	10	11	12	13	14	15	16	17	18	19	20	21	22	23	24	25	26	27	28	29	30
☉	8♏	9	10	11	12	13	14	15	16	17	18	19	20	21	22	23	24	25	26	27	28	29	0♐	1	2	3	4	5	6	7
☽	24♓	8♈	23	8♉	22	6♊	20	3♋	16	28	10♌	22	4♍	16	28	10♎	22	4♏	17	0♐	13	27	10♑	24	8♒	22	6♓	20	4♈	18
☿	2♐	2	3	4	4	5	5	6	6	6	6	5	5	4	3	2	1	0	29♏	28	26	25	24	23	22	21	20	20	20	20
♀	26♏	27	28	29	1♐	2	3	4	6	7	8	9	11	12	13	14	16	17	18	19	21	22	23	24	26	27	28	29	1♑	2
♂	21♌	21	22	22	23	23	24	24	25	25	26	26	27	27	28	28	29	29	30	0♍	0	1	1	2	2	3	3	4	4	4
	1	6	11	16	21	26			1	11	21			1	11	21			1	16		1	16		1	16		1	11	21
♃	6♍	6	7	8	8	9		♄	23♍	24	25		⚷	12♉	11	11		♅	20♏	21	♆	19♐	19	♇	20♎	20	☊	5♍	5	4

DEC

	1	2	3	4	5	6	7	8	9	10	11	12	13	14	15	16	17	18	19	20	21	22	23	24	25	26	27	28	29	30	31
☉	8♐	9	10	11	12	13	14	15	16	17	18	19	20	21	22	23	24	25	26	27	29	30	1♑	2	3	4	5	6	7	8	9
☽	2♉	17	1♊	14	28	11♋	24	6♌	18	0♍	12	24	6♎	18	30	12♏	25	8♐	22	6♑	20	4♒	18	2♓	17	1♈	15	29	13♉	26	10♊
☿	20♏	20	21	21	22	23	24	25	26	27	28	29	1♐	2	3	5	6	7	9	10	12	13	14	16	17	19	20	22	23	25	26
♀	3♑	4	5	7	8	9	10	12	13	14	15	17	18	19	20	22	23	24	25	27	28	29	0♒	2	3	4	5	6	8	9	10
♂	5♍	5	6	6	6	7	7	7	8	8	8	9	9	9	10	10	10	11	11	11	12	12	12	12	13	13	13	13	13	14	14
	1	6	11	16	21	26	31		1	11	21	31		1	11	21	31		1	16		1	16		1	16		1	11	21	31
♃	9♍	10	10	10	10	10	10	♄	26♍	26	27	27	⚷	10♉	10	10	9	♅	22♏	23	♆	20♐	20	♇	21♎	21	☊	4♍	3	2	2

EPHEMERIS

1980

JAN

	1	2	3	4	5	6	7	8	9	10	11	12	13	14	15	16	17	18	19	20	21	22	23	24	25	26	27	28	29	30	31
☉	10♑	11	12	13	14	15	16	17	18	19	20	21	22	23	24	25	26	27	28	29	0♒	1	2	3	4	5	6	7	8	9	10
☽	23♊	6♋	19	2♌	14	26	8♍	20	2♎	13	25	8♏	20	3♐	16	0♑	14	29	13♒	28	12♓	27	11♈	26	10♉	23	7♊	20	3♋	15	28
☿	28♐	29	1♑	3	4	6	7	9	10	12	14	15	17	18	20	22	23	25	27	28	30	2♒	3	5	7	8	10	12	14	15	17
♀	11♒	13	14	15	16	18	19	20	21	22	24	25	26	27	29	30	1♓	2	3	5	6	7	8	10	11	12	13	14	16	17	18
♂	14♍	14	14	14	15	15	15	15	15	15	15	15	15	15	15	15	15	15	15	15	15	15	15	15	15	15	15	14	14	14	14
	1	6	11	16	21	26	31		1	11	21	31		1	11	21	31		1	16		1	16		1	16		1	11	21	31
♃	10♍	10	10	10	9	9	8	♄	27♍	27	27	27	⚷	9♉	9	9	9	♅	24♏	25	♆	21♐	21	♇	22♎	22	☊	2♍	1	1	0

FEB

	1	2	3	4	5	6	7	8	9	10	11	12	13	14	15	16	17	18	19	20	21	22	23	24	25	26	27	28	29		
☉	11♒	12	13	14	15	16	17	18	19	20	21	22	23	24	25	26	27	28	29	1♓	2	3	4	5	6	7	8	9	10		
☽	10♌	22	4♍	16	28	10♎	22	4♏	16	28	11♐	24	8♑	22	6♒	21	6♓	21	6♈	21	6♉	20	3♊	17	30	12♋	25	7♌	19		
☿	19♒	21	22	24	26	28	29	1♓	3	5	6	8	9	11	13	14	15	16	18	19	19	20	21	21	21	22	21	21	21		
♀	19♓	20	22	23	24	25	26	28	29	0♈	1	2	4	5	6	7	8	9	11	12	13	14	15	16	18	19	20	21	22		
♂	14♍	14	13	13	13	13	12	12	12	11	11	11	10	10	10	9	9	9	8	8	7	7	7	6	6	5	5	5	4		
	1	6	11	16	21	26			1	11	21			1	11	21			1	16		1	16		1	16		1	11	21	
♃	8♍	8	7	6	6	5		♄	26♍	26	25		⚷	9♉	9	10		♅	25♏	25	♆	22♐	22	♇	22♎	22	☊	0♍	30♌	29	

MAR

	1	2	3	4	5	6	7	8	9	10	11	12	13	14	15	16	17	18	19	20	21	22	23	24	25	26	27	28	29	30	31
☉	11♓	12	13	14	15	16	17	18	19	20	21	22	23	24	25	26	27	28	29	30	1♈	2	3	4	4	5	6	7	8	9	10
☽	1♍	13	25	7♎	18	0♏	12	25	7♐	20	3♑	16	0♒	15	29	14♓	30	15♈	30	15♉	29	13♊	26	9♋	22	4♌	16	28	10♍	22	4♎
☿	20♓	20	19	18	17	16	15	14	13	12	11	10	10	9	8	8	8	8	7	7	8	8	8	8	9	9	10	10	11	12	13
♀	23♈	25	26	27	28	29	0♉	1	2	4	5	6	7	8	9	10	11	12	14	15	16	17	18	19	20	21	22	23	24	25	26
♂	4♍	4	3	3	2	2	2	1	1	1	0	30♌	30	29	29	29	29	28	28	28	28	27	27	27	27	27	27	26	26	26	26
	1	6	11	16	21	26	31		1	11	21	31		1	11	21	31		1	16		1	16		1	16		1	11	21	31
♃	5♍	4	3	3	2	2	1	♄	25♍	24	23	22	⚷	10♉	10	11	11	♅	26♏	25	♆	23♐	23	♇	21♎	21	☊	29♌	28	28	27

APR

	1	2	3	4	5	6	7	8	9	10	11	12	13	14	15	16	17	18	19	20	21	22	23	24	25	26	27	28	29	30	
☉	11♈	12	13	14	15	16	17	18	19	20	21	22	23	24	25	26	27	28	29	0♉	1	2	3	4	5	6	7	8	9	10	
☽	15♎	27	9♏	22	4♐	16	29	12♑	25	9♒	23	8♓	23	8♈	23	8♉	23	7♊	21	5♋	18	1♌	13	25	7♍	19	0♎	12	24	6♏	
☿	14♓	15	16	17	18	19	20	21	22	24	25	26	28	29	0♈	2	3	5	6	8	10	11	13	15	16	18	20	22	23	25	
♀	27♉	28	29	0♊	1	2	3	4	5	6	7	8	9	10	11	12	12	13	14	15	16	17	17	18	19	20	21	21	22	23	
♂	26♌	26	26	26	26	26	26	26	26	26	26	26	26	26	26	26	27	27	27	27	27	27	27	28	28	28	28	28	29	29	
	1	6	11	16	21	26			1	11	21			1	11	21			1	16		1	16		1	16		1	11	21	
♃	1♍	1	1	0	0	0		♄	22♍	22	21		⚷	12♉	12	13		♅	25♏	25	♆	23♐	23	♇	21♎	20	☊	27♌	27	26	

MAY

	1	2	3	4	5	6	7	8	9	10	11	12	13	14	15	16	17	18	19	20	21	22	23	24	25	26	27	28	29	30	31
☉	11♉	12	13	14	15	16	17	18	19	19	20	21	22	23	24	25	26	27	28	29	0♊	1	2	3	4	5	6	7	8	9	10
☽	18♏	1♐	13	26	9♑	22	6♒	19	3♓	17	2♈	17	2♉	16	1♊	16	29	13♋	26	9♌	21	3♍	15	27	9♎	21	3♏	15	27	10♐	23
☿	27♈	29	1♉	3	5	7	9	11	13	15	18	20	22	24	26	28	1♊	3	5	7	9	11	13	15	17	19	21	23	25	27	28
♀	23♊	24	25	25	26	27	27	28	28	29	29	30	0♋	0	1	1	1	2	2	2	2	2	3	3	3	3	2	2	2	2	2
♂	29♌	29	30	30	0♍	1	1	1	1	2	2	2	3	3	3	4	4	4	5	5	6	6	6	7	7	8	8	8	9	9	10
	1	6	11	16	21	26	31		1	11	21	31		1	11	21	31		1	16		1	16		1	16		1	11	21	31
♃	0♍	0	1	1	1	2	2	♄	21♍	20	20	20	⚷	13♉	14	15	15	♅	24♏	23	♆	22♐	22	♇	20♎	19	☊	25♌	25	24	24

JUN

	1	2	3	4	5	6	7	8	9	10	11	12	13	14	15	16	17	18	19	20	21	22	23	24	25	26	27	28	29	30	
☉	11♊	12	13	14	14	15	16	17	18	19	20	21	22	23	24	25	26	27	28	29	30	1♋	2	3	4	5	5	6	7	8	
☽	6♑	19	3♒	16	30	14♓	28	12♈	27	11♉	26	10♊	24	8♋	21	4♌	17	29	11♍	23	5♎	17	29	11♏	23	6♐	19	2♑	15	29	
☿	0♋	2	3	5	6	8	9	11	12	13	14	15	17	18	19	19	20	21	22	22	23	24	24	24	25	25	25	25	25	25	
♀	2♋	1	1	1	0	30♊	29	29	28	28	27	26	26	25	25	24	23	23	22	21	21	20	20	19	19	18	18	18	17	17	
♂	10♍	11	11	11	12	12	13	13	14	14	15	15	16	16	17	17	17	18	18	19	19	20	21	21	22	22	23	23	24	24	
	1	6	11	16	21	26			1	11	21			1	11	21			1	16		1	16		1	16		1	11	21	
♃	2♍	3	3	4	5	5		♄	20♍	21	21		⚷	15♉	16	17		♅	23♏	22	♆	22♐	21	♇	19♎	19	☊	24♌	23	23	

1980

JUL

	1	2	3	4	5	6	7	8	9	10	11	12	13	14	15	16	17	18	19	20	21	22	23	24	25	26	27	28	29	30	31
☉	9♋	10	11	12	13	14	15	16	17	18	19	20	21	22	23	24	25	26	26	27	28	29	0♌	1	2	3	4	5	6	7	8
☽	13♒	27	11♓	25	9♈	23	7♉	21	5♊	19	3♋	16	29	12♌	25	7♍	19	1♎	13	25	7♏	19	1♐	14	27	10♑	24	8♒	22	7♓	21
☿	25♋	25	24	24	24	23	23	22	21	21	20	19	19	18	18	17	17	16	16	16	15	15	15	15	15	16	16	17	17	18	19
♀	17♊	17	16	16	16	16	16	16	16	16	16	17	17	17	17	18	18	18	19	19	20	20	20	21	22	22	23	23	24	25	25
♂	25♍	25	26	26	27	27	28	28	29	30	0♎	1	1	2	2	3	4	4	5	5	6	6	7	8	8	9	9	10	11	11	12
	1	6	11	16	21	26	31		1	11	21	31		1	11	21	31		1	16		1	16		1	16		1	11	21	31
♃	6♍	7	8	9	10	10	11	♄	21♍	22	23	24	⚷	17♉	17	18	18	♅	22♏	22	♆	21♐	20	♇	19♎	19	☊	22♌	22	21	21

AUG

	1	2	3	4	5	6	7	8	9	10	11	12	13	14	15	16	17	18	19	20	21	22	23	24	25	26	27	28	29	30	31
☉	9♌	10	11	12	13	14	15	16	17	18	18	19	20	21	22	23	24	25	26	27	28	29	0♍	1	2	3	4	5	6	7	8
☽	5♈	20	4♉	18	2♊	16	29	13♋	26	8♌	21	3♍	15	27	9♎	21	3♏	15	27	9♐	22	5♑	18	2♒	16	1♓	16	1♈	15	0♉	15
☿	19♋	20	22	23	24	25	27	28	30	1♌	3	5	7	9	10	12	14	16	18	20	22	24	26	28	0♍	2	4	6	8	10	12
♀	26♊	27	27	28	29	30	0♋	1	2	3	4	4	5	6	7	8	9	10	11	11	12	13	14	15	16	17	18	19	20	21	22
♂	12♎	13	14	14	15	15	16	17	17	18	18	19	20	20	21	22	22	23	23	24	25	25	26	27	27	28	29	29	30	0♏	1
	1	6	11	16	21	26	31		1	11	21	31		1	11	21	31		1	16		1	16		1	16		1	11	21	31
♃	12♍	13	14	15	16	17	18	♄	24♍	25	26	27	⚷	18♉	18	18	18	♅	22♏	22	♆	20♐	20	♇	19♎	20	☊	21♌	20	20	19

SEP

	1	2	3	4	5	6	7	8	9	10	11	12	13	14	15	16	17	18	19	20	21	22	23	24	25	26	27	28	29	30	
☉	9♍	10	11	12	13	14	15	15	16	17	18	19	20	21	22	23	24	25	26	27	28	29	0♎	1	2	3	4	5	6	7	
☽	29♉	13♊	26	9♋	22	5♌	17	30	12♍	24	6♎	18	29	11♏	23	5♐	18	0♑	13	26	10♒	24	9♓	24	9♈	24	9♉	24	9♊	23	
☿	14♍	16	18	19	21	23	25	26	28	30	2♎	3	5	6	8	10	11	13	14	16	17	19	20	22	23	24	26	27	29	30	
♀	23♋	24	25	26	27	28	29	0♌	1	2	3	4	6	7	8	9	10	11	12	13	14	15	16	18	19	20	21	22	23	24	
♂	2♏	2	3	4	4	5	6	6	7	8	8	9	10	10	11	12	12	13	14	14	15	16	17	17	18	19	19	20	21	21	
	1	6	11	16	21	26			1	11	21			1	11	21			1	16		1	16		1	16		1	11	21	
♃	18♍	19	20	21	22	23		♄	27♍	29	30		⚷	18♉	18	18		♅	22♏	22	♆	20♐	20	♇	20♎	21	☊	19♌	18	18	

OCT

	1	2	3	4	5	6	7	8	9	10	11	12	13	14	15	16	17	18	19	20	21	22	23	24	25	26	27	28	29	30	31
☉	8♎	9	10	11	12	13	14	15	16	17	18	19	20	21	22	23	24	25	26	27	28	29	30	1♏	2	3	4	5	6	7	8
☽	6♋	19	2♌	15	27	9♍	21	3♎	15	26	8♏	20	2♐	14	27	9♑	22	5♒	19	3♓	17	2♈	17	3♉	18	3♊	18	2♋	15	29	11♌
☿	1♏	3	4	5	6	7	9	10	11	12	13	14	15	16	16	17	18	18	19	19	20	20	20	20	20	19	19	18	17	16	15
♀	25♌	27	28	29	0♍	1	2	3	5	6	7	8	9	10	12	13	14	15	16	18	19	20	21	22	23	25	26	27	28	29	1♎
♂	22♏	23	23	24	25	26	26	27	28	28	29	30	1♐	1	2	3	3	4	5	6	6	7	8	8	9	10	11	11	12	13	14
	1	6	11	16	21	26	31		1	11	21	31		1	11	21	31		1	16		1	16		1	16		1	11	21	31
♃	25♍	26	27	28	29	30	1♎	♄	1♎	2	4	5	⚷	18♉	17	17	16	♅	23♏	24	♆	20♐	20	♇	21♎	22	☊	17♌	17	16	16

NOV

	1	2	3	4	5	6	7	8	9	10	11	12	13	14	15	16	17	18	19	20	21	22	23	24	25	26	27	28	29	30	
☉	9♏	10	11	12	13	14	15	16	17	18	19	20	21	22	23	24	25	26	27	28	29	30	1♐	2	3	4	5	6	7	8	
☽	24♌	6♍	18	30	12♎	23	5♏	17	29	11♐	24	6♑	19	2♒	15	28	12♓	26	11♈	26	11♉	26	11♊	26	10♋	24	7♌	20	2♍	14	
☿	14♏	13	12	10	9	8	7	6	5	5	4	4	4	4	5	5	6	6	7	8	9	11	12	13	14	16	17	18	20	21	
♀	2♎	3	4	5	7	8	9	10	12	13	14	15	16	18	19	20	21	23	24	25	26	27	29	30	1♏	2	4	5	6	7	
♂	14♐	15	16	16	17	18	19	19	20	21	22	22	23	24	25	25	26	27	28	28	29	30	1♑	1	2	3	4	5	5	6	
	1	6	11	16	21	26			1	11	21			1	11	21			1	16		1	16		1	16		1	11	21	
♃	1♎	2	3	4	4	5		♄	5♎	6	7		⚷	16♉	16	15		♅	25♏	26	♆	21♐	21	♇	22♎	23	☊	16♌	15	15	

DEC

	1	2	3	4	5	6	7	8	9	10	11	12	13	14	15	16	17	18	19	20	21	22	23	24	25	26	27	28	29	30	31
☉	9♐	10	11	12	13	14	15	16	17	18	19	20	21	22	23	24	25	26	27	28	29	0♑	1	2	3	4	5	6	7	8	9
☽	26♍	8♎	20	2♏	14	26	8♐	21	3♑	16	29	12♒	25	8♓	22	6♈	21	5♉	20	4♊	19	4♋	18	1♌	15	28	10♍	22	4♎	16	28
☿	23♏	24	26	27	29	0♐	2	3	5	6	8	9	11	13	14	16	17	19	20	22	23	25	27	28	30	1♑	3	4	6	8	9
♀	9♏	10	11	12	14	15	16	17	18	20	21	22	23	25	26	27	28	30	1♐	2	3	5	6	7	8	10	11	12	13	15	16
♂	7♑	8	8	9	10	11	11	12	13	14	14	15	16	17	18	18	19	20	21	21	22	23	24	25	25	26	27	28	28	29	0♒
	1	6	11	16	21	26	31		1	11	21	31		1	11	21	31		1	16		1	16		1	16		1	11	21	31
♃	6♎	7	7	8	9	9	9	♄	8♎	8	9	9	⚷	15♉	14	14	14	♅	27♏	28	♆	22♐	22	♇	23♎	24	☊	14♌	14	13	13

1981

EPHEMERIS

JAN

	1	2	3	4	5	6	7	8	9	10	11	12	13	14	15	16	17	18	19	20	21	22	23	24	25	26	27	28	29	30	31
☉	10♑	12	13	14	15	16	17	18	19	20	21	22	23	24	25	26	27	28	29	30	1♒	2	3	4	5	6	7	8	9	10	11
☽	10♏	22	4♐	17	29	12♑	25	8♒	22	5♓	19	3♈	17	1♉	16	30	14♊	28	12♋	26	9♌	22	5♍	18	0♎	12	24	6♏	18	30	12♐
☿	11♑	12	14	16	17	19	21	22	24	26	27	29	1♒	2	4	6	7	9	11	12	14	16	17	19	21	22	24	25	27	28	29
♀	17♐	18	20	21	22	23	25	26	27	28	30	1♑	2	3	5	6	7	8	10	11	12	13	15	16	17	18	20	21	22	23	25
♂	1♒	2	2	3	4	5	6	6	7	8	9	9	10	11	12	13	13	14	15	16	17	17	18	19	20	21	21	22	23	24	24
	1	6	11	16	21	26	31		1	11	21	31		1	11	21	31		1	16		1	16		1	16		1	11	21	31
♃	10♎	10	10	10	10	10	10	♄	10♎	10	10	10	⚷	14♉	13	13	13	♅	28♏	29	♆	23♐	24	♇	24♎	24	☊	13♌	12	11	11

FEB

	1	2	3	4	5	6	7	8	9	10	11	12	13	14	15	16	17	18	19	20	21	22	23	24	25	26	27	28			
☉	12♒	13	14	15	16	17	18	19	20	21	22	23	24	25	26	27	28	29	0♓	1	2	3	4	5	6	7	8	9			
☽	24♐	7♑	20	3♒	17	1♓	15	29	14♈	28	12♉	27	11♊	24	8♋	22	5♌	18	1♍	13	26	8♎	20	2♏	14	26	8♐	20			
☿	0♓	1	2	3	4	4	5	5	5	5	4	4	3	2	1	0	29♒	28	27	26	25	24	23	22	21	21	20	20			
♀	26♑	27	28	30	1♒	2	3	5	6	7	8	10	11	12	13	15	16	17	18	20	21	22	23	25	26	27	28	30			
♂	25♒	26	27	28	28	29	0♓	1	2	2	3	4	5	6	6	7	8	9	10	10	11	12	13	13	14	15	16	17			
	1	6	11	16	21	26			1	11	21			1	11	21			1	16		1	16		1	16		1	11	21	
♃	10♎	10	10	10	9	9		♄	10♎	9	9		⚷	13♉	14	14		♅	30♏	30	♆	24♐	24	♇	24♎	24	☊	11♌	10	10	

MAR

	1	2	3	4	5	6	7	8	9	10	11	12	13	14	15	16	17	18	19	20	21	22	23	24	25	26	27	28	29	30	31
☉	10♓	11	12	13	14	15	16	17	18	19	20	21	22	23	24	25	26	27	28	29	0♈	1	2	3	4	5	6	7	8	9	10
☽	2♑	15	28	11♒	25	9♓	24	9♈	24	8♉	23	7♊	21	5♋	18	2♌	15	27	10♍	22	4♎	16	28	10♏	22	4♐	16	28	10♑	23	6♒
☿	20♒	20	20	20	20	21	21	21	22	23	23	24	25	26	27	28	29	30	1♓	2	3	4	6	7	8	10	11	12	14	15	17
♀	1♓	2	3	5	6	7	8	10	11	12	13	15	16	17	18	20	21	22	23	25	26	27	28	30	1♈	2	3	5	6	7	8
♂	17♓	18	19	20	21	21	22	23	24	24	25	26	27	28	28	29	30	1♈	1	2	3	4	5	5	6	7	8	8	9	10	11
	1	6	11	16	21	26	31		1	11	21	31		1	11	21	31		1	16		1	16		1	16		1	11	21	31
♃	9♎	8	7	7	6	6	5	♄	8♎	8	7	6	⚷	14♉	15	15	16	♅	0♐	0	♆	25♐	25	♇	24♎	24	☊	9♌	9	8	8

APR

	1	2	3	4	5	6	7	8	9	10	11	12	13	14	15	16	17	18	19	20	21	22	23	24	25	26	27	28	29	30	
☉	11♈	12	13	14	15	16	17	18	19	20	21	22	23	24	25	26	27	28	29	30	1♉	2	3	4	5	6	7	8	9	10	
☽	19♒	3♓	17	2♈	17	2♉	18	3♊	17	1♋	15	29	12♌	24	7♍	19	1♎	13	25	7♏	19	1♐	13	25	7♑	19	2♒	14	28	12♓	
☿	18♓	20	21	23	24	26	28	29	1♈	3	5	6	8	10	12	14	16	17	19	21	23	25	27	30	2♉	4	6	8	10	12	
♀	10♈	11	12	13	15	16	17	18	19	21	22	23	24	26	27	28	29	1♉	2	3	4	6	7	8	9	10	12	13	14	15	
♂	12♈	12	13	14	15	15	16	17	18	18	19	20	21	21	22	23	24	24	25	26	27	28	28	29	30	1♉	1	2	3	4	
	1	6	11	16	21	26			1	11	21			1	11	21			1	16		1	16		1	16		1	11	21	
♃	5♎	4	4	3	2	2		♄	6♎	5	5		⚷	16♉	16	17		♅	30♏	29	♆	25♐	25	♇	23♎	23	☊	8♌	7	7	

MAY

	1	2	3	4	5	6	7	8	9	10	11	12	13	14	15	16	17	18	19	20	21	22	23	24	25	26	27	28	29	30	31
☉	11♉	12	12	13	14	15	16	17	18	19	20	21	22	23	24	25	26	27	28	29	30	1♊	2	3	4	5	6	7	8	8	9
☽	26♓	10♈	26	11♉	26	11♊	26	11♋	25	8♌	21	4♍	16	28	10♎	22	4♏	16	28	10♐	22	4♑	16	28	11♒	24	7♓	21	5♈	19	4♉
☿	14♉	17	19	21	23	25	27	29	1♊	3	5	7	9	11	12	14	16	17	19	20	21	23	24	25	26	27	28	29	0♋	1	2
♀	17♉	18	19	20	22	23	24	25	27	28	29	0♊	1	3	4	5	6	8	9	10	11	13	14	15	16	17	19	20	21	22	24
♂	4♉	5	6	6	7	8	9	9	10	11	12	12	13	14	15	15	16	17	18	18	19	20	20	21	22	23	23	24	25	26	26
	1	6	11	16	21	26	31		1	11	21	31		1	11	21	31		1	16		1	16		1	16		1	11	21	31
♃	2♎	1	1	1	1	0	0	♄	4♎	4	3	3	⚷	17♉	18	19	19	♅	29♏	28	♆	25♐	24	♇	22♎	22	☊	6♌	6	5	5

JUN

	1	2	3	4	5	6	7	8	9	10	11	12	13	14	15	16	17	18	19	20	21	22	23	24	25	26	27	28	29	30	
☉	10♊	11	12	13	14	15	16	17	18	19	20	21	22	23	24	25	26	27	28	29	30	0♋	1	2	3	4	5	6	7	8	
☽	19♉	5♊	20	5♋	19	3♌	17	30	13♍	25	7♎	19	1♏	13	25	7♐	19	1♑	13	26	8♒	21	4♓	17	1♈	15	29	14♉	29	13♊	
☿	2♋	3	4	4	4	5	5	5	5	5	5	5	5	4	4	4	3	3	2	2	1	1	30♊	29	29	28	28	27	27	27	
♀	25♊	26	27	28	30	1♋	2	3	5	6	7	8	9	11	12	13	14	16	17	18	19	20	22	23	24	25	27	28	29	0♌	
♂	27♉	28	28	29	30	1♊	1	2	3	3	4	5	6	6	7	8	8	9	10	10	11	12	13	13	14	15	15	16	17	17	
	1	6	11	16	21	26			1	11	21			1	11	21			1	16		1	16		1	16		1	11	21	
♃	0♎	1	1	1	1	2		♄	3♎	3	3		⚷	20♉	20	21		♅	28♏	27	♆	24♐	23	♇	22♎	22	☊	5♌	4	3	

1981

EPHEMERIS

JUL	1	2	3	4	5	6	7	8	9	10	11	12	13	14	15	16	17	18	19	20	21	22	23	24	25	26	27	28	29	30	31
☉	9♋	10	11	12	13	14	15	16	17	18	19	20	21	21	22	23	24	25	26	27	28	29	0♌	1	2	3	4	5	6	7	8
☽	28♊	13♋	27	11♌	25	8♍	21	3♎	15	27	9♏	21	3♐	15	27	10♑	22	5♒	18	1♓	14	28	12♈	26	10♉	24	9♊	23	7♋	22	6♌
☿	27♊	26	26	26	26	27	27	27	28	28	29	29	0♋	1	2	3	4	5	6	8	9	11	12	14	15	17	19	21	23	24	26
♀	1♌	3	4	5	6	7	9	10	11	12	14	15	16	17	18	20	21	22	23	24	26	27	28	29	0♍	2	3	4	5	7	8
♂	18♊	19	20	20	21	22	22	23	24	24	25	26	26	27	28	28	29	30	0♋	1	2	2	3	4	4	5	6	6	7	8	8
	1	6	11	16	21	26	31		1	11	21	31		1	11	21	31		1	16		1	16		1	16		1	11	21	31
♃	2♎	3	3	4	4	5	6	♄	4♎	4	5	5	⚷	21♉	22	22	22	♅	27♏	26	♆	23♐	23	♇	22♎	22	☊	3♌	2	2	1

AUG	1	2	3	4	5	6	7	8	9	10	11	12	13	14	15	16	17	18	19	20	21	22	23	24	25	26	27	28	29	30	31
☉	9♌	10	11	12	12	13	14	15	16	17	18	19	20	21	22	23	24	25	26	27	28	29	30	1♍	2	3	4	5	6	7	7
☽	19♌	3♍	16	29	11♎	23	6♏	17	29	11♐	23	5♑	18	1♒	14	27	10♓	24	8♈	22	7♉	21	5♊	19	3♋	17	1♌	15	28	11♍	24
☿	28♋	0♌	3	5	7	9	11	13	15	17	19	21	23	25	27	29	1♍	3	5	7	8	10	12	14	15	17	19	21	22	24	25
♀	9♍	10	11	13	14	15	16	17	19	20	21	22	23	25	26	27	28	29	1♎	2	3	4	5	6	8	9	10	11	12	14	15
♂	9♋	10	10	11	12	12	13	14	14	15	16	16	17	18	18	19	20	20	21	22	22	23	24	24	25	25	26	27	27	28	29
	1	6	11	16	21	26	31		1	11	21	31		1	11	21	31		1	16		1	16		1	16		1	11	21	31
♃	6♎	7	8	9	10	11	11	♄	6♎	6	7	9	⚷	23♉	23	23	23	♅	26♏	26	♆	22♐	22	♇	22♎	22	☊	1♌	1	0	30♋

SEP	1	2	3	4	5	6	7	8	9	10	11	12	13	14	15	16	17	18	19	20	21	22	23	24	25	26	27	28	29	30
☉	8♍	9	10	11	12	13	14	15	16	17	18	19	20	21	22	23	24	25	26	27	28	29	30	1♎	2	3	4	5	6	7
☽	7♎	19	1♏	13	25	7♐	19	1♑	13	26	9♒	22	5♓	19	4♈	18	3♉	17	2♊	16	0♋	14	28	11♌	24	7♍	20	3♎	15	28
☿	27♍	29	0♎	2	3	5	6	7	9	10	12	13	14	16	17	18	19	21	22	23	24	25	26	27	28	29	30	0♏	1	2
♀	16♎	17	18	19	21	22	23	24	25	27	28	29	0♏	1	2	4	5	6	7	8	9	11	12	13	14	15	16	17	19	20
♂	29♋	30	1♌	1	2	2	3	4	4	5	6	6	7	8	8	9	9	10	11	11	12	12	13	14	14	15	16	16	17	17
	1	6	11	16	21	26			1	11	21			1	11	21			1	16		1	16		1	16		1	11	21
♃	12♎	13	14	15	16	17		♄	9♎	10	11		⚷	23♉	23	23		♅	26♏	27	♆	22♐	22	♇	23♎	23	☊	30♋	29	29

OCT	1	2	3	4	5	6	7	8	9	10	11	12	13	14	15	16	17	18	19	20	21	22	23	24	25	26	27	28	29	30	31
☉	8♎	9	10	11	12	13	14	15	16	17	18	19	20	21	22	23	24	25	26	27	28	28	29	0♏	1	2	3	4	5	6	7
☽	10♏	22	3♐	15	27	9♑	21	4♒	16	30	13♓	28	12♈	27	12♉	27	12♊	26	11♋	25	8♌	21	4♍	17	30	12♎	24	6♏	18	0♐	12
☿	2♏	3	3	4	4	4	4	4	3	3	2	2	1	0	29♎	28	27	25	24	23	22	21	20	19	19	18	18	18	18	19	19
♀	21♏	22	23	24	25	27	28	29	30	1♐	2	3	4	6	7	8	9	10	11	12	13	14	16	17	18	19	20	21	22	23	24
♂	18♌	19	19	20	20	21	22	22	23	23	24	25	25	26	26	27	28	28	29	29	30	1♍	1	2	2	3	3	4	5	5	6
	1	6	11	16	21	26	31		1	11	21	31		1	11	21	31		1	16		1	16		1	16		1	11	21	31
♃	18♎	19	20	21	22	23	24	♄	12♎	13	15	16	⚷	22♉	22	22	21	♅	27♏	28	♆	22♐	23	♇	24♎	24	☊	28♋	28	27	26

NOV	1	2	3	4	5	6	7	8	9	10	11	12	13	14	15	16	17	18	19	20	21	22	23	24	25	26	27	28	29	30
☉	8♏	9	10	11	12	13	14	15	16	18	19	20	21	22	23	24	25	26	27	28	29	30	1♐	2	3	4	5	6	7	8
☽	24♐	6♑	17	30	12♒	25	8♓	21	6♈	20	5♉	20	6♊	21	6♋	20	4♌	18	1♍	14	27	9♎	21	3♏	15	27	9♐	21	3♑	14
☿	20♎	21	22	23	24	25	27	28	29	1♏	2	4	5	7	8	10	11	13	14	16	18	19	21	22	24	25	27	29	0♐	2
♀	25♐	26	27	28	29	0♑	2	3	4	5	6	7	8	9	10	11	12	12	13	14	15	16	17	18	19	20	21	22	22	23
♂	6♍	7	7	8	9	9	10	10	11	11	12	12	13	14	14	15	15	16	16	17	17	18	18	19	19	20	21	21	22	22
	1	6	11	16	21	26			1	11	21			1	11	21			1	16		1	16		1	16		1	11	21
♃	25♎	26	27	28	29	30		♄	16♎	17	18		⚷	21♉	20	20		♅	29♏	30	♆	23♐	23	♇	25♎	25	☊	26♋	26	25

DEC	1	2	3	4	5	6	7	8	9	10	11	12	13	14	15	16	17	18	19	20	21	22	23	24	25	26	27	28	29	30	31
☉	9♐	10	11	12	13	14	15	16	17	18	19	20	21	22	23	24	25	26	27	28	29	0♑	1	2	3	4	5	6	7	8	9
☽	26♑	9♒	21	4♓	17	0♈	14	28	13♉	28	14♊	29	14♋	29	13♌	27	10♍	23	6♎	18	0♏	12	24	6♐	18	30	11♑	23	6♒	18	1♓
☿	3♐	5	7	8	10	11	13	14	16	17	19	21	22	24	25	27	29	0♑	2	3	5	6	8	10	11	13	14	16	18	19	21
♀	24♑	25	26	26	27	28	29	29	0♒	1	1	2	3	3	4	4	5	5	6	6	7	7	7	8	8	8	8	9	9	9	9
♂	23♍	23	24	24	25	25	26	26	27	27	28	28	29	29	30	30	0♎	1	1	2	2	3	3	4	4	5	5	5	6	6	7
	1	6	11	16	21	26	31		1	11	21	31		1	11	21	31		1	16		1	16		1	16		1	11	21	31
♃	1♏	2	3	4	4	5	6	♄	19♎	20	21	21	⚷	19♉	19	19	18	♅	1♐	2	♆	24♐	25	♇	26♎	26	☊	25♋	24	24	23

1982

JAN

	1	2	3	4	5	6	7	8	9	10	11	12	13	14	15	16	17	18	19	20	21	22	23	24	25	26	27	28	29	30	31
☉	10♑	11	12	13	14	15	16	17	18	19	20	21	22	23	25	26	27	28	29	30	1♒	2	3	4	5	6	7	8	9	10	11
☽	13♓	26	10♈	24	8♉	22	7♊	22	7♋	22	6♌	21	5♍	18	1♎	14	27	9♏	21	2♐	14	26	8♑	20	2♒	15	27	10♓	23	7♈	20
☿	23♑	24	26	27	29	0♒	2	4	5	7	8	9	11	12	13	14	15	16	17	18	18	18	19	19	18	18	17	17	16	15	13
♀	9♒	9	9	9	9	8	8	8	8	7	7	6	6	5	5	4	4	3	3	2	1	1	0	29♑	29	28	28	27	27	26	26
♂	7♎	7	8	8	9	9	9	10	10	11	11	11	12	12	12	13	13	13	14	14	14	14	15	15	15	16	16	16	16	17	17
	1	6	11	16	21	26	31		1	11	21	31		1	11	21	31		1	16		1	16		1	16		1	11	21	31
♃	6♏	7	7	8	9	9	9	♄	21♎	22	22	22	⚷	18♉	18	18	18	♅	3♐	3	♆	25♐	26	♇	27♎	27	☊	23♋	23	22	22

FEB

	1	2	3	4	5	6	7	8	9	10	11	12	13	14	15	16	17	18	19	20	21	22	23	24	25	26	27	28			
☉	12♒	13	14	15	16	17	18	19	20	21	22	23	24	25	26	27	28	29	0♓	1	2	3	4	5	6	7	8	9			
☽	4♉	18	2♊	17	1♋	16	0♌	14	29	13♍	26	9♎	22	4♏	17	29	10♐	22	4♑	16	28	11♒	23	6♓	20	3♈	17	1♉			
☿	12♒	11	10	9	7	6	6	5	4	4	3	3	3	3	3	3	4	4	5	5	6	7	7	8	9	10	11	12			
♀	25♑	25	25	24	24	24	24	24	23	23	23	23	23	24	24	24	24	24	25	25	25	26	26	27	27	27	28	29			
♂	17♎	17	17	18	18	18	18	18	18	18	19	19	19	19	19	19	19	19	19	19	19	19	19	19	19	19	19	19			
	1	6	11	16	21	26			1	11	21			1	11	21			1	16		1	16		1	16		1	11	21	
♃	9♏	10	10	10	10	10		♄	22♎	22	22		⚷	18♉	18	18		♅	4♐	4	♆	26♐	27	♇	27♎	27	☊	22♋	21	20	

MAR

	1	2	3	4	5	6	7	8	9	10	11	12	13	14	15	16	17	18	19	20	21	22	23	24	25	26	27	28	29	30	31
☉	10♓	11	12	13	14	15	16	17	18	19	20	21	22	23	24	25	26	27	28	29	0♈	1	2	3	4	5	6	7	8	9	10
☽	15♉	29	13♊	27	11♋	25	9♌	23	7♍	21	4♎	17	30	12♏	24	6♐	18	0♑	12	24	6♒	19	2♓	15	28	12♈	27	11♉	25	10♊	24
☿	13♒	14	16	17	18	19	21	22	23	25	26	27	29	0♓	2	3	5	6	8	9	11	13	14	16	18	19	21	23	25	27	28
♀	29♑	30	0♒	1	2	2	3	4	4	5	6	7	7	8	9	10	11	12	12	13	14	15	16	17	18	19	20	21	22	23	24
♂	19♎	19	19	18	18	18	18	18	18	17	17	17	17	16	16	16	15	15	15	15	14	14	14	13	13	12	12	12	11	11	11
	1	6	11	16	21	26	31		1	11	21	31		1	11	21	31		1	16		1	16		1	16		1	11	21	31
♃	10♏	10	10	10	9	9	9	♄	22♎	21	20	20	⚷	18♉	19	19	20	♅	5♐	5	♆	27♐	27	♇	27♎	26	☊	20♋	20	19	18

APR

	1	2	3	4	5	6	7	8	9	10	11	12	13	14	15	16	17	18	19	20	21	22	23	24	25	26	27	28	29	30	
☉	11♈	12	13	14	15	16	17	18	19	20	21	22	23	24	25	26	27	28	29	30	1♉	2	3	3	4	5	6	7	8	9	
☽	8♋	22	6♌	20	3♍	17	30	13♎	26	8♏	20	2♐	14	26	8♑	20	2♒	14	27	10♓	23	7♈	21	5♉	20	5♊	20	4♋	19	3♌	
☿	0♈	2	4	6	8	10	12	14	16	18	20	22	24	26	28	0♉	3	5	7	9	11	13	15	17	19	21	22	24	26	28	
♀	25♒	25	26	27	28	29	0♓	2	3	4	5	6	7	8	9	10	11	12	13	14	15	16	17	18	20	21	22	23	24	25	
♂	10♎	10	9	9	9	8	8	7	7	7	6	6	6	5	5	5	4	4	4	3	3	3	3	2	2	2	2	2	1	1	
	1	6	11	16	21	26			1	11	21			1	11	21			1	16		1	16		1	16		1	11	21	
♃	8♏	8	7	7	6	5		♄	20♎	19	18		⚷	20♉	20	21		♅	4♐	4	♆	27♐	27	♇	26♎	26	☊	18♋	18	17	

MAY

	1	2	3	4	5	6	7	8	9	10	11	12	13	14	15	16	17	18	19	20	21	22	23	24	25	26	27	28	29	30	31
☉	10♉	11	12	13	14	15	16	17	18	19	20	21	22	23	24	25	26	27	28	29	30	1♊	2	3	3	4	5	6	7	8	9
☽	17♌	0♍	13	26	9♎	22	4♏	17	29	11♐	23	4♑	16	28	10♒	22	5♓	18	1♈	15	29	14♉	29	14♊	29	14♋	29	13♌	27	10♍	23
☿	29♉	1♊	2	3	5	6	7	8	9	10	11	12	13	13	14	14	15	15	15	15	15	15	15	15	15	14	14	13	13	13	12
♀	26♓	27	28	29	1♈	2	3	4	5	6	7	8	10	11	12	13	14	15	16	17	19	20	21	22	23	24	26	27	28	29	0♉
♂	1♎	1	1	1	1	1	1	0	0	0	0	0	0	0	0	0	1	1	1	1	1	1	1	1	1	2	2	2	2	2	3
	1	6	11	16	21	26	31		1	11	21	31		1	11	21	31		1	16		1	16		1	16		1	11	21	31
♃	5♏	4	4	3	2	2	2	♄	17♎	17	16	16	⚷	22♉	22	23	24	♅	4♐	3	♆	27♐	26	♇	25♎	25	☊	17♋	16	16	15

JUN

	1	2	3	4	5	6	7	8	9	10	11	12	13	14	15	16	17	18	19	20	21	22	23	24	25	26	27	28	29	30	
☉	10♊	11	12	13	14	15	16	17	18	19	20	21	22	23	24	25	25	26	27	28	29	0♋	1	2	3	4	5	6	7	8	
☽	6♎	19	1♏	14	26	8♐	20	1♑	13	25	7♒	19	1♓	14	27	10♈	23	8♉	22	7♊	22	7♋	23	7♌	22	6♍	20	3♎	16	28	
☿	11♊	11	10	10	9	9	8	8	7	7	7	7	7	7	7	7	7	7	8	8	8	9	10	10	11	12	13	14	15	16	
♀	1♉	2	4	5	6	7	8	9	11	12	13	14	15	16	18	19	20	21	22	23	25	26	27	28	29	1♊	2	3	4	5	
♂	3♎	3	3	3	4	4	4	5	5	5	5	6	6	6	7	7	7	8	8	9	9	9	10	10	10	11	11	12	12	13	
	1	6	11	16	21	26			1	11	21			1	11	21			1	16		1	16		1	16		1	11	21	
♃	1♏	1	1	1	1	0		♄	16♎	16	16		⚷	24♉	25	25		♅	2♐	2	♆	26♐	26	♇	24♎	24	☊	15♋	15	14	

1982

JUL

	1	2	3	4	5	6	7	8	9	10	11	12	13	14	15	16	17	18	19	20	21	22	23	24	25	26	27	28	29	30	31
☉	9♋	10	11	12	13	14	15	16	16	17	18	19	20	21	22	23	24	25	26	27	28	29	30	1♌	2	3	4	5	6	7	7
☽	11♏	23	5♐	17	28	10♑	22	4♒	16	28	11♓	23	6♈	19	3♉	17	1♊	16	1♋	16	1♌	16	0♍	15	28	12♎	25	7♏	20	2♐	13
☿	17♊	19	20	21	23	24	26	27	29	1♋	3	5	6	8	10	12	14	16	19	21	23	25	27	29	1♌	3	6	8	10	12	14
♀	7♊	8	9	10	11	12	14	15	16	17	18	20	21	22	23	24	26	27	28	29	0♋	2	3	4	5	6	8	9	10	11	12
♂	13♎	13	14	14	15	15	16	16	17	17	18	18	19	19	20	20	21	21	22	22	23	23	24	24	25	25	26	26	27	27	28
	1	6	11	16	21	26	31		1	11	21	31		1	11	21	31		1	16		1	16		1	16		1	11	21	31
♃	0♏	1	1	1	1	2	2	♄	16♎	16	16	17	⚷	26♉	26	27	27	♅	1♐	1	♆	25♐	25	♇	24♎	24	☊	14♋	13	13	12

AUG

	1	2	3	4	5	6	7	8	9	10	11	12	13	14	15	16	17	18	19	20	21	22	23	24	25	26	27	28	29	30	31
☉	8♌	9	10	11	12	13	14	15	16	17	18	19	20	21	22	23	24	25	26	27	28	29	30	1♍	1	2	3	4	5	6	7
☽	25♐	7♑	19	1♒	13	25	8♓	20	3♈	16	29	13♉	27	11♊	25	10♋	25	9♌	24	9♍	23	7♎	20	3♏	16	28	10♐	22	4♑	15	27
☿	16♌	18	20	22	23	25	27	29	1♍	2	4	6	8	9	11	13	14	16	17	19	20	22	23	24	26	27	29	30	1♎	2	4
♀	14♋	15	16	17	18	20	21	22	23	25	26	27	28	29	1♌	2	3	4	6	7	8	9	10	12	13	14	15	17	18	19	20
♂	29♎	29	30	0♏	1	1	2	3	3	4	4	5	6	6	7	7	8	9	9	10	10	11	12	12	13	14	14	15	15	16	17
	1	6	11	16	21	26	31		1	11	21	31		1	11	21	31		1	16		1	16		1	16		1	11	21	31
♃	2♏	3	3	4	4	5	6	♄	17♎	18	19	20	⚷	27♉	27	28	28	♅	1♐	1	♆	25♐	24	♇	24♎	25	☊	12♋	11	11	10

SEP

	1	2	3	4	5	6	7	8	9	10	11	12	13	14	15	16	17	18	19	20	21	22	23	24	25	26	27	28	29	30	
☉	8♍	9	10	11	12	13	14	15	16	17	18	19	20	21	22	23	24	25	26	27	28	29	30	1♎	2	3	4	5	6	7	
☽	9♒	22	4♓	17	30	13♈	26	10♉	24	8♊	22	6♋	20	4♌	19	3♍	17	1♎	15	28	11♏	24	6♐	18	30	12♑	23	5♒	17	30	
☿	5♎	6	7	8	9	10	11	12	13	14	14	15	16	16	17	17	17	17	18	18	17	17	17	16	16	15	14	13	12	11	
♀	21♌	23	24	25	26	28	29	0♍	1	3	4	5	6	8	9	10	11	13	14	15	16	17	19	20	21	22	24	25	26	27	
♂	17♏	18	19	19	20	21	21	22	23	23	24	25	25	26	27	27	28	29	29	30	1♐	1	2	3	3	4	5	5	6	7	
	1	6	11	16	21	26			1	11	21			1	11	21			1	16		1	16		1	16		1	11	21	
♃	6♏	7	8	9	10	11		♄	20♎	21	22		⚷	28♉	28	28		♅	1♐	1	♆	24♐	24	♇	25♎	26	☊	10♋	10	9	

OCT

	1	2	3	4	5	6	7	8	9	10	11	12	13	14	15	16	17	18	19	20	21	22	23	24	25	26	27	28	29	30	31
☉	7♎	8	9	10	11	12	13	14	15	16	17	18	19	20	21	22	23	24	25	26	27	28	29	0♏	1	2	3	4	5	6	7
☽	13♓	26	9♈	22	6♉	20	4♊	18	3♋	17	1♌	15	29	13♍	26	10♎	23	6♏	19	2♐	14	26	8♑	19	1♒	13	25	8♓	20	4♈	17
☿	10♎	9	8	7	6	5	4	3	3	3	2	2	3	3	4	4	5	6	7	8	10	11	12	14	15	17	19	20	22	23	25
♀	29♍	30	1♎	2	4	5	6	7	9	10	11	12	14	15	16	17	19	20	21	22	24	25	26	27	29	30	1♏	2	4	5	6
♂	8♐	8	9	10	10	11	12	13	13	14	15	15	16	17	18	18	19	20	20	21	22	23	23	24	25	26	26	27	28	29	29
	1	6	11	16	21	26	31		1	11	21	31		1	11	21	31		1	16		1	16		1	16		1	11	21	31
♃	12♏	13	14	15	16	17	18	♄	23♎	24	25	27	⚷	27♉	27	27	26	♅	2♐	2	♆	24♐	25	♇	26♎	27	☊	9♋	8	8	7

NOV

	1	2	3	4	5	6	7	8	9	10	11	12	13	14	15	16	17	18	19	20	21	22	23	24	25	26	27	28	29	30	
☉	8♏	9	10	11	12	13	14	15	16	17	18	19	20	21	22	23	24	25	26	27	28	29	0♐	1	2	3	4	5	6	7	
☽	1♉	15	30	14♊	29	13♋	28	12♌	26	9♍	23	6♎	19	2♏	15	27	10♐	22	4♑	16	27	9♒	21	3♓	16	28	11♈	25	9♉	24	
☿	27♎	28	30	2♏	3	5	7	8	10	11	13	15	16	18	19	21	23	24	26	27	29	1♐	2	4	5	7	8	10	12	13	
♀	7♏	9	10	11	12	14	15	16	17	19	20	21	23	24	25	26	28	29	0♐	1	3	4	5	6	8	9	10	11	13	14	
♂	0♑	1	2	2	3	4	5	5	6	7	8	8	9	10	11	11	12	13	14	14	15	16	17	17	18	19	20	21	21	22	
	1	6	11	16	21	26			1	11	21			1	11	21			1	16		1	16		1	16		1	11	21	
♃	18♏	19	20	21	23	24		♄	27♎	28	29		⚷	26♉	26	25		♅	3♐	4	♆	25♐	26	♇	27♎	28	☊	7♋	7	6	

DEC

	1	2	3	4	5	6	7	8	9	10	11	12	13	14	15	16	17	18	19	20	21	22	23	24	25	26	27	28	29	30	31
☉	8♐	9	10	11	13	14	15	16	17	18	19	20	21	22	23	24	25	26	27	28	29	30	1♑	2	3	4	5	6	7	8	9
☽	8♊	23	8♋	23	8♌	22	6♍	20	3♎	16	29	12♏	24	6♐	18	0♑	12	24	6♒	18	30	12♓	24	7♈	20	3♉	17	1♊	16	1♋	16
☿	15♐	16	18	19	21	22	24	26	27	29	0♑	2	3	5	6	8	9	11	13	14	15	17	18	20	21	23	24	25	26	27	29
♀	15♐	16	18	19	20	21	23	24	25	26	28	29	0♑	1	3	4	5	6	8	9	10	11	13	14	15	17	18	19	20	22	23
♂	23♑	24	24	25	26	27	27	28	29	30	1♒	1	2	3	4	4	5	6	7	8	8	9	10	11	12	12	13	14	15	15	16
	1	6	11	16	21	26	31		1	11	21	31		1	11	21	31		1	16		1	16		1	16		1	11	21	31
♃	25♏	26	27	28	29	30	1♐	♄	0♏	1	2	3	⚷	25♉	24	24	23	♅	5♐	6	♆	26♐	27	♇	28♎	29	☊	5♋	5	4	4

1983

EPHEMERIS

JAN	1	2	3	4	5	6	7	8	9	10	11	12	13	14	15	16	17	18	19	20	21	22	23	24	25	26	27	28	29	30	31
☉	10♑	11	12	13	14	15	16	17	18	19	20	21	22	23	24	25	26	27	28	29	0♒	1	2	3	4	5	6	7	9	10	11
☽	2♌	17	1♍	16	30	13♎	26	9♏	21	3♐	15	27	9♑	21	3♒	15	26	9♓	21	3♈	16	29	12♉	26	10♊	24	9♋	24	9♌	25	10♍
☿	30♑	0♒	1	2	2	2	3	3	2	2	1	0	29♑	28	27	26	24	23	22	21	20	19	18	17	17	17	16	16	17	17	17
♀	24♑	25	27	28	29	0♒	2	3	4	5	7	8	9	10	12	13	14	15	17	18	19	20	22	23	24	25	27	28	29	0♓	2
♂	17♒	18	19	19	20	21	22	22	23	24	25	26	26	27	28	29	30	0♓	1	2	3	3	4	5	6	7	7	8	9	10	11
	1	6	11	16	21	26	31		1	11	21	31		1	11	21	31		1	16		1	16		1	16		1	11	21	31
♃	1♐	2	3	4	5	6	6	♄	3♏	4	4	4	⚷	23♉	23	23	23	♅	7♐	8	♆	27♐	28	♇	29♎	29	☊	4♋	3	3	2

FEB	1	2	3	4	5	6	7	8	9	10	11	12	13	14	15	16	17	18	19	20	21	22	23	24	25	26	27	28			
☉	12♒	13	14	15	16	17	18	19	20	21	22	23	24	25	26	27	28	29	30	1♓	2	3	4	5	6	7	8	9			
☽	24♍	8♎	22	5♏	18	0♐	12	24	6♑	18	30	12♒	23	6♓	18	0♈	13	25	8♉	22	5♊	19	3♋	18	3♌	18	3♍	17			
☿	18♑	18	19	20	20	21	22	23	24	25	26	27	28	30	1♒	2	3	5	6	7	9	10	11	13	14	16	17	19			
♀	3♓	4	5	7	8	9	10	12	13	14	15	17	18	19	20	21	23	24	25	26	28	29	0♈	1	3	4	5	6			
♂	11♓	12	13	14	14	15	16	17	18	18	19	20	21	21	22	23	24	25	25	26	27	28	28	29	30	1♈	2	2			
	1	6	11	16	21	26			1	11	21			1	11	21			1	16		1	16		1	16		1	11	21	
♃	7♐	7	8	9	9	10		♄	4♏	4	4		⚷	23♉	23	23		♅	8♐	9	♆	28♐	29	♇	30♎	29	☊	2♋	2	1	

MAR	1	2	3	4	5	6	7	8	9	10	11	12	13	14	15	16	17	18	19	20	21	22	23	24	25	26	27	28	29	30	31
☉	10♓	11	12	13	14	15	16	17	18	19	20	21	22	23	24	25	26	27	28	29	30	1♈	2	3	4	5	6	7	8	9	10
☽	2♎	16	0♏	13	26	9♐	21	3♑	15	26	8♒	20	2♓	14	27	10♈	22	5♉	19	2♊	16	29	14♋	28	12♌	27	11♍	26	10♎	24	8♏
☿	20♒	22	23	25	26	28	30	1♓	3	5	6	8	10	12	13	15	17	19	21	23	24	26	28	0♈	2	4	6	8	10	12	14
♀	8♈	9	10	11	12	14	15	16	17	19	20	21	22	23	25	26	27	28	30	1♉	2	3	4	6	7	8	9	10	12	13	14
♂	3♈	4	5	5	6	7	8	8	9	10	11	11	12	13	14	15	15	16	17	18	18	19	20	21	21	22	23	24	24	25	26
	1	6	11	16	21	26	31		1	11	21	31		1	11	21	31		1	16		1	16		1	16		1	11	21	31
♃	10♐	10	10	11	11	11	11	♄	4♏	4	3	3	⚷	23♉	23	24	24	♅	9♐	9	♆	29♐	29	♇	29♎	29	☊	1♋	0	30♊	29

APR	1	2	3	4	5	6	7	8	9	10	11	12	13	14	15	16	17	18	19	20	21	22	23	24	25	26	27	28	29	30	
☉	11♈	12	13	14	15	16	17	18	19	20	21	22	23	23	24	25	26	27	28	29	0♉	1	2	3	4	5	6	7	8	9	
☽	21♏	4♐	17	29	11♑	23	4♒	16	28	10♓	23	6♈	18	2♉	15	29	12♊	26	10♋	24	9♌	23	7♍	21	5♎	19	3♏	16	29	12♐	
☿	16♈	19	21	23	25	27	29	1♉	2	4	6	8	10	11	13	14	16	17	18	19	20	21	22	23	23	24	25	25	25	25	
♀	15♉	16	18	19	20	21	22	24	25	26	27	28	29	1♊	2	3	4	5	6	8	9	10	11	12	13	15	16	17	18	19	
♂	27♈	27	28	29	30	0♉	1	2	3	3	4	5	5	6	7	8	8	9	10	11	11	12	13	14	14	15	16	16	17	18	
	1	6	11	16	21	26			1	11	21			1	11	21			1	16		1	16		1	16		1	11	21	
♃	11♐	11	11	10	10	10		♄	3♏	2	1		⚷	24♉	25	26		♅	9♐	9	♆	29♐	29	♇	29♎	28	☊	29♊	29	28	

MAY	1	2	3	4	5	6	7	8	9	10	11	12	13	14	15	16	17	18	19	20	21	22	23	24	25	26	27	28	29	30	31
☉	10♉	11	12	13	14	15	16	17	18	19	20	21	22	23	24	25	26	27	27	28	29	0♊	1	2	3	4	5	6	7	8	9
☽	24♐	7♑	19	0♒	12	24	6♓	18	1♈	14	27	10♉	24	8♊	22	7♋	21	5♌	20	4♍	18	2♎	15	29	12♏	25	8♐	20	2♑	15	27
☿	26♉	26	25	25	25	25	24	24	23	23	22	22	21	21	20	19	19	18	18	18	17	17	17	17	16	16	16	17	17	17	18
♀	20♊	22	23	24	25	26	27	28	29	1♋	2	3	4	5	6	7	8	10	11	12	13	14	15	16	17	18	19	20	21	22	24
♂	19♉	19	20	21	22	22	23	24	24	25	26	27	27	28	29	29	0♊	1	1	2	3	4	4	5	6	6	7	8	9	9	10
	1	6	11	16	21	26	31		1	11	21	31		1	11	21	31		1	16		1	16		1	16		1	11	21	31
♃	9♐	9	8	8	7	6	6	♄	0♏	30♎	29	29	⚷	26♉	27	28	29	♅	8♐	8	♆	29♐	29	♇	28♎	27	☊	28♊	27	26	26

JUN	1	2	3	4	5	6	7	8	9	10	11	12	13	14	15	16	17	18	19	20	21	22	23	24	25	26	27	28	29	30	
☉	10♊	11	12	13	14	15	16	17	18	19	20	20	21	22	23	24	25	26	27	28	29	0♋	1	2	3	4	5	6	7	8	
☽	8♒	20	2♓	14	26	9♈	22	5♉	19	3♊	17	1♋	16	1♌	16	0♍	14	28	12♎	26	9♏	22	4♐	17	29	11♑	23	5♒	17	29	
☿	18♉	18	19	20	20	21	22	23	24	25	26	27	28	30	1♊	2	4	5	7	8	10	11	13	15	17	18	20	22	24	26	
♀	25♋	26	27	28	29	30	1♌	2	3	4	5	6	7	8	9	10	11	12	13	13	14	15	16	17	18	19	20	21	21	22	
♂	11♊	11	12	13	13	14	15	15	16	17	18	18	19	20	20	21	22	22	23	24	24	25	26	26	27	28	28	29	30	0♋	
	1	6	11	16	21	26			1	11	21			1	11	21			1	16		1	16		1	16		1	11	21	
♃	6♐	5	4	4	3	3		♄	28♎	28	28		⚷	29♉	29	30		♅	7♐	6	♆	28♐	28	♇	27♎	27	☊	26♊	25	25	

EPHEMERIS

1983

JUL

	1	2	3	4	5	6	7	8	9	10	11	12	13	14	15	16	17	18	19	20	21	22	23	24	25	26	27	28	29	30	31
☉	9♋	10	11	11	12	13	14	15	16	17	18	19	20	21	22	23	24	25	26	27	28	29	30	1♌	2	2	3	4	5	6	7
☽	10♓	22	5♈	17	30	13♉	27	11♊	25	10♋	25	10♌	25	10♍	25	9♎	22	6♏	19	1♐	14	26	8♑	20	2♒	14	25	7♓	19	1♈	14
☿	28♊	0♋	3	5	7	9	11	13	15	18	20	22	24	26	28	0♌	2	4	6	8	10	12	14	16	18	19	21	23	24	26	28
♀	23♌	24	25	25	26	27	28	28	29	30	1♍	1	2	2	3	4	4	5	5	6	6	7	7	7	8	8	8	9	9	9	9
♂	1♋	2	3	3	4	5	5	6	7	7	8	9	9	10	11	11	12	13	13	14	15	15	16	16	17	18	18	19	20	20	21
	1	6	11	16	21	26	31		1	11	21	31		1	11	21	31		1	16		1	16		1	16		1	11	21	31
♃	2♐	2	2	1	1	1	1	♄	28♎	28	28	28	⚷	1♊	1	2	2	♅	6♐	5	♆	28♐	27	♇	27♎	27	☊	24♊	24	23	23

AUG

	1	2	3	4	5	6	7	8	9	10	11	12	13	14	15	16	17	18	19	20	21	22	23	24	25	26	27	28	29	30	31
☉	8♌	9	10	11	12	13	14	15	16	17	18	19	20	21	22	23	24	25	25	26	27	28	29	0♍	1	2	3	4	5	6	7
☽	26♈	9♉	22	5♊	19	4♋	18	3♌	19	4♍	19	4♎	18	2♏	15	28	11♐	23	5♑	17	29	11♒	22	4♓	16	28	11♈	23	5♉	18	1♊
☿	29♌	1♍	2	4	5	7	8	10	11	12	14	15	16	17	19	20	21	22	23	24	25	26	26	27	28	28	29	29	30	0♎	1
♀	9♍	9	9	9	9	9	9	9	9	9	8	8	8	7	7	7	6	6	5	5	4	3	3	2	2	1	0	30♌	29	28	28
♂	22♋	22	23	24	24	25	26	26	27	28	28	29	30	0♌	1	1	2	3	3	4	5	5	6	7	7	8	9	9	10	10	11
	1	6	11	16	21	26	31		1	11	21	31		1	11	21	31		1	16		1	16		1	16		1	11	21	31
♃	1♐	1	1	2	2	2	3	♄	28♎	29	30	1♏	⚷	2♊	3	3	3	♅	5♐	5	♆	27♐	27	♇	27♎	27	☊	23♊	22	22	21

SEP

	1	2	3	4	5	6	7	8	9	10	11	12	13	14	15	16	17	18	19	20	21	22	23	24	25	26	27	28	29	30	
☉	8♍	9	10	11	12	13	14	15	16	17	18	19	20	21	22	23	24	25	25	26	27	28	29	0♎	1	2	3	4	5	6	
☽	15♊	28	12♋	27	12♌	27	12♍	27	12♎	27	10♏	24	7♐	19	2♑	14	26	8♒	19	1♓	13	25	8♈	20	3♉	15	28	11♊	25	8♋	
☿	1♎	1	1	1	0	0	30♍	29	28	28	27	26	25	24	23	22	21	20	19	18	18	17	17	16	16	16	17	17	18	19	
♀	27♌	27	26	26	25	25	25	24	24	24	24	23	23	23	23	23	23	23	23	24	24	24	24	24	25	25	26	26	26	27	
♂	12♌	12	13	14	14	15	16	16	17	17	18	19	19	20	21	21	22	22	23	24	24	25	26	26	27	28	28	29	29	30	
	1	6	11	16	21	26			1	11	21			1	11	21			1	16		1	16		1	16		1	11	21	
♃	3♐	3	4	4	5	6		♄	1♏	2	3		⚷	3♊	3	3		♅	5♐	6	♆	26♐	26	♇	28♎	28	☊	21♊	20	20	

OCT

	1	2	3	4	5	6	7	8	9	10	11	12	13	14	15	16	17	18	19	20	21	22	23	24	25	26	27	28	29	30	31
☉	7♎	8	9	10	11	12	13	14	15	16	17	18	19	20	21	22	23	24	25	26	27	28	29	0♏	1	2	3	4	5	6	7
☽	22♋	7♌	21	6♍	21	6♎	20	5♏	19	2♐	15	28	10♑	22	4♒	16	28	10♓	22	4♈	16	29	12♉	25	8♊	22	5♋	19	3♌	17	1♍
☿	19♍	20	22	23	24	25	27	28	0♎	2	3	5	7	8	10	12	14	15	17	19	20	22	24	26	27	29	1♏	2	4	6	7
♀	27♌	28	28	29	30	0♍	1	1	2	3	3	4	5	6	6	7	8	9	10	11	11	12	13	14	15	16	17	18	19	20	21
♂	1♍	1	2	2	3	4	4	5	6	6	7	7	8	9	9	10	10	11	12	12	13	14	14	15	15	16	17	17	18	18	19
	1	6	11	16	21	26	31		1	11	21	31		1	11	21	31		1	16		1	16		1	16		1	11	21	31
♃	7♐	8	8	9	10	11	12	♄	4♏	5	6	7	⚷	3♊	2	2	2	♅	6♐	7	♆	27♐	27	♇	29♎	29	☊	19♊	19	18	18

NOV

	1	2	3	4	5	6	7	8	9	10	11	12	13	14	15	16	17	18	19	20	21	22	23	24	25	26	27	28	29	30	
☉	8♏	9	10	11	12	13	14	15	16	17	18	19	20	21	22	23	24	25	26	27	28	29	0♐	1	2	3	4	5	6	7	
☽	16♍	0♎	15	29	13♏	27	10♐	23	5♑	18	30	12♒	24	6♓	18	30	12♈	25	7♉	21	4♊	18	2♋	16	30	14♌	28	12♍	27	11♎	
☿	9♏	10	12	14	15	17	18	20	22	23	25	26	28	29	1♐	3	4	6	7	9	10	12	13	15	16	18	19	21	22	24	
♀	21♍	22	23	24	25	26	27	29	30	1♎	2	3	4	5	6	7	8	9	10	11	12	13	15	16	17	18	19	20	21	22	
♂	20♍	20	21	21	22	23	23	24	24	25	26	26	27	27	28	29	29	30	0♎	1	2	2	3	3	4	4	5	6	6	7	
	1	6	11	16	21	26			1	11	21			1	11	21			1	16		1	16		1	16		1	11	21	
♃	12♐	13	14	16	17	18		♄	7♏	9	10		⚷	2♊	1	0		♅	8♐	8	♆	27♐	28	♇	30♎	0♏	☊	18♊	17	17	

DEC

	1	2	3	4	5	6	7	8	9	10	11	12	13	14	15	16	17	18	19	20	21	22	23	24	25	26	27	28	29	30	31
☉	8♐	9	10	11	12	13	14	15	16	17	18	19	20	21	22	23	24	25	27	28	29	30	1♑	2	3	4	5	6	7	8	9
☽	24♎	8♏	22	5♐	18	1♑	13	26	8♒	20	2♓	13	25	7♈	20	2♉	15	29	12♊	26	11♋	25	10♌	25	9♍	23	7♎	21	5♏	18	1♐
☿	25♐	26	28	29	1♑	2	3	5	6	7	9	10	11	12	13	14	15	15	16	16	17	17	17	16	16	15	14	13	12	11	9
♀	24♎	25	26	27	28	29	0♏	2	3	4	5	6	7	9	10	11	12	13	14	16	17	18	19	20	22	23	24	25	26	27	29
♂	7♎	8	8	9	10	10	11	11	12	12	13	14	14	15	15	16	16	17	18	18	19	19	20	20	21	21	22	23	23	24	24
	1	6	11	16	21	26	31		1	11	21	31		1	11	21	31		1	16		1	16		1	16		1	11	21	31
♃	19♐	20	21	22	23	25	26	♄	11♏	12	13	14	⚷	30♉	29	29	28	♅	9♐	10	♆	28♐	29	♇	1♏	1	☊	16♊	16	15	15

1984

EPHEMERIS

JAN

	1	2	3	4	5	6	7	8	9	10	11	12	13	14	15	16	17	18	19	20	21	22	23	24	25	26	27	28	29	30	31
☉	10♑	11	12	13	14	15	16	17	18	19	20	21	22	23	24	25	26	27	28	29	0♒	1	2	3	4	5	6	7	8	9	10
☽	14♐	27	9♑	22	4♒	16	28	10♓	21	3♈	15	28	10♉	23	6♊	20	4♋	19	4♌	19	4♍	19	4♎	18	2♏	15	28	11♐	24	6♑	18
☿	8♑	7	6	4	3	2	2	1	1	0	0	0	1	1	1	2	3	3	4	5	6	7	8	9	10	11	12	14	15	16	17
♀	30♏	1♐	2	4	5	6	7	8	10	11	12	13	14	16	17	18	19	20	22	23	24	25	27	28	29	0♑	1	3	4	5	6
♂	25♎	25	26	26	27	27	28	28	29	29	30	0♏	1	1	2	2	3	3	4	4	5	5	6	6	7	7	8	8	9	9	10
	1	6	11	16	21	26	31		1	11	21	31		1	11	21	31		1	16		1	16		1	16		1	11	21	31
♃	26♐	27	28	29	0♑	1	2	♄	14♏	15	15	16	⚷	28♉	28	28	28	♅	11♐	12	♆	29♐	30	♇	2♏	2	☊	15♊	14	13	13

FEB

	1	2	3	4	5	6	7	8	9	10	11	12	13	14	15	16	17	18	19	20	21	22	23	24	25	26	27	28	29		
☉	11♒	12	13	14	15	16	17	18	19	20	21	22	23	24	25	26	28	29	30	1♓	2	3	4	5	6	7	8	9	10		
☽	0♒	12	24	6♓	18	30	12♈	24	6♉	18	1♊	14	28	12♋	27	12♌	27	12♍	28	13♎	27	11♏	25	8♐	21	3♑	15	27	9♒		
☿	19♑	20	21	23	24	26	27	28	30	1♒	3	4	6	7	9	11	12	14	15	17	19	20	22	24	25	27	29	0♓	2		
♀	8♑	9	10	11	13	14	15	16	17	19	20	21	22	24	25	26	27	29	30	1♒	2	3	5	6	7	8	10	11	12		
♂	10♏	11	11	12	12	12	13	13	14	14	15	15	16	16	16	17	17	18	18	18	19	19	19	20	20	21	21	21	22		
	1	6	11	16	21	26			1	11	21			1	11	21			1	16		1	16		1	16		1	11	21	
♃	3♑	4	5	5	6	7		♄	16♏	16	16		⚷	28♉	28	28		♅	13♐	13	♆	0♑	1	♇	2♏	2	☊	13♊	12	12	

MAR

	1	2	3	4	5	6	7	8	9	10	11	12	13	14	15	16	17	18	19	20	21	22	23	24	25	26	27	28	29	30	31
☉	11♓	12	13	14	15	16	17	18	19	20	21	22	23	24	25	26	27	28	29	30	1♈	2	3	4	5	6	7	7	8	9	10
☽	21♒	3♓	15	27	9♈	21	3♉	15	28	10♊	23	7♋	21	5♌	20	5♍	21	6♎	21	6♏	20	4♐	17	30	12♑	24	6♒	18	0♓	12	24
☿	4♓	6	8	9	11	13	15	17	19	21	23	25	27	29	1♈	3	5	7	9	10	12	14	16	18	20	21	23	25	26	28	29
♀	13♒	15	16	17	18	19	21	22	23	24	26	27	28	29	1♓	2	3	4	6	7	8	9	10	12	13	14	15	17	18	19	20
♂	22♏	22	23	23	23	23	24	24	24	25	25	25	25	26	26	26	26	26	27	27	27	27	27	27	28	28	28	28	28	28	28
	1	6	11	16	21	26	31		1	11	21	31		1	11	21	31		1	16		1	16		1	16		1	11	21	31
♃	8♑	9	9	10	11	11	12	♄	16♏	16	16	15	⚷	28♉	28	29	29	♅	13♐	14	♆	1♑	1	♇	2♏	2	☊	11♊	11	10	10

APR

	1	2	3	4	5	6	7	8	9	10	11	12	13	14	15	16	17	18	19	20	21	22	23	24	25	26	27	28	29	30	
☉	11♈	12	13	14	15	16	17	18	19	20	21	22	23	24	25	26	27	28	29	0♉	1	2	3	4	5	6	7	8	9	10	
☽	6♈	18	0♉	12	25	7♊	20	3♋	17	1♌	15	29	14♍	29	14♎	29	14♏	28	12♐	25	8♑	21	3♒	15	27	9♓	21	2♈	14	27	
☿	0♉	1	2	3	4	5	5	6	6	7	7	7	7	6	6	6	5	5	4	4	3	2	2	1	0	30♈	29	28	28	28	
♀	22♓	23	24	25	26	28	29	0♈	1	3	4	5	6	8	9	10	11	13	14	15	16	17	19	20	21	22	24	25	26	27	
♂	28♏	28	28	28	28	28	28	28	28	28	28	28	28	28	28	28	28	27	27	27	27	27	26	26	26	26	25	25	25	25	
	1	6	11	16	21	26			1	11	21			1	11	21			1	16		1	16		1	16		1	11	21	
♃	12♑	12	12	13	13	13		♄	15♏	15	14		⚷	29♉	30	1♊		♅	13♐	13	♆	1♑	1	♇	1♏	1	☊	10♊	9	9	

MAY

	1	2	3	4	5	6	7	8	9	10	11	12	13	14	15	16	17	18	19	20	21	22	23	24	25	26	27	28	29	30	31
☉	11♉	12	13	14	15	16	17	18	19	20	20	21	22	23	24	25	26	27	28	29	0♊	1	2	3	4	5	6	7	8	9	10
☽	9♉	22	4♊	17	0♋	14	27	11♌	25	10♍	24	9♎	23	8♏	22	6♐	20	3♑	16	28	11♒	23	5♓	17	29	11♈	23	5♉	18	0♊	13
☿	27♈	27	27	26	26	26	26	27	27	27	27	28	28	29	30	0♉	1	2	3	4	5	6	7	8	9	11	12	13	15	16	17
♀	29♈	30	1♉	2	3	5	6	7	8	10	11	12	13	15	16	17	18	19	21	22	23	24	26	27	28	29	0♊	2	3	4	5
♂	24♏	24	24	23	23	23	22	22	22	21	21	21	20	20	20	19	19	18	18	18	17	17	17	16	16	16	15	15	15	15	14
	1	6	11	16	21	26	31		1	11	21	31		1	11	21	31		1	16		1	16		1	16		1	11	21	31
♃	13♑	13	13	13	12	12	11	♄	13♏	13	12	11	⚷	1♊	2	3	4	♅	13♐	12	♆	1♑	1	♇	0♏	0	☊	8♊	8	7	7

JUN

	1	2	3	4	5	6	7	8	9	10	11	12	13	14	15	16	17	18	19	20	21	22	23	24	25	26	27	28	29	30	
☉	11♊	12	13	14	15	15	16	17	18	19	20	21	22	23	24	25	26	27	28	29	30	1♋	2	3	4	5	6	6	7	8	
☽	27♊	10♋	24	8♌	22	6♍	20	5♎	19	3♏	17	1♐	15	28	11♑	24	6♒	19	1♓	13	25	7♈	19	1♉	13	26	9♊	22	6♋	20	
☿	19♉	20	22	24	25	27	29	1♊	2	4	6	8	10	12	14	16	19	21	23	25	27	29	2♋	4	6	8	10	12	15	17	
♀	7♊	8	9	10	12	13	14	15	16	18	19	20	21	23	24	25	26	28	29	30	1♋	2	4	5	6	7	9	10	11	12	
♂	14♏	14	14	13	13	13	13	13	12	12	12	12	12	12	12	12	12	12	12	12	12	12	12	12	12	12	12	12	12	12	
	1	6	11	16	21	26			1	11	21			1	11	21			1	16		1	16		1	16		1	11	21	
♃	11♑	11	10	10	9	9		♄	11♏	11	10		⚷	4♊	4	5		♅	12♐	11	♆	1♑	0	♇	30♎	29	☊	6♊	6	5	

1984

JUL

	1	2	3	4	5	6	7	8	9	10	11	12	13	14	15	16	17	18	19	20	21	22	23	24	25	26	27	28	29	30	31
☉	9♋	10	11	12	13	14	15	16	17	18	19	20	21	22	23	24	25	26	27	27	28	29	0♌	1	2	3	4	5	6	7	8
☽	4♌	18	3♍	17	2♎	16	30	14♏	27	11♐	24	7♑	20	2♒	15	27	9♓	21	3♈	15	27	9♉	21	4♊	17	0♋	14	28	13♌	28	13♍
☿	19♋	21	23	25	27	29	0♌	2	4	6	8	9	11	13	14	16	17	19	20	22	23	25	26	27	28	30	1♍	2	3	4	5
♀	13♋	15	16	17	18	20	21	22	23	25	26	27	28	29	1♌	2	3	4	6	7	8	9	11	12	13	14	15	17	18	19	20
♂	13♏	13	13	13	13	13	14	14	14	14	15	15	15	15	16	16	16	17	17	17	18	18	18	19	19	19	20	20	21	21	21
	1	6	11	16	21	26	31		1	11	21	31		1	11	21	31		1	16		1	16		1	16		1	11	21	31
♃	8♑	7	7	6	5	5	4	♄	10♏	10	10	10	⚷	6♊	6	7	7	♅	10♐	10	♆	30♐	29	♇	29♎	29	☊	5♊	4	4	3

AUG

	1	2	3	4	5	6	7	8	9	10	11	12	13	14	15	16	17	18	19	20	21	22	23	24	25	26	27	28	29	30	31
☉	9♌	10	11	12	13	14	15	16	17	18	19	19	20	21	22	23	24	25	26	27	28	29	0♍	1	2	3	4	5	6	7	8
☽	28♍	12♎	26	10♏	24	7♐	21	4♑	16	29	11♒	23	5♓	17	29	11♈	23	5♉	17	29	12♊	25	8♋	22	7♌	21	7♍	22	7♎	22	6♏
☿	6♍	7	8	9	10	10	11	11	12	12	13	13	13	13	13	13	13	13	13	12	12	11	10	10	9	8	7	6	5	4	3
♀	22♌	23	24	25	27	28	29	0♍	1	3	4	5	6	8	9	10	11	13	14	15	16	17	19	20	21	22	24	25	26	27	29
♂	22♏	22	23	23	24	24	25	25	26	26	27	27	28	28	29	29	30	0♐	1	1	2	2	3	3	4	4	5	6	6	7	7
	1	6	11	16	21	26	31		1	11	21	31		1	11	21	31		1	16		1	16		1	16		1	11	21	31
♃	4♑	4	4	3	3	3	3	♄	10♏	10	11	12	⚷	8♊	8	8	8	♅	10♐	10	♆	29♐	29	♇	29♎	30	☊	3♊	3	2	2

SEP

	1	2	3	4	5	6	7	8	9	10	11	12	13	14	15	16	17	18	19	20	21	22	23	24	25	26	27	28	29	30
☉	9♍	10	11	12	13	14	15	16	16	17	18	19	20	21	22	23	24	25	26	27	28	29	0♎	1	2	3	4	5	6	7
☽	21♏	4♐	18	1♑	13	26	8♒	20	2♓	14	26	8♈	20	2♉	14	26	8♊	21	3♋	17	1♌	15	30	15♍	0♎	15	1♏	15	30	14♐
☿	3♍	2	1	1	0	0	0	0	0	1	1	2	3	3	4	6	7	8	10	11	13	14	16	18	20	21	23	25	27	29
♀	30♍	1♎	2	3	5	6	7	8	10	11	12	13	14	16	17	18	19	21	22	23	24	26	27	28	29	0♏	2	3	4	5
♂	8♐	9	9	10	10	11	12	12	13	13	14	15	15	16	17	17	18	18	19	20	20	21	22	22	23	24	24	25	26	26
	1	6	11	16	21	26			1	11	21			1	11	21			1	16		1	16		1	16		1	11	21
♃	3♑	3	3	4	4	4		♄	12♏	12	13		⚷	8♊	9	9		♅	10♐	10	♆	29♐	29	♇	0♏	1	☊	2♊	1	1

OCT

	1	2	3	4	5	6	7	8	9	10	11	12	13	14	15	16	17	18	19	20	21	22	23	24	25	26	27	28	29	30	31
☉	8♎	9	10	11	12	13	14	15	16	17	18	19	20	21	22	23	24	25	26	27	28	29	30	1♏	2	3	4	5	6	7	8
☽	27♐	10♑	23	5♒	17	29	11♓	23	5♈	17	29	11♉	23	5♊	17	30	13♋	26	10♌	24	9♍	23	8♎	24	9♏	23	8♐	22	6♑	19	1♒
☿	0♎	2	4	6	8	9	11	13	15	16	18	20	21	23	25	26	28	30	1♏	3	5	6	8	9	11	13	14	16	17	19	20
♀	7♏	8	9	10	11	13	14	15	16	18	19	20	21	22	24	25	26	27	28	30	1♐	2	3	5	6	7	8	9	11	12	13
♂	27♐	28	28	29	30	1♑	1	2	3	3	4	5	5	6	7	8	8	9	10	10	11	12	13	13	14	15	15	16	17	18	18
	1	6	11	16	21	26	31		1	11	21	31		1	11	21	31		1	16		1	16		1	16		1	11	21	31
♃	5♑	5	6	6	7	8	9	♄	14♏	15	17	18	⚷	8♊	8	8	7	♅	10♐	11	♆	29♐	29	♇	1♏	2	☊	0♊	29♉	29	28

NOV

	1	2	3	4	5	6	7	8	9	10	11	12	13	14	15	16	17	18	19	20	21	22	23	24	25	26	27	28	29	30
☉	9♏	10	11	12	13	14	15	16	17	18	19	20	21	22	23	24	25	26	27	28	29	30	1♐	2	3	4	5	6	7	8
☽	14♒	26	8♓	20	2♈	14	26	8♉	20	2♊	14	27	10♋	23	6♌	20	4♍	18	3♎	17	2♏	17	1♐	16	30	13♑	27	10♒	22	4♓
☿	22♏	23	25	26	28	29	1♐	2	4	5	7	8	9	11	12	13	15	16	17	19	20	21	22	23	25	26	27	27	28	29
♀	14♐	16	17	18	19	20	22	23	24	25	26	28	29	0♑	1	2	4	5	6	7	8	10	11	12	13	14	16	17	18	19
♂	19♑	20	21	21	22	23	23	24	25	26	26	27	28	29	29	0♒	1	2	2	3	4	5	5	6	7	8	8	9	10	11
	1	6	11	16	21	26			1	11	21			1	11	21			1	16		1	16		1	16		1	11	21
♃	9♑	10	11	12	12	14		♄	18♏	19	20		⚷	7♊	7	6		♅	12♐	13	♆	29♐	30	♇	2♏	3	☊	28♉	28	27

DEC

	1	2	3	4	5	6	7	8	9	10	11	12	13	14	15	16	17	18	19	20	21	22	23	24	25	26	27	28	29	30	31
☉	9♐	10	11	12	13	14	15	16	17	18	19	20	21	22	23	24	25	26	27	28	29	0♑	1	2	3	4	5	6	7	8	9
☽	16♓	28	10♈	22	4♉	16	28	11♊	24	7♋	20	3♌	17	1♍	15	29	13♎	27	12♏	26	10♐	24	8♑	21	4♒	17	30	12♓	24	6♈	18
☿	30♐	0♑	1	1	1	1	0	30♐	29	28	27	26	25	24	22	21	20	18	17	16	16	15	15	15	15	15	15	15	16	16	17
♀	20♑	22	23	24	25	26	27	29	30	1♒	2	3	5	6	7	8	9	10	12	13	14	15	16	17	18	20	21	22	23	24	25
♂	11♒	12	13	14	15	15	16	17	18	18	19	20	21	21	22	23	24	24	25	26	27	27	28	29	30	1♓	1	2	3	4	4
	1	6	11	16	21	26	31		1	11	21	31		1	11	21	31		1	16		1	16		1	16		1	11	21	31
♃	15♑	16	17	18	19	20	21	♄	21♏	23	24	25	⚷	6♊	5	5	4	♅	14♐	14	♆	0♑	1	♇	3♏	4	☊	27♉	26	26	25

1985

JAN

	1	2	3	4	5	6	7	8	9	10	11	12	13	14	15	16	17	18	19	20	21	22	23	24	25	26	27	28	29	30	31
☉	11♑	12	13	14	15	16	17	18	19	20	21	22	23	24	25	26	27	28	29	30	1♒	2	3	4	5	6	7	8	9	10	11
☽	30♈	12♉	24	6♊	19	2♋	15	29	13♌	27	11♍	26	10♎	24	8♏	22	6♐	20	3♑	16	30	13♒	25	8♓	20	2♈	14	26	7♉	19	2♊
☿	18♐	19	20	21	22	23	24	25	26	28	29	0♑	2	3	4	6	7	8	10	11	13	14	16	17	19	20	22	23	25	26	28
♀	26♒	27	29	30	1♓	2	3	4	5	6	7	8	10	11	12	13	14	15	16	17	18	19	20	21	22	23	24	25	26	27	28
♂	5♓	6	7	7	8	9	10	10	11	12	13	14	14	15	16	17	17	18	19	20	20	21	22	23	23	24	25	26	26	27	28
	1	6	11	16	21	26	31		1	11	21	31		1	11	21	31		1	16		1	16		1	16		1	11	21	31
♃	21♑	23	24	25	26	27	28	♄	25♏	26	26	27	⚷	4♊	4	3	3	♅	15♐	16	♆	1♑	2	♇	4♏	5	☊	25♉	25	24	24

FEB

	1	2	3	4	5	6	7	8	9	10	11	12	13	14	15	16	17	18	19	20	21	22	23	24	25	26	27	28			
☉	12♒	13	14	15	16	17	18	19	20	21	22	23	24	25	26	27	28	29	0♓	1	2	3	4	5	6	7	8	9			
☽	14♊	27	10♋	24	8♌	22	7♍	21	6♎	21	5♏	19	3♐	16	30	13♑	26	9♒	21	4♓	16	28	10♈	22	4♉	15	27	9♊			
☿	29♑	1♒	3	4	6	8	9	11	13	14	16	18	19	21	23	25	26	28	0♓	2	4	6	7	9	11	13	15	17			
♀	29♓	30	1♈	2	2	3	4	5	6	7	8	8	9	10	11	11	12	13	14	14	15	16	16	17	17	18	18	19			
♂	29♓	29	0♈	1	2	2	3	4	5	5	6	7	8	8	9	10	11	11	12	13	14	14	15	16	17	17	18	19			
	1	6	11	16	21	26			1	11	21			1	11	21			1	16		1	16		1	16		1	11	21	
♃	29♑	30	1♒	2	3	4		♄	27♏	28	28		⚷	3♊	3	3		♅	17♐	17	♆	3♑	3	♇	5♏	5	☊	24♉	23	22	

MAR

	1	2	3	4	5	6	7	8	9	10	11	12	13	14	15	16	17	18	19	20	21	22	23	24	25	26	27	28	29	30	31
☉	10♓	11	12	13	14	15	16	17	18	19	20	21	22	23	24	25	26	27	28	29	0♈	1	2	3	4	5	6	7	8	9	10
☽	22♊	5♋	18	1♌	16	0♍	15	0♎	15	0♏	15	29	13♐	27	10♑	23	6♒	18	1♓	13	25	7♈	19	0♉	12	24	6♊	18	0♋	13	26
☿	19♓	21	23	24	26	28	30	2♈	3	5	7	8	10	11	12	14	15	16	16	17	18	18	18	19	19	19	18	18	18	17	16
♀	19♈	20	20	20	21	21	21	22	22	22	22	22	22	22	22	22	22	22	22	21	21	21	21	20	20	19	19	18	18	17	17
♂	20♈	20	21	22	23	23	24	25	25	26	27	28	28	29	30	1♉	1	2	3	3	4	5	6	6	7	8	9	9	10	11	11
	1	6	11	16	21	26	31		1	11	21	31		1	11	21	31		1	16		1	16		1	16		1	11	21	31
♃	5♒	6	7	8	9	10	11	♄	28♏	28	28	28	⚷	3♊	4	4	5	♅	18♐	18	♆	3♑	4	♇	5♏	4	☊	22♉	21	21	20

APR

	1	2	3	4	5	6	7	8	9	10	11	12	13	14	15	16	17	18	19	20	21	22	23	24	25	26	27	28	29	30	
☉	11♈	12	13	14	15	16	17	18	19	20	21	22	23	24	25	26	27	28	29	30	1♉	2	3	4	5	6	7	8	9	10	
☽	10♌	24	8♍	23	8♎	24	9♏	24	8♐	23	6♑	20	3♒	15	28	10♓	22	4♈	16	27	9♉	21	3♊	15	27	10♋	22	5♌	19	3♍	
☿	16♈	15	14	13	13	12	11	10	10	9	8	8	8	7	7	7	7	7	7	7	7	8	8	9	9	10	10	11	12	13	
♀	16♈	15	15	14	13	13	12	12	11	10	10	9	9	8	8	8	7	7	7	7	6	6	6	6	6	6	6	6	6	6	
♂	12♉	13	14	14	15	16	16	17	18	19	19	20	21	21	22	23	23	24	25	26	26	27	28	28	29	30	0♊	1	2	3	
	1	6	11	16	21	26			1	11	21			1	11	21			1	16		1	16		1	16		1	11	21	
♃	11♒	12	13	13	14	15		♄	28♏	27	27		⚷	5♊	5	6		♅	18♐	18	♆	4♑	4	♇	4♏	4	☊	20♉	20	19	

MAY

	1	2	3	4	5	6	7	8	9	10	11	12	13	14	15	16	17	18	19	20	21	22	23	24	25	26	27	28	29	30	31
☉	11♉	12	13	13	14	15	16	17	18	19	20	21	22	23	24	25	26	27	28	29	30	1♊	2	3	4	5	6	7	8	9	9
☽	17♍	2♎	17	2♏	17	2♐	17	1♑	15	29	12♒	24	7♓	19	1♈	13	24	6♉	18	30	12♊	24	7♋	19	2♌	15	29	13♍	27	11♎	26
☿	14♈	15	16	17	18	19	20	22	23	24	26	27	28	30	1♉	3	5	6	8	9	11	13	15	17	18	20	22	24	26	28	0♊
♀	7♈	7	7	7	8	8	9	9	9	10	10	11	11	12	13	13	14	15	15	16	17	17	18	19	20	20	21	22	23	24	24
♂	3♊	4	5	5	6	7	7	8	9	9	10	11	11	12	13	14	14	15	16	16	17	18	18	19	20	20	21	22	22	23	24
	1	6	11	16	21	26	31		1	11	21	31		1	11	21	31		1	16		1	16		1	16		1	11	21	31
♃	15♒	16	16	16	17	17	17	♄	26♏	25	24	24	⚷	7♊	7	8	9	♅	17♐	17	♆	3♑	3	♇	3♏	3	☊	19♉	18	18	17

JUN

	1	2	3	4	5	6	7	8	9	10	11	12	13	14	15	16	17	18	19	20	21	22	23	24	25	26	27	28	29	30	
☉	10♊	11	12	13	14	15	16	17	18	19	20	21	22	23	24	25	26	27	28	29	30	1♋	1	2	3	4	5	6	7	8	
☽	10♏	25	10♐	25	9♑	23	7♒	20	3♓	15	27	9♈	21	3♉	15	27	9♊	21	3♋	16	29	12♌	26	9♍	23	7♎	21	6♏	20	5♐	
☿	2♊	5	7	9	11	13	15	18	20	22	24	26	29	1♋	3	5	7	9	11	13	15	17	18	20	22	24	25	27	29	0♌	
♀	25♈	26	27	28	29	30	1♉	1	2	3	4	5	6	7	8	9	10	11	12	13	14	15	16	17	18	19	20	21	22	23	
♂	24♊	25	26	26	27	28	28	29	30	0♋	1	2	2	3	4	4	5	6	6	7	8	8	9	10	10	11	12	12	13	14	
	1	6	11	16	21	26			1	11	21			1	11	21			1	16		1	16		1	16		1	11	21	
♃	17♒	17	17	17	17	16		♄	24♏	23	22		⚷	9♊	10	11		♅	16♐	16	♆	3♑	2	♇	2♏	2	☊	17♉	17	16	

EPHEMERIS

1985

JUL

	1	2	3	4	5	6	7	8	9	10	11	12	13	14	15	16	17	18	19	20	21	22	23	24	25	26	27	28	29	30	31
☉	9♋	10	11	12	13	14	15	16	17	18	19	20	21	22	22	23	24	25	26	27	28	29	0♌	1	2	3	4	5	6	7	8
☽	19♐	3♑	18	1♒	15	28	11♓	23	5♈	17	29	11♉	23	5♊	17	30	12♋	25	9♌	22	6♍	20	4♎	18	2♏	16	0♐	15	29	13♑	26
☿	2♌	3	5	6	8	9	10	11	13	14	15	16	17	18	19	20	21	21	22	23	23	24	24	25	25	25	25	25	25	25	25
♀	24♉	25	26	28	29	30	1♊	2	3	4	5	6	7	8	9	11	12	13	14	15	16	17	18	19	21	22	23	24	25	26	27
♂	14♋	15	16	16	17	18	18	19	19	20	21	21	22	23	23	24	25	25	26	27	27	28	29	29	30	1♌	1	2	2	3	4
	1	6	11	16	21	26	31		1	11	21	31		1	11	21	31		1	16		1	16		1	16		1	11	21	31
♃	16♒	15	15	14	14	13	13	♄	22♏	22	21	21	⚷	11♊	12	13	13	♅	15♐	15	♆	2♑	2	♇	2♏	2	☊	16♉	15	15	14

AUG

	1	2	3	4	5	6	7	8	9	10	11	12	13	14	15	16	17	18	19	20	21	22	23	24	25	26	27	28	29	30	31
☉	9♌	10	11	12	13	13	14	15	16	17	18	19	20	21	22	23	24	25	26	27	28	29	30	1♍	2	3	4	5	6	7	8
☽	10♒	23	6♓	19	1♈	13	25	7♉	19	1♊	13	25	8♋	21	4♌	18	2♍	16	0♎	15	29	13♏	27	11♐	25	9♑	22	6♒	19	2♓	15
☿	25♌	24	24	23	23	22	21	21	20	19	18	17	17	16	15	15	14	14	13	13	13	13	13	14	14	15	16	16	17	18	20
♀	28♊	30	1♋	2	3	4	5	6	8	9	10	11	12	13	15	16	17	18	19	20	22	23	24	25	26	27	29	30	1♌	2	3
♂	4♌	5	6	6	7	8	8	9	10	10	11	11	12	13	13	14	15	15	16	17	17	18	19	19	20	20	21	22	22	23	24
	1	6	11	16	21	26	31		1	11	21	31		1	11	21	31		1	16		1	16		1	16		1	11	21	31
♃	12♒	12	11	11	10	9	9	♄	21♏	22	22	23	⚷	13♊	14	14	14	♅	14♐	14	♆	1♑	1	♇	2♏	2	☊	14♉	13	13	12

SEP

	1	2	3	4	5	6	7	8	9	10	11	12	13	14	15	16	17	18	19	20	21	22	23	24	25	26	27	28	29	30
☉	9♍	9	10	11	12	13	14	15	16	17	18	19	20	21	22	23	24	25	26	27	28	29	30	1♎	2	3	4	5	6	7
☽	27♓	9♈	21	3♉	15	27	9♊	21	3♋	16	29	12♌	26	10♍	25	9♎	24	9♏	24	8♐	22	6♑	19	3♒	16	28	11♓	23	6♈	18
☿	21♌	22	24	25	27	29	0♍	2	4	6	8	9	11	13	15	17	19	21	23	25	26	28	0♎	2	4	5	7	9	11	12
♀	5♌	6	7	8	9	11	12	13	14	15	17	18	19	20	21	23	24	25	26	27	29	30	1♍	2	4	5	6	7	8	10
♂	24♌	25	26	26	27	27	28	29	29	30	1♍	1	2	2	3	4	4	5	6	6	7	8	8	9	9	10	11	11	12	13
	1	6	11	16	21	26			1	11	21			1	11	21			1	16		1	16		1	16		1	11	21
♃	9♒	8	8	8	7	7		♄	23♏	23	24		⚷	14♊	15	15		♅	14♐	14	♆	1♑	1	♇	3♏	3	☊	12♉	12	11

OCT

	1	2	3	4	5	6	7	8	9	10	11	12	13	14	15	16	17	18	19	20	21	22	23	24	25	26	27	28	29	30	31
☉	8♎	9	10	11	12	13	14	15	16	17	18	19	20	21	22	23	24	25	26	27	28	29	30	1♏	2	3	4	5	6	7	8
☽	30♈	12♉	23	5♊	17	29	11♋	24	7♌	20	4♍	18	3♎	18	3♏	18	3♐	18	2♑	16	29	13♒	26	8♓	20	3♈	15	27	8♉	20	2♊
☿	14♎	16	17	19	21	22	24	26	27	29	0♏	2	3	5	6	8	9	11	12	14	15	17	18	20	21	22	24	25	26	28	29
♀	11♍	12	13	15	16	17	18	19	21	22	23	24	26	27	28	29	1♎	2	3	4	6	7	8	9	10	12	13	14	15	17	18
♂	13♍	14	15	15	16	16	17	18	18	19	20	20	21	21	22	23	23	24	25	25	26	26	27	28	28	29	30	0♎	1	1	2
	1	6	11	16	21	26	31		1	11	21	31		1	11	21	31		1	16		1	16		1	16		1	11	21	31
♃	7♒	7	7	7	8	8	8	♄	25♏	26	27	28	⚷	15♊	14	14	14	♅	15♐	15	♆	1♑	1	♇	4♏	4	☊	11♉	10	10	9

NOV

	1	2	3	4	5	6	7	8	9	10	11	12	13	14	15	16	17	18	19	20	21	22	23	24	25	26	27	28	29	30
☉	9♏	10	11	12	13	14	15	16	17	18	19	20	21	22	23	24	25	26	27	28	29	30	1♐	2	3	4	5	6	7	8
☽	14♊	26	8♋	20	3♌	15	29	12♍	26	11♎	26	11♏	26	11♐	26	11♑	25	9♒	22	5♓	17	30	12♈	24	5♉	17	29	11♊	23	5♋
☿	0♐	2	3	4	5	6	7	9	10	10	11	12	13	14	14	14	15	15	15	15	15	14	13	13	12	10	9	8	7	5
♀	19♎	20	22	23	24	25	27	28	29	0♏	2	3	4	5	7	8	9	10	12	13	14	16	17	18	19	21	22	23	24	26
♂	3♎	3	4	5	5	6	6	7	8	8	9	10	10	11	11	12	13	13	14	15	15	16	16	17	18	18	19	20	20	21
	1	6	11	16	21	26			1	11	21			1	11	21			1	16		1	16		1	16		1	11	21
♃	8♒	9	9	10	11	12		♄	28♏	29	0♐		⚷	14♊	13	13		♅	16♐	17	♆	2♑	2	♇	5♏	5	☊	9♉	9	8

DEC

	1	2	3	4	5	6	7	8	9	10	11	12	13	14	15	16	17	18	19	20	21	22	23	24	25	26	27	28	29	30	31
☉	9♐	10	11	12	13	14	15	16	17	18	19	20	21	22	23	24	25	26	27	28	29	0♑	1	2	3	4	5	6	7	8	9
☽	17♋	29	12♌	25	8♍	22	5♎	20	4♏	19	4♐	19	4♑	19	3♒	17	1♓	14	26	8♈	20	2♉	14	26	8♊	20	2♋	14	26	9♌	22
☿	4♐	3	2	1	30♏	29	29	29	29	29	29	30	0♐	1	2	3	4	5	6	7	8	9	11	12	13	14	16	17	19	20	21
♀	27♏	28	29	1♐	2	3	4	6	7	8	9	11	12	13	14	16	17	18	19	21	22	23	24	26	27	28	30	1♑	2	3	5
♂	21♎	22	23	23	24	25	25	26	26	27	28	28	29	30	0♏	1	1	2	3	3	4	4	5	6	6	7	8	8	9	9	10
	1	6	11	16	21	26	31		1	11	21	31		1	11	21	31		1	16		1	16		1	16		1	11	21	31
♃	12♒	13	14	15	16	17	18	♄	2♐	3	4	5	⚷	12♊	12	11	10	♅	18♐	19	♆	2♑	3	♇	6♏	6	☊	7♉	7	6	6

1986

JAN

	1	2	3	4	5	6	7	8	9	10	11	12	13	14	15	16	17	18	19	20	21	22	23	24	25	26	27	28	29	30	31
☉	10♑	11	12	13	14	15	16	17	18	19	20	21	22	24	25	26	27	28	29	30	1♒	2	3	4	5	6	7	8	9	10	11
☽	5♍	18	2♎	16	30	14♏	28	13♐	28	12♑	27	11♒	25	9♓	22	4♈	16	28	10♉	22	4♊	16	28	10♋	23	5♌	18	2♍	15	29	12♎
☿	23♐	24	26	27	29	0♑	2	3	5	6	8	9	11	12	14	15	17	19	20	22	23	25	27	28	30	2♒	3	5	7	8	10
♀	6♑	7	8	10	11	12	13	15	16	17	18	20	21	22	23	25	26	27	28	30	1♒	2	3	5	6	7	9	10	11	12	14
♂	11♏	11	12	12	13	14	14	15	15	16	17	17	18	18	19	20	20	21	21	22	23	23	24	24	25	26	26	27	27	28	29
	1	6	11	16	21	26	31		1	11	21	31		1	11	21	31		1	16		1	16		1	16		1	11	21	31
♃	18♒	19	20	22	23	24	25	♄	5♐	6	7	8	⚷	10♊	10	10	9	♅	20♐	20	♆	4♑	4	♇	7♏	7	☊	6♉	5	5	4

FEB

	1	2	3	4	5	6	7	8	9	10	11	12	13	14	15	16	17	18	19	20	21	22	23	24	25	26	27	28			
☉	12♒	13	14	15	16	17	18	19	20	21	22	23	24	25	26	27	28	29	0♓	1	2	3	4	5	6	7	8	9			
☽	26♎	10♏	24	9♐	23	7♑	21	6♒	19	3♓	16	29	12♈	24	6♉	18	30	12♊	24	6♋	18	1♌	14	27	11♍	25	9♎	23			
☿	12♒	14	15	17	19	21	22	24	26	28	30	1♓	3	5	7	9	10	12	14	16	17	19	21	22	23	25	26	27			
♀	15♒	16	17	19	20	21	22	24	25	26	27	29	30	1♓	2	4	5	6	7	9	10	11	12	14	15	16	17	19			
♂	29♏	30	0♐	1	2	2	3	3	4	5	5	6	6	7	7	8	9	9	10	10	11	11	12	13	13	14	14	15			
	1	6	11	16	21	26			1	11	21			1	11	21			1	16		1	16		1	16		1	11	21	
♃	25♒	26	28	29	0♓	1		♄	8♐	9	9		⚷	9♊	9	9		♅	21♐	22	♆	5♑	5	♇	7♏	7	☊	4♉	4	3	

MAR

	1	2	3	4	5	6	7	8	9	10	11	12	13	14	15	16	17	18	19	20	21	22	23	24	25	26	27	28	29	30	31
☉	10♓	11	12	13	14	15	16	17	18	19	20	21	22	23	24	25	26	27	28	29	0♈	1	2	3	4	5	6	7	8	9	10
☽	7♏	21	5♐	19	4♑	17	1♒	15	28	12♓	25	7♈	20	2♉	14	26	8♊	20	1♋	14	26	9♌	22	5♍	19	3♎	18	2♏	17	2♐	16
☿	28♓	29	30	0♈	1	1	1	1	1	1	0	30♓	29	28	28	27	26	25	24	23	22	21	21	20	19	19	18	18	18	18	18
♀	20♓	21	22	24	25	26	27	29	30	1♈	2	4	5	6	7	9	10	11	12	13	15	16	17	18	20	21	22	23	25	26	27
♂	15♐	16	17	17	18	18	19	19	20	20	21	22	22	23	23	24	24	25	25	26	26	27	27	28	28	29	29	30	0♑	1	1
	1	6	11	16	21	26	31		1	11	21	31		1	11	21	31		1	16		1	16		1	16		1	11	21	31
♃	2♓	3	4	6	7	8	9	♄	9♐	10	10	10	⚷	9♊	10	10	10	♅	22♐	22	♆	5♑	6	♇	7♏	7	☊	3♉	2	2	1

APR

	1	2	3	4	5	6	7	8	9	10	11	12	13	14	15	16	17	18	19	20	21	22	23	24	25	26	27	28	29	30	
☉	11♈	12	13	14	15	16	17	18	19	20	21	22	23	24	25	26	27	28	29	30	1♉	2	3	4	4	5	6	7	8	9	
☽	0♑	14	28	12♒	25	8♓	21	4♈	16	28	10♉	22	4♊	16	28	10♋	22	4♌	17	30	13♍	27	11♎	26	11♏	26	11♐	26	10♑	25	
☿	18♓	18	19	19	19	20	20	21	22	23	23	24	25	26	27	28	29	1♈	2	3	4	6	7	8	10	11	13	14	16	17	
♀	28♈	30	1♉	2	3	5	6	7	8	9	11	12	13	14	16	17	18	19	20	22	23	24	25	27	28	29	0♊	1	3	4	
♂	2♑	2	3	3	4	4	5	5	6	6	7	7	8	8	9	9	9	10	10	11	11	12	12	12	13	13	14	14	14	15	
	1	6	11	16	21	26			1	11	21			1	11	21			1	16		1	16		1	16		1	11	21	
♃	9♓	10	11	12	13	14		♄	10♐	9	9		⚷	10♊	11	12		♅	22♐	22	♆	6♑	6	♇	7♏	6	☊	1♉	1	30♈	

MAY

	1	2	3	4	5	6	7	8	9	10	11	12	13	14	15	16	17	18	19	20	21	22	23	24	25	26	27	28	29	30	31
☉	10♉	11	12	13	14	15	16	17	18	19	20	21	22	23	24	25	26	27	28	29	30	1♊	2	3	4	4	5	6	7	8	9
☽	9♒	22	5♓	18	1♈	13	25	7♉	19	1♊	13	24	6♋	18	0♌	13	25	8♍	22	5♎	20	4♏	19	4♐	20	5♑	20	4♒	18	2♓	15
☿	19♈	20	22	24	26	27	29	1♉	3	5	7	8	10	12	14	17	19	21	23	25	27	29	2♊	4	6	8	10	12	15	17	19
♀	5♊	6	8	9	10	11	12	14	15	16	17	18	20	21	22	23	24	26	27	28	29	1♋	2	3	4	5	7	8	9	10	11
♂	15♑	15	16	16	17	17	17	17	18	18	18	19	19	19	20	20	20	20	21	21	21	21	21	22	22	22	22	22	22	23	23
	1	6	11	16	21	26	31		1	11	21	31		1	11	21	31		1	16		1	16		1	16		1	11	21	31
♃	15♓	16	17	18	19	19	20	♄	8♐	8	7	6	⚷	12♊	13	14	15	♅	22♐	21	♆	6♑	5	♇	6♏	5	☊	29♈	29	28	28

JUN

	1	2	3	4	5	6	7	8	9	10	11	12	13	14	15	16	17	18	19	20	21	22	23	24	25	26	27	28	29	30	
☉	10♊	11	12	13	14	15	16	17	18	19	20	21	22	23	24	25	26	26	27	28	29	0♋	1	2	3	4	5	6	7	8	
☽	28♓	10♈	22	4♉	16	28	10♊	21	3♋	15	27	10♌	22	5♍	18	1♎	14	28	13♏	28	13♐	28	13♑	28	13♒	27	11♓	24	7♈	19	
☿	21♊	23	25	27	29	1♋	3	4	6	8	10	11	13	14	16	17	19	20	22	23	24	25	26	27	28	29	0♌	1	2	3	
♀	12♋	14	15	16	17	18	20	21	22	23	24	26	27	28	29	0♌	1	3	4	5	6	7	8	10	11	12	13	14	15	17	
♂	23♑	23	23	23	23	23	23	23	23	23	23	23	23	23	23	23	23	23	22	22	22	22	22	22	22	21	21	21	21	20	
	1	6	11	16	21	26			1	11	21			1	11	21			1	16		1	16		1	16		1	11	21	
♃	20♓	21	21	22	22	22		♄	6♐	5	5		⚷	15♊	16	16		♅	21♐	20	♆	5♑	5	♇	5♏	5	☊	28♈	27	27	

1986

JUL

	1	2	3	4	5	6	7	8	9	10	11	12	13	14	15	16	17	18	19	20	21	22	23	24	25	26	27	28	29	30	31
☉	9♋	10	11	12	13	14	15	16	17	17	18	19	20	21	22	23	24	25	26	27	28	29	30	1♌	2	3	4	5	6	7	8
☽	1♉	13	25	7♊	18	0♋	12	24	7♌	19	2♍	14	27	11♎	24	8♏	22	7♐	22	7♑	22	7♒	21	5♓	19	2♈	15	27	9♉	21	3♊
☿	3♌	4	5	5	6	6	6	6	6	6	6	6	6	6	5	5	4	4	3	3	2	1	1	30♋	29	29	28	27	27	27	26
♀	18♌	19	20	21	22	24	25	26	27	28	29	0♍	1	3	4	5	6	7	8	9	11	12	13	14	15	16	17	18	19	20	22
♂	20♑	20	20	19	19	19	19	18	18	18	17	17	17	17	16	16	16	15	15	15	15	14	14	14	14	13	13	13	13	13	12
	1	6	11	16	21	26	31		1	11	21	31		1	11	21	31		1	16		1	16		1	16		1	11	21	31
♃	23♓	23	23	23	23	23	22	♄	4♐	4	3	3	⚷	17♊	18	19	19	♅	20♐	19	♆	4♑	4	♇	5♏	5	☊	26♈	26	25	25

AUG

	1	2	3	4	5	6	7	8	9	10	11	12	13	14	15	16	17	18	19	20	21	22	23	24	25	26	27	28	29	30	31
☉	8♌	9	10	11	12	13	14	15	16	17	18	19	20	21	22	23	24	25	26	27	28	29	30	1♍	2	2	3	4	5	6	7
☽	15♊	27	9♋	21	3♌	16	29	11♍	24	8♎	21	5♏	19	3♐	17	2♑	16	1♒	15	29	13♓	27	10♈	23	5♉	18	29	11♊	23	5♋	17
☿	26♋	26	26	26	26	26	27	27	28	28	29	0♌	1	2	3	5	6	8	9	11	13	14	16	18	20	22	24	26	28	30	2♍
♀	23♍	24	25	26	27	28	29	0♎	1	2	3	4	5	6	7	9	10	11	12	13	14	15	16	17	18	19	19	20	21	22	23
♂	12♑	12	12	12	12	12	12	12	11	11	11	11	11	11	11	12	12	12	12	12	12	12	12	12	13	13	13	13	13	14	14
	1	6	11	16	21	26	31		1	11	21	31		1	11	21	31		1	16		1	16		1	16		1	11	21	31
♃	22♓	22	22	21	20	20	19	♄	3♐	3	3	4	⚷	19♊	20	20	21	♅	19♐	18	♆	4♑	3	♇	5♏	5	☊	25♈	24	24	23

SEP

	1	2	3	4	5	6	7	8	9	10	11	12	13	14	15	16	17	18	19	20	21	22	23	24	25	26	27	28	29	30
☉	8♍	9	10	11	12	13	14	15	16	17	18	19	20	21	22	23	24	25	26	27	28	29	30	1♎	2	3	4	5	6	7
☽	29♋	12♌	25	8♍	21	4♎	18	2♏	16	30	14♐	28	12♑	26	11♒	25	8♓	22	5♈	18	1♉	13	25	7♊	19	1♋	13	25	7♌	20
☿	4♍	6	8	10	11	13	15	17	19	21	23	25	26	28	30	2♎	3	5	7	8	10	12	13	15	16	18	20	21	23	24
♀	24♎	25	26	27	28	29	30	0♏	1	2	3	4	5	5	6	7	8	9	9	10	11	11	12	13	13	14	14	15	16	16
♂	14♑	14	15	15	15	15	16	16	16	17	17	17	18	18	19	19	19	20	20	21	21	21	22	22	23	23	24	24	25	25
	1	6	11	16	21	26			1	11	21			1	11	21			1	16		1	16		1	16		1	11	21
♃	19♓	19	18	17	17	16		♄	4♐	4	5		⚷	21♊	21	21		♅	18♐	19	♆	3♑	3	♇	5♏	6	☊	23♈	22	22

OCT

	1	2	3	4	5	6	7	8	9	10	11	12	13	14	15	16	17	18	19	20	21	22	23	24	25	26	27	28	29	30	31
☉	8♎	9	9	10	11	12	13	14	15	16	17	18	19	20	21	22	23	24	25	26	27	28	29	0♏	1	2	3	4	5	6	7
☽	3♍	16	29	13♎	27	12♏	26	10♐	25	9♑	23	7♒	21	4♓	18	1♈	14	27	9♉	21	3♊	15	27	9♋	21	3♌	15	28	11♍	24	7♎
☿	26♎	27	29	30	1♏	3	4	6	7	8	10	11	12	14	15	16	17	18	19	21	22	23	24	24	25	26	27	27	28	28	29
♀	17♏	17	18	18	18	19	19	19	20	20	20	20	20	20	20	20	20	20	20	20	20	20	19	19	19	18	18	17	17	16	16
♂	26♑	26	27	27	28	28	29	29	30	1♒	1	2	2	3	3	4	4	5	6	6	7	7	8	9	9	10	10	11	12	12	13
	1	6	11	16	21	26	31		1	11	21	31		1	11	21	31		1	16		1	16		1	16		1	11	21	31
♃	15♓	15	14	14	14	13	13	♄	5♐	6	7	8	⚷	21♊	21	21	21	♅	19♐	19	♆	3♑	3	♇	6♏	7	☊	21♈	21	20	20

NOV

	1	2	3	4	5	6	7	8	9	10	11	12	13	14	15	16	17	18	19	20	21	22	23	24	25	26	27	28	29	30
☉	8♏	9	10	11	12	13	14	15	16	17	18	19	20	21	22	23	24	25	26	27	28	29	0♐	1	2	3	4	5	6	7
☽	21♎	6♏	21	5♐	20	5♑	20	4♒	18	1♓	15	28	10♈	23	5♉	18	30	12♊	24	6♋	17	29	11♌	23	6♍	19	2♎	15	29	14♏
☿	29♏	29	29	29	29	28	27	27	26	25	23	22	21	19	18	17	16	15	14	14	13	13	13	13	14	14	15	16	16	17
♀	15♏	15	14	14	13	12	12	11	11	10	9	9	8	8	7	7	7	6	6	6	5	5	5	5	5	5	5	5	5	5
♂	14♒	14	15	15	16	17	17	18	19	19	20	21	21	22	23	23	24	25	25	26	27	27	28	29	29	30	1♓	1	2	3
	1	6	11	16	21	26			1	11	21			1	11	21			1	16		1	16		1	16		1	11	21
♃	13♓	13	13	13	13	13		♄	8♐	9	11		⚷	21♊	20	20		♅	20♐	21	♆	4♑	4	♇	7♏	8	☊	20♈	19	19

DEC

	1	2	3	4	5	6	7	8	9	10	11	12	13	14	15	16	17	18	19	20	21	22	23	24	25	26	27	28	29	30	31
☉	8♐	10	11	12	13	14	15	16	17	18	19	20	21	22	23	24	25	26	27	28	29	30	1♑	2	3	4	5	6	7	8	9
☽	29♏	14♐	29	14♑	29	14♒	28	11♓	25	8♈	20	2♉	15	27	9♊	21	2♋	14	26	8♌	20	2♍	15	27	10♎	24	7♏	22	7♐	22	7♑
☿	18♏	20	21	22	23	24	26	27	29	30	1♐	3	4	6	7	9	10	12	13	15	16	18	19	21	22	24	25	27	28	0♑	2
♀	5♏	6	6	6	6	7	7	8	8	8	9	9	10	11	11	12	12	13	14	14	15	16	17	17	18	19	20	21	21	22	23
♂	3♓	4	5	5	6	7	7	8	9	9	10	11	12	12	13	14	14	15	16	16	17	18	18	19	20	21	21	22	23	23	24
	1	6	11	16	21	26	31		1	11	21	31		1	11	21	31		1	16		1	16		1	16		1	11	21	31
♃	14♓	14	15	15	16	17	17	♄	12♐	13	14	15	⚷	19♊	19	18	17	♅	22♐	23	♆	5♑	5	♇	9♏	9	☊	18♈	18	17	17

1987

EPHEMERIS

JAN

	1	2	3	4	5	6	7	8	9	10	11	12	13	14	15	16	17	18	19	20	21	22	23	24	25	26	27	28	29	30	31
☉	10♑	11	12	13	14	15	16	17	18	19	20	21	22	23	24	25	26	27	28	29	0♒	1	2	3	4	5	6	8	9	10	11
☽	22♑	8♒	22	7♓	21	4♈	17	29	12♉	24	6♊	17	29	11♋	23	5♌	17	29	12♍	24	7♎	20	3♏	17	1♐	15	0♑	15	0♒	16	0♓
☿	3♑	5	6	8	9	11	13	14	16	18	19	21	22	24	26	27	29	1♒	2	4	6	8	9	11	13	14	16	18	20	21	23
♀	24♏	25	26	27	28	29	30	1♐	2	2	3	4	5	6	7	8	9	10	12	13	14	15	16	17	18	19	20	21	22	23	24
♂	25♓	25	26	27	28	28	29	30	0♈	1	2	2	3	4	5	5	6	7	7	8	9	9	10	11	12	12	13	14	14	15	16
	1	6	11	16	21	26	31		1	11	21	31		1	11	21	31		1	16		1	16		1	16		1	11	21	31
♃	18♓	18	19	20	21	22	23	♄	15♐	16	17	18	⚷	17♊	17	16	16	♅	24♐	24	♆	6♑	6	♇	9♏	10	☊	16♈	16	15	15

FEB

	1	2	3	4	5	6	7	8	9	10	11	12	13	14	15	16	17	18	19	20	21	22	23	24	25	26	27	28			
☉	12♒	13	14	15	16	17	18	19	20	21	22	23	24	25	26	27	28	29	30	1♓	2	3	4	5	6	7	8	9			
☽	15♓	29	12♈	25	8♉	20	2♊	14	26	8♋	20	2♌	14	26	9♍	21	4♎	17	30	13♏	27	11♐	25	10♑	24	9♒	24	8♓			
☿	25♒	27	28	30	1♓	3	4	6	7	9	10	11	12	13	13	14	14	14	14	14	14	14	13	12	11	10	9	8			
♀	25♐	27	28	29	30	1♑	2	3	4	5	7	8	9	10	11	12	13	15	16	17	18	19	20	21	23	24	25	26			
♂	16♈	17	18	18	19	20	21	21	22	23	23	24	25	25	26	27	28	28	29	30	0♉	1	2	2	3	4	4	5			
	1	6	11	16	21	26			1	11	21			1	11	21			1	16		1	16		1	16		1	11	21	
♃	23♓	24	25	27	28	29		♄	18♐	19	20		⚷	16♊	16	16		♅	25♐	26	♆	7♑	7	♇	10♏	10	☊	15♈	14	14	

MAR

	1	2	3	4	5	6	7	8	9	10	11	12	13	14	15	16	17	18	19	20	21	22	23	24	25	26	27	28	29	30	31
☉	10♓	11	12	13	14	15	16	17	18	19	20	21	22	23	24	25	26	27	28	29	30	1♈	2	3	4	5	6	7	8	9	10
☽	23♓	7♈	20	3♉	16	28	10♊	22	4♋	16	28	10♌	22	5♍	17	0♎	13	27	10♏	24	8♐	22	6♑	20	5♒	19	3♓	17	1♈	15	28
☿	7♓	6	5	4	3	3	2	1	1	0	0	30♒	30	0♓	0	0	1	1	2	2	3	4	4	5	6	7	8	9	10	11	12
♀	27♑	28	30	1♒	2	3	4	5	7	8	9	10	11	13	14	15	16	17	18	20	21	22	23	24	26	27	28	29	0♓	2	3
♂	6♉	6	7	8	9	9	10	11	11	12	13	13	14	15	15	16	17	17	18	19	19	20	21	21	22	23	23	24	25	26	26
	1	6	11	16	21	26	31		1	11	21	31		1	11	21	31		1	16		1	16		1	16		1	11	21	31
♃	30♓	1♈	2	3	4	6	7	♄	20♐	21	21	21	⚷	16♊	16	16	17	♅	26♐	27	♆	8♑	8	♇	10♏	10	☊	13♈	13	12	12

APR

	1	2	3	4	5	6	7	8	9	10	11	12	13	14	15	16	17	18	19	20	21	22	23	24	25	26	27	28	29	30	
☉	11♈	12	13	14	15	16	17	18	19	20	21	22	23	24	25	25	26	27	28	29	0♉	1	2	3	4	5	6	7	8	9	
☽	11♉	24	6♊	18	0♋	12	24	6♌	18	0♍	13	26	9♎	22	6♏	20	4♐	18	3♑	17	1♒	15	29	13♓	27	10♈	23	6♉	19	2♊	
☿	14♓	15	16	17	19	20	21	23	24	26	27	29	0♈	2	3	5	7	8	10	12	14	15	17	19	21	23	25	27	29	1♉	
♀	4♓	5	6	8	9	10	11	12	14	15	16	17	18	20	21	22	23	24	26	27	28	29	0♈	2	3	4	5	6	8	9	
♂	27♉	28	28	29	30	0♊	1	2	2	3	4	4	5	6	6	7	8	8	9	10	10	11	12	12	13	14	14	15	15	16	
	1	6	11	16	21	26			1	11	21			1	11	21			1	16		1	16		1	16		1	11	21	
♃	7♈	8	9	11	12	13		♄	21♐	21	21		⚷	17♊	17	18		♅	27♐	27	♆	8♑	8	♇	9♏	9	☊	12♈	11	11	

MAY

	1	2	3	4	5	6	7	8	9	10	11	12	13	14	15	16	17	18	19	20	21	22	23	24	25	26	27	28	29	30	31
☉	10♉	11	12	13	14	15	16	17	18	19	20	21	22	23	24	25	26	27	28	28	29	0♊	1	2	3	4	5	6	7	8	9
☽	14♊	26	8♋	20	2♌	14	26	8♍	21	4♎	17	0♏	15	29	14♐	28	13♑	28	12♒	26	10♓	24	7♈	20	3♉	15	28	10♊	22	5♋	16
☿	3♉	5	7	9	11	13	15	18	20	22	24	26	28	1♊	3	5	7	9	11	13	15	17	18	20	22	24	25	27	28	30	1♋
♀	10♈	11	12	14	15	16	17	19	20	21	22	23	25	26	27	28	29	1♉	2	3	4	5	7	8	9	10	12	13	14	15	16
♂	17♊	17	18	19	19	20	21	21	22	23	23	24	25	25	26	27	27	28	29	29	30	1♋	1	2	3	3	4	4	5	6	6
	1	6	11	16	21	26	31		1	11	21	31		1	11	21	31		1	16		1	16		1	16		1	11	21	31
♃	14♈	15	16	17	19	20	21	♄	20♐	20	19	19	⚷	19♊	19	20	21	♅	26♐	26	♆	8♑	8	♇	9♏	8	☊	10♈	10	9	9

JUN

	1	2	3	4	5	6	7	8	9	10	11	12	13	14	15	16	17	18	19	20	21	22	23	24	25	26	27	28	29	30	
☉	10♊	11	12	13	14	15	16	17	18	19	20	21	21	22	23	24	25	26	27	28	29	0♋	1	2	3	4	5	6	7	8	
☽	28♋	10♌	22	4♍	16	29	12♎	25	9♏	23	7♐	22	8♑	23	8♒	22	7♓	20	4♈	17	30	13♉	25	7♊	19	1♋	13	25	7♌	19	
☿	3♋	4	5	6	7	8	10	10	11	12	13	14	14	15	15	16	16	16	17	17	17	17	17	17	16	16	16	15	15	14	
♀	18♉	19	20	21	22	24	25	26	27	29	30	1♊	2	3	5	6	7	8	9	11	12	13	14	16	17	18	19	20	22	23	
♂	7♋	8	8	9	10	10	11	12	12	13	14	14	15	15	16	17	17	18	19	19	20	21	21	22	23	23	24	24	25	26	
	1	6	11	16	21	26			1	11	21			1	11	21			1	16		1	16		1	16		1	11	21	
♃	21♈	22	23	24	24	25		♄	18♐	18	17		⚷	21♊	22	23		♅	25♐	25	♆	7♑	7	♇	8♏	7	☊	8♈	8	7	

1987

JUL

	1	2	3	4	5	6	7	8	9	10	11	12	13	14	15	16	17	18	19	20	21	22	23	24	25	26	27	28	29	30	31
☉	9♋	10	11	12	12	13	14	15	16	17	18	19	20	21	22	23	24	25	26	27	28	29	30	1♌	2	3	3	4	5	6	7
☽	1♍	13	25	7♎	20	3♏	17	1♐	16	1♑	16	1♒	17	1♓	16	30	14♈	27	10♉	22	4♊	16	28	10♋	22	4♌	16	28	10♍	22	4♎
☿	14♋	13	12	12	11	11	10	9	9	9	8	8	8	7	7	7	8	8	8	8	9	9	10	11	12	13	14	15	16	17	19
♀	24♊	25	27	28	29	0♋	1	3	4	5	6	8	9	10	11	12	14	15	16	17	19	20	21	22	23	25	26	27	28	30	1♌
♂	26♋	27	28	28	29	30	0♌	1	1	2	3	3	4	5	5	6	7	7	8	8	9	10	10	11	12	12	13	14	14	15	15
	1	6	11	16	21	26	31		1	11	21	31		1	11	21	31		1	16		1	16		1	16		1	11	21	31
♃	26♈	27	27	28	28	29	29	♄	16♐	16	15	15	⚷	24♊	25	25	26	♅	24♐	24	♆	7♑	6	♇	7♏	7	☊	7♈	6	6	5

AUG

	1	2	3	4	5	6	7	8	9	10	11	12	13	14	15	16	17	18	19	20	21	22	23	24	25	26	27	28	29	30	31
☉	8♌	9	10	11	12	13	14	15	16	17	18	19	20	21	22	23	24	25	25	26	27	28	29	0♍	1	2	3	4	5	6	7
☽	17♎	29	13♏	26	10♐	25	9♑	25	10♒	25	10♓	25	9♈	22	6♉	19	1♊	13	25	7♋	19	1♌	13	25	7♍	19	1♎	14	26	9♏	22
☿	20♋	22	23	25	27	28	0♌	2	4	6	8	10	12	14	16	18	20	22	24	26	28	0♍	2	4	6	8	10	12	13	15	17
♀	2♌	3	5	6	7	8	10	11	12	13	14	16	17	18	19	21	22	23	24	26	27	28	29	1♍	2	3	4	5	7	8	9
♂	16♌	17	17	18	19	19	20	21	21	22	22	23	24	24	25	26	26	27	28	28	29	29	0♍	1	1	2	3	3	4	5	5
	1	6	11	16	21	26	31		1	11	21	31		1	11	21	31		1	16		1	16		1	16		1	11	21	31
♃	29♈	29	30	30	30	30	30	♄	15♐	15	15	15	⚷	26♊	27	27	28	♅	23♐	23	♆	6♑	6	♇	7♏	7	☊	5♈	5	4	4

SEP

	1	2	3	4	5	6	7	8	9	10	11	12	13	14	15	16	17	18	19	20	21	22	23	24	25	26	27	28	29	30
☉	8♍	9	10	11	12	13	14	15	16	17	18	19	20	21	22	23	24	25	26	27	27	28	29	0♎	1	2	3	4	5	6
☽	6♐	20	4♑	19	3♒	18	3♓	18	3♈	17	1♉	14	27	9♊	22	4♋	16	28	9♌	21	3♍	16	28	10♎	23	6♏	19	3♐	17	0♑
☿	19♍	21	22	24	26	27	29	1♎	2	4	5	7	9	10	12	13	14	16	17	19	20	21	23	24	25	27	28	29	0♏	1
♀	10♍	12	13	14	15	17	18	19	20	22	23	24	25	27	28	29	0♎	2	3	4	5	7	8	9	10	11	13	14	15	16
♂	6♍	6	7	8	8	9	10	10	11	12	12	13	13	14	15	15	16	17	17	18	19	19	20	21	21	22	22	23	24	24
	1	6	11	16	21	26			1	11	21			1	11	21			1	16		1	16		1	16		1	11	21
♃	29♈	29	29	29	28	28		♄	15♐	15	15		⚷	28♊	28	29		♅	23♐	23	♆	5♑	5	♇	8♏	8	☊	4♈	3	3

OCT

	1	2	3	4	5	6	7	8	9	10	11	12	13	14	15	16	17	18	19	20	21	22	23	24	25	26	27	28	29	30	31
☉	7♎	8	9	10	11	12	13	14	15	16	17	18	19	20	21	22	23	24	25	26	27	28	29	0♏	1	2	3	4	5	6	7
☽	15♑	29	13♒	28	12♓	27	11♈	25	9♉	22	5♊	17	30	12♋	24	6♌	18	29	12♍	24	6♎	19	2♏	16	29	13♐	27	11♑	26	10♒	24
☿	3♏	4	5	6	7	8	9	9	10	11	11	12	12	13	13	13	13	13	13	12	12	11	10	10	8	7	6	5	4	2	1
♀	18♎	19	20	21	23	24	25	26	28	29	0♏	1	3	4	5	6	8	9	10	11	13	14	15	16	18	19	20	21	23	24	25
♂	25♍	26	26	27	28	28	29	29	0♎	1	1	2	3	3	4	5	5	6	7	7	8	8	9	10	10	11	12	12	13	14	14
	1	6	11	16	21	26	31		1	11	21	31		1	11	21	31		1	16		1	16		1	16		1	11	21	31
♃	27♈	26	26	25	24	24	23	♄	16♐	17	18	18	⚷	29♊	29	29	28	♅	23♐	24	♆	5♑	5	♇	9♏	9	☊	2♈	2	1	0

NOV

	1	2	3	4	5	6	7	8	9	10	11	12	13	14	15	16	17	18	19	20	21	22	23	24	25	26	27	28	29	30
☉	8♏	9	10	11	12	13	14	15	16	17	18	19	20	21	22	23	24	25	26	27	28	29	0♐	1	2	3	4	5	6	7
☽	8♓	22	6♈	20	3♉	17	30	13♊	25	8♋	20	2♌	13	25	7♍	19	2♎	14	27	11♏	25	9♐	23	8♑	22	6♒	21	5♓	19	2♈
☿	0♏	29♎	28	28	28	27	27	28	28	29	29	0♏	1	2	3	4	6	7	8	10	11	12	14	15	17	18	20	21	23	24
♀	26♏	28	29	0♐	1	3	4	5	6	8	9	10	11	12	14	15	16	17	19	20	21	22	24	25	26	27	29	30	1♑	2
♂	15♎	16	16	17	18	18	19	19	20	21	21	22	23	23	24	25	25	26	27	27	28	29	29	30	1♏	1	2	3	3	4
	1	6	11	16	21	26			1	11	21			1	11	21			1	16		1	16		1	16		1	11	21
♃	23♈	22	22	21	21	20		♄	19♐	20	21		⚷	28♊	28	28		♅	24♐	25	♆	6♑	6	♇	10♏	10	☊	0♈	30♓	29

DEC

	1	2	3	4	5	6	7	8	9	10	11	12	13	14	15	16	17	18	19	20	21	22	23	24	25	26	27	28	29	30	31
☉	8♐	9	10	11	12	13	14	15	16	17	18	19	20	21	22	23	24	26	27	28	29	30	1♑	2	3	4	5	6	7	8	9
☽	16♈	29	13♉	26	8♊	21	3♋	16	28	10♌	21	3♍	15	27	9♎	22	5♏	19	3♐	17	2♑	17	2♒	16	1♓	15	29	13♈	26	9♉	22
☿	26♏	28	29	1♐	2	4	5	7	8	10	12	13	15	16	18	19	21	23	24	26	27	29	0♑	2	4	5	7	8	10	12	13
♀	4♑	5	6	7	9	10	11	12	14	15	16	17	19	20	21	22	23	25	26	27	28	30	1♒	2	3	5	6	7	8	10	11
♂	4♏	5	6	6	7	8	8	9	10	10	11	12	12	13	14	14	15	16	16	17	18	18	19	20	20	21	22	22	23	24	24
	1	6	11	16	21	26	31		1	11	21	31		1	11	21	31		1	16		1	16		1	16		1	11	21	31
♃	20♈	20	20	20	20	20	20	♄	22♐	23	24	25	⚷	27♊	26	26	25	♅	26♐	27	♆	7♑	7	♇	11♏	12	☊	29♓	28	28	27

1988

EPHEMERIS

JAN

	1	2	3	4	5	6	7	8	9	10	11	12	13	14	15	16	17	18	19	20	21	22	23	24	25	26	27	28	29	30	31
☉	10♑	11	12	13	14	15	16	17	18	19	20	21	22	23	24	25	26	27	28	29	0♒	1	2	3	4	5	6	7	8	9	10
☽	5♊	18	30	12♋	24	6♌	18	30	12♍	23	5♎	18	0♏	13	27	11♐	25	10♑	25	10♒	25	10♓	25	9♈	23	6♉	19	2♊	15	27	9♋
☿	15♑	16	18	20	21	23	25	26	28	30	1♒	3	5	6	8	9	11	13	14	16	17	19	20	21	23	24	25	26	26	27	28
♀	12♒	13	14	16	17	18	19	21	22	23	24	26	27	28	29	0♓	2	3	4	5	6	8	9	10	11	13	14	15	16	17	19
♂	25♏	26	26	27	28	28	29	30	0♐	1	2	2	3	4	4	5	6	6	7	8	8	9	10	10	11	12	12	13	14	14	15
	1	6	11	16	21	26	31		1	11	21	31		1	11	21	31		1	16		1	16		1	16		1	11	21	31
♃	20♈	21	21	21	22	23	23	♄	25♐	27	28	29	⚷	25♊	25	24	24	♅	28♐	29	♆	8♑	8	♇	12♏	12	☊	27♓	27	26	26

FEB

	1	2	3	4	5	6	7	8	9	10	11	12	13	14	15	16	17	18	19	20	21	22	23	24	25	26	27	28	29		
☉	11♒	12	13	14	15	16	17	18	19	20	21	22	23	25	26	27	28	29	30	1♓	2	3	4	5	6	7	8	9	10		
☽	21♋	3♌	15	27	8♍	20	2♎	14	27	9♏	22	5♐	19	3♑	18	3♒	18	3♓	18	3♈	18	2♉	15	29	11♊	24	6♋	18	30		
☿	28♒	28	28	28	27	27	26	25	24	23	22	21	20	18	17	16	15	15	14	14	13	13	13	13	13	13	13	14	14		
♀	20♓	21	22	23	25	26	27	28	29	1♈	2	3	4	5	6	8	9	10	11	12	13	15	16	17	18	19	20	22	23		
♂	16♐	16	17	18	18	19	20	20	21	22	22	23	24	24	25	26	26	27	28	28	29	30	0♑	1	2	2	3	4	4		
	1	6	11	16	21	26			1	11	21			1	11	21			1	16		1	16		1	16		1	11	21	
♃	23♈	24	25	26	27	28		♄	29♐	30	1♑		⚷	24♊	23	23		♅	29♐	0♑	♆	9♑	9	♇	13♏	13	☊	26♓	25	24	

MAR

	1	2	3	4	5	6	7	8	9	10	11	12	13	14	15	16	17	18	19	20	21	22	23	24	25	26	27	28	29	30	31
☉	11♓	12	13	14	15	16	17	18	19	20	21	22	23	24	25	26	27	28	29	30	1♈	2	3	4	5	6	7	8	9	10	10
☽	12♌	24	5♍	17	29	11♎	24	6♏	19	2♐	15	29	13♑	27	12♒	26	11♓	26	11♈	26	10♉	24	7♊	20	2♋	15	27	8♌	20	2♍	14
☿	15♒	15	16	17	18	18	19	20	21	22	23	25	26	27	28	29	1♓	2	3	5	6	8	9	11	12	14	15	17	18	20	22
♀	24♈	25	26	27	28	30	1♉	2	3	4	5	6	7	8	9	11	12	13	14	15	16	17	18	19	20	21	22	23	24	25	26
♂	5♑	6	6	7	8	8	9	10	11	11	12	13	13	14	15	15	16	17	17	18	19	19	20	21	21	22	23	23	24	25	25
	1	6	11	16	21	26	31		1	11	21	31		1	11	21	31		1	16		1	16		1	16		1	11	21	31
♃	28♈	29	0♉	2	3	4	5	♄	1♑	2	2	2	⚷	23♊	23	23	24	♅	1♑	1	♆	10♑	10	♇	13♏	12	☊	24♓	23	23	22

APR

	1	2	3	4	5	6	7	8	9	10	11	12	13	14	15	16	17	18	19	20	21	22	23	24	25	26	27	28	29	30	
☉	11♈	12	13	14	15	16	17	18	19	20	21	22	23	24	25	26	27	28	29	0♉	1	2	3	4	5	6	7	8	9	10	
☽	26♍	8♎	20	3♏	16	29	12♐	25	9♑	23	7♒	21	6♓	20	5♈	20	4♉	18	2♊	15	28	10♋	23	5♌	17	28	10♍	22	4♎	17	
☿	23♓	25	27	28	0♈	2	4	6	7	9	11	13	15	17	19	21	23	25	27	29	2♉	4	6	8	10	12	14	16	19	21	
♀	27♉	28	29	0♊	1	2	3	4	5	6	7	8	9	10	11	11	12	13	14	15	16	16	17	18	19	19	20	21	21	22	
♂	26♑	27	27	28	29	29	0♒	1	1	2	3	3	4	5	5	6	7	7	8	9	9	10	11	11	12	13	13	14	15	15	
	1	6	11	16	21	26			1	11	21			1	11	21			1	16		1	16		1	16		1	11	21	
♃	5♉	6	7	9	10	11		♄	2♑	3	2		⚷	24♊	24	25		♅	1♑	1	♆	10♑	10	♇	12♏	12	☊	22♓	22	21	

MAY

	1	2	3	4	5	6	7	8	9	10	11	12	13	14	15	16	17	18	19	20	21	22	23	24	25	26	27	28	29	30	31
☉	11♉	12	13	14	15	16	17	18	19	20	21	21	22	23	24	25	26	27	28	29	0♊	1	2	3	4	5	6	7	8	9	10
☽	29♎	12♏	25	8♐	22	6♑	20	4♒	18	2♓	16	0♈	15	29	13♉	26	10♊	23	6♋	18	1♌	13	24	6♍	18	0♎	12	25	7♏	21	4♐
☿	23♉	25	27	28	0♊	2	4	6	7	9	10	12	13	15	16	17	18	19	20	21	22	23	24	24	25	25	26	26	26	27	27
♀	23♊	23	24	25	25	26	26	27	27	28	28	28	29	29	29	30	30	0♋	0	0	0	0	0	0	0	0	0	30♊	30	29	29
♂	16♒	17	17	18	19	19	20	21	21	22	23	23	24	25	25	26	27	27	28	29	29	30	0♓	1	2	2	3	4	4	5	5
	1	6	11	16	21	26	31		1	11	21	31		1	11	21	31		1	16		1	16		1	16		1	11	21	31
♃	12♉	13	15	16	17	18	19	♄	2♑	2	1	1	⚷	26♊	26	27	28	♅	1♑	0	♆	10♑	10	♇	11♏	11	☊	21♓	20	20	19

JUN

	1	2	3	4	5	6	7	8	9	10	11	12	13	14	15	16	17	18	19	20	21	22	23	24	25	26	27	28	29	30	
☉	11♊	12	13	14	15	16	16	17	18	19	20	21	22	23	24	25	26	27	28	29	30	1♋	2	3	4	5	6	7	7	8	
☽	18♐	2♑	16	0♒	15	29	13♓	27	11♈	25	9♉	22	5♊	19	1♋	14	26	9♌	21	2♍	14	26	8♎	20	3♏	15	29	12♐	26	11♑	
☿	27♊	27	27	26	26	26	25	25	25	24	24	23	22	22	21	21	20	20	19	19	19	18	18	18	18	18	18	19	19	19	
♀	29♊	28	28	27	27	26	26	25	25	24	24	23	22	22	21	20	20	19	19	18	18	17	17	16	16	15	15	15	15	14	
♂	6♓	7	7	8	9	9	10	10	11	12	12	13	13	14	15	15	16	16	17	18	18	19	19	20	20	21	21	22	23	23	
	1	6	11	16	21	26			1	11	21			1	11	21			1	16		1	16		1	16		1	11	21	
♃	20♉	21	22	23	24	25		♄	1♑	30♐	29		⚷	28♊	29	30		♅	30♐	29	♆	10♑	9	♇	10♏	10	☊	19♓	19	18	

1988

EPHEMERIS

JUL

	1	2	3	4	5	6	7	8	9	10	11	12	13	14	15	16	17	18	19	20	21	22	23	24	25	26	27	28	29	30	31
☉	9♋	10	11	12	13	14	15	16	17	18	19	20	21	22	23	24	25	26	27	27	28	29	0♌	1	2	3	4	5	6	7	8
☽	25♑	10♒	25	9♓	24	8♈	22	5♉	19	2♊	15	28	10♋	23	5♌	17	29	11♍	22	4♎	16	28	11♏	24	7♐	21	5♑	19	4♒	19	4♓
☿	20♊	20	21	21	22	23	24	25	26	27	28	30	1♋	2	4	5	7	9	10	12	14	16	18	20	22	24	26	28	0♌	2	4
♀	14♊	14	14	14	14	14	14	14	14	14	15	15	15	16	16	16	17	17	18	18	19	19	20	20	21	21	22	23	23	24	25
♂	24♓	24	25	25	26	26	27	27	28	28	29	29	30	0♈	1	1	1	2	2	3	3	4	4	4	5	5	5	6	6	7	7
	1	6	11	16	21	26	31		1	11	21	31		1	11	21	31		1	16		1	16		1	16		1	11	21	31
♃	26♉	27	28	29	30	1♊	1	♄	28♐	28	27	27	⚷	1♋	2	3	4	♅	29♐	28	♆	9♑	8	♇	10♏	10	☊	18♓	17	16	16

AUG

	1	2	3	4	5	6	7	8	9	10	11	12	13	14	15	16	17	18	19	20	21	22	23	24	25	26	27	28	29	30	31
☉	9♌	10	11	12	13	14	15	16	17	18	19	20	20	21	22	23	24	25	26	27	28	29	0♍	1	2	3	4	5	6	7	8
☽	19♓	4♈	18	2♉	16	29	12♊	25	7♋	20	2♌	14	26	7♍	19	1♎	13	25	7♏	19	2♐	15	29	13♑	27	12♒	27	13♓	28	13♈	27
☿	7♌	9	11	13	15	17	19	21	23	25	27	29	1♍	2	4	6	8	10	11	13	15	16	18	20	21	23	24	26	27	29	0♎
♀	25♊	26	27	28	28	29	0♋	1	2	3	3	4	5	6	7	8	9	10	11	11	12	13	14	15	16	17	18	19	20	21	22
♂	7♈	7	8	8	8	9	9	9	9	10	10	10	10	10	11	11	11	11	11	11	11	11	11	11	11	11	11	11	11	11	11
	1	6	11	16	21	26	31		1	11	21	31		1	11	21	31		1	16		1	16		1	16		1	11	21	31
♃	2♊	2	3	4	4	5	5	♄	27♐	26	26	26	⚷	4♋	4	5	6	♅	28♐	27	♆	8♑	8	♇	10♏	10	☊	16♓	15	15	14

SEP

	1	2	3	4	5	6	7	8	9	10	11	12	13	14	15	16	17	18	19	20	21	22	23	24	25	26	27	28	29	30
☉	9♍	10	11	12	13	14	15	16	17	18	18	19	20	21	22	23	24	25	26	27	28	29	0♎	1	2	3	4	5	6	7
☽	12♉	25	9♊	22	4♋	17	29	11♌	23	5♍	16	28	10♎	22	4♏	16	29	11♐	25	8♑	22	6♒	21	6♓	21	6♈	21	6♉	20	4♊
☿	2♎	3	4	6	7	8	10	11	12	13	15	16	17	18	19	20	21	22	23	23	24	25	25	26	26	27	27	27	27	27
♀	23♋	24	25	26	27	28	29	1♌	2	3	4	5	6	7	8	9	10	11	12	14	15	16	17	18	19	20	21	23	24	25
♂	11♈	11	11	11	11	11	11	10	10	10	10	10	9	9	9	9	8	8	8	8	7	7	7	6	6	6	6	5	5	5
	1	6	11	16	21	26			1	11	21			1	11	21			1	16		1	16		1	16		1	11	21
♃	5♊	6	6	6	6	6		♄	26♐	26	26		⚷	6♋	6	7		♅	27♐	27	♆	8♑	7	♇	10♏	11	☊	14♓	14	13

OCT

	1	2	3	4	5	6	7	8	9	10	11	12	13	14	15	16	17	18	19	20	21	22	23	24	25	26	27	28	29	30	31
☉	8♎	9	10	11	12	13	14	15	16	17	18	19	20	21	22	23	24	25	26	27	28	29	30	1♏	2	3	4	5	6	7	8
☽	18♊	1♋	13	26	8♌	20	1♍	13	25	7♎	19	1♏	13	26	8♐	21	5♑	18	2♒	16	0♓	15	29	14♈	29	14♉	28	12♊	26	9♋	22
☿	27♎	26	26	25	25	24	23	22	21	20	18	17	16	15	14	13	13	12	12	12	12	12	12	13	14	14	15	16	18	19	20
♀	26♌	27	28	29	1♍	2	3	4	5	6	7	9	10	11	12	13	15	16	17	18	19	20	22	23	24	25	26	28	29	0♎	1
♂	4♈	4	4	4	3	3	3	3	2	2	2	2	1	1	1	1	1	1	0	0	0	0	0	30♓	30	30	30	30	30	30	30
	1	6	11	16	21	26	31		1	11	21	31		1	11	21	31		1	16		1	16		1	16		1	11	21	31
♃	6♊	6	6	5	5	5	4	♄	27♐	27	28	29	⚷	7♋	7	7	7	♅	27♐	28	♆	7♑	8	♇	11♏	12	☊	13♓	12	12	11

NOV

	1	2	3	4	5	6	7	8	9	10	11	12	13	14	15	16	17	18	19	20	21	22	23	24	25	26	27	28	29	30
☉	9♏	10	11	12	13	14	15	16	17	18	19	20	21	22	23	24	25	26	27	28	29	30	1♐	2	3	4	5	6	7	8
☽	4♌	16	28	10♍	22	3♎	15	28	10♏	22	5♐	18	2♑	15	29	12♒	26	10♓	24	9♈	23	8♉	22	6♊	20	4♋	17	30	12♌	24
☿	22♎	23	24	26	27	29	1♏	2	4	5	7	9	10	12	13	15	17	18	20	21	23	25	26	28	29	1♐	2	4	6	7
♀	2♎	4	5	6	7	8	10	11	12	13	15	16	17	18	19	21	22	23	24	26	27	28	29	1♏	2	3	4	5	7	8
♂	30♓	0♈	0	0	0	0	0	1	1	1	1	1	1	2	2	2	2	3	3	3	3	4	4	4	4	5	5	5	6	6
	1	6	11	16	21	26			1	11	21			1	11	21			1	16		1	16		1	16		1	11	21
♃	4♊	3	3	2	1	1		♄	29♐	30	1♑		⚷	7♋	7	6		♅	28♐	29	♆	8♑	8	♇	12♏	13	☊	11♓	10	10

DEC

	1	2	3	4	5	6	7	8	9	10	11	12	13	14	15	16	17	18	19	20	21	22	23	24	25	26	27	28	29	30	31
☉	9♐	10	11	12	13	14	15	16	17	18	19	20	21	22	23	24	25	26	27	28	29	0♑	1	2	3	4	5	6	7	9	10
☽	6♍	18	30	11♎	23	6♏	18	1♐	14	28	11♑	25	9♒	23	7♓	21	5♈	19	3♉	17	1♊	15	29	12♋	25	7♌	20	2♍	14	25	7♎
☿	9♐	10	12	14	15	17	18	20	21	23	24	26	28	29	1♑	2	4	6	7	9	10	12	13	15	17	18	20	21	23	24	26
♀	9♏	10	12	13	14	15	17	18	19	20	22	23	24	25	27	28	29	0♐	2	3	4	5	7	8	9	10	12	13	14	15	17
♂	6♈	7	7	8	8	8	9	9	10	10	10	11	11	12	12	13	13	13	14	14	15	15	16	16	17	17	18	18	19	19	20
	1	6	11	16	21	26	31		1	11	21	31		1	11	21	31		1	16		1	16		1	16		1	11	21	31
♃	30♉	29	29	28	28	27	27	♄	2♑	3	4	5	⚷	6♋	5	5	4	♅	30♐	1♑	♆	9♑	9	♇	14♏	14	☊	9♓	9	8	8

EPHEMERIS

JAN

JAN	1	2	3	4	5	6	7	8	9	10	11	12	13	14	15	16	17	18	19	20	21	22	23	24	25	26	27	28	29	30	31
☉	11♑	12	13	14	15	16	17	18	19	20	21	22	23	24	25	26	27	28	29	30	1♒	2	3	4	5	6	7	8	9	10	11
☽	19♎	1♏	14	26	9♐	22	6♑	20	4♒	19	3♓	18	2♈	16	0♉	14	28	11♊	25	8♋	20	3♌	16	28	10♍	22	3♎	15	27	9♏	21
☿	27♑	29	0♒	2	3	4	6	7	8	9	10	10	11	11	12	12	12	12	11	10	10	9	7	6	5	4	2	1	0	29♑	28
♀	18♐	19	20	22	23	24	25	27	28	29	0♑	2	3	4	5	7	8	9	10	12	13	14	15	17	18	19	20	22	23	24	25
♂	20♈	21	21	22	22	23	23	24	24	25	25	26	27	27	28	28	29	29	30	0♉	1	1	2	3	3	4	4	5	5	6	7
	1	6	11	16	21	26	31		1	11	21	31		1	11	21	31		1	16		1	16		1	16		1	11	21	31
♃	27♉	26	26	26	26	26	26	♄	6♑	7	8	9	⚷	4♋	3	3	2	♅	2♑	3	♆	10♑	10	♇	15♏	15	☊	8♓	7	7	6

FEB

FEB	1	2	3	4	5	6	7	8	9	10	11	12	13	14	15	16	17	18	19	20	21	22	23	24	25	26	27	28			
☉	12♒	13	14	15	16	17	18	19	20	21	22	23	24	25	26	27	28	29	0♓	1	2	3	4	5	6	7	8	9			
☽	4♐	17	0♑	14	28	13♒	28	12♓	27	12♈	27	11♉	25	8♊	21	4♋	17	30	12♌	24	6♍	18	30	12♎	24	5♏	18	30			
☿	28♑	27	27	26	26	26	26	26	27	27	27	28	29	29	0♒	1	2	3	4	5	6	7	8	9	11	12	13	15			
♀	27♑	28	29	0♒	2	3	4	5	7	8	9	10	12	13	14	15	17	18	19	20	22	23	24	25	27	28	29	0♓			
♂	7♉	8	8	9	9	10	11	11	12	12	13	14	14	15	15	16	17	17	18	18	19	20	20	21	21	22	23	23			
	1	6	11	16	21	26			1	11	21			1	11	21			1	16		1	16		1	16		1	11	21	
♃	26♉	27	27	27	28	28		♄	9♑	10	11		⚷	2♋	2	1		♅	3♑	4	♆	11♑	12	♇	15♏	15	☊	6♓	6	5	

MAR

MAR	1	2	3	4	5	6	7	8	9	10	11	12	13	14	15	16	17	18	19	20	21	22	23	24	25	26	27	28	29	30	31
☉	10♓	11	12	13	14	15	16	17	18	19	20	21	22	23	24	25	26	27	28	29	0♈	1	2	3	4	5	6	7	8	9	10
☽	12♐	25	8♑	22	6♒	21	6♓	21	6♈	21	6♉	20	4♊	18	1♋	14	27	9♌	21	3♍	15	27	9♎	20	2♏	14	26	9♐	21	4♑	17
☿	16♒	17	19	20	21	23	24	26	27	29	0♓	2	4	5	7	8	10	12	13	15	17	19	20	22	24	26	28	30	2♈	4	6
♀	2♓	3	4	5	7	8	9	10	12	13	14	15	17	18	19	20	22	23	24	25	27	28	29	0♈	2	3	4	5	6	8	9
♂	24♉	24	25	26	26	27	27	28	29	29	30	0♊	1	2	2	3	3	4	5	5	6	6	7	8	8	9	10	10	11	11	12
	1	6	11	16	21	26	31		1	11	21	31		1	11	21	31		1	16		1	16		1	16		1	11	21	31
♃	29♉	29	30	1♊	2	2	3	♄	12♑	12	13	13	⚷	1♋	1	1	2	♅	5♑	5	♆	12♑	12	♇	15♏	15	☊	5♓	4	4	3

APR

APR	1	2	3	4	5	6	7	8	9	10	11	12	13	14	15	16	17	18	19	20	21	22	23	24	25	26	27	28	29	30	
☉	11♈	12	13	14	15	16	17	18	19	20	21	22	23	24	25	26	27	28	29	30	1♉	2	3	4	5	6	7	8	9	10	
☽	1♒	15	29	14♓	29	14♈	29	14♉	29	13♊	27	11♋	23	6♌	18	0♍	12	24	6♎	17	29	11♏	24	6♐	18	1♑	14	27	10♒	24	
☿	8♈	10	12	14	16	18	20	22	24	26	28	0♉	2	4	6	8	10	12	14	16	18	19	21	22	24	25	27	28	29	0♊	
♀	10♈	11	13	14	15	16	18	19	20	21	23	24	25	26	28	29	0♉	1	3	4	5	6	7	9	10	11	12	14	15	16	
♂	13♊	13	14	14	15	16	16	17	18	18	19	19	20	21	21	22	22	23	24	24	25	26	26	27	27	28	29	29	30	0♋	
	1	6	11	16	21	26			1	11	21			1	11	21			1	16		1	16		1	16		1	11	21	
♃	3♊	4	5	6	7	8		♄	14♑	14	14		⚷	2♋	2	3		♅	5♑	5	♆	12♑	12	♇	15♏	14	☊	3♓	2	2	

MAY

MAY	1	2	3	4	5	6	7	8	9	10	11	12	13	14	15	16	17	18	19	20	21	22	23	24	25	26	27	28	29	30	31
☉	11♉	12	13	14	14	15	16	17	18	19	20	21	22	23	24	25	26	27	28	29	30	1♊	2	3	4	5	6	7	8	9	10
☽	8♓	23	8♈	23	8♉	23	7♊	22	6♋	19	2♌	14	27	9♍	21	2♎	14	26	8♏	20	3♐	15	28	11♑	24	7♒	21	4♓	18	3♈	17
☿	1♊	2	3	4	4	5	6	6	6	7	7	7	7	7	7	6	6	6	5	5	4	4	3	3	2	2	1	0	30♉	30	29
♀	17♉	19	20	21	22	24	25	26	27	28	30	1♊	2	3	5	6	7	8	10	11	12	13	14	16	17	18	19	21	22	23	24
♂	1♋	2	2	3	4	4	5	5	6	7	7	8	9	9	10	10	11	12	12	13	13	14	15	15	16	17	17	18	18	19	20
	1	6	11	16	21	26	31		1	11	21	31		1	11	21	31		1	16		1	16		1	16		1	11	21	31
♃	10♊	11	12	13	14	15	16	♄	14♑	14	13	13	⚷	3♋	4	5	6	♅	5♑	5	♆	12♑	12	♇	14♏	13	☊	1♓	1	0	30♒

JUN

JUN	1	2	3	4	5	6	7	8	9	10	11	12	13	14	15	16	17	18	19	20	21	22	23	24	25	26	27	28	29	30	
☉	10♊	11	12	13	14	15	16	17	18	19	20	21	22	23	24	25	26	27	28	29	30	1♋	2	2	3	4	5	6	7	8	
☽	2♉	17	1♊	16	30	14♋	27	10♌	23	5♍	17	29	11♎	22	4♏	17	29	11♐	24	7♑	21	4♒	18	1♓	15	29	14♈	28	12♉	26	
☿	29♉	29	28	28	28	28	28	28	29	29	29	30	0♊	1	2	2	3	4	5	6	7	8	9	11	12	13	15	16	18	19	
♀	25♊	27	28	29	0♋	2	3	4	5	6	8	9	10	11	13	14	15	16	17	19	20	21	22	24	25	26	27	28	30	1♌	
♂	20♋	21	22	22	23	23	24	25	25	26	27	27	28	28	29	30	0♌	1	1	2	3	3	4	5	5	6	6	7	8	8	
	1	6	11	16	21	26			1	11	21			1	11	21			1	16		1	16		1	16		1	11	21	
♃	17♊	18	19	20	21	22		♄	13♑	12	11		⚷	6♋	7	8		♅	4♑	4	♆	12♑	11	♇	13♏	13	☊	30♒	29	29	

1989

JUL

	1	2	3	4	5	6	7	8	9	10	11	12	13	14	15	16	17	18	19	20	21	22	23	24	25	26	27	28	29	30	31
☉	9♋	10	11	12	13	14	15	16	17	18	19	20	21	22	22	23	24	25	26	27	28	29	0♌	1	2	3	4	5	6	7	8
☽	11♊	25	8♋	22	5♌	18	0♍	13	25	7♎	19	0♏	12	25	7♐	20	3♑	16	30	14♒	28	12♓	26	10♈	25	9♉	23	7♊	21	4♋	18
☿	21♊	23	24	26	28	30	2♋	4	6	8	10	12	14	16	19	21	23	25	27	29	1♌	3	5	7	10	12	13	15	17	19	21
♀	2♌	3	4	6	7	8	9	11	12	13	14	15	17	18	19	20	21	23	24	25	26	28	29	30	1♍	2	4	5	6	7	8
♂	9♌	10	10	11	11	12	13	13	14	15	15	16	16	17	18	18	19	20	20	21	21	22	23	23	24	25	25	26	26	27	28
	1	6	11	16	21	26	31		1	11	21	31		1	11	21	31		1	16		1	16		1	16		1	11	21	31
♃	23♊	25	26	27	28	29	0♋	♄	11♑	10	9	9	⚷	9♋	10	11	12	♅	3♑	3	♆	11♑	11	♇	13♏	12	☊	28♒	28	27	27

AUG

	1	2	3	4	5	6	7	8	9	10	11	12	13	14	15	16	17	18	19	20	21	22	23	24	25	26	27	28	29	30	31
☉	9♌	10	11	12	13	14	14	15	16	17	18	19	20	21	22	23	24	25	26	27	28	29	30	1♍	2	3	4	5	6	7	8
☽	1♌	14	26	9♍	21	3♎	15	26	8♏	20	3♐	15	28	11♑	24	8♒	22	7♓	21	6♈	21	5♉	20	4♊	17	1♋	14	27	10♌	23	5♍
☿	23♌	25	26	28	30	2♍	3	5	7	8	10	11	13	14	16	17	18	20	21	23	24	25	26	27	29	30	1♎	2	3	4	5
♀	10♍	11	12	13	14	16	17	18	19	20	22	23	24	25	26	28	29	30	1♎	2	3	5	6	7	8	9	11	12	13	14	15
♂	28♌	29	30	0♍	1	2	2	3	3	4	5	5	6	7	7	8	8	9	10	10	11	12	12	13	14	14	15	15	16	17	17
	1	6	11	16	21	26	31		1	11	21	31		1	11	21	31		1	16		1	16		1	16		1	11	21	31
♃	0♋	1	2	3	4	5	6	♄	9♑	8	8	7	⚷	12♋	13	14	14	♅	2♑	2	♆	10♑	10	♇	12♏	13	☊	27♒	26	26	25

SEP

	1	2	3	4	5	6	7	8	9	10	11	12	13	14	15	16	17	18	19	20	21	22	23	24	25	26	27	28	29	30
☉	9♍	10	10	11	12	13	14	15	16	17	18	19	20	21	22	23	24	25	26	27	28	29	30	1♎	2	3	4	5	6	7
☽	17♍	29	11♎	23	5♏	17	29	11♐	23	6♑	19	2♒	16	1♓	15	0♈	15	0♉	15	30	14♊	28	11♋	24	7♌	19	2♍	14	26	8♎
☿	6♎	6	7	8	8	9	9	10	10	10	11	11	10	10	10	10	9	8	8	7	6	5	4	3	2	1	30♍	29	28	27
♀	16♎	18	19	20	21	22	24	25	26	27	28	29	1♏	2	3	4	5	6	8	9	10	11	12	13	14	16	17	18	19	20
♂	18♍	19	19	20	21	21	22	23	23	24	24	25	26	26	27	28	28	29	30	0♎	1	2	2	3	3	4	5	5	6	7
	1	6	11	16	21	26			1	11	21			1	11	21			1	16		1	16		1	16		1	11	21
♃	6♋	7	7	8	9	9		♄	7♑	7	7		⚷	14♋	15	16		♅	1♑	1	♆	10♑	10	♇	13♏	13	☊	25♒	24	24

OCT

	1	2	3	4	5	6	7	8	9	10	11	12	13	14	15	16	17	18	19	20	21	22	23	24	25	26	27	28	29	30	31
☉	8♎	9	10	11	12	13	14	15	16	17	18	19	20	21	22	23	24	25	26	27	28	29	30	1♏	2	3	4	5	6	7	8
☽	20♎	2♏	13	25	7♐	19	2♑	14	27	11♒	24	9♓	23	8♈	24	9♉	24	9♊	23	7♋	21	4♌	17	29	11♍	23	5♎	17	29	10♏	22
☿	27♍	26	26	26	26	26	27	27	28	29	30	1♎	2	3	5	6	8	9	11	12	14	16	17	19	21	22	24	26	27	29	1♏
♀	21♏	22	24	25	26	27	28	29	0♐	1	3	4	5	6	7	8	9	10	11	13	14	15	16	17	18	19	20	21	22	23	24
♂	7♎	8	9	9	10	11	11	12	13	13	14	15	15	16	17	17	18	19	19	20	21	21	22	23	23	24	25	25	26	27	27
	1	6	11	16	21	26	31		1	11	21	31		1	11	21	31		1	16		1	16		1	16		1	11	21	31
♃	10♋	10	10	11	11	11	11	♄	8♑	8	9	9	⚷	16♋	16	17	17	♅	2♑	2	♆	10♑	10	♇	14♏	14	☊	23♒	23	22	22

NOV

	1	2	3	4	5	6	7	8	9	10	11	12	13	14	15	16	17	18	19	20	21	22	23	24	25	26	27	28	29	30
☉	9♏	10	11	12	13	14	15	16	17	18	19	20	21	22	23	24	25	26	27	28	29	30	1♐	2	3	4	5	6	7	8
☽	4♐	16	29	11♑	24	6♒	20	3♓	17	2♈	17	2♉	17	2♊	17	2♋	16	30	13♌	25	8♍	20	2♎	14	25	7♏	19	1♐	13	26
☿	2♏	4	6	7	9	11	12	14	15	17	19	20	22	23	25	27	28	30	1♐	3	4	6	8	9	11	12	14	15	17	18
♀	25♐	26	28	29	30	1♑	2	3	4	5	6	7	8	9	10	10	11	12	13	14	15	16	17	18	19	19	20	21	22	23
♂	28♎	29	29	30	1♏	1	2	3	3	4	5	5	6	7	7	8	9	9	10	11	11	12	13	13	14	15	15	16	17	17
	1	6	11	16	21	26			1	11	21			1	11	21			1	16		1	16		1	16		1	11	21
♃	11♋	11	11	10	10	10		♄	9♑	10	11		⚷	17♋	16	16		♅	2♑	3	♆	10♑	10	♇	15♏	15	☊	22♒	21	21

DEC

	1	2	3	4	5	6	7	8	9	10	11	12	13	14	15	16	17	18	19	20	21	22	23	24	25	26	27	28	29	30	31
☉	9♐	10	11	12	13	14	15	16	17	18	19	20	21	22	23	24	25	26	27	28	29	0♑	1	2	3	4	5	6	7	8	9
☽	8♑	21	3♒	16	30	13♓	27	11♈	26	11♉	25	10♊	25	10♋	24	8♌	21	4♍	16	28	10♎	22	4♏	16	28	10♐	22	5♑	17	0♒	13
☿	20♐	21	23	25	26	28	29	1♑	2	4	5	7	8	9	11	12	14	15	16	18	19	20	21	22	23	24	25	25	26	26	26
♀	24♑	24	25	26	27	27	28	29	29	30	0♒	1	2	2	3	3	4	4	4	5	5	5	6	6	6	6	6	6	6	6	6
♂	18♏	19	19	20	21	22	22	23	24	24	25	26	26	27	28	28	29	30	1♐	1	2	3	3	4	5	5	6	7	8	8	9
	1	6	11	16	21	26	31		1	11	21	31		1	11	21	31		1	16		1	16		1	16		1	11	21	31
♃	9♋	9	8	7	7	6	5	♄	12♑	13	14	15	⚷	16♋	15	15	14	♅	4♑	5	♆	11♑	11	♇	16♏	17	☊	20♒	20	19	19

1990

EPHEMERIS

JAN

	1	2	3	4	5	6	7	8	9	10	11	12	13	14	15	16	17	18	19	20	21	22	23	24	25	26	27	28	29	30	31
☉	10♑	11	12	13	14	15	16	17	18	19	20	22	23	24	25	26	27	28	29	30	1♒	2	3	4	5	6	7	8	9	10	11
☽	27♒	10♓	24	8♈	22	6♉	20	5♊	19	4♋	18	2♌	15	28	11♍	24	6♎	18	30	12♏	24	6♐	18	0♑	13	26	9♒	23	6♓	20	4♈
☿	26♑	26	25	24	23	22	21	20	19	17	16	15	14	13	12	11	10	10	10	10	10	10	10	11	11	12	12	13	14	15	16
♀	6♒	6	6	6	6	5	5	5	4	4	3	3	2	2	1	0	30♑	29	29	28	27	27	26	26	25	25	24	24	23	23	22
♂	10♐	10	11	12	12	13	14	15	15	16	17	17	18	19	20	20	21	22	22	23	24	25	25	26	27	27	28	29	30	0♑	1
	1	6	11	16	21	26	31		1	11	21	31		1	11	21	31		1	16		1	16		1	16		1	11	21	31
♃	5♋	5	4	3	3	2	2	♄	16♑	17	18	19	⚷	14♋	13	12	12	♅	6♑	7	♆	12♑	13	♇	17♏	17	☊	18♒	18	17	17

FEB

	1	2	3	4	5	6	7	8	9	10	11	12	13	14	15	16	17	18	19	20	21	22	23	24	25	26	27	28			
☉	12♒	13	14	15	16	17	18	19	20	21	22	23	24	25	26	27	28	29	0♓	1	2	3	4	5	6	7	8	9			
☽	18♈	3♉	17	1♊	15	29	13♋	27	10♌	23	6♍	19	1♎	14	26	8♏	20	1♐	13	26	8♑	21	4♒	17	1♓	15	30	14♈			
☿	17♑	18	19	20	21	22	23	25	26	27	29	30	1♒	3	4	5	7	8	10	11	13	14	16	17	19	21	22	24			
♀	22♑	22	22	21	21	21	21	21	21	21	21	21	21	22	22	22	22	23	23	23	24	24	25	25	26	26	27	28			
♂	2♑	2	3	4	5	5	6	7	8	8	9	10	10	11	12	13	13	14	15	16	16	17	18	18	19	20	21	21			
	1	6	11	16	21	26			1	11	21			1	11	21			1	16		1	16		1	16		1	11	21	
♃	2♋	1	1	1	1	1		♄	19♑	20	21		⚷	12♋	11	11		♅	8♑	8	♆	13♑	14	♇	18♏	18	☊	17♒	16	16	

MAR

	1	2	3	4	5	6	7	8	9	10	11	12	13	14	15	16	17	18	19	20	21	22	23	24	25	26	27	28	29	30	31
☉	10♓	11	12	13	14	15	16	17	18	19	20	21	22	23	24	25	26	27	28	29	0♈	1	2	3	4	5	6	7	8	9	10
☽	29♈	13♉	28	12♊	26	10♋	23	6♌	19	2♍	15	27	10♎	22	4♏	16	28	9♐	21	4♑	16	29	12♒	25	9♓	24	8♈	23	8♉	23	8♊
☿	25♒	27	29	0♓	2	4	6	7	9	11	13	15	16	18	20	22	24	26	28	30	2♈	4	6	8	10	12	14	16	18	20	22
♀	28♑	29	29	0♒	1	2	2	3	4	5	5	6	7	8	9	10	10	11	12	13	14	15	16	17	18	19	20	21	22	23	24
♂	22♑	23	24	24	25	26	27	27	28	29	30	0♒	1	2	2	3	4	5	5	6	7	8	8	9	10	11	11	12	13	14	14
	1	6	11	16	21	26	31		1	11	21	31		1	11	21	31		1	16		1	16		1	16		1	11	21	31
♃	1♋	1	1	1	2	2	3	♄	22♑	23	24	24	⚷	11♋	11	11	11	♅	9♑	9	♆	14♑	14	♇	18♏	18	☊	15♒	15	14	14

APR

	1	2	3	4	5	6	7	8	9	10	11	12	13	14	15	16	17	18	19	20	21	22	23	24	25	26	27	28	29	30	
☉	11♈	12	13	14	15	16	17	18	19	20	21	22	23	24	25	26	27	28	29	30	1♉	2	3	4	5	6	6	7	8	9	
☽	22♊	6♋	20	3♌	16	29	12♍	24	6♎	18	0♏	12	24	6♐	18	30	12♑	24	7♒	20	3♓	17	2♈	17	2♉	17	2♊	17	2♋	16	
☿	24♈	26	28	29	1♉	3	4	6	7	9	10	11	12	13	14	15	16	16	17	17	17	17	18	18	17	17	17	17	16	16	
♀	25♒	26	27	28	29	30	1♓	2	3	4	5	6	7	8	9	10	11	12	13	14	15	17	18	19	20	21	22	23	24	25	
♂	15♒	16	17	17	18	19	20	20	21	22	23	23	24	25	26	26	27	28	29	29	0♓	1	2	2	3	4	5	5	6	7	
	1	6	11	16	21	26			1	11	21			1	11	21			1	16		1	16		1	16		1	11	21	
♃	3♋	3	4	5	5	6		♄	24♑	25	25		⚷	11♋	11	12		♅	10♑	10	♆	15♑	15	♇	17♏	17	☊	14♒	13	13	

MAY

	1	2	3	4	5	6	7	8	9	10	11	12	13	14	15	16	17	18	19	20	21	22	23	24	25	26	27	28	29	30	31
☉	10♉	11	12	13	14	15	16	17	18	19	20	21	22	23	24	25	26	27	28	29	30	1♊	2	3	4	5	5	6	7	8	9
☽	30♋	13♌	26	9♍	21	3♎	15	27	9♏	21	3♐	15	27	9♑	21	3♒	16	29	12♓	26	10♈	25	10♉	26	11♊	26	11♋	25	9♌	22	5♍
☿	15♉	15	14	13	13	12	11	11	10	10	9	9	9	8	8	8	8	8	8	8	9	9	9	10	10	11	12	12	13	14	15
♀	26♓	28	29	30	1♈	2	3	4	5	7	8	9	10	11	12	13	15	16	17	18	19	20	21	23	24	25	26	27	28	30	1♉
♂	8♓	8	9	10	11	11	12	13	13	14	15	16	16	17	18	19	19	20	21	22	22	23	24	25	25	26	27	28	28	29	30
	1	6	11	16	21	26	31		1	11	21	31		1	11	21	31		1	16		1	16		1	16		1	11	21	31
♃	7♋	8	9	10	11	12	13	♄	25♑	25	25	25	⚷	12♋	13	14	15	♅	9♑	9	♆	15♑	14	♇	17♏	16	☊	12♒	12	11	11

JUN

	1	2	3	4	5	6	7	8	9	10	11	12	13	14	15	16	17	18	19	20	21	22	23	24	25	26	27	28	29	30	
☉	10♊	11	12	13	14	15	16	17	18	19	20	21	22	23	24	25	26	27	27	28	29	0♋	1	2	3	4	5	6	7	8	
☽	18♍	0♎	12	24	6♏	18	30	12♐	24	6♑	18	0♒	13	26	9♓	22	6♈	20	4♉	19	4♊	19	4♋	19	3♌	17	1♍	14	26	9♎	
☿	16♉	17	18	19	20	22	23	24	26	27	28	30	2♊	3	5	7	8	10	12	14	16	18	20	22	24	26	28	0♋	2	5	
♀	2♉	3	4	5	6	8	9	10	11	12	13	15	16	17	18	19	21	22	23	24	25	26	28	29	30	1♊	2	4	5	6	
♂	1♈	1	2	3	3	4	5	6	6	7	8	9	9	10	11	11	12	13	14	14	15	16	16	17	18	19	19	20	21	21	
	1	6	11	16	21	26			1	11	21			1	11	21			1	16		1	16		1	16		1	11	21	
♃	13♋	14	15	16	17	18		♄	25♑	24	24		⚷	15♋	16	17		♅	9♑	8	♆	14♑	14	♇	16♏	15	☊	10♒	10	9	

1990

EPHEMERIS

JUL

	1	2	3	4	5	6	7	8	9	10	11	12	13	14	15	16	17	18	19	20	21	22	23	24	25	26	27	28	29	30	31
☉	9♋	10	11	12	13	14	15	16	17	18	18	19	20	21	22	23	24	25	26	27	28	29	30	1♌	2	3	4	5	6	7	8
☽	21♎	3♏	15	27	9♐	21	3♑	15	27	10♒	23	6♓	19	2♈	16	0♉	15	29	14♊	28	13♋	27	11♌	25	9♍	22	5♎	17	29	11♏	23
☿	7♋	9	11	13	15	18	20	22	24	26	28	0♌	2	4	6	8	10	11	13	15	17	18	20	22	23	25	26	28	29	1♍	2
♀	7♊	8	9	11	12	13	14	15	17	18	19	20	21	23	24	25	26	27	29	30	1♋	2	3	5	6	7	8	9	11	12	13
♂	22♈	23	23	24	25	25	26	27	28	28	29	30	0♉	1	2	2	3	4	4	5	6	6	7	8	8	9	9	10	11	11	12
	1	6	11	16	21	26	31		1	11	21	31		1	11	21	31		1	16		1	16		1	16		1	11	21	31
♃	19♋	20	22	23	24	25	26	♄	23♑	22	22	21	⚷	18♋	19	20	21	♅	8♑	7	♆	13♑	13	♇	15♏	15	☊	9♒	8	8	7

AUG

	1	2	3	4	5	6	7	8	9	10	11	12	13	14	15	16	17	18	19	20	21	22	23	24	25	26	27	28	29	30	31
☉	9♌	9	10	11	12	13	14	15	16	17	18	19	20	21	22	23	24	25	26	27	28	29	30	1♍	2	3	3	4	5	6	7
☽	5♐	17	29	11♑	24	6♒	19	2♓	16	29	13♈	27	11♉	25	10♊	24	8♋	22	6♌	20	4♍	17	30	13♎	25	7♏	19	1♐	13	25	7♑
☿	4♍	5	6	8	9	10	11	12	13	14	15	16	17	18	19	20	20	21	22	22	23	23	23	23	24	24	23	23	23	23	22
♀	14♋	16	17	18	19	20	22	23	24	25	26	28	29	0♌	1	3	4	5	6	7	9	10	11	12	14	15	16	17	18	20	21
♂	13♉	13	14	15	15	16	16	17	18	18	19	19	20	21	21	22	22	23	23	24	24	25	26	26	27	27	28	28	29	29	30
	1	6	11	16	21	26	31		1	11	21	31		1	11	21	31		1	16		1	16		1	16		1	11	21	31
♃	26♋	27	28	30	1♌	2	3	♄	21♑	20	20	19	⚷	21♋	22	23	24	♅	6♑	6	♆	13♑	12	♇	15♏	15	☊	7♒	7	6	6

SEP

	1	2	3	4	5	6	7	8	9	10	11	12	13	14	15	16	17	18	19	20	21	22	23	24	25	26	27	28	29	30
☉	8♍	9	10	11	12	13	14	15	16	17	18	19	20	21	22	23	24	25	26	27	28	29	30	1♎	2	3	4	5	6	7
☽	19♑	2♒	15	28	11♓	25	9♈	23	8♉	22	6♊	21	5♋	19	2♌	16	29	12♍	25	8♎	21	3♏	15	27	9♐	21	3♑	15	27	9♒
☿	22♍	21	20	19	18	17	16	15	14	14	13	12	11	11	10	10	10	10	10	10	11	11	12	13	14	15	16	18	19	21
♀	22♌	23	25	26	27	28	30	1♍	2	3	5	6	7	8	9	11	12	13	14	16	17	18	19	21	22	23	24	26	27	28
♂	0♊	1	1	2	2	3	3	4	4	4	5	5	6	6	7	7	7	8	8	8	9	9	10	10	10	10	11	11	11	12
	1	6	11	16	21	26			1	11	21			1	11	21			1	16		1	16		1	16		1	11	21
♃	3♌	4	5	6	7	7		♄	19♑	19	19		⚷	24♋	25	26		♅	6♑	6	♆	12♑	12	♇	15♏	16	☊	6♒	5	5

OCT

	1	2	3	4	5	6	7	8	9	10	11	12	13	14	15	16	17	18	19	20	21	22	23	24	25	26	27	28	29	30	31
☉	8♎	9	10	11	11	12	13	14	15	16	17	18	19	20	21	22	23	24	25	26	27	28	29	0♏	1	2	3	4	5	6	7
☽	22♒	6♓	20	4♈	18	3♉	18	3♊	17	1♋	16	29	13♌	26	9♍	22	4♎	17	29	11♏	23	5♐	17	29	11♑	23	5♒	17	0♓	14	27
☿	22♍	24	25	27	29	0♎	2	4	6	7	9	11	13	15	16	18	20	21	23	25	27	28	30	2♏	3	5	6	8	10	11	13
♀	29♍	1♎	2	3	4	6	7	8	9	11	12	13	14	16	17	18	19	21	22	23	24	26	27	28	29	1♏	2	3	4	6	7
♂	12♊	12	12	13	13	13	13	13	14	14	14	14	14	14	14	14	14	15	15	15	15	15	15	14	14	14	14	14	14	14	14
	1	6	11	16	21	26	31		1	11	21	31		1	11	21	31		1	16		1	16		1	16		1	11	21	31
♃	8♌	9	10	10	11	12	12	♄	19♑	19	19	20	⚷	26♋	27	27	27	♅	6♑	6	♆	12♑	12	♇	16♏	17	☊	4♒	3	3	2

NOV

	1	2	3	4	5	6	7	8	9	10	11	12	13	14	15	16	17	18	19	20	21	22	23	24	25	26	27	28	29	30
☉	8♏	9	10	11	12	13	14	15	16	17	18	19	20	21	22	23	24	25	26	27	28	29	0♐	1	2	3	4	5	6	8
☽	12♈	27	12♉	27	12♊	27	11♋	26	10♌	23	6♍	19	1♎	14	26	8♏	20	2♐	14	26	8♑	19	1♒	14	26	9♓	22	6♈	20	5♉
☿	14♏	16	18	19	21	22	24	25	27	28	30	2♐	3	5	6	8	9	10	12	13	15	16	18	19	21	22	23	25	26	27
♀	8♏	9	11	12	13	14	16	17	18	19	21	22	23	24	26	27	28	29	1♐	2	3	5	6	7	8	10	11	12	13	15
♂	14♊	13	13	13	13	13	12	12	12	12	11	11	11	10	10	10	9	9	9	8	8	8	7	7	6	6	6	5	5	5
	1	6	11	16	21	26			1	11	21			1	11	21			1	16		1	16		1	16		1	11	21
♃	12♌	13	13	13	13	14		♄	20♑	21	21		⚷	27♋	27	27		♅	7♑	7	♆	12♑	13	♇	17♏	18	☊	2♒	2	1

DEC

	1	2	3	4	5	6	7	8	9	10	11	12	13	14	15	16	17	18	19	20	21	22	23	24	25	26	27	28	29	30	31
☉	9♐	10	11	12	13	14	15	16	17	18	19	20	21	22	23	24	25	26	27	28	29	30	1♑	2	3	4	5	6	7	8	9
☽	20♉	5♊	20	5♋	20	5♌	19	2♍	16	28	11♎	23	5♏	17	29	11♐	23	5♑	17	28	11♒	23	5♓	18	1♈	15	29	13♉	28	13♊	28
☿	29♐	30	1♑	2	4	5	6	7	7	8	9	9	10	10	10	10	10	9	8	8	6	5	4	3	1	30♐	29	27	26	26	25
♀	16♐	17	18	20	21	22	23	25	26	27	28	30	1♑	2	3	5	6	7	8	10	11	12	13	15	16	17	18	20	21	22	23
♂	4♊	4	3	3	3	2	2	2	1	1	1	1	0	0	30♉	30	29	29	29	29	29	28	28	28	28	28	28	28	28	28	28
	1	6	11	16	21	26	31		1	11	21	31		1	11	21	31		1	16		1	16		1	16		1	11	21	31
♃	14♌	14	13	13	13	13	12	♄	22♑	23	24	26	⚷	27♋	27	26	25	♅	8♑	9	♆	13♑	14	♇	19♏	19	☊	1♒	0	30♑	29

1991

EPHEMERIS

JAN

	1	2	3	4	5	6	7	8	9	10	11	12	13	14	15	16	17	18	19	20	21	22	23	24	25	26	27	28	29	30	31
☉	10♑	11	12	13	14	15	16	17	18	19	20	21	22	23	24	25	26	27	28	29	0♒	1	2	3	5	6	7	8	9	10	11
☽	13♋	28	13♌	27	11♍	24	7♎	20	2♏	14	26	8♐	20	1♑	13	25	8♒	20	2♓	15	28	11♈	25	9♉	23	7♊	22	7♋	21	6♌	21
☿	24♐	24	24	24	24	24	24	25	26	26	27	28	29	30	1♑	2	3	4	5	6	8	9	10	11	13	14	16	17	18	20	21
♀	25♑	26	27	28	30	1♒	2	3	5	6	7	9	10	11	12	14	15	16	17	19	20	21	22	24	25	26	27	29	30	1♓	2
♂	28♉	28	28	28	28	28	28	28	28	28	28	28	29	29	29	29	29	29	30	30	30	0♊	0	1	1	1	1	2	2	2	3
	1	6	11	16	21	26	31		1	11	21	31		1	11	21	31		1	16		1	16		1	16		1	11	21	31
♃	12♌	11	11	10	10	9	8	♄	26♑	27	28	29	⚷	25♋	25	24	23	♅	10♑	11	♆	14♑	15	♇	20♏	20	☊	29♑	29	28	28

FEB

	1	2	3	4	5	6	7	8	9	10	11	12	13	14	15	16	17	18	19	20	21	22	23	24	25	26	27	28			
☉	12♒	13	14	15	16	17	18	19	20	21	22	23	24	25	26	27	28	29	30	1♓	2	3	4	5	6	7	8	9			
☽	5♍	19	2♎	15	28	10♏	22	4♐	16	28	10♑	22	4♒	16	29	12♓	25	8♈	22	5♉	19	3♊	18	2♋	16	0♌	15	29			
☿	23♑	24	26	27	29	0♒	2	3	5	6	8	9	11	13	14	16	18	19	21	23	25	26	28	30	2♓	3	5	7			
♀	3♓	5	6	7	8	10	11	12	13	15	16	17	18	20	21	22	23	25	26	27	28	30	1♈	2	3	4	6	7			
♂	3♊	3	4	4	4	5	5	5	6	6	6	7	7	7	8	8	9	9	9	10	10	11	11	11	12	12	13	13			
	1	6	11	16	21	26			1	11	21			1	11	21			1	16		1	16		1	16		1	11	21	
♃	8♌	8	7	6	6	5		♄	29♑	0♒	2		⚷	23♋	22	22		♅	12♑	12	♆	15♑	16	♇	20♏	20	☊	27♑	27	26	

MAR

	1	2	3	4	5	6	7	8	9	10	11	12	13	14	15	16	17	18	19	20	21	22	23	24	25	26	27	28	29	30	31
☉	10♓	11	12	13	14	15	16	17	18	19	20	21	22	23	24	25	26	27	28	29	30	1♈	2	3	4	5	6	7	8	9	10
☽	13♍	27	10♎	23	6♏	18	0♐	12	24	6♑	18	30	12♒	25	7♓	21	4♈	18	2♉	16	0♊	14	29	13♋	27	11♌	24	8♍	22	5♎	18
☿	9♓	11	13	15	17	18	20	22	24	26	28	0♈	2	4	6	8	10	11	13	15	16	18	19	21	22	23	24	25	26	27	28
♀	8♈	9	11	12	13	14	16	17	18	19	20	22	23	24	25	26	28	29	0♉	1	3	4	5	6	7	9	10	11	12	13	15
♂	14♊	14	15	15	16	16	16	17	17	18	18	19	19	20	20	21	21	22	22	23	23	24	24	25	25	26	26	27	27	28	28
	1	6	11	16	21	26	31		1	11	21	31		1	11	21	31		1	16		1	16		1	16		1	11	21	31
♃	5♌	5	4	4	4	4	4	♄	2♒	3	4	5	⚷	22♋	21	21	21	♅	13♑	13	♆	16♑	16	♇	20♏	20	☊	26♑	25	25	24

APR

	1	2	3	4	5	6	7	8	9	10	11	12	13	14	15	16	17	18	19	20	21	22	23	24	25	26	27	28	29	30	
☉	11♈	12	13	14	15	16	17	18	19	20	21	22	23	24	25	26	26	27	28	29	0♉	1	2	3	4	5	6	7	8	9	
☽	1♏	14	26	8♐	20	2♑	14	25	8♒	20	2♓	16	29	13♈	27	11♉	26	11♊	25	9♋	24	7♌	21	5♍	18	1♎	14	27	10♏	22	
☿	28♈	29	29	29	29	29	29	28	28	28	27	26	26	25	24	24	24	23	22	21	21	20	20	19	19	18	18	18	18	18	
♀	16♉	17	18	19	21	22	23	24	25	26	28	29	30	1♊	2	4	5	6	7	8	9	11	12	13	14	15	16	17	19	20	
♂	29♊	29	30	1♋	1	2	2	3	3	4	4	5	5	6	6	7	8	8	9	9	10	10	11	11	12	13	13	14	14	15	
	1	6	11	16	21	26			1	11	21			1	11	21			1	16		1	16		1	16		1	11	21	
♃	4♌	4	4	4	4	5		♄	5♒	6	6		⚷	21♋	21	22		♅	14♑	14	♆	17♑	17	♇	20♏	20	☊	24♑	24	23	

MAY

	1	2	3	4	5	6	7	8	9	10	11	12	13	14	15	16	17	18	19	20	21	22	23	24	25	26	27	28	29	30	31
☉	10♉	11	12	13	14	15	16	17	18	19	20	21	22	23	24	25	26	27	28	29	29	0♊	1	2	3	4	5	6	7	8	9
☽	4♐	16	28	10♑	22	4♒	16	28	11♓	24	7♈	21	5♉	20	5♊	20	5♋	19	4♌	18	2♍	15	28	11♎	24	6♏	19	1♐	13	25	7♑
☿	18♈	19	19	19	20	20	21	22	22	23	24	25	26	27	28	29	0♉	1	2	4	5	6	8	9	11	12	14	16	17	19	21
♀	21♊	22	23	24	25	27	28	29	30	1♋	2	3	4	6	7	8	9	10	11	12	13	14	15	16	17	19	20	21	22	23	24
♂	15♋	16	16	17	18	18	19	19	20	20	21	22	22	23	23	24	24	25	26	26	27	27	28	29	29	30	0♌	1	1	2	3
	1	6	11	16	21	26	31		1	11	21	31		1	11	21	31		1	16		1	16		1	16		1	11	21	31
♃	5♌	6	6	7	7	8	9	♄	7♒	7	7	7	⚷	22♋	23	24	24	♅	14♑	14	♆	17♑	17	♇	19♏	19	☊	23♑	22	22	21

JUN

	1	2	3	4	5	6	7	8	9	10	11	12	13	14	15	16	17	18	19	20	21	22	23	24	25	26	27	28	29	30	
☉	10♊	11	12	13	14	15	16	17	18	19	20	21	22	22	23	24	25	26	27	28	29	0♋	1	2	3	4	5	6	7	8	
☽	18♑	0♒	12	24	6♓	19	2♈	15	29	14♉	28	13♊	29	14♋	29	13♌	28	12♍	25	8♎	21	3♏	16	28	10♐	22	4♑	15	27	9♒	
☿	22♉	24	26	28	30	2♊	4	6	8	10	12	14	16	19	21	23	25	27	29	2♋	4	6	8	10	12	14	16	18	20	22	
♀	25♋	26	27	28	29	30	1♌	2	3	4	5	6	7	8	9	10	11	12	13	13	14	15	16	17	18	19	20	20	21	22	
♂	3♌	4	4	5	6	6	7	7	8	9	9	10	10	11	12	12	13	13	14	15	15	16	16	17	18	18	19	19	20	21	
	1	6	11	16	21	26			1	11	21			1	11	21			1	16		1	16		1	16		1	11	21	
♃	9♌	10	11	12	12	13		♄	7♒	6	6		⚷	25♋	26	27		♅	13♑	13	♆	16♑	16	♇	18♏	18	☊	21♑	21	20	

EPHEMERIS

1991

JUL

	1	2	3	4	5	6	7	8	9	10	11	12	13	14	15	16	17	18	19	20	21	22	23	24	25	26	27	28	29	30	31
☉	9♋	10	11	12	13	13	14	15	16	17	18	19	20	21	22	23	24	25	26	27	28	29	30	1♌	2	3	3	4	5	6	7
☽	21♒	3♓	15	28	11♈	24	8♉	22	7♊	22	7♋	22	7♌	22	6♍	21	4♎	17	0♏	13	25	7♐	19	1♑	12	24	6♒	18	0♓	13	25
☿	24♋	26	28	30	1♌	3	5	6	8	10	11	13	14	15	17	18	20	21	22	23	24	26	27	28	29	30	0♍	1	2	3	3
♀	23♌	24	24	25	26	27	27	28	29	29	30	0♍	1	2	2	3	3	4	4	5	5	5	6	6	6	7	7	7	7	7	7
♂	21♌	22	22	23	24	24	25	25	26	27	27	28	28	29	30	0♍	1	2	2	3	3	4	5	5	6	6	7	8	8	9	10
	1	6	11	16	21	26	31		1	11	21	31		1	11	21	31		1	16		1	16		1	16		1	11	21	31
♃	14♌	15	16	17	18	20	21	♄	5♒	5	4	3	⚷	28♋	29	30	1♌	♅	12♑	11	♆	16♑	15	♇	18♏	18	☊	20♑	19	18	18

AUG

	1	2	3	4	5	6	7	8	9	10	11	12	13	14	15	16	17	18	19	20	21	22	23	24	25	26	27	28	29	30	31
☉	8♌	9	10	11	12	13	14	15	16	17	18	19	20	21	22	23	24	25	26	27	27	28	29	0♍	1	2	3	4	5	6	7
☽	8♈	21	4♉	18	2♊	16	1♋	16	1♌	15	0♍	15	29	13♎	26	9♏	21	3♐	15	27	9♑	21	3♒	15	27	9♓	22	5♈	18	1♉	15
☿	4♍	4	5	5	6	6	6	6	6	6	6	5	5	4	4	3	2	2	1	30♌	29	28	27	27	26	25	24	24	24	23	23
♀	7♍	7	7	7	7	7	7	6	6	6	6	5	5	4	4	3	3	2	2	1	0	30♌	29	29	28	27	27	26	26	25	24
♂	10♍	11	11	12	13	13	14	15	15	16	16	17	18	18	19	20	20	21	22	22	23	23	24	25	25	26	27	27	28	29	29
	1	6	11	16	21	26	31		1	11	21	31		1	11	21	31		1	16		1	16		1	16		1	11	21	31
♃	21♌	22	23	24	25	26	27	♄	3♒	2	2	1	⚷	1♌	2	3	5	♅	11♑	10	♆	15♑	14	♇	18♏	18	☊	18♑	17	17	16

SEP

	1	2	3	4	5	6	7	8	9	10	11	12	13	14	15	16	17	18	19	20	21	22	23	24	25	26	27	28	29	30
☉	8♍	9	10	11	12	13	14	15	16	17	18	19	20	21	22	23	24	25	26	27	28	28	29	0♎	1	2	3	4	5	6
☽	28♉	12♊	26	11♋	25	10♌	24	9♍	23	7♎	21	4♏	17	29	12♐	24	5♑	17	29	11♒	23	6♓	18	1♈	14	28	11♉	25	9♊	23
☿	23♌	23	23	24	24	25	26	27	28	29	0♍	2	3	5	6	8	10	11	13	15	17	19	21	22	24	26	28	30	2♎	3
♀	24♌	24	23	23	22	22	22	22	21	21	21	21	21	21	21	21	21	21	22	22	22	22	23	23	23	24	24	25	25	26
♂	30♍	0♎	1	2	2	3	4	4	5	6	6	7	8	8	9	10	10	11	12	12	13	13	14	15	15	16	17	17	18	19
	1	6	11	16	21	26			1	11	21			1	11	21			1	16		1	16		1	16		1	11	21
♃	28♌	29	30	1♍	2	3		♄	1♒	1	0		⚷	5♌	6	7		♅	10♑	10	♆	14♑	14	♇	18♏	18	☊	16♑	16	15

OCT

	1	2	3	4	5	6	7	8	9	10	11	12	13	14	15	16	17	18	19	20	21	22	23	24	25	26	27	28	29	30	31
☉	7♎	8	9	10	11	12	13	14	15	16	17	18	19	20	21	22	23	24	25	26	27	28	29	0♏	1	2	3	4	5	6	7
☽	7♋	21	5♌	20	4♍	18	2♎	15	29	12♏	25	7♐	19	1♑	13	25	7♒	19	1♓	14	26	10♈	23	7♉	21	5♊	20	4♋	18	2♌	16
☿	5♎	7	9	11	12	14	16	17	19	21	22	24	26	27	29	1♏	2	4	5	7	9	10	12	13	15	16	18	19	21	22	24
♀	26♌	27	28	28	29	29	0♍	1	1	2	3	4	4	5	6	7	8	9	9	10	11	12	13	14	15	16	17	18	19	20	21
♂	19♎	20	21	21	22	23	23	24	25	25	26	27	27	28	29	29	0♏	1	1	2	3	4	4	5	6	6	7	8	8	9	10
	1	6	11	16	21	26	31		1	11	21	31		1	11	21	31		1	16		1	16		1	16		1	11	21	31
♃	4♍	5	6	7	8	8	9	♄	0♒	0	0	1	⚷	7♌	8	9	9	♅	10♑	10	♆	14♑	14	♇	19♏	19	☊	15♑	14	14	13

NOV

	1	2	3	4	5	6	7	8	9	10	11	12	13	14	15	16	17	18	19	20	21	22	23	24	25	26	27	28	29	30
☉	8♏	9	10	11	12	13	14	15	16	17	18	19	20	21	22	23	24	25	26	27	28	29	0♐	1	2	3	4	5	6	7
☽	0♍	14	28	11♎	24	8♏	20	3♐	15	27	9♑	21	3♒	15	27	9♓	21	4♈	18	1♉	15	30	14♊	29	14♋	28	13♌	27	11♍	25
☿	25♏	27	28	29	1♐	2	4	5	6	8	9	10	11	13	14	15	16	17	18	19	20	21	22	23	23	24	24	24	24	24
♀	22♍	23	24	25	26	27	28	29	30	1♎	2	3	4	5	6	7	8	9	10	12	13	14	15	16	17	18	19	20	22	23
♂	10♏	11	12	12	13	14	15	15	16	17	17	18	19	19	20	21	21	22	23	24	24	25	26	26	27	28	29	29	30	1♐
	1	6	11	16	21	26			1	11	21			1	11	21			1	16		1	16		1	16		1	11	21
♃	9♍	10	11	12	12	13		♄	1♒	1	2		⚷	9♌	9	10		♅	11♑	11	♆	14♑	15	♇	20♏	20	☊	13♑	13	12

DEC

	1	2	3	4	5	6	7	8	9	10	11	12	13	14	15	16	17	18	19	20	21	22	23	24	25	26	27	28	29	30	31
☉	8♐	9	10	11	12	13	14	15	16	17	18	19	20	21	22	24	25	26	27	28	29	30	1♑	2	3	4	5	6	7	8	9
☽	8♎	21	4♏	17	29	12♐	24	6♑	17	29	11♒	23	5♓	17	29	12♈	25	9♉	23	8♊	23	8♋	23	8♌	22	7♍	21	5♎	18	1♏	14
☿	24♐	23	23	22	21	20	18	17	15	14	13	12	11	10	9	8	8	8	8	8	8	9	9	10	11	12	13	14	15	16	17
♀	24♎	25	26	27	28	30	1♏	2	3	4	5	7	8	9	10	11	13	14	15	16	17	18	20	21	22	23	24	26	27	28	29
♂	1♐	2	3	3	4	5	6	6	7	8	9	9	10	11	11	12	13	14	14	15	16	16	17	18	19	19	20	21	22	22	23
	1	6	11	16	21	26	31		1	11	21	31		1	11	21	31		1	16		1	16		1	16		1	11	21	31
♃	13♍	14	14	14	14	15	15	♄	3♒	4	5	6	⚷	10♌	9	9	8	♅	12♑	13	♆	15♑	16	♇	21♏	22	☊	11♑	11	10	10

1992

JAN

	1	2	3	4	5	6	7	8	9	10	11	12	13	14	15	16	17	18	19	20	21	22	23	24	25	26	27	28	29	30	31
☉	10♑	11	12	13	14	15	16	17	18	19	20	21	22	23	24	25	26	27	28	29	0♒	1	2	3	4	5	6	7	8	9	10
☽	26♏	8♐	20	2♑	14	26	8♒	20	2♓	14	26	8♈	21	4♉	17	1♊	16	0♋	15	1♌	16	1♍	16	0♎	14	28	11♏	23	5♐	18	29
☿	18♐	19	21	22	23	24	26	27	29	30	1♑	3	4	6	7	9	10	12	13	15	16	18	19	21	22	24	25	27	29	0♒	2
♀	0♐	2	3	4	5	6	8	9	10	11	13	14	15	16	17	19	20	21	22	24	25	26	27	28	30	1♑	2	3	5	6	7
♂	24♐	25	25	26	27	27	28	29	30	0♑	1	2	3	3	4	5	6	6	7	8	9	9	10	11	12	12	13	14	15	15	16
	1	6	11	16	21	26	31		1	11	21	31		1	11	21	31		1	16		1	16		1	16		1	11	21	31
♃	15♍	15	14	14	14	14	13	♄	6♒	7	8	9	⚷	8♌	8	7	6	♅	14♑	15	♆	16♑	17	♇	22♏	22	☊	10♑	9	9	8

FEB

	1	2	3	4	5	6	7	8	9	10	11	12	13	14	15	16	17	18	19	20	21	22	23	24	25	26	27	28	29	
☉	11♒	12	13	14	15	16	17	18	19	20	22	23	24	25	26	27	28	29	30	1♓	2	3	4	5	6	7	8	9	10	
☽	11♑	23	5♒	17	29	11♓	23	5♈	17	0♉	13	27	10♊	24	9♋	24	9♌	24	9♍	24	8♎	22	6♏	19	2♐	14	26	8♑	20	
☿	3♒	5	7	8	10	12	14	15	17	19	20	22	24	26	28	29	1♓	3	5	7	9	11	12	14	16	18	20	22	23	
♀	8♑	9	11	12	13	14	16	17	18	19	21	22	23	24	25	27	28	29	0♒	2	3	4	5	7	8	9	10	11	13	
♂	17♑	18	18	19	20	21	21	22	23	24	25	25	26	27	28	28	29	30	1♒	1	2	3	4	4	5	6	7	8	8	
	1	6	11	16	21	26			1	11	21			1	11	21			1	16		1	16		1	16		1	11	21
♃	13♍	13	12	11	11	10		♄	9♒	11	12		⚷	6♌	5	5		♅	15♑	16	♆	17♑	18	♇	23♏	23	☊	8♑	8	7

MAR

	1	2	3	4	5	6	7	8	9	10	11	12	13	14	15	16	17	18	19	20	21	22	23	24	25	26	27	28	29	30	31
☉	11♓	12	13	14	15	16	17	18	19	20	21	22	23	24	25	26	27	28	29	30	1♈	2	3	4	5	6	7	8	9	10	11
☽	2♒	13	25	7♓	20	2♈	15	27	10♉	23	7♊	20	4♋	18	3♌	18	2♍	17	2♎	16	0♏	14	27	10♐	22	4♑	16	28	10♒	22	4♓
☿	25♓	27	29	0♈	2	3	4	6	7	8	9	10	10	11	11	11	11	11	11	11	10	10	9	8	8	7	6	5	4	3	3
♀	14♒	15	16	18	19	20	21	23	24	25	26	28	29	0♓	1	2	4	5	6	7	9	10	11	12	14	15	16	17	19	20	21
♂	9♒	10	11	11	12	13	14	14	15	16	17	18	18	19	20	21	21	22	23	24	25	25	26	27	28	28	29	30	1♓	1	2
	1	6	11	16	21	26	31		1	11	21	31		1	11	21	31		1	16		1	16		1	16		1	11	21	31
♃	10♍	9	8	8	7	7	6	♄	13♒	14	15	16	⚷	4♌	4	3	3	♅	17♑	17	♆	18♑	19	♇	23♏	23	☊	7♑	6	6	5

APR

	1	2	3	4	5	6	7	8	9	10	11	12	13	14	15	16	17	18	19	20	21	22	23	24	25	26	27	28	29	30
☉	12♈	13	13	14	15	16	17	18	19	20	21	22	23	24	25	26	27	28	29	0♉	1	2	3	4	5	6	7	8	9	10
☽	16♓	28	11♈	24	7♉	20	4♊	17	1♋	15	29	13♌	28	12♍	26	11♎	25	8♏	22	5♐	18	0♑	12	24	6♒	18	30	12♓	24	7♈
☿	2♈	1	1	30♓	30	29	29	29	29	29	29	29	29	30	0♈	1	1	2	3	3	4	5	6	7	8	9	10	11	12	14
♀	22♓	23	25	26	27	28	30	1♈	2	3	5	6	7	8	9	11	12	13	14	16	17	18	19	21	22	23	24	26	27	28
♂	3♓	4	5	5	6	7	8	8	9	10	11	12	12	13	14	15	15	16	17	18	19	19	20	21	22	22	23	24	25	25
	1	6	11	16	21	26			1	11	21			1	11	21			1	16		1	16		1	16		1	11	21
♃	6♍	6	5	5	5	5		♄	16♒	17	17		⚷	3♌	3	4		♅	18♑	18	♆	19♑	19	♇	23♏	22	☊	5♑	4	4

MAY

	1	2	3	4	5	6	7	8	9	10	11	12	13	14	15	16	17	18	19	20	21	22	23	24	25	26	27	28	29	30	31
☉	11♉	12	13	14	15	16	17	18	19	20	21	22	22	23	24	25	26	27	28	29	0♊	1	2	3	4	5	6	7	8	9	10
☽	20♈	3♉	16	30	14♊	28	12♋	26	10♌	24	8♍	22	6♎	20	4♏	17	0♐	13	26	8♑	20	2♒	14	26	8♓	20	2♈	15	28	11♉	25
☿	15♈	16	18	19	20	22	23	25	26	28	30	1♉	3	5	7	8	10	12	14	16	18	20	22	24	26	28	0♊	2	5	7	9
♀	29♈	0♉	2	3	4	5	7	8	9	10	11	13	14	15	16	18	19	20	21	23	24	25	26	27	29	30	1♊	2	4	5	6
♂	26♓	27	28	29	29	0♈	1	2	2	3	4	5	5	6	7	8	8	9	10	11	12	12	13	14	15	15	16	17	18	18	19
	1	6	11	16	21	26	31		1	11	21	31		1	11	21	31		1	16		1	16		1	16		1	11	21	31
♃	5♍	5	5	5	5	6	6	♄	18♒	18	18	18	⚷	4♌	4	5	6	♅	18♑	18	♆	19♑	19	♇	22♏	21	☊	3♑	3	2	2

JUN

	1	2	3	4	5	6	7	8	9	10	11	12	13	14	15	16	17	18	19	20	21	22	23	24	25	26	27	28	29	30
☉	11♊	12	13	14	15	16	16	17	18	19	20	21	22	23	24	25	26	27	28	29	30	1♋	2	3	4	5	6	7	8	8
☽	9♊	23	7♋	22	6♌	21	5♍	19	3♎	17	0♏	14	27	9♐	22	4♑	16	28	10♒	22	4♓	16	28	10♈	23	6♉	19	3♊	17	1♋
☿	11♊	13	16	18	20	22	24	26	28	0♋	2	4	6	8	10	12	14	16	17	19	21	22	24	25	27	28	30	1♌	2	4
♀	7♊	9	10	11	12	13	15	16	17	18	20	21	22	23	25	26	27	28	29	1♋	2	3	4	6	7	8	9	10	12	13
♂	20♈	21	21	22	23	24	24	25	26	27	27	28	29	30	0♉	1	2	2	3	4	5	5	6	7	8	8	9	10	10	11
	1	6	11	16	21	26			1	11	21			1	11	21			1	16		1	16		1	16		1	11	21
♃	6♍	7	7	8	8	9		♄	18♒	18	18		⚷	6♌	7	8		♅	17♑	17	♆	19♑	18	♇	21♏	21	☊	2♑	1	1

1992

JUL

	1	2	3	4	5	6	7	8	9	10	11	12	13	14	15	16	17	18	19	20	21	22	23	24	25	26	27	28	29	30	31
☉	9♋	10	11	12	13	14	15	16	17	18	19	20	21	22	23	24	25	26	27	28	28	29	0♌	1	2	3	4	5	6	7	8
☽	16♋	1♌	16	1♍	15	30	14♎	27	11♏	23	6♐	19	1♑	13	25	7♒	19	1♓	12	24	6♈	19	1♉	14	27	11♊	25	10♋	25	10♌	25
☿	5♌	6	7	8	9	10	11	12	13	14	14	15	16	16	16	17	17	17	17	17	17	17	17	17	16	16	16	15	14	14	13
♀	14♋	15	17	18	19	20	22	23	24	25	26	28	29	0♌	1	3	4	5	6	8	9	10	11	12	14	15	16	17	19	20	21
♂	12♉	13	13	14	15	15	16	17	18	18	19	20	20	21	22	23	23	24	25	25	26	27	27	28	29	29	0♊	1	2	2	3
	1	6	11	16	21	26	31		1	11	21	31		1	11	21	31		1	16		1	16		1	16		1	11	21	31
♃	10♍	11	11	12	13	14	15	♄	18♒	17	16	16	⚷	9♌	10	11	13	♅	16♑	16	♆	18♑	17	♇	20♏	20	☊	0♑	30♐	29	29

AUG

	1	2	3	4	5	6	7	8	9	10	11	12	13	14	15	16	17	18	19	20	21	22	23	24	25	26	27	28	29	30	31
☉	9♌	10	11	12	13	14	15	16	17	18	19	20	20	21	22	23	24	25	26	27	28	29	0♍	1	2	3	4	5	6	7	8
☽	10♍	25	9♎	24	7♏	20	3♐	16	28	10♑	22	4♒	16	28	9♓	21	3♈	16	28	10♉	23	6♊	20	4♋	18	3♌	18	3♍	19	4♎	18
☿	12♌	11	11	10	9	9	8	7	7	7	6	6	6	6	6	6	7	7	8	9	10	11	12	13	14	16	17	19	20	22	24
♀	22♌	24	25	26	27	28	30	1♍	2	3	5	6	7	8	10	11	12	13	14	16	17	18	19	21	22	23	24	25	27	28	29
♂	4♊	4	5	6	6	7	8	8	9	10	10	11	11	12	13	13	14	15	15	16	17	17	18	18	19	20	20	21	22	22	23
	1	6	11	16	21	26	31		1	11	21	31		1	11	21	31		1	16		1	16		1	16		1	11	21	31
♃	15♍	16	17	18	19	20	21	♄	16♒	15	14	13	⚷	13♌	14	15	16	♅	15♑	15	♆	17♑	17	♇	20♏	20	☊	29♐	28	27	27

SEP

	1	2	3	4	5	6	7	8	9	10	11	12	13	14	15	16	17	18	19	20	21	22	23	24	25	26	27	28	29	30
☉	9♍	10	11	12	13	14	15	16	17	18	19	19	20	21	22	23	24	25	26	27	28	29	0♎	1	2	3	4	5	6	7
☽	3♏	16	30	12♐	25	7♑	19	1♒	13	25	6♓	18	0♈	13	25	7♉	20	3♊	16	29	13♋	27	12♌	27	12♍	27	12♎	27	11♏	25
☿	26♌	28	29	1♍	3	5	7	9	11	13	15	17	19	20	22	24	26	28	30	1♎	3	5	7	8	10	12	13	15	17	18
♀	0♎	2	3	4	5	7	8	9	10	11	13	14	15	16	18	19	20	21	22	24	25	26	27	29	30	1♏	2	3	5	6
♂	23♊	24	25	25	26	26	27	28	28	29	29	30	0♋	1	2	2	3	3	4	4	5	5	6	6	7	8	8	9	9	10
	1	6	11	16	21	26			1	11	21			1	11	21			1	16		1	16		1	16		1	11	21
♃	21♍	23	24	25	26	27		♄	13♒	13	12		⚷	17♌	18	19		♅	14♑	14	♆	16♑	16	♇	20♏	21	☊	27♐	26	26

OCT

	1	2	3	4	5	6	7	8	9	10	11	12	13	14	15	16	17	18	19	20	21	22	23	24	25	26	27	28	29	30	31
☉	8♎	9	10	11	12	13	14	15	16	17	18	19	20	21	22	23	24	25	26	27	28	29	30	1♏	2	3	4	5	6	7	8
☽	8♐	21	3♑	16	28	9♒	21	3♓	15	27	9♈	22	4♉	17	30	13♊	26	10♋	24	8♌	22	6♍	21	6♎	20	5♏	19	3♐	16	29	11♑
☿	20♎	22	23	25	26	28	29	1♏	2	4	5	7	8	10	11	13	14	15	17	18	19	21	22	23	25	26	27	28	29	0♐	1
♀	7♏	8	10	11	12	13	14	16	17	18	19	21	22	23	24	25	27	28	29	0♐	2	3	4	5	6	8	9	10	11	12	14
♂	10♋	11	11	12	12	13	13	13	14	14	15	15	16	16	17	17	17	18	18	19	19	19	20	20	21	21	21	22	22	22	23
	1	6	11	16	21	26	31		1	11	21	31		1	11	21	31		1	16		1	16		1	16		1	11	21	31
♃	28♍	29	0♎	1	2	3	4	♄	12♒	12	12	12	⚷	20♌	21	22	22	♅	14♑	14	♆	16♑	16	♇	21♏	22	☊	25♐	25	24	24

NOV

	1	2	3	4	5	6	7	8	9	10	11	12	13	14	15	16	17	18	19	20	21	22	23	24	25	26	27	28	29	30
☉	9♏	10	11	12	13	14	15	16	17	18	19	20	21	22	23	24	25	26	27	28	29	30	1♐	2	3	4	5	6	7	8
☽	24♑	6♒	18	29	11♓	23	5♈	18	0♉	13	26	10♊	23	7♋	20	4♌	19	3♍	17	1♎	15	29	13♏	27	11♐	24	7♑	19	1♒	13
☿	2♐	3	4	5	6	7	7	8	8	8	8	8	8	8	7	7	6	5	4	2	1	30♏	28	27	26	25	24	23	23	22
♀	15♐	16	17	19	20	21	22	23	25	26	27	28	29	1♑	2	3	4	5	7	8	9	10	11	13	14	15	16	17	18	20
♂	23♋	23	24	24	24	24	25	25	25	25	26	26	26	26	26	27	27	27	27	27	27	27	27	27	28	28	28	28	28	28
	1	6	11	16	21	26			1	11	21			1	11	21			1	16		1	16		1	16		1	11	21
♃	4♎	5	6	7	8	9		♄	12♒	12	13		⚷	22♌	23	23		♅	15♑	15	♆	17♑	17	♇	22♏	23	☊	24♐	23	23

DEC

	1	2	3	4	5	6	7	8	9	10	11	12	13	14	15	16	17	18	19	20	21	22	23	24	25	26	27	28	29	30	31
☉	9♐	10	11	12	13	14	15	16	17	18	19	20	21	22	23	24	25	26	27	28	29	0♑	1	2	3	4	5	7	8	9	10
☽	25♒	7♓	19	1♈	13	26	8♉	21	5♊	18	2♋	16	1♌	15	29	14♍	28	12♎	26	9♏	23	6♐	19	2♑	15	27	9♒	21	3♓	15	27
☿	22♏	22	22	23	23	24	25	25	26	27	28	30	1♐	2	3	5	6	7	9	10	11	13	14	16	17	19	20	22	23	25	26
♀	21♑	22	23	24	26	27	28	29	0♒	1	3	4	5	6	7	8	10	11	12	13	14	15	17	18	19	20	21	22	23	24	26
♂	28♋	28	28	27	27	27	27	27	27	27	27	26	26	26	26	26	25	25	25	25	24	24	24	23	23	23	22	22	22	21	21
	1	6	11	16	21	26	31		1	11	21	31		1	11	21	31		1	16		1	16		1	16		1	11	21	31
♃	10♎	10	11	12	12	13	13	♄	14♒	14	15	16	⚷	24♌	24	23	23	♅	16♑	17	♆	17♑	18	♇	24♏	24	☊	22♐	22	21	20

1993

EPHEMERIS

JAN

	1	2	3	4	5	6	7	8	9	10	11	12	13	14	15	16	17	18	19	20	21	22	23	24	25	26	27	28	29	30	31
☉	11♑	12	13	14	15	16	17	18	19	20	21	22	23	24	25	26	27	28	29	30	1♒	2	3	4	5	6	7	8	9	10	11
☽	9♈	21	3♉	16	29	12♊	26	11♋	25	10♌	25	10♍	24	9♎	23	6♏	20	3♐	16	29	11♑	23	6♒	18	30	11♓	23	5♈	17	29	11♉
☿	28♐	29	1♑	2	4	5	7	8	10	11	13	15	16	18	19	21	23	24	26	28	29	1♒	3	4	6	8	9	11	13	15	16
♀	27♒	28	29	0♓	1	2	3	4	5	7	8	9	10	11	12	13	14	15	16	17	18	19	20	21	22	23	24	25	26	27	28
♂	20♋	20	20	19	19	18	18	18	17	17	16	16	16	15	15	15	14	14	14	13	13	13	12	12	12	11	11	11	11	10	10
	1	6	11	16	21	26	31		1	11	21	31		1	11	21	31		1	16		1	16		1	16		1	11	21	31
♃	13♎	14	14	14	15	15	15	♄	16♒	17	19	20	⚷	23♌	22	22	21	♅	18♑	19	♆	18♑	19	♇	25♏	25	☊	20♐	20	19	19

FEB

	1	2	3	4	5	6	7	8	9	10	11	12	13	14	15	16	17	18	19	20	21	22	23	24	25	26	27	28			
☉	12♒	13	14	15	16	17	18	19	20	21	22	23	24	25	26	27	28	29	0♓	1	2	3	4	5	6	7	8	9			
☽	24♉	7♊	20	4♋	18	3♌	18	3♍	19	4♎	18	3♏	17	30	13♐	26	8♑	20	2♒	14	26	8♓	20	2♈	14	26	8♉	20			
☿	18♒	20	22	23	25	27	29	1♓	2	4	6	8	9	11	12	14	15	17	18	19	20	21	22	23	24	24	24	24			
♀	29♓	30	0♈	1	2	3	4	5	6	6	7	8	9	9	10	11	12	12	13	13	14	15	15	16	16	17	17	18			
♂	10♋	10	10	10	9	9	9	9	9	9	9	9	9	9	9	9	9	9	9	9	9	9	9	9	9	9	9	10			
	1	6	11	16	21	26			1	11	21			1	11	21			1	16		1	16		1	16		1	11	21	
♃	15♎	15	14	14	14	13		♄	20♒	21	22		⚷	21♌	20	20		♅	19♑	20	♆	20♑	20	♇	25♏	25	☊	19♐	18	18	

MAR

	1	2	3	4	5	6	7	8	9	10	11	12	13	14	15	16	17	18	19	20	21	22	23	24	25	26	27	28	29	30	31
☉	10♓	11	12	13	14	15	16	17	18	19	20	21	22	23	24	25	26	27	28	29	0♈	1	2	3	4	5	6	7	8	9	10
☽	3♊	16	29	12♋	27	11♌	26	12♍	27	12♎	27	12♏	26	9♐	22	5♑	17	30	12♒	23	5♓	17	29	11♈	23	5♉	17	30	12♊	25	8♋
☿	24♓	24	23	23	22	22	21	20	19	18	17	16	15	14	13	12	12	11	11	11	10	10	10	10	11	11	11	12	12	13	13
♀	18♈	18	19	19	19	19	20	20	20	20	20	20	20	20	20	20	19	19	19	19	18	18	17	17	16	16	15	15	14	13	13
♂	10♋	10	10	10	10	11	11	11	11	12	12	12	12	13	13	13	13	14	14	14	15	15	15	16	16	16	17	17	17	18	18
	1	6	11	16	21	26	31		1	11	21	31		1	11	21	31		1	16		1	16		1	16		1	11	21	31
♃	13♎	13	12	12	11	10	10	♄	23♒	24	25	27	⚷	19♌	18	18	17	♅	21♑	21	♆	20♑	21	♇	26♏	25	☊	17♐	17	16	16

APR

	1	2	3	4	5	6	7	8	9	10	11	12	13	14	15	16	17	18	19	20	21	22	23	24	25	26	27	28	29	30	
☉	11♈	12	13	14	15	16	17	18	19	20	21	22	23	24	25	26	27	28	29	30	1♉	2	3	4	5	6	7	8	9	10	
☽	22♋	6♌	20	5♍	20	5♎	20	5♏	20	4♐	18	1♑	14	26	8♒	20	2♓	14	26	8♈	20	2♉	14	27	9♊	22	5♋	18	2♌	16	
☿	14♓	15	16	17	17	18	19	21	22	23	24	25	27	28	29	0♈	2	3	5	6	8	9	11	13	14	16	18	19	21	23	
♀	12♈	12	11	10	10	9	8	8	7	7	6	6	6	5	5	5	4	4	4	4	4	4	4	4	4	4	4	4	5	5	
♂	18♋	19	19	20	20	20	21	21	22	22	22	23	23	24	24	25	25	25	26	26	27	27	28	28	29	29	30	0♌	0	1	
	1	6	11	16	21	26			1	11	21			1	11	21			1	16		1	16		1	16		1	11	21	
♃	10♎	9	8	8	7	7		♄	27♒	28	28		⚷	17♌	17	17		♅	22♑	22	♆	21♑	21	♇	25♏	25	☊	16♐	15	15	

MAY

	1	2	3	4	5	6	7	8	9	10	11	12	13	14	15	16	17	18	19	20	21	22	23	24	25	26	27	28	29	30	31
☉	11♉	12	13	14	15	15	16	17	18	19	20	21	22	23	24	25	26	27	28	29	30	1♊	2	3	4	5	6	7	8	9	10
☽	30♌	14♍	29	14♎	29	13♏	28	12♐	26	9♑	22	4♒	17	29	10♓	22	4♈	16	28	11♉	23	6♊	19	2♋	15	29	13♌	27	11♍	25	9♎
☿	25♈	26	28	0♉	2	4	6	8	10	12	14	16	18	21	23	25	27	29	2♊	4	6	8	10	12	14	16	18	20	22	24	26
♀	5♈	5	6	6	6	7	7	8	8	9	9	10	11	11	12	13	13	14	15	15	16	17	18	18	19	20	21	22	23	23	24
♂	1♌	2	2	3	3	4	4	5	5	6	6	7	7	8	8	9	9	10	11	11	12	12	13	13	14	14	15	15	16	16	17
	1	6	11	16	21	26	31		1	11	21	31		1	11	21	31		1	16		1	16		1	16		1	11	21	31
♃	6♎	6	5	5	5	5	5	♄	29♒	30	30	0♓	⚷	17♌	18	18	19	♅	22♑	22	♆	21♑	21	♇	25♏	24	☊	14♐	14	13	12

JUN

	1	2	3	4	5	6	7	8	9	10	11	12	13	14	15	16	17	18	19	20	21	22	23	24	25	26	27	28	29	30	
☉	11♊	11	12	13	14	15	16	17	18	19	20	21	22	23	24	25	26	27	28	29	30	1♋	2	3	3	4	5	6	7	8	
☽	24♎	8♏	22	6♐	20	4♑	17	30	12♒	24	7♓	18	0♈	12	24	6♉	19	1♊	14	28	11♋	25	9♌	23	8♍	22	6♎	20	4♏	18	
☿	28♊	30	1♋	3	5	6	8	9	11	12	14	15	16	17	18	19	21	21	22	23	24	25	25	26	27	27	27	28	28	28	
♀	25♈	26	27	28	29	30	1♉	1	2	3	4	5	6	7	8	9	10	11	12	13	14	15	16	17	18	19	20	21	23	24	
♂	17♌	18	19	19	20	20	21	21	22	22	23	24	24	25	25	26	26	27	28	28	29	29	30	0♍	1	2	2	3	3	4	
	1	6	11	16	21	26			1	11	21			1	11	21			1	16		1	16		1	16		1	11	21	
♃	5♎	5	5	5	5	6		♄	0♓	0	0		⚷	19♌	20	21		♅	22♑	21	♆	21♑	20	♇	24♏	23	☊	12♐	12	11	

1993

EPHEMERIS

JUL

	1	2	3	4	5	6	7	8	9	10	11	12	13	14	15	16	17	18	19	20	21	22	23	24	25	26	27	28	29	30	31
☉	9♋	10	11	12	13	14	15	16	17	18	19	20	21	22	23	23	24	25	26	27	28	29	0♌	1	2	3	4	5	6	7	8
☽	2♐	16	29	12♑	25	8♒	20	2♓	15	26	8♈	20	2♉	14	27	10♊	23	6♋	20	4♌	19	3♍	18	3♎	17	1♏	15	29	12♐	25	8♑
☿	28♋	28	28	28	28	28	27	27	26	26	25	25	24	23	23	22	21	21	20	20	19	19	19	18	18	18	18	18	19	19	19
♀	25♉	26	27	28	29	30	1♊	2	3	4	5	7	8	9	10	11	12	13	14	15	16	18	19	20	21	22	23	24	26	27	28
♂	4♍	5	6	6	7	7	8	9	9	10	10	11	12	12	13	13	14	15	15	16	16	17	18	18	19	19	20	21	21	22	22
	1	6	11	16	21	26	31		1	11	21	31		1	11	21	31		1	16		1	16		1	16		1	11	21	31
♃	6♎	7	7	8	8	9	10	♄	30♒	30	29	28	⚷	22♌	23	24	25	♅	21♑	20	♆	20♑	20	♇	23♏	23	☊	11♐	10	10	9

AUG

	1	2	3	4	5	6	7	8	9	10	11	12	13	14	15	16	17	18	19	20	21	22	23	24	25	26	27	28	29	30	31
☉	9♌	10	11	12	13	14	15	15	16	17	18	19	20	21	22	23	24	25	26	27	28	29	30	1♍	2	3	4	5	6	7	8
☽	21♑	4♒	16	29	11♓	23	5♈	16	28	10♉	22	5♊	18	1♋	14	28	13♌	28	13♍	28	13♎	27	12♏	26	9♐	22	5♑	18	1♒	13	25
☿	20♋	21	21	22	23	24	26	27	28	30	1♌	3	4	6	8	10	12	14	15	17	19	21	23	25	27	29	1♍	3	5	7	9
♀	29♊	0♋	1	2	4	5	6	7	8	9	10	12	13	14	15	16	17	19	20	21	22	23	24	26	27	28	29	0♌	2	3	4
♂	23♍	24	24	25	26	26	27	27	28	29	29	30	1♎	1	2	2	3	4	4	5	6	6	7	8	8	9	10	10	11	11	12
	1	6	11	16	21	26	31		1	11	21	31		1	11	21	31		1	16		1	16		1	16		1	11	21	31
♃	10♎	11	11	12	13	14	15	♄	28♒	28	27	26	⚷	26♌	27	28	30	♅	19♑	19	♆	19♑	19	♇	23♏	23	☊	9♐	9	8	8

SEP

	1	2	3	4	5	6	7	8	9	10	11	12	13	14	15	16	17	18	19	20	21	22	23	24	25	26	27	28	29	30
☉	9♍	10	11	11	12	13	14	15	16	17	18	19	20	21	22	23	24	25	26	27	28	29	30	1♎	2	3	4	5	6	7
☽	7♓	19	1♈	13	25	7♉	19	1♊	13	26	9♋	23	7♌	21	6♍	21	7♎	22	7♏	21	5♐	19	2♑	15	28	10♒	22	4♓	16	28
☿	11♍	13	15	17	19	20	22	24	26	27	29	1♎	3	4	6	8	9	11	12	14	15	17	18	20	21	23	24	26	27	29
♀	5♌	6	8	9	10	11	12	14	15	16	17	18	20	21	22	23	24	26	27	28	29	0♍	2	3	4	5	7	8	9	10
♂	13♎	13	14	15	15	16	17	17	18	19	19	20	21	21	22	23	23	24	25	25	26	27	27	28	29	29	30	1♏	1	2
	1	6	11	16	21	26			1	11	21			1	11	21			1	16		1	16		1	16		1	11	21
♃	15♎	16	17	18	19	20		♄	26♒	25	25		⚷	30♌	1♍	2		♅	19♑	18	♆	19♑	18	♇	23♏	23	☊	8♐	7	6

OCT

	1	2	3	4	5	6	7	8	9	10	11	12	13	14	15	16	17	18	19	20	21	22	23	24	25	26	27	28	29	30	31
☉	8♎	9	10	11	12	13	14	15	16	17	18	19	20	21	22	23	24	25	26	27	28	29	30	1♏	2	3	4	5	6	7	8
☽	10♈	22	4♉	16	28	10♊	22	5♋	18	1♌	15	30	14♍	29	15♎	30	15♏	30	14♐	28	11♑	24	7♒	19	1♓	13	25	7♈	19	1♉	13
☿	30♎	1♏	3	4	5	6	8	9	10	11	12	13	14	16	16	17	18	19	20	20	21	22	22	22	22	23	22	22	22	21	21
♀	11♍	13	14	15	16	18	19	20	21	23	24	25	26	28	29	30	1♎	2	4	5	6	7	9	10	11	12	14	15	16	17	19
♂	3♏	3	4	5	5	6	7	7	8	9	9	10	11	12	12	13	14	14	15	16	16	17	18	18	19	20	21	21	22	23	23
	1	6	11	16	21	26	31		1	11	21	31		1	11	21	31		1	16		1	16		1	16		1	11	21	31
♃	21♎	22	23	25	26	27	28	♄	24♒	24	24	24	⚷	3♍	5	6	7	♅	18♑	18	♆	18♑	18	♇	24♏	24	☊	6♐	5	5	4

NOV

	1	2	3	4	5	6	7	8	9	10	11	12	13	14	15	16	17	18	19	20	21	22	23	24	25	26	27	28	29	30
☉	9♏	10	11	12	13	14	15	16	17	18	19	20	21	22	23	24	25	26	27	28	29	30	1♐	2	3	4	5	6	7	8
☽	25♉	7♊	19	2♋	15	28	11♌	25	9♍	23	8♎	23	8♏	23	8♐	22	6♑	20	3♒	15	28	10♓	22	4♈	16	27	9♉	21	4♊	16
☿	20♏	19	18	17	15	14	13	11	10	9	8	8	7	7	7	7	7	7	8	8	9	10	11	12	13	15	16	17	18	20
♀	20♎	21	22	24	25	26	27	29	30	1♏	2	4	5	6	7	9	10	11	12	14	15	16	17	19	20	21	22	24	25	26
♂	24♏	25	26	26	27	28	28	29	30	1♐	1	2	3	3	4	5	6	6	7	8	9	9	10	11	11	12	13	14	14	15
	1	6	11	16	21	26			1	11	21			1	11	21			1	16		1	16		1	16		1	11	21
♃	28♎	29	0♏	1	2	3		♄	24♒	24	24		⚷	7♍	8	8		♅	19♑	19	♆	19♑	19	♇	25♏	25	☊	4♐	4	3

DEC

	1	2	3	4	5	6	7	8	9	10	11	12	13	14	15	16	17	18	19	20	21	22	23	24	25	26	27	28	29	30	31
☉	9♐	10	11	12	13	14	15	16	17	18	19	20	21	22	23	24	25	26	27	28	29	0♑	1	2	3	4	5	6	7	8	9
☽	29♊	12♋	25	8♌	22	5♍	19	4♎	18	2♏	17	1♐	16	30	14♑	27	10♒	23	6♓	18	30	12♈	24	5♉	17	30	12♊	25	8♋	21	5♌
☿	21♏	23	24	25	27	28	30	1♐	3	4	6	7	9	11	12	14	15	17	18	20	21	23	24	26	28	29	1♑	2	4	5	7
♀	27♏	29	0♐	1	3	4	5	6	8	9	10	11	13	14	15	16	18	19	20	21	23	24	25	26	28	29	0♑	1	3	4	5
♂	16♐	17	17	18	19	20	20	21	22	22	23	24	25	25	26	27	28	28	29	30	1♑	1	2	3	4	5	5	6	7	8	8
	1	6	11	16	21	26	31		1	11	21	31		1	11	21	31		1	16		1	16		1	16		1	11	21	31
♃	4♏	5	6	7	8	9	10	♄	25♒	25	26	27	⚷	9♍	9	9	9	♅	20♑	21	♆	19♑	20	♇	26♏	27	☊	3♐	2	2	1

1994

JAN

	1	2	3	4	5	6	7	8	9	10	11	12	13	14	15	16	17	18	19	20	21	22	23	24	25	26	27	28	29	30	31
☉	10♑	11	12	13	14	15	16	17	18	20	21	22	23	24	25	26	27	28	29	30	1♒	2	3	4	5	6	7	8	9	10	11
☽	18♌	2♍	16	0♎	14	29	13♏	27	11♐	25	8♑	22	5♒	18	1♓	13	26	8♈	19	1♉	13	25	7♊	20	3♋	16	30	14♌	28	12♍	27
☿	9♑	10	12	13	15	17	18	20	22	23	25	27	28	30	2♒	3	5	7	8	10	12	14	15	17	19	20	22	23	25	27	28
♀	6♑	8	9	10	12	13	14	15	17	18	19	20	22	23	24	25	27	28	29	0♒	2	3	4	5	7	8	9	10	12	13	14
♂	9♑	10	11	11	12	13	14	14	15	16	17	17	18	19	20	21	21	22	23	24	24	25	26	27	28	28	29	30	1♒	1	2
	1	6	11	16	21	26	31		1	11	21	31		1	11	21	31		1	16		1	16		1	16		1	11	21	31
♃	10♏	11	11	12	12	13	13	♄	27♒	28	29	0♓	⚷	9♍	9	9	8	♅	22♑	22	♆	20♑	21	♇	27♏	28	☊	1♐	1	0	30♏

FEB

	1	2	3	4	5	6	7	8	9	10	11	12	13	14	15	16	17	18	19	20	21	22	23	24	25	26	27	28			
☉	12♒	13	14	15	16	17	18	19	20	21	22	23	24	25	26	27	28	29	0♓	1	2	3	4	5	6	7	8	9			
☽	11♎	25	10♏	23	7♐	21	4♑	18	1♒	14	27	9♓	21	4♈	16	27	9♉	21	3♊	15	28	11♋	24	8♌	22	6♍	21	6♎			
☿	29♒	1♓	2	3	4	5	6	7	7	7	8	8	7	7	6	6	5	4	3	2	1	30♒	29	27	27	26	25	24			
♀	15♒	17	18	19	20	22	23	24	26	27	28	29	1♓	2	3	4	6	7	8	9	11	12	13	14	16	17	18	19			
♂	3♒	4	5	5	6	7	8	8	9	10	11	12	12	13	14	15	15	16	17	18	19	19	20	21	22	23	23	24			
	1	6	11	16	21	26			1	11	21			1	11	21			1	16		1	16		1	16		1	11	21	
♃	13♏	14	14	14	15	15		♄	0♓	2	3		⚷	8♍	7	6		♅	23♑	24	♆	22♑	22	♇	28♏	28	☊	29♏	29	28	

MAR

	1	2	3	4	5	6	7	8	9	10	11	12	13	14	15	16	17	18	19	20	21	22	23	24	25	26	27	28	29	30	31
☉	10♓	11	12	13	14	15	16	17	18	19	20	21	22	23	24	25	26	27	28	29	0♈	1	2	3	4	5	6	7	8	9	10
☽	21♎	6♏	20	4♐	18	1♑	15	28	11♒	23	6♓	18	0♈	12	24	6♉	17	29	11♊	23	6♋	19	2♌	16	30	15♍	30	15♎	30	15♏	30
☿	24♒	23	23	23	23	23	23	23	23	24	24	25	25	26	27	28	29	30	0♓	2	3	4	5	6	7	8	10	11	12	14	15
♀	21♓	22	23	24	26	27	28	29	0♈	2	3	4	5	7	8	9	10	12	13	14	15	17	18	19	20	22	23	24	25	27	28
♂	25♒	26	26	27	28	29	30	0♓	1	2	3	4	4	5	6	7	8	8	9	10	11	11	12	13	14	15	15	16	17	18	18
	1	6	11	16	21	26	31		1	11	21	31		1	11	21	31		1	16		1	16		1	16		1	11	21	31
♃	15♏	15	14	14	14	14	13	♄	4♓	5	6	7	⚷	6♍	5	4	4	♅	25♑	25	♆	23♑	23	♇	28♏	28	☊	28♏	27	27	26

APR

	1	2	3	4	5	6	7	8	9	10	11	12	13	14	15	16	17	18	19	20	21	22	23	24	25	26	27	28	29	30	
☉	11♈	12	13	14	15	16	17	18	19	20	21	22	23	24	25	26	27	28	29	30	1♉	2	3	4	5	6	7	7	8	9	
☽	14♐	28	11♑	25	8♒	20	3♓	15	27	9♈	21	3♉	14	26	8♊	20	2♋	15	27	11♌	24	8♍	23	8♎	23	8♏	23	8♐	23	7♑	
☿	17♓	18	19	21	23	24	26	27	29	1♈	2	4	6	7	9	11	13	15	17	18	20	22	24	26	28	0♉	3	5	7	9	
♀	29♈	0♉	1	3	4	5	6	8	9	10	11	13	14	15	16	17	19	20	21	22	24	25	26	27	28	30	1♊	2	3	5	
♂	19♓	20	21	22	22	23	24	25	26	26	27	28	29	29	0♈	1	2	3	3	4	5	6	6	7	8	9	9	10	11	12	
	1	6	11	16	21	26			1	11	21			1	11	21			1	16		1	16		1	16		1	11	21	
♃	13♏	13	12	12	11	10		♄	7♓	8	9		⚷	4♍	3	3		♅	26♑	26	♆	23♑	23	♇	28♏	28	☊	26♏	26	25	

MAY

	1	2	3	4	5	6	7	8	9	10	11	12	13	14	15	16	17	18	19	20	21	22	23	24	25	26	27	28	29	30	31
☉	10♉	11	12	13	14	15	16	17	18	19	20	21	22	23	24	25	26	27	28	29	30	1♊	2	3	4	5	5	6	7	8	9
☽	21♑	4♒	17	30	12♓	24	6♈	18	30	11♉	23	5♊	17	29	12♋	24	7♌	20	4♍	18	2♎	16	1♏	16	1♐	16	1♑	15	29	13♒	26
☿	11♉	13	15	18	20	22	24	26	28	0♊	2	4	6	8	10	12	14	15	17	19	20	22	23	24	26	27	28	29	0♋	1	2
♀	6♊	7	8	9	11	12	13	14	15	17	18	19	20	22	23	24	25	26	28	29	30	1♋	2	4	5	6	7	8	10	11	12
♂	13♈	13	14	15	16	16	17	18	19	19	20	21	22	22	23	24	25	26	26	27	28	29	29	0♉	1	2	2	3	4	5	5
	1	6	11	16	21	26	31		1	11	21	31		1	11	21	31		1	16		1	16		1	16		1	11	21	31
♃	10♏	9	8	8	7	7	6	♄	10♓	11	12	12	⚷	3♍	3	3	4	♅	26♑	26	♆	23♑	23	♇	27♏	27	☊	25♏	24	24	23

JUN

	1	2	3	4	5	6	7	8	9	10	11	12	13	14	15	16	17	18	19	20	21	22	23	24	25	26	27	28	29	30	
☉	10♊	11	12	13	14	15	16	17	18	19	20	21	22	23	24	25	26	27	28	28	29	0♋	1	2	3	4	5	6	7	8	
☽	8♓	21	3♈	15	26	8♉	20	2♊	14	26	9♋	21	4♌	17	0♍	14	28	12♎	26	11♏	25	10♐	25	9♑	23	7♒	21	4♓	17	29	
☿	3♋	4	5	6	6	7	7	8	8	8	8	8	8	8	8	8	8	7	7	7	6	6	5	4	4	3	3	2	2	1	
♀	13♋	14	15	17	18	19	20	21	23	24	25	26	27	28	30	1♌	2	3	4	5	7	8	9	10	11	12	14	15	16	17	
♂	6♉	7	8	8	9	10	10	11	12	13	13	14	15	16	16	17	18	19	19	20	21	21	22	23	24	24	25	26	26	27	
	1	6	11	16	21	26			1	11	21			1	11	21			1	16		1	16		1	16		1	11	21	
♃	6♏	6	5	5	5	5		♄	12♓	12	12		⚷	4♍	4	5		♅	26♑	26	♆	23♑	23	♇	26♏	26	☊	23♏	23	22	

1994

JUL

	1	2	3	4	5	6	7	8	9	10	11	12	13	14	15	16	17	18	19	20	21	22	23	24	25	26	27	28	29	30	31
☉	9♋	10	11	12	13	14	15	16	17	18	18	19	20	21	22	23	24	25	26	27	28	29	30	1♌	2	3	4	5	6	7	8
☽	11♈	23	5♉	17	28	10♊	23	5♋	18	1♌	14	27	11♍	25	9♎	23	7♏	21	5♐	20	4♑	18	2♒	16	29	12♓	25	7♈	19	1♉	13
☿	1♋	0	30♊	30	30	29	29	29	30	30	0♋	1	1	2	2	3	4	5	6	7	8	9	11	12	13	15	17	18	20	22	24
♀	18♌	19	21	22	23	24	25	26	27	29	30	1♍	2	3	4	5	6	8	9	10	11	12	13	14	15	16	18	19	20	21	22
♂	28♉	29	29	0♊	1	1	2	3	4	4	5	6	6	7	8	8	9	10	11	11	12	13	13	14	15	15	16	17	17	18	19
	1	6	11	16	21	26	31		1	11	21	31		1	11	21	31		1	16		1	16		1	16		1	11	21	31
♃	5♏	5	5	5	5	6	6	♄	12♓	12	12	11	⚷	6♍	7	8	9	♅	25♑	24	♆	22♑	22	♇	26♏	25	☊	22♏	21	20	20

AUG

	1	2	3	4	5	6	7	8	9	10	11	12	13	14	15	16	17	18	19	20	21	22	23	24	25	26	27	28	29	30	31
☉	9♌	9	10	11	12	13	14	15	16	17	18	19	20	21	22	23	24	25	26	27	28	29	30	1♍	2	3	4	4	5	6	7
☽	25♉	6♊	19	1♋	13	26	10♌	23	7♍	21	5♎	19	4♏	18	2♐	16	30	14♑	27	11♒	24	7♓	20	3♈	15	27	9♉	21	2♊	14	26
☿	26♋	28	29	1♌	4	6	8	10	12	14	16	18	20	22	24	26	28	30	2♍	4	6	8	9	11	13	15	16	18	20	22	23
♀	23♍	24	25	26	27	28	29	0♎	1	3	4	5	6	7	8	9	10	11	12	13	14	15	16	17	18	19	19	20	21	22	23
♂	19♊	20	21	21	22	23	24	24	25	26	26	27	27	28	29	29	0♋	1	1	2	3	3	4	5	5	6	7	7	8	9	9
	1	6	11	16	21	26	31		1	11	21	31		1	11	21	31		1	16		1	16		1	16		1	11	21	31
♃	6♏	7	7	8	8	9	10	♄	11♓	11	10	9	⚷	10♍	11	12	14	♅	24♑	23	♆	22♑	21	♇	25♏	25	☊	20♏	19	19	18

SEP

	1	2	3	4	5	6	7	8	9	10	11	12	13	14	15	16	17	18	19	20	21	22	23	24	25	26	27	28	29	30	
☉	8♍	9	10	11	12	13	14	15	16	17	18	19	20	21	22	23	24	25	26	27	28	29	30	1♎	2	3	4	5	6	7	
☽	9♋	22	5♌	18	2♍	16	1♎	15	30	14♏	29	13♐	27	10♑	24	7♒	21	3♓	16	29	11♈	23	5♉	17	29	10♊	22	4♋	17	29	
☿	25♍	27	28	30	1♎	3	4	6	7	9	10	12	13	14	16	17	18	20	21	22	23	24	26	27	28	29	30	1♏	1	2	
♀	24♎	25	26	27	28	29	29	0♏	1	2	3	3	4	5	6	7	7	8	9	9	10	11	11	12	12	13	13	14	14	15	
♂	10♋	10	11	12	12	13	14	14	15	15	16	17	17	18	18	19	20	20	21	21	22	23	23	24	24	25	26	26	27	27	
	1	6	11	16	21	26			1	11	21			1	11	21			1	16		1	16		1	16		1	11	21	
♃	10♏	11	11	12	13	14		♄	9♓	8	8		⚷	14♍	15	17		♅	23♑	22	♆	21♑	21	♇	25♏	26	☊	18♏	18	17	

OCT

	1	2	3	4	5	6	7	8	9	10	11	12	13	14	15	16	17	18	19	20	21	22	23	24	25	26	27	28	29	30	31
☉	8♎	9	10	11	12	13	13	14	15	16	17	18	19	20	21	22	23	24	25	26	27	28	29	0♏	1	2	3	4	5	6	7
☽	13♌	26	10♍	25	9♎	24	9♏	24	9♐	23	7♑	21	4♒	17	0♓	13	25	8♈	20	2♉	14	25	7♊	19	1♋	13	25	8♌	21	4♍	18
☿	3♏	4	4	5	5	6	6	6	6	6	6	6	6	5	4	3	3	1	0	29♎	28	27	25	24	23	22	22	21	21	21	21
♀	15♏	16	16	16	17	17	17	17	18	18	18	18	18	18	18	18	18	18	17	17	17	16	16	16	15	15	14	14	13	13	12
♂	28♋	28	29	30	0♌	1	1	2	2	3	4	4	5	5	6	6	7	7	8	8	9	9	10	10	11	11	12	12	13	13	14
	1	6	11	16	21	26	31		1	11	21	31		1	11	21	31		1	16		1	16		1	16		1	11	21	31
♃	15♏	16	17	18	19	20	21	♄	7♓	6	6	6	⚷	18♍	19	21	22	♅	22♑	22	♆	21♑	21	♇	26♏	27	☊	17♏	16	16	15

NOV

	1	2	3	4	5	6	7	8	9	10	11	12	13	14	15	16	17	18	19	20	21	22	23	24	25	26	27	28	29	30	
☉	8♏	9	10	11	12	13	14	15	16	17	18	19	20	21	22	23	24	25	26	27	28	29	0♐	1	2	3	5	6	7	8	
☽	3♎	17	2♏	17	3♐	18	2♑	17	1♒	14	27	10♓	22	5♈	17	29	10♉	22	4♊	16	28	10♋	22	4♌	17	30	13♍	27	11♎	25	
☿	21♎	22	22	23	24	25	26	27	28	29	1♏	2	3	5	6	8	9	11	12	14	16	17	19	20	22	23	25	27	28	30	
♀	11♏	11	10	10	9	8	8	7	7	6	6	5	5	4	4	4	3	3	3	3	3	3	2	2	3	3	3	3	3	3	
♂	14♌	15	15	16	16	17	17	18	18	19	19	19	20	20	21	21	22	22	22	23	23	24	24	24	25	25	25	26	26	26	
	1	6	11	16	21	26			1	11	21			1	11	21			1	16		1	16		1	16		1	11	21	
♃	22♏	23	24	25	26	27		♄	6♓	6	6		⚷	22♍	23	24		♅	23♑	23	♆	21♑	21	♇	27♏	28	☊	15♏	14	14	

DEC

	1	2	3	4	5	6	7	8	9	10	11	12	13	14	15	16	17	18	19	20	21	22	23	24	25	26	27	28	29	30	31
☉	9♐	10	11	12	13	14	15	16	17	18	19	20	21	22	23	24	25	26	27	28	29	30	1♑	2	3	4	5	6	7	8	9
☽	10♏	25	11♐	26	11♑	25	9♒	23	6♓	19	1♈	14	26	7♉	19	1♊	13	25	7♋	19	1♌	14	27	10♍	23	7♎	20	5♏	19	4♐	19
☿	1♐	3	4	6	8	9	11	12	14	15	17	19	20	22	23	25	26	28	30	1♑	3	4	6	8	9	11	12	14	16	17	19
♀	4♏	4	4	4	5	5	6	6	7	7	8	8	9	10	10	11	12	12	13	14	15	15	16	17	18	19	19	20	21	22	23
♂	27♌	27	27	28	28	28	29	29	29	29	30	30	0♍	0	1	1	1	1	1	1	2	2	2	2	2	2	2	2	3	3	3
	1	6	11	16	21	26	31		1	11	21	31		1	11	21	31		1	16		1	16		1	16		1	11	21	31
♃	28♏	29	0♐	1	2	4	5	♄	6♓	7	7	8	⚷	25♍	26	26	26	♅	24♑	25	♆	22♑	22	♇	28♏	29	☊	13♏	13	12	12

1995

EPHEMERIS

JAN

	1	2	3	4	5	6	7	8	9	10	11	12	13	14	15	16	17	18	19	20	21	22	23	24	25	26	27	28	29	30	31
☉	10♑	11	12	13	14	15	16	17	18	19	20	21	22	23	24	25	26	27	28	29	0♒	1	3	4	5	6	7	8	9	10	11
☽	4♑	19	3♒	17	1♓	15	27	10♈	22	4♉	16	28	9♊	21	3♋	16	28	11♌	24	7♍	20	3♎	17	1♏	15	29	13♐	28	12♑	27	11♒
☿	20♑	22	24	25	27	29	0♒	2	3	5	6	8	9	11	12	14	15	16	17	18	19	20	20	21	21	21	21	21	20	20	19
♀	24♏	25	26	27	28	29	30	0♐	1	2	3	4	5	6	8	9	10	11	12	13	14	15	16	17	18	19	20	21	22	24	25
♂	3♍	3	3	3	3	3	3	2	2	2	2	2	2	2	2	2	1	1	1	1	1	0	30♌	30	29	29	29	29	28	28	28
	1	6	11	16	21	26	31		1	11	21	31		1	11	21	31		1	16		1	16		1	16		1	11	21	31
♃	5♐	6	7	8	9	9	10	♄	8♓	9	10	11	⚷	26♍	26	26	26	♅	25♑	26	♆	23♑	23	♇	30♏	30	☊	12♏	11	11	10

FEB

	1	2	3	4	5	6	7	8	9	10	11	12	13	14	15	16	17	18	19	20	21	22	23	24	25	26	27	28			
☉	12♒	13	14	15	16	17	18	19	20	21	22	23	24	25	26	27	28	29	30	1♓	2	3	4	5	6	7	8	9			
☽	25♒	9♓	22	5♈	18	30	12♉	24	6♊	17	29	12♋	24	7♌	20	3♍	16	30	14♎	28	12♏	26	10♐	24	8♑	22	6♒	20			
☿	18♒	17	16	15	13	12	11	10	9	8	7	7	6	6	6	6	6	6	6	6	7	7	8	9	9	10	11	12			
♀	26♐	27	28	29	0♑	1	2	4	5	6	7	8	9	10	12	13	14	15	16	17	18	20	21	22	23	24	25	27			
♂	27♌	27	26	26	26	25	25	25	24	24	23	23	23	22	22	21	21	21	20	20	19	19	19	18	18	18	17	17			
	1	6	11	16	21	26			1	11	21			1	11	21			1	16		1	16		1	16		1	11	21	
♃	10♐	11	12	12	13	14		♄	11♓	12	13		⚷	26♍	26	25		♅	27♑	28	♆	24♑	24	♇	0♐	1	☊	10♏	10	9	

MAR

	1	2	3	4	5	6	7	8	9	10	11	12	13	14	15	16	17	18	19	20	21	22	23	24	25	26	27	28	29	30	31
☉	10♓	11	12	13	14	15	16	17	18	19	20	21	22	23	24	25	26	27	28	29	30	1♈	2	3	4	5	6	7	8	9	10
☽	4♓	17	0♈	13	25	8♉	20	2♊	13	25	7♋	19	2♌	15	28	11♍	25	9♎	23	8♏	22	7♐	21	5♑	19	3♒	16	30	13♓	26	9♈
☿	13♒	14	15	16	17	18	20	21	22	23	25	26	27	29	0♓	2	3	5	6	8	9	11	12	14	16	17	19	21	22	24	26
♀	28♑	29	0♒	1	2	4	5	6	7	8	10	11	12	13	14	15	17	18	19	20	21	23	24	25	26	27	29	30	1♓	2	3
♂	17♌	16	16	16	16	15	15	15	15	15	14	14	14	14	14	14	14	13	13	13	13	13	13	13	13	13	13	13	13	13	13
	1	6	11	16	21	26	31		1	11	21	31		1	11	21	31		1	16		1	16		1	16		1	11	21	31
♃	14♐	14	15	15	15	15	15	♄	14♓	16	17	18	⚷	24♍	24	23	22	♅	29♑	29	♆	25♑	25	♇	1♐	1	☊	9♏	8	8	7

APR

	1	2	3	4	5	6	7	8	9	10	11	12	13	14	15	16	17	18	19	20	21	22	23	24	25	26	27	28	29	30	
☉	11♈	12	13	14	15	16	17	18	19	20	21	22	23	24	25	26	27	28	28	29	0♉	1	2	3	4	5	6	7	8	9	
☽	21♈	4♉	16	28	9♊	21	3♋	15	27	10♌	23	6♍	19	3♎	18	2♏	17	2♐	17	1♑	16	30	13♒	27	10♓	23	5♈	18	0♉	12	
☿	28♓	29	1♈	3	5	7	9	11	13	15	17	19	21	23	25	27	29	1♉	4	6	8	10	12	14	16	18	20	22	24	26	
♀	5♓	6	7	8	9	11	12	13	14	15	17	18	19	20	21	23	24	25	26	27	29	30	1♈	2	3	5	6	7	8	9	
♂	13♌	14	14	14	14	14	14	14	15	15	15	15	15	15	16	16	16	16	17	17	17	17	18	18	18	19	19	19	20	20	
	1	6	11	16	21	26			1	11	21			1	11	21			1	16		1	16		1	16		1	11	21	
♃	15♐	15	15	15	15	14		♄	18♓	19	20		⚷	22♍	21	21		♅	30♑	0♒	♆	25♑	26	♇	0♐	0	☊	7♏	6	6	

MAY

	1	2	3	4	5	6	7	8	9	10	11	12	13	14	15	16	17	18	19	20	21	22	23	24	25	26	27	28	29	30	31
☉	10♉	11	12	13	14	15	16	17	18	19	20	21	22	23	24	25	26	27	28	29	29	0♊	1	2	3	4	5	6	7	8	9
☽	24♉	6♊	18	30	11♋	23	6♌	18	1♍	14	27	11♎	26	11♏	26	11♐	26	11♑	25	10♒	23	7♓	20	2♈	15	27	9♉	21	3♊	15	27
☿	27♉	29	1♊	2	4	5	6	8	9	10	11	12	13	14	15	16	16	17	17	18	18	18	18	18	18	18	18	18	18	17	17
♀	11♈	12	13	14	16	17	18	19	20	22	23	24	25	26	28	29	0♉	1	2	4	5	6	7	9	10	11	12	13	15	16	17
♂	20♌	21	21	21	22	22	22	23	23	23	24	24	25	25	25	26	26	27	27	28	28	28	29	29	30	0♍	1	1	2	2	2
	1	6	11	16	21	26	31		1	11	21	31		1	11	21	31		1	16		1	16		1	16		1	11	21	31
♃	14♐	14	13	13	12	11	11	♄	21♓	22	23	24	⚷	20♍	20	20	20	♅	0♒	0	♆	26♑	25	♇	30♏	29	☊	5♏	5	4	4

JUN

	1	2	3	4	5	6	7	8	9	10	11	12	13	14	15	16	17	18	19	20	21	22	23	24	25	26	27	28	29	30	
☉	10♊	11	12	13	14	15	16	17	18	19	20	21	22	22	23	24	25	26	27	28	29	0♋	1	2	3	4	5	6	7	8	
☽	8♋	20	2♌	15	27	10♍	23	6♎	20	4♏	19	4♐	19	4♑	20	4♒	19	3♓	16	29	12♈	24	6♉	18	30	12♊	24	5♋	17	29	
☿	16♊	16	15	15	14	14	13	13	12	12	11	11	10	10	10	10	10	10	10	10	10	11	11	12	12	13	13	14	15	16	
♀	18♉	19	21	22	23	24	26	27	28	29	0♊	2	3	4	5	6	8	9	10	11	13	14	15	16	17	19	20	21	22	24	
♂	3♍	3	4	4	5	5	6	6	7	7	8	8	9	9	10	10	11	11	12	12	13	13	14	15	15	16	16	17	17	18	
	1	6	11	16	21	26			1	11	21			1	11	21			1	16		1	16		1	16		1	11	21	
♃	11♐	10	9	9	8	8		♄	24♓	24	25		⚷	20♍	21	21		♅	0♒	30♑	♆	25♑	25	♇	29♏	29	☊	4♏	3	3	

1995

EPHEMERIS

JUL

	1	2	3	4	5	6	7	8	9	10	11	12	13	14	15	16	17	18	19	20	21	22	23	24	25	26	27	28	29	30	31
☉	9♋	10	11	12	13	13	14	15	16	17	18	19	20	21	22	23	24	25	26	27	28	29	30	1♌	2	3	4	4	5	6	7
☽	12♌	24	6♍	19	2♎	16	29	13♏	28	13♐	28	13♑	28	13♒	27	11♓	25	8♈	21	3♉	15	27	9♊	20	2♋	14	26	9♌	21	4♍	16
☿	17♊	18	19	20	22	23	24	26	27	29	0♋	2	4	6	8	9	11	13	15	17	20	22	24	26	28	0♌	2	4	6	9	11
♀	25♊	26	27	28	30	1♋	2	3	5	6	7	8	9	11	12	13	14	16	17	18	19	20	22	23	24	25	27	28	29	0♌	2
♂	18♍	19	19	20	21	21	22	22	23	23	24	25	25	26	26	27	27	28	29	29	30	0♎	1	2	2	3	3	4	5	5	6
	1	6	11	16	21	26	31		1	11	21	31		1	11	21	31		1	16		1	16		1	16		1	11	21	31
♃	7♐	7	6	6	6	6	6	♄	25♓	25	25	24	⚷	22♍	23	24	25	♅	29♑	29	♆	25♑	24	♇	28♏	28	☊	2♏	2	1	1

AUG

	1	2	3	4	5	6	7	8	9	10	11	12	13	14	15	16	17	18	19	20	21	22	23	24	25	26	27	28	29	30	31
☉	8♌	9	10	11	12	13	14	15	16	17	18	19	20	21	22	23	24	25	26	27	27	28	29	0♍	1	2	3	4	5	6	7
☽	29♍	12♎	26	9♏	23	8♐	22	7♑	22	6♒	21	5♓	19	3♈	16	29	11♉	23	5♊	17	29	11♋	23	5♌	17	0♍	13	26	9♎	23	6♏
☿	13♌	15	17	19	21	23	24	26	28	30	2♍	4	5	7	9	10	12	14	15	17	18	20	21	23	24	26	27	29	30	1♎	3
♀	3♌	4	5	6	8	9	10	11	13	14	15	16	18	19	20	21	23	24	25	26	27	29	30	1♍	2	4	5	6	7	9	10
♂	6♎	7	8	8	9	9	10	11	11	12	12	13	14	14	15	16	16	17	18	18	19	19	20	21	21	22	23	23	24	25	25
	1	6	11	16	21	26	31		1	11	21	31		1	11	21	31		1	16		1	16		1	16		1	11	21	31
♃	6♐	6	6	6	6	6	7	♄	24♓	24	23	22	⚷	25♍	26	27	29	♅	28♑	28	♆	24♑	23	♇	28♏	28	☊	1♏	0	29♎	29

SEP

	1	2	3	4	5	6	7	8	9	10	11	12	13	14	15	16	17	18	19	20	21	22	23	24	25	26	27	28	29	30
☉	8♍	9	10	11	12	13	14	15	16	17	18	19	20	21	22	23	24	25	26	27	28	29	30	0♎	1	2	3	4	5	6
☽	20♏	4♐	18	3♑	17	1♒	16	30	14♓	28	11♈	24	7♉	19	1♊	13	25	7♋	19	1♌	13	26	9♍	22	5♎	19	3♏	17	1♐	15
☿	4♎	5	6	7	9	10	11	12	13	14	15	15	16	17	18	18	19	19	20	20	20	20	20	20	20	19	19	18	18	17
♀	11♍	12	14	15	16	17	19	20	21	22	24	25	26	27	28	30	1♎	2	3	5	6	7	8	10	11	12	13	15	16	17
♂	26♎	27	27	28	28	29	30	0♏	1	2	2	3	4	4	5	6	6	7	8	8	9	10	11	11	12	13	13	14	15	15
	1	6	11	16	21	26			1	11	21			1	11	21			1	16		1	16		1	16		1	11	21
♃	7♐	7	8	8	9	10		♄	22♓	22	21		⚷	29♍	0♎	2		♅	27♑	27	♆	23♑	23	♇	28♏	28	☊	29♎	28	28

OCT

	1	2	3	4	5	6	7	8	9	10	11	12	13	14	15	16	17	18	19	20	21	22	23	24	25	26	27	28	29	30	31
☉	7♎	8	9	10	11	12	13	14	15	16	17	18	19	20	21	22	23	24	25	26	27	28	29	0♏	1	2	3	4	5	6	7
☽	29♐	13♑	28	12♒	26	9♓	23	6♈	19	2♉	15	27	9♊	21	3♋	15	27	9♌	21	4♍	17	30	14♎	28	12♏	26	11♐	26	10♑	24	9♒
☿	16♎	15	14	13	11	10	9	8	7	6	6	5	5	5	5	5	6	6	7	8	9	10	11	13	14	15	17	18	20	21	23
♀	18♎	20	21	22	23	25	26	27	28	30	1♏	2	3	5	6	7	8	10	11	12	13	15	16	17	18	20	21	22	23	24	26
♂	16♏	17	17	18	19	19	20	21	22	22	23	24	24	25	26	27	27	28	29	29	0♐	1	2	2	3	4	4	5	6	7	7
	1	6	11	16	21	26	31		1	11	21	31		1	11	21	31		1	16		1	16		1	16		1	11	21	31
♃	10♐	11	12	13	14	15	16	♄	20♓	19	19	18	⚷	3♎	5	6	7	♅	27♑	27	♆	23♑	23	♇	29♏	29	☊	27♎	27	26	26

NOV

	1	2	3	4	5	6	7	8	9	10	11	12	13	14	15	16	17	18	19	20	21	22	23	24	25	26	27	28	29	30
☉	8♏	9	10	11	12	13	14	15	16	17	18	19	20	21	22	23	24	25	26	27	28	29	0♐	1	2	3	4	5	6	7
☽	22♒	6♓	19	3♈	15	28	11♉	23	5♊	17	29	11♋	23	5♌	17	29	11♍	24	8♎	21	6♏	20	5♐	20	5♑	20	5♒	19	3♓	16
☿	25♎	26	28	29	1♏	3	4	6	8	9	11	12	14	16	17	19	21	22	24	25	27	28	0♐	2	3	5	6	8	10	11
♀	27♏	28	29	1♐	2	3	4	6	7	8	9	11	12	13	14	16	17	18	19	21	22	23	24	26	27	28	29	1♑	2	3
♂	8♐	9	9	10	11	12	12	13	14	15	15	16	17	18	18	19	20	21	21	22	23	24	24	25	26	27	27	28	29	30
	1	6	11	16	21	26			1	11	21			1	11	21			1	16		1	16		1	16		1	11	21
♃	16♐	17	18	19	20	21		♄	18♓	18	18		⚷	7♎	9	10		♅	27♑	27	♆	23♑	23	♇	30♏	0♐	☊	26♎	25	25

DEC

	1	2	3	4	5	6	7	8	9	10	11	12	13	14	15	16	17	18	19	20	21	22	23	24	25	26	27	28	29	30	31
☉	8♐	9	10	11	12	13	14	15	16	17	18	19	20	22	23	24	25	26	27	28	29	30	1♑	2	3	4	5	6	7	8	9
☽	30♓	12♈	25	7♉	20	2♊	14	26	8♋	19	1♌	13	25	7♍	20	3♎	16	29	13♏	28	13♐	28	14♑	29	14♒	28	12♓	26	9♈	22	4♉
☿	13♐	14	16	17	19	20	22	24	25	27	28	30	1♑	3	4	6	8	9	11	12	14	15	17	18	20	21	23	24	25	27	28
♀	4♑	6	7	8	9	10	12	13	14	15	17	18	19	20	22	23	24	25	27	28	29	0♒	2	3	4	5	6	8	9	10	11
♂	0♑	1	2	3	3	4	5	6	6	7	8	9	9	10	11	12	13	13	14	15	16	16	17	18	19	20	20	21	22	23	23
	1	6	11	16	21	26	31		1	11	21	31		1	11	21	31		1	16		1	16		1	16		1	11	21	31
♃	22♐	24	25	26	27	28	29	♄	18♓	18	19	19	⚷	11♎	12	13	14	♅	28♑	28	♆	24♑	24	♇	1♐	1	☊	24♎	24	23	22

1996

EPHEMERIS

JAN

	1	2	3	4	5	6	7	8	9	10	11	12	13	14	15	16	17	18	19	20	21	22	23	24	25	26	27	28	29	30	31
☉	10♑	11	12	13	14	15	16	17	18	19	20	21	22	23	24	25	26	27	28	29	0♒	1	2	3	4	5	6	7	8	9	10
☽	17♉	29	11♊	23	4♋	16	28	10♌	22	4♍	17	29	12♎	25	8♏	22	6♐	21	6♑	22	7♒	22	7♓	21	5♈	18	1♉	13	26	8♊	20
☿	29♑	0♒	1	2	3	4	4	5	5	5	5	5	4	4	3	2	0	29♑	28	27	25	24	23	22	21	20	20	20	19	19	19
♀	13♒	14	15	16	18	19	20	21	22	24	25	26	27	29	30	1♓	2	3	5	6	7	8	9	11	12	13	14	16	17	18	19
♂	24♑	25	26	27	27	28	29	30	0♒	1	2	3	4	4	5	6	7	7	8	9	10	11	11	12	13	14	15	15	16	17	18
	1	6	11	16	21	26	31		1	11	21	31		1	11	21	31		1	16		1	16		1	16		1	11	21	31
♃	29♐	1♑	2	3	4	5	6	♄	19♓	20	21	22	⚷	14♎	14	14	14	♅	29♑	0♒	♆	25♑	25	♇	2♐	2	☊	22♎	22	21	21

FEB

	1	2	3	4	5	6	7	8	9	10	11	12	13	14	15	16	17	18	19	20	21	22	23	24	25	26	27	28	29		
☉	11♒	12	13	14	15	16	17	18	20	21	22	23	24	25	26	27	28	29	30	1♓	2	3	4	5	6	7	8	9	10		
☽	1♋	13	25	7♌	19	1♍	14	26	9♎	22	5♏	18	2♐	16	0♑	15	30	15♒	30	15♓	29	13♈	26	9♉	22	4♊	16	28	10♋		
☿	19♑	20	20	20	21	22	22	23	24	25	26	27	28	29	30	1♒	2	3	5	6	7	9	10	11	13	14	15	17	18		
♀	20♓	22	23	24	25	26	28	29	30	1♈	2	3	5	6	7	8	9	10	12	13	14	15	16	17	19	20	21	22	23		
♂	19♒	19	20	21	22	22	23	24	25	26	26	27	28	29	30	0♓	1	2	3	4	4	5	6	7	8	8	9	10	11		
	1	6	11	16	21	26			1	11	21			1	11	21			1	16		1	16		1	16		1	11	21	
♃	6♑	7	8	9	10	11		♄	22♓	23	24		⚷	14♎	14	14		♅	1♒	2	♆	26♑	26	♇	3♐	3	☊	21♎	20	20	

MAR

	1	2	3	4	5	6	7	8	9	10	11	12	13	14	15	16	17	18	19	20	21	22	23	24	25	26	27	28	29	30	31
☉	11♓	12	13	14	15	16	17	18	19	20	21	22	23	24	25	26	27	28	29	30	1♈	2	3	4	5	6	7	8	9	10	11
☽	22♋	4♌	16	28	10♍	23	6♎	18	2♏	15	29	12♐	26	11♑	25	10♒	24	9♓	23	7♈	21	4♉	17	29	12♊	24	6♋	18	30	12♌	24
☿	20♒	21	23	24	26	28	29	1♓	2	4	6	7	9	11	13	14	16	18	20	22	24	25	27	29	1♈	3	5	7	9	11	13
♀	24♈	25	27	28	29	30	1♉	2	3	4	5	7	8	9	10	11	12	13	14	15	16	17	18	19	20	21	22	23	24	25	26
♂	11♓	12	13	14	15	15	16	17	18	19	19	20	21	22	22	23	24	25	26	26	27	28	29	30	0♈	1	2	3	3	4	5
	1	6	11	16	21	26	31		1	11	21	31		1	11	21	31		1	16		1	16		1	16		1	11	21	31
♃	12♑	13	13	14	15	15	16	♄	25♓	27	28	29	⚷	13♎	13	12	11	♅	3♒	3	♆	27♑	27	♇	3♐	3	☊	19♎	19	18	18

APR

	1	2	3	4	5	6	7	8	9	10	11	12	13	14	15	16	17	18	19	20	21	22	23	24	25	26	27	28	29	30	
☉	12♈	13	14	15	15	16	17	18	19	20	21	22	23	24	25	26	27	28	29	0♉	1	2	3	4	5	6	7	8	9	10	
☽	6♍	19	1♎	14	28	11♏	25	9♐	23	7♑	22	6♒	20	4♓	18	2♈	15	29	12♉	25	7♊	20	2♋	14	26	8♌	20	2♍	14	27	
☿	15♈	17	20	22	24	26	28	30	2♉	4	6	7	9	11	13	14	16	17	19	20	21	22	23	24	25	26	26	27	28	28	
♀	27♉	28	29	0♊	1	2	3	4	5	6	7	8	9	9	10	11	12	13	14	14	15	16	17	17	18	19	20	20	21	21	
♂	6♈	6	7	8	9	10	10	11	12	13	13	14	15	16	17	17	18	19	20	20	21	22	23	23	24	25	26	26	27	28	
	1	6	11	16	21	26			1	11	21			1	11	21			1	16		1	16		1	16		1	11	21	
♃	16♑	16	17	17	17	18		♄	29♓	0♈	2		⚷	11♎	10	10		♅	4♒	4	♆	28♑	28	♇	3♐	3	☊	18♎	17	17	

MAY

	1	2	3	4	5	6	7	8	9	10	11	12	13	14	15	16	17	18	19	20	21	22	23	24	25	26	27	28	29	30	31
☉	11♉	12	13	14	15	16	17	18	19	20	21	22	23	23	24	25	26	27	28	29	0♊	1	2	3	4	5	6	7	8	9	10
☽	9♎	23	6♏	20	5♐	19	4♑	18	3♒	17	1♓	15	28	12♈	25	8♉	21	3♊	16	28	10♋	22	4♌	16	28	10♍	22	4♎	17	1♏	15
☿	28♉	28	29	29	29	28	28	28	28	27	27	26	26	25	25	24	23	23	22	22	21	21	20	20	20	20	20	20	20	20	20
♀	22♊	23	23	24	24	25	25	26	26	26	27	27	27	28	28	28	28	28	28	28	28	28	28	28	28	28	27	27	27	26	26
♂	29♈	29	0♉	1	2	2	3	4	5	5	6	7	8	8	9	10	11	11	12	13	14	14	15	16	17	17	18	19	19	20	21
	1	6	11	16	21	26	31		1	11	21	31		1	11	21	31		1	16		1	16		1	16		1	11	21	31
♃	18♑	18	18	17	17	17	17	♄	3♈	4	5	5	⚷	9♎	8	8	8	♅	5♒	5	♆	28♑	28	♇	2♐	2	☊	16♎	16	15	14

JUN

	1	2	3	4	5	6	7	8	9	10	11	12	13	14	15	16	17	18	19	20	21	22	23	24	25	26	27	28	29	30	
☉	11♊	12	13	14	15	16	17	17	18	19	20	21	22	23	24	25	26	27	28	29	30	1♋	2	3	4	5	6	7	8	8	
☽	29♏	14♐	28	13♑	28	13♒	27	12♓	25	9♈	22	5♉	17	30	12♊	24	6♋	18	0♌	12	24	6♍	18	0♎	13	26	9♏	23	7♐	22	
☿	20♉	21	21	22	22	23	23	24	25	26	27	28	29	0♊	1	3	4	5	7	8	10	11	13	14	16	18	20	22	23	25	
♀	26♊	25	25	24	23	23	22	22	21	20	20	19	19	18	17	17	16	16	15	15	14	14	13	13	13	13	12	12	12	12	
♂	22♉	22	23	24	25	25	26	27	27	28	29	30	0♊	1	2	2	3	4	5	5	6	7	7	8	9	9	10	11	12	12	
	1	6	11	16	21	26			1	11	21			1	11	21			1	16		1	16		1	16		1	11	21	
♃	17♑	16	16	15	14	14		♄	6♈	6	7		⚷	8♎	8	8		♅	4♒	4	♆	27♑	27	♇	1♐	1	☊	14♎	14	13	

1996

JUL

	1	2	3	4	5	6	7	8	9	10	11	12	13	14	15	16	17	18	19	20	21	22	23	24	25	26	27	28	29	30	31
☉	9♋	10	11	12	13	14	15	16	17	18	19	20	21	22	23	24	25	26	27	28	29	29	0♌	1	2	3	4	5	6	7	8
☽	7♑	22	8♒	23	7♓	21	5♈	19	2♉	14	27	9♊	21	3♋	15	27	9♌	21	3♍	15	27	9♎	22	4♏	18	2♐	16	0♑	15	1♒	16
☿	27♊	29	1♋	3	6	8	10	12	14	16	19	21	23	25	27	29	1♌	3	5	7	9	11	13	15	17	19	20	22	24	26	27
♀	12♊	12	12	12	12	12	12	12	13	13	13	13	14	14	15	15	16	16	17	17	18	18	19	19	20	21	21	22	23	23	24
♂	13♊	14	14	15	16	16	17	18	19	19	20	21	21	22	23	23	24	25	25	26	27	27	28	29	29	0♋	1	1	2	3	4
	1	6	11	16	21	26	31		1	11	21	31		1	11	21	31		1	16		1	16		1	16		1	11	21	31
♃	13♑	13	12	11	11	10	10	♄	7♈	7	7	7	⚷	9♎	9	10	11	♅	4♒	3	♆	27♑	26	♇	1♐	1	☊	13♎	12	12	11

AUG

	1	2	3	4	5	6	7	8	9	10	11	12	13	14	15	16	17	18	19	20	21	22	23	24	25	26	27	28	29	30	31
☉	9♌	10	11	12	13	14	15	16	17	18	19	20	21	21	22	23	24	25	26	27	28	29	0♍	1	2	3	4	5	6	7	8
☽	1♓	16	1♈	15	28	11♉	24	6♊	18	1♋	12	24	6♌	18	30	12♍	24	6♎	19	1♏	14	27	11♐	25	9♑	24	9♒	24	10♓	24	9♈
☿	29♌	1♍	2	4	5	7	8	10	11	12	14	15	16	18	19	20	21	22	23	25	26	27	27	28	29	30	1♎	1	2	2	3
♀	25♊	26	27	27	28	29	30	1♋	1	2	3	4	5	6	7	8	9	10	11	12	12	13	14	15	16	17	18	19	20	21	22
♂	4♋	5	6	6	7	8	8	9	9	10	11	11	12	13	13	14	15	15	16	17	17	18	19	19	20	21	21	22	22	23	24
	1	6	11	16	21	26	31		1	11	21	31		1	11	21	31		1	16		1	16		1	16		1	11	21	31
♃	10♑	9	9	8	8	8	8	♄	7♈	7	7	6	⚷	11♎	12	13	14	♅	2♒	2	♆	26♑	26	♇	0♐	0	☊	11♎	11	10	10

SEP

	1	2	3	4	5	6	7	8	9	10	11	12	13	14	15	16	17	18	19	20	21	22	23	24	25	26	27	28	29	30
☉	9♍	10	11	12	13	14	15	16	17	18	19	20	20	21	22	23	24	25	26	27	28	29	0♎	1	2	3	4	5	6	7
☽	23♈	7♉	20	3♊	15	27	9♋	21	3♌	15	27	9♍	21	3♎	16	28	11♏	24	8♐	21	5♑	19	4♒	18	3♓	18	3♈	17	1♉	15
☿	3♎	3	3	3	3	3	3	3	2	2	1	0	29♍	29	28	27	25	24	23	22	22	21	20	20	19	19	19	19	19	20
♀	23♋	25	26	27	28	29	30	1♌	2	3	4	5	6	7	8	10	11	12	13	14	15	16	17	18	20	21	22	23	24	25
♂	24♋	25	26	26	27	28	28	29	29	0♌	1	1	2	3	3	4	4	5	6	6	7	8	8	9	9	10	11	11	12	12
	1	6	11	16	21	26			1	11	21			1	11	21			1	16		1	16		1	16		1	11	21
♃	8♑	8	8	8	8	9		♄	6♈	5	4		⚷	14♎	16	17		♅	1♒	1	♆	25♑	25	♇	0♐	1	☊	10♎	9	8

OCT

	1	2	3	4	5	6	7	8	9	10	11	12	13	14	15	16	17	18	19	20	21	22	23	24	25	26	27	28	29	30	31
☉	8♎	9	10	11	12	13	14	15	16	17	18	19	20	21	22	23	24	25	26	27	28	29	30	1♏	2	3	4	5	6	7	8
☽	28♉	11♊	23	5♋	17	29	11♌	23	5♍	17	29	12♎	25	8♏	21	4♐	18	2♑	16	0♒	14	29	13♓	27	11♈	25	9♉	23	6♊	19	1♋
☿	21♍	21	22	23	24	26	27	28	30	1♎	3	5	6	8	9	11	13	15	16	18	20	21	23	25	27	28	30	2♏	3	5	7
♀	26♌	28	29	30	1♍	2	3	4	6	7	8	9	10	12	13	14	15	16	17	19	20	21	22	23	25	26	27	28	29	1♎	2
♂	13♌	14	14	15	15	16	17	17	18	18	19	20	20	21	21	22	22	23	24	24	25	25	26	26	27	28	28	29	29	30	0♍
	1	6	11	16	21	26	31		1	11	21	31		1	11	21	31		1	16		1	16		1	16		1	11	21	31
♃	9♑	9	10	11	11	12	13	♄	4♈	3	2	2	⚷	19♎	20	21	23	♅	1♒	1	♆	25♑	25	♇	1♐	2	☊	8♎	7	7	6

NOV

	1	2	3	4	5	6	7	8	9	10	11	12	13	14	15	16	17	18	19	20	21	22	23	24	25	26	27	28	29	30
☉	9♏	10	11	12	13	14	15	16	17	18	19	20	21	22	23	24	25	26	27	28	29	30	1♐	2	3	4	5	6	7	8
☽	13♋	25	7♌	19	1♍	13	25	8♎	20	3♏	17	0♐	14	28	13♑	27	11♒	25	9♓	23	7♈	21	4♉	18	1♊	14	27	9♋	21	3♌
☿	8♏	10	11	13	15	16	18	19	21	23	24	26	27	29	0♐	2	4	5	7	8	10	11	13	14	16	17	19	20	22	23
♀	3♎	4	5	7	8	9	10	12	13	14	15	16	18	19	20	21	23	24	25	26	27	29	30	1♏	2	4	5	6	7	9
♂	1♍	1	2	3	3	4	4	5	5	6	6	7	7	8	8	9	10	10	11	11	12	12	13	13	14	14	15	15	16	16
	1	6	11	16	21	26			1	11	21			1	11	21			1	16		1	16		1	16		1	11	21
♃	13♑	14	14	15	16	17		♄	2♈	1	1		⚷	23♎	24	26		♅	1♒	1	♆	25♑	25	♇	2♐	3	☊	6♎	6	5

DEC

	1	2	3	4	5	6	7	8	9	10	11	12	13	14	15	16	17	18	19	20	21	22	23	24	25	26	27	28	29	30	31
☉	9♐	10	11	12	13	14	15	16	17	18	19	20	21	22	23	24	25	26	27	28	29	0♑	1	2	3	4	6	7	8	9	10
☽	15♌	27	9♍	21	3♎	15	28	11♏	25	9♐	23	8♑	22	7♒	22	6♓	20	4♈	18	1♉	14	27	10♊	23	5♋	17	29	11♌	23	5♍	17
☿	25♐	26	28	29	1♑	2	3	5	6	8	9	10	11	13	14	15	16	17	17	18	19	19	19	19	19	19	18	18	17	16	14
♀	10♏	11	12	14	15	16	17	19	20	21	22	23	25	26	27	28	30	1♐	2	3	5	6	7	8	10	11	12	13	15	16	17
♂	16♍	17	17	18	18	19	19	20	20	21	21	21	22	22	23	23	24	24	24	25	25	26	26	26	27	27	27	28	28	29	29
	1	6	11	16	21	26	31		1	11	21	31		1	11	21	31		1	16		1	16		1	16		1	11	21	31
♃	18♑	19	20	22	23	24	25	♄	1♈	1	1	1	⚷	27♎	28	29	0♏	♅	2♒	2	♆	26♑	26	♇	3♐	4	☊	5♎	4	4	3

1997

JAN

	1	2	3	4	5	6	7	8	9	10	11	12	13	14	15	16	17	18	19	20	21	22	23	24	25	26	27	28	29	30	31
☉	11♑	12	13	14	15	16	17	18	19	20	21	22	23	24	25	26	27	28	29	30	1♒	2	3	4	5	6	7	8	9	10	11
☽	29♍	11♎	23	6♏	19	3♐	17	1♑	16	1♒	16	1♓	16	0♈	14	28	11♉	24	7♊	19	2♋	14	26	8♌	20	2♍	14	25	7♎	19	2♏
☿	13♑	12	10	9	8	7	6	5	4	4	3	3	3	3	3	4	4	5	5	6	7	8	9	10	11	12	13	14	15	16	17
♀	18♐	20	21	22	23	25	26	27	28	30	1♑	2	3	5	6	7	8	10	11	12	13	15	16	17	18	20	21	22	24	25	26
♂	29♍	30	30	0♎	1	1	1	1	2	2	2	2	3	3	3	3	4	4	4	4	4	5	5	5	5	5	5	5	6	6	6
	1	6	11	16	21	26	31		1	11	21	31		1	11	21	31		1	16		1	16		1	16		1	11	21	31
♃	25♑	26	27	29	30	1♒	2	♄	1♈	2	3	4	⚷	0♏	1	2	2	♅	3♒	4	♆	27♑	27	♇	4♐	5	☊	3♎	3	2	1

FEB

	1	2	3	4	5	6	7	8	9	10	11	12	13	14	15	16	17	18	19	20	21	22	23	24	25	26	27	28			
☉	12♒	13	14	15	16	17	18	19	20	21	22	23	24	25	26	27	28	29	0♓	1	2	3	4	5	6	7	8	9			
☽	14♏	27	11♐	25	9♑	24	9♒	25	10♓	25	9♈	24	7♉	21	4♊	16	29	11♋	23	5♌	17	29	11♍	22	4♎	16	28	11♏			
☿	19♑	20	21	23	24	25	27	28	30	1♒	3	4	6	7	9	10	12	13	15	16	18	20	21	23	25	26	28	30			
♀	27♑	29	30	1♒	2	4	5	6	7	9	10	11	12	14	15	16	17	19	20	21	22	24	25	26	27	29	30	1♓			
♂	6♎	6	6	6	6	6	6	6	6	6	6	6	6	6	5	5	5	5	5	5	4	4	4	4	4	3	3	3			
	1	6	11	16	21	26			1	11	21			1	11	21			1	16		1	16		1	16		1	11	21	
♃	2♒	4	5	6	7	8		♄	4♈	5	6		⚷	2♏	2	2		♅	5♒	6	♆	28♑	29	♇	5♐	5	☊	1♎	1	0	

MAR

	1	2	3	4	5	6	7	8	9	10	11	12	13	14	15	16	17	18	19	20	21	22	23	24	25	26	27	28	29	30	31
☉	10♓	11	12	13	14	15	16	17	18	19	20	21	22	23	24	25	26	27	28	29	0♈	1	2	3	4	5	6	7	8	9	10
☽	24♏	7♐	20	4♑	18	3♒	17	3♓	18	3♈	18	2♉	16	30	13♊	25	8♋	20	2♌	14	26	7♍	19	1♎	13	26	8♏	21	3♐	17	30
☿	1♓	3	5	7	9	10	12	14	16	18	20	22	24	26	28	30	2♈	4	6	8	10	12	14	15	17	19	21	23	24	26	28
♀	2♓	4	5	6	7	9	10	11	12	14	15	16	17	19	20	21	22	23	25	26	27	28	30	1♈	2	3	5	6	7	8	10
♂	3♎	2	2	2	1	1	1	0	30♍	30	29	29	28	28	28	27	27	27	26	26	25	25	25	24	24	23	23	23	22	22	22
	1	6	11	16	21	26	31		1	11	21	31		1	11	21	31		1	16		1	16		1	16		1	11	21	31
♃	9♒	10	11	12	13	14	15	♄	7♈	8	9	10	⚷	2♏	2	1	0	♅	7♒	7	♆	29♑	29	♇	6♐	6	☊	30♍	29	29	28

APR

	1	2	3	4	5	6	7	8	9	10	11	12	13	14	15	16	17	18	19	20	21	22	23	24	25	26	27	28	29	30	
☉	11♈	12	13	14	15	16	17	18	19	20	21	22	23	24	25	26	27	28	29	30	1♉	2	3	4	5	6	7	8	9	10	
☽	14♑	28	12♒	27	11♓	26	11♈	26	10♉	24	8♊	21	4♋	16	28	10♌	22	4♍	16	28	10♎	22	5♏	17	0♐	13	27	10♑	24	8♒	
☿	29♈	1♉	2	3	4	5	6	7	8	8	9	9	9	10	10	10	9	9	9	8	8	7	7	6	6	5	4	4	3	2	
♀	11♈	12	13	15	16	17	18	20	21	22	23	25	26	27	28	29	1♉	2	3	4	6	7	8	9	11	12	13	14	16	17	
♂	21♍	21	21	20	20	20	20	19	19	19	19	18	18	18	18	18	17	17	17	17	17	17	17	17	17	17	17	17	17	17	
	1	6	11	16	21	26			1	11	21			1	11	21			1	16		1	16		1	16		1	11	21	
♃	15♒	16	17	17	18	19		♄	10♈	12	13		⚷	0♏	30♎	29		♅	8♒	8	♆	30♑	30	♇	5♐	5	☊	28♍	28	27	

MAY

	1	2	3	4	5	6	7	8	9	10	11	12	13	14	15	16	17	18	19	20	21	22	23	24	25	26	27	28	29	30	31
☉	11♉	12	13	14	15	16	16	17	18	19	20	21	22	23	24	25	26	27	28	29	30	1♊	2	3	4	5	6	7	8	9	10
☽	22♒	7♓	21	5♈	20	4♉	18	2♊	16	29	12♋	24	6♌	18	0♍	12	24	6♎	18	0♏	13	26	10♐	23	7♑	21	5♒	19	3♓	17	2♈
☿	2♉	1	1	0	0	30♈	30	29	29	30	30	30	0♉	1	1	1	2	3	3	4	5	6	7	8	9	10	11	12	13	15	16
♀	18♉	19	20	22	23	24	25	27	28	29	0♊	2	3	4	5	6	8	9	10	11	13	14	15	16	18	19	20	21	22	24	25
♂	17♍	17	17	17	17	17	17	17	17	18	18	18	18	18	18	19	19	19	19	20	20	20	20	21	21	21	21	22	22	22	23
	1	6	11	16	21	26	31		1	11	21	31		1	11	21	31		1	16		1	16		1	16		1	11	21	31
♃	20♒	20	21	21	21	22	22	♄	14♈	15	16	17	⚷	28♎	27	27	26	♅	9♒	9	♆	30♑	30	♇	5♐	4	☊	27♍	26	26	25

JUN

	1	2	3	4	5	6	7	8	9	10	11	12	13	14	15	16	17	18	19	20	21	22	23	24	25	26	27	28	29	30	
☉	11♊	12	12	13	14	15	16	17	18	19	20	21	22	23	24	25	26	27	28	29	30	1♋	2	3	3	4	5	6	7	8	
☽	16♈	30	13♉	27	11♊	24	7♋	20	2♌	14	26	8♍	20	2♎	14	26	8♏	21	5♐	18	2♑	17	1♒	15	30	14♓	28	12♈	26	10♉	
☿	17♉	19	20	22	23	25	27	28	0♊	2	4	5	7	9	11	13	15	17	19	22	24	26	28	0♋	2	5	7	9	11	13	
♀	26♊	27	29	30	1♋	2	3	5	6	7	8	10	11	12	13	14	16	17	18	19	21	22	23	24	25	27	28	29	0♌	1	
♂	23♍	23	24	24	24	25	25	25	26	26	27	27	27	28	28	29	29	29	30	0♎	1	1	2	2	3	3	3	4	4	5	
	1	6	11	16	21	26			1	11	21			1	11	21			1	16		1	16		1	16		1	11	21	
♃	22♒	22	22	22	22	22		♄	17♈	18	19		⚷	26♎	26	26		♅	9♒	8	♆	30♑	29	♇	4♐	4	☊	25♍	25	24	

1997

JUL

	1	2	3	4	5	6	7	8	9	10	11	12	13	14	15	16	17	18	19	20	21	22	23	24	25	26	27	28	29	30	31
☉	9♋	10	11	12	13	14	15	16	17	18	19	20	21	22	23	24	24	25	26	27	28	29	0♌	1	2	3	4	5	6	7	8
☽	24♉	7♊	20	3♋	16	28	10♌	22	4♍	16	28	10♎	22	4♏	16	29	13♐	27	11♑	25	10♒	25	10♓	25	9♈	23	7♉	21	4♊	17	30
☿	15♋	18	20	22	24	26	28	30	1♌	3	5	7	9	10	12	14	15	17	19	20	22	23	25	26	27	29	30	1♍	2	4	5
♀	3♌	4	5	6	8	9	10	11	12	14	15	16	17	18	20	21	22	23	25	26	27	28	29	1♍	2	3	4	5	7	8	9
♂	5♎	6	6	7	7	8	8	9	9	10	10	11	11	12	13	13	14	14	15	15	16	16	17	17	18	19	19	20	20	21	21
	1	6	11	16	21	26	31		1	11	21	31		1	11	21	31		1	16		1	16		1	16		1	11	21	31
♃	21♒	21	20	20	19	19	18	♄	20♈	20	20	20	⚷	26♎	26	26	27	♅	8♒	7	♆	29♑	29	♇	3♐	3	☊	23♍	23	22	22

AUG

	1	2	3	4	5	6	7	8	9	10	11	12	13	14	15	16	17	18	19	20	21	22	23	24	25	26	27	28	29	30	31
☉	9♌	10	11	12	13	14	15	15	16	17	18	19	20	21	22	23	24	25	26	27	28	29	30	1♍	2	3	4	5	6	7	8
☽	12♋	25	7♌	19	1♍	13	24	6♎	18	0♏	12	25	8♐	21	5♑	19	4♒	19	4♓	19	4♈	19	3♉	17	1♊	14	27	9♋	22	4♌	16
☿	6♍	7	8	9	10	11	12	12	13	14	14	15	15	16	16	16	16	16	16	16	16	15	15	14	14	13	12	11	11	10	9
♀	10♍	11	13	14	15	16	17	19	20	21	22	23	25	26	27	28	29	0♎	2	3	4	5	6	8	9	10	11	12	13	15	16
♂	22♎	23	23	24	24	25	26	26	27	27	28	29	29	30	0♏	1	2	2	3	3	4	5	5	6	7	7	8	9	9	10	11
	1	6	11	16	21	26	31		1	11	21	31		1	11	21	31		1	16		1	16		1	16		1	11	21	31
♃	18♒	17	17	16	16	15	14	♄	20♈	20	20	20	⚷	27♎	28	29	30	♅	7♒	6	♆	28♑	28	♇	3♐	3	☊	22♍	21	21	20

SEP

	1	2	3	4	5	6	7	8	9	10	11	12	13	14	15	16	17	18	19	20	21	22	23	24	25	26	27	28	29	30	
☉	9♍	10	11	12	12	13	14	15	16	17	18	19	20	21	22	23	24	25	26	27	28	29	0♎	1	2	3	4	5	6	7	
☽	28♌	10♍	21	3♎	15	27	9♏	21	4♐	17	30	13♑	28	12♒	27	12♓	27	12♈	27	12♉	26	10♊	23	6♋	19	1♌	13	25	7♍	18	
☿	8♍	7	6	5	4	4	3	3	3	3	3	3	3	4	5	5	6	7	8	10	11	13	14	16	17	19	21	22	24	26	
♀	17♎	18	19	21	22	23	24	25	26	28	29	30	1♏	2	3	5	6	7	8	9	10	11	13	14	15	16	17	18	19	21	
♂	11♏	12	12	13	14	14	15	16	16	17	18	18	19	20	20	21	22	22	23	24	25	25	26	27	27	28	29	29	0♐	1	
	1	6	11	16	21	26			1	11	21			1	11	21			1	16		1	16		1	16		1	11	21	
♃	14♒	14	13	13	13	12		♄	20♈	19	18		⚷	30♎	1♏	2		♅	5♒	5	♆	28♑	27	♇	3♐	3	☊	20♍	20	19	

OCT

	1	2	3	4	5	6	7	8	9	10	11	12	13	14	15	16	17	18	19	20	21	22	23	24	25	26	27	28	29	30	31
☉	8♎	9	10	11	12	13	14	15	16	17	18	19	20	21	22	23	24	25	26	27	28	29	30	1♏	2	3	4	5	6	7	8
☽	0♎	12	24	6♏	18	1♐	13	26	9♑	23	7♒	21	5♓	20	5♈	20	5♉	20	4♊	18	2♋	15	27	10♌	22	3♍	15	27	9♎	21	3♏
☿	28♍	30	1♎	3	5	7	9	10	12	14	16	17	19	21	22	24	26	28	29	1♏	2	4	6	7	9	10	12	14	15	17	18
♀	22♏	23	24	25	26	27	28	30	1♐	2	3	4	5	6	7	8	10	11	12	13	14	15	16	17	18	19	20	21	22	23	25
♂	1♐	2	3	4	4	5	6	6	7	8	9	9	10	11	11	12	13	14	14	15	16	16	17	18	19	19	20	21	22	22	23
	1	6	11	16	21	26	31		1	11	21	31		1	11	21	31		1	16		1	16		1	16		1	11	21	31
♃	12♒	12	12	12	12	13	13	♄	18♈	17	16	15	⚷	3♏	5	6	8	♅	5♒	5	♆	27♑	27	♇	3♐	4	☊	19♍	18	18	17

NOV

	1	2	3	4	5	6	7	8	9	10	11	12	13	14	15	16	17	18	19	20	21	22	23	24	25	26	27	28	29	30	
☉	9♏	10	11	12	13	14	15	16	17	18	19	20	21	22	23	24	25	26	27	28	29	30	1♐	2	3	4	5	6	7	8	
☽	15♏	28	10♐	23	6♑	20	3♒	17	1♓	15	30	14♈	29	14♉	28	12♊	26	10♋	23	5♌	18	30	12♍	23	5♎	17	29	11♏	24	7♐	
☿	20♏	21	23	24	26	27	29	0♐	2	3	5	6	8	9	11	12	13	15	16	17	19	20	21	23	24	25	26	27	28	29	
♀	26♐	27	28	29	30	1♑	2	3	4	5	6	7	7	8	9	10	11	12	13	14	15	16	17	17	18	19	20	21	21	22	
♂	24♐	25	25	26	27	28	28	29	30	1♑	1	2	3	4	4	5	6	7	7	8	9	10	10	11	12	13	14	14	15	16	
	1	6	11	16	21	26			1	11	21			1	11	21			1	16		1	16		1	16		1	11	21	
♃	13♒	13	14	14	15	16		♄	15♈	15	14		⚷	8♏	9	11		♅	5♒	5	♆	27♑	28	♇	4♐	5	☊	17♍	16	16	

DEC

	1	2	3	4	5	6	7	8	9	10	11	12	13	14	15	16	17	18	19	20	21	22	23	24	25	26	27	28	29	30	31
☉	9♐	10	11	12	13	14	15	16	17	18	19	20	21	22	23	24	25	26	27	28	29	0♑	1	2	3	4	5	6	7	8	9
☽	20♐	3♑	16	0♒	14	28	12♓	26	10♈	24	8♉	23	7♊	21	4♋	18	1♌	13	25	8♍	19	1♎	13	25	7♏	19	2♐	15	28	12♑	26
☿	0♑	1	2	2	3	3	3	3	3	3	2	2	1	30♐	29	27	26	24	23	22	21	20	19	18	18	17	17	17	17	18	18
♀	23♑	24	24	25	26	26	27	28	28	29	29	30	0♒	1	1	2	2	2	3	3	3	3	4	4	4	4	4	4	4	4	4
♂	17♑	17	18	19	20	20	21	22	23	24	24	25	26	27	27	28	29	30	1♒	1	2	3	4	4	5	6	7	8	8	9	10
	1	6	11	16	21	26	31		1	11	21	31		1	11	21	31		1	16		1	16		1	16		1	11	21	31
♃	17♒	17	18	19	20	21	22	♄	14♈	14	14	14	⚷	12♏	13	14	15	♅	6♒	6	♆	28♑	28	♇	6♐	6	☊	15♍	15	14	14

1998

JAN

	1	2	3	4	5	6	7	8	9	10	11	12	13	14	15	16	17	18	19	20	21	22	23	24	25	26	27	28	29	30	31
☉	10♑	11	12	13	14	15	16	17	19	20	21	22	23	24	25	26	27	28	29	30	1♒	2	3	4	5	6	7	8	9	10	11
☽	10♒	24	8♓	22	7♈	21	5♉	19	2♊	16	30	13♋	26	9♌	21	3♍	15	27	9♎	21	3♏	15	27	10♐	23	6♑	20	4♒	19	4♓	18
☿	18♐	19	20	21	22	22	23	25	26	27	28	29	0♑	2	3	4	6	7	8	10	11	13	14	15	17	18	20	21	23	24	26
♀	3♒	3	3	3	2	2	1	1	0	30♑	29	29	28	28	27	26	26	25	25	24	23	23	22	22	21	21	20	20	20	19	19
♂	11♒	12	12	13	14	15	15	16	17	18	19	19	20	21	22	23	23	24	25	26	27	27	28	29	30	0♓	1	2	3	4	4
	1	6	11	16	21	26	31		1	11	21	31		1	11	21	31		1	16		1	16		1	16		1	11	21	31
♃	22♒	23	24	25	27	28	29	♄	14♈	14	15	15	⚷	16♏	16	17	18	♅	7♒	8	♆	29♑	30	♇	7♐	7	☊	14♍	13	13	12

FEB

	1	2	3	4	5	6	7	8	9	10	11	12	13	14	15	16	17	18	19	20	21	22	23	24	25	26	27	28			
☉	12♒	13	14	15	16	17	18	19	20	21	22	23	24	25	26	27	28	29	0♓	1	2	3	4	5	6	7	8	9			
☽	3♈	17	2♉	16	29	13♊	26	9♋	22	5♌	17	29	11♍	23	5♎	17	29	11♏	23	5♐	18	1♑	14	28	12♒	27	12♓	27			
☿	27♑	29	1♒	2	4	5	7	9	10	12	14	15	17	19	20	22	24	26	27	29	1♓	3	5	7	8	10	12	14			
♀	19♑	19	19	19	18	18	18	19	19	19	19	19	19	20	20	20	21	21	22	22	23	23	24	24	25	25	26	27			
♂	5♓	6	7	8	8	9	10	11	12	12	13	14	15	15	16	17	18	19	19	20	21	22	22	23	24	25	26	26			
	1	6	11	16	21	26			1	11	21			1	11	21			1	16		1	16		1	16		1	11	21	
♃	29♒	0♓	2	3	4	5		♄	15♈	16	17		⚷	18♏	18	19		♅	9♒	10	♆	0♒	1	♇	8♐	8	☊	12♍	12	11	

MAR

	1	2	3	4	5	6	7	8	9	10	11	12	13	14	15	16	17	18	19	20	21	22	23	24	25	26	27	28	29	30	31
☉	10♓	11	12	13	14	15	16	17	18	19	20	21	22	23	24	25	26	27	28	29	0♈	1	2	3	4	5	6	7	8	9	10
☽	12♈	27	12♉	26	10♊	23	6♋	19	2♌	14	26	8♍	20	2♎	14	26	7♏	19	2♐	14	26	9♑	23	6♒	20	5♓	20	5♈	20	6♉	20
☿	16♓	18	20	22	24	26	27	29	1♈	3	5	6	8	10	11	13	14	15	17	18	19	19	20	21	21	21	21	21	21	21	21
♀	27♑	28	29	29	0♒	1	2	3	3	4	5	6	7	8	8	9	10	11	12	13	14	15	16	17	18	19	20	21	22	23	24
♂	27♓	28	29	29	0♈	1	2	3	3	4	5	6	6	7	8	9	10	10	11	12	13	13	14	15	16	16	17	18	19	19	20
	1	6	11	16	21	26	31		1	11	21	31		1	11	21	31		1	16		1	16		1	16		1	11	21	31
♃	6♓	7	8	9	11	12	13	♄	18♈	19	20	22	⚷	19♏	19	18	18	♅	10♒	11	♆	1♒	2	♇	8♐	8	☊	11♍	10	10	9

APR

	1	2	3	4	5	6	7	8	9	10	11	12	13	14	15	16	17	18	19	20	21	22	23	24	25	26	27	28	29	30	
☉	11♈	12	13	14	15	16	17	18	19	20	21	22	23	24	25	26	27	28	29	30	1♉	2	3	4	5	6	7	8	8	9	
☽	5♊	19	3♋	16	29	11♌	23	5♍	17	29	11♎	23	4♏	16	29	11♐	23	6♑	19	2♒	15	29	14♓	28	13♈	29	14♉	29	13♊	28	
☿	20♈	20	19	19	18	17	16	16	15	14	13	13	12	11	11	11	10	10	10	10	10	10	10	10	11	11	12	12	13	13	
♀	25♒	26	27	28	29	30	1♓	2	3	4	5	6	7	8	9	10	11	13	14	15	16	17	18	19	20	21	22	24	25	26	
♂	21♈	22	22	23	24	25	25	26	27	28	28	29	30	1♉	1	2	3	4	4	5	6	7	7	8	9	10	10	11	12	13	
	1	6	11	16	21	26			1	11	21			1	11	21			1	16		1	16		1	16		1	11	21	
♃	13♓	14	15	16	18	19		♄	22♈	23	24		⚷	18♏	17	17		♅	12♒	12	♆	2♒	2	♇	8♐	8	☊	9♍	8	8	

MAY

	1	2	3	4	5	6	7	8	9	10	11	12	13	14	15	16	17	18	19	20	21	22	23	24	25	26	27	28	29	30	31
☉	10♉	11	12	13	14	15	16	17	18	19	20	21	22	23	24	25	26	27	28	29	30	1♊	2	3	4	5	6	6	7	8	9
☽	11♋	25	8♌	20	2♍	14	26	8♎	20	1♏	13	26	8♐	20	3♑	16	29	12♒	25	9♓	23	8♈	23	7♉	22	7♊	22	6♋	20	3♌	16
☿	14♈	15	16	17	18	19	20	21	22	23	25	26	27	28	30	1♉	3	4	6	7	9	11	12	14	16	18	20	21	23	25	27
♀	27♓	28	29	0♈	1	2	4	5	6	7	8	9	10	12	13	14	15	16	17	18	20	21	22	23	24	25	27	28	29	0♉	1
♂	13♉	14	15	15	16	17	18	18	19	20	21	21	22	23	23	24	25	26	26	27	28	28	29	30	1♊	1	2	3	3	4	5
	1	6	11	16	21	26	31		1	11	21	31		1	11	21	31		1	16		1	16		1	16		1	11	21	31
♃	20♓	20	21	22	23	24	25	♄	26♈	27	28	29	⚷	16♏	15	15	14	♅	13♒	13	♆	2♒	2	♇	7♐	7	☊	7♍	7	6	6

JUN

	1	2	3	4	5	6	7	8	9	10	11	12	13	14	15	16	17	18	19	20	21	22	23	24	25	26	27	28	29	30	
☉	10♊	11	12	13	14	15	16	17	18	19	20	21	22	23	24	25	26	27	28	28	29	0♋	1	2	3	4	5	6	7	8	
☽	28♌	10♍	22	4♎	16	28	10♏	22	4♐	17	30	12♑	26	9♒	22	6♓	20	4♈	18	3♉	17	2♊	16	0♋	14	28	11♌	24	6♍	18	
☿	29♉	1♊	3	6	8	10	12	14	16	19	21	23	25	27	30	2♋	4	6	8	10	12	14	16	18	20	21	23	25	27	28	
♀	2♉	4	5	6	7	8	9	11	12	13	14	15	16	18	19	20	21	22	23	25	26	27	28	29	1♊	2	3	4	5	7	
♂	6♊	6	7	8	8	9	10	10	11	12	13	13	14	15	15	16	17	17	18	19	20	20	21	22	22	23	24	24	25	26	
	1	6	11	16	21	26			1	11	21			1	11	21			1	16		1	16		1	16		1	11	21	
♃	25♓	25	26	26	27	27		♄	29♈	0♉	1		⚷	14♏	13	13		♅	13♒	12	♆	2♒	2	♇	7♐	6	☊	6♍	5	5	

1998

JUL

	1	2	3	4	5	6	7	8	9	10	11	12	13	14	15	16	17	18	19	20	21	22	23	24	25	26	27	28	29	30	31
☉	9♋	10	11	12	13	14	15	16	17	18	19	19	20	21	22	23	24	25	26	27	28	29	30	1♌	2	3	4	5	6	7	8
☽	0♎	12	24	6♏	18	0♐	13	25	8♑	22	5♒	19	3♓	17	1♈	15	29	13♉	27	12♊	26	9♋	23	6♌	19	2♍	14	26	8♎	20	2♏
☿	0♌	2	3	5	6	8	9	10	12	13	14	16	17	18	19	20	21	22	23	24	24	25	26	26	27	27	28	28	28	28	28
♀	8♊	9	10	11	12	14	15	16	17	18	20	21	22	23	24	26	27	28	29	0♋	2	3	4	5	6	8	9	10	11	13	14
♂	26♊	27	28	28	29	30	0♋	1	2	2	3	4	4	5	6	6	7	8	8	9	10	10	11	12	12	13	14	14	15	16	16
	1	6	11	16	21	26	31		1	11	21	31		1	11	21	31		1	16		1	16		1	16		1	11	21	31
♃	28♓	28	28	28	28	28	28	♄	2♉	3	3	3	⚷	13♏	12	12	13	♅	12♒	11	♆	1♒	1	♇	6♐	6	☊	4♍	4	3	3

AUG

	1	2	3	4	5	6	7	8	9	10	11	12	13	14	15	16	17	18	19	20	21	22	23	24	25	26	27	28	29	30	31
☉	9♌	10	10	11	12	13	14	15	16	17	18	19	20	21	22	23	24	25	26	27	28	29	30	1♍	2	3	4	5	5	6	7
☽	14♏	26	8♐	21	4♑	17	0♒	14	28	12♓	27	11♈	26	10♉	24	8♊	22	6♋	19	2♌	15	28	10♍	22	4♎	16	28	10♏	22	4♐	16
☿	28♌	28	28	28	27	27	26	26	25	24	23	23	22	21	20	19	19	18	17	17	16	16	16	16	16	16	17	17	18	18	19
♀	15♋	16	17	19	20	21	22	23	25	26	27	28	30	1♌	2	3	4	6	7	8	9	11	12	13	14	15	17	18	19	20	22
♂	17♋	18	18	19	20	20	21	22	22	23	24	24	25	26	26	27	28	28	29	29	0♌	1	1	2	3	3	4	5	5	6	7
	1	6	11	16	21	26	31		1	11	21	31		1	11	21	31		1	16		1	16		1	16		1	11	21	31
♃	28♓	27	27	27	26	26	25	♄	3♉	4	4	3	⚷	13♏	13	14	15	♅	11♒	10	♆	1♒	0	♇	5♐	5	☊	2♍	2	1	1

SEP

	1	2	3	4	5	6	7	8	9	10	11	12	13	14	15	16	17	18	19	20	21	22	23	24	25	26	27	28	29	30
☉	8♍	9	10	11	12	13	14	15	16	17	18	19	20	21	22	23	24	25	26	27	28	29	30	1♎	2	3	4	5	6	7
☽	29♐	12♑	25	8♒	22	7♓	21	6♈	21	6♉	21	5♊	19	3♋	16	29	12♌	24	7♍	19	1♎	13	25	7♏	19	0♐	12	25	7♑	20
☿	20♌	21	23	24	25	27	28	30	2♍	3	5	7	9	11	12	14	16	18	20	22	24	26	27	29	1♎	3	5	6	8	10
♀	23♌	24	25	27	28	29	0♍	1	3	4	5	6	8	9	10	11	13	14	15	16	18	19	20	21	23	24	25	26	28	29
♂	7♌	8	8	9	10	10	11	12	12	13	14	14	15	15	16	17	17	18	19	19	20	20	21	22	22	23	24	24	25	25
	1	6	11	16	21	26			1	11	21			1	11	21			1	16		1	16		1	16		1	11	21
♃	25♓	24	24	23	22	22		♄	3♉	3	3		⚷	15♏	16	17		♅	10♒	9	♆	30♑	30	♇	5♐	6	☊	1♍	0	30♌

OCT

	1	2	3	4	5	6	7	8	9	10	11	12	13	14	15	16	17	18	19	20	21	22	23	24	25	26	27	28	29	30	31
☉	8♎	9	10	11	12	13	14	15	15	16	17	18	19	20	21	22	23	24	25	26	27	28	29	0♏	1	2	3	4	5	6	7
☽	3♒	16	0♓	15	30	15♈	0♉	15	0♊	15	29	13♋	26	9♌	21	4♍	16	28	10♎	22	4♏	15	27	9♐	21	4♑	16	29	12♒	25	9♓
☿	12♎	13	15	17	18	20	22	23	25	27	28	30	1♏	3	5	6	8	9	11	12	14	15	17	18	19	21	22	24	25	26	28
♀	0♎	1	3	4	5	6	8	9	10	11	13	14	15	16	18	19	20	21	23	24	25	26	28	29	0♏	1	3	4	5	6	8
♂	26♌	27	27	28	28	29	30	0♍	1	2	2	3	3	4	5	5	6	6	7	8	8	9	9	10	11	11	12	12	13	14	14
	1	6	11	16	21	26	31		1	11	21	31		1	11	21	31		1	16		1	16		1	16		1	11	21	31
♃	21♓	21	20	20	19	19	18	♄	2♉	1	0	30♈	⚷	18♏	19	20	21	♅	9♒	9	♆	29♑	29	♇	6♐	6	☊	29♌	29	28	28

NOV

	1	2	3	4	5	6	7	8	9	10	11	12	13	14	15	16	17	18	19	20	21	22	23	24	25	26	27	28	29	30
☉	8♏	9	10	11	12	13	14	15	16	17	18	19	20	21	22	23	24	25	26	27	28	29	0♐	1	3	4	5	6	7	8
☽	23♓	8♈	23	8♉	24	9♊	24	8♋	22	5♌	18	1♍	13	25	7♎	19	1♏	12	24	6♐	18	1♑	13	25	8♒	21	4♓	18	2♈	16
☿	29♏	0♐	2	3	4	6	7	8	9	10	11	12	13	14	15	16	16	17	17	17	18	18	17	17	17	16	15	14	13	11
♀	9♏	10	11	13	14	15	16	18	19	20	21	23	24	25	26	28	29	0♐	1	3	4	5	6	8	9	10	11	13	14	15
♂	15♍	15	16	17	17	18	18	19	19	20	21	21	22	22	23	24	24	25	25	26	26	27	28	28	29	29	30	0♎	1	1
	1	6	11	16	21	26			1	11	21			1	11	21			1	16		1	16		1	16		1	11	21
♃	18♓	18	18	18	18	18		♄	30♈	29	28		⚷	21♏	23	24		♅	9♒	9	♆	30♑	30	♇	7♐	7	☊	28♌	27	27

DEC

	1	2	3	4	5	6	7	8	9	10	11	12	13	14	15	16	17	18	19	20	21	22	23	24	25	26	27	28	29	30	31
☉	9♐	10	11	12	13	14	15	16	17	18	19	20	21	22	23	24	25	26	27	28	29	30	1♑	2	3	4	5	6	7	8	9
☽	1♉	16	2♊	17	2♋	16	0♌	14	27	9♍	22	4♎	16	27	9♏	21	3♐	15	27	10♑	22	5♒	18	1♓	15	28	12♈	26	11♉	25	10♊
☿	10♐	9	7	6	5	4	3	2	2	1	1	1	2	2	2	3	4	4	5	6	7	8	10	11	12	13	15	16	17	19	20
♀	16♐	18	19	20	21	23	24	25	27	28	29	0♑	2	3	4	5	7	8	9	10	12	13	14	15	17	18	19	20	22	23	24
♂	2♎	3	3	4	4	5	5	6	6	7	7	8	9	9	10	10	11	11	12	12	13	13	14	14	15	15	16	16	17	17	18
	1	6	11	16	21	26	31		1	11	21	31		1	11	21	31		1	16		1	16		1	16		1	11	21	31
♃	19♓	19	19	20	20	21	22	♄	28♈	27	27	27	⚷	25♏	27	28	29	♅	10♒	10	♆	0♒	1	♇	8♐	9	☊	26♌	26	25	24

1999

EPHEMERIS

JAN

	1	2	3	4	5	6	7	8	9	10	11	12	13	14	15	16	17	18	19	20	21	22	23	24	25	26	27	28	29	30	31
☉	10♑	11	12	13	14	15	16	17	18	19	20	21	22	23	24	25	26	27	28	29	0♒	1	3	4	5	6	7	8	9	10	11
☽	25♊	10♋	24	8♌	21	4♍	17	30	12♎	24	6♏	17	29	11♐	24	6♑	19	2♒	15	28	11♓	25	9♈	23	7♉	21	6♊	20	4♋	18	2♌
☿	21♐	23	24	26	27	28	30	1♑	3	4	6	7	9	10	12	13	15	17	18	20	21	23	24	26	28	29	1♒	3	4	6	8
♀	25♑	27	28	29	0♒	2	3	4	5	7	8	9	10	12	13	14	15	17	18	19	20	22	23	24	25	27	28	29	0♓	2	3
♂	18♎	19	19	20	20	21	21	22	22	23	23	24	24	25	25	25	26	26	27	27	28	28	29	29	29	30	0♏	1	1	1	2
	1	6	11	16	21	26	31		1	11	21	31		1	11	21	31		1	16		1	16		1	16		1	11	21	31
♃	22♓	23	24	24	25	26	27	♄	27♈	27	27	28	⚷	29♏	0♐	1	2	♅	11♒	12	♆	1♒	2	♇	9♐	10	☊	24♌	24	23	23

FEB

	1	2	3	4	5	6	7	8	9	10	11	12	13	14	15	16	17	18	19	20	21	22	23	24	25	26	27	28			
☉	12♒	13	14	15	16	17	18	19	20	21	22	23	24	25	26	27	28	29	30	1♓	2	3	4	5	6	7	8	9			
☽	16♌	29	12♍	25	7♎	19	1♏	13	25	7♐	19	1♑	14	27	10♒	23	7♓	21	5♈	20	4♉	18	2♊	17	0♋	14	28	11♌			
☿	9♒	11	13	15	16	18	20	22	23	25	27	29	1♓	2	4	6	8	10	12	13	15	17	19	20	22	24	25	26			
♀	4♓	5	7	8	9	10	12	13	14	15	17	18	19	20	22	23	24	25	26	28	29	0♈	1	3	4	5	6	8			
♂	2♏	3	3	3	4	4	4	5	5	5	6	6	6	7	7	7	8	8	8	8	9	9	9	9	10	10	10	10			
	1	6	11	16	21	26			1	11	21			1	11	21			1	16		1	16		1	16		1	11	21	
♃	27♓	28	30	1♈	2	3		♄	28♈	28	29		⚷	2♐	3	3		♅	13♒	14	♆	2♒	3	♇	10♐	10	☊	23♌	22	22	

MAR

	1	2	3	4	5	6	7	8	9	10	11	12	13	14	15	16	17	18	19	20	21	22	23	24	25	26	27	28	29	30	31
☉	10♓	11	12	13	14	15	16	17	18	19	20	21	22	23	24	25	26	27	28	29	30	1♈	2	3	4	5	6	7	8	9	10
☽	25♌	8♍	20	3♎	15	27	9♏	21	3♐	15	27	9♑	22	5♒	18	1♓	15	30	15♈	29	14♉	29	13♊	27	11♋	25	8♌	21	4♍	17	29
☿	28♓	29	0♈	1	2	3	3	4	4	4	4	4	4	3	3	2	1	0	29♓	29	28	27	26	25	24	23	23	22	22	21	21
♀	9♈	10	11	12	14	15	16	17	19	20	21	22	23	25	26	27	28	29	1♉	2	3	4	6	7	8	9	10	12	13	14	15
♂	10♏	11	11	11	11	11	11	12	12	12	12	12	12	12	12	12	12	12	12	12	12	12	12	12	12	12	12	12	12	11	11
	1	6	11	16	21	26	31		1	11	21	31		1	11	21	31		1	16		1	16		1	16		1	11	21	31
♃	4♈	5	6	7	8	10	11	♄	30♈	1♉	2	3	⚷	4♐	4	4	4	♅	14♒	15	♆	3♒	4	♇	10♐	10	☊	21♌	21	20	20

APR

	1	2	3	4	5	6	7	8	9	10	11	12	13	14	15	16	17	18	19	20	21	22	23	24	25	26	27	28	29	30	
☉	11♈	12	13	14	15	16	17	18	19	20	21	22	23	24	25	26	27	28	29	29	0♉	1	2	3	4	5	6	7	8	9	
☽	11♎	24	6♏	18	29	11♐	23	5♑	17	30	13♒	26	9♓	24	8♈	23	8♉	23	8♊	23	7♋	21	5♌	18	1♍	14	26	8♎	20	2♏	
☿	21♓	21	21	21	21	21	22	22	23	23	24	25	25	26	27	28	29	0♈	1	2	3	5	6	7	8	10	11	13	14	15	
♀	16♉	18	19	20	21	22	23	25	26	27	28	29	1♊	2	3	4	5	6	8	9	10	11	12	13	14	16	17	18	19	20	
♂	11♏	11	11	11	10	10	10	10	9	9	9	8	8	8	8	7	7	7	6	6	5	5	5	4	4	4	3	3	3	2	
	1	6	11	16	21	26			1	11	21			1	11	21			1	16		1	16		1	16		1	11	21	
♃	11♈	12	13	15	16	17		♄	3♉	5	6		⚷	4♐	3	3		♅	16♒	16	♆	4♒	4	♇	10♐	10	☊	20♌	19	19	

MAY

	1	2	3	4	5	6	7	8	9	10	11	12	13	14	15	16	17	18	19	20	21	22	23	24	25	26	27	28	29	30	31
☉	10♉	11	12	13	14	15	16	17	18	19	20	21	22	23	24	25	26	27	28	29	30	0♊	1	2	3	4	5	6	7	8	9
☽	14♏	26	8♐	20	2♑	14	26	8♒	21	4♓	18	2♈	16	1♉	17	2♊	17	2♋	17	1♌	14	28	11♍	23	5♎	17	29	11♏	23	5♐	17
☿	17♈	19	20	22	23	25	27	28	0♉	2	4	6	8	9	11	13	15	17	20	22	24	26	28	0♊	2	5	7	9	11	13	16
♀	21♊	22	24	25	26	27	28	29	0♋	1	3	4	5	6	7	8	9	10	11	12	14	15	16	17	18	19	20	21	22	23	24
♂	2♏	1	1	1	0	30♎	30	29	29	29	28	28	28	27	27	27	27	26	26	26	26	26	25	25	25	25	25	25	25	25	25
	1	6	11	16	21	26	31		1	11	21	31		1	11	21	31		1	16		1	16		1	16		1	11	21	31
♃	18♈	19	20	22	23	24	25	♄	7♉	8	10	11	⚷	2♐	2	1	0	♅	17♒	17	♆	4♒	4	♇	10♐	10	☊	18♌	18	17	16

JUN

	1	2	3	4	5	6	7	8	9	10	11	12	13	14	15	16	17	18	19	20	21	22	23	24	25	26	27	28	29	30	
☉	10♊	11	12	13	14	15	16	17	18	19	20	21	22	23	23	24	25	26	27	28	29	0♋	1	2	3	4	5	6	7	8	
☽	29♐	11♑	23	5♒	18	1♓	14	27	11♈	25	10♉	25	10♊	25	10♋	25	9♌	23	6♍	19	2♎	14	26	8♏	20	2♐	14	26	8♑	20	
☿	18♊	20	22	24	26	28	30	2♋	4	6	7	9	11	13	14	16	17	19	20	22	23	24	26	27	28	29	0♌	1	2	3	
♀	25♋	26	27	28	29	0♌	1	2	3	4	5	6	7	8	9	10	11	12	12	13	14	15	16	17	18	18	19	20	21	22	
♂	25♎	24	24	24	24	24	24	25	25	25	25	25	25	25	25	25	25	26	26	26	26	26	27	27	27	27	28	28	28	28	
	1	6	11	16	21	26			1	11	21			1	11	21			1	16		1	16		1	16		1	11	21	
♃	25♈	26	27	28	29	30		♄	11♉	12	13		⚷	0♐	29♏	29		♅	17♒	17	♆	4♒	4	♇	9♐	9	☊	16♌	16	15	

1999

JUL

	1	2	3	4	5	6	7	8	9	10	11	12	13	14	15	16	17	18	19	20	21	22	23	24	25	26	27	28	29	30	31
☉	9♋	10	11	12	13	14	14	15	16	17	18	19	20	21	22	23	24	25	26	27	28	29	30	1♌	2	3	4	5	5	6	7
☽	2♒	15	28	10♓	24	7♈	21	5♉	20	4♊	19	4♋	19	3♌	18	1♍	15	28	10♎	23	5♏	17	29	10♐	22	4♑	17	29	12♒	24	7♓
☿	4♌	5	6	6	7	8	8	9	9	9	9	9	9	9	9	9	9	8	8	8	7	6	6	5	4	4	3	2	2	1	0
♀	22♌	23	24	25	25	26	27	27	28	29	29	30	0♍	1	1	2	2	3	3	3	4	4	4	4	5	5	5	5	5	5	5
♂	29♎	29	29	30	30	0♏	1	1	1	2	2	2	3	3	4	4	4	5	5	6	6	7	7	8	8	8	9	9	10	10	11
	1	6	11	16	21	26	31		1	11	21	31		1	11	21	31		1	16		1	16		1	16		1	11	21	31
♃	0♉	1	2	2	3	4	4	♄	14♉	15	16	16	⚷	28♏	28	28	28	♅	16♒	16	♆	4♒	3	♇	8♐	8	☊	15♌	14	14	13

AUG

	1	2	3	4	5	6	7	8	9	10	11	12	13	14	15	16	17	18	19	20	21	22	23	24	25	26	27	28	29	30	31
☉	8♌	9	10	11	12	13	14	15	16	17	18	19	20	21	22	23	24	25	26	27	28	28	29	0♍	1	2	3	4	5	6	7
☽	21♓	4♈	18	2♉	16	0♊	14	29	13♋	28	12♌	26	9♍	23	6♎	18	1♏	13	25	7♐	19	0♑	13	25	7♒	20	3♓	17	0♈	14	28
☿	30♋	29	29	29	29	29	29	29	29	29	30	0♌	1	2	3	4	5	6	8	9	11	12	14	16	17	19	21	23	25	27	29
♀	5♍	5	5	5	4	4	4	4	3	3	2	2	1	1	0	30♌	29	29	28	27	27	26	25	25	24	24	23	23	22	22	21
♂	11♏	12	12	13	13	14	14	15	16	16	17	17	18	18	19	19	20	21	21	22	22	23	23	24	25	25	26	26	27	28	28
	1	6	11	16	21	26	31		1	11	21	31		1	11	21	31		1	16		1	16		1	16		1	11	21	31
♃	4♉	4	5	5	5	5	5	♄	16♉	17	17	17	⚷	28♏	28	28	28	♅	15♒	14	♆	3♒	2	♇	8♐	8	☊	13♌	13	12	12

SEP

	1	2	3	4	5	6	7	8	9	10	11	12	13	14	15	16	17	18	19	20	21	22	23	24	25	26	27	28	29	30	
☉	8♍	9	10	11	12	13	14	15	16	17	18	19	20	21	22	23	24	25	26	27	28	29	30	1♎	1	2	3	4	5	6	
☽	13♉	27	11♊	25	9♋	23	7♌	21	5♍	18	1♎	14	26	9♏	21	3♐	15	26	8♑	20	3♒	15	28	12♓	26	10♈	24	9♉	23	8♊	
☿	1♍	3	5	7	9	10	12	14	16	18	20	22	24	25	27	29	1♎	3	4	6	8	9	11	13	14	16	17	19	21	22	
♀	21♌	20	20	20	20	19	19	19	19	19	19	19	19	19	19	19	19	20	20	20	21	21	21	22	22	23	23	24	24	25	
♂	29♏	29	0♐	1	1	2	3	3	4	5	5	6	7	7	8	8	9	10	10	11	12	12	13	14	15	15	16	17	17	18	
	1	6	11	16	21	26			1	11	21			1	11	21			1	16		1	16		1	16		1	11	21	
♃	5♉	5	5	4	4	3		♄	17♉	17	17		⚷	29♏	29	30		♅	14♒	13	♆	2♒	2	♇	8♐	8	☊	12♌	11	10	

OCT

	1	2	3	4	5	6	7	8	9	10	11	12	13	14	15	16	17	18	19	20	21	22	23	24	25	26	27	28	29	30	31
☉	7♎	8	9	10	11	12	13	14	15	16	17	18	19	20	21	22	23	24	25	26	27	28	29	0♏	1	2	3	4	5	6	7
☽	22♊	6♋	20	4♌	17	1♍	14	27	10♎	22	5♏	17	29	11♐	23	4♑	16	28	11♒	23	6♓	20	4♈	18	3♉	18	3♊	18	2♋	17	1♌
☿	24♎	25	27	28	30	1♏	3	4	5	7	8	10	11	12	14	15	16	17	19	20	21	22	23	24	25	26	27	28	29	29	0♐
♀	25♌	26	27	27	28	29	29	0♍	1	2	3	3	4	5	6	7	7	8	9	10	11	12	13	14	15	16	17	18	19	20	21
♂	19♐	19	20	21	21	22	23	24	24	25	26	26	27	28	29	29	30	1♑	1	2	3	4	4	5	6	6	7	8	9	9	10
	1	6	11	16	21	26	31		1	11	21	31		1	11	21	31		1	16		1	16		1	16		1	11	21	31
♃	3♉	2	2	1	0	30♈	29	♄	16♉	16	15	14	⚷	1♐	2	3	4	♅	13♒	13	♆	2♒	2	♇	8♐	9	☊	10♌	9	9	8

NOV

	1	2	3	4	5	6	7	8	9	10	11	12	13	14	15	16	17	18	19	20	21	22	23	24	25	26	27	28	29	30	
☉	8♏	9	10	11	12	13	14	15	16	17	18	19	20	21	22	23	24	25	26	27	28	29	0♐	1	2	3	4	5	6	7	
☽	14♌	28	11♍	24	6♎	19	1♏	13	25	7♐	19	1♑	13	25	7♒	19	1♓	14	28	12♈	26	11♉	26	11♊	27	12♋	26	10♌	24	8♍	
☿	1♐	1	1	2	2	2	1	1	1	30♏	29	28	27	26	24	23	22	20	19	18	17	17	16	16	16	16	16	16	17	17	
♀	22♍	23	24	25	26	27	28	29	30	1♎	2	3	4	5	6	7	9	10	11	12	13	14	15	16	17	19	20	21	22	23	
♂	11♑	12	12	13	14	15	15	16	17	18	18	19	20	21	21	22	23	24	24	25	26	27	27	28	29	30	1♒	1	2	3	
	1	6	11	16	21	26			1	11	21			1	11	21			1	16		1	16		1	16		1	11	21	
♃	29♈	28	28	27	26	26		♄	14♉	13	13		⚷	4♐	5	7		♅	13♒	13	♆	2♒	2	♇	9♐	10	☊	8♌	8	7	

DEC

	1	2	3	4	5	6	7	8	9	10	11	12	13	14	15	16	17	18	19	20	21	22	23	24	25	26	27	28	29	30	31
☉	8♐	9	10	11	12	13	14	15	16	17	18	19	21	22	23	24	25	26	27	28	29	30	1♑	2	3	4	5	6	7	8	9
☽	21♍	3♎	16	28	10♏	22	4♐	16	28	10♑	22	3♒	16	28	10♓	23	6♈	20	4♉	19	4♊	19	5♋	20	5♌	19	3♍	17	30	13♎	25
☿	18♏	19	20	21	22	23	25	26	27	29	30	1♐	3	4	6	7	8	10	11	13	14	16	17	19	20	22	23	25	26	28	30
♀	24♎	25	27	28	29	0♏	1	2	4	5	6	7	8	9	11	12	13	14	15	17	18	19	20	21	23	24	25	26	27	29	30
♂	4♒	4	5	6	7	7	8	9	10	11	11	12	13	14	14	15	16	17	17	18	19	20	21	21	22	23	24	24	25	26	27
	1	6	11	16	21	26	31		1	11	21	31		1	11	21	31		1	16		1	16		1	16		1	11	21	31
♃	26♈	25	25	25	25	25	25	♄	12♉	11	11	10	⚷	8♐	9	10	11	♅	13♒	14	♆	2♒	3	♇	10♐	11	☊	7♌	6	6	5

2000

EPHEMERIS

JAN

	1	2	3	4	5	6	7	8	9	10	11	12	13	14	15	16	17	18	19	20	21	22	23	24	25	26	27	28	29	30	31
☉	10♑	11	12	13	14	15	16	17	18	19	20	21	22	23	24	25	26	27	28	29	0♒	1	2	3	4	5	6	7	8	9	10
☽	7♏	19	1♐	13	25	7♑	19	1♒	13	25	7♓	20	3♈	16	30	14♉	28	13♊	27	13♋	28	12♌	27	11♍	25	8♎	21	4♏	16	28	10♐
☿	1♑	3	4	6	7	9	11	12	14	15	17	19	20	22	23	25	27	28	0♒	2	3	5	7	9	10	12	14	16	17	19	21
♀	1♐	2	3	5	6	7	8	9	11	12	13	14	16	17	18	19	20	22	23	24	25	27	28	29	0♑	1	3	4	5	6	8
♂	28♒	28	29	30	1♓	1	2	3	4	5	5	6	7	8	8	9	10	11	12	12	13	14	15	15	16	17	18	18	19	20	21
	1	6	11	16	21	26	31		1	11	21	31		1	11	21	31		1	16		1	16		1	16		1	11	21	31
♃	25♈	25	26	26	27	27	28	♄	10♉	10	10	11	⚷	12♐	13	14	15	♅	15♒	16	♆	3♒	4	♇	11♐	12	☊	5♌	5	4	3

FEB

	1	2	3	4	5	6	7	8	9	10	11	12	13	14	15	16	17	18	19	20	21	22	23	24	25	26	27	28	29		
☉	11♒	12	13	14	15	16	18	19	20	21	22	23	24	25	26	27	28	29	30	1♓	2	3	4	5	6	7	8	9	10		
☽	22♐	3♑	15	27	9♒	22	4♓	17	30	13♈	26	10♉	24	8♊	22	7♋	21	6♌	20	5♍	19	3♎	16	29	12♏	24	6♐	18	30		
☿	23♒	24	26	28	29	1♓	3	4	6	7	9	10	11	13	14	15	15	16	17	17	17	17	17	17	16	16	15	14	13		
♀	9♑	10	11	13	14	15	16	17	19	20	21	22	24	25	26	27	29	30	1♒	2	3	5	6	7	8	10	11	12	13		
♂	22♓	22	23	24	25	25	26	27	28	28	29	30	1♈	1	2	3	4	5	5	6	7	8	8	9	10	11	11	12	13		
	1	6	11	16	21	26			1	11	21			1	11	21			1	16		1	16		1	16		1	11	21	
♃	28♈	29	29	0♉	1	2		♄	11♉	11	12		⚷	15♐	16	16		♅	16♒	17	♆	4♒	5	♇	12♐	13	☊	3♌	3	2	

MAR

	1	2	3	4	5	6	7	8	9	10	11	12	13	14	15	16	17	18	19	20	21	22	23	24	25	26	27	28	29	30	31
☉	11♓	12	13	14	15	16	17	18	19	20	21	22	23	24	25	26	27	28	29	30	1♈	2	3	4	5	6	7	8	9	10	11
☽	11♑	23	5♒	18	0♓	13	26	10♈	23	7♉	21	5♊	19	3♋	17	1♌	15	30	13♍	27	11♎	24	7♏	19	2♐	14	26	7♑	19	1♒	13
☿	12♓	11	10	9	8	7	6	5	5	4	4	3	3	3	3	3	3	3	4	4	5	5	6	6	7	8	9	10	11	12	13
♀	15♒	16	17	18	20	21	22	23	24	26	27	28	29	1♓	2	3	4	6	7	8	9	11	12	13	14	15	17	18	19	20	22
♂	14♈	14	15	16	17	17	18	19	20	20	21	22	23	23	24	25	26	26	27	28	28	29	30	1♉	1	2	3	4	4	5	6
	1	6	11	16	21	26	31		1	11	21	31		1	11	21	31		1	16		1	16		1	16		1	11	21	31
♃	3♉	4	5	6	7	8	9	♄	12♉	13	14	15	⚷	17♐	17	17	17	♅	18♒	19	♆	5♒	6	♇	13♐	13	☊	2♌	1	1	0

APR

	1	2	3	4	5	6	7	8	9	10	11	12	13	14	15	16	17	18	19	20	21	22	23	24	25	26	27	28	29	30	
☉	12♈	13	14	15	16	16	17	18	19	20	21	22	23	24	25	26	27	28	29	0♉	1	2	3	4	5	6	7	8	9	10	
☽	26♒	8♓	21	5♈	19	3♉	17	1♊	16	30	14♋	28	12♌	26	9♍	23	6♎	19	2♏	15	27	10♐	22	4♑	15	27	9♒	21	4♓	16	
☿	14♓	15	16	18	19	20	21	23	24	26	27	28	30	2♈	3	5	6	8	10	11	13	15	16	18	20	22	24	26	28	30	
♀	23♓	24	25	27	28	29	0♈	2	3	4	5	6	8	9	10	11	13	14	15	16	18	19	20	21	22	24	25	26	27	29	
♂	7♉	7	8	9	9	10	11	12	12	13	14	15	15	16	17	17	18	19	20	20	21	22	22	23	24	24	25	26	27	27	
	1	6	11	16	21	26			1	11	21			1	11	21			1	16		1	16		1	16		1	11	21	
♃	9♉	10	11	13	14	15		♄	16♉	17	18		⚷	17♐	17	17		♅	20♒	20	♆	6♒	6	♇	13♐	13	☊	0♌	30♋	29	

MAY

	1	2	3	4	5	6	7	8	9	10	11	12	13	14	15	16	17	18	19	20	21	22	23	24	25	26	27	28	29	30	31
☉	11♉	12	13	14	15	16	17	18	19	20	21	22	23	24	24	25	26	27	28	29	0♊	1	2	3	4	5	6	7	8	9	10
☽	29♓	13♈	27	11♉	26	11♊	26	10♋	25	9♌	23	6♍	20	3♎	16	29	11♏	24	6♐	18	30	12♑	24	5♒	17	29	12♓	25	8♈	21	5♉
☿	2♉	4	6	8	10	12	14	16	18	21	23	25	27	29	2♊	4	6	8	10	12	14	16	18	20	21	23	25	27	28	30	1♋
♀	30♈	1♉	2	4	5	6	7	8	10	11	12	13	15	16	17	18	20	21	22	23	24	26	27	28	29	1♊	2	3	4	6	7
♂	28♉	29	29	0♊	1	2	2	3	4	4	5	6	6	7	8	9	9	10	11	11	12	13	13	14	15	15	16	17	17	18	19
	1	6	11	16	21	26	31		1	11	21	31		1	11	21	31		1	16		1	16		1	16		1	11	21	31
♃	16♉	17	19	20	21	22	23	♄	19♉	20	22	23	⚷	16♐	16	15	14	♅	21♒	21	♆	7♒	7	♇	12♐	12	☊	29♋	28	28	27

JUN

	1	2	3	4	5	6	7	8	9	10	11	12	13	14	15	16	17	18	19	20	21	22	23	24	25	26	27	28	29	30	
☉	11♊	12	13	14	15	16	17	18	18	19	20	21	22	23	24	25	26	27	28	29	30	1♋	2	3	4	5	6	7	8	9	
☽	20♉	5♊	20	5♋	20	4♌	19	3♍	17	0♎	13	26	8♏	21	3♐	15	27	9♑	20	2♒	14	26	8♓	21	3♈	16	30	14♉	28	13♊	
☿	3♋	4	5	7	8	9	10	11	12	13	14	15	16	17	17	18	18	19	19	20	20	20	20	20	20	20	19	19	19	18	
♀	8♊	9	10	12	13	14	15	17	18	19	20	21	23	24	25	26	28	29	0♋	1	3	4	5	6	7	9	10	11	12	14	
♂	20♊	20	21	22	22	23	24	24	25	26	26	27	28	28	29	30	0♋	1	2	2	3	4	4	5	6	6	7	8	8	9	
	1	6	11	16	21	26			1	11	21			1	11	21			1	16		1	16		1	16		1	11	21	
♃	23♉	25	26	27	28	29		♄	23♉	24	26		⚷	14♐	14	13		♅	21♒	21	♆	6♒	6	♇	12♐	11	☊	27♋	26	26	

2000

EPHEMERIS

JUL

	1	2	3	4	5	6	7	8	9	10	11	12	13	14	15	16	17	18	19	20	21	22	23	24	25	26	27	28	29	30	31
☉	9♋	10	11	12	13	14	15	16	17	18	19	20	21	22	23	24	25	26	27	28	29	29	0♌	1	2	3	4	5	6	7	8
☽	28♊	13♋	28	13♌	28	12♍	26	10♎	23	5♏	18	30	12♐	24	6♑	17	29	11♒	23	5♓	17	30	13♈	26	9♉	23	7♊	22	7♋	22	7♌
☿	18♋	17	17	16	16	15	14	14	13	13	12	12	11	11	11	10	10	10	10	11	11	11	12	12	13	14	15	16	17	18	19
♀	15♋	16	17	19	20	21	22	23	25	26	27	28	30	1♌	2	3	5	6	7	8	9	11	12	13	14	16	17	18	19	20	22
♂	10♋	10	11	12	12	13	14	14	15	16	16	17	18	18	19	20	20	21	22	22	23	23	24	25	25	26	27	27	28	29	29
	1	6	11	16	21	26	31		1	11	21	31		1	11	21	31		1	16		1	16		1	16		1	11	21	31
♃	0♊	1	2	3	4	5	6	♄	27♉	28	29	29	⚷	12♐	12	11	11	♅	20♒	20	♆	6♒	6	♇	11♐	10	☊	25♋	25	24	24

AUG

	1	2	3	4	5	6	7	8	9	10	11	12	13	14	15	16	17	18	19	20	21	22	23	24	25	26	27	28	29	30	31
☉	9♌	10	11	12	13	14	15	16	17	18	19	20	21	22	22	23	24	25	26	27	28	29	0♍	1	2	3	4	5	6	7	8
☽	22♌	6♍	21	5♎	18	2♏	14	27	9♐	21	3♑	14	26	8♒	20	2♓	14	27	10♈	23	6♉	19	3♊	17	1♋	16	0♌	15	0♍	15	29
☿	20♋	22	23	25	26	28	30	1♌	3	5	7	9	11	13	15	17	19	21	23	25	27	29	1♍	3	5	7	9	11	13	14	16
♀	23♌	24	25	27	28	29	0♍	2	3	4	5	6	8	9	10	11	13	14	15	16	18	19	20	21	22	24	25	26	27	29	30
♂	30♋	1♌	1	2	3	3	4	4	5	6	6	7	8	8	9	10	10	11	12	12	13	13	14	15	15	16	17	17	18	19	19
	1	6	11	16	21	26	31		1	11	21	31		1	11	21	31		1	16		1	16		1	16		1	11	21	31
♃	6♊	7	7	8	9	9	10	♄	29♉	0♊	1	1	⚷	11♐	11	11	11	♅	19♒	19	♆	5♒	5	♇	10♐	10	☊	24♋	23	23	22

SEP

	1	2	3	4	5	6	7	8	9	10	11	12	13	14	15	16	17	18	19	20	21	22	23	24	25	26	27	28	29	30
☉	9♍	10	11	12	13	14	15	16	17	18	19	20	21	21	22	23	24	25	26	27	28	29	0♎	1	2	3	4	5	6	7
☽	13♎	27	10♏	23	5♐	17	29	11♑	23	5♒	17	29	11♓	24	6♈	19	3♉	16	30	14♊	27	12♋	26	10♌	25	9♍	23	7♎	21	5♏
☿	18♍	20	22	23	25	27	28	0♎	2	3	5	7	8	10	11	13	14	16	17	19	20	21	23	24	25	27	28	29	1♏	2
♀	1♎	2	3	5	6	7	8	10	11	12	13	15	16	17	18	19	21	22	23	24	26	27	28	29	0♏	2	3	4	5	7
♂	20♌	20	21	22	22	23	24	24	25	26	26	27	27	28	29	29	30	1♍	1	2	3	3	4	4	5	6	6	7	8	8
	1	6	11	16	21	26			1	11	21			1	11	21			1	16		1	16		1	16		1	11	21
♃	10♊	10	11	11	11	11		♄	1♊	1	1		⚷	11♐	12	12		♅	18♒	18	♆	4♒	4	♇	10♐	10	☊	22♋	22	21

OCT

	1	2	3	4	5	6	7	8	9	10	11	12	13	14	15	16	17	18	19	20	21	22	23	24	25	26	27	28	29	30	31
☉	8♎	9	10	11	12	13	14	15	16	17	18	19	20	21	22	23	24	25	26	27	28	29	30	1♏	2	3	4	5	6	7	8
☽	18♏	1♐	13	25	7♑	19	1♒	13	25	7♓	19	2♈	15	29	12♉	26	10♊	24	8♋	23	7♌	21	5♍	19	3♎	16	30	13♏	26	9♐	21
☿	3♏	4	5	6	7	8	9	10	11	12	13	13	14	15	15	15	16	16	16	16	15	15	14	14	13	12	11	10	8	7	6
♀	8♏	9	10	11	13	14	15	16	18	19	20	21	22	24	25	26	27	28	30	1♐	2	3	5	6	7	8	9	11	12	13	14
♂	9♍	9	10	11	11	12	13	13	14	14	15	16	16	17	18	18	19	19	20	21	21	22	23	23	24	24	25	26	26	27	27
	1	6	11	16	21	26	31		1	11	21	31		1	11	21	31		1	16		1	16		1	16		1	11	21	31
♃	11♊	11	11	11	10	10	10	♄	1♊	0	30♉	29	⚷	13♐	14	15	16	♅	17♒	17	♆	4♒	4	♇	11♐	11	☊	21♋	20	19	19

NOV

	1	2	3	4	5	6	7	8	9	10	11	12	13	14	15	16	17	18	19	20	21	22	23	24	25	26	27	28	29	30
☉	9♏	10	11	12	13	14	15	16	17	18	19	20	21	22	23	24	25	26	27	28	29	30	1♐	2	3	4	5	6	7	8
☽	3♑	15	27	9♒	20	2♓	15	27	10♈	24	7♉	21	6♊	20	5♋	19	3♌	18	2♍	15	29	13♎	26	9♏	22	4♐	17	29	11♑	23
☿	5♏	3	2	2	1	0	0	30♎	0♏	0	1	1	2	3	4	5	6	7	8	10	11	12	14	15	17	18	20	21	23	24
♀	15♐	17	18	19	20	21	23	24	25	26	27	29	30	1♑	2	3	5	6	7	8	9	11	12	13	14	15	17	18	19	20
♂	28♍	29	29	30	1♎	1	2	2	3	4	4	5	5	6	7	7	8	9	9	10	10	11	12	12	13	13	14	15	15	16
	1	6	11	16	21	26			1	11	21			1	11	21			1	16		1	16		1	16		1	11	21
♃	10♊	9	8	8	7	6		♄	29♉	28	27		⚷	16♐	17	18		♅	17♒	17	♆	4♒	4	♇	11♐	12	☊	19♋	18	18

DEC

	1	2	3	4	5	6	7	8	9	10	11	12	13	14	15	16	17	18	19	20	21	22	23	24	25	26	27	28	29	30	31
☉	9♐	10	11	12	13	14	15	16	17	18	19	20	21	22	23	24	25	26	27	28	29	0♑	1	2	3	5	6	7	8	9	10
☽	5♒	16	28	10♓	23	5♈	18	1♉	15	29	14♊	29	14♋	29	13♌	28	12♍	26	10♎	23	6♏	19	1♐	13	26	8♑	19	1♒	13	25	7♓
☿	26♏	27	29	0♐	2	3	5	6	8	10	11	13	14	16	17	19	20	22	24	25	27	28	30	1♑	3	5	6	8	9	11	13
♀	21♑	23	24	25	26	27	28	30	1♒	2	3	4	5	7	8	9	10	11	12	13	15	16	17	18	19	20	21	23	24	25	26
♂	16♎	17	18	18	19	19	20	21	21	22	22	23	24	24	25	25	26	27	27	28	28	29	30	0♏	1	1	2	3	3	4	4
	1	6	11	16	21	26	31		1	11	21	31		1	11	21	31		1	16		1	16		1	16		1	11	21	31
♃	6♊	5	4	4	3	3	2	♄	27♉	26	25	25	⚷	19♐	20	21	22	♅	17♒	18	♆	4♒	5	♇	13♐	13	☊	17♋	17	16	16

2001

JAN	1	2	3	4	5	6	7	8	9	10	11	12	13	14	15	16	17	18	19	20	21	22	23	24	25	26	27	28	29	30	31
☉	11♑	12	13	14	15	16	17	18	19	20	21	22	23	24	25	26	27	28	29	30	1♒	2	3	4	5	6	7	8	9	10	11
☽	19♓	1♈	13	26	9♉	23	7♊	22	7♋	22	7♌	22	7♍	22	6♎	19	3♏	16	28	10♐	23	4♑	16	28	10♒	22	4♓	16	28	10♈	22
☿	14♑	16	18	19	21	22	24	26	27	29	1♒	2	4	6	7	9	11	12	14	15	17	19	20	22	23	24	25	27	28	28	29
♀	27♒	28	29	0♓	1	2	4	5	6	7	8	9	10	11	12	13	14	15	16	17	18	19	20	21	22	23	24	25	26	27	28
♂	5♏	6	6	7	7	8	8	9	10	10	11	11	12	12	13	14	14	15	15	16	16	17	18	18	19	19	20	20	21	21	22
	1	6	11	16	21	26	31		1	11	21	31		1	11	21	31		1	16		1	16		1	16		1	11	21	31
♃	2♊	2	2	1	1	1	1	♄	25♉	24	24	24	⚷	23♐	24	25	26	♅	19♒	19	♆	5♒	6	♇	14♐	14	☊	16♋	15	15	14

FEB	1	2	3	4	5	6	7	8	9	10	11	12	13	14	15	16	17	18	19	20	21	22	23	24	25	26	27	28		
☉	12♒	13	14	15	16	17	18	19	20	21	22	23	24	25	26	27	28	29	0♓	1	2	3	4	5	6	7	8	9		
☽	5♉	18	2♊	16	30	15♋	30	15♌	0♍	15	0♎	14	28	12♏	25	7♐	19	1♑	13	25	7♒	19	1♓	13	25	7♈	19	2♉		
☿	30♒	0♓	1	1	1	0	30♒	29	29	28	27	26	24	23	22	21	20	19	18	17	17	16	16	16	15	15	16	16		
♀	28♓	29	0♈	1	2	3	4	4	5	6	7	7	8	9	9	10	11	11	12	13	13	14	14	15	15	15	16	16		
♂	23♏	23	24	24	25	25	26	26	27	27	28	29	29	30	0♐	1	1	2	2	3	3	4	4	5	5	6	6	7		
	1	6	11	16	21	26			1	11	21			1	11	21			1	16		1	16		1	16		1	11	21
♃	1♊	1	2	2	2	3		♄	24♉	24	25		⚷	26♐	27	27		♅	20♒	21	♆	6♒	7	♇	15♐	15	☊	14♋	14	13

MAR	1	2	3	4	5	6	7	8	9	10	11	12	13	14	15	16	17	18	19	20	21	22	23	24	25	26	27	28	29	30	31
☉	10♓	11	12	13	14	15	16	17	18	19	20	21	22	23	24	25	26	27	28	29	0♈	1	2	3	4	5	6	7	8	9	10
☽	15♉	28	11♊	25	9♋	24	8♌	23	8♍	23	8♎	23	7♏	20	3♐	16	28	10♑	22	4♒	15	27	9♓	21	4♈	16	29	12♉	25	8♊	22
☿	16♒	16	17	17	18	19	19	20	21	22	23	24	25	26	27	28	30	1♓	2	3	5	6	8	9	10	12	13	15	16	18	20
♀	16♈	17	17	17	17	18	18	18	18	18	18	18	17	17	17	17	16	16	16	15	15	14	14	13	13	12	12	11	10	10	9
♂	7♐	8	8	9	9	10	10	11	11	11	12	12	13	13	14	14	15	15	15	16	16	17	17	18	18	18	19	19	20	20	20
	1	6	11	16	21	26	31		1	11	21	31		1	11	21	31		1	16		1	16		1	16		1	11	21	31
♃	3♊	4	4	5	6	7	7	♄	25♉	26	27	28	⚷	28♐	28	29	29	♅	22♒	23	♆	7♒	8	♇	15♐	15	☊	13♋	12	12	11

APR	1	2	3	4	5	6	7	8	9	10	11	12	13	14	15	16	17	18	19	20	21	22	23	24	25	26	27	28	29	30
☉	11♈	12	13	14	15	16	17	18	19	20	21	22	23	24	25	26	27	28	29	30	1♉	2	3	4	5	6	7	8	9	10
☽	6♋	19	4♌	18	3♍	17	2♎	16	1♏	14	28	11♐	24	6♑	18	30	12♒	24	5♓	18	30	12♈	25	8♉	21	5♊	19	2♋	16	0♌
☿	21♓	23	24	26	28	29	1♈	3	5	7	8	10	12	14	16	18	20	22	24	26	28	0♉	2	5	7	9	11	13	15	17
♀	8♈	8	7	7	6	5	5	4	4	4	3	3	3	2	2	2	2	2	1	1	1	2	2	2	2	2	2	3	3	3
♂	21♐	21	21	22	22	22	23	23	23	24	24	24	25	25	25	25	26	26	26	26	27	27	27	27	27	28	28	28	28	28
	1	6	11	16	21	26			1	11	21			1	11	21			1	16		1	16		1	16		1	11	21
♃	8♊	9	9	10	11	12		♄	28♉	29	0♊		⚷	29♐	29	29		♅	23♒	24	♆	8♒	9	♇	15♐	15	☊	11♋	10	10

MAY	1	2	3	4	5	6	7	8	9	10	11	12	13	14	15	16	17	18	19	20	21	22	23	24	25	26	27	28	29	30	31
☉	11♉	12	13	14	15	16	17	17	18	19	20	21	22	23	24	25	26	27	28	29	0♊	1	2	3	4	5	6	7	8	9	10
☽	14♌	29	13♍	27	11♎	25	9♏	23	6♐	19	1♑	14	26	8♒	20	1♓	13	26	8♈	21	4♉	17	0♊	14	28	13♋	27	11♌	25	10♍	24
☿	20♉	22	24	26	28	30	2♊	3	5	7	9	10	12	13	15	16	18	19	20	21	22	23	24	25	26	27	27	28	28	29	29
♀	4♈	4	4	5	5	6	6	7	7	8	9	9	10	11	11	12	13	13	14	15	16	16	17	18	19	20	21	21	22	23	24
♂	28♐	28	29	29	29	29	29	29	29	29	29	29	29	29	29	29	29	29	29	29	28	28	28	28	28	28	28	27	27	27	27
	1	6	11	16	21	26	31		1	11	21	31		1	11	21	31		1	16		1	16		1	16		1	11	21	31
♃	13♊	15	16	17	18	19	20	♄	1♊	2	4	5	⚷	29♐	28	28	27	♅	25♒	25	♆	9♒	9	♇	15♐	14	☊	9♋	9	8	8

JUN	1	2	3	4	5	6	7	8	9	10	11	12	13	14	15	16	17	18	19	20	21	22	23	24	25	26	27	28	29	30
☉	11♊	12	12	13	14	15	16	17	18	19	20	21	22	23	24	25	26	27	28	29	30	1♋	2	3	4	4	5	6	7	8
☽	8♎	22	5♏	18	2♐	15	27	10♑	22	4♒	16	28	9♓	21	4♈	16	29	12♉	25	9♊	23	7♋	22	7♌	21	6♍	20	5♎	18	2♏
☿	30♊	30	30	30	30	30	30	29	29	29	28	28	27	27	26	26	25	25	24	24	23	23	22	22	22	21	21	21	21	21
♀	25♈	26	27	28	29	30	1♉	1	2	3	4	5	6	7	8	9	10	11	12	13	14	15	17	18	19	20	21	22	23	24
♂	26♐	26	26	26	25	25	25	25	24	24	24	23	23	23	22	22	22	21	21	21	20	20	20	19	19	19	19	18	18	18
	1	6	11	16	21	26			1	11	21			1	11	21			1	16		1	16		1	16		1	11	21
♃	20♊	22	23	24	25	26		♄	5♊	6	8		⚷	27♐	26	26		♅	25♒	25	♆	9♒	8	♇	14♐	14	☊	8♋	7	7

2001

EPHEMERIS

JUL

	1	2	3	4	5	6	7	8	9	10	11	12	13	14	15	16	17	18	19	20	21	22	23	24	25	26	27	28	29	30	31
☉	9♋	10	11	12	13	14	15	16	17	18	19	20	21	22	23	24	24	25	26	27	28	29	0♌	1	2	3	4	5	6	7	8
☽	15♏	28	11♐	24	6♑	18	0♒	12	24	6♓	18	30	12♈	24	7♉	20	3♊	17	1♋	16	1♌	16	1♍	16	1♎	15	29	12♏	25	8♐	21
☿	22♊	22	22	23	23	24	24	25	26	27	28	29	0♋	1	3	4	5	7	8	10	12	13	15	17	19	21	23	25	27	29	1♌
♀	25♉	26	27	28	29	0♊	1	3	4	5	6	7	8	9	10	11	12	14	15	16	17	18	19	20	21	23	24	25	26	27	28
♂	18♐	17	17	17	17	16	16	16	16	16	16	16	15	15	15	15	15	15	15	15	15	15	15	15	15	15	15	16	16	16	16
	1	6	11	16	21	26	31		1	11	21	31		1	11	21	31		1	16		1	16		1	16		1	11	21	31
♃	27♊	28	30	1♋	2	3	4	♄	9♊	10	11	12	⚷	25♐	24	24	23	♅	24♒	24	♆	8♒	8	♇	13♐	13	☊	6♋	6	5	5

AUG

	1	2	3	4	5	6	7	8	9	10	11	12	13	14	15	16	17	18	19	20	21	22	23	24	25	26	27	28	29	30	31
☉	9♌	10	11	12	13	14	15	16	16	17	18	19	20	21	22	23	24	25	26	27	28	29	30	1♍	2	3	4	5	6	7	8
☽	3♑	15	27	9♒	21	3♓	15	26	8♈	21	3♉	15	28	12♊	25	10♋	24	9♌	24	10♍	25	10♎	24	8♏	22	5♐	18	30	12♑	24	6♒
☿	3♌	5	7	10	12	14	16	18	20	22	24	26	28	30	1♍	3	5	7	9	11	12	14	16	17	19	21	22	24	25	27	28
♀	29♊	1♋	2	3	4	5	6	7	9	10	11	12	13	14	16	17	18	19	20	22	23	24	25	26	27	29	30	1♌	2	3	5
♂	16♐	16	16	17	17	17	17	18	18	18	18	19	19	19	20	20	20	21	21	21	22	22	22	23	23	24	24	24	25	25	26
	1	6	11	16	21	26	31		1	11	21	31		1	11	21	31		1	16		1	16		1	16		1	11	21	31
♃	4♋	5	6	7	8	9	10	♄	12♊	13	14	14	⚷	23♐	23	23	23	♅	23♒	23	♆	7♒	7	♇	13♐	13	☊	4♋	4	3	3

SEP

	1	2	3	4	5	6	7	8	9	10	11	12	13	14	15	16	17	18	19	20	21	22	23	24	25	26	27	28	29	30
☉	9♍	10	11	12	13	13	14	15	16	17	18	19	20	21	22	23	24	25	26	27	28	29	0♎	1	2	3	4	5	6	7
☽	18♒	30	12♓	24	6♈	18	30	12♉	25	8♊	21	4♋	18	3♌	18	3♍	18	3♎	18	3♏	17	1♐	14	26	9♑	21	3♒	15	27	8♓
☿	30♍	1♎	3	4	6	7	8	10	11	12	14	15	16	17	18	19	21	22	23	23	24	25	26	27	27	28	28	29	29	30
♀	6♌	7	8	9	11	12	13	14	15	17	18	19	20	21	23	24	25	26	27	29	30	1♍	2	4	5	6	7	8	10	11
♂	26♐	27	27	28	28	29	29	30	0♑	1	1	2	2	3	3	4	4	5	6	6	7	7	8	8	9	10	10	11	11	12
	1	6	11	16	21	26			1	11	21			1	11	21			1	16		1	16		1	16		1	11	21
♃	10♋	11	12	12	13	13		♄	14♊	15	15		⚷	23♐	23	23		♅	22♒	22	♆	7♒	6	♇	13♐	13	☊	3♋	2	2

OCT

	1	2	3	4	5	6	7	8	9	10	11	12	13	14	15	16	17	18	19	20	21	22	23	24	25	26	27	28	29	30	31
☉	8♎	9	10	11	12	13	14	15	16	17	18	19	20	21	22	23	24	25	26	27	28	29	30	1♏	2	3	4	5	6	7	8
☽	20♓	2♈	15	27	9♉	22	5♊	18	1♋	14	28	12♌	27	12♍	27	12♎	26	11♏	25	9♐	22	5♑	17	29	11♒	23	5♓	17	29	11♈	23
☿	30♎	30	30	29	29	29	28	27	26	25	24	23	22	21	20	19	17	17	16	15	15	14	14	14	15	15	16	16	17	18	19
♀	12♍	13	15	16	17	18	20	21	22	23	24	26	27	28	29	1♎	2	3	4	6	7	8	9	11	12	13	14	16	17	18	19
♂	13♑	13	14	14	15	16	16	17	18	18	19	20	20	21	21	22	23	23	24	25	25	26	27	27	28	29	30	0♒	1	2	2
	1	6	11	16	21	26	31		1	11	21	31		1	11	21	31		1	16		1	16		1	16		1	11	21	31
♃	14♋	14	15	15	15	16	16	♄	15♊	15	14	14	⚷	24♐	24	25	26	♅	21♒	21	♆	6♒	6	♇	13♐	13	☊	1♋	1	0	30♊

NOV

	1	2	3	4	5	6	7	8	9	10	11	12	13	14	15	16	17	18	19	20	21	22	23	24	25	26	27	28	29	30
☉	9♏	10	11	12	13	14	15	16	17	18	19	20	21	22	23	24	25	26	27	28	29	30	1♐	2	3	4	5	6	7	8
☽	6♉	19	2♊	15	28	11♋	25	9♌	23	7♍	22	6♎	21	5♏	19	3♐	16	30	12♑	25	7♒	19	1♓	13	25	7♈	19	2♉	14	27
☿	20♎	22	23	24	26	27	29	0♏	2	3	5	6	8	10	11	13	14	16	18	19	21	22	24	26	27	29	0♐	2	4	5
♀	21♎	22	23	24	26	27	28	29	1♏	2	3	4	6	7	8	9	11	12	13	14	16	17	18	19	21	22	23	24	26	27
♂	3♒	4	4	5	6	6	7	8	9	9	10	11	11	12	13	13	14	15	16	16	17	18	18	19	20	21	21	22	23	24
	1	6	11	16	21	26			1	11	21			1	11	21			1	16		1	16		1	16		1	11	21
♃	16♋	16	16	15	15	15		♄	14♊	13	12		⚷	26♐	27	28		♅	21♒	21	♆	6♒	6	♇	14♐	14	☊	30♊	29	29

DEC

	1	2	3	4	5	6	7	8	9	10	11	12	13	14	15	16	17	18	19	20	21	22	23	24	25	26	27	28	29	30	31
☉	9♐	10	11	12	13	14	15	16	17	18	19	20	21	22	23	24	25	26	27	28	29	0♑	1	2	3	4	5	6	7	8	9
☽	10♊	24	8♋	22	6♌	20	4♍	18	2♎	16	0♏	14	28	11♐	25	8♑	20	3♒	15	27	9♓	21	3♈	15	27	9♉	22	5♊	19	3♋	17
☿	7♐	8	10	11	13	15	16	18	19	21	22	24	26	27	29	0♑	2	3	5	7	8	10	11	13	15	16	18	19	21	22	24
♀	28♏	29	1♐	2	3	4	6	7	8	9	11	12	13	15	16	17	18	20	21	22	23	25	26	27	28	30	1♑	2	3	5	6
♂	24♒	25	26	26	27	28	29	29	0♓	1	2	2	3	4	4	5	6	7	7	8	9	10	10	11	12	12	13	14	15	15	16
	1	6	11	16	21	26	31		1	11	21	31		1	11	21	31		1	16		1	16		1	16		1	11	21	31
♃	14♋	14	13	13	12	11	11	♄	12♊	11	10	9	⚷	29♐	30	1♑	2	♅	21♒	22	♆	7♒	7	♇	15♐	15	☊	28♊	27	27	26

2002

JAN

	1	2	3	4	5	6	7	8	9	10	11	12	13	14	15	16	17	18	19	20	21	22	23	24	25	26	27	28	29	30	31
☉	10♑	11	12	13	14	15	16	18	19	20	21	22	23	24	25	26	27	28	29	30	1♒	2	3	4	5	6	7	8	9	10	11
☽	1♌	16	0♍	15	29	13♎	27	11♏	24	8♐	21	4♑	16	29	11♒	23	5♓	17	29	11♈	23	5♉	17	30	13♊	26	10♋	25	10♌	25	10♍
☿	26♑	27	29	0♒	2	3	4	6	7	8	10	11	12	12	13	14	14	14	14	14	14	14	13	12	11	10	9	7	6	5	4
♀	7♑	8	10	11	12	13	15	16	17	18	20	21	22	24	25	26	27	29	30	1♒	2	4	5	6	7	9	10	11	12	14	15
♂	17♓	18	18	19	20	21	21	22	23	23	24	25	26	26	27	28	29	29	0♈	1	1	2	3	4	4	5	6	7	7	8	9
	1	6	11	16	21	26	31		1	11	21	31		1	11	21	31		1	16		1	16		1	16		1	11	21	31
♃	11♋	10	9	9	8	8	7	♄	9♊	9	8	8	⚷	2♑	3	4	5	♅	22♒	23	♆	7♒	8	♇	16♐	17	☊	26♊	26	25	25

FEB

	1	2	3	4	5	6	7	8	9	10	11	12	13	14	15	16	17	18	19	20	21	22	23	24	25	26	27	28			
☉	12♒	13	14	15	16	17	18	19	20	21	22	23	24	25	26	27	28	29	0♓	1	2	3	4	5	6	7	8	9			
☽	25♍	9♎	24	8♏	21	5♐	18	0♑	13	25	7♒	20	2♓	13	25	7♈	19	1♉	13	25	8♊	21	4♋	18	3♌	17	3♍	18			
☿	3♒	2	1	0	30♑	29	29	29	29	29	29	29	30	0♒	1	1	2	3	4	5	6	7	8	9	10	11	12	13			
♀	16♒	17	19	20	21	22	24	25	26	27	29	30	1♓	2	4	5	6	7	9	10	11	12	14	15	16	17	19	20			
♂	9♈	10	11	12	12	13	14	15	15	16	17	17	18	19	20	20	21	22	22	23	24	25	25	26	27	27	28	29			
	1	6	11	16	21	26			1	11	21			1	11	21			1	16		1	16		1	16		1	11	21	
♃	7♋	7	6	6	6	6		♄	8♊	8	8		⚷	5♑	6	7		♅	24♒	25	♆	9♒	9	♇	17♐	17	☊	25♊	24	24	

MAR

	1	2	3	4	5	6	7	8	9	10	11	12	13	14	15	16	17	18	19	20	21	22	23	24	25	26	27	28	29	30	31
☉	10♓	11	12	13	14	15	16	17	18	19	20	21	22	23	24	25	26	27	28	29	0♈	1	2	3	4	5	6	7	8	9	10
☽	3♎	18	3♏	17	1♐	15	27	10♑	22	5♒	17	29	10♓	22	4♈	16	28	10♉	22	4♊	17	30	13♋	27	11♌	26	11♍	26	11♎	27	12♏
☿	15♒	16	17	19	20	21	23	24	26	27	29	0♓	2	3	5	6	8	10	11	13	15	16	18	20	22	23	25	27	29	1♈	3
♀	21♓	22	24	25	26	27	29	30	1♈	2	4	5	6	7	9	10	11	12	14	15	16	17	19	20	21	22	23	25	26	27	28
♂	30♈	0♉	1	2	2	3	4	5	5	6	7	7	8	9	9	10	11	12	12	13	14	14	15	16	16	17	18	18	19	20	21
	1	6	11	16	21	26	31		1	11	21	31		1	11	21	31		1	16		1	16		1	16		1	11	21	31
♃	6♋	6	6	6	6	7	7	♄	8♊	9	10	10	⚷	8♑	8	9	9	♅	26♒	27	♆	10♒	10	♇	18♐	18	☊	23♊	23	22	22

APR

	1	2	3	4	5	6	7	8	9	10	11	12	13	14	15	16	17	18	19	20	21	22	23	24	25	26	27	28	29	30	
☉	11♈	12	13	14	15	16	17	18	19	20	21	22	23	24	25	26	27	28	29	30	1♉	2	3	4	5	6	7	8	9	9	
☽	26♏	10♐	23	6♑	19	1♒	14	26	7♓	19	1♈	13	25	7♉	19	2♊	14	27	10♋	23	7♌	21	5♍	20	5♎	20	5♏	20	4♐	18	
☿	5♈	7	9	10	13	15	17	19	21	23	25	27	29	1♉	3	5	7	9	11	13	15	17	19	21	22	24	25	27	28	30	
♀	30♈	1♉	2	3	5	6	7	8	10	11	12	13	14	16	17	18	19	21	22	23	24	25	27	28	29	0♊	2	3	4	5	
♂	21♉	22	23	23	24	25	25	26	27	27	28	29	29	0♊	1	2	2	3	4	4	5	6	6	7	8	8	9	10	10	11	
	1	6	11	16	21	26			1	11	21			1	11	21			1	16		1	16		1	16		1	11	21	
♃	7♋	8	8	9	9	10		♄	10♊	11	12		⚷	9♑	9	9		♅	27♒	28	♆	10♒	11	♇	18♐	17	☊	22♊	21	21	

MAY

	1	2	3	4	5	6	7	8	9	10	11	12	13	14	15	16	17	18	19	20	21	22	23	24	25	26	27	28	29	30	31
☉	10♉	11	12	13	14	15	16	17	18	19	20	21	22	23	24	25	26	27	28	29	30	1♊	2	3	4	5	6	7	7	8	9
☽	2♑	15	28	10♒	22	4♓	16	28	10♈	22	4♉	16	28	11♊	24	7♋	20	3♌	17	1♍	15	30	14♎	29	14♏	28	12♐	26	10♑	23	5♒
☿	1♊	2	3	4	5	6	7	7	8	9	9	9	10	10	10	10	10	10	10	9	9	9	8	8	7	7	6	5	5	4	4
♀	6♊	8	9	10	11	12	14	15	16	17	18	20	21	22	23	25	26	27	28	29	1♋	2	3	4	5	7	8	9	10	11	12
♂	12♊	12	13	14	14	15	16	16	17	18	18	19	20	20	21	22	22	23	24	24	25	26	26	27	28	28	29	30	0♋	1	2
	1	6	11	16	21	26	31		1	11	21	31		1	11	21	31		1	16		1	16		1	16		1	11	21	31
♃	11♋	12	13	13	14	15	16	♄	14♊	15	16	17	⚷	9♑	9	8	8	♅	28♒	29	♆	11♒	11	♇	17♐	17	☊	20♊	19	19	18

JUN

	1	2	3	4	5	6	7	8	9	10	11	12	13	14	15	16	17	18	19	20	21	22	23	24	25	26	27	28	29	30	
☉	10♊	11	12	13	14	15	16	17	18	19	20	21	22	23	24	25	26	27	28	29	29	0♋	1	2	3	4	5	6	7	8	
☽	18♒	0♓	12	24	6♈	18	30	12♉	25	7♊	20	3♋	17	0♌	14	28	12♍	26	11♎	25	9♏	23	7♐	21	4♑	18	1♒	13	26	8♓	
☿	3♊	3	2	2	2	2	1	1	1	1	2	2	2	2	3	3	4	5	5	6	7	8	9	10	11	12	14	15	16	18	
♀	14♋	15	16	17	18	20	21	22	23	24	25	27	28	29	0♌	1	3	4	5	6	7	8	10	11	12	13	14	15	16	18	
♂	2♋	3	4	4	5	6	6	7	8	8	9	10	10	11	11	12	13	13	14	15	15	16	17	17	18	19	19	20	21	21	
	1	6	11	16	21	26			1	11	21			1	11	21			1	16		1	16		1	16		1	11	21	
♃	17♋	18	19	20	21	22		♄	17♊	19	20		⚷	8♑	7	7		♅	29♒	29	♆	11♒	11	♇	16♐	16	☊	18♊	18	17	

2002

EPHEMERIS

JUL

	1	2	3	4	5	6	7	8	9	10	11	12	13	14	15	16	17	18	19	20	21	22	23	24	25	26	27	28	29	30	31
☉	9♋	10	11	12	13	14	15	16	17	18	19	19	20	21	22	23	24	25	26	27	28	29	30	1♌	2	3	4	5	6	7	8
☽	20♓	2♈	14	26	8♉	20	3♊	15	29	12♋	26	10♌	24	9♍	23	7♎	22	6♏	20	3♐	17	0♑	13	26	9♒	22	4♓	16	28	10♈	22
☿	19♊	21	22	24	26	27	29	1♋	3	5	7	9	11	13	15	17	19	22	24	26	28	0♌	2	4	6	8	10	12	14	16	18
♀	19♌	20	21	22	23	24	26	27	28	29	0♍	1	2	4	5	6	7	8	9	10	11	12	14	15	16	17	18	19	20	21	22
♂	22♋	22	23	24	24	25	26	26	27	28	28	29	30	0♌	1	2	2	3	3	4	5	5	6	7	7	8	9	9	10	10	11
	1	6	11	16	21	26	31		1	11	21	31		1	11	21	31		1	16		1	16		1	16		1	11	21	31
♃	23♋	24	25	26	27	29	30	♄	21♊	22	24	25	⚷	6♑	5	5	4	♅	29♒	28	♆	10♒	10	♇	16♐	15	☊	17♊	16	16	15

AUG

	1	2	3	4	5	6	7	8	9	10	11	12	13	14	15	16	17	18	19	20	21	22	23	24	25	26	27	28	29	30	31
☉	9♌	10	11	11	12	13	14	15	16	17	18	19	20	21	22	23	24	25	26	27	28	29	30	1♍	2	3	4	5	5	6	7
☽	4♉	16	28	11♊	23	7♋	20	4♌	19	4♍	18	3♎	18	2♏	16	0♐	14	27	10♑	23	6♒	18	0♓	13	25	7♈	18	0♉	12	24	6♊
☿	20♌	22	24	26	28	29	1♍	3	4	6	8	9	11	12	14	15	17	18	20	21	23	24	25	26	28	29	0♎	1	2	3	5♀
♀	23♍	24	25	26	28	29	30	1♎	2	3	4	5	6	7	8	9	10	11	12	13	14	15	16	17	18	19	19	20	21	22	23
♂	12♌	12	13	14	14	15	16	16	17	18	18	19	19	20	21	21	22	23	23	24	25	25	26	26	27	28	28	29	30	0♍	1
	1	6	11	16	21	26	31		1	11	21	31		1	11	21	31		1	16		1	16		1	16		1	11	21	31
♃	30♋	1♌	2	3	4	5	6	♄	25♊	26	27	28	⚷	4♑	4	3	3	♅	28♒	27	♆	10♒	9	♇	15♐	15	☊	15♊	15	14	14

SEP

	1	2	3	4	5	6	7	8	9	10	11	12	13	14	15	16	17	18	19	20	21	22	23	24	25	26	27	28	29	30
☉	8♍	9	10	11	12	13	14	15	16	17	18	19	20	21	22	23	24	25	26	27	28	29	30	1♎	2	3	4	5	6	7
☽	19♊	1♋	15	28	13♌	27	12♍	27	13♎	28	12♏	27	11♐	24	7♑	20	3♒	15	27	9♓	21	3♈	15	27	9♉	21	3♊	15	27	10♋
☿	6♎	6	7	8	9	10	10	11	12	12	13	13	13	13	13	13	13	13	12	12	11	10	9	9	8	6	5	4	3	2
♀	24♎	25	26	27	27	28	29	30	1♏	1	2	3	4	4	5	6	7	7	8	9	9	10	10	11	11	12	12	13	13	14
♂	2♍	2	3	3	4	5	5	6	7	7	8	9	9	10	10	11	12	12	13	14	14	15	16	16	17	17	18	19	19	20
	1	6	11	16	21	26			1	11	21			1	11	21			1	16		1	16		1	16		1	11	21
♃	6♌	8	8	9	10	11		♄	28♊	28	29		⚷	3♑	3	3		♅	26♒	26	♆	9♒	9	♇	15♐	15	☊	13♊	13	12

OCT

	1	2	3	4	5	6	7	8	9	10	11	12	13	14	15	16	17	18	19	20	21	22	23	24	25	26	27	28	29	30	31
☉	8♎	9	10	11	12	13	14	15	16	17	18	18	19	20	21	22	23	24	25	26	27	28	29	0♏	1	2	3	4	5	6	7
☽	23♋	7♌	21	6♍	21	6♎	21	6♏	21	6♐	20	3♑	17	30	12♒	24	6♓	18	0♈	12	24	6♉	18	30	12♊	24	7♋	19	3♌	16	30
☿	1♎	0	30♍	29	29	28	28	28	29	29	30	1♎	1	3	4	5	6	8	9	10	12	14	15	17	18	20	22	23	25	27	28
♀	14♏	14	14	15	15	15	15	15	16	16	16	16	16	15	15	15	15	15	14	14	14	13	13	12	12	11	11	10	9	9	8
♂	21♍	21	22	23	23	24	24	25	26	26	27	28	28	29	30	0♎	1	1	2	3	3	4	5	5	6	7	7	8	8	9	10
	1	6	11	16	21	26	31		1	11	21	31		1	11	21	31		1	16		1	16		1	16		1	11	21	31
♃	12♌	13	14	14	15	16	16	♄	29♊	29	29	29	⚷	4♑	4	5	5	♅	25♒	25	♆	8♒	8	♇	15♐	16	☊	12♊	11	11	10

NOV

	1	2	3	4	5	6	7	8	9	10	11	12	13	14	15	16	17	18	19	20	21	22	23	24	25	26	27	28	29	30
☉	8♏	9	10	11	12	13	14	15	16	17	18	19	20	21	22	23	24	25	26	27	28	29	1♐	2	3	4	5	6	7	8
☽	14♍	29	14♎	29	14♏	29	14♐	28	12♑	25	8♒	21	3♓	15	27	9♈	21	3♉	15	27	9♊	21	4♋	16	29	13♌	26	10♍	24	8♎
☿	0♏	2	3	5	7	8	10	12	13	15	17	18	20	21	23	25	26	28	29	1♐	2	4	6	7	9	10	12	13	15	16
♀	8♏	7	6	6	5	5	4	4	3	3	2	2	1	1	1	1	0	0	0	0	0	0	0	0	0	0	1	1	1	2
♂	10♎	11	12	12	13	14	14	15	16	16	17	17	18	19	19	20	21	21	22	23	23	24	24	25	26	26	27	28	28	29
	1	6	11	16	21	26			1	11	21			1	11	21			1	16		1	16		1	16		1	11	21
♃	16♌	17	17	18	18	18		♄	29♊	28	28		⚷	5♑	6	7		♅	25♒	25	♆	8♒	8	♇	16♐	17	☊	10♊	10	9

DEC

	1	2	3	4	5	6	7	8	9	10	11	12	13	14	15	16	17	18	19	20	21	22	23	24	25	26	27	28	29	30	31
☉	9♐	10	11	12	13	14	15	16	17	18	19	20	21	22	23	24	25	26	27	28	29	30	1♑	2	3	4	5	6	7	8	9
☽	23♎	8♏	23	7♐	22	6♑	20	3♒	16	29	11♓	24	5♈	17	29	11♉	23	5♊	18	0♋	13	26	10♌	23	7♍	21	5♎	19	3♏	17	2♐
☿	18♐	19	21	23	24	26	27	29	0♑	2	3	5	6	8	9	11	12	14	15	16	18	19	20	22	23	24	25	26	27	27	28
♀	2♏	2	3	3	4	4	5	5	6	6	7	7	8	9	9	10	11	12	12	13	14	15	16	17	17	18	19	20	21	22	23
♂	30♎	0♏	1	2	2	3	3	4	5	5	6	7	7	8	9	9	10	11	11	12	12	13	14	14	15	16	16	17	18	18	19
	1	6	11	16	21	26	31		1	11	21	31		1	11	21	31		1	16		1	16		1	16		1	11	21	31
♃	18♌	18	18	18	18	17	17	♄	27♊	26	25	25	⚷	8♑	9	10	11	♅	25♒	26	♆	9♒	9	♇	17♐	18	☊	9♊	8	8	7

2003

EPHEMERIS

JAN

	1	2	3	4	5	6	7	8	9	10	11	12	13	14	15	16	17	18	19	20	21	22	23	24	25	26	27	28	29	30	31
☉	10♑	11	12	13	14	15	16	17	18	19	20	21	22	23	24	25	26	27	28	29	1♒	2	3	4	5	6	7	8	9	10	11
☽	16♐	0♑	14	28	11♒	24	7♓	19	1♈	13	25	7♉	19	1♊	13	26	9♋	22	5♌	19	3♍	17	2♎	16	30	14♏	28	12♐	26	9♑	23
☿	28♑	28	28	28	28	27	27	26	25	24	22	21	20	18	17	16	15	14	13	13	13	12	12	12	13	13	13	14	14	15	16
♀	24♏	25	26	27	27	28	29	0♐	1	2	3	4	6	7	8	9	10	11	12	13	14	15	16	17	18	19	20	22	23	24	25
♂	20♏	20	21	22	22	23	23	24	25	25	26	27	27	28	29	29	30	1♐	1	2	2	3	4	4	5	6	6	7	8	8	9
	1	6	11	16	21	26	31		1	11	21	31		1	11	21	31		1	16		1	16		1	16		1	11	21	31
♃	17♌	16	16	15	15	14	13	♄	24♊	24	23	23	⚷	11♑	12	13	14	♅	26♒	27	♆	10♒	10	♇	18♐	19	☊	7♊	7	6	5

FEB

	1	2	3	4	5	6	7	8	9	10	11	12	13	14	15	16	17	18	19	20	21	22	23	24	25	26	27	28			
☉	12♒	13	14	15	16	17	18	19	20	21	22	23	24	25	26	27	28	29	30	1♓	2	3	4	5	6	7	8	9			
☽	6♒	19	2♓	15	27	9♈	21	3♉	15	27	9♊	21	4♋	17	30	14♌	28	12♍	27	12♎	26	11♏	25	9♐	23	6♑	19	2♒			
☿	17♑	17	18	19	20	22	23	24	25	26	27	29	30	1♒	3	4	5	7	8	10	11	13	14	16	17	19	20	22			
♀	26♐	27	28	29	0♑	2	3	4	5	6	7	8	10	11	12	13	14	15	17	18	19	20	21	22	24	25	26	27			
♂	10♐	10	11	11	12	13	13	14	15	15	16	17	17	18	19	19	20	20	21	22	22	23	24	24	25	26	26	27			
	1	6	11	16	21	26			1	11	21			1	11	21			1	16		1	16		1	16		1	11	21	
♃	13♌	13	12	11	11	10		♄	23♊	22	22		⚷	14♑	15	15		♅	28♒	29	♆	11♒	11	♇	19♐	20	☊	5♊	5	4	

MAR

	1	2	3	4	5	6	7	8	9	10	11	12	13	14	15	16	17	18	19	20	21	22	23	24	25	26	27	28	29	30	31
☉	10♓	11	12	13	14	15	16	17	18	19	20	21	22	23	24	25	26	27	28	29	30	1♈	2	3	4	5	6	7	8	9	10
☽	15♒	28	11♓	23	5♈	17	29	11♉	23	5♊	17	29	11♋	24	8♌	22	6♍	21	6♎	21	6♏	21	5♐	19	3♑	16	30	12♒	25	8♓	20
☿	23♒	25	27	28	30	2♓	3	5	7	8	10	12	14	16	17	19	21	23	25	27	29	1♈	3	5	7	9	11	13	15	17	19
♀	28♑	29	1♒	2	3	4	5	6	8	9	10	11	12	14	15	16	17	18	20	21	22	23	24	25	27	28	29	0♓	1	3	4
♂	28♐	28	29	29	0♑	1	1	2	3	3	4	5	5	6	6	7	8	8	9	10	10	11	11	12	13	13	14	15	15	16	16
	1	6	11	16	21	26	31		1	11	21	31		1	11	21	31		1	16		1	16		1	16		1	11	21	31
♃	10♌	9	9	9	8	8	8	♄	22♊	22	23	23	⚷	16♑	17	17	18	♅	29♒	0♓	♆	12♒	12	♇	20♐	20	☊	4♊	3	3	2

APR

	1	2	3	4	5	6	7	8	9	10	11	12	13	14	15	16	17	18	19	20	21	22	23	24	25	26	27	28	29	30	
☉	11♈	12	13	14	15	16	17	18	19	20	21	22	23	24	25	26	27	28	29	30	0♉	1	2	3	4	5	6	7	8	9	
☽	2♈	14	26	8♉	19	1♊	13	25	7♋	20	3♌	16	30	14♍	29	14♎	29	14♏	29	14♐	29	13♑	26	9♒	22	5♓	17	29	11♈	23	
☿	21♈	23	25	27	29	1♉	2	4	6	7	9	10	12	13	14	15	16	17	18	19	19	20	20	20	20	21	21	20	20	20	
♀	5♓	6	7	9	10	11	12	14	15	16	17	18	20	21	22	23	24	26	27	28	29	0♈	2	3	4	5	6	8	9	10	
♂	17♑	18	18	19	20	20	21	21	22	23	23	24	25	25	26	26	27	28	28	29	29	0♒	1	1	2	2	3	4	4	5	
	1	6	11	16	21	26			1	11	21			1	11	21			1	16		1	16		1	16		1	11	21	
♃	8♌	8	8	8	9	9		♄	23♊	24	25		⚷	18♑	18	18		♅	1♓	2	♆	13♒	13	♇	20♐	20	☊	2♊	2	1	

MAY

	1	2	3	4	5	6	7	8	9	10	11	12	13	14	15	16	17	18	19	20	21	22	23	24	25	26	27	28	29	30	31
☉	10♉	11	12	13	14	15	16	17	18	19	20	21	22	23	24	25	26	27	28	29	30	1♊	1	2	3	4	5	6	7	8	9
☽	5♉	16	28	10♊	22	4♋	16	29	12♌	25	9♍	23	7♎	22	7♏	23	8♐	23	7♑	21	5♒	18	1♓	14	26	8♈	20	2♉	13	25	7♊
☿	20♉	19	19	18	18	17	17	16	15	15	14	14	13	13	12	12	12	11	11	11	11	11	11	12	12	12	13	13	14	15	15
♀	11♈	12	14	15	16	17	19	20	21	22	23	25	26	27	28	29	1♉	2	3	4	6	7	8	9	10	12	13	14	15	16	18
♂	5♒	6	7	7	8	8	9	9	10	11	11	12	12	13	13	14	15	15	16	16	17	17	18	18	19	19	20	20	21	21	22
	1	6	11	16	21	26	31		1	11	21	31		1	11	21	31		1	16		1	16		1	16		1	11	21	31
♃	9♌	10	10	11	11	12	13	♄	26♊	27	28	29	⚷	18♑	18	18	17	♅	2♓	3	♆	13♒	13	♇	20♐	19	☊	1♊	0	30♉	29

JUN

	1	2	3	4	5	6	7	8	9	10	11	12	13	14	15	16	17	18	19	20	21	22	23	24	25	26	27	28	29	30	
☉	10♊	11	12	13	14	15	16	17	18	19	20	21	22	23	24	24	25	26	27	28	29	0♋	1	2	3	4	5	6	7	8	
☽	19♊	1♋	14	26	9♌	22	5♍	19	3♎	17	1♏	16	1♐	16	1♑	15	30	13♒	27	10♓	22	5♈	17	28	10♉	22	4♊	16	28	10♋	
☿	16♉	17	18	19	20	21	22	23	24	26	27	28	30	1♊	3	5	6	8	10	11	13	15	17	19	21	23	25	27	29	1♋	
♀	19♉	20	21	23	24	25	26	27	29	30	1♊	2	3	5	6	7	8	10	11	12	13	14	16	17	18	19	21	22	23	24	
♂	22♒	23	23	24	24	25	25	26	26	27	27	28	28	29	29	30	30	0♓	1	1	2	2	2	3	3	4	4	4	5	5	
	1	6	11	16	21	26			1	11	21			1	11	21			1	16		1	16		1	16		1	11	21	
♃	13♌	14	14	15	16	17		♄	30♊	1♋	2		⚷	17♑	17	16		♅	3♓	3	♆	13♒	13	♇	19♐	18	☊	29♉	29	28	

2003

JUL

	1	2	3	4	5	6	7	8	9	10	11	12	13	14	15	16	17	18	19	20	21	22	23	24	25	26	27	28	29	30	31
☉	9♋	10	11	12	13	14	14	15	16	17	18	19	20	21	22	23	24	25	26	27	28	29	30	1♌	2	3	4	5	5	6	7
☽	23♋	6♌	19	2♍	16	29	13♎	27	11♏	26	10♐	25	9♑	24	8♒	21	5♓	18	0♈	13	25	7♉	18	0♊	12	24	7♋	19	2♌	15	29
☿	3♋	6	8	10	12	14	16	19	21	23	25	27	29	1♌	3	5	7	9	11	12	14	16	18	19	21	23	24	26	28	29	1♍
♀	25♊	27	28	29	0♋	2	3	4	5	6	8	9	10	11	13	14	15	16	17	19	20	21	22	24	25	26	27	29	30	1♌	2
♂	5♓	6	6	6	6	7	7	7	8	8	8	8	8	9	9	9	9	9	9	10	10	10	10	10	10	10	10	10	10	10	10
	1	6	11	16	21	26	31		1	11	21	31		1	11	21	31		1	16		1	16		1	16		1	11	21	31
♃	18♌	19	20	21	22	23	24	♄	3♋	5	6	7	⚷	16♑	15	14	14	♅	3♓	2	♆	13♒	12	♇	18♐	18	☊	27♉	27	26	26

AUG

	1	2	3	4	5	6	7	8	9	10	11	12	13	14	15	16	17	18	19	20	21	22	23	24	25	26	27	28	29	30	31
☉	8♌	9	10	11	12	13	14	15	16	17	18	19	20	21	22	23	24	25	26	27	28	29	29	0♍	1	2	3	4	5	6	7
☽	12♍	26	10♎	24	8♏	22	6♐	21	5♑	19	3♒	16	30	13♓	26	8♈	21	3♉	14	26	8♊	20	2♋	15	27	11♌	24	8♍	22	6♎	20
☿	2♍	4	5	6	8	9	10	12	13	14	15	16	17	18	19	20	21	22	23	23	24	24	25	25	26	26	26	26	26	26	26
♀	3♌	5	6	7	8	10	11	12	13	15	16	17	18	20	21	22	23	24	26	27	28	29	1♍	2	3	4	6	7	8	9	11
♂	10♓	10	10	10	10	10	10	10	9	9	9	9	9	9	8	8	8	8	8	7	7	7	7	6	6	6	5	5	5	5	4
	1	6	11	16	21	26	31		1	11	21	31		1	11	21	31		1	16		1	16		1	16		1	11	21	31
♃	24♌	25	26	28	29	30	1♍	♄	7♋	9	10	11	⚷	14♑	13	13	13	♅	2♓	1	♆	12♒	11	♇	17♐	17	☊	26♉	25	25	24

SEP

	1	2	3	4	5	6	7	8	9	10	11	12	13	14	15	16	17	18	19	20	21	22	23	24	25	26	27	28	29	30
☉	8♍	9	10	11	12	13	14	15	16	17	18	19	20	21	22	23	24	25	26	27	28	29	30	1♎	2	2	3	4	5	6
☽	5♏	19	3♐	17	1♑	15	29	12♒	26	9♓	21	4♈	16	29	11♉	22	4♊	16	28	10♋	23	5♌	19	2♍	16	1♎	15	0♏	15	29
☿	26♍	25	25	24	24	23	22	21	20	19	18	17	16	15	14	14	13	13	12	12	12	12	13	13	14	15	16	17	18	19
♀	12♍	13	14	16	17	18	19	20	22	23	24	25	27	28	29	0♎	2	3	4	5	7	8	9	10	12	13	14	15	17	18
♂	4♓	4	4	3	3	3	3	2	2	2	2	2	1	1	1	1	1	1	1	0	0	0	0	0	0	0	0	0	0	0
	1	6	11	16	21	26			1	11	21			1	11	21			1	16		1	16		1	16		1	11	21
♃	1♍	2	3	4	5	6		♄	11♋	11	12		⚷	13♑	12	12		♅	1♓	30♒	♆	11♒	11	♇	17♐	17	☊	24♉	24	23

OCT

	1	2	3	4	5	6	7	8	9	10	11	12	13	14	15	16	17	18	19	20	21	22	23	24	25	26	27	28	29	30	31
☉	7♎	8	9	10	11	12	13	14	15	16	17	18	19	20	21	22	23	24	25	26	27	28	29	0♏	1	2	3	4	5	6	7
☽	14♐	28	12♑	26	9♒	22	5♓	18	0♈	13	25	7♉	19	1♊	12	24	6♋	18	1♌	13	27	10♍	24	9♎	24	9♏	24	9♐	24	8♑	22
☿	20♍	22	23	25	27	28	30	2♎	3	5	7	9	10	12	14	16	17	19	21	22	24	26	28	29	1♏	3	4	6	7	9	11
♀	19♎	20	22	23	24	25	27	28	29	0♏	2	3	4	5	6	8	9	10	11	13	14	15	16	18	19	20	21	23	24	25	26
♂	0♓	0	0	0	1	1	1	1	1	1	1	2	2	2	2	2	3	3	3	3	4	4	4	5	5	5	6	6	6	7	7
	1	6	11	16	21	26	31		1	11	21	31		1	11	21	31		1	16		1	16		1	16		1	11	21	31
♃	7♍	8	9	10	11	12	13	♄	13♋	13	13	13	⚷	12♑	13	13	14	♅	29♒	29	♆	11♒	10	♇	18♐	18	☊	23♉	22	22	21

NOV

	1	2	3	4	5	6	7	8	9	10	11	12	13	14	15	16	17	18	19	20	21	22	23	24	25	26	27	28	29	30
☉	8♏	9	10	11	12	13	14	15	16	17	18	19	20	21	22	23	24	25	26	27	28	29	0♐	1	2	3	4	5	6	7
☽	6♒	19	2♓	15	27	10♈	22	4♉	16	27	9♊	21	3♋	15	27	9♌	22	5♍	19	3♎	17	2♏	17	2♐	17	2♑	17	1♒	15	29
☿	12♏	14	16	17	19	20	22	23	25	26	28	30	1♐	3	4	6	7	9	10	12	13	15	16	18	19	20	22	23	25	26
♀	28♏	29	0♐	1	3	4	5	6	8	9	10	11	13	14	15	16	18	19	20	21	22	24	25	26	27	29	30	1♑	2	4
♂	7♓	8	8	8	9	9	10	10	11	11	11	12	12	13	13	14	14	15	15	16	16	17	17	18	18	19	19	20	20	21
	1	6	11	16	21	26			1	11	21			1	11	21			1	16		1	16		1	16		1	11	21
♃	13♍	14	15	15	16	17		♄	13♋	13	13		⚷	14♑	14	15		♅	29♒	29	♆	10♒	11	♇	18♐	19	☊	21♉	20	20

DEC

	1	2	3	4	5	6	7	8	9	10	11	12	13	14	15	16	17	18	19	20	21	22	23	24	25	26	27	28	29	30	31
☉	8♐	9	10	11	12	13	14	15	16	17	19	20	21	22	23	24	25	26	27	28	29	30	1♑	2	3	4	5	6	7	8	9
☽	12♓	24	7♈	19	1♉	13	24	6♊	18	30	12♋	24	6♌	19	2♍	15	28	12♎	26	10♏	25	10♐	25	10♑	25	10♒	24	7♓	20	3♈	15
☿	27♐	29	0♑	1	3	4	5	6	7	8	9	10	11	11	12	12	13	13	12	12	12	11	10	9	8	6	5	4	2	1	30♐
♀	5♑	6	7	9	10	11	12	14	15	16	17	19	20	21	22	23	25	26	27	28	30	1♒	2	3	5	6	7	8	10	11	12
♂	21♓	22	22	23	23	24	25	25	26	26	27	27	28	29	29	30	0♈	1	1	2	3	3	4	4	5	6	6	7	7	8	9
	1	6	11	16	21	26	31		1	11	21	31		1	11	21	31		1	16		1	16		1	16		1	11	21	31
♃	17♍	18	18	18	19	19	19	♄	12♋	11	11	10	⚷	16♑	17	17	18	♅	29♒	29	♆	11♒	11	♇	19♐	20	☊	19♉	19	18	18

2004

JAN	1	2	3	4	5	6	7	8	9	10	11	12	13	14	15	16	17	18	19	20	21	22	23	24	25	26	27	28	29	30	31
☉	10♑	11	12	13	14	15	16	17	18	19	20	21	22	23	24	25	26	27	28	29	0♒	1	2	3	4	5	6	7	8	9	10
☽	27♈	9♉	21	3♊	15	27	9♋	21	3♌	16	29	12♍	25	8♎	22	5♏	20	4♐	19	3♑	18	3♒	17	1♓	15	28	11♈	24	6♉	18	29
☿	29♐	28	27	27	26	26	26	26	27	27	28	28	29	30	0♑	1	2	3	4	6	7	8	9	10	12	13	14	15	17	18	20
♀	13♒	14	16	17	18	19	21	22	23	24	25	27	28	29	0♓	2	3	4	5	6	8	9	10	11	12	14	15	16	17	18	20
♂	9♈	10	10	11	12	12	13	13	14	15	15	16	17	17	18	18	19	20	20	21	22	22	23	23	24	25	25	26	27	27	28
	1	6	11	16	21	26	31		1	11	21	31		1	11	21	31		1	16		1	16		1	16		1	11	21	31
♃	19♍	19	19	19	18	18	18	♄	10♋	9	8	7	⚷	18♑	19	20	21	♅	0♓	1	♆	12♒	12	♇	20♐	21	☊	18♉	17	17	16

FEB	1	2	3	4	5	6	7	8	9	10	11	12	13	14	15	16	17	18	19	20	21	22	23	24	25	26	27	28	29		
☉	11♒	12	13	14	16	17	18	19	20	21	22	23	24	25	26	27	28	29	30	1♓	2	3	4	5	6	7	8	9	10		
☽	11♊	23	5♋	17	30	12♌	25	8♍	21	5♎	19	2♏	16	0♐	14	29	13♑	27	12♒	26	9♓	23	6♈	19	1♉	13	25	7♊	19		
☿	21♑	22	24	25	27	28	30	1♒	3	4	6	7	9	11	12	14	15	17	19	20	22	24	26	27	29	1♓	3	4	6		
♀	21♓	22	23	24	26	27	28	29	0♈	2	3	4	5	6	7	9	10	11	12	13	14	16	17	18	19	20	21	22	24		
♂	28♈	29	30	0♉	1	2	2	3	4	4	5	5	6	7	7	8	9	9	10	11	11	12	12	13	14	14	15	16	16		
	1	6	11	16	21	26			1	11	21			1	11	21			1	16		1	16		1	16		1	11	21	
♃	18♍	17	17	16	16	15		♄	7♋	7	7		⚷	21♑	22	23		♅	2♓	2	♆	13♒	13	♇	21♐	22	☊	16♉	16	15	

MAR	1	2	3	4	5	6	7	8	9	10	11	12	13	14	15	16	17	18	19	20	21	22	23	24	25	26	27	28	29	30	31
☉	11♓	12	13	14	15	16	17	18	19	20	21	22	23	24	25	26	27	28	29	30	1♈	2	3	4	5	6	7	8	9	10	11
☽	1♋	13	25	8♌	21	4♍	17	1♎	15	29	13♏	27	11♐	25	9♑	23	7♒	21	5♓	18	1♈	14	27	9♉	21	3♊	15	27	9♋	21	3♌
☿	8♓	10	12	14	16	18	19	21	23	25	27	29	1♈	3	5	7	9	11	13	14	16	18	19	21	22	24	25	26	27	28	29
♀	25♈	26	27	28	29	0♉	1	2	4	5	6	7	8	9	10	11	12	13	14	15	16	17	18	20	21	22	23	24	25	26	27
♂	17♉	18	18	19	20	20	21	21	22	23	23	24	25	25	26	27	27	28	29	29	30	0♊	1	2	2	3	4	4	5	6	6
	1	6	11	16	21	26	31		1	11	21	31		1	11	21	31		1	16		1	16		1	16		1	11	21	31
♃	14♍	14	13	12	12	11	11	♄	6♋	6	6	7	⚷	24♑	24	25	25	♅	3♓	4	♆	14♒	14	♇	22♐	22	☊	15♉	14	13	13

APR	1	2	3	4	5	6	7	8	9	10	11	12	13	14	15	16	17	18	19	20	21	22	23	24	25	26	27	28	29	30	
☉	12♈	13	14	15	16	17	18	18	19	20	21	22	23	24	25	26	27	28	29	0♉	1	2	3	4	5	6	7	8	9	10	
☽	16♌	28	12♍	25	9♎	24	8♏	23	7♐	22	6♑	20	4♒	18	1♓	15	28	10♈	23	5♉	17	29	11♊	23	5♋	17	29	11♌	24	6♍	
☿	30♈	1♉	1	1	2	2	2	2	2	1	1	1	0	29♈	29	28	27	27	26	25	25	24	23	23	22	22	22	21	21	21	
♀	27♉	28	29	0♊	1	2	3	4	5	6	7	8	8	9	10	11	12	12	13	14	15	16	16	17	18	18	19	19	20	21	
♂	7♊	7	8	9	9	10	11	11	12	13	13	14	15	15	16	16	17	18	18	19	20	20	21	22	22	23	23	24	25	25	
	1	6	11	16	21	26			1	11	21			1	11	21			1	16		1	16		1	16		1	11	21	
♃	11♍	10	10	9	9	9		♄	7♋	7	8		⚷	26♑	26	26		♅	5♓	6	♆	15♒	15	♇	22♐	22	☊	13♉	12	12	

MAY	1	2	3	4	5	6	7	8	9	10	11	12	13	14	15	16	17	18	19	20	21	22	23	24	25	26	27	28	29	30	31
☉	11♉	12	13	14	15	16	17	18	19	20	21	22	23	24	24	25	26	27	28	29	0♊	1	2	3	4	5	6	7	8	9	10
☽	20♍	3♎	18	2♏	17	2♐	17	2♑	16	1♒	15	28	12♓	25	7♈	20	2♉	14	26	8♊	20	2♋	14	25	7♌	20	2♍	15	28	12♎	26
☿	21♈	21	21	22	22	22	23	23	24	25	25	26	27	28	29	30	1♉	2	3	4	5	7	8	9	11	12	14	15	17	18	20
♀	21♊	22	22	23	23	24	24	24	25	25	25	25	26	26	26	26	26	26	26	26	26	26	26	25	25	25	24	24	24	23	23
♂	26♊	27	27	28	28	29	30	0♋	1	2	2	3	4	4	5	5	6	7	7	8	9	9	10	11	11	12	12	13	14	14	15
	1	6	11	16	21	26	31		1	11	21	31		1	11	21	31		1	16		1	16		1	16		1	11	21	31
♃	9♍	9	9	9	9	10	10	♄	9♋	10	11	12	⚷	26♑	26	26	26	♅	6♓	7	♆	15♒	15	♇	22♐	22	☊	11♉	11	10	10

JUN	1	2	3	4	5	6	7	8	9	10	11	12	13	14	15	16	17	18	19	20	21	22	23	24	25	26	27	28	29	30	
☉	11♊	12	13	14	15	16	17	18	18	19	20	21	22	23	24	25	26	27	28	29	30	1♋	2	3	4	5	6	7	8	9	
☽	10♏	25	10♐	25	11♑	26	10♒	24	8♓	21	4♈	17	29	11♉	23	5♊	17	29	11♋	22	4♌	17	29	11♍	24	7♎	21	5♏	19	4♐	
☿	22♉	24	25	27	29	1♊	3	5	7	9	11	13	15	17	19	22	24	26	28	0♋	3	5	7	9	11	13	15	17	19	21	
♀	22♊	22	21	21	20	19	19	18	17	17	16	16	15	14	14	13	13	12	12	12	11	11	11	10	10	10	10	10	10	10	
♂	16♋	16	17	17	18	19	19	20	21	21	22	23	23	24	24	25	26	26	27	28	28	29	29	0♌	1	1	2	3	3	4	
	1	6	11	16	21	26			1	11	21			1	11	21			1	16		1	16		1	16		1	11	21	
♃	10♍	10	11	11	12	13		♄	12♋	13	15		⚷	26♑	25	25		♅	7♓	7	♆	15♒	15	♇	21♐	21	☊	10♉	9	9	

2004

JUL

	1	2	3	4	5	6	7	8	9	10	11	12	13	14	15	16	17	18	19	20	21	22	23	24	25	26	27	28	29	30	31
☉	9♋	10	11	12	13	14	15	16	17	18	19	20	21	22	23	24	25	26	27	28	29	30	0♌	1	2	3	4	5	6	7	8
☽	19♐	4♑	19	4♒	19	3♓	17	1♈	13	26	8♉	20	2♊	14	26	8♋	19	2♌	14	26	8♍	21	4♎	17	0♏	14	28	13♐	28	13♑	28
☿	23♋	25	27	29	1♌	2	4	6	8	9	11	12	14	15	17	18	20	21	22	24	25	26	27	28	29	0♍	1	2	3	4	5
♀	10♊	10	10	10	10	10	11	11	11	11	12	12	13	13	14	14	15	15	16	16	17	17	18	19	19	20	21	22	22	23	24
♂	4♌	5	6	6	7	8	8	9	10	10	11	11	12	13	13	14	15	15	16	16	17	18	18	19	20	20	21	22	22	23	23
	1	6	11	16	21	26	31		1	11	21	31		1	11	21	31		1	16		1	16		1	16		1	11	21	31
♃	13♍	14	15	16	17	17	18	♄	16♋	17	18	20	⚷	24♑	24	23	22	♅	7♓	6	♆	15♒	15	♇	20♐	20	☊	8♉	8	7	6

AUG

	1	2	3	4	5	6	7	8	9	10	11	12	13	14	15	16	17	18	19	20	21	22	23	24	25	26	27	28	29	30	31
☉	9♌	10	11	12	13	14	15	16	17	18	19	20	21	22	23	23	24	25	26	27	28	29	0♍	1	2	3	4	5	6	7	8
☽	13♒	27	12♓	25	9♈	22	4♉	17	29	11♊	22	4♋	16	28	10♌	23	5♍	18	1♎	14	27	11♏	25	9♐	23	7♑	22	7♒	21	6♓	20
☿	6♍	6	7	7	8	8	8	9	9	9	9	9	8	8	8	7	7	6	5	4	4	3	2	1	0	29♌	28	28	27	27	26
♀	25♊	25	26	27	28	29	30	0♋	1	2	3	4	5	6	7	8	9	10	11	12	13	14	15	16	17	18	19	20	21	22	23
♂	24♌	25	25	26	27	27	28	28	29	30	0♍	1	2	2	3	4	4	5	5	6	7	7	8	9	9	10	11	11	12	12	13
	1	6	11	16	21	26	31		1	11	21	31		1	11	21	31		1	16		1	16		1	16		1	11	21	31
♃	19♍	20	20	21	23	24	25	♄	20♋	21	22	23	⚷	22♑	22	21	21	♅	6♓	5	♆	14♒	14	♇	20♐	20	☊	6♉	6	5	5

SEP

	1	2	3	4	5	6	7	8	9	10	11	12	13	14	15	16	17	18	19	20	21	22	23	24	25	26	27	28	29	30	
☉	9♍	10	11	12	13	14	15	16	17	18	19	20	21	22	22	23	24	25	26	27	28	29	0♎	1	2	3	4	5	6	7	
☽	4♈	17	30	12♉	25	7♊	19	1♋	12	24	7♌	19	1♍	14	27	11♎	24	8♏	22	6♐	20	4♑	18	2♒	16	1♓	15	28	12♈	25	
☿	26♌	26	26	26	26	27	27	28	29	30	1♍	2	3	5	6	8	9	11	13	14	16	18	20	22	23	25	27	29	1♎	3	
♀	24♋	25	26	27	28	29	0♌	1	2	3	4	5	7	8	9	10	11	12	13	14	15	17	18	19	20	21	22	23	25	26	
♂	14♍	14	15	16	16	17	18	18	19	19	20	21	21	22	23	23	24	25	25	26	27	27	28	28	29	30	0♎	1	2	2	
	1	6	11	16	21	26			1	11	21			1	11	21			1	16		1	16		1	16		1	11	21	
♃	25♍	26	27	28	29	0♎		♄	23♋	24	25		⚷	21♑	21	21		♅	5♓	4	♆	13♒	13	♇	20♐	20	☊	5♉	4	4	

OCT

	1	2	3	4	5	6	7	8	9	10	11	12	13	14	15	16	17	18	19	20	21	22	23	24	25	26	27	28	29	30	31
☉	8♎	9	10	11	12	13	14	15	16	17	18	19	20	21	22	23	24	25	26	27	28	29	30	1♏	2	3	4	5	6	7	8
☽	8♉	20	3♊	15	27	8♋	20	2♌	14	27	10♍	23	6♎	19	3♏	18	2♐	16	1♑	15	29	13♒	27	11♓	24	7♈	21	3♉	16	28	11♊
☿	4♎	6	8	10	11	13	15	17	18	20	22	23	25	27	28	0♏	2	3	5	6	8	10	11	13	14	16	17	19	20	22	23
♀	27♌	28	29	0♍	1	3	4	5	6	7	8	10	11	12	13	14	16	17	18	19	20	22	23	24	25	26	28	29	30	1♎	2
♂	3♎	4	4	5	6	6	7	8	8	9	9	10	11	11	12	13	13	14	15	15	16	17	17	18	19	19	20	21	21	22	23
	1	6	11	16	21	26	31		1	11	21	31		1	11	21	31		1	16		1	16		1	16		1	11	21	31
♃	1♎	2	3	4	6	7	8	♄	26♋	27	27	27	⚷	21♑	21	21	21	♅	4♓	3	♆	13♒	13	♇	20♐	20	☊	3♉	3	2	2

NOV

	1	2	3	4	5	6	7	8	9	10	11	12	13	14	15	16	17	18	19	20	21	22	23	24	25	26	27	28	29	30	
☉	9♏	10	11	12	13	14	15	16	17	18	19	20	21	22	23	24	25	26	27	28	29	0♐	1	2	3	4	5	6	7	8	
☽	23♊	5♋	16	28	10♌	22	5♍	17	0♎	14	28	12♏	26	11♐	26	11♑	25	10♒	24	8♓	21	4♈	17	30	12♉	25	7♊	19	1♋	13	
☿	25♏	26	28	29	1♐	2	3	5	6	8	9	10	12	13	14	15	17	18	19	20	21	22	23	24	25	25	26	26	27	27	
♀	4♎	5	6	7	8	10	11	12	13	15	16	17	18	19	21	22	23	24	26	27	28	29	1♏	2	3	4	5	7	8	9	
♂	23♎	24	25	25	26	27	27	28	29	29	30	1♏	1	2	3	3	4	5	5	6	7	7	8	9	9	10	11	11	12	13	
	1	6	11	16	21	26			1	11	21			1	11	21			1	16		1	16		1	16		1	11	21	
♃	8♎	9	10	11	12	12		♄	27♋	27	27		⚷	21♑	22	22		♅	3♓	3	♆	13♒	13	♇	21♐	21	☊	2♉	1	0	

DEC

	1	2	3	4	5	6	7	8	9	10	11	12	13	14	15	16	17	18	19	20	21	22	23	24	25	26	27	28	29	30	31
☉	9♐	10	11	12	13	14	15	16	17	18	19	20	21	22	23	24	25	26	27	28	29	0♑	1	3	4	5	6	7	8	9	10
☽	25♋	7♌	18	0♍	13	25	8♎	22	5♏	20	4♐	19	5♑	20	5♒	20	4♓	18	1♈	14	27	9♉	22	4♊	16	28	10♋	21	3♌	15	27
☿	27♐	27	26	26	25	24	23	22	20	19	18	16	15	14	13	12	11	11	11	10	10	11	11	11	12	13	14	14	15	16	17
♀	10♏	12	13	14	15	17	18	19	20	22	23	24	25	27	28	29	0♐	2	3	4	5	7	8	9	10	12	13	14	15	17	18
♂	13♏	14	15	15	16	17	17	18	19	19	20	21	21	22	23	23	24	25	25	26	27	27	28	29	30	0♐	1	2	2	3	4
	1	6	11	16	21	26	31		1	11	21	31		1	11	21	31		1	16		1	16		1	16		1	11	21	31
♃	13♎	14	15	15	16	17	17	♄	27♋	26	26	25	⚷	23♑	24	25	25	♅	3♓	3	♆	13♒	13	♇	22♐	22	☊	30♈	29	29	28

2005

EPHEMERIS

JAN

	1	2	3	4	5	6	7	8	9	10	11	12	13	14	15	16	17	18	19	20	21	22	23	24	25	26	27	28	29	30	31
☉	11♑	12	13	14	15	16	17	18	19	20	21	22	23	24	25	26	27	28	29	0♒	1	2	3	4	5	6	7	8	9	10	11
☽	9♍	22	4♎	17	30	14♏	28	12♐	27	13♑	28	13♒	28	13♓	27	10♈	24	6♉	19	1♊	13	25	7♋	18	0♌	12	24	6♍	19	1♎	13
☿	18♐	20	21	22	23	24	26	27	28	30	1♑	3	4	5	7	8	10	11	13	14	16	17	19	20	22	23	25	26	28	30	1♒
♀	19♐	20	22	23	24	25	27	28	29	0♑	2	3	4	5	7	8	9	10	12	13	14	15	17	18	19	20	22	23	24	25	27
♂	4♐	5	6	6	7	8	8	9	10	11	11	12	13	13	14	15	15	16	17	18	18	19	20	20	21	22	22	23	24	25	25
	1	6	11	16	21	26	31		1	11	21	31		1	11	21	31		1	16		1	16		1	16		1	11	21	31
♃	17♎	18	18	18	19	19	19	♄	25♋	24	23	23	⚷	26♑	26	27	28	♅	4♓	5	♆	14♒	14	♇	23♐	23	☊	28♈	28	27	27

FEB

	1	2	3	4	5	6	7	8	9	10	11	12	13	14	15	16	17	18	19	20	21	22	23	24	25	26	27	28			
☉	12♒	13	14	15	16	17	18	19	20	21	22	23	24	25	26	27	28	29	0♓	1	2	3	4	5	6	7	8	9			
☽	26♎	9♏	23	7♐	21	6♑	21	6♒	21	6♓	21	5♈	19	2♉	15	27	9♊	21	3♋	15	27	9♌	21	3♍	15	28	11♎	23			
☿	3♒	4	6	8	9	11	13	15	16	18	20	21	23	25	27	29	0♓	2	4	6	8	10	12	14	15	17	19	21			
♀	28♑	29	0♒	2	3	4	5	7	8	9	10	12	13	14	15	17	18	19	20	22	23	24	25	27	28	29	0♓	2			
♂	26♐	27	27	28	29	29	0♑	1	2	2	3	4	4	5	6	7	7	8	9	9	10	11	12	12	13	14	14	15			
	1	6	11	16	21	26			1	11	21			1	11	21			1	16		1	16		1	16		1	11	21	
♃	19♎	19	19	19	18	18		♄	22♋	22	21		⚷	28♑	29	30		♅	5♓	6	♆	15♒	16	♇	24♐	24	☊	27♈	26	26	

MAR

	1	2	3	4	5	6	7	8	9	10	11	12	13	14	15	16	17	18	19	20	21	22	23	24	25	26	27	28	29	30	31
☉	10♓	12	13	14	15	16	17	18	19	20	21	22	23	24	25	26	26	27	28	29	0♈	1	2	3	4	5	6	7	8	9	10
☽	6♏	20	3♐	17	1♑	15	0♒	15	30	14♓	29	13♈	27	10♉	23	5♊	18	30	12♋	23	5♌	17	29	12♍	24	7♎	20	3♏	16	0♐	14
☿	23♓	25	26	28	30	2♈	3	5	6	7	9	10	11	12	12	13	13	14	14	14	14	14	14	13	13	12	11	10	10	9	8
♀	3♓	4	5	7	8	9	10	12	13	14	15	17	18	19	20	22	23	24	25	27	28	29	0♈	2	3	4	5	7	8	9	10
♂	16♑	17	17	18	19	19	20	21	22	22	23	24	24	25	26	27	27	28	29	29	0♒	1	2	2	3	4	5	5	6	7	7
	1	6	11	16	21	26	31		1	11	21	31		1	11	21	31		1	16		1	16		1	16		1	11	21	31
♃	18♎	17	17	16	16	15	14	♄	21♋	21	20	20	⚷	1♒	1	2	2	♅	7♓	8	♆	16♒	17	♇	24♐	24	☊	25♈	25	24	24

APR

	1	2	3	4	5	6	7	8	9	10	11	12	13	14	15	16	17	18	19	20	21	22	23	24	25	26	27	28	29	30	
☉	11♈	12	13	14	15	16	17	18	19	20	21	22	23	24	25	26	27	28	29	0♉	1	2	3	4	5	6	7	8	9	10	
☽	28♐	12♑	26	10♒	25	9♓	23	7♈	21	5♉	18	1♊	13	25	7♋	19	1♌	13	25	7♍	20	2♎	15	29	12♏	26	10♐	24	9♑	23	
☿	7♈	6	6	5	4	4	3	3	2	2	2	2	2	2	2	2	3	3	4	4	5	5	6	7	8	9	10	11	12	13	
♀	12♈	13	14	15	17	18	19	20	22	23	24	25	26	28	29	0♉	1	3	4	5	6	8	9	10	11	13	14	15	16	17	
♂	8♒	9	10	10	11	12	12	13	14	15	15	16	17	18	18	19	20	20	21	22	23	23	24	25	26	26	27	28	28	29	
	1	6	11	16	21	26			1	11	21			1	11	21			1	16		1	16		1	16		1	11	21	
♃	14♎	14	13	12	12	11		♄	20♋	21	21		⚷	2♒	3	3		♅	9♓	9	♆	17♒	17	♇	25♐	24	☊	24♈	23	22	

MAY

	1	2	3	4	5	6	7	8	9	10	11	12	13	14	15	16	17	18	19	20	21	22	23	24	25	26	27	28	29	30	31
☉	11♉	12	13	14	15	16	17	18	18	19	20	21	22	23	24	25	26	27	28	29	0♊	1	2	3	4	5	6	7	8	9	10
☽	7♒	21	5♓	19	3♈	17	30	13♉	26	9♊	21	3♋	15	27	9♌	21	3♍	15	28	10♎	23	7♏	21	5♐	19	4♑	19	4♒	18	2♓	16
☿	14♈	15	17	18	19	21	22	23	25	26	28	29	1♉	3	4	6	8	10	11	13	15	17	19	21	23	25	27	29	1♊	3	5
♀	19♉	20	21	22	24	25	26	27	29	30	1♊	2	3	5	6	7	8	10	11	12	13	15	16	17	18	19	21	22	23	24	26
♂	30♒	1♓	1	2	3	4	4	5	6	6	7	8	9	9	10	11	11	12	13	14	14	15	16	16	17	18	19	19	20	21	21
	1	6	11	16	21	26	31		1	11	21	31		1	11	21	31		1	16		1	16		1	16		1	11	21	31
♃	11♎	10	10	10	9	9	9	♄	22♋	23	23	24	⚷	3♒	3	3	3	♅	10♓	10	♆	18♒	18	♇	24♐	24	☊	22♈	21	21	20

JUN

	1	2	3	4	5	6	7	8	9	10	11	12	13	14	15	16	17	18	19	20	21	22	23	24	25	26	27	28	29	30	
☉	11♊	12	13	13	14	15	16	17	18	19	20	21	22	23	24	25	26	27	28	29	30	1♋	2	3	4	4	5	6	7	8	
☽	30♓	13♈	27	10♉	22	5♊	17	30	12♋	24	6♌	17	29	11♍	23	6♎	18	1♏	15	29	13♐	28	13♑	28	13♒	28	13♓	27	10♈	24	
☿	8♊	10	12	14	16	19	21	23	25	27	29	1♋	4	6	7	9	11	13	15	17	19	20	22	24	25	27	28	30	1♌	3	
♀	27♊	28	29	0♋	2	3	4	5	7	8	9	10	11	13	14	15	16	18	19	20	21	22	24	25	26	27	28	30	1♌	2	
♂	22♓	23	24	24	25	26	26	27	28	29	29	30	1♈	1	2	3	3	4	5	5	6	7	8	8	9	10	10	11	12	12	
	1	6	11	16	21	26			1	11	21			1	11	21			1	16		1	16		1	16		1	11	21	
♃	9♎	9	9	9	9	10		♄	25♋	26	27		⚷	3♒	3	2		♅	11♓	11	♆	18♒	17	♇	24♐	23	☊	20♈	20	19	

EPHEMERIS

2005

JUL

	1	2	3	4	5	6	7	8	9	10	11	12	13	14	15	16	17	18	19	20	21	22	23	24	25	26	27	28	29	30	31
☉	9♋	10	11	12	13	14	15	16	17	18	19	20	21	22	23	24	25	25	26	27	28	29	0♌	1	2	3	4	5	6	7	8
☽	7♉	19	2♊	14	26	8♋	20	2♌	14	26	8♍	20	2♎	14	27	10♏	23	7♐	22	7♑	22	7♒	22	7♓	22	6♈	20	3♉	16	29	11♊
☿	4♌	5	7	8	9	10	11	12	13	14	15	16	17	17	18	18	19	19	20	20	20	20	20	20	20	20	20	19	19	19	18
♀	3♌	5	6	7	8	9	11	12	13	14	15	17	18	19	20	22	23	24	25	26	28	29	30	1♍	2	4	5	6	7	8	10
♂	13♈	14	14	15	16	16	17	17	18	19	19	20	21	21	22	23	23	24	24	25	26	26	27	28	28	29	29	30	0♉	1	2
	1	6	11	16	21	26	31		1	11	21	31		1	11	21	31		1	16		1	16		1	16		1	11	21	31
♃	10♎	10	11	11	12	12	13	♄	28♋	29	1♌	2	⚷	2♒	1	1	0	♅	11♓	10	♆	17♒	17	♇	23♐	22	☊	19♈	18	18	17

AUG

	1	2	3	4	5	6	7	8	9	10	11	12	13	14	15	16	17	18	19	20	21	22	23	24	25	26	27	28	29	30	31
☉	9♌	10	11	12	13	14	15	16	17	17	18	19	20	21	22	23	24	25	26	27	28	29	30	1♍	2	3	4	5	6	7	8
☽	24♊	6♋	18	29	11♌	23	5♍	17	29	11♎	23	6♏	19	2♐	16	0♑	15	0♒	15	1♓	16	1♈	15	29	12♉	25	8♊	20	3♋	15	26
☿	17♌	17	16	15	14	14	13	12	11	11	10	10	9	9	9	9	9	9	9	10	10	11	12	13	14	15	16	17	19	20	22
♀	11♍	12	13	14	16	17	18	19	20	22	23	24	25	26	27	29	30	1♎	2	3	5	6	7	8	9	10	12	13	14	15	16
♂	2♉	3	3	4	4	5	6	6	7	7	8	8	9	9	10	10	11	11	12	12	13	13	13	14	14	15	15	16	16	16	17
	1	6	11	16	21	26	31		1	11	21	31		1	11	21	31		1	16		1	16		1	16		1	11	21	31
♃	13♎	14	15	16	17	17	18	♄	2♌	3	5	6	⚷	0♒	29♑	29	29	♅	10♓	9	♆	16♒	16	♇	22♐	22	☊	17♈	17	16	16

SEP

	1	2	3	4	5	6	7	8	9	10	11	12	13	14	15	16	17	18	19	20	21	22	23	24	25	26	27	28	29	30	
☉	9♍	10	11	12	13	14	14	15	16	17	18	19	20	21	22	23	24	25	26	27	28	29	0♎	1	2	3	4	5	6	7	
☽	8♌	20	2♍	14	26	8♎	21	3♏	16	29	12♐	26	10♑	24	9♒	24	9♓	24	9♈	23	7♉	21	4♊	16	29	11♋	23	5♌	17	29	
☿	23♌	25	27	29	0♍	2	4	6	8	10	12	14	16	18	19	21	23	25	27	29	1♎	2	4	6	8	9	11	13	14	16	
♀	18♎	19	20	21	22	23	25	26	27	28	29	0♏	2	3	4	5	6	7	8	10	11	12	13	14	15	16	18	19	20	21	
♂	17♉	17	18	18	19	19	19	19	20	20	20	21	21	21	21	22	22	22	22	22	23	23	23	23	23	23	23	23	23	23	
	1	6	11	16	21	26			1	11	21			1	11	21			1	16		1	16		1	16		1	11	21	
♃	19♎	19	20	21	22	24		♄	6♌	7	8		⚷	28♑	28	28		♅	9♓	8	♆	16♒	15	♇	22♐	22	☊	15♈	15	14	

OCT

	1	2	3	4	5	6	7	8	9	10	11	12	13	14	15	16	17	18	19	20	21	22	23	24	25	26	27	28	29	30	31
☉	8♎	9	10	11	12	13	14	15	16	17	18	19	20	21	22	23	24	25	26	27	28	29	30	1♏	2	3	4	5	6	7	8
☽	11♍	23	5♎	17	30	13♏	26	9♐	23	6♑	20	5♒	19	4♓	18	3♈	17	1♉	15	28	12♊	24	7♋	19	1♌	13	25	7♍	19	1♎	13
☿	18♎	19	21	23	24	26	27	29	0♏	2	3	5	6	8	9	11	12	14	15	17	18	19	21	22	23	25	26	27	28	30	1♐
♀	22♏	23	24	25	27	28	29	30	1♐	2	3	4	5	7	8	9	10	11	12	13	14	15	16	17	18	19	20	22	23	24	25
♂	23♉	23	23	23	23	23	23	23	23	23	23	23	22	22	22	22	22	21	21	21	21	20	20	20	20	19	19	19	18	18	18
	1	6	11	16	21	26	31		1	11	21	31		1	11	21	31		1	16		1	16		1	16		1	11	21	31
♃	25♎	26	27	28	29	30	1♏	♄	9♌	10	10	11	⚷	28♑	28	28	28	♅	8♓	7	♆	15♒	15	♇	22♐	22	☊	14♈	13	13	12

NOV

	1	2	3	4	5	6	7	8	9	10	11	12	13	14	15	16	17	18	19	20	21	22	23	24	25	26	27	28	29	30	
☉	9♏	10	11	12	13	14	15	16	17	18	19	20	21	22	23	24	25	26	27	28	29	30	1♐	2	3	4	5	6	7	8	
☽	26♎	9♏	22	6♐	19	3♑	17	1♒	16	30	14♓	28	12♈	26	10♉	23	7♊	20	2♋	15	27	9♌	21	3♍	14	26	9♎	21	4♏	17	
☿	2♐	3	4	5	6	7	8	8	9	10	10	11	11	11	11	11	10	10	9	8	7	6	5	3	2	1	29♏	28	27	26	
♀	26♐	27	28	29	30	1♑	2	3	4	5	5	6	7	8	9	10	11	12	13	14	15	15	16	17	18	19	19	20	21	22	
♂	17♉	17	17	16	16	15	15	15	14	14	14	13	13	13	12	12	12	12	11	11	11	10	10	10	10	10	9	9	9	9	
	1	6	11	16	21	26			1	11	21			1	11	21			1	16		1	16		1	16		1	11	21	
♃	1♏	2	3	5	6	7		♄	11♌	11	11		⚷	28♑	29	29		♅	7♓	7	♆	15♒	15	♇	23♐	23	☊	12♈	12	11	

DEC

	1	2	3	4	5	6	7	8	9	10	11	12	13	14	15	16	17	18	19	20	21	22	23	24	25	26	27	28	29	30	31
☉	9♐	10	11	12	13	14	15	16	17	18	19	20	21	22	23	24	25	26	27	28	29	0♑	1	2	3	4	5	6	7	8	9
☽	1♐	15	29	13♑	28	12♒	27	11♓	25	9♈	22	6♉	19	2♊	15	28	10♋	23	5♌	17	29	10♍	22	4♎	16	29	12♏	25	9♐	23	8♑
☿	26♏	25	25	25	25	25	25	26	27	27	28	29	0♐	1	2	3	5	6	7	9	10	11	13	14	15	17	18	20	21	23	24
♀	22♑	23	24	24	25	25	26	27	27	28	28	29	29	29	30	0♒	0	1	1	1	1	1	1	1	1	1	1	1	1	1	1
♂	9♉	9	9	8	8	8	8	8	8	8	8	8	8	8	8	8	9	9	9	9	9	9	9	9	10	10	10	10	10	11	11
	1	6	11	16	21	26	31		1	11	21	31		1	11	21	31		1	16		1	16		1	16		1	11	21	31
♃v	8♏	9	10	11	11	12	13	♄	11♌	11	11	10	⚷	30♑	0♒	1	2	♅	7♓	7	♆	15♒	16	♇	24♐	24	☊	11♈	10	10	9

2006

JAN

	1	2	3	4	5	6	7	8	9	10	11	12	13	14	15	16	17	18	19	20	21	22	23	24	25	26	27	28	29	30	31
☉	10♑	11	12	13	14	16	17	18	19	20	21	22	23	24	25	26	27	28	29	30	1♒	2	3	4	5	6	7	8	9	10	11
☽	22♑	7♒	22	7♓	21	5♈	19	3♉	16	29	12♊	24	7♋	19	1♌	13	25	7♍	19	1♎	13	25	7♏	20	3♐	17	1♑	16	1♒	16	1♓
☿	26♐	27	29	0♑	2	3	5	6	8	9	11	12	14	16	17	19	20	22	24	25	27	29	0♒	2	4	5	7	9	10	12	14
♀	0♒	30♑	30	29	29	28	28	27	27	26	26	25	24	24	23	22	22	21	21	20	20	19	19	18	18	17	17	17	17	16	16
♂	11♉	11	12	12	12	12	13	13	13	14	14	14	15	15	15	16	16	16	17	17	18	18	18	19	19	19	20	20	21	21	22
	1	6	11	16	21	26	31		1	11	21	31		1	11	21	31		1	16		1	16		1	16		1	11	21	31
♃	13♏	14	15	16	16	17	17	♄	10♌	9	8	8	⚷	2♒	3	4	4	♅	8♓	8	♆	16♒	16	♇	25♐	25	☊	9♈	8	8	7

FEB

	1	2	3	4	5	6	7	8	9	10	11	12	13	14	15	16	17	18	19	20	21	22	23	24	25	26	27	28			
☉	12♒	13	14	15	16	17	18	19	20	21	22	23	24	25	26	27	28	29	0♓	1	2	3	4	5	6	7	8	9			
☽	16♓	1♈	15	29	13♉	26	9♊	21	4♋	16	28	10♌	22	4♍	16	27	9♎	21	3♏	16	29	12♐	25	9♑	24	9♒	24	9♓			
☿	16♒	17	19	21	23	25	26	28	30	2♓	3	5	7	9	10	12	14	15	17	18	20	21	22	23	24	25	26	26			
♀	16♑	16	16	16	16	16	16	16	17	17	17	17	18	18	19	19	19	20	20	21	21	22	23	23	24	25	25	26			
♂	22♉	22	23	23	24	24	25	25	26	26	27	27	28	28	29	29	30	0♊	1	1	2	2	3	3	4	4	5	5			
	1	6	11	16	21	26			1	11	21			1	11	21			1	16		1	16		1	16		1	11	21	
♃	17♏	18	18	18	19	19		♄	8♌	7	6		⚷	4♒	5	6		♅	9♓	10	♆	17♒	18	♇	26♐	26	☊	7♈	7	6	

MAR

	1	2	3	4	5	6	7	8	9	10	11	12	13	14	15	16	17	18	19	20	21	22	23	24	25	26	27	28	29	30	31
☉	10♓	11	12	13	14	15	16	17	18	19	20	21	22	23	24	25	26	27	28	29	0♈	1	2	3	4	5	6	7	8	9	10
☽	24♓	9♈	24	8♉	22	5♊	18	1♋	13	25	7♌	19	1♍	13	24	6♎	18	1♏	13	25	8♐	21	5♑	19	3♒	17	2♓	17	2♈	17	2♉
☿	27♓	27	27	27	27	26	26	25	24	23	22	21	21	20	19	18	17	16	15	15	14	14	14	13	13	13	13	13	14	14	15
♀	27♑	27	28	29	30	1♒	1	2	3	4	5	6	6	7	8	9	10	11	12	13	14	15	16	17	18	19	20	21	22	23	24
♂	6♊	6	7	7	8	8	9	9	10	10	11	11	12	13	13	14	14	15	15	16	16	17	17	18	19	19	20	20	21	21	22
	1	6	11	16	21	26	31		1	11	21	31		1	11	21	31		1	16		1	16		1	16		1	11	21	31
♃	19♏	19	19	19	18	18	18	♄	5♌	5	5	4	⚷	7♒	7	8	9	♅	11♓	12	♆	18♒	19	♇	27♐	27	☊	6♈	5	5	4

APR

	1	2	3	4	5	6	7	8	9	10	11	12	13	14	15	16	17	18	19	20	21	22	23	24	25	26	27	28	29	30	
☉	11♈	12	13	14	15	16	17	18	19	20	21	22	23	24	25	26	27	28	29	30	1♉	2	3	4	5	6	7	8	9	10	
☽	16♉	0♊	14	27	9♋	22	4♌	16	28	9♍	21	3♎	15	27	10♏	22	5♐	18	2♑	15	29	13♒	27	12♓	26	11♈	25	10♉	24	8♊	
☿	15♓	16	16	17	18	19	19	20	21	22	23	25	26	27	28	29	1♈	2	3	5	6	8	9	11	12	14	15	17	19	20	
♀	25♒	26	27	28	29	30	1♓	2	3	4	5	6	7	8	10	11	12	13	14	15	16	17	18	19	21	22	23	24	25	26	
♂	23♊	23	24	24	25	25	26	27	27	28	28	29	29	30	1♋	1	2	2	3	3	4	5	5	6	6	7	8	8	9	9	
	1	6	11	16	21	26			1	11	21			1	11	21			1	16		1	16		1	16		1	11	21	
♃	18♏	17	17	16	16	15		♄	4♌	4	5		⚷	9♒	9	9		♅	12♓	13	♆	19♒	19	♇	27♐	27	☊	4♈	4	3	

MAY

	1	2	3	4	5	6	7	8	9	10	11	12	13	14	15	16	17	18	19	20	21	22	23	24	25	26	27	28	29	30	31
☉	10♉	11	12	13	14	15	16	17	18	19	20	21	22	23	24	25	26	27	28	29	30	1♊	2	3	4	5	6	7	8	8	9
☽	22♊	5♋	17	30	12♌	24	6♍	18	29	11♎	24	6♏	19	2♐	15	28	12♑	26	10♒	24	8♓	22	6♈	21	5♉	19	3♊	16	30	13♋	25
☿	22♈	24	26	27	29	1♉	3	5	7	9	11	13	15	17	19	22	24	26	28	0♊	2	5	7	9	11	13	15	17	20	22	23
♀	27♓	28	30	1♈	2	3	4	5	6	7	9	10	11	12	13	14	15	17	18	19	20	21	22	24	25	26	27	28	29	1♉	2
♂	10♋	10	11	12	12	13	13	14	15	15	16	16	17	18	18	19	19	20	21	21	22	22	23	24	24	25	25	26	27	27	28
	1	6	11	16	21	26	31		1	11	21	31		1	11	21	31		1	16		1	16		1	16		1	11	21	31
♃	14♏	14	13	13	12	11	11	♄	5♌	5	6	7	⚷	10♒	10	10	10	♅	14♓	14	♆	20♒	20	♇	26♐	26	☊	3♈	2	2	1

JUN

	1	2	3	4	5	6	7	8	9	10	11	12	13	14	15	16	17	18	19	20	21	22	23	24	25	26	27	28	29	30	
☉	10♊	11	12	13	14	15	16	17	18	19	20	21	22	23	24	25	26	27	28	29	30	0♋	1	2	3	4	5	6	7	8	
☽	8♌	20	2♍	14	25	7♎	19	2♏	14	27	10♐	24	8♑	22	6♒	20	5♓	19	3♈	17	1♉	15	28	12♊	25	8♋	21	4♌	16	28	
☿	25♊	27	29	1♋	3	4	6	8	9	11	12	14	15	16	18	19	20	21	22	23	24	25	26	27	28	28	29	30	0♌	0	
♀	3♉	4	5	6	8	9	10	11	12	13	15	16	17	18	19	21	22	23	24	25	26	28	29	30	1♊	2	4	5	6	7	
♂	28♋	29	30	0♌	1	1	2	3	3	4	4	5	6	6	7	7	8	9	9	10	10	11	12	12	13	13	14	15	15	16	
	1	6	11	16	21	26			1	11	21			1	11	21			1	16		1	16		1	16		1	11	21	
♃	11♏	10	10	10	9	9		♄	7♌	8	9		⚷	10♒	9	9		♅	15♓	15	♆	20♒	20	♇	26♐	25	☊	1♈	0	30♓	

2006

JUL	1	2	3	4	5	6	7	8	9	10	11	12	13	14	15	16	17	18	19	20	21	22	23	24	25	26	27	28	29	30	31
☉	9♋	10	11	12	13	14	15	16	17	18	19	20	20	21	22	23	24	25	26	27	28	29	0♌	1	2	3	4	5	6	7	8
☽	10♍	22	3♎	15	27	10♏	22	5♐	19	3♑	17	1♒	16	1♓	15	30	14♈	28	12♉	25	9♊	22	5♋	17	30	12♌	24	6♍	18	30	12♎
☿	1♌	1	1	1	1	1	1	1	1	0	30♋	29	29	28	28	27	26	26	25	24	24	23	23	22	22	21	21	21	21	21	21
♀	8♊	9	11	12	13	14	15	17	18	19	20	21	23	24	25	26	27	29	30	1♋	2	3	5	6	7	8	10	11	12	13	14
♂	17♌	17	18	18	19	20	20	21	21	22	23	23	24	25	25	26	26	27	28	28	29	30	0♍	1	1	2	3	3	4	4	5
	1	6	11	16	21	26	31		1	11	21	31		1	11	21	31		1	16		1	16		1	16		1	11	21	31
♃	9♏	9	9	9	9	10	10	♄	10♌	11	13	14	⚷	9♒	8	8	7	♅	15♓	14	♆	19♒	19	♇	25♐	25	☊	29♓	29	28	28

AUG	1	2	3	4	5	6	7	8	9	10	11	12	13	14	15	16	17	18	19	20	21	22	23	24	25	26	27	28	29	30	31
☉	9♌	10	11	12	12	13	14	15	16	17	18	19	20	21	22	23	24	25	26	27	28	29	30	1♍	2	3	4	5	6	7	7
☽	23♎	5♏	18	0♐	13	27	11♑	25	10♒	25	10♓	25	10♈	24	8♉	22	6♊	19	2♋	14	27	9♌	21	3♍	15	27	8♎	20	2♏	14	26
☿	22♋	22	22	23	24	24	25	26	27	28	30	1♌	3	4	6	7	9	11	13	15	17	18	20	22	24	26	28	0♍	2	4	6
♀	16♋	17	18	19	20	22	23	24	25	27	28	29	0♌	1	3	4	5	6	8	9	10	11	12	14	15	16	17	19	20	21	22
♂	6♍	6	7	8	8	9	10	10	11	11	12	13	13	14	15	15	16	16	17	18	18	19	20	20	21	22	22	23	23	24	25
	1	6	11	16	21	26	31		1	11	21	31		1	11	21	31		1	16		1	16		1	16		1	11	21	31
♃	10♏	10	11	11	12	13	13	♄	14♌	15	17	18	⚷	7♒	6	6	5	♅	14♓	14	♆	19♒	18	♇	24♐	24	☊	28♓	27	27	26

SEP	1	2	3	4	5	6	7	8	9	10	11	12	13	14	15	16	17	18	19	20	21	22	23	24	25	26	27	28	29	30
☉	8♍	9	10	11	12	13	14	15	16	17	18	19	20	21	22	23	24	25	26	27	28	29	30	1♎	2	3	4	5	6	7
☽	9♐	22	5♑	19	3♒	18	3♓	18	4♈	19	3♉	18	2♊	15	28	11♋	24	6♌	18	30	12♍	24	5♎	17	29	11♏	23	6♐	18	1♑
☿	8♍	10	12	14	16	18	20	21	23	25	27	28	0♎	2	4	5	7	9	10	12	13	15	16	18	20	21	23	24	25	27
♀	24♌	25	26	27	28	30	1♍	2	3	5	6	7	8	10	11	12	13	15	16	17	18	20	21	22	23	24	26	27	28	29
♂	25♍	26	27	27	28	29	29	30	1♎	1	2	2	3	4	4	5	6	6	7	8	8	9	10	10	11	12	12	13	14	14
	1	6	11	16	21	26			1	11	21			1	11	21			1	16		1	16		1	16		1	11	21
♃	13♏	14	15	16	17	18		♄	18♌	19	20		⚷	5♒	5	5		♅	13♓	12	♆	18♒	18	♇	24♐	24	☊	26♓	26	25

OCT	1	2	3	4	5	6	7	8	9	10	11	12	13	14	15	16	17	18	19	20	21	22	23	24	25	26	27	28	29	30	31
☉	8♎	9	10	11	12	13	14	15	16	17	18	19	20	21	21	22	23	24	25	26	27	28	29	0♏	1	2	3	4	5	6	7
☽	14♑	28	12♒	27	11♓	26	12♈	27	12♉	26	11♊	24	7♋	20	3♌	15	27	9♍	21	2♎	14	26	8♏	20	3♐	15	28	11♑	24	8♒	22
☿	28♎	30	1♏	2	4	5	6	8	9	10	11	13	14	15	16	17	18	19	20	21	22	22	23	24	24	25	25	25	25	25	25
♀	1♎	2	3	4	6	7	8	9	11	12	13	14	16	17	18	19	21	22	23	24	26	27	28	29	1♏	2	3	4	6	7	8
♂	15♎	16	16	17	18	18	19	20	20	21	21	22	23	23	24	25	26	26	27	28	28	29	30	0♏	1	2	2	3	4	4	5
	1	6	11	16	21	26	31		1	11	21	31		1	11	21	31		1	16		1	16		1	16		1	11	21	31
♃	18♏	19	20	21	23	24	25	♄	21♌	22	23	24	⚷	4♒	4	4	5	♅	12♓	11	♆	17♒	17	♇	24♐	25	☊	25♓	24	23	23

NOV	1	2	3	4	5	6	7	8	9	10	11	12	13	14	15	16	17	18	19	20	21	22	23	24	25	26	27	28	29	30
☉	8♏	9	10	11	12	13	14	15	16	17	18	19	20	21	22	23	24	25	27	28	29	30	1♐	2	3	4	5	6	7	8
☽	6♓	20	5♈	20	5♉	20	4♊	19	2♋	16	29	11♌	23	5♍	17	29	11♎	23	5♏	17	29	12♐	25	8♑	21	5♒	18	2♓	16	0♈
☿	24♏	24	23	22	21	20	19	18	16	15	14	12	11	11	10	9	9	9	9	9	10	10	11	12	13	14	15	16	17	19
♀	10♏	11	12	13	15	16	17	18	20	21	22	23	25	26	27	28	30	1♐	2	3	5	6	7	8	10	11	12	13	15	16
♂	6♏	6	7	8	8	9	10	10	11	12	12	13	14	15	15	16	17	17	18	19	19	20	21	21	22	23	24	24	25	26
	1	6	11	16	21	26			1	11	21			1	11	21			1	16		1	16		1	16		1	11	21
♃	25♏	26	27	28	29	0♐		♄	24♌	24	25		⚷	5♒	5	5		♅	11♓	11	♆	17♒	17	♇	25♐	25	☊	23♓	22	22

DEC	1	2	3	4	5	6	7	8	9	10	11	12	13	14	15	16	17	18	19	20	21	22	23	24	25	26	27	28	29	30	31
☉	9♐	10	11	12	13	14	15	16	17	18	19	20	21	22	23	24	25	26	27	28	29	30	1♑	2	3	4	5	6	7	8	9
☽	15♈	29	14♉	28	12♊	27	10♋	24	6♌	19	1♍	13	25	7♎	19	1♏	13	25	8♐	21	4♑	18	1♒	15	29	13♓	27	11♈	25	9♉	23
☿	20♏	21	22	24	25	27	28	30	1♐	3	4	6	7	9	10	12	13	15	16	18	19	21	22	24	26	27	29	0♑	2	3	5
♀	17♐	18	20	21	22	23	25	26	27	28	30	1♑	2	3	5	6	7	8	10	11	12	14	15	16	17	19	20	21	22	24	25
♂	26♏	27	28	28	29	30	1♐	1	2	3	3	4	5	6	6	7	8	8	9	10	11	11	12	13	13	14	15	16	16	17	18
	1	6	11	16	21	26	31		1	11	21	31		1	11	21	31		1	16		1	16		1	16		1	11	21	31
♃	2♐	3	4	5	6	7	8	♄	25♌	25	25	25	⚷	6♒	6	7	8	♅	11♓	11	♆	17♒	18	♇	26♐	26	☊	21♓	21	20	20

2007

JAN

	1	2	3	4	5	6	7	8	9	10	11	12	13	14	15	16	17	18	19	20	21	22	23	24	25	26	27	28	29	30	31
☉	10♑	11	12	13	14	15	16	17	18	19	20	21	22	23	24	25	26	27	29	30	1♒	2	3	4	5	6	7	8	9	10	11
☽	7♊	21	5♋	18	1♌	14	27	9♍	21	3♎	15	26	8♏	21	3♐	16	29	12♑	26	10♒	25	9♓	23	8♈	22	6♉	20	4♊	18	1♋	14
☿	7♑	8	10	11	13	15	16	18	19	21	23	24	26	28	29	1♒	3	4	6	8	10	11	13	15	16	18	20	21	23	25	26
♀	26♑	27	29	30	1♒	2	4	5	6	7	9	10	11	12	14	15	16	17	19	20	21	22	24	25	26	27	29	30	1♓	2	4
♂	18♐	19	20	21	21	22	23	24	24	25	26	26	27	28	29	29	0♑	1	2	2	3	4	5	5	6	7	7	8	9	10	10
	1	6	11	16	21	26	31		1	11	21	31		1	11	21	31		1	16		1	16		1	16		1	11	21	31
♃	8♐	9	10	11	12	13	14	♄	24♌	24	23	23	⚷	8♒	9	9	10	♅	12♓	12	♆	18♒	19	♇	27♐	28	☊	20♓	19	19	18

FEB

	1	2	3	4	5	6	7	8	9	10	11	12	13	14	15	16	17	18	19	20	21	22	23	24	25	26	27	28			
☉	12♒	13	14	15	16	17	18	19	20	21	22	23	24	25	26	27	28	29	30	1♓	2	3	4	5	6	7	8	9			
☽	27♋	10♌	22	5♍	17	29	11♎	23	4♏	16	28	11♐	24	7♑	20	4♒	19	3♓	18	3♈	18	2♉	17	1♊	14	28	11♋	24			
☿	28♒	29	1♓	2	4	5	6	7	8	9	9	10	10	10	10	10	10	9	8	7	6	5	4	3	2	1	0	29♒			
♀	5♓	6	7	9	10	11	12	13	15	16	17	18	20	21	22	23	25	26	27	28	30	1♈	2	3	4	6	7	8			
♂	11♑	12	13	13	14	15	16	16	17	18	19	19	20	21	22	22	23	24	25	25	26	27	28	28	29	30	1♒	1			
	1	6	11	16	21	26			1	11	21			1	11	21			1	16		1	16		1	16		1	11	21	
♃	14♐	15	16	16	17	17		♄	22♌	22	21		⚷	10♒	11	12		♅	13♓	14	♆	19♒	20	♇	28♐	28	☊	18♓	17	17	

MAR

	1	2	3	4	5	6	7	8	9	10	11	12	13	14	15	16	17	18	19	20	21	22	23	24	25	26	27	28	29	30	31
☉	10♓	11	12	13	14	15	16	17	18	19	20	21	22	23	24	25	26	27	28	29	30	1♈	2	3	4	5	6	7	8	9	10
☽	7♌	19	1♍	13	25	7♎	19	1♏	13	25	7♐	19	2♑	15	28	12♒	27	11♓	26	12♈	27	12♉	26	11♊	24	8♋	21	4♌	16	28	10♍
☿	28♒	28	27	26	26	26	25	25	25	26	26	26	27	27	28	28	29	30	0♓	1	2	3	4	5	6	8	9	10	11	12	14
♀	9♈	11	12	13	14	16	17	18	19	20	22	23	24	25	26	28	29	0♉	1	3	4	5	6	7	9	10	11	12	13	15	16
♂	2♒	3	4	4	5	6	7	8	8	9	10	11	11	12	13	14	14	15	16	17	17	18	19	20	21	21	22	23	24	24	25
	1	6	11	16	21	26	31		1	11	21	31		1	11	21	31		1	16		1	16		1	16		1	11	21	31
♃	18♐	18	19	19	19	20	20	♄	20♌	20	19	19	⚷	12♒	13	14	14	♅	14♓	15	♆	20♒	21	♇	29♐	29	☊	17♓	16	15	15

APR

	1	2	3	4	5	6	7	8	9	10	11	12	13	14	15	16	17	18	19	20	21	22	23	24	25	26	27	28	29	30	
☉	11♈	12	13	14	15	16	17	18	19	20	21	22	23	24	25	26	27	28	29	30	1♉	1	2	3	4	5	6	7	8	9	
☽	22♍	4♎	16	28	10♏	22	4♐	16	28	11♑	24	7♒	21	5♓	20	5♈	20	5♉	20	5♊	20	4♋	17	0♌	13	25	7♍	19	1♎	13	
☿	15♓	17	18	19	21	22	24	25	27	28	0♈	2	3	5	7	8	10	12	14	16	18	19	21	23	25	27	29	1♉	4	6	
♀	17♉	18	19	20	22	23	24	25	26	28	29	30	1♊	2	3	5	6	7	8	9	10	12	13	14	15	16	17	18	20	21	
♂	26♒	27	27	28	29	30	0♓	1	2	3	4	4	5	6	7	7	8	9	10	10	11	12	13	14	14	15	16	17	17	18	
	1	6	11	16	21	26			1	11	21			1	11	21			1	16		1	16		1	16		1	11	21	
♃	20♐	20	20	20	19	19		♄	18♌	18	18		⚷	14♒	15	15		♅	16♓	17	♆	21♒	22	♇	29♐	29	☊	15♓	14	14	

MAY

	1	2	3	4	5	6	7	8	9	10	11	12	13	14	15	16	17	18	19	20	21	22	23	24	25	26	27	28	29	30	31
☉	10♉	11	12	13	14	15	16	17	18	19	20	21	22	23	24	25	26	27	28	29	30	1♊	2	2	3	4	5	6	7	8	9
☽	25♎	7♏	19	1♐	13	25	8♑	20	3♒	17	0♓	14	29	13♈	28	13♉	28	13♊	28	12♋	26	9♌	21	4♍	16	28	10♎	22	3♏	15	27
☿	8♉	10	12	14	16	18	21	23	25	27	29	1♊	3	5	7	9	11	13	15	17	18	20	22	23	25	26	27	29	30	1♋	2
♀	22♊	23	24	25	26	27	29	30	1♋	2	3	4	5	6	7	8	10	11	12	13	14	15	16	17	18	19	20	21	22	23	24
♂	19♓	20	20	21	22	23	23	24	25	26	27	27	28	29	30	0♈	1	2	3	3	4	5	6	6	7	8	9	9	10	11	12
	1	6	11	16	21	26	31		1	11	21	31		1	11	21	31		1	16		1	16		1	16		1	11	21	31
♃	19♐	18	18	17	17	16	16	♄	18♌	19	19	20	⚷	15♒	16	16	16	♅	18♓	18	♆	22♒	22	♇	29♐	28	☊	13♓	13	12	12

JUN

	1	2	3	4	5	6	7	8	9	10	11	12	13	14	15	16	17	18	19	20	21	22	23	24	25	26	27	28	29	30	
☉	10♊	11	12	13	14	15	16	17	18	19	20	21	22	23	24	25	25	26	27	28	29	0♋	1	2	3	4	5	6	7	8	
☽	10♐	22	5♑	17	0♒	14	27	11♓	24	9♈	23	8♉	22	7♊	22	6♋	20	4♌	17	30	12♍	24	6♎	18	30	12♏	24	6♐	18	1♑	
☿	3♋	4	5	6	7	8	9	9	10	10	11	11	11	11	12	12	12	11	11	11	11	10	10	9	9	8	8	7	7	6	
♀	25♋	26	27	28	29	0♌	1	2	3	4	5	6	7	8	9	10	11	11	12	13	14	15	16	17	17	18	19	20	20	21	
♂	12♈	13	14	15	15	16	17	18	18	19	20	21	21	22	23	24	24	25	26	26	27	28	29	29	0♉	1	2	2	3	4	
	1	6	11	16	21	26			1	11	21			1	11	21			1	16		1	16		1	16		1	11	21	
♃	16♐	15	14	14	13	12		♄	20♌	20	21		⚷	16♒	15	15		♅	18♓	19	♆	22♒	22	♇	28♐	28	☊	12♓	11	11	

2007

EPHEMERIS

JUL

	1	2	3	4	5	6	7	8	9	10	11	12	13	14	15	16	17	18	19	20	21	22	23	24	25	26	27	28	29	30	31
☉	9♋	10	11	12	13	14	15	15	16	17	18	19	20	21	22	23	24	25	26	27	28	29	30	1♌	2	3	4	5	6	6	7
☽	14♑	27	10♒	24	7♓	21	5♈	19	4♉	18	2♊	17	1♋	15	28	12♌	25	8♍	20	2♎	14	26	8♏	20	2♐	14	27	9♑	23	6♒	20
☿	5♋	5	4	4	3	3	3	3	3	2	3	3	3	3	4	4	5	5	6	7	8	9	10	11	12	14	15	16	18	20	21
♀	22♌	23	23	24	25	25	26	27	27	28	28	29	29	30	0♍	1	1	1	2	2	2	2	3	3	3	3	3	3	3	3	3
♂	4♉	5	6	7	7	8	9	9	10	11	12	12	13	14	14	15	16	16	17	18	18	19	20	21	21	22	23	23	24	25	25
	1	6	11	16	21	26	31		1	11	21	31		1	11	21	31		1	16		1	16		1	16		1	11	21	31
♃	12♐	11	11	11	10	10	10	♄	22♌	23	25	26	⚷	15♒	14	14	13	♅	19♓	18	♆	22♒	21	♇	27♐	27	☊	10♓	10	9	8

AUG

	1	2	3	4	5	6	7	8	9	10	11	12	13	14	15	16	17	18	19	20	21	22	23	24	25	26	27	28	29	30	31
☉	8♌	9	10	11	12	13	14	15	16	17	18	19	20	21	22	23	24	25	26	27	28	29	30	0♍	1	2	3	4	5	6	7
☽	4♓	18	2♈	16	0♉	15	29	13♊	27	11♋	24	7♌	20	3♍	16	28	10♎	22	4♏	16	28	10♐	22	5♑	17	1♒	14	28	13♓	27	12♈
☿	23♋	25	27	29	1♌	3	5	7	9	11	13	15	17	19	21	23	25	27	29	1♍	3	5	7	8	10	12	14	16	17	19	21
♀	3♍	2	2	2	2	1	1	0	0	30♌	29	29	28	27	27	26	26	25	24	24	23	22	22	21	21	20	20	19	19	18	18
♂	26♉	27	27	28	29	29	30	0♊	1	2	2	3	4	4	5	6	6	7	7	8	9	9	10	11	11	12	12	13	14	14	15
	1	6	11	16	21	26	31		1	11	21	31		1	11	21	31		1	16		1	16		1	16		1	11	21	31
♃	10♐	10	10	10	10	10	11	♄	26♌	27	28	30	⚷	13♒	13	12	12	♅	18♓	18	♆	21♒	21	♇	27♐	26	☊	8♓	8	7	7

SEP

	1	2	3	4	5	6	7	8	9	10	11	12	13	14	15	16	17	18	19	20	21	22	23	24	25	26	27	28	29	30
☉	8♍	9	10	11	12	13	14	15	16	17	18	19	20	21	22	23	24	25	26	27	28	29	30	1♎	2	3	4	4	5	6
☽	27♈	11♉	26	10♊	24	7♋	21	4♌	17	29	12♍	24	6♎	18	0♏	12	24	6♐	18	0♑	13	25	9♒	22	7♓	21	6♈	21	6♉	21
☿	23♍	24	26	28	29	1♎	2	4	5	7	8	10	11	13	14	16	17	18	20	21	22	23	25	26	27	28	29	0♏	1	2
♀	18♌	17	17	17	17	17	17	17	17	17	17	17	17	17	17	18	18	18	19	19	19	20	20	21	21	22	22	23	23	24
♂	15♊	16	16	17	18	18	19	19	20	20	21	21	22	23	23	24	24	25	25	26	26	27	27	28	28	29	29	30	0♋	0
	1	6	11	16	21	26			1	11	21			1	11	21			1	16		1	16		1	16		1	11	21
♃	11♐	11	12	12	13	14		♄	30♌	1♍	2		⚷	12♒	11	11		♅	17♓	16	♆	20♒	20	♇	26♐	26	☊	7♓	6	6

OCT

	1	2	3	4	5	6	7	8	9	10	11	12	13	14	15	16	17	18	19	20	21	22	23	24	25	26	27	28	29	30	31
☉	7♎	8	9	10	11	12	13	14	15	16	17	18	19	20	21	22	23	24	25	26	27	28	29	0♏	1	2	3	4	5	6	7
☽	6♊	20	4♋	18	1♌	14	26	9♍	21	3♎	15	27	9♏	21	2♐	14	26	9♑	21	4♒	17	1♓	15	29	14♈	29	15♉	30	15♊	29	14♋
☿	3♏	4	5	6	6	7	8	8	9	9	9	9	9	9	9	8	8	7	6	5	4	3	1	0	29♎	28	27	26	25	24	24
♀	25♌	25	26	27	28	28	29	30	1♍	1	2	3	4	5	6	6	7	8	9	10	11	12	13	14	15	16	17	18	19	20	21
♂	1♋	1	2	2	3	3	3	4	4	5	5	5	6	6	6	7	7	7	8	8	8	9	9	9	10	10	10	10	10	11	11
	1	6	11	16	21	26	31		1	11	21	31		1	11	21	31		1	16		1	16		1	16		1	11	21	31
♃	14♐	15	16	17	18	18	19	♄	3♍	5	6	6	⚷	11♒	11	10	11	♅	16♓	15	♆	20♒	19	♇	26♐	27	☊	5♓	5	4	4

NOV

	1	2	3	4	5	6	7	8	9	10	11	12	13	14	15	16	17	18	19	20	21	22	23	24	25	26	27	28	29	30
☉	8♏	9	10	11	12	13	14	15	16	17	18	19	20	21	22	23	24	25	26	27	28	29	0♐	1	2	3	4	5	6	7
☽	27♋	11♌	23	6♍	18	0♎	12	24	6♏	18	30	11♐	23	6♑	18	0♒	13	26	9♓	23	8♈	22	7♉	23	8♊	23	8♋	22	6♌	19
☿	23♎	23	23	24	24	25	26	26	27	28	30	1♏	2	3	5	6	8	9	11	12	14	15	17	18	20	21	23	24	26	28
♀	22♍	23	24	25	26	27	28	29	0♎	1	2	3	4	6	7	8	9	10	11	12	13	14	16	17	18	19	20	21	22	24
♂	11♋	11	11	12	12	12	12	12	12	12	12	12	12	12	12	12	12	12	12	12	12	12	12	12	12	12	11	11	11	11
	1	6	11	16	21	26			1	11	21			1	11	21			1	16		1	16		1	16		1	11	21
♃	20♐	21	22	23	24	25		♄	6♍	7	8		⚷	11♒	11	11		♅	15♓	15	♆	19♒	19	♇	27♐	28	☊	4♓	3	3

DEC

	1	2	3	4	5	6	7	8	9	10	11	12	13	14	15	16	17	18	19	20	21	22	23	24	25	26	27	28	29	30	31
☉	8♐	9	10	11	12	13	14	15	17	18	19	20	21	22	23	24	25	26	27	28	29	30	1♑	2	3	4	5	6	7	8	9
☽	2♍	15	27	9♎	21	3♏	15	26	8♐	20	3♑	15	27	10♒	23	6♓	19	3♈	17	1♉	16	1♊	16	1♋	16	0♌	14	27	10♍	23	5♎
☿	29♏	1♐	2	4	5	7	9	10	12	13	15	16	18	20	21	23	24	26	27	29	1♑	2	4	5	7	9	10	12	13	15	17
♀	25♎	26	27	28	29	1♏	2	3	4	5	6	8	9	10	11	12	13	15	16	17	18	19	21	22	23	24	25	27	28	29	0♐
♂	11♋	10	10	10	10	9	9	9	9	8	8	8	7	7	6	6	6	5	5	5	4	4	3	3	3	2	2	1	1	1	0
	1	6	11	16	21	26	31		1	11	21	31		1	11	21	31		1	16		1	16		1	16		1	11	21	31
♃	26♐	27	28	29	0♑	2	3	♄	8♍	8	9	8	⚷	11♒	12	13	13	♅	15♓	15	♆	20♒	20	♇	28♐	29	☊	2♓	1	1	0

2008

EPHEMERIS

JAN

	1	2	3	4	5	6	7	8	9	10	11	12	13	14	15	16	17	18	19	20	21	22	23	24	25	26	27	28	29	30	31
☉	10♑	11	12	13	14	15	16	17	18	19	20	21	22	23	24	25	26	27	28	29	0♒	1	2	3	4	5	6	7	8	9	10
☽	17♎	29	11♏	23	5♐	17	29	11♑	24	7♒	20	3♓	16	30	14♈	28	12♉	26	11♊	25	10♋	24	8♌	22	5♍	18	1♎	13	25	7♏	19
☿	18♑	20	22	23	25	26	28	30	1♒	3	5	6	8	9	11	12	14	15	16	18	19	20	21	22	23	23	24	24	24	24	23
♀	2♐	3	4	5	6	8	9	10	11	12	14	15	16	17	19	20	21	22	23	25	26	27	28	30	1♑	2	3	4	6	7	8
♂	30♊	30	29	29	28	28	28	28	27	27	27	26	26	26	26	26	25	25	25	25	25	25	24	24	24	24	24	24	24	24	24
	1	6	11	16	21	26	31		1	11	21	31		1	11	21	31		1	16		1	16		1	16		1	11	21	31
♃	3♑	4	5	6	8	9	10	♄	8♍	8	8	7	⚷	13♒	14	15	15	♅	15♓	16	♆	20♒	21	♇	29♐	30	☊	0♓	30♒	29	29

FEB

	1	2	3	4	5	6	7	8	9	10	11	12	13	14	15	16	17	18	19	20	21	22	23	24	25	26	27	28	29		
☉	11♒	13	14	15	16	17	18	19	20	21	22	23	24	25	26	27	28	29	30	1♓	2	3	4	5	6	7	8	9	10		
☽	1♐	13	25	7♑	20	3♒	16	29	13♓	26	10♈	24	9♉	23	7♊	21	5♋	19	3♌	17	30	13♍	26	8♎	21	3♏	15	27	9♐		
☿	23♒	22	21	20	19	18	17	16	15	14	12	12	11	10	9	9	9	8	8	8	9	9	9	10	10	11	11	12	13		
♀	9♑	11	12	13	14	16	17	18	19	21	22	23	24	25	27	28	29	0♒	2	3	4	5	7	8	9	10	12	13	14		
♂	24♊	24	24	24	24	24	24	24	25	25	25	25	25	25	25	26	26	26	26	26	27	27	27	27	28	28	28	28	29		
	1	6	11	16	21	26			1	11	21			1	11	21			1	16		1	16		1	16		1	11	21	
♃	10♑	11	12	13	14	15		♄	7♍	6	5		⚷	15♒	16	17		♅	17♓	17	♆	21♒	22	♇	0♑	1	☊	29♒	28	28	

MAR

	1	2	3	4	5	6	7	8	9	10	11	12	13	14	15	16	17	18	19	20	21	22	23	24	25	26	27	28	29	30	31
☉	11♓	12	13	14	15	16	17	18	19	20	21	22	23	24	25	26	27	28	29	30	1♈	2	3	4	5	6	7	8	9	10	11
☽	21♐	3♑	15	28	11♒	24	7♓	21	6♈	20	5♉	19	4♊	18	2♋	16	29	13♌	26	9♍	22	4♎	17	29	11♏	23	5♐	17	29	11♑	23
☿	14♒	15	16	17	18	19	20	21	22	24	25	26	27	29	0♓	1	3	4	6	7	9	10	12	13	15	17	18	20	22	23	25
♀	15♒	16	18	19	20	21	23	24	25	26	28	29	0♓	1	3	4	5	6	7	9	10	11	12	14	15	16	17	19	20	21	22
♂	29♊	29	30	30	0♋	1	1	1	2	2	2	3	3	3	4	4	4	5	5	6	6	6	7	7	8	8	9	9	9	10	10
	1	6	11	16	21	26	31		1	11	21	31		1	11	21	31		1	16		1	16		1	16		1	11	21	31
♃	16♑	16	17	18	19	19	20	♄	5♍	4	3	3	⚷	18♒	18	19	20	♅	18♓	19	♆	22♒	23	♇	1♑	1	☊	27♒	27	26	26

APR

	1	2	3	4	5	6	7	8	9	10	11	12	13	14	15	16	17	18	19	20	21	22	23	24	25	26	27	28	29	30	
☉	12♈	13	14	15	16	17	18	19	20	21	21	22	23	24	25	26	27	28	29	0♉	1	2	3	4	5	6	7	8	9	10	
☽	5♒	18	2♓	16	30	14♈	29	14♉	29	14♊	28	13♋	26	10♌	23	6♍	18	1♎	13	25	8♏	20	1♐	13	25	7♑	19	1♒	14	27	
☿	27♓	29	0♈	2	4	6	8	10	12	14	16	18	20	22	24	26	28	0♉	2	4	7	9	11	13	15	17	19	21	23	25	
♀	24♓	25	26	27	28	30	1♈	2	3	5	6	7	8	10	11	12	13	15	16	17	18	19	21	22	23	24	26	27	28	29	
♂	11♋	11	12	12	13	13	13	14	14	15	15	16	16	17	17	18	18	19	19	20	20	21	21	22	22	23	23	24	24	25	
	1	6	11	16	21	26			1	11	21			1	11	21			1	16		1	16		1	16		1	11	21	
♃	20♑	21	21	22	22	22		♄	3♍	2	2		⚷	20♒	20	21		♅	20♓	21	♆	23♒	24	♇	1♑	1	☊	26♒	25	24	

MAY

	1	2	3	4	5	6	7	8	9	10	11	12	13	14	15	16	17	18	19	20	21	22	23	24	25	26	27	28	29	30	31
☉	11♉	12	13	14	15	16	17	18	19	20	21	22	23	24	25	26	26	27	28	29	0♊	1	2	3	4	5	6	7	8	9	10
☽	10♓	24	8♈	23	8♉	23	8♊	23	8♋	22	6♌	20	3♍	16	28	10♎	22	4♏	16	28	10♐	22	4♑	16	28	10♒	23	6♓	19	2♈	16
☿	27♉	29	0♊	2	4	5	7	8	9	11	12	13	14	15	16	17	18	19	19	20	20	21	21	21	21	22	22	21	21	21	21
♀	1♉	2	3	4	5	7	8	9	10	12	13	14	15	17	18	19	20	21	23	24	25	26	28	29	0♊	1	3	4	5	6	7
♂	25♋	26	26	27	27	28	28	29	30	0♌	1	1	2	2	3	3	4	4	5	6	6	7	7	8	8	9	9	10	11	11	12
	1	6	11	16	21	26	31		1	11	21	31		1	11	21	31		1	16		1	16		1	16		1	11	21	31
♃	22♑	22	22	22	22	22	22	♄	2♍	2	2	2	⚷	21♒	21	21	21	♅	21♓	22	♆	24♒	24	♇	1♑	1	☊	24♒	23	23	22

JUN

	1	2	3	4	5	6	7	8	9	10	11	12	13	14	15	16	17	18	19	20	21	22	23	24	25	26	27	28	29	30	
☉	11♊	12	13	14	15	16	17	18	19	19	20	21	22	23	24	25	26	27	28	29	30	1♋	2	3	4	5	6	7	8	9	
☽	1♉	16	1♊	17	2♋	17	1♌	15	29	12♍	25	7♎	19	2♏	13	25	7♐	19	1♑	13	25	7♒	20	2♓	15	28	12♈	26	10♉	25	
☿	21♊	20	20	19	19	18	18	17	16	16	15	15	14	14	14	13	13	13	13	13	13	13	13	14	14	15	15	16	16	17	
♀	9♊	10	11	12	14	15	16	17	18	20	21	22	23	25	26	27	28	30	1♋	2	3	4	6	7	8	9	11	12	13	14	
♂	12♌	13	13	14	14	15	16	16	17	17	18	18	19	20	20	21	21	22	23	23	24	24	25	25	26	27	27	28	28	29	
	1	6	11	16	21	26			1	11	21			1	11	21			1	16		1	16		1	16		1	11	21	
♃	22♑	21	21	20	20	19		♄	2♍	3	4		⚷	21♒	21	21		♅	22♓	23	♆	24♒	24	♇	0♑	30♐	☊	22♒	22	21	

2008

EPHEMERIS

JUL

	1	2	3	4	5	6	7	8	9	10	11	12	13	14	15	16	17	18	19	20	21	22	23	24	25	26	27	28	29	30	31
☉	10♋	10	11	12	13	14	15	16	17	18	19	20	21	22	23	24	25	26	27	28	29	30	1♌	1	2	3	4	5	6	7	8
☽	10♊	25	10♋	25	9♌	24	7♍	21	3♎	16	28	10♏	22	4♐	16	28	10♑	22	4♒	17	29	12♓	25	9♈	22	6♉	20	5♊	19	4♋	19
☿	18♊	19	20	21	22	23	25	26	27	29	0♋	2	3	5	7	9	11	13	14	16	19	21	23	25	27	29	1♌	3	5	7	9
♀	16♋	17	18	19	20	22	23	24	25	27	28	29	0♌	2	3	4	5	6	8	9	10	11	13	14	15	16	17	19	20	21	22
♂	30♌	0♍	1	1	2	3	3	4	4	5	6	6	7	7	8	9	9	10	10	11	12	12	13	13	14	15	15	16	17	17	18
	1	6	11	16	21	26	31		1	11	21	31		1	11	21	31		1	16		1	16		1	16		1	11	21	31
♃	19♑	18	17	17	16	15	15	♄	5♍	5	7	8	⚷	20♒	20	20	19	♅	23♓	23	♆	24♒	24	♇	30♐	29	☊	21♒	20	20	19

AUG

	1	2	3	4	5	6	7	8	9	10	11	12	13	14	15	16	17	18	19	20	21	22	23	24	25	26	27	28	29	30	31
☉	9♌	10	11	12	13	14	15	16	17	18	19	20	21	22	23	24	24	25	26	27	28	29	0♍	1	2	3	4	5	6	7	8
☽	3♌	18	2♍	15	29	12♎	24	6♏	18	0♐	12	24	6♑	18	1♒	13	26	9♓	22	6♈	19	3♉	17	1♊	16	30	14♋	28	12♌	26	10♍
☿	12♌	14	16	18	20	22	24	25	27	29	1♍	3	5	6	8	10	11	13	15	16	18	20	21	23	24	26	27	28	30	1♎	3
♀	24♌	25	26	27	29	30	1♍	2	3	5	6	7	8	10	11	12	13	15	16	17	18	19	21	22	23	24	26	27	28	29	0♎
♂	18♍	19	20	20	21	22	22	23	23	24	25	25	26	27	27	28	28	29	30	0♎	1	2	2	3	4	4	5	5	6	7	7
	1	6	11	16	21	26	31		1	11	21	31		1	11	21	31		1	16		1	16		1	16		1	11	21	31
♃	15♑	14	14	13	13	13	13	♄	8♍	9	10	11	⚷	19♒	19	18	18	♅	22♓	22	♆	23♒	23	♇	29♐	29	☊	19♒	19	18	17

SEP

	1	2	3	4	5	6	7	8	9	10	11	12	13	14	15	16	17	18	19	20	21	22	23	24	25	26	27	28	29	30	
☉	9♍	10	11	12	13	14	15	16	17	18	19	20	21	22	23	23	24	25	26	27	28	29	0♎	1	2	3	4	5	6	7	
☽	24♍	7♎	20	2♏	14	26	8♐	20	2♑	14	26	9♒	21	4♓	18	1♈	15	29	14♉	28	12♊	27	11♋	25	8♌	22	6♍	19	2♎	15	
☿	4♎	5	6	8	9	10	11	12	13	14	15	16	17	18	19	20	20	21	21	22	22	23	23	23	23	23	22	22	22	21	
♀	2♎	3	4	5	7	8	9	10	12	13	14	15	16	18	19	20	21	23	24	25	26	27	29	30	1♏	2	4	5	6	7	
♂	8♎	9	9	10	11	11	12	13	13	14	15	15	16	17	17	18	19	19	20	21	21	22	22	23	24	24	25	26	27	27	
	1	6	11	16	21	26			1	11	21			1	11	21			1	16		1	16		1	16		1	11	21	
♃	13♑	13	13	13	13	13		♄	12♍	13	14		⚷	17♒	17	17		♅	21♓	21	♆	22♒	22	♇	29♐	29	☊	17♒	17	16	

OCT

	1	2	3	4	5	6	7	8	9	10	11	12	13	14	15	16	17	18	19	20	21	22	23	24	25	26	27	28	29	30	31
☉	8♎	9	10	11	12	13	14	15	16	17	18	19	20	21	22	23	24	25	26	27	28	29	30	1♏	2	3	4	5	6	7	8
☽	28♎	10♏	22	4♐	16	28	10♑	22	4♒	16	29	12♓	26	10♈	24	9♉	24	8♊	23	7♋	22	5♌	19	2♍	16	28	11♎	24	6♏	19	1♐
☿	20♎	19	18	17	16	15	14	13	12	11	10	9	8	8	8	8	8	8	8	9	10	11	12	13	14	15	17	18	20	21	23
♀	8♏	10	11	12	13	14	16	17	18	19	21	22	23	24	25	27	28	29	0♐	1	3	4	5	6	8	9	10	11	12	14	15
♂	28♎	29	29	30	1♏	1	2	3	3	4	5	5	6	7	7	8	9	9	10	11	11	12	13	14	14	15	16	16	17	18	18
	1	6	11	16	21	26	31		1	11	21	31		1	11	21	31		1	16		1	16		1	16		1	11	21	31
♃	13♑	14	14	15	15	16	17	♄	15♍	16	18	19	⚷	16♒	16	16	16	♅	20♓	19	♆	22♒	22	♇	29♐	29	☊	16♒	15	15	14

NOV

	1	2	3	4	5	6	7	8	9	10	11	12	13	14	15	16	17	18	19	20	21	22	23	24	25	26	27	28	29	30	
☉	9♏	10	11	12	13	14	15	16	17	18	19	20	21	22	23	24	25	26	27	28	29	0♐	1	2	3	4	5	6	7	8	
☽	13♐	24	6♑	18	30	12♒	24	7♓	20	4♈	18	2♉	17	2♊	18	3♋	17	2♌	16	29	13♍	26	8♎	21	3♏	15	27	9♐	21	3♑	
☿	24♎	26	27	29	1♏	2	4	5	7	9	10	12	14	15	17	18	20	22	23	25	26	28	30	1♐	3	4	6	7	9	11	
♀	16♐	17	18	20	21	22	23	24	26	27	28	29	0♑	2	3	4	5	6	8	9	10	11	12	14	15	16	17	18	19	21	
♂	19♏	20	21	21	22	23	23	24	25	25	26	27	28	28	29	30	0♐	1	2	3	3	4	5	5	6	7	8	8	9	10	
	1	6	11	16	21	26			1	11	21			1	11	21			1	16		1	16		1	16		1	11	21	
♃	17♑	18	18	19	20	21		♄	19♍	20	20		⚷	16♒	16	16		♅	19♓	19	♆	21♒	22	♇	29♐	30	☊	14♒	14	13	

DEC

	1	2	3	4	5	6	7	8	9	10	11	12	13	14	15	16	17	18	19	20	21	22	23	24	25	26	27	28	29	30	31
☉	9♐	10	11	12	13	14	15	16	17	18	19	20	21	22	23	24	25	26	27	28	29	1♑	2	3	4	5	6	7	8	9	10
☽	15♑	27	9♒	21	3♓	15	28	12♈	26	10♉	25	10♊	26	11♋	26	11♌	25	9♍	22	5♎	18	0♏	12	24	6♐	18	0♑	12	24	6♒	18
☿	12♐	14	15	17	18	20	22	23	25	26	28	29	1♑	2	4	6	7	9	10	12	13	15	16	18	20	21	23	24	25	27	28
♀	22♑	23	24	25	27	28	29	0♒	1	2	4	5	6	7	8	9	10	12	13	14	15	16	17	18	19	21	22	23	24	25	26
♂	11♐	11	12	13	13	14	15	16	16	17	18	19	19	20	21	22	22	23	24	25	25	26	27	28	28	29	30	1♑	1	2	3
	1	6	11	16	21	26	31		1	11	21	31		1	11	21	31		1	16		1	16		1	16		1	11	21	31
♃	22♑	23	24	25	26	28	29	♄	21♍	21	22	22	⚷	17♒	17	18	18	♅	19♓	19	♆	22♒	22	♇	0♑	1	☊	13♒	12	12	11

2009

EPHEMERIS

JAN

	1	2	3	4	5	6	7	8	9	10	11	12	13	14	15	16	17	18	19	20	21	22	23	24	25	26	27	28	29	30	31
☉	11♑	12	13	14	15	16	17	18	19	20	21	22	23	24	25	26	27	28	29	0♒	1	2	3	4	5	6	7	8	9	10	11
☽	30♒	12♓	25	8♈	21	5♉	19	4♊	18	4♋	19	4♌	19	3♍	17	1♎	14	27	9♏	21	3♐	15	27	9♑	21	3♒	15	27	9♓	22	5♈
☿	29♑	1♒	2	3	4	5	6	7	7	7	8	8	8	7	7	6	5	4	3	2	0	29♑	28	27	25	25	24	23	22	22	22
♀	27♒	28	29	1♓	2	3	4	5	6	7	8	9	10	11	12	13	14	15	16	17	18	19	20	21	22	23	24	25	26	26	27
♂	4♑	4	5	6	7	7	8	9	10	10	11	12	13	13	14	15	16	16	17	18	19	19	20	21	22	23	23	24	25	26	26
	1	6	11	16	21	26	31		1	11	21	31		1	11	21	31		1	16		1	16		1	16		1	11	21	31
♃	29♑	0♒	1	2	4	5	6	♄	22♍	22	21	21	⚷	18♒	19	20	20	♅	19♓	20	♆	22♒	23	♇	1♑	2	☊	11♒	10	10	9

FEB

	1	2	3	4	5	6	7	8	9	10	11	12	13	14	15	16	17	18	19	20	21	22	23	24	25	26	27	28			
☉	12♒	13	14	15	16	17	18	19	20	21	22	23	24	25	26	27	28	29	0♓	1	2	3	5	6	7	8	9	10			
☽	18♈	1♉	15	29	13♊	27	12♋	27	12♌	27	11♍	25	9♎	22	5♏	17	30	12♐	23	5♑	17	29	11♒	23	6♓	18	1♈	15			
☿	22♑	22	22	22	23	23	24	24	25	26	27	27	28	29	0♒	1	3	4	5	6	7	9	10	11	13	14	15	17			
♀	28♓	29	30	1♈	2	2	3	4	5	5	6	7	7	8	9	9	10	10	11	11	12	12	13	13	14	14	14	15			
♂	27♑	28	29	29	0♒	1	2	3	3	4	5	6	6	7	8	9	10	10	11	12	13	13	14	15	16	17	17	18			
	1	6	11	16	21	26			1	11	21			1	11	21			1	16		1	16		1	16		1	11	21	
♃	6♒	7	9	10	11	12		♄	21♍	20	20		⚷	20♒	21	22		♅	20♓	21	♆	24♒	24	♇	2♑	3	☊	9♒	9	8	

MAR

	1	2	3	4	5	6	7	8	9	10	11	12	13	14	15	16	17	18	19	20	21	22	23	24	25	26	27	28	29	30	31
☉	11♓	12	13	14	15	16	17	18	19	20	21	22	23	24	25	26	27	28	29	30	1♈	2	2	3	4	5	6	7	8	9	10
☽	28♈	12♉	25	9♊	23	8♋	22	6♌	21	5♍	19	3♎	17	30	13♏	25	7♐	19	1♑	13	25	7♒	19	1♓	14	27	11♈	24	8♉	22	6♊
☿	18♒	20	21	23	24	26	27	29	0♓	2	4	5	7	9	10	12	14	15	17	19	21	23	25	26	28	0♈	2	4	6	8	10
♀	15♈	15	15	15	15	15	15	15	15	15	15	15	15	14	14	14	13	13	12	12	11	11	10	10	9	8	8	7	7	6	5
♂	19♒	20	20	21	22	23	24	24	25	26	27	28	28	29	30	1♓	1	2	3	4	5	5	6	7	8	9	9	10	11	12	12
	1	6	11	16	21	26	31		1	11	21	31		1	11	21	31		1	16		1	16		1	16		1	11	21	31
♃	13♒	14	15	16	17	18	19	♄	19♍	18	17	17	⚷	23♒	23	24	24	♅	22♓	23	♆	25♒	25	♇	3♑	3	☊	8♒	7	7	6

APR

	1	2	3	4	5	6	7	8	9	10	11	12	13	14	15	16	17	18	19	20	21	22	23	24	25	26	27	28	29	30	
☉	11♈	12	13	14	15	16	17	18	19	20	21	22	23	24	25	26	27	28	29	0♉	1	2	3	4	5	6	7	8	9	10	
☽	20♊	4♋	19	3♌	17	1♍	14	28	12♎	25	8♏	21	3♐	15	27	9♑	21	3♒	15	27	9♓	22	5♈	19	3♉	17	2♊	16	1♋	15	
☿	12♈	14	16	18	21	23	25	27	29	1♉	3	5	7	9	10	12	14	16	17	19	20	21	23	24	25	26	27	28	29	29	
♀	5♈	4	4	3	2	2	2	1	1	0	0	30♓	30	29	29	29	29	29	29	29	29	30	30	30	0♈	0	1	1	1	2	
♂	13♓	14	15	16	16	17	18	19	19	20	21	22	23	23	24	25	26	26	27	28	29	30	0♈	1	2	3	3	4	5	6	
	1	6	11	16	21	26			1	11	21			1	11	21			1	16		1	16		1	16		1	11	21	
♃	19♒	20	21	22	23	23		♄	17♍	16	15		⚷	24♒	25	25		♅	24♓	24	♆	26♒	26	♇	3♑	3	☊	6♒	6	5	

MAY

	1	2	3	4	5	6	7	8	9	10	11	12	13	14	15	16	17	18	19	20	21	22	23	24	25	26	27	28	29	30	31
☉	11♉	12	13	14	15	16	17	18	19	19	20	21	22	23	24	25	26	27	28	29	0♊	1	2	3	4	5	6	7	8	9	10
☽	29♋	13♌	27	11♍	25	8♎	21	4♏	17	29	11♐	23	5♑	17	29	11♒	23	5♓	17	0♈	14	27	11♉	26	11♊	26	11♋	25	10♌	24	8♍
☿	0♊	1	1	1	2	2	2	2	2	1	1	1	0	30♉	30	29	28	28	27	27	26	26	25	25	24	24	23	23	23	23	23
♀	2♈	3	3	4	4	5	5	6	7	7	8	9	9	10	11	11	12	13	14	15	15	16	17	18	19	20	20	21	22	23	24
♂	7♈	7	8	9	10	10	11	12	13	13	14	15	16	16	17	18	19	20	20	21	22	23	23	24	25	26	26	27	28	29	29
	1	6	11	16	21	26	31		1	11	21	31		1	11	21	31		1	16		1	16		1	16		1	11	21	31
♃	24♒	25	25	26	26	26	27	♄	15♍	15	15	15	⚷	26♒	26	26	26	♅	25♓	26	♆	26♒	26	♇	3♑	3	☊	5♒	4	4	3

JUN

	1	2	3	4	5	6	7	8	9	10	11	12	13	14	15	16	17	18	19	20	21	22	23	24	25	26	27	28	29	30	
☉	11♊	12	13	14	14	15	16	17	18	19	20	21	22	23	24	25	26	27	28	29	30	1♋	2	3	4	5	5	6	7	8	
☽	21♍	5♎	18	1♏	13	26	8♐	20	2♑	14	26	7♒	19	1♓	13	26	9♈	22	6♉	20	4♊	19	4♋	19	4♌	19	4♍	18	1♎	15	
☿	23♉	23	23	23	24	24	25	25	26	27	27	28	29	30	1♊	2	3	4	5	7	8	10	11	12	14	16	17	19	21	23	
♀	25♈	26	27	28	29	30	1♉	2	3	4	5	6	7	8	9	10	11	12	13	14	15	16	17	18	19	20	21	22	23	24	
♂	0♉	1	2	2	3	4	5	5	6	7	8	8	9	10	10	11	12	13	13	14	15	16	16	17	18	18	19	20	21	21	
	1	6	11	16	21	26			1	11	21			1	11	21			1	16		1	16		1	16		1	11	21	
♃	27♒	27	27	27	27	27		♄	15♍	15	16		⚷	26♒	26	26		♅	26♓	27	♆	26♒	26	♇	3♑	2	☊	3♒	2	2	

EPHEMERIS

2009

JUL

	1	2	3	4	5	6	7	8	9	10	11	12	13	14	15	16	17	18	19	20	21	22	23	24	25	26	27	28	29	30	31
☉	9♋	10	11	12	13	14	15	16	17	18	19	20	21	22	23	24	25	26	26	27	28	29	0♌	1	2	3	4	5	6	7	8
☽	28♎	10♏	23	5♐	17	29	11♑	23	4♒	16	28	10♓	22	5♈	18	1♉	14	28	13♊	28	13♋	28	13♌	28	13♍	27	11♎	24	7♏	20	2♐
☿	25♊	26	28	0♋	2	4	7	9	11	13	15	17	19	22	24	26	28	0♌	2	4	6	8	10	12	14	16	18	20	21	23	25
♀	25♉	26	27	29	30	1♊	2	3	4	5	6	7	8	10	11	12	13	14	15	16	17	19	20	21	22	23	24	25	26	28	29
♂	22♉	23	24	24	25	26	26	27	28	29	29	30	1♊	1	2	3	3	4	5	6	6	7	8	8	9	10	10	11	12	12	13
	1	6	11	16	21	26	31		1	11	21	31		1	11	21	31		1	16		1	16		1	16		1	11	21	31
♃	27♒	26	26	26	25	25	24	♄	17♍	17	18	19	⚷	26♒	25	25	25	♅	27♓	27	♆	26♒	26	♇	2♑	1	☊	1♒	1	0	30♑

AUG

	1	2	3	4	5	6	7	8	9	10	11	12	13	14	15	16	17	18	19	20	21	22	23	24	25	26	27	28	29	30	31
☉	9♌	10	11	12	13	14	15	16	17	18	18	19	20	21	22	23	24	25	26	27	28	29	0♍	1	2	3	4	5	6	7	8
☽	14♐	26	8♑	20	1♒	13	25	7♓	19	2♈	14	27	11♉	24	8♊	22	7♋	21	6♌	21	6♍	21	5♎	19	3♏	16	28	11♐	23	5♑	16
☿	27♌	28	0♍	2	3	5	6	8	9	11	12	14	15	17	18	19	20	22	23	24	25	26	27	28	29	0♎	1	2	3	3	4
♀	30♊	1♋	2	3	5	6	7	8	9	10	12	13	14	15	16	17	19	20	21	22	23	24	26	27	28	29	0♌	2	3	4	5
♂	14♊	14	15	16	16	17	18	18	19	20	20	21	22	22	23	24	24	25	26	26	27	28	28	29	30	0♋	1	1	2	3	3
	1	6	11	16	21	26	31		1	11	21	31		1	11	21	31		1	16		1	16		1	16		1	11	21	31
♃	24♒	23	23	22	21	21	20	♄	19♍	20	22	23	⚷	24♒	24	23	23	♅	26♓	26	♆	26♒	25	♇	1♑	1	☊	30♑	29	29	28

SEP

	1	2	3	4	5	6	7	8	9	10	11	12	13	14	15	16	17	18	19	20	21	22	23	24	25	26	27	28	29	30
☉	9♍	10	11	12	13	14	15	15	16	17	18	19	20	21	22	23	24	25	26	27	28	29	0♎	1	2	3	4	5	6	7
☽	28♑	10♒	22	4♓	16	29	11♈	24	8♉	21	4♊	18	2♋	16	1♌	15	0♍	15	29	13♎	27	11♏	24	6♐	19	1♑	13	25	6♒	18
☿	4♎	5	5	6	6	6	6	6	6	6	5	5	4	4	3	2	1	0	29♍	28	27	26	25	24	23	23	22	22	22	22
♀	6♌	8	9	10	11	12	14	15	16	17	18	20	21	22	23	24	26	27	28	29	1♍	2	3	4	5	7	8	9	10	12
♂	4♋	5	5	6	6	7	8	8	9	10	10	11	11	12	13	13	14	14	15	15	16	17	17	18	18	19	19	20	21	21
	1	6	11	16	21	26			1	11	21			1	11	21			1	16		1	16		1	16		1	11	21
♃	20♒	19	19	18	18	18		♄	23♍	24	25		⚷	23♒	22	22		♅	25♓	25	♆	25♒	24	♇	1♑	1	☊	28♑	28	27

OCT

	1	2	3	4	5	6	7	8	9	10	11	12	13	14	15	16	17	18	19	20	21	22	23	24	25	26	27	28	29	30	31
☉	8♎	9	10	11	12	13	14	15	16	17	18	19	20	21	22	23	24	25	26	27	28	29	30	1♏	2	3	4	5	6	7	8
☽	0♓	13	25	8♈	21	4♉	18	1♊	15	29	13♋	27	11♌	25	10♍	24	8♎	22	5♏	19	2♐	14	27	9♑	21	2♒	14	26	8♓	21	3♈
☿	22♍	22	23	23	24	25	26	27	28	30	1♎	3	4	6	7	9	11	12	14	16	17	19	21	23	24	26	28	29	1♏	3	4
♀	13♍	14	15	16	18	19	20	21	23	24	25	26	28	29	0♎	1	3	4	5	6	8	9	10	11	12	14	15	16	17	19	20
♂	22♋	22	23	23	24	24	25	26	26	27	27	28	28	29	29	30	0♌	1	1	2	2	3	3	4	4	5	5	5	6	6	7
	1	6	11	16	21	26	31		1	11	21	31		1	11	21	31		1	16		1	16		1	16		1	11	21	31
♃	17♒	17	17	17	17	17	18	♄	27♍	28	29	0♎	⚷	22♒	21	21	21	♅	24♓	24	♆	24♒	24	♇	1♑	1	☊	27♑	26	25	25

NOV

	1	2	3	4	5	6	7	8	9	10	11	12	13	14	15	16	17	18	19	20	21	22	23	24	25	26	27	28	29	30
☉	9♏	10	11	12	13	14	15	16	17	18	19	20	21	22	23	24	25	26	27	28	29	30	1♐	2	3	4	5	6	7	8
☽	16♈	30	13♉	27	11♊	25	10♋	24	8♌	22	6♍	20	4♎	17	1♏	14	27	10♐	22	5♑	17	28	10♒	22	4♓	16	28	11♈	24	8♉
☿	6♏	8	9	11	12	14	16	17	19	21	22	24	25	27	28	30	2♐	3	5	6	8	9	11	12	14	15	17	18	20	21
♀	21♎	22	24	25	26	27	29	30	1♏	2	4	5	6	7	9	10	11	13	14	15	16	18	19	20	21	23	24	25	26	28
♂	7♌	8	8	8	9	9	10	10	11	11	11	12	12	12	13	13	13	14	14	14	15	15	15	16	16	16	16	17	17	17
	1	6	11	16	21	26			1	11	21			1	11	21			1	16		1	16		1	16		1	11	21
♃	18♒	18	19	19	20	20		♄	0♎	1	2		⚷	21♒	21	21		♅	23♓	23	♆	24♒	24	♇	1♑	2	☊	25♑	24	24

DEC

	1	2	3	4	5	6	7	8	9	10	11	12	13	14	15	16	17	18	19	20	21	22	23	24	25	26	27	28	29	30	31
☉	9♐	10	11	12	13	14	15	16	17	18	19	20	21	22	23	24	25	26	27	28	29	0♑	1	2	3	4	5	6	7	8	9
☽	21♉	6♊	20	5♋	20	4♌	19	3♍	17	1♎	14	28	11♏	23	6♐	18	1♑	13	25	7♒	18	0♓	12	24	6♈	19	2♉	15	29	14♊	28
☿	23♐	24	26	27	29	0♑	2	3	5	6	8	9	10	12	13	14	15	16	17	18	19	20	21	21	22	22	22	22	21	21	20
♀	29♏	0♐	1	3	4	5	6	8	9	10	11	13	14	15	16	18	19	20	21	23	24	25	27	28	29	0♑	2	3	4	5	7
♂	17♌	18	18	18	18	18	19	19	19	19	19	19	19	19	19	20	20	20	20	20	20	20	20	20	20	19	19	19	19	19	19
	1	6	11	16	21	26	31		1	11	21	31		1	11	21	31		1	16		1	16		1	16		1	11	21	31
♃	21♒	22	22	23	24	25	26	♄	3♎	4	4	4	⚷	22♒	22	23	23	♅	23♓	23	♆	24♒	24	♇	2♑	3	☊	23♑	23	22	22

2010

JAN

	1	2	3	4	5	6	7	8	9	10	11	12	13	14	15	16	17	18	19	20	21	22	23	24	25	26	27	28	29	30	31
☉	10♑	11	12	14	15	16	17	18	19	20	21	22	23	24	25	26	27	28	29	30	1♒	2	3	4	5	6	7	8	9	10	11
☽	13♋	28	13♌	28	13♍	27	11♎	24	8♏	20	3♐	15	28	10♑	21	3♒	15	27	9♓	21	3♈	15	28	10♉	24	7♊	22	6♋	21	6♌	22
☿	19♑	18	17	15	14	13	11	10	9	8	7	7	6	6	6	6	6	6	6	7	7	8	9	9	10	11	12	13	14	15	17
♀	8♑	9	10	12	13	14	15	17	18	19	20	22	23	24	25	27	28	29	0♒	2	3	4	6	7	8	9	11	12	13	14	16
♂	19♌	19	18	18	18	18	18	17	17	17	17	16	16	16	15	15	15	14	14	14	13	13	12	12	12	11	11	11	10	10	9
	1	6	11	16	21	26	31		1	11	21	31		1	11	21	31		1	16		1	16		1	16		1	11	21	31
♃	26♒	27	28	30	1♓	2	3	♄	5♎	5	5	4	⚷	23♒	24	24	25	♅	23♓	24	♆	25♒	25	♇	3♑	4	☊	22♑	21	21	20

FEB

	1	2	3	4	5	6	7	8	9	10	11	12	13	14	15	16	17	18	19	20	21	22	23	24	25	26	27	28		
☉	12♒	13	14	15	16	17	18	19	20	21	22	23	24	25	26	27	28	29	0♓	1	2	3	4	5	6	7	8	9		
☽	7♍	22	6♎	20	4♏	17	30	12♐	25	7♑	18	0♒	12	24	6♓	18	30	12♈	24	7♉	20	3♊	16	0♋	15	29	14♌	29		
☿	18♑	19	20	21	23	24	25	27	28	29	1♒	2	4	5	7	8	10	11	13	14	16	17	19	21	22	24	26	27		
♀	17♒	18	19	21	22	23	24	26	27	28	29	1♓	2	3	4	6	7	8	9	11	12	13	14	16	17	18	19	21		
♂	9♌	9	8	8	7	7	7	6	6	6	5	5	5	4	4	4	3	3	3	3	2	2	2	2	1	1	1	1		
	1	6	11	16	21	26			1	11	21			1	11	21			1	16		1	16		1	16		1	11	21
♃	3♓	4	6	7	8	9		♄	4♎	4	3		⚷	25♒	26	27		♅	24♓	25	♆	26♒	26	♇	4♑	5	☊	20♑	19	19

MAR

	1	2	3	4	5	6	7	8	9	10	11	12	13	14	15	16	17	18	19	20	21	22	23	24	25	26	27	28	29	30	31
☉	10♓	11	12	13	14	15	16	17	18	19	20	21	22	23	24	25	26	27	28	29	0♈	1	2	3	4	5	6	7	8	9	10
☽	15♍	30	14♎	29	13♏	26	9♐	21	3♑	15	27	9♒	21	3♓	15	27	9♈	21	4♉	17	30	13♊	26	10♋	24	9♌	23	8♍	23	8♎	22
☿	29♒	1♓	2	4	6	8	10	11	13	15	17	19	21	23	25	27	29	1♈	3	5	7	9	11	13	15	17	19	20	22	24	26
♀	22♓	23	24	26	27	28	29	1♈	2	3	4	6	7	8	9	11	12	13	14	15	17	18	19	20	22	23	24	25	27	28	29
♂	1♌	1	1	1	0	0	0	0	0	0	0	0	0	0	0	0	1	1	1	1	1	1	1	1	1	2	2	2	2	2	3
	1	6	11	16	21	26	31		1	11	21	31		1	11	21	31		1	16		1	16		1	16		1	11	21	31
♃	10♓	11	12	13	15	16	17	♄	3♎	2	1	1	⚷	27♒	28	28	29	♅	26♓	26	♆	27♒	27	♇	5♑	5	☊	19♑	18	17	17

APR

	1	2	3	4	5	6	7	8	9	10	11	12	13	14	15	16	17	18	19	20	21	22	23	24	25	26	27	28	29	30
☉	11♈	12	13	14	15	16	17	18	19	20	21	22	23	24	25	26	27	28	29	30	1♉	2	3	4	5	6	7	8	9	10
☽	7♏	21	4♐	17	29	12♑	24	5♒	17	29	11♓	23	5♈	18	1♉	13	27	10♊	23	7♋	21	5♌	19	3♍	18	2♎	17	1♏	15	29
☿	28♈	29	1♉	2	4	5	6	7	8	9	10	11	11	12	12	12	13	13	13	12	12	12	12	11	11	10	9	9	8	7
♀	0♉	2	3	4	5	6	8	9	10	11	13	14	15	16	18	19	20	21	22	24	25	26	27	29	30	1♊	2	3	5	6
♂	3♌	3	3	4	4	4	4	5	5	5	5	6	6	6	7	7	7	8	8	8	9	9	9	10	10	11	11	11	12	12
	1	6	11	16	21	26			1	11	21			1	11	21			1	16		1	16		1	16		1	11	21
♃	17♓	18	20	21	22	23		♄	1♎	30♍	29		⚷	29♒	30	0♓		♅	27♓	28	♆	28♒	28	♇	5♑	5	☊	17♑	16	16

MAY

	1	2	3	4	5	6	7	8	9	10	11	12	13	14	15	16	17	18	19	20	21	22	23	24	25	26	27	28	29	30	31
☉	11♉	11	12	13	14	15	16	17	18	19	20	21	22	23	24	25	26	27	28	29	30	1♊	2	3	4	5	6	7	8	8	9
☽	12♐	25	7♑	20	2♒	13	25	7♓	19	1♈	14	26	9♉	23	6♊	20	4♋	18	2♌	16	0♍	14	28	12♎	26	10♏	24	7♐	20	3♑	15
☿	7♉	6	6	5	4	4	4	3	3	3	3	3	3	3	3	3	4	4	5	5	6	6	7	8	9	10	11	12	13	14	15
♀	7♊	8	9	11	12	13	14	16	17	18	19	20	22	23	24	25	26	28	29	30	1♋	2	4	5	6	7	8	9	11	12	13
♂	13♌	13	13	14	14	15	15	15	16	16	17	17	18	18	19	19	19	20	20	21	21	22	22	23	23	24	24	25	25	26	26
	1	6	11	16	21	26	31		1	11	21	31		1	11	21	31		1	16		1	16		1	16		1	11	21	31
♃	24♓	25	26	27	28	28	29	♄	29♍	28	28	28	⚷	0♓	1	1	1	♅	29♓	30	♆	28♒	29	♇	5♑	5	☊	15♑	15	14	14

JUN

	1	2	3	4	5	6	7	8	9	10	11	12	13	14	15	16	17	18	19	20	21	22	23	24	25	26	27	28	29	30
☉	10♊	11	12	13	14	15	16	17	18	19	20	21	22	23	24	25	26	27	28	29	30	0♋	1	2	3	4	5	6	7	8
☽	27♑	9♒	21	3♓	15	27	9♈	22	4♉	18	1♊	15	29	13♋	28	12♌	27	11♍	25	9♎	23	7♏	20	3♐	16	29	11♑	23	6♒	18
☿	16♉	18	19	20	22	23	25	26	28	30	1♊	3	5	7	8	10	12	14	16	18	20	23	25	27	29	1♋	3	6	8	10
♀	14♋	15	17	18	19	20	21	23	24	25	26	27	28	30	1♌	2	3	4	5	7	8	9	10	11	12	14	15	16	17	18
♂	27♌	27	28	28	29	29	30	0♍	1	1	2	2	3	4	4	5	5	6	6	7	7	8	8	9	10	10	11	11	12	12
	1	6	11	16	21	26			1	11	21			1	11	21			1	16		1	16		1	16		1	11	21
♃	29♓	30	1♈	1	2	2		♄	28♍	28	28		⚷	1♓	1	1		♅	0♈	0	♆	29♒	29	♇	5♑	4	☊	14♑	13	13

EPHEMERIS

2010

JUL

	1	2	3	4	5	6	7	8	9	10	11	12	13	14	15	16	17	18	19	20	21	22	23	24	25	26	27	28	29	30	31
☉	9♋	10	11	12	13	14	15	16	17	18	19	20	21	21	22	23	24	25	26	27	28	29	0♌	1	2	3	4	5	6	7	8
☽	29♒	11♓	23	5♈	17	30	12♉	26	9♊	23	7♋	22	7♌	22	7♍	21	6♎	20	4♏	17	0♐	13	26	8♑	20	2♒	14	26	8♓	20	2♈
☿	12♋	14	16	19	21	23	25	27	29	1♌	3	4	6	8	10	12	13	15	17	18	20	21	23	24	26	27	29	0♍	1	3	4
♀	19♌	20	22	23	24	25	26	27	28	29	1♍	2	3	4	5	6	7	8	9	11	12	13	14	15	16	17	18	19	20	21	22
♂	13♍	14	14	15	15	16	16	17	18	18	19	19	20	20	21	22	22	23	23	24	25	25	26	26	27	28	28	29	29	0♎	1
	1	6	11	16	21	26	31		1	11	21	31		1	11	21	31		1	16		1	16		1	16		1	11	21	31
♃	3♈	3	3	3	3	3	3	♄	29♍	29	30	1♎	⚷	1♓	0	30♒	30	♅	1♈	1	♆	28♒	28	♇	4♑	4	☊	12♑	12	11	10

AUG

	1	2	3	4	5	6	7	8	9	10	11	12	13	14	15	16	17	18	19	20	21	22	23	24	25	26	27	28	29	30	31
☉	9♌	10	11	12	12	13	14	15	16	17	18	19	20	21	22	23	24	25	26	27	28	29	30	1♍	2	3	4	5	6	7	8
☽	14♈	26	8♉	21	4♊	17	1♋	16	0♌	15	1♍	16	1♎	15	30	14♏	27	10♐	23	5♑	17	29	11♒	23	5♓	17	29	11♈	23	5♉	17
☿	5♍	6	8	9	10	11	12	13	14	14	15	16	16	17	18	18	18	19	19	19	19	19	19	19	18	18	17	17	16	15	14
♀	24♍	25	26	27	28	29	30	1♎	2	3	4	5	6	7	8	9	10	11	12	13	14	15	16	17	18	18	19	20	21	22	23
♂	1♎	2	2	3	4	4	5	6	6	7	7	8	9	9	10	11	11	12	12	13	14	14	15	16	16	17	18	18	19	20	20
	1	6	11	16	21	26	31		1	11	21	31		1	11	21	31		1	16		1	16		1	16		1	11	21	31
♃	3♈	3	3	3	2	2	1	♄	1♎	2	3	4	⚷	30♒	29	29	28	♅	0♈	30♓	♆	28♒	27	♇	3♑	3	☊	10♑	10	9	9

SEP

	1	2	3	4	5	6	7	8	9	10	11	12	13	14	15	16	17	18	19	20	21	22	23	24	25	26	27	28	29	30
☉	8♍	9	10	11	12	13	14	15	16	17	18	19	20	21	22	23	24	25	26	27	28	29	30	1♎	2	3	4	5	6	7
☽	30♉	13♊	26	10♋	24	9♌	24	9♍	24	9♎	24	9♏	23	6♐	19	2♑	14	26	8♒	20	2♓	14	26	8♈	20	2♉	14	27	9♊	22
☿	13♍	12	11	10	10	9	8	7	7	6	6	5	5	5	6	6	7	7	8	9	10	11	13	14	15	17	19	20	22	24
♀	24♎	25	25	26	27	28	29	29	0♏	1	2	2	3	4	5	5	6	6	7	8	8	9	9	10	10	11	11	11	12	12
♂	21♎	21	22	23	23	24	25	25	26	27	27	28	29	29	0♏	1	1	2	3	3	4	5	5	6	7	7	8	9	9	10
	1	6	11	16	21	26			1	11	21			1	11	21			1	16		1	16		1	16		1	11	21
♃	1♈	0	30♓	29	28	28		♄	4♎	5	7		⚷	28♒	28	27		♅	29♓	29	♆	27♒	27	♇	3♑	3	☊	9♑	8	8

OCT

	1	2	3	4	5	6	7	8	9	10	11	12	13	14	15	16	17	18	19	20	21	22	23	24	25	26	27	28	29	30	31
☉	8♎	9	10	11	12	13	14	15	16	17	18	19	20	21	22	23	24	25	26	26	27	28	29	0♏	1	2	3	4	5	6	7
☽	6♋	19	3♌	18	2♍	17	3♎	18	3♏	17	1♐	15	28	10♑	23	5♒	17	29	10♓	22	4♈	16	29	11♉	24	7♊	19	3♋	16	30	14♌
☿	25♍	27	29	1♎	2	4	6	8	10	11	13	15	17	18	20	22	23	25	27	29	0♏	2	3	5	7	8	10	12	13	15	16
♀	12♏	12	13	13	13	13	13	13	13	13	13	13	13	13	12	12	12	11	11	11	10	10	9	8	8	7	7	6	6	5	4
♂	11♏	12	12	13	14	14	15	16	16	17	18	18	19	20	21	21	22	23	23	24	25	26	26	27	28	28	29	30	1♐	1	2
	1	6	11	16	21	26	31		1	11	21	31		1	11	21	31		1	16		1	16		1	16		1	11	21	31
♃	27♓	27	26	25	25	24	24	♄	8♎	9	10	11	⚷	27♒	26	26	26	♅	28♓	28	♆	26♒	26	♇	3♑	3	☊	7♑	7	6	6

NOV

	1	2	3	4	5	6	7	8	9	10	11	12	13	14	15	16	17	18	19	20	21	22	23	24	25	26	27	28	29	30
☉	8♏	9	10	11	12	13	14	15	16	17	18	19	20	22	23	24	25	26	27	28	29	30	1♐	2	3	4	5	6	7	8
☽	28♌	12♍	27	11♎	26	11♏	25	9♐	23	6♑	18	1♒	13	25	7♓	19	1♈	13	25	7♉	20	3♊	16	29	13♋	27	10♌	24	8♍	23
☿	18♏	19	21	22	24	25	27	29	0♐	2	3	4	6	7	9	10	12	13	15	16	17	19	20	21	23	24	25	27	28	29
♀	4♏	3	3	2	1	1	0	0	30♎	29	29	29	28	28	28	28	28	28	28	28	28	28	28	28	28	29	29	29	30	30
♂	3♐	3	4	5	6	6	7	8	8	9	10	11	11	12	13	14	14	15	16	17	17	18	19	20	20	21	22	22	23	24
	1	6	11	16	21	26			1	11	21			1	11	21			1	16		1	16		1	16		1	11	21
♃	24♓	24	24	24	24	24		♄	11♎	13	14		⚷	26♒	26	26		♅	27♓	27	♆	26♒	26	♇	3♑	4	☊	6♑	5	4

DEC

	1	2	3	4	5	6	7	8	9	10	11	12	13	14	15	16	17	18	19	20	21	22	23	24	25	26	27	28	29	30	31
☉	9♐	10	11	12	13	14	15	16	17	18	19	20	21	22	23	24	25	26	27	28	29	0♑	1	2	3	4	5	6	7	8	9
☽	7♎	21	5♏	20	3♐	17	0♑	13	26	8♒	21	3♓	15	26	8♈	20	3♉	15	28	11♊	25	8♋	22	7♌	21	5♍	20	4♎	18	2♏	16
☿	30♐	1♑	2	3	4	4	5	5	6	6	6	6	5	5	4	3	2	1	29♐	28	27	25	24	23	22	21	21	20	20	20	20
♀	0♏	1	1	2	2	3	3	4	5	5	6	7	7	8	9	10	10	11	12	13	14	14	15	16	17	18	19	20	21	22	23
♂	25♐	25	26	27	28	28	29	0♑	1	2	2	3	4	5	5	6	7	8	8	9	10	11	11	12	13	14	15	15	16	17	18
	1	6	11	16	21	26	31		1	11	21	31		1	11	21	31		1	16		1	16		1	16		1	11	21	31
♃	24♓	24	24	25	25	26	26	♄	15♎	15	16	17	⚷	26♒	27	27	28	♅	27♓	27	♆	26♒	26	♇	4♑	5	☊	4♑	3	3	2

SIDEREAL TIMES

Master Table

	JAN	FEB	MAR	APR	MAY	JUN	JUL	AUG	SEP	OCT	NOV	DEC
1	6 41	8 43	10 34	12 36	14 34	16 36	18 35	20 37	22 39	0 37	2 40	4 38
2	6 45	8 47	10 38	12 40	14 38	16 40	18 39	20 41	22 43	0 41	2 43	4 42
3	6 49	8 51	10 41	12 44	14 42	16 44	18 42	20 45	22 47	0 45	2 47	4 46
4	6 53	8 55	10 45	12 48	14 46	16 48	18 46	20 49	22 51	0 49	2 51	4 50
5	6 57	8 59	10 49	12 52	14 50	16 52	18 50	20 53	22 55	0 53	2 55	4 54
6	7 01	9 03	10 53	12 56	14 54	16 56	18 54	20 57	22 59	0 57	2 59	4 58
7	7 05	9 07	10 57	12 59	14 58	16 60	18 58	21 00	23 03	1 01	3 03	5 01
8	7 09	9 11	11 01	13 03	15 02	17 04	19 02	21 04	23 07	1 05	3 07	5 05
9	7 13	9 15	11 05	13 07	15 06	17 08	19 06	21 08	23 11	1 09	3 11	5 09
10	7 16	9 19	11 09	13 11	15 10	17 12	19 10	21 12	23 15	1 13	3 15	5 13
11	7 20	9 23	11 13	13 15	15 14	17 16	19 14	21 16	23 18	1 17	3 19	5 17
12	7 24	9 27	11 17	13 19	15 17	17 20	19 18	21 20	23 22	1 21	3 23	5 21
13	7 28	9 31	11 21	13 23	15 21	17 24	19 22	21 24	23 26	1 25	3 27	5 25
14	7 32	9 34	11 25	13 27	15 25	17 28	19 26	21 28	23 30	1 29	3 31	5 29
15	7 36	9 38	11 29	13 31	15 29	17 32	19 30	21 32	23 34	1 33	3 35	5 33
16	7 40	9 42	11 33	13 35	15 33	17 35	19 34	21 36	23 38	1 36	3 39	5 37
17	7 44	9 46	11 37	13 39	15 37	17 39	19 38	21 40	23 42	1 40	3 43	5 41
18	7 48	9 50	11 41	13 43	15 41	17 43	19 42	21 44	23 46	1 44	3 47	5 45
19	7 52	9 54	11 45	13 47	15 45	17 47	19 46	21 48	23 50	1 48	3 51	5 49
20	7 56	9 58	11 49	13 51	15 49	17 51	19 50	21 52	23 54	1 52	3 54	5 53
21	7 60	10 02	11 52	13 55	15 53	17 55	19 53	21 56	23 58	1 56	3 58	5 57
22	8 04	10 06	11 56	13 59	15 57	17 59	19 57	21 60	0 02	2 00	4 02	6 01
23	8 08	10 10	12 00	14 03	16 01	18 03	20 01	22 04	0 06	2 04	4 06	6 05
24	8 12	10 14	12 04	14 07	16 05	18 07	20 05	22 08	0 10	2 08	4 10	6 09
25	8 16	10 18	12 08	14 10	16 09	18 11	20 09	22 11	0 14	2 12	4 14	6 12
26	8 20	10 22	12 12	14 14	16 13	18 15	20 13	22 15	0 18	2 16	4 18	6 16
27	8 24	10 26	12 16	14 18	16 17	18 19	20 17	22 19	0 22	2 20	4 22	6 20
28	8 27	10 30	12 20	14 22	16 21	18 23	20 21	22 23	0 26	2 24	4 26	6 24
29	8 31	10 34	12 24	14 26	16 25	18 27	20 25	22 27	0 29	2 28	4 30	6 28
30	8 35		12 28	14 30	16 28	18 31	20 29	22 31	0 33	2 32	4 34	6 32
31	8 39		12 32		16 32		20 33	22 35		2 36		6 36

The master table provides the sidereal time (ST) for each day of the year, but these need to be modified to match the specific year. The following table provides these values.

Example for Sept 12, 2005

Sept 12 = 23h22m

2005 + 2m

23h24m is ST at 0h GMT

Individual Year Table

leap year	*Jan-Feb*	*Mar-Dec*	*year*	*Jan-Dec*	*year*	*Jan-Dec*	*year*	*Jan-Dec*
1960	-2	2	1961	1	1962	0	1963	-1
1964	-2	2	1965	1	1966	0	1967	-1
1968	-2	2	1969	1	1970	0	1971	-1
1972	-2	2	1973	1	1974	0	1975	-1
1976	-2	2	1977	1	1978	0	1979	-1
1980	-2	2	1981	1	1982	0	1983	-1
1984	-2	2	1985	1	1986	0	1987	-1
1988	-1	3	1989	2	1990	1	1991	0
1992	-2	2	1993	2	1994	1	1995	0
1996	-1	3	1997	2	1998	1	1999	0
2000	-1	3	2001	2	2002	1	2003	0
2004	-1	3	2005	2	2006	1	2007	0
2008	-1	3	2009	2	2010	1		

TABLES OF HOUSES

ST		0N	5N	10N	15N	20N	25N	30N	33N	36N	39N	42N	45N	48N	50N	52N	54N	56N	58N	60N
h m	Mc	As	As	As	As	As	As	As	As	As	As	As	As	As	As	As	As	As	As	As
0 0	0♈	0♋	2♋	4♋	6♋	8♋	11♋	13♋	14♋	16♋	18♋	20♋	22♋	24♋	25♋	27♋	29♋	1♌	2♌	5♌
0 4	1	1	3	5	7	9	11	14	15	17	19	21	22	25	26	28	29	1	3	5
0 8	2	2	4	6	8	10	12	15	16	18	20	21	23	25	27	28	0♌	2	4	6
0 12	3	3	5	7	9	11	13	16	17	19	20	22	24	26	28	29	1	3	4	6
0 16	4	4	6	8	10	12	14	16	18	19	21	23	25	27	28	30	2	3	5	7
0 20	5	5	7	9	11	13	15	17	19	20	22	24	26	28	29	1♌	2	4	6	8
0 24	7	6	7	9	12	14	16	18	20	21	23	25	26	28	30	1	3	5	6	8
0 28	8	6	8	10	12	14	17	19	20	22	24	25	27	29	1♌	2	4	5	7	9
0 32	9	7	9	11	13	15	18	20	21	23	24	26	28	30	1	3	4	6	8	10
0 36	10	8	10	12	14	16	18	21	22	24	25	27	29	1♌	2	3	5	7	8	10
0 40	11	9	11	13	15	17	19	22	23	24	26	28	29	1	3	4	6	7	9	11
0 44	12	10	12	14	16	18	20	22	24	25	27	29	0♌	2	3	5	6	8	10	11
0 48	13	11	13	15	17	19	21	23	25	26	28	29	1	3	4	6	7	9	10	12
0 52	14	12	14	16	18	20	22	24	25	27	28	0♌	2	4	5	6	8	9	11	13
0 56	15	13	15	17	19	21	23	25	26	28	29	1	3	4	6	7	8	10	12	13
1 0	16	14	16	18	20	22	24	26	27	29	0♌	2	3	5	6	8	9	11	12	14
1 4	17	15	17	19	21	22	25	27	28	29	1	2	4	6	7	8	10	11	13	14
1 8	18	16	18	19	21	23	25	28	29	0♌	2	3	5	7	8	9	10	12	13	15
1 12	20	17	19	20	22	24	26	28	30	1	2	4	6	7	9	10	11	13	14	16
1 16	21	18	19	21	23	25	27	29	1♌	2	3	5	6	8	9	11	12	13	15	16
1 20	22	18	20	22	24	26	28	0♌	1	3	4	6	7	9	10	11	13	14	15	17
1 24	23	19	21	23	25	27	29	1	2	3	5	6	8	10	11	12	13	15	16	17
1 28	24	20	22	24	26	28	30	2	3	4	6	7	9	10	11	13	14	15	17	18
1 32	25	21	23	25	27	29	1♌	3	4	5	6	8	9	11	12	13	15	16	17	19
1 36	26	22	24	26	28	30	1	3	5	6	7	9	10	12	13	14	15	17	18	19
1 40	27	23	25	27	29	0♌	2	4	5	7	8	9	11	12	14	15	16	17	19	20
1 44	28	24	26	28	30	1	3	5	6	8	9	10	12	13	14	15	17	18	19	21
1 48	29	25	27	29	0♌	2	4	6	7	8	10	11	12	14	15	16	17	18	20	21
1 52	0♉	26	28	30	1	3	5	7	8	9	10	12	13	15	16	17	18	19	20	22
1 56	1	27	29	0♌	2	4	6	8	9	10	11	13	14	15	16	17	19	20	21	22
2 0	2	28	30	1	3	5	7	8	10	11	12	13	15	16	17	18	19	20	22	23
2 4	3	29	1♌	2	4	6	8	9	10	12	13	14	15	17	18	19	20	21	22	24
2 8	4	30	2	3	5	7	8	10	11	12	14	15	16	18	19	20	21	22	23	24
2 12	5	1♌	3	4	6	8	9	11	12	13	14	16	17	18	19	20	21	22	24	25
2 16	6	2	3	5	7	8	10	12	13	14	15	16	18	19	20	21	22	23	24	25
2 20	7	3	4	6	8	9	11	13	14	15	16	17	18	20	21	22	23	24	25	26
2 24	8	4	5	7	9	10	12	14	15	16	17	18	19	20	21	22	23	24	25	27
2 28	9	5	6	8	10	11	13	14	15	16	18	19	20	21	22	23	24	25	26	27
2 32	10	6	7	9	10	12	14	15	16	17	18	20	21	22	23	24	25	26	27	28
2 36	11	7	8	10	11	13	14	16	17	18	19	20	21	23	24	24	25	26	27	28
2 40	12	8	9	11	12	14	15	17	18	19	20	21	22	23	24	25	26	27	28	29
2 44	13	9	10	12	13	15	16	18	19	20	21	22	23	24	25	26	27	28	29	30
2 48	14	10	11	13	14	16	17	19	20	21	22	23	24	25	26	27	27	28	29	0♍
2 52	15	11	12	14	15	16	18	19	20	21	22	23	24	26	26	27	28	29	30	1
2 56	16	12	13	15	16	17	19	20	21	22	23	24	25	26	27	28	29	30	1♍	2
3 0	17	13	14	15	17	18	20	21	22	23	24	25	26	27	28	29	29	0♍	1	2
3 4	18	14	15	16	18	19	21	22	23	24	25	26	27	28	29	29	0♍	1	2	3
3 8	19	15	16	17	19	20	21	23	24	25	26	26	27	28	29	30	1	2	2	3
3 12	20	16	17	18	20	21	22	24	25	25	26	27	28	29	30	1♍	1	2	3	4
3 16	21	17	18	19	21	22	23	25	25	26	27	28	29	30	1♍	1	2	3	4	5
3 20	22	18	19	20	22	23	24	25	26	27	28	29	30	1♍	1	2	3	4	4	5
3 24	23	19	20	21	22	24	25	26	27	28	29	30	0♍	1	2	3	3	4	5	6
3 28	24	20	21	22	23	25	26	27	28	29	29	0♍	1	2	3	3	4	5	6	6
3 32	25	21	22	23	24	26	27	28	29	30	0♍	1	2	3	3	4	5	6	6	7
3 36	26	22	23	24	25	26	28	29	30	0♍	1	2	3	4	4	5	6	6	7	8
3 40	27	23	24	25	26	27	29	30	0♍	1	2	3	3	4	5	6	6	7	8	8
3 44	28	24	25	26	27	28	29	1♍	1	2	3	3	4	5	6	6	7	8	8	9
3 48	29	25	26	27	28	29	0♍	1	2	3	3	4	5	6	6	7	8	8	9	10
3 52	0♊	26	27	28	29	0♍	1	2	3	4	4	5	6	7	7	8	8	9	9	10
3 56	1	27	28	29	0♍	1	2	3	4	4	5	6	6	7	8	8	9	9	10	11
4 0	2♊	28♌	29♌	30♌	1♍	2♍	3♍	4♍	5♍	5♍	6♍	7♍	7♍	8♍	8♍	9♍	10♍	10♍	11♍	11♍

TABLES OF HOUSES

ST		0N	5N	10N	15N	20N	25N	30N	33N	36N	39N	42N	45N	48N	50N	52N	54N	56N	58N	60N
h m	Mc	As	As	As	As	As	As	As	As	As	As	As	As	As	As	As	As	As	As	As
4 0	2♊	28♌	29♌	30♌	1♍	2♍	3♍	4♍	5♍	5♍	6♍	7♍	7♍	8♍	8♍	9♍	10♍	10♍	11♍	11♍
4 4	3	29	30	1♍	2	3	4	5	5	6	7	7	8	9	9	10	10	11	11	12
4 8	4	30	1♍	2	3	4	5	6	6	7	7	8	9	9	10	10	11	11	12	13
4 12	5	1♍	2	3	4	5	6	7	7	8	8	9	10	10	11	11	12	12	13	13
4 16	6	2	3	4	5	6	7	7	8	9	9	10	10	11	11	12	12	13	13	14
4 20	7	3	4	5	6	7	7	8	9	9	10	10	11	12	12	13	13	13	14	14
4 24	8	4	5	6	7	8	8	9	10	10	11	11	12	12	13	13	14	14	15	15
4 28	9	5	6	7	8	8	9	10	10	11	11	12	13	13	13	14	14	15	15	16
4 32	10	6	7	8	9	9	10	11	11	12	12	13	13	14	14	15	15	15	16	16
4 36	11	7	8	9	10	10	11	12	12	13	13	14	14	15	15	15	16	16	17	17
4 40	12	8	9	10	11	11	12	13	13	13	14	14	15	15	16	16	16	17	17	18
4 44	12	9	10	11	12	12	13	13	14	14	15	15	16	16	16	17	17	17	18	18
4 48	13	10	11	12	12	13	14	14	15	15	15	16	16	17	17	17	18	18	18	19
4 52	14	12	12	13	13	14	15	15	16	16	16	17	17	18	18	18	18	19	19	19
4 56	15	13	13	14	14	15	16	16	16	17	17	17	18	18	19	19	19	19	20	20
5 0	16	14	14	15	15	16	16	17	17	18	18	18	19	19	19	19	20	20	20	21
5 4	17	15	15	16	16	17	17	18	18	18	19	19	19	20	20	20	20	21	21	21
5 8	18	16	16	17	17	18	18	19	19	19	20	20	20	20	21	21	21	21	22	22
5 12	19	17	17	18	18	19	19	20	20	20	20	21	21	21	21	22	22	22	22	23
5 16	20	18	18	19	19	20	20	20	21	21	21	21	22	22	22	22	22	23	23	23
5 20	21	19	20	20	20	21	21	21	21	22	22	22	22	23	23	23	23	23	24	24
5 24	22	20	21	21	21	22	22	22	22	23	23	23	23	23	24	24	24	24	24	24
5 28	23	21	22	22	22	22	23	23	23	23	24	24	24	24	24	24	25	25	25	25
5 32	24	22	23	23	23	23	24	24	24	24	24	25	25	25	25	25	25	25	25	26
5 36	24	23	24	24	24	24	25	25	25	25	25	25	25	26	26	26	26	26	26	26
5 40	25	25	25	25	25	25	25	26	26	26	26	26	26	26	26	26	27	27	27	27
5 44	26	26	26	26	26	26	26	27	27	27	27	27	27	27	27	27	27	27	27	28
5 48	27	27	27	27	27	27	27	27	27	28	28	28	28	28	28	28	28	28	28	28
5 52	28	28	28	28	28	28	28	28	28	28	28	28	28	29	29	29	29	29	29	29
5 56	29	29	29	29	29	29	29	29	29	29	29	29	29	29	29	29	29	29	29	29
6 0	0♋	0♎	0♎	0♎	0♎	0♎	0♎	0♎	0♎	0♎	0♎	0♎	0♎	0♎	0♎	0♎	0♎	0♎	0♎	0♎
6 4	1	1	1	1	1	1	1	1	1	1	1	1	1	1	1	1	1	1	1	1
6 8	2	2	2	2	2	2	2	2	2	2	2	2	2	1	1	1	1	1	1	1
6 12	3	3	3	3	3	3	3	3	3	2	2	2	2	2	2	2	2	2	2	2
6 16	4	4	4	4	4	4	4	3	3	3	3	3	3	3	3	3	3	3	3	2
6 20	5	5	5	5	5	5	5	4	4	4	4	4	4	4	4	4	3	3	3	3
6 24	6	7	6	6	6	6	5	5	5	5	5	5	5	4	4	4	4	4	4	4
6 28	6	8	7	7	7	7	6	6	6	6	6	5	5	5	5	5	5	5	5	4
6 32	7	9	8	8	8	8	7	7	7	7	6	6	6	6	6	6	5	5	5	5
6 36	8	10	9	9	9	8	8	8	8	7	7	7	7	7	6	6	6	6	6	6
6 40	9	11	10	10	10	9	9	9	9	8	8	8	8	7	7	7	7	7	6	6
6 44	10	12	12	11	11	10	10	10	9	9	9	9	8	8	8	8	8	7	7	7
6 48	11	13	13	12	12	11	11	10	10	10	10	9	9	9	9	8	8	8	8	7
6 52	12	14	14	13	13	12	12	11	11	11	10	10	10	10	9	9	9	9	8	8
6 56	13	15	15	14	14	13	13	12	12	12	11	11	11	10	10	10	10	9	9	9
7 0	14	16	16	15	15	14	14	13	13	12	12	12	11	11	11	11	10	10	10	9
7 4	15	17	17	16	16	15	14	14	14	13	13	13	12	12	11	11	11	11	10	10
7 8	16	18	18	17	17	16	15	15	14	14	14	13	13	12	12	12	12	11	11	11
7 12	17	20	19	18	18	17	16	16	15	15	15	14	14	13	13	13	12	12	12	11
7 16	18	21	20	19	18	18	17	17	16	16	15	15	14	14	14	13	13	13	12	12
7 20	18	22	21	20	19	19	18	17	17	17	16	16	15	15	14	14	14	13	13	12
7 24	19	23	22	21	20	20	19	18	18	17	17	16	16	15	15	15	14	14	13	13
7 28	20	24	23	22	21	21	20	19	19	18	18	17	17	16	16	15	15	15	14	14
7 32	21	25	24	23	22	22	21	20	20	19	19	18	17	17	17	16	16	15	15	14
7 36	22	26	25	24	23	22	22	21	20	20	19	19	18	18	17	17	16	16	15	15
7 40	23	27	26	25	24	23	23	22	21	21	20	20	19	18	18	17	17	17	16	16
7 44	24	28	27	26	25	24	23	23	22	21	21	20	20	19	19	18	18	17	17	16
7 48	25	29	28	27	26	25	24	23	23	22	22	21	20	20	19	19	18	18	17	17
7 52	26	0♏	29	28	27	26	25	24	24	23	23	22	21	21	20	20	19	19	18	17
7 56	27	1	0♏	29	28	27	26	25	25	24	23	23	22	21	21	20	20	19	19	18
8 0	28♋	2♏	1♏	0♏	29♎	28♎	27♎	26♎	25♎	25♎	24♎	23♎	23♎	22♎	22♎	21♎	20♎	20♎	19♎	19♎

TABLES OF HOUSES

ST		0N	5N	10N	15N	20N	25N	30N	33N	36N	39N	42N	45N	48N	50N	52N	54N	56N	58N	60N
h m	Mc	As	As	As	As	As	As	As	As	As	As	As	As	As	As	As	As	As	As	As
8 0	28♋	2♏	1♏	0♏	29♎	28♎	27♎	26♎	25♎	25♎	24♎	23♎	23♎	22♎	22♎	21♎	20♎	20♎	19♎	19♎
8 4	29	3	2	1	30	29	28	27	26	26	25	24	24	23	22	22	21	21	20	19
8 8	30	4	3	2	1♏	30	29	28	27	26	26	25	24	23	23	22	22	21	21	20
8 12	1♌	5	4	3	2	1♏	30	29	28	27	27	26	25	24	24	23	22	22	21	20
8 16	2	6	5	4	3	2	1♏	29	29	28	27	27	26	25	24	24	23	22	22	21
8 20	3	7	6	5	4	3	1	0♏	30	29	28	27	27	26	25	24	24	23	22	22
8 24	4	8	7	6	5	4	2	1	0♏	30	29	28	27	26	26	25	24	24	23	22
8 28	5	9	8	7	6	4	3	2	1	0♏	30	29	28	27	27	26	25	24	24	23
8 32	6	10	9	8	7	5	4	3	2	1	1♏	30	29	28	27	27	26	25	24	24
8 36	7	11	10	9	8	6	5	4	3	2	1	0♏	30	29	28	27	27	26	25	24
8 40	8	12	11	10	8	7	6	5	4	3	2	1	0♏	29	29	28	27	26	26	25
8 44	9	13	12	11	9	8	7	5	5	4	3	2	1	0♏	29	29	28	27	26	25
8 48	10	14	13	12	10	9	8	6	5	5	4	3	2	1	0♏	29	29	28	27	26
8 52	11	15	14	13	11	10	9	7	6	5	4	4	3	2	1	0♏	29	28	28	27
8 56	12	16	15	14	12	11	9	8	7	6	5	4	3	2	1	1	30	29	28	27
9 0	13	17	16	15	13	12	10	9	8	7	6	5	4	3	2	1	1♏	30	29	28
9 4	14	18	17	15	14	13	11	10	9	8	7	6	5	4	3	2	1	0♏	29	28
9 8	15	19	18	16	15	14	12	11	10	9	8	7	6	4	4	3	2	1	0♏	29
9 12	16	20	19	17	16	14	13	11	10	9	8	7	6	5	4	3	3	2	1	30
9 16	17	21	20	18	17	15	14	12	11	10	9	8	7	6	5	4	3	2	1	0♏
9 20	18	22	21	19	18	16	15	13	12	11	10	9	8	7	6	5	4	3	2	1
9 24	19	23	22	20	19	17	16	14	13	12	11	10	9	7	6	6	5	4	3	2
9 28	20	24	23	21	20	18	16	15	14	13	12	10	9	8	7	6	5	4	3	2
9 32	21	25	24	22	20	19	17	16	15	14	12	11	10	9	8	7	6	5	4	3
9 36	22	26	25	23	21	20	18	16	15	14	13	12	11	10	9	8	7	6	5	3
9 40	23	27	26	24	22	21	19	17	16	15	14	13	12	10	9	8	7	6	5	4
9 44	24	28	27	25	23	22	20	18	17	16	15	14	12	11	10	9	8	7	6	5
9 48	25	29	27	26	24	22	21	19	18	17	16	14	13	12	11	10	9	8	6	5
9 52	26	0♐	28	27	25	23	22	20	19	18	16	15	14	12	11	10	9	8	7	6
9 56	27	1	29	28	26	24	22	21	20	18	17	16	15	13	12	11	10	9	8	6
10 0	28	2	0♐	29	27	25	23	22	20	19	18	17	15	14	13	12	11	10	8	7
10 4	29	3	1	30	28	26	24	22	21	20	19	17	16	15	14	13	11	10	9	8
10 8	30	4	2	0♐	29	27	25	23	22	21	20	18	17	15	14	13	12	11	10	8
10 12	1♍	5	3	1	30	28	26	24	23	22	20	19	18	16	15	14	13	12	10	9
10 16	2	6	4	2	0♐	29	27	25	24	22	21	20	18	17	16	15	13	12	11	9
10 20	3	7	5	3	1	30	28	26	25	23	22	21	19	18	16	15	14	13	11	10
10 24	4	8	6	4	2	0♐	29	27	25	24	23	21	20	18	17	16	15	13	12	11
10 28	5	9	7	5	3	1	29	27	26	25	24	22	21	19	18	17	15	14	13	11
10 32	6	10	8	6	4	2	0♐	28	27	26	24	23	21	20	19	17	16	15	13	12
10 36	7	11	9	7	5	3	1	29	28	27	25	24	22	20	19	18	17	15	14	13
10 40	8	12	10	8	6	4	2	30	29	27	26	24	23	21	20	19	17	16	15	13
10 44	9	12	11	9	7	5	3	1♐	29	28	27	25	24	22	21	19	18	17	15	14
10 48	10	13	11	10	8	6	4	2	0♐	29	28	26	24	23	21	20	19	17	16	14
10 52	12	14	12	11	9	7	5	2	1	30	28	27	25	23	22	21	20	18	17	15
10 56	13	15	13	11	9	8	5	3	2	1♐	29	28	26	24	23	22	20	19	17	16
11 0	14	16	14	12	10	8	6	4	3	1	30	28	27	25	24	22	21	19	18	16
11 4	15	17	15	13	11	9	7	5	4	2	1♐	29	27	26	24	23	22	20	18	17
11 8	16	18	16	14	12	10	8	6	5	3	2	30	28	26	25	24	22	21	19	17
11 12	17	19	17	15	13	11	9	7	5	4	2	1♐	29	27	26	24	23	21	20	18
11 16	18	20	18	16	14	12	10	8	6	5	3	1	30	28	27	25	24	22	20	19
11 20	19	21	19	17	15	13	11	8	7	6	4	2	1♐	29	27	26	24	23	21	19
11 24	20	22	20	18	16	14	12	9	8	6	5	3	1	29	28	27	25	23	22	20
11 28	21	23	21	19	17	15	12	10	9	7	6	4	2	0♐	29	27	26	24	22	20
11 32	22	24	22	20	18	16	13	11	10	8	6	5	3	1	29	28	26	25	23	21
11 36	23	24	23	21	18	16	14	12	10	9	7	5	4	2	0♐	29	27	25	24	22
11 40	25	25	23	21	19	17	15	13	11	10	8	6	4	2	1	29	28	26	24	22
11 44	26	26	24	22	20	18	16	14	12	11	9	7	5	3	2	0♐	28	27	25	23
11 48	27	27	25	23	21	19	17	14	13	11	10	8	6	4	2	1	29	27	26	24
11 52	28	28	26	24	22	20	18	15	14	12	10	9	7	5	3	2	30	28	26	24
11 56	29	29	27	25	23	21	19	16	15	13	11	9	8	5	4	2	1♐	29	27	25
12 0	0♎	0♑	28♐	26♐	24♐	22♐	19♐	17♐	16♐	14♐	12♐	10♐	8♐	6♐	5♐	3♐	1♐	29♏	28♏	25♏

TABLES OF HOUSES

ST		0N	5N	10N	15N	20N	25N	30N	33N	36N	39N	42N	45N	48N	50N	52N	54N	56N	58N	60N
h m	Mc	As	As	As	As	As	As	As	As	As	As	As	As	As	As	As	As	As	As	As
12 0	0♎	0♑	28♐	26♐	24♐	22♐	19♐	17♐	16♐	14♐	12♐	10♐	8♐	6♐	5♐	3♐	1♐	29♏	28♏	25♏
12 4	1	1	29	27	25	23	20	18	16	15	13	11	9	7	5	4	2	0♐	28	26
12 8	2	2	30	28	26	24	21	19	17	16	14	12	10	8	6	4	3	1	29	27
12 12	3	3	1♑	29	27	24	22	20	18	16	15	13	11	8	7	5	3	2	29	27
12 16	4	4	2	30	28	25	23	21	19	17	15	14	11	9	8	6	4	2	0♐	28
12 20	5	5	3	1♑	28	26	24	21	20	18	16	14	12	10	8	7	5	3	1	29
12 24	7	6	4	1	29	27	25	22	21	19	17	15	13	11	9	7	6	4	1	29
12 28	8	6	4	2	0♑	28	26	23	22	20	18	16	14	12	10	8	6	4	2	30
12 32	9	7	5	3	1	29	27	24	22	21	19	17	15	12	11	9	7	5	3	0♐
12 36	10	8	6	4	2	30	28	25	23	22	20	18	16	13	11	10	8	6	3	1
12 40	11	9	7	5	3	1♑	28	26	24	22	21	19	16	14	12	10	8	6	4	2
12 44	12	10	8	6	4	2	29	27	25	23	21	19	17	15	13	11	9	7	5	2
12 48	13	11	9	7	5	3	0♑	28	26	24	22	20	18	16	14	12	10	8	5	3
12 52	14	12	10	8	6	4	1	29	27	25	23	21	19	16	15	13	11	9	6	4
12 56	15	13	11	9	7	5	2	30	28	26	24	22	20	17	15	14	11	9	7	4
13 0	16	14	12	10	8	5	3	0♑	29	27	25	23	21	18	16	14	12	10	8	5
13 4	17	15	13	11	9	6	4	1	30	28	26	24	21	19	17	15	13	11	8	6
13 8	18	16	14	12	10	7	5	2	1♑	29	27	25	22	20	18	16	14	11	9	6
13 12	20	17	15	13	11	8	6	3	2	30	28	26	23	21	19	17	14	12	10	7
13 16	21	18	16	14	11	9	7	4	2	1♑	29	26	24	21	19	17	15	13	10	8
13 20	22	18	17	15	12	10	8	5	3	2	29	27	25	22	20	18	16	14	11	8
13 24	23	19	17	15	13	11	9	6	4	2	0♑	28	26	23	21	19	17	14	12	9
13 28	24	20	18	16	14	12	10	7	5	3	1	29	27	24	22	20	18	15	12	10
13 32	25	21	19	17	15	13	11	8	6	4	2	0♑	28	25	23	21	18	16	13	10
13 36	26	22	20	18	16	14	12	9	7	5	3	1	28	26	24	22	19	17	14	11
13 40	27	23	21	19	17	15	13	10	8	6	4	2	29	27	25	22	20	17	15	12
13 44	28	24	22	20	18	16	14	11	9	7	5	3	0♑	27	25	23	21	18	15	12
13 48	29	25	23	21	19	17	15	12	10	8	6	4	1	28	26	24	22	19	16	13
13 52	0♏	26	24	22	20	18	16	13	11	9	7	5	2	29	27	25	22	20	17	14
13 56	1	27	25	23	21	19	17	14	12	10	8	6	3	0♑	28	26	23	21	18	14
14 0	2	28	26	24	22	20	18	15	13	11	9	7	4	1	29	27	24	21	18	15
14 4	3	29	27	25	23	21	19	16	14	12	10	8	5	2	30	28	25	22	19	16
14 8	4	30	28	26	24	22	20	17	15	13	11	9	6	3	1♑	28	26	23	20	17
14 12	5	1♒	29	27	25	23	21	18	16	14	12	10	7	4	2	29	27	24	21	17
14 16	6	2	30	28	26	24	22	19	17	15	13	11	8	5	3	0♑	28	25	22	18
14 20	7	3	1♒	29	27	25	23	20	18	16	14	12	9	6	4	1	29	26	22	19
14 24	8	4	2	0♒	28	26	24	21	19	17	15	13	10	7	5	2	29	26	23	20
14 28	9	5	3	1	29	27	25	22	20	18	16	14	11	8	6	3	0♑	27	24	20
14 32	10	6	4	2	0♒	28	26	23	21	19	17	15	12	9	7	4	1	28	25	21
14 36	11	7	5	3	1	29	27	24	22	20	18	16	13	10	8	5	2	29	26	22
14 40	12	8	6	4	2	0♒	28	25	23	21	19	17	14	11	9	6	3	30	26	23
14 44	13	9	7	5	3	1	29	26	24	23	20	18	15	12	10	7	4	1♑	27	23
14 48	14	10	8	6	4	2	30	27	26	24	21	19	16	13	11	8	5	2	28	24
14 52	15	11	9	7	5	3	1♒	28	27	25	23	20	17	14	12	9	6	3	29	25
14 56	16	12	10	8	6	4	2	30	28	26	24	21	18	15	13	10	7	4	0♑	26
15 0	17	13	11	9	7	5	3	1♒	29	27	25	22	20	16	14	11	8	5	1	27
15 4	18	14	12	10	9	7	4	2	0♒	28	26	23	21	17	15	12	9	6	2	28
15 8	19	15	13	11	10	8	5	3	1	29	27	25	22	19	16	13	10	7	3	28
15 12	20	16	14	12	11	9	7	4	2	0♒	28	26	23	20	17	14	11	8	4	29
15 16	21	17	15	13	12	10	8	5	3	2	29	27	24	21	18	16	12	9	5	0♑
15 20	22	18	16	15	13	11	9	6	5	3	1♒	28	25	22	20	17	14	10	6	1
15 24	23	19	17	16	14	12	10	8	6	4	2	29	27	23	21	18	15	11	7	2
15 28	24	20	18	17	15	13	11	9	7	5	3	1♒	28	25	22	19	16	12	8	3
15 32	25	21	19	18	16	14	12	10	8	6	4	2	29	26	23	20	17	13	9	4
15 36	26	22	20	19	17	15	13	11	9	8	6	3	0♒	27	25	22	18	15	10	5
15 40	27	23	21	20	18	17	15	12	11	9	7	4	2	28	26	23	20	16	11	6
15 44	28	24	22	21	19	18	16	14	12	10	8	6	3	30	27	24	21	17	12	7
15 48	29	25	23	22	21	19	17	15	13	11	9	7	4	1♒	28	26	22	18	14	8
15 52	0♐	26	25	23	22	20	18	16	14	13	11	8	6	2	30	27	24	20	15	10
15 56	1	27	26	24	23	21	19	17	16	14	12	10	7	4	1♒	28	25	21	16	11
16 0	2♐	28♒	27♒	25♒	24♒	22♒	21♒	18♒	17♒	15♒	13♒	11♒	8♒	5♒	3♒	30♑	26♑	22♑	18♑	12♑

TABLES OF HOUSES

ST		0N	5N	10N	15N	20N	25N	30N	33N	36N	39N	42N	45N	48N	50N	52N	54N	56N	58N	60N
h m	Mc	As	As	As	As	As	As	As	As	As	As	As	As	As	As	As	As	As	As	As
16 0	2♐	28♒	27♒	25♒	24♒	22♒	21♒	18♒	17♒	15♒	13♒	11♒	8♒	5♒	3♒	30♑	26♑	22♑	18♑	12♑
16 4	3	29	28	26	25	24	22	20	18	17	15	12	10	7	4	1♒	28	24	19	13
16 8	4	30	29	28	26	25	23	21	20	18	16	14	11	8	6	3	29	25	20	14
16 12	5	1♓	30	29	27	26	24	22	21	19	17	15	13	10	7	4	1♒	27	22	16
16 16	6	2	1♓	30	29	27	26	24	22	21	19	17	14	11	9	6	2	28	23	17
16 20	7	3	2	1♓	30	28	27	25	24	22	20	18	16	13	10	7	4	30	25	19
16 24	8	4	3	2	1♓	30	28	26	25	23	22	20	17	14	12	9	6	1♒	26	20
16 28	9	5	4	3	2	1♓	29	28	26	25	23	21	19	16	13	11	7	3	28	22
16 32	10	6	5	4	3	2	1♓	29	28	26	25	23	20	17	15	12	9	5	30	23
16 36	11	7	6	5	4	3	2	0♓	29	28	26	24	22	19	17	14	11	7	2♒	25
16 40	12	8	8	7	6	5	3	2	0♓	29	28	26	24	21	19	16	13	9	3	27
16 44	12	9	9	8	7	6	4	3	2	1♓	29	27	25	23	20	18	14	10	5	29
16 48	13	10	10	9	8	7	6	4	3	2	1♓	29	27	24	22	20	16	12	7	1♒
16 52	14	12	11	10	9	8	7	6	5	4	2	1♓	29	26	24	22	18	15	9	3
16 56	15	13	12	11	10	9	8	7	6	5	4	2	0♓	28	26	24	20	17	12	5
17 0	16	14	13	12	12	11	10	8	8	7	5	4	2	30	28	26	23	19	14	7
17 4	17	15	14	14	13	12	11	10	9	8	7	6	4	2♓	30	28	25	21	16	10
17 8	18	16	15	15	14	13	12	11	11	10	9	7	6	4	2♓	30	27	24	19	12
17 12	19	17	16	16	15	15	14	13	12	11	10	9	7	5	4	2♓	29	26	21	15
17 16	20	18	18	17	16	16	15	14	13	13	12	11	9	7	6	4	2♓	28	24	18
17 20	21	19	19	18	18	17	16	16	15	14	13	12	11	9	8	6	4	1♓	27	21
17 24	22	20	20	19	19	18	18	17	16	16	15	14	13	11	10	8	6	4	30	24
17 28	23	21	21	21	20	20	19	18	18	17	17	16	15	13	12	11	9	6	3♓	28
17 32	24	22	22	22	21	21	20	20	19	19	18	18	17	15	14	13	11	9	6	1♓
17 36	24	23	23	23	23	22	22	21	21	20	20	19	19	17	17	15	14	12	9	5
17 40	25	25	24	24	24	24	23	23	22	22	22	21	20	20	19	18	17	15	13	9
17 44	26	26	25	25	25	25	25	24	24	24	23	23	22	22	21	20	19	18	16	13
17 48	27	27	27	26	26	26	26	26	25	25	25	25	24	24	23	23	22	21	19	17
17 52	28	28	28	28	28	27	27	27	27	27	27	26	26	26	25	25	25	24	23	21
17 56	29	29	29	29	29	29	29	29	28	28	28	28	28	28	28	28	27	27	26	26
18 0	0♑	0♈	0♈	0♈	0♈	0♈	0♈	0♈	0♈	0♈	0♈	0♈	0♈	0♈	0♈	0♈	0♈	0♈	0♈	0♈
18 4	1	1	1	1	1	1	1	1	2	2	2	2	2	2	2	2	3	3	4	4
18 8	2	2	2	2	2	3	3	3	3	3	3	4	4	4	5	5	5	6	7	9
18 12	3	3	3	4	4	4	4	4	5	5	5	5	6	6	7	7	8	9	11	13
18 16	4	4	5	5	5	5	5	6	6	6	7	7	8	8	9	10	11	12	14	17
18 20	5	5	6	6	6	6	7	7	8	8	8	9	10	10	11	12	13	15	17	21
18 24	6	7	7	7	7	8	8	9	9	10	10	11	11	13	13	15	16	18	21	25
18 28	6	8	8	8	9	9	10	10	11	11	12	12	13	15	16	17	19	21	24	29
18 32	7	9	9	9	10	10	11	12	12	13	13	14	15	17	18	19	21	24	27	2♉
18 36	8	10	10	11	11	12	12	13	14	14	15	16	17	19	20	22	24	26	0♉	6
18 40	9	11	11	12	12	13	14	14	15	16	17	18	19	21	22	24	26	29	3	9
18 44	10	12	12	13	14	14	15	16	17	17	18	19	21	23	24	26	28	2♉	6	12
18 48	11	13	14	14	15	15	16	17	18	19	20	21	23	25	26	28	1♉	4	9	15
18 52	12	14	15	15	16	17	18	19	19	20	21	23	24	26	28	0♉	3	6	11	18
18 56	13	15	16	16	17	18	19	20	21	22	23	24	26	28	0♉	2	5	9	14	20
19 0	14	16	17	18	18	19	20	22	22	23	25	26	28	0♉	2	4	7	11	16	23
19 4	15	17	18	19	20	21	22	23	24	25	26	28	30	2	4	6	10	13	18	25
19 8	16	18	19	20	21	22	23	24	25	26	28	29	1♉	4	6	8	12	15	21	27
19 12	17	20	20	21	22	23	24	26	27	28	29	1♉	3	6	8	10	14	18	23	29
19 16	18	21	21	22	23	24	26	27	28	29	1♉	3	5	7	10	12	16	20	25	1♊
19 20	18	22	22	23	24	25	27	28	30	1♉	2	4	6	9	11	14	17	21	27	3
19 24	19	23	24	25	26	27	28	30	1♉	2	4	6	8	11	13	16	19	23	28	5
19 28	20	24	25	26	27	28	29	1♉	2	4	5	7	10	13	15	18	21	25	0♊	7
19 32	21	25	26	27	28	29	1♉	2	4	5	7	9	11	14	17	19	23	27	2	8
19 36	22	26	27	28	29	0♉	2	4	5	7	8	10	13	16	18	21	24	29	4	10
19 40	23	27	28	29	0♉	2	3	5	6	8	10	12	14	17	20	23	26	0♊	5	11
19 44	24	28	29	0♉	1	3	4	6	8	9	11	13	16	19	21	24	28	2	7	13
19 48	25	29	0♉	1	3	4	6	8	9	11	13	15	17	20	23	26	29	3	8	14
19 52	26	0♉	1	2	4	5	7	9	10	12	14	16	19	22	24	27	1♊	5	10	16
19 56	27	1	2	4	5	6	8	10	12	13	15	18	20	23	26	29	2	6	11	17
20 0	28♑	2♉	3♉	5♉	6♉	8♉	9♉	12♉	13♉	15♉	17♉	19♉	22♉	25♉	27♉	0♊	4♊	8♊	12♊	18♊

TABLES OF HOUSES

ST		0N	5N	10N	15N	20N	25N	30N	33N	36N	39N	42N	45N	48N	50N	52N	54N	56N	58N	60N
h m	Mc	As	As	As	As	As	As	As	As	As	As	As	As	As	As	As	As	As	As	As
20 0	28♑	2♉	3♉	5♉	6♉	8♉	9♉	12♉	13♉	15♉	17♉	19♉	22♉	25♉	27♉	0♊	4♊	8♊	12♊	18♊
20 4	29	3	4	6	7	9	11	13	14	16	18	20	23	26	29	2	5	9	14	19
20 8	30	4	5	7	8	10	12	14	16	17	19	22	24	28	0♊	3	6	10	15	20
20 12	1♒	5	7	8	9	11	13	15	17	19	21	23	26	29	2	4	8	12	16	22
20 16	2	6	8	9	11	12	14	16	18	20	22	24	27	0♊	3	6	9	13	18	23
20 20	3	7	9	10	12	13	15	18	19	21	23	26	28	2	4	7	10	14	19	24
20 24	4	8	10	11	13	15	17	19	21	22	24	27	30	3	5	8	12	15	20	25
20 28	5	9	11	12	14	16	18	20	22	24	26	28	1♊	4	7	10	13	17	21	26
20 32	6	10	12	13	15	17	19	21	23	25	27	29	2	5	8	11	14	18	22	27
20 36	7	11	13	14	16	18	20	22	24	26	28	1♊	3	7	9	12	15	19	23	28
20 40	8	12	14	15	17	19	21	24	25	27	29	2	5	8	10	13	16	20	24	29
20 44	9	13	15	17	18	20	22	25	27	28	1♊	3	6	9	12	14	18	21	25	30
20 48	10	14	16	18	19	21	23	26	28	30	2	4	7	10	13	16	19	22	26	1♋
20 52	11	15	17	19	20	22	25	27	29	1♊	3	5	8	11	14	17	20	23	27	2
20 56	12	16	18	20	21	23	26	28	30	2	4	7	9	13	15	18	21	24	28	2
21 0	13	17	19	21	23	25	27	29	1♊	3	5	8	10	14	16	19	22	25	29	3
21 4	14	18	20	22	24	26	28	0♊	2	4	6	9	12	15	17	20	23	26	30	4
21 8	15	19	21	23	25	27	29	2	3	5	7	10	13	16	18	21	24	27	1♋	5
21 12	16	20	22	24	26	28	0♊	3	4	6	9	11	14	17	19	22	25	28	2	6
21 16	17	21	23	25	27	29	1	4	6	7	10	12	15	18	20	23	26	29	3	7
21 20	18	22	24	26	28	30	2	5	7	9	11	13	16	19	21	24	27	0♋	4	7
21 24	19	23	25	27	29	1♊	3	6	8	10	12	14	17	20	22	25	28	1	4	8
21 28	20	24	26	28	30	2	4	7	9	11	13	15	18	21	23	26	29	2	5	9
21 32	21	25	27	29	1♊	3	5	8	10	12	14	16	19	22	24	27	30	3	6	10
21 36	22	26	28	30	2	4	6	9	11	13	15	17	20	23	25	28	1♋	4	7	10
21 40	23	27	29	1♊	3	5	7	10	12	14	16	18	21	24	26	29	1	4	8	11
21 44	24	28	0♊	2	4	6	8	11	13	15	17	19	22	25	27	30	2	5	8	12
21 48	25	29	1	3	5	7	9	12	14	16	18	20	23	26	28	1♋	3	6	9	13
21 52	26	0♊	2	4	6	8	10	13	15	17	19	21	24	27	29	2	4	7	10	13
21 56	27	1	3	5	7	9	11	14	16	18	20	22	25	28	0♋	2	5	8	11	14
22 0	28	2	4	6	8	10	12	15	17	19	21	23	26	29	1	3	6	9	12	15
22 4	29	3	5	7	9	11	13	16	18	20	22	24	27	30	2	4	7	9	12	16
22 8	30	4	6	8	10	12	14	17	19	21	23	25	28	1♋	3	5	8	10	13	16
22 12	1♓	5	7	9	11	13	15	18	20	22	24	26	29	2	4	6	8	11	14	17
22 16	2	6	8	10	12	14	16	19	21	23	25	27	30	3	5	7	9	12	15	18
22 20	3	7	9	11	13	15	17	20	22	24	26	28	1♋	3	5	8	10	13	15	18
22 24	4	8	10	12	14	16	18	21	23	25	27	29	2	4	6	8	11	13	16	19
22 28	5	9	11	13	15	17	19	22	24	26	28	30	2	5	7	9	12	14	17	20
22 32	6	10	12	14	16	18	20	23	25	27	29	1♋	3	6	8	10	12	15	18	20
22 36	7	11	13	15	17	19	21	24	26	28	30	2	4	7	9	11	13	16	18	21
22 40	8	12	13	15	18	20	22	25	27	28	1♋	3	5	8	10	12	14	16	19	22
22 44	9	12	14	16	19	21	23	26	28	29	1	4	6	9	11	13	15	17	20	22
22 48	10	13	15	17	19	22	24	27	28	0♋	2	4	7	9	11	13	16	18	20	23
22 52	12	14	16	18	20	23	25	28	29	1	3	5	8	10	12	14	16	19	21	24
22 56	13	15	17	19	21	24	26	29	0♋	2	4	6	9	11	13	15	17	19	22	24
23 0	14	16	18	20	22	25	27	30	1	3	5	7	9	12	14	16	18	20	22	25
23 4	15	17	19	21	23	25	28	0♋	2	4	6	8	10	13	15	16	19	21	23	26
23 8	16	18	20	22	24	26	29	1	3	5	7	9	11	14	15	17	19	21	24	26
23 12	17	19	21	23	25	27	30	2	4	6	8	10	12	14	16	18	20	22	25	27
23 16	18	20	22	24	26	28	1♋	3	5	7	9	11	13	15	17	19	21	23	25	28
23 20	19	21	23	25	27	29	2	4	6	8	9	11	14	16	18	20	22	24	26	28
23 24	20	22	24	26	28	0♋	2	5	7	8	10	12	14	17	19	20	22	24	27	29
23 28	21	23	25	27	29	1	3	6	8	9	11	13	15	18	19	21	23	25	27	30
23 32	22	24	26	28	30	2	4	7	8	10	12	14	16	18	20	22	24	26	28	0♌
23 36	23	24	26	29	1♋	3	5	8	9	11	13	15	17	19	21	23	24	26	29	1
23 40	25	25	27	29	2	4	6	9	10	12	14	16	18	20	22	23	25	27	29	1
23 44	26	26	28	0♋	2	5	7	9	11	13	15	16	19	21	22	24	26	28	30	2
23 48	27	27	29	1	3	6	8	10	12	14	15	17	19	22	23	25	27	28	1♌	3
23 52	28	28	0♋	2	4	6	9	11	13	14	16	18	20	22	24	26	27	29	1	3
23 56	29	29	1	3	5	7	10	12	14	15	17	19	21	23	25	26	28	30	2	4
24 0	0	0♋	2♋	4♋	6♋	8♋	11♋	13♋	14♋	16♋	18♋	20♋	22♋	24♋	25♋	27♋	29♋	1♌	2♌	5♌

SUN-SIGN CHANGES

Year	Jan	Feb	Mar	Apr	May	Jun	Jul	Aug	Sep	Oct	Nov	Dec
1960	21 ♒ 1:10	19 ♓ 15:26	20 ♈ 14:43	20 ♉ 2:07	21 ♊ 1:34	21 ♋ 9:43	22 ♌ 20:38	23 ♍ 3:35	23 ♎ 0:59	23 ♏ 10:02	22 ♐ 7:19	21 ♑ 20:26
1961	20 ♒ 7:02	18 ♓ 21:17	20 ♈ 20:32	20 ♉ 7:56	21 ♊ 7:23	21 ♋ 15:31	23 ♌ 2:24	23 ♍ 9:19	23 ♎ 6:43	23 ♏ 15:48	22 ♐ 13:08	22 ♑ 2:20
1962	20 ♒ 12:59	19 ♓ 3:15	21 ♈ 2:30	20 ♉ 13:51	21 ♊ 13:17	21 ♋ 21:25	23 ♌ 8:18	23 ♍ 15:13	23 ♎ 12:36	23 ♏ 21:41	22 ♐ 19:02	22 ♑ 8:16
1963	20 ♒ 18:55	19 ♓ 9:09	21 ♈ 8:20	20 ♉ 19:37	21 ♊ 18:58	22 ♋ 3:04	23 ♌ 13:60	23 ♍ 20:58	23 ♎ 18:24	24 ♏ 3:30	23 ♐ 0:50	22 ♑ 14:03
1964	21 ♒ 0:42	19 ♓ 14:58	20 ♈ 14:10	20 ♉ 1:28	21 ♊ 0:51	21 ♋ 8:57	22 ♌ 19:53	23 ♍ 2:52	23 ♎ 0:17	23 ♏ 9:21	22 ♐ 6:40	21 ♑ 19:51
1965	20 ♒ 6:30	18 ♓ 20:49	20 ♈ 20:05	20 ♉ 7:27	21 ♊ 6:51	21 ♋ 14:56	23 ♌ 1:49	23 ♍ 8:44	23 ♎ 6:07	23 ♏ 15:11	22 ♐ 12:30	22 ♑ 1:42
1966	20 ♒ 12:21	19 ♓ 2:39	21 ♈ 1:54	20 ♉ 13:12	21 ♊ 12:32	21 ♋ 20:34	23 ♌ 7:24	23 ♍ 14:19	23 ♎ 11:44	23 ♏ 20:52	22 ♐ 18:15	22 ♑ 7:29
1967	20 ♒ 18:09	19 ♓ 8:24	21 ♈ 7:38	20 ♉ 18:56	21 ♊ 18:18	22 ♋ 2:23	23 ♌ 13:17	23 ♍ 20:13	23 ♎ 17:39	24 ♏ 2:45	23 ♐ 0:06	22 ♑ 13:17
1968	20 ♒ 23:55	19 ♓ 14:10	20 ♈ 13:22	20 ♉ 0:42	21 ♊ 0:07	21 ♋ 8:14	22 ♌ 19:08	23 ♍ 2:04	22 ♎ 23:27	23 ♏ 8:30	22 ♐ 5:49	21 ♑ 19:01
1969	20 ♒ 5:39	18 ♓ 19:55	20 ♈ 19:09	20 ♉ 6:27	21 ♊ 5:51	21 ♋ 13:56	23 ♌ 0:49	23 ♍ 7:44	23 ♎ 5:08	23 ♏ 14:12	22 ♐ 11:31	22 ♑ 0:44
1970	20 ♒ 11:24	19 ♓ 1:42	21 ♈ 0:57	20 ♉ 12:15	21 ♊ 11:38	21 ♋ 19:43	23 ♌ 6:37	23 ♍ 13:34	23 ♎ 10:60	23 ♏ 20:05	22 ♐ 17:25	22 ♑ 6:36
1971	20 ♒ 17:13	19 ♓ 7:27	21 ♈ 6:39	20 ♉ 17:55	21 ♊ 17:16	22 ♋ 1:21	23 ♌ 12:16	23 ♍ 19:16	23 ♎ 16:45	24 ♏ 1:54	22 ♐ 23:15	22 ♑ 12:24
1972	20 ♒ 22:59	19 ♓ 13:12	20 ♈ 12:22	19 ♉ 23:38	20 ♊ 23:01	21 ♋ 7:07	22 ♌ 18:03	23 ♍ 1:04	22 ♎ 22:34	23 ♏ 7:42	22 ♐ 5:03	21 ♑ 18:14
1973	20 ♒ 4:49	18 ♓ 19:02	20 ♈ 18:13	20 ♉ 5:31	21 ♊ 4:55	21 ♋ 13:01	22 ♌ 23:56	23 ♍ 6:54	23 ♎ 4:22	23 ♏ 13:31	22 ♐ 10:55	22 ♑ 0:09
1974	20 ♒ 10:47	19 ♓ 0:60	21 ♈ 0:08	20 ♉ 11:20	21 ♊ 10:37	21 ♋ 18:39	23 ♌ 5:32	23 ♍ 12:30	23 ♎ 9:60	23 ♏ 19:12	22 ♐ 16:40	22 ♑ 5:57
1975	20 ♒ 16:37	19 ♓ 6:51	21 ♈ 5:58	20 ♉ 17:08	21 ♊ 16:25	22 ♋ 0:28	23 ♌ 11:24	23 ♍ 18:25	23 ♎ 15:56	24 ♏ 1:07	22 ♐ 22:32	22 ♑ 11:47
1976	20 ♒ 22:26	19 ♓ 12:41	20 ♈ 11:51	19 ♉ 23:04	20 ♊ 22:22	21 ♋ 6:25	22 ♌ 17:20	23 ♍ 0:20	22 ♎ 21:50	23 ♏ 6:59	22 ♐ 4:22	21 ♑ 17:36
1977	20 ♒ 4:16	18 ♓ 18:31	20 ♈ 17:43	20 ♉ 4:58	21 ♊ 4:15	21 ♋ 12:15	22 ♌ 23:05	23 ♍ 6:01	23 ♎ 3:31	23 ♏ 12:42	22 ♐ 10:08	21 ♑ 23:24
1978	20 ♒ 10:05	19 ♓ 0:22	20 ♈ 23:34	20 ♉ 10:50	21 ♊ 10:09	21 ♋ 18:11	23 ♌ 5:02	23 ♍ 11:58	23 ♎ 9:26	23 ♏ 18:38	22 ♐ 16:06	22 ♑ 5:22
1979	20 ♒ 16:01	19 ♓ 6:14	21 ♈ 5:23	20 ♉ 16:36	21 ♊ 15:55	21 ♋ 23:57	23 ♌ 10:50	23 ♍ 17:48	23 ♎ 15:17	24 ♏ 0:28	22 ♐ 21:55	22 ♑ 11:11
1980	20 ♒ 21:50	19 ♓ 12:02	20 ♈ 11:10	19 ♉ 22:23	20 ♊ 21:43	21 ♋ 5:48	22 ♌ 16:42	22 ♍ 23:41	22 ♎ 21:10	23 ♏ 6:18	22 ♐ 3:42	21 ♑ 16:57
1981	20 ♒ 3:37	18 ♓ 17:53	20 ♈ 17:04	20 ♉ 4:19	21 ♊ 3:40	21 ♋ 11:45	22 ♌ 22:40	23 ♍ 5:38	23 ♎ 3:06	23 ♏ 12:14	22 ♐ 9:37	21 ♑ 22:51
1982	20 ♒ 9:32	18 ♓ 23:48	20 ♈ 22:57	20 ♉ 10:08	21 ♊ 9:24	21 ♋ 17:24	23 ♌ 4:16	23 ♍ 11:16	23 ♎ 8:47	23 ♏ 17:59	22 ♐ 15:25	22 ♑ 4:40
1983	20 ♒ 15:18	19 ♓ 5:32	21 ♈ 4:40	20 ♉ 15:51	21 ♊ 15:07	21 ♋ 23:09	23 ♌ 10:05	23 ♍ 17:09	23 ♎ 14:43	23 ♏ 23:56	22 ♐ 21:20	22 ♑ 10:32
1984	20 ♒ 21:07	19 ♓ 11:17	20 ♈ 10:25	19 ♉ 21:39	20 ♊ 20:59	21 ♋ 5:03	22 ♌ 15:59	22 ♍ 23:01	22 ♎ 20:34	23 ♏ 5:47	22 ♐ 3:12	21 ♑ 16:24
1985	20 ♒ 2:59	18 ♓ 17:09	20 ♈ 16:15	20 ♉ 3:27	21 ♊ 2:44	21 ♋ 10:45	22 ♌ 21:38	23 ♍ 4:37	23 ♎ 2:09	23 ♏ 11:23	22 ♐ 8:52	21 ♑ 22:09
1986	20 ♒ 8:47	18 ♓ 22:59	20 ♈ 22:04	20 ♉ 9:13	21 ♊ 8:29	21 ♋ 16:31	23 ♌ 3:26	23 ♍ 10:27	23 ♎ 8:00	23 ♏ 17:16	22 ♐ 14:46	22 ♑ 4:04
1987	20 ♒ 14:42	19 ♓ 4:51	21 ♈ 3:53	20 ♉ 14:59	21 ♊ 14:11	21 ♋ 22:12	23 ♌ 9:07	23 ♍ 16:11	23 ♎ 13:46	23 ♏ 23:02	22 ♐ 20:30	22 ♑ 9:47
1988	20 ♒ 20:26	19 ♓ 10:36	20 ♈ 9:39	19 ♉ 20:46	20 ♊ 19:58	21 ♋ 3:58	22 ♌ 14:52	22 ♍ 21:55	22 ♎ 19:30	23 ♏ 4:45	22 ♐ 2:13	21 ♑ 15:28
1989	20 ♒ 2:08	18 ♓ 16:22	20 ♈ 15:29	20 ♉ 2:40	21 ♊ 1:54	21 ♋ 9:54	22 ♌ 20:47	23 ♍ 3:47	23 ♎ 1:21	23 ♏ 10:36	22 ♐ 8:06	21 ♑ 21:23
1990	20 ♒ 8:02	18 ♓ 22:15	20 ♈ 21:20	20 ♉ 8:27	21 ♊ 7:38	21 ♋ 15:34	23 ♌ 2:23	23 ♍ 9:22	23 ♎ 6:56	23 ♏ 16:15	22 ♐ 13:48	22 ♑ 3:08
1991	20 ♒ 13:48	19 ♓ 3:59	21 ♈ 3:03	20 ♉ 14:10	21 ♊ 13:22	21 ♋ 21:20	23 ♌ 8:12	23 ♍ 15:14	23 ♎ 12:49	23 ♏ 22:06	22 ♐ 19:37	22 ♑ 8:55
1992	20 ♒ 19:34	19 ♓ 9:45	20 ♈ 8:49	19 ♉ 19:58	20 ♊ 19:14	21 ♋ 3:16	22 ♌ 14:10	22 ♍ 21:11	22 ♎ 18:44	23 ♏ 3:58	22 ♐ 1:27	21 ♑ 14:44
1993	20 ♒ 1:24	18 ♓ 15:37	20 ♈ 14:42	20 ♉ 1:50	21 ♊ 1:03	21 ♋ 9:01	22 ♌ 19:52	23 ♍ 2:52	23 ♎ 0:24	23 ♏ 9:39	22 ♐ 7:08	21 ♑ 20:27
1994	20 ♒ 7:08	18 ♓ 21:23	20 ♈ 20:30	20 ♉ 7:38	21 ♊ 6:50	21 ♋ 14:49	23 ♌ 1:42	23 ♍ 8:45	23 ♎ 6:21	23 ♏ 15:38	22 ♐ 13:07	22 ♑ 2:24
1995	20 ♒ 13:02	19 ♓ 3:12	21 ♈ 2:15	20 ♉ 13:23	21 ♊ 12:36	21 ♋ 20:36	23 ♌ 7:31	23 ♍ 14:37	23 ♎ 12:15	23 ♏ 21:33	22 ♐ 19:03	22 ♑ 8:18
1996	20 ♒ 18:54	19 ♓ 9:02	20 ♈ 8:04	19 ♉ 19:11	20 ♊ 18:24	21 ♋ 2:25	22 ♌ 13:20	22 ♍ 20:24	22 ♎ 18:02	23 ♏ 3:20	22 ♐ 0:51	21 ♑ 14:07
1997	20 ♒ 0:43	18 ♓ 14:53	20 ♈ 13:56	20 ♉ 1:04	21 ♊ 0:19	21 ♋ 8:21	22 ♌ 19:17	23 ♍ 2:20	22 ♎ 23:57	23 ♏ 9:16	22 ♐ 6:49	21 ♑ 20:09
1998	20 ♒ 6:47	18 ♓ 20:56	20 ♈ 19:56	20 ♉ 6:58	21 ♊ 6:07	21 ♋ 14:04	23 ♌ 0:57	23 ♍ 8:00	23 ♎ 5:38	23 ♏ 14:60	22 ♐ 12:36	22 ♑ 1:58
1999	20 ♒ 12:39	19 ♓ 2:48	21 ♈ 1:47	20 ♉ 12:47	21 ♊ 11:54	21 ♋ 19:51	23 ♌ 6:45	23 ♍ 13:52	23 ♎ 11:33	23 ♏ 20:53	22 ♐ 18:26	22 ♑ 7:45
2000	20 ♒ 18:24	19 ♓ 8:35	20 ♈ 7:36	19 ♉ 18:40	20 ♊ 17:50	21 ♋ 1:49	22 ♌ 12:43	22 ♍ 19:49	22 ♎ 17:29	23 ♏ 2:49	22 ♐ 0:21	21 ♑ 13:39
2001	20 ♒ 0:18	18 ♓ 14:29	20 ♈ 13:32	20 ♉ 0:37	20 ♊ 23:45	21 ♋ 7:39	22 ♌ 18:27	23 ♍ 1:28	22 ♎ 23:06	23 ♏ 8:27	22 ♐ 6:02	21 ♑ 19:23
2002	20 ♒ 6:04	18 ♓ 20:15	20 ♈ 19:18	20 ♉ 6:22	21 ♊ 5:30	21 ♋ 13:25	23 ♌ 0:16	23 ♍ 7:19	23 ♎ 4:57	23 ♏ 14:19	22 ♐ 11:56	22 ♑ 1:17
2003	20 ♒ 11:55	19 ♓ 2:02	21 ♈ 1:01	20 ♉ 12:04	21 ♊ 11:14	21 ♋ 19:11	23 ♌ 6:05	23 ♍ 13:10	23 ♎ 10:49	23 ♏ 20:10	22 ♐ 17:45	22 ♑ 7:06
2004	20 ♒ 17:44	19 ♓ 7:52	20 ♈ 6:50	19 ♉ 17:52	20 ♊ 17:00	21 ♋ 0:58	22 ♌ 11:51	22 ♍ 18:55	22 ♎ 16:32	23 ♏ 1:51	21 ♐ 23:23	21 ♑ 12:43
2005	19 ♒ 23:23	18 ♓ 13:33	20 ♈ 12:35	19 ♉ 23:39	20 ♊ 22:48	21 ♋ 6:47	22 ♌ 17:42	23 ♍ 0:47	22 ♎ 22:24	23 ♏ 7:44	22 ♐ 5:17	21 ♑ 18:36
2006	20 ♒ 5:17	18 ♓ 19:27	20 ♈ 18:27	20 ♉ 5:27	21 ♊ 4:33	21 ♋ 12:27	22 ♌ 23:19	23 ♍ 6:24	23 ♎ 4:05	23 ♏ 13:28	22 ♐ 11:03	22 ♑ 0:24
2007	20 ♒ 11:02	19 ♓ 1:10	21 ♈ 0:08	20 ♉ 11:08	21 ♊ 10:13	21 ♋ 18:08	23 ♌ 5:01	23 ♍ 12:09	23 ♎ 9:53	23 ♏ 19:17	22 ♐ 16:51	22 ♑ 6:09
2008	20 ♒ 16:44	19 ♓ 6:50	20 ♈ 5:49	19 ♉ 16:52	20 ♊ 16:02	21 ♋ 0:01	22 ♌ 10:56	22 ♍ 18:03	22 ♎ 15:46	23 ♏ 1:10	21 ♐ 22:46	21 ♑ 12:05
2009	19 ♒ 22:41	18 ♓ 12:47	20 ♈ 11:45	19 ♉ 22:46	20 ♊ 21:53	21 ♋ 5:47	22 ♌ 16:37	22 ♍ 23:40	22 ♎ 21:20	23 ♏ 6:45	22 ♐ 4:24	21 ♑ 17:48
2010	20 ♒ 4:29	18 ♓ 18:37	20 ♈ 17:33	20 ♉ 4:31	21 ♊ 3:36	21 ♋ 11:30	22 ♌ 22:23	23 ♍ 5:29	23 ♎ 3:11	23 ♏ 12:36	22 ♐ 10:16	21 ♑ 23:40

The Longitude Equivalent in Time

The Longitude Equivalent in time is based upon the earth's rotation on its axis. Every 15° is equivalent to an hour.
The tables give the equivalent in time that the geographic latitude affects in relation to Greenwich.

°	h m	°	h m	°	h m	°	h m	°	h m	°	h m
1	0 04	31	2 04	61	4 04	91	6 04	121	8 04	151	10 04
2	0 08	32	2 08	62	4 08	92	6 08	122	8 08	152	10 08
3	0 12	33	2 12	63	4 12	93	6 12	123	8 12	153	10 12
4	0 16	34	2 16	64	4 16	94	6 16	124	8 16	154	10 16
5	0 20	35	2 20	65	4 20	95	6 20	125	8 20	155	10 20
6	0 24	36	2 24	66	4 24	96	6 24	126	8 24	156	10 24
7	0 28	37	2 28	67	4 28	97	6 28	127	8 28	157	10 28
8	0 32	38	2 32	68	4 32	98	6 32	128	8 32	158	10 32
9	0 36	39	2 36	69	4 36	99	6 36	129	8 36	159	10 36
10	0 40	40	2 40	70	4 40	100	6 40	130	8 40	160	10 40
11	0 44	41	2 44	71	4 44	101	6 44	131	8 44	161	10 44
12	0 48	42	2 48	72	4 48	102	6 48	132	8 48	162	10 48
13	0 52	43	2 52	73	4 52	103	6 52	133	8 52	163	10 52
14	0 56	44	2 56	74	4 56	104	6 56	134	8 56	164	10 56
15	1 00	45	3 00	75	5 00	105	7 00	135	9 00	165	11 00
16	1 04	46	3 04	76	5 04	106	7 04	136	9 04	166	11 04
17	1 08	47	3 08	77	5 08	107	7 08	137	9 08	167	11 08
18	1 12	48	3 12	78	5 12	108	7 12	138	9 12	168	11 12
19	1 16	49	3 16	79	5 16	109	7 16	139	9 16	169	11 16
20	1 20	50	3 20	80	5 20	110	7 20	140	9 20	170	11 20
21	1 24	51	3 24	81	5 24	111	7 24	141	9 24	171	11 24
22	1 28	52	3 28	82	5 28	112	7 28	142	9 28	172	11 28
23	1 32	53	3 32	83	5 32	113	7 32	143	9 32	173	11 32
24	1 36	54	3 36	84	5 36	114	7 36	144	9 36	174	11 36
25	1 40	55	3 40	85	5 40	115	7 40	145	9 40	175	11 40
26	1 44	56	3 44	86	5 44	116	7 44	146	9 44	176	11 44
27	1 48	57	3 48	87	5 48	117	7 48	147	9 48	177	11 48
28	1 52	58	3 52	88	5 52	118	7 52	148	9 52	178	11 52
29	1 56	59	3 56	89	5 56	119	7 56	149	9 56	179	11 56
30	2 00	60	4 00	90	6 00	120	8 00	150	10 00	180	12 00

0' - 07'	0 00
8' - 22'	0 01
23' - 37'	0 02
38' - 52'	0 03
53' - 59'	0 04

Example for Chicago 87° 39' N

87° = 5h 48m
39' = 3m
5h 51m

The Acceleration on the Interval

In every 24 hours, the sidereal time accelerates past the clock time by nearly 4 minutes. During the day a small correction must be made to allow for this increase.
This simple table provides the time adjustment.

Time range in hours/minutes	*Corrections in minutes*
0 00 - 3 03	0 00
3 04 - 9 07	0 01
9 08 - 15 13	0 02
15 14 - 21 18	0 03
21 19 - 24 00	0 04

Examples:
Acceleration on 5h 36m is 1 minute.
Acceleration on 22h 04m is 4 minutes.

Daylight Saving Time (Summer Time)

UK

Since 1998 the formula for summer times is: begins last Sunday in March (1 A.M.), ends last Sunday in October (2 A.M.).

1960	Apr 10 – Oct 2	**1977**	Mar 20 – Oct 23	**1994**	Mar 27 – Oct 23
1961	Mar 26 – Oct 29	**1978**	Mar 19 – Oct 22	**1995**	Mar 26 – Oct 22
1962	Mar 25 – Oct 28	**1979**	Mar 18 – Oct 28	**1996**	Mar 31 – Oct 27
1963	Mar 31 – Oct 27	**1980**	Mar 16 – Oct 26	**1997**	Mar 30 – Oct 26
1964	Mar 22 – Oct 25	**1981**	Mar 29 – Oct 25	**1998**	Mar 29 – Oct 25
1965	Mar 21 – 24 Oct	**1982**	Mar 28 – Oct 24	**1999**	Mar 28 – Oct 31
1966	Mar 20 – Oct 23	**1983**	Mar 27 – Oct 23	**2000**	Mar 26 – Oct 29
1967	Mar 19 – Oct 29	**1984**	Mar 25 – Oct 28	**2001**	Mar 25 – Oct 28
1968	Feb 18 – Dec 31	**1985**	Mar 31 – Oct 27	**2002**	Mar 31 – Oct 27
1969	Jan 1 – Dec 31	**1986**	Mar 30 – Oct 26	**2003**	Mar 30 – Oct 26
1970	Jan 1 – Dec 31	**1987**	Mar 29 – Oct 25	**2004**	Mar 28 – Oct 31
1971	Jan 1 – Oct 31	**1988**	Mar 27 – Oct 23	**2005**	Mar 27 – Oct 30
1972	Mar 19 – Oct 29	**1989**	Mar 26 – Oct 29	**2006**	Mar 26 – Oct 29
1973	Mar 18 – Oct 28	**1990**	Mar 25 – Oct 28	**2007**	Mar 25 – Oct 28
1974	Mar 17 – Oct 27	**1991**	Mar 31 – Oct 27	**2008**	Mar 30 – Oct 26
1975	Mar 16 – Oct 26	**1992**	Mar 29 – Oct 25	**2009**	Mar 29 – Oct 25
1976	Mar 21 – Oct 24	**1993**	Mar 28 – Oct 24	**2010**	Mar 28 – Oct 31

USA

Since 1987 the formula for summer times is: begins first Sunday in April (2 A.M.), ends last Sunday in October (2 A.M.).

* *Prior to 1966 it may be difficult to find out when daylight saving time was used in some areas* (rough guide provided)

1960 *	Apr 24 – Oct 30	**1977**	Apr 24 – Oct 30	**1994**	Apr 3 – Oct 30
1961 *	Apr 30 – Oct 29	**1978**	Apr 30 – Oct 29	**1995**	Apr 2 – Oct 29
1962 *	Apr 29 – Oct 28	**1979**	Apr 29 – Oct 28	**1996**	Apr 7 – Oct 27
1963 *	Apr 28 – Oct 27	**1980**	Apr 27 – Oct 26	**1997**	Apr 6 – Oct 26
1964 *	Apr 26 – Oct 25	**1981**	Apr 26 – Oct 25	**1998**	Apr 5 – Oct 25
1965 *	Apr 25 – Oct 31	**1982**	Apr 25 – Oct 31	**1999**	Apr 4 – Oct 31
1966	Apr 24 – Oct 30	**1983**	Apr 24 – Oct 30	**2000**	Apr 2 – Oct 29
1967	Apr 30 – Oct 29	**1984**	Apr 29 – Oct 28	**2001**	Apr 1 – Oct 28
1968	Apr 28 – Oct 27	**1985**	Apr 28 – Oct 27	**2002**	Apr 7 – Oct 27
1969	Apr 27 – Oct 26	**1986**	Apr 27 – Oct 26	**2003**	Apr 6 – Oct 26
1970	Apr 26 – Oct 25	**1987**	Apr 5 – Oct 25	**2004**	Apr 4 – Oct 31
1971	Apr 25 – Oct 31	**1988**	Apr 3 – Oct 30	**2005**	Apr 3 – Oct 30
1972	Apr 30 – Oct 29	**1989**	Apr 2 – Oct 29	**2006**	Apr 2 – Oct 29
1973	Apr 29 – Oct 28	**1990**	Apr 1 – Oct 28	**2007**	Apr 1 – Oct 28
1974	Jan 6 – Oct 27	**1991**	Apr 7 – Oct 27	**2008**	Apr 6 – Oct 26
1975	Feb 23 – Oct 26	**1992**	Apr 5 – Oct 25	**2009**	Apr 5 – Oct 25
1976	Apr 25 – Oct 31	**1993**	Apr 4 – Oct 31	**2010**	Apr 4 – Oct 31

♈ ♉ ♊

We hope you enjoyed this Astro Room/Hay House book.
If you would like to receive a free catalog featuring additional
Hay House books and products, or if you would like information
about the Hay Foundation, please contact:

Hay House, Inc.
P.O. Box 5100
Carlsbad, CA 92018-5100

(760) 431-7695 or **(800) 654-5126**
(760) 431-6948 (fax) or **(800) 650-5115 (fax)**
www.hayhouse.com

♈ ♉ ♊

Distributed in Canada by: Raincoast, 9050 Shaughnessy St.,
Vancouver, B.C., Canada V6P 6E5

♈ ♉ ♊